WEALTH FOREVER

The Analytics of Stock Markets

WEALTH FOREVER

The Analytics of Stock Markets

Sarkis Joseph Khoury
University of California, Riverside, USA

Poorna Pal
Glendale Community College, USA

Chunsheng Zhou
Peking University, China

John Karayan
California State Polytechnic University, USA

World Scientific
New Jersey • London • Singapore • Hong Kong

Published by

World Scientific Publishing Co. Pte. Ltd.
5 Toh Tuck Link, Singapore 596224
USA office: Suite 202, 1060 Main Street, River Edge, NJ 07661
UK office: 57 Shelton Street, Covent Garden, London WC2H 9HE

British Library Cataloguing-in-Publication Data
A catalogue record for this book is available from the British Library.

WEALTH FOREVER: THE ANALYTICS OF STOCK MARKETS

ISBN 981-238-443-X
ISBN 981-238-444-8 (pbk)

Printed in Singapore by World Scientific Printers (S) Pte Ltd

FOREWORD

This book seeks to answer many a question about the stock market: why invest in stocks, how to invest in stocks, how to value stocks, how to change the risk profile of portfolios, how to analyze the results of stock investing, and how to minimize estate taxes and to maximize control, even after death.

The book covers all aspects of the stock market to include the basic tools that will allow the reader to understand the stock market basics, the history of the stock market performance in the US and overseas, the various ways to value stocks and to assess their risk, and the various methods that have been proposed to capitalize on the inefficiencies of the stock market, be they temporary or permanent.

The book debunks many of the convenient theories to explain the performance and the behavior of the stock market. It does so in very rigorous ways. It analyzes every aspect of past performance of the stock market. There are many books on this last issue alone. We match them and exceed them in many cases. We show the serious problem in the various stock valuation techniques that typically yield different results. This may explain the price bubble that had recently burst. The book presents also a comprehensive, easy to understand chapter on stock options and deals effectively with tax planning and setting up trusts. Hedging, speculative, and arbitrage strategies and tools involving stock options market are examined as an integral part of a system that will permit the investor to establish optimal risk/return tradeoffs meeting his/her risk profile.

The section on estate planning is necessary in order to critically examine the methods for maximizing intergenerational wealth transfer, largely through tax planning devices, and to make sure, if and when necessary, that transferred wealth is controlled by the person who generated it, even after his or her death.

The book has a simple and very rigorous way for presenting the materials and for settling, if only nominally in some cases, long standing controversies or myths about the stock market.

The book is very rigorous and often mathematical. The latter is kept to a minimum in order to maximize the readability and the accessibility of the book. The book settles many an argument and strongly supports many a hypothesis about the capacity of certain strategies to beat the market. The historical analyses of stock market performances all over the world leave no doubt that that the stock market is the investment vehicle of choice when compared with inflation and any other investment vehicle. The lessons for developing economies in all of this is to improve economic efficiency and to foster the development of financial markets as this is the fastest way to wealth creation and for spreading democratic, capitalism all over the world.

The book will be useful to educators, professionals, and sophisticated investors. It will be useful in investment courses, corporate finance courses, speculative market courses, and courses on the stock market. It will also be useful in financial certification courses as well.

Two colleagues at UCR examined different portions of the book. We are grateful to Jerry Liu and to Vasilis Polimenis. We are also grateful to many reviewers whose comments improved the structure, the flow and the contents of the book. Of course, we remain responsible for any and all remaining errors.

CONTENTS

Chapter 1

THE FASCINATING WORLD OF THE STOCK MARKET: BASIC KNOWLEDGE AND CONSIDERATIONS

1.1 Introduction

<u>Time Line</u>: *June 26, 2000*

Scientists from the National Institute of Health and from Celera Genomics Group, a division of PE Corporation, announced that they have a map for the sequencing of the human genome. The decoding involved three billion chemical bases (letters) that make up the human DNA, and allows scientists to find and understand the more than 60,000 human genes. The announced draft allows for the identification of 95% of the genes known to cause disease.

This colossal discovery, some argue the most significant ever in human history, has incalculable consequences on the quality of life, and on the longevity of life. The computers are churning to find out what companies will in fact benefit from this discovery, what will be the impact on their revenue and their profits, and ultimately on their market price. Do you know what company to invest in? Do you know what group of companies you should invest in so even if only one of them is a big winner, you will reap huge profits? How much of your investable funds would you put in genome based-companies?

The answers may astound you, as will the fact that there is an accessible, easy to understand way for systematically going about answering the above questions to prepare you and your family for a better working life and a better retirement.

Time Line: April 2000

Financial industry titan, Julian Robertson of the Tiger Fund calls it quit. Mr. Stanley F. Druckenmiller of the $8.2 billion Quantum Fund, another hedge fund run by the legendary W. Soros, calls it quit. Nicholos Roditi of the London-based Quota Fund, which had lost a third of its value by the end of April 2000, calls it quit. Many others followed suit. All claimed that they could no longer make money for their clients in the ever more unpredictable and gyrating stock market.

And you thought that the stock market is easy to figure out!!!

"Down markets may represent the greatest buying opportunity for the investor."

The twentieth century has been very kind to America, especially the last twenty years of the century. Ninety percent of US wealth has been created since 1980, most of it from emerging firms. The trends appeared to be continuing in the early months of the twenty-first century. Standing in January 2003 and looking in the rearview mirror over the last two years, one is hard pressed to write an optimistic book about the stock market, however. Investors are typically fickle and their circumstances and attitudes often shift, either because of changing personal experiences or because of an altered (unpredictably) environment in which they function.

The US stock market, not unlike practically all stock markets in the developed countries, has turned in a negative performance in 2000, 2001 and 2002 (Exhibit 1.1). These data are surely the fodder for the stock market bears, and are likely to keep some investors at bay.

The state of the stock market reflects itself in the venture capital industry. In 2002, venture capitalists raised $5 billion compared to $20 billion in the fourth quarter of 2000. The stock market also impacts

Exhibit 1.1: Top panel compares the performances of the three major US stock market indexes — the Dow, the NASDAQ and the S&P 500 — from January 1, 2000 to December 31, 2002 and the bottom panel compares the Dow and the Dow Jones World Stock Index over this period.

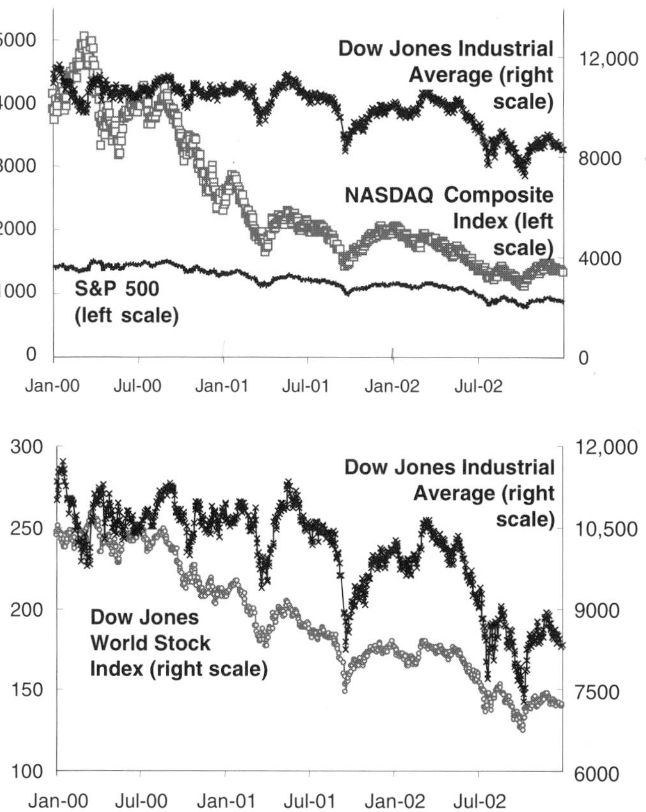

consumer confidence, as it is a leading indicator for economic performance. It also affects consumer spending, as some argue. The latter is referred to as the "wealth effect".

Pessimism about the stock market ignores the fact that never in its history has the stock market moved straight up or down. The cyclical nature of the market is a historical constant, and is hardly an aberration. The issue is the depth and the length of the downturns and the upturns.

The myopic view of the stock market is precisely what this book is intended to discredit. The evidence we present in the following pages is compelling when stock market returns are analyzed over sufficiently long periods, say about 20 years or longer, and are compared with returns from alternative investments.

The data from the last century dwarf those of the one preceding it. GDP per capita grew at between 1% and 1.5% per year in the US during the 19th century. This caught the attention of many leading economists. Even Karl Marx was impressed by these results. However, the sustainable growth in per capita GDP in the United States rose to about 2% and some believe that it can easily be at 3% if the pace of technological innovation in the last decade stay the same or accelerate. Those adherents to this belief point to the pace of innovation in networked computers and in telecommunications as the foundation for their optimism. But the investment in information technology has only begun as Exhibit 1.2 shows. There is ample room for growth in the United States and in the world despite a massive rise in corporate spending on technology (Exhibit 1.3). The effects of these technologies do show up in US macro economic data, but their full impact has yet to be accounted for, as existing technology makes its way through the operations of the corporate world, and as new frontiers in technology continue to open. The genome project is just one of many of these new frontiers.

The pace of technological innovation accelerated enormously in the last ten years. The shelf life of computer-related products and software

Exhibit 1.2: IT spending as a % of GDP.

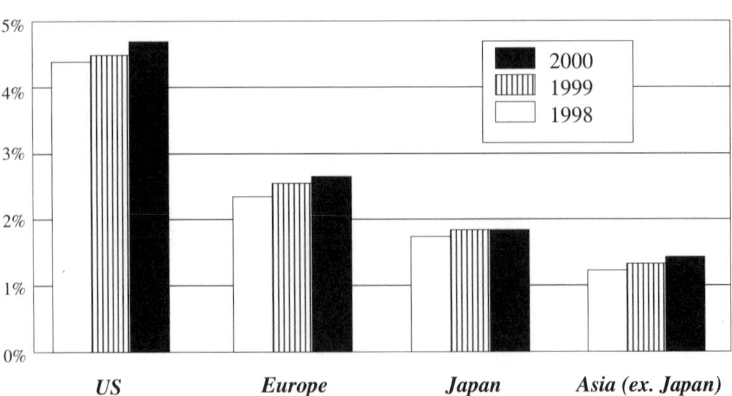

Source: IDC

Exhibit 1.3: US informational technology spending — Investment in equipment, computers and peripheral equipment as percentage of investment in equipment/industrial equipment.

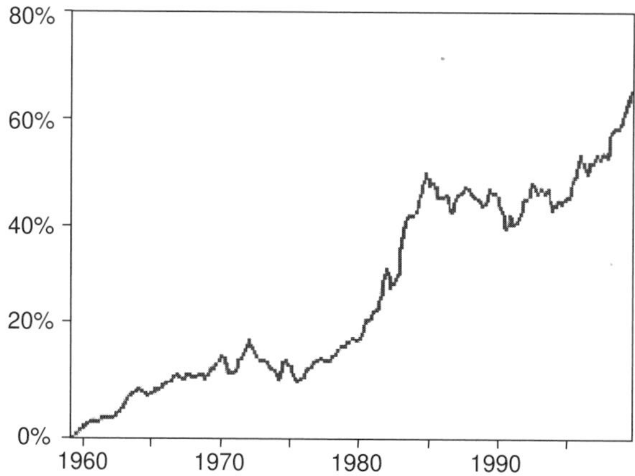

Source: US Department of Commerce

has decreased from years to few months. In the computer area Moore's law still holds, albeit tenuously. The capacity of computers: speed, processing power and storage, according to Gordon Moore, doubles every 18 months. The Internet has speeded up the innovation process to a point where a web year is now three months, that is, the time it takes from concept, to development to innovation has shrunk to three months. The entire technological foundation, on which Microsoft managed to increase the wealth of its shareholders at rates unprecedented in human history, is being revisited and reengineered. Mr. Gates is often on television boosting the transformation of Microsoft. The old paradigm may forever be replaced with a new one that will most certainly have a shorter life span. Competition in the twenty first century will be based on this simple reality, and on the firm's capacity to manage innovation and keep a competitive edge either through internal growth or through acquisition.

The adoption of technology has almost kept pace with the pace of innovation. It is driven by the need to support business ventures, improving performance, improving the flexibility of the firm, improving price/performance, end-user demand, the reengineering of business processes, and the need for a shorter payback period.

All of these developments are ultimately reflected in the economic data measuring the well being of Americans and their optimism about the future. The United States, which accounts for only 4.2% of the world population (Exhibit 1.4), accounts for 21% of the world GDP in real terms and has led the world in productivity gains throughout the twentieth century. Our current per capita GDP is the highest in the world except for that of few small countries like Switzerland and Luxembourg. It stands currently at about $29,000. Our stock market capitalization (the value of all outstanding stocks in the United States) stands at over $20 trillion, the highest in the world. The stock market, especially the bull trend of the last 18 years, has allowed the American people to accumulate more wealth than ever, in absolute and in relative terms. Exhibit 1.5 shows the enormous wealth accumulated in the United States, followed by Japan. Notice how little of the world wealth China (Chine) is controlling. This will be changing dramatically during the early part of the twenty-first century. At the heart of this data is an open system that is transparent, where the role of government is fundamental sustaining of business expansion, and where the spirit of entrepreneurship is soaring. Small and medium size businesses created over 1.8 million jobs between 1988 and 1993 alone, while only 100,000 jobs were created by the FORTUNE 1000 during the same period.

America had solved, or so it appeared, its budget deficit problems until the September 11, 2001 disaster occurred. Budget deficits are now projected well into 2005. The US also has massive deficits in its trade account, and potentially in its Social Security and Medicare accounts. These problems are being addressed. There is no shortage of commitment to solutions by either political party, despite their considerable differences in approach. But, there are some trends that are somewhat disconcerting.

Leading economists have been expressing their concerns over the falling saving rate in the United States, the excessive consumption of the American citizen, and the excessive debt incurred in the process. Total consumer debt reached $1589.2 billion in July 2000. During the year 2000, consumer debt was rising at a rate of 7.5%, about the

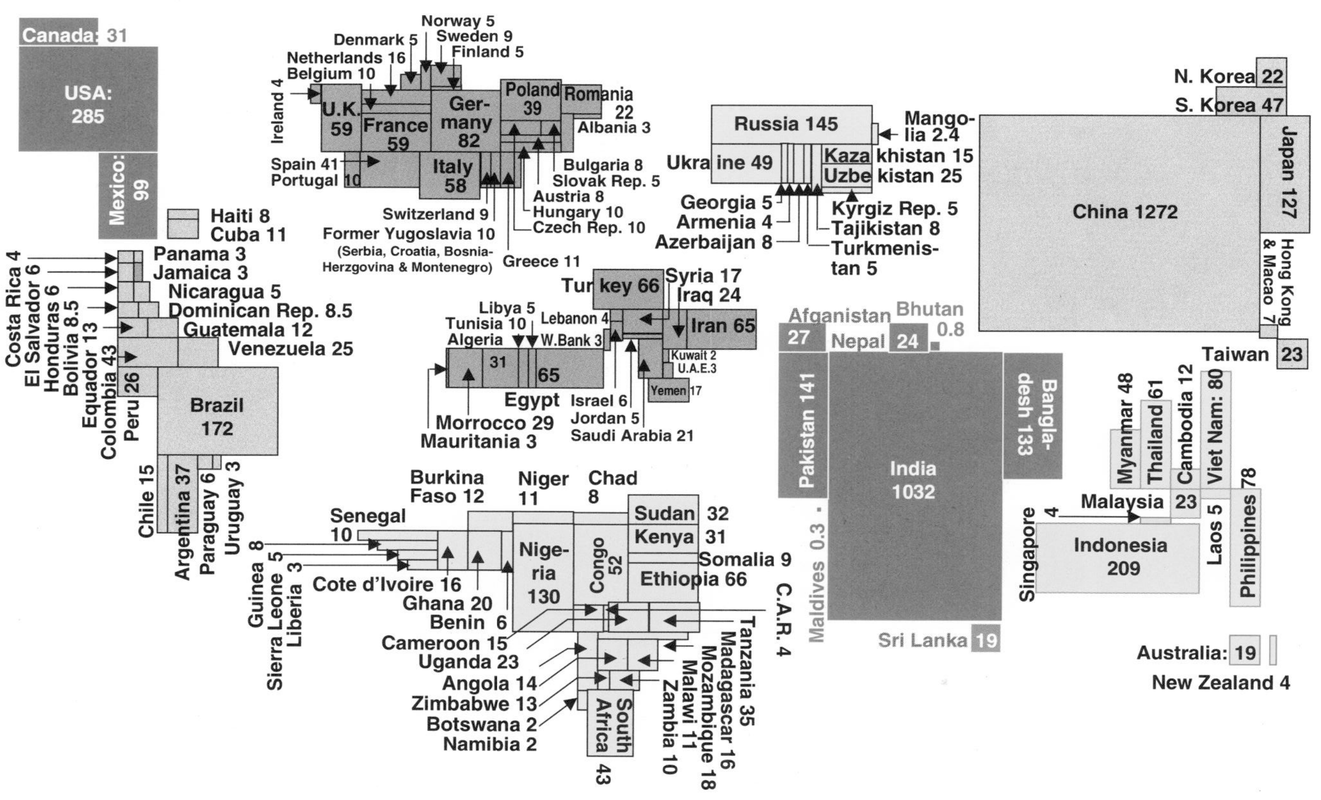

Exhibit 1.4: The dynamics of world population.

Exhibit 1.5: The uneven distribution of world's wealth.

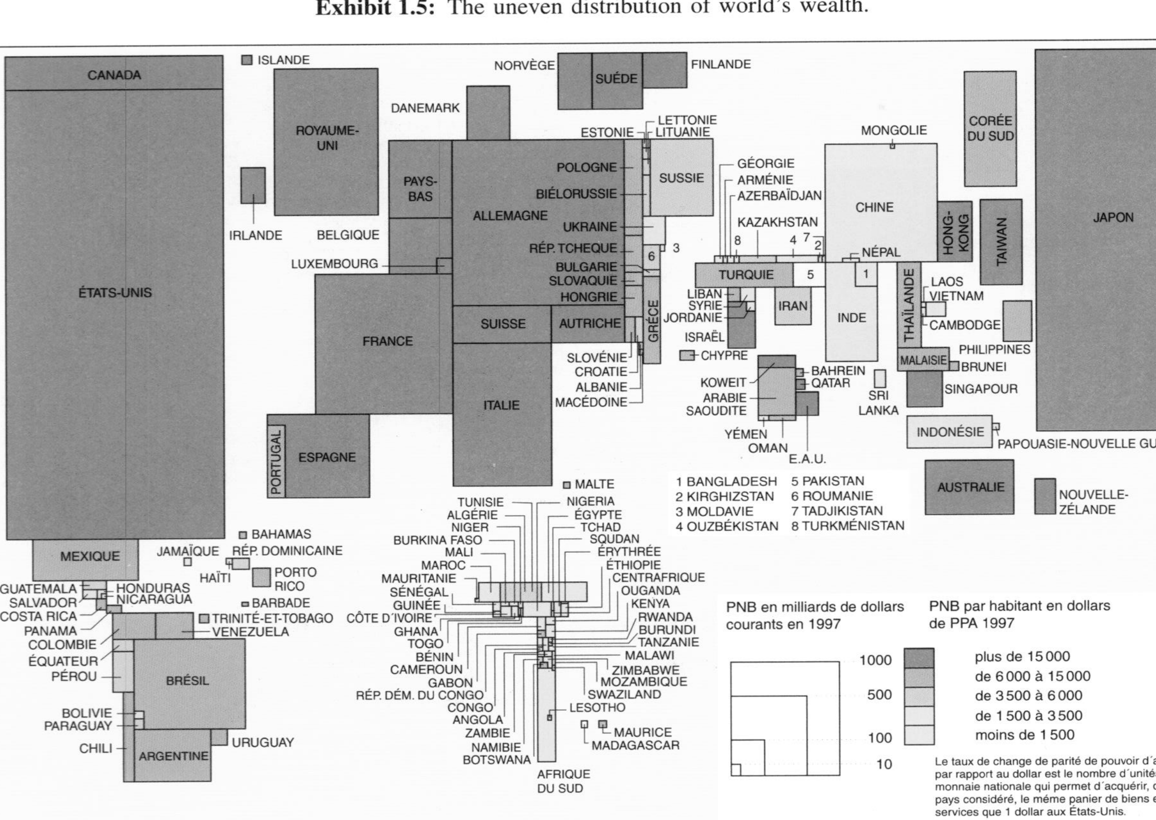

same rate of growth between 1980 and 2000. This debt growth exceeded the growth in personal income, which averaged 5.57% during the same period. We are more leveraged than ever before, and this is bound to aggravate the fall when the economic downturn comes. A falling saving rate is deemed disquieting because, over the last twenty years, it has been associated with a fall in new investment as percentage of GDP. This will ultimately lower the capital stock available to an American worker and with it the productivity of the American worker.

Exhibit 1.6 shows the precipitous decline in the saving rate in the United States. By 2001, the US saving rate was still dismal, while the

Exhibit 1.6: (a) Personal saving rate (percentage). (b) Real personal consumption expenditures (percentage change from preceding period).

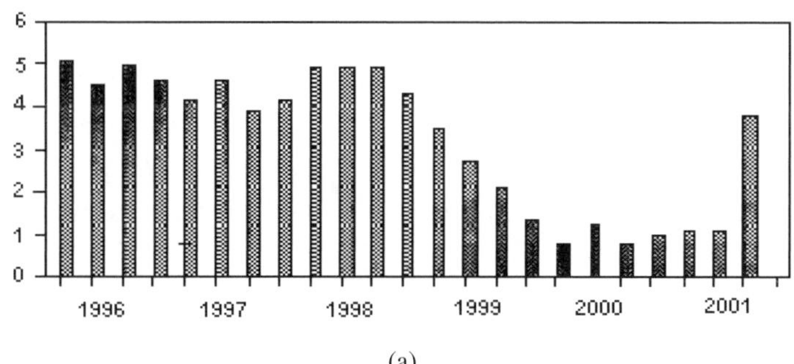

(a)

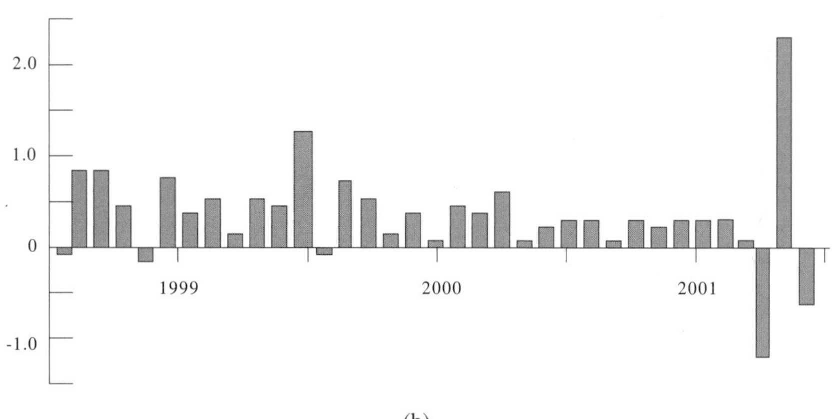

(b)

Source: Bureau of Economic Analysis

average personal saving rate in Europe was 12% and that in Japan was 13.6%. A technical correction is in order, however. Personal saving takes into account wages, dividends, interest and rental income and subtracts taxes and households expenditures on goods and services. The capital gains on stocks and other assets are excluded, however. This makes the saving rate lower than it otherwise would be, and it denied the existence of any "wealth effect", which has been shown to have some influence to one degree or another over the consumption of Americans.

In a recent massive study on the subject by Jonathan A. Parker prepared for N-BER Working Paper Series, the following surprises were disclosed:

1. *Aggregate wealth to income ratio in the United States has actually increased as consumption rose.*
2. *The saving rate including capital gains has not fallen.*
3. *Only one fifth of the increase of consumption to income can be explained by the wealth effect. Between 1994 and 1999, the stock market added over $6 trillion to household wealth. However, even a 10% spending of this addition could increase consumption by $600 billion a year.*
4. *Perhaps federal transfers in the form of Social Security and Medicare are increasing the consumption of the elderly, while relaxed liquidity constraints are allowing the young to consume more of their income. The effective discount rate for the representative agent has actually risen which increases current consumption.*

The low saving rate is a problem, but not apparently as serious a problem as originally thought. The other concern expressed by an increasing minority of economists deals with the distribution of wealth in the United States, especially that resulting from the bull stock market. Exhibit 1.7 shows that the richest 1% of Americans took the lion share (51.4%) of the huge increases in wealth. This skewness in wealth distribution could have long term destabilizing effects on the US economy, but is well beyond the scope of analysis of this book.

We now examine the many considerations for investing in equity securities.

Exhibit 1.7: Percentage of stock shares owned in 1997 by different income groups.

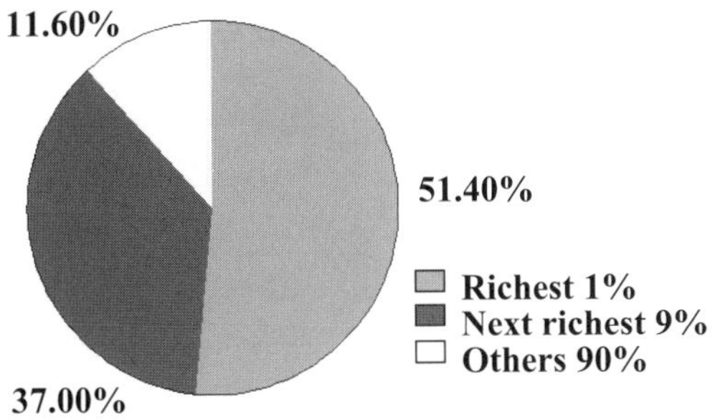

Source: *The Wall Street Journal*, September 13, 1999.

1.2 Stock Ownership Has Never Been Easier

Stock ownership in the United States has soared from merely 2.2 million individuals holding shares in 1900 to almost 80 million people in 1999 holding shares directly or indirectly. The active participation by small investors and their rather steady nerves in the market, particularly in downturns, have contributed to further stabilizing the market and to lowering volatility.

Individual investors execute either through their own accounts, through their advisors and through investment clubs which are proliferating.

Exhibit 1.8 shows the marked increase in the median size of the portfolio unadjusted for inflation. It had reached $27.5 million by the end of 1999. Capital gains may explain much of that increase, as would inflation. The activity level on the NYSE and on the NASDAQ also increased dramatically. A billion-share-day is now common on both venues. The annual volume on the NASDAQ was higher by almost 73 billion shares than that on the NYSE. And the Dow Jones Industrial Average (DJIA) had risen from a 235.41 level in 1950 to 11,497.1 at the end of 1999, an increase of 4800%. This impressive increase led an active participation in the mutual fund industry as well, from $2.5 billion in 1950 to $92.1 billion in 1999.

This is particularly highlighted in the results of the Federal Reserve Board's triennial "Survey of Consumer Finances". Exhibit 1.9 compares these data for 1992, 1995, 1998 and 2001. Note the appreciable rise in an average family's stock holdings. It is not only that over one-half of

Exhibit 1.8: Stock market data.

	1900	1950	1975	1999
Ind. shares owners	2.2 mil.	6.3 mil.	25.3 mil.	79.4 mil.
Median portfolio value	$1200	$3800	$10,100	$27,500
Annual volume				
NYSE	102.4 mil.	524.8 mil.	4693.4 mil.	204 bil.
NASDAQ (started in 1971)			1394 mil.	272.6 bil.
Market capitalization				
NYSE	$3972 mil.	$93.8 bil.	$685.1 bil.	$12.3 tril.
NASDAQ (started in 1971)			$78,190 mil.	$5204 bil.
Dow Jones levels				
High		236.63	888.85	11,568.8
Low		193.94	619.13	9611.33
Close	70.71	235.41	852.41	11,497.1
Size of the mutual fund assets		$2531 mil.	$41,720 mil.	$92,126 mil.

Exhibit 1.9: A comparison of the results of the Federal Reserve Board's triennial "Survey of Consumer Finances".

	1992	1995	1998	2001
Families having stock holdings (direct or indirect*)	36.7%	40.4%	48.9%	51.9%
Median value among families with holdings†	$13,000	$16,900	$27,200	$34,300
Stock holdings as share of				
(a) financial assets	33.7%	39.9%	53.9%	56.0%
(b) total assets	10.7%	14.6%	21.9%	23.5%
Family net-worth†	$61,300	$66,400	$78,000	$81,100
Median family income (before tax)†	$33,000	$35,000	$36,400	$39,900

*Indirect holdings are those in mutual funds, retirement accounts and other managed assets.
†The median values are in 2001 dollars.

Source: Ana M. Aizorbe, Arthur B. Kennickell and Kevin B. Moore: "Recent Changes in US Family Finances: Evidence from the 1998 and 2001 Surveys of Consumer Finances", *Federal Reserve Bulletin*, vol. 86, pp. 1–32, January, 2003.

Exhibit 1.10: Discount brokerages.

Brokerage	Minimum to open account	Average cost per trade
1st Discount Brokerage, Inc.	None	$14.75
1st Global, Inc.	None	$35.00
Access Brokerage Limited	$5000	$29.50
American Express Financial Dir	$15,000	$14.95
Ameritrade Holding Company	$2000	$8.00
Andrew Peck Associates, Inc.	$3000	$13.50
Bank of San Francisco Brokerage	None	$29 + 1.7% (gross)
Bidwell & Company	$2000	$12 (1500 shares or less)
Bright Trading, Inc	None	$0.01/share
Brown & Company	$15,000 (cash account)	$5 + $0.01/share
Bull & Bear Securities, Inc.	$3000	$19.95
Burke, Christensen and Lewin S	None	$13 (5000 shares or less)
Charles Schwab & Co.	$5000	$20.00 (2c/shares over 1000)
CompuTEL Securities	HIGH SECURITY RATE	HIGH SECURITY SITE
CT Market Partner	$15,000	$29 (1000 shares or less) + depends on shares prices
Cutter & Co. Brokerage, Inc.	None	$40
Dashin Securities Co., Ltd.	FOREIGN SITE	FOREIGN SITE
Datek	None	$9.99 (1–5000 shares)
Day-Traders Network	$100,000	N/A
Discount Direct AG	FOREIGN SITE	FOREIGN SITE
DJF Discount Brokerage	None	$35 (100 shares)
DLJdirect	None	$19.95 ($14.95 NYSE/ AMEX only)
Downstate Discounts Direct	None	$30.00 + $0.03/share (up to 1000)
Dreylus Brokerage Services	None	$15.00 (Flat Rate)
E*Trade	$1000	$14.95 (2000 shares or less)
Empire Financial Discounts Direct	$1000	$6.95 (5000 shares or less)

Exhibit 1.10 (*Continued*)

Brokerage	Minimum to open account	Average cost per trade
FCNIS Brokerage	None	$14.95
Fidelity	$5000	$14.95
Financial Discounts Direct	3000 pounds	No handling fee
First Midwest Securities, Inc.	None	$24 (10,000 shares or less)
Firstrade.com	None	$6.95
Freeman Welwood	None	$14.95 (2000 shares)
Frontier Futuras, Inc.	None	$29 (2999 shares or less)
Green Line Investor Services	See TD Waterhouse	See TD Waterhouse
HongKong Bank Discount Tradi	FOREIGN SITE	FOREIGN SITE
Investex Securities Group	$5000 to cover first purchase	$13.95
InvestNet	FOREIGN SITE	FOREIGN SITE
InvesTrade Discount Securities	$2000	$7.95
Jack White & Company	$2000 + $10,000 net worth	See TD Waterhouse
JB Oxford & Company	$2000	$14.50 (1000 shares) + $0.04/share
Killik & Co	None	40 pounds
Livebroker.com	None	$39 (1000 shares) + $0.04/share
Marquette de Bary Co., Inc.	FOREIGN SITE	$50
Midwest Discount Brokers, Inc.	None	$40 (depends on price)
Morgan Stanley Dean Witter	None	$29.95 (1000 shares or less)
Mr. Stock	100% coverage of first purchase	$14.95 (5000 shares or less)
Muriel Sibert & Co.		
National Discount Brokers, Inc.	None	$14.75 (100–2500 shares)
Nestlerode & Co., Inc	None	$52 (1000 shares or less)
Net Investor	$5000	$19.95 + (100 shares)
Netstock Direct Corporation	None	$19.95
Newport Discount Brokerage	None	$19 (100 shares)

Exhibit 1.10 (*Continued*)

Brokerage	Minimum to open account	Average cost per trade
NexTrend	$25,000 (daytraders account)	$12 (5000 shares or less)
OLDE Discount	$500,000 (cash/securities)	$20 ($1–5; 1–100 shares)
Online Trading, Inc.	$100,000	$24.95 (1000 or less)
Pennaiuna & Company	None	$45 (1000 shares or less)
Pont Securities	See TD Waterhouse	See TD Waterhouse
Prime Time Trading, Inc.	5000	Free Trial; $19.95
Quick & Relly	None	$14.95
RML Trading and Stock Cam Ins.	$250,000	$14.95 + $2220/month
Royal Bank Action Direct	None	$40
Sanford Securities, Inc.	None	$19.95
Scotia Discount Brokerage	None	$28
Scottrade	$500 equity	$7.00
Self Trading Securities	$25,000	$9.50 + $0.02/share
Shamrock Financial Services	$5000	$5 (300 shares or less)
Shochet Securities	None	$14.95 (2000 shares or less)
Sovereign Securities	None	$12 (5000 shares or less)
STA Research	None	$14 (5000 shares or less)
Stock Power	None	Direct trade w/ company
Sunlogic Securities	$2000	$15.99 + $0.02/share
SuperTradeUSA	None	$14.95 (5000 shares or less)
Suretrade.com	None	$7.95
T. Rowe Price	$500	$24.95
TD Waterhouse Group	$1000	$19.95
Trade Securities	$50,000	N/A
TradeStar Investments, Inc.	$2000 equity	N/A
Tradewell	$500 (cash account)	$22.00
US RICA Financial Inc.	None	$4.95 + $29.95/month

Exhibit 1.10 (*Continued*)

Brokerage	Minimum to open account	Average cost per trade
Wall Street Access	$10,000	$25 (5000 shares or less)
Wall Street Discount Corporation	None	$19.95
Wall Street Equities, Inc.	$2000	$12.00
WallStreet Electronica Online	$5000	$24.95 (1000 shares or less)
Web Street Securities	$0 (cash account) $2000 (margin)	$14.95 (1000 shares or less)
Westminister Securities Coroporation	None	$39 (1000 shares or less)
White Discount Securities/Thom	$2000 (IRA)	N/A
Wilshire Capital Management	$10,000 (cash/securities)	$20 (0–50 trades) + $300/month
Yamner & Co., Inc.	$50,000 equity	$35 + $0.02/share
York Securities	25% of first purchase	$25.00

*Market Orders Limit orders are on average $2–5 additional costs.
Note: IRA accounts on average requires an initial minimum deposit of $2000.

American families held stocks in 2001, compared to a little over a third in 1992, but also that the proportion of family's assets held in stocks has more than doubled in this period.

The massive interest in the stock market has led to the proliferation of discount brokers, documented in Exhibit 1.10, who offered for the most part discounted trading (execution systems) with little or no investment advice, and often no contact with a broker. Most of the systems allowed for direct orders to be placed by the client using the Internet. Small investors responded with great enthusiasm as the average per unit trading costs fell sharply, as computer and Internet availability and usage soared, as the information about stocks and stock markets proliferated through a multitude of venues (the Internet, television (CNBC, CNN-fn, etc…), newspapers) and as the performance of the stock market left the non-participant feeling left out, if not outright stupid. The psychology of "you cannot be helping yourself and your family if you are out of the market" became dominant. Meanwhile, technology and its costs were getting more accessible and ever cheaper to the point that there currently exist Internet connections that are literally free. By the end of 1999, 40% of stock trades completed by individuals were done online. Some companies have experienced much higher rates of Internet usage for stock purposes. Schwab International gets 70 to 80% of its trading activity from outside the United States through the Internet. Some firms have added even more interesting features in order to facilitate further the use of technology. Ameritrade, a discount broker, now uses InterVoice, a speech-enabled system that allows its customers to act on their investment decisions via telephone using natural speech recognition.

Note that many of the discount brokers documented in Exhibit 1.10 do not require a minimum amount to open an account, and those that do are cutting their minimum on a regular basis. The costs do vary depending on the size of the order, how it is placed, and how much information

Exhibit 1.11: Mean implied roundtrip transaction costs.

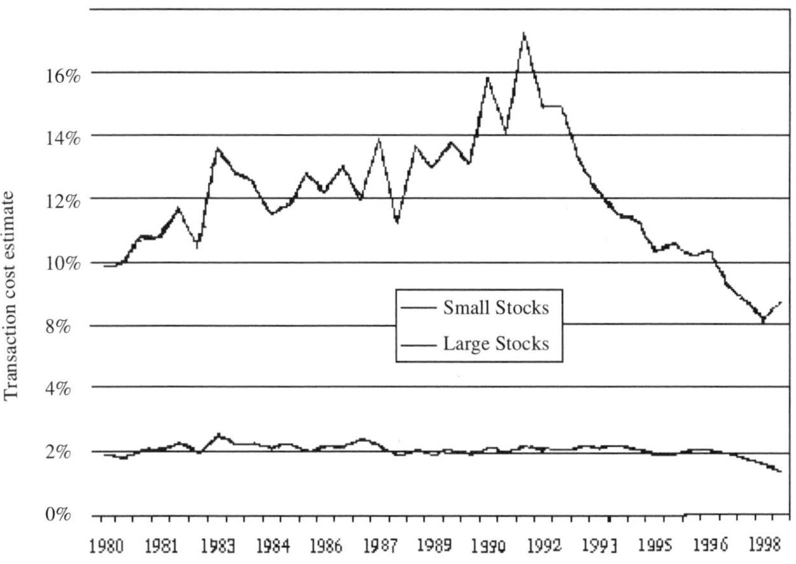

Note: Estimates based on Lesmond, Ogden, Trzcinka, RFS, 1999.

and service components are included in the transaction. Many of these companies have yet to show profitability, and many are said to be on the extinction block. No matter, they never anticipated. The winner in all of this has been the investor, the small one, especially. The mean, implied roundtrip transaction costs (all costs) for small and large stocks have fallen steadily as Exhibit 1.11 shows.

The traditional broker/investment advisor had also to see his preeminent position as the sole, or primary, provider of investment information eroded because of the avalanche of new sources of information, especially on the Internet, available at no cost to practically everyone. Exhibit 1.12 lists some of the most often used sources and the quality of their coverage.

The ability of investors to invest internationally has also been enhanced by technology and with the development of sophisticated exchanges and trading systems all over the world. Exchanges, London and New York especially, have been adding a lot of foreign stocks to their listings. Daily trading in foreign stocks (non-British stocks) account for a third, at least, of all daily trading volume. The New York Stock Exchange (NYSE) has twelve foreign stocks listed directly and 326 stocks listed through ADR's (American Depository Receipts, an alternative "stock certificate" issued in the US against a foreign stock). The latter allows foreign stock values to be denominated in US dollars, but does not eliminate, contrary to public perception, foreign exchange risk, as the returns on the underlying stock are still influenced by exchange rate changes.

The cross listing of securities across exchanges is becoming the order of the day in Europe as the move toward economic and financial integration, one Europe, accelerates. Similar conversions are taking place in the rest of the world as cross listing improves the image of a stock and in the process the interest of the investor in it. Mercedes Corporation saw a major appreciation (about 30%) in the value of its stock the moment it listed on the New York Stock Exchange. The cross-listed securities across financial markets are shown in Exhibit 1.13. The list is very dynamic. It even changes from one day to the next.

All of these developments in the financial markets are a reflection of an incredible movement toward globalization (Exhibit 1.14). Although potent and almost all-inclusive, globalization is not as deep, yet, as many

Exhibit 1.12: Data sources — Fast and costless.

Rank	Name	Location	Content	Degree of thoroughness	Sub	Raw data
1	CompuStat, a.k.a. Research Insight	Computer Labs	Company specific data	10	No	Yes
			Industry specific data	10	No	Yes
2	Data Stream	Computer Labs	Company specific data	10	No	Yes
			Industry specific data	10	No	Yes
			Country specific data	10	No	Yes
			Macroeconomic data	10	No	Yes
Rank	**Name**	**Web site**	**Content**	**Degree of thoroughness**	**Sub**	**Raw data**
1	Bloomberg	www.bloomberg.com	Market information	7	Yes	No
			Macroeconomic data	7		
			Stock quotes and research	7		
			Investment tools	9		
2	CNN Financial	www.cnnfn.com	Market information	8	No	No
			Macroeconomic data	7		
	CNN Money	Money.cnn.com	Stock quotes and research	8		
			Investment tools	6		
3	Quicken	www.quicken.com	Stock quotes and research	8	No	No
			Investment tools	8		
4	Big Charts	www.bigcharts.com	Technical analysis tools	8	No	No

Exhibit 1.12 (*Continued*)

Rank	Name	Web site	Content	Degree of thoroughness	Sub	Raw data
5	CNBC	www.cnbc.com	Market information	9		
			Macroeconomic data	9		
			Stock quotes and research	9		
			Investment tools	6		
6	Yahoo Finance	finance.yahoo.com	Market news	6	No	Yes
			Marcoeconomic data	6		
			Stock quotes and research	7		
			Investment tools	3		
7	Hoovers	www.hoovers.com	Stock quotes and research	10	Yes	No
8	Red Herring	www.redherring.com	IPO data	10	Yes	No
9	Motley Fool	www.fool.com	Personal investing education	9	No	No
10	Quote.com	www.quote.com	Real time quote and news	9	Yes	No
11	SEC	www.sec.gov	Company filings	10	No	No
12	Prophet Finance	www.prohpetcharts.com	Technical analysis tools	10	No	No

Exhibit 1.13: (a) The country-to-country distribution of foreign listings.

This table provides the country-to-country frequency distribution of cross listings as of 1998 obtained from the individual exchanges. The total sample is comprised of 2367 overseas listings. The listings in the US include foreign companies traded only on the NYSE and NASDAQ. Only those countries with non-zero sample cross listings are listed as host markets.

	Host country																									
Home country	**Australia**	**Austria**	**Belgium**	**Brazil**	**Canada**	**Denmark**	**Finland**	**France**	**Germany**	**H. Kong**	**Ireland**	**Italy**	**Japan**	**Luxem.**	**Malaysia**	**Nether.**	**N. Zealand**	**Norway**	**Peru**	**Singapore**	**S. Africe**	**Spain**	**Sweden**	**Switz.**	**UK**	**USA**
Argentina				1										3										1	1	12
Australia					5				3				4	1			25			2				2	9	30
Austria			1					1	8																	
Belgium								7	3					6		7		1		2			1	5	2	1
Brazil														5											1	21
Canada	3		7					6	2				1			3				1	1			6	21	213
Chile																										21
Colombia														3												2
Czech R.																									4	
Denmark							1							1				2					1	1	3	6
Finland								1	1														3		2	4
France			11						8			1	2	3		10						1	3	5	6	23
Germany		15	8					13				2	9	6		13				1		2	1	31	10	11
Greece														1		1		1							8	5
H. Kong	3				1								1					1		4						24
Hungary		2												5											5	1
India														48											17	
Indonesia														1						1					2	4
Ireland																									56	17
Israel																									4	84
Italy			2					4	5							3						1				22
Japan			5		1			31	54					21		19				6				15	29	28
Korea		1												12											12	3
Luxem.			2					4	1							2							1	2	2	4
Malaysia													1							1					4	
Mexico																										31
Nether.		6	14					13	23				1	8						1		1	1	19	17	36
N. Zealand	19																								1	4
Norway						2		1	2							1							2	1	5	5
Peru																										3
Philippines														6												1
Poland														1											9	
Portugal									1																1	4
Singapore	2														3										1	3
S. Africa	1							15	6					4										5	37	13
Spain								4	4				4			3								2	4	5
Sweden						5		3	4				2					2						4	12	16
Switz.		1	1					5	12				4	2		1									2	5
Taiwan														15						1					13	3
Thailand														2											1	
Turkey														1											6	
UK	4				4	1		15	11	1	16		8	2		12		4		2	3			5		89
USA	5	2	34		29			33	43				23	3		75		4	2	1			5	74	92	
Venezuela					1									1												3

Exhibit 1.13: (b) Aggregate market data and accounting standards.

This table provides aggregate economic, equity market, and exchange listing standards data for the sample countries. GDP is from the 1999 *CIA World Factbook*. Market capitalization is from the International Federation of Stock Exchanges (FIBV). Volatility is the market's estimate of the standard deviation of monthly US dollar denominated returns over the period 1990–1998. Turnover is the ratio of average trading volume of domestic shares in 1998 over the home market capitalization reported by either the FIBV or respective stock exchange. Aggregate imports and exports for each country are also from the 1999 *CIA World Factbook*. IAS GAAP is a dummy variable which is set to one if the country allows foreign firms to list with IAS GAAP-based financial statements and zero otherwise. US GAAP is a dummy variable which is set to one if the country allows foreign firms to list with US GAAP-based financial statements and zero otherwise.

	Market size		**Liquidity**		**Trade**	**Listing standards**	
	GDP ($B)	**Market cap ($B)**	**Volatility (%)**	**Turnover (%)**	**Imports ($B)**	**IAS GAAP**	**US GAAP**
Argentina	374	45	15.71	51	32	0	0
Australia	393	329	5.34	53	61	1	0
Austria	185	36	6.27	42	66	1	1
Belgium	236	246	4.27	28	137	1	0
Brazil	1035	161	16.27	66	58	0	0
Canada	688	543	4.69	59	202	0	0
Chile	185	52	8.11	7	17	0	0
Columbia	255	11	10.16	11	14	1	1
Czech Rep.	117	10	9.66	206	27	0	0
Denmark	124	99	4.65	65	46	1	1
Finland	103	155	7.90	55	31	1	0
France	1320	992	5.10	66	255	1	0
Germany	1813	1094	4.58	138	426	1	0
Greece	143	80	11.64	83	28	1	0
Hong Kong	168	344	8.66	62	208	0	0
Hungary	75	14	12.55	436	23	1	0
India	1689	93	9.93	52	41	1	0
Indonesia	602	22	13.93	57	24	1	0

Exhibit 1.13 *(Continued)*

	Market size		Liquidity		Trade	Listing standards	
	GDP ($B)	Market cap ($B)	Volatility (%)	Turnover (%)	Imports ($B)	IAS GAAP	US GAAP
Ireland	339	67	6.05	60	43	0	0
Israel	101	39	8.07	34	26	0	1
Italy	1181	570	6.70	102	202	1	0
Japan	2903	2440	7.93	34	319	1	0
Korea	584	115	13.13	207	94	0	0
Luxembourg	14	38	4.89	4	10	1	1
Malaysia	215	96	11.40	30	59	1	0
Mexico	815	92	10.26	27	111	1	0
Netherlands	348	603	4.11	71	142	1	1
New Zealand	61	25	6.33	48	13	1	1
Norway	109	46	7.45	66	37	1	1
Peru	112	10	9.87	23	10	1	0
Philippines	270	35	11.15	32	29	0	0
Poland	263	21	14.79	58	38	0	0
Portugal	145	63	6.45	82	34	1	0
Singapore	91	97	6.53	64	133	1	0
South Africa	290	151	7.45	27	27	1	0
Spain	645	402	6.27	170	132	0	0
Sweden	175	279	6.95	70	67	0	0
Switzerland	191	689	4.97	100	95	1	1
Taiwan	363	261	12.36	314	114	0	0
Thailand	369	34	13.01	69	73	1	1
Turkey	425	34	17.14	143	47	1	1
UK	1252	2373	4.48	47	304	1	0
USA	8511	12,926	3.68	152*	912	0	1
Venezuela	194	8	15.28	19	12	0	0

*The turnover rate in the US is the market capitalization weighted turnover rates on the NYSE and NASDAQ.

Exhibit 1.14: Globalization — Virtuous cycle.

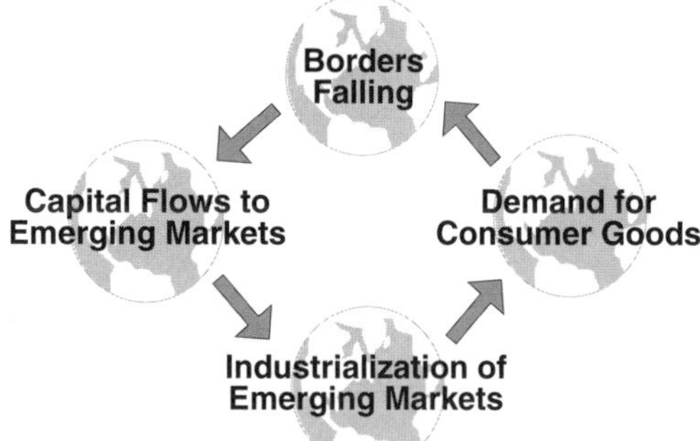

assume it to be. There are still numerous regional monopolies, and considerable differences in rates and transactions costs across national borders. The disappearance of the power of the state is premature despite the fact that many transactions across national borders are seamless.

The talk now is shifting, interestingly, from globalization into regionalism. The Europeans, the Asians and the Americans are all becoming more regional in their focus. We may well be moving toward a tri-polar world where borders are still relevant, but are less relevant only within a specific region. The North American Free Trade Agreement (NAFTA) has allowed for this kind of development between the member states (US, Mexico, and Canada), as has the Maastricht treaty between the member states of the European Union.

1.3 Markets and Their Indices

Each market is like the human body. Complex as it is, you need not examine every part in order to determine whether it is healthy or not. You are generally satisfied with taking its temperature, or the heartbeat or the blood pressure, or a combination of these three indicators to determine its health. Similarly, the health of the stock market and its direction may be inferred from a small sample of stocks included in an average or an index. The average is simply the adjusted arithmetic average of a carefully selected group of stocks, and the index is the value of a carefully selected group of stocks in relation to a base period chosen with history and efficiency in mind. Typically, the standard value picked for the base period is 100.

The most famous and the oldest of the averages is the Dow Jones Industrial Average (DJIA) made up of thirty stocks, most of which are listed on the New York Stock Exchange and representing a wide set of industries without, unfortunately, being very representative. The average is price weighted which means that you add the price of the component stocks and you divide by the divisor, which is the number of shares adjusted for stock splits, stock dividends, etc. The higher price stocks will have, by the very nature of the mathematics, a greater impact on the movement of the average.

Despite the obvious drawbacks, the DJIA remains the most followed average (index) in the world. It is well inculcated in the minds of investors as it dates back to 1896, as it is constantly updated during trading hours, as it is published in every financial publication and through every financial information transmission medium, and as it is an average constantly pushed by *The Wall Street Journal*, the dominant business publication owned by the Dow Jones News Services. Also, the Dow theory which has many adherents in the wild world of technical analysts relies on the DJIA and on the Dow Jones Transportation Average (DJTA). The transportation average covers 20 stocks in the airline and railroad sectors and is used as a tool for the confirmation of developments (trends) in the DJIA. The Dow Jones Company has developed averages similar to the DJIA for the world and for many of the leading financial markets of the world. They are reported on regularly in *The Wall Street Journal*.

The second most popular market indicator is the Standard and Poor's 500 index (S&P 500). This index is value weighted. The index is calculated by summing across the total market value of each of the 500 shares that make up the index, and dividing by the value of the index in the base period (1950). The reservation about this index is its representativeness of the US economy and its mathematical construct that allows for a larger impact for price movements in the high capitalization stocks in the index.

The third most commonly followed index is the NASDAQ index which contains the value of all shares of each company traded on the NASDAQ divided by the base period. Like the S&P 500, it is a value-weighted index (value being the market value of all the shares), where companies with the highest capitalization have a disproportionate impact on the movement of the index.

The NASDAQ is the where the "hottest" companies in America are traded. It is where the tech companies are traded and represents to many the future of America's industry. These companies include Microsoft, eBay, Dell, Yahoo, etc... The NASDAQ is also a value-weighted index, like the S&P, and is an index.

The conservative investor with a rather narrow portfolio of traditional stocks (old time securities) would look at the DJIA as a good indicator of price movements for the portfolio. The investor with a broader portfolio would look at the S&P 500. That with a high tech portfolio would look at the NASDAQ for direction or at any of its subparts as shown in Exhibit 1.15. The specific industry indices are very helpful for those who do not have a diversified portfolio across sectors. It is wise to look at all of the indices and try to develop a sense of where the market is. One should also consider whether the market is advancing or falling based on heavy or weak volume, and whether the advance is persistent in face of some bad news, or some good news, if the direction is downward.

The financial markets have developed instruments that track these and other indices that are traded just like any stock is. The NASDAQ is tracked by a stock called QQQ, which mirrors its movements. We discuss these issues in the next chapter.

The market indicators are not limited to these three. Exhibit 1.15 presents a rather exhaustive list of indices, their coverage and the method used for their calculation.

Exhibit 1.15: Major stock market indices, their coverage and the method used for their calculation.

Market index	Coverage	Equation
Dow Jones Industrial Average	30 "blue-chip" US stocks	The sum of all the closing prices of the component stocks divided by the divisor (30 adjusted for stock splits and stock dividends, etc.).
Dow Jones Transportation Average	20 stocks of airline, trucking, railroad, and shipping business	The sum of all the closing prices of the component stocks divided by the divisor (20 adjusted for stock splits and stock dividends, etc.).
Dow Jones Utilities Average	15 stocks of gas and electric utilities industries	The sum of all the closing prices of the component stocks divided by the divisor (15 adjusted for stock splits and stock dividends, etc.).
Dow Jones Global Average	3000 separate indexes; 2900 companies in 33 countries, ten world regions, nine market sectors containing 122 industry groups	The sum of all the closing prices of the component stocks divided by the divisor (3000 adjusted for stock splits and stock dividends, etc.).
Dow Jones STOXX Average	Joint venture with French, German, and Swiss stock exchanges	The sum of all the closing prices of the component stocks divided by the divisor (number of adjusted stocks in joint ventures).
NYSE Composite	Includes subgroups: industrial, transportation, utility, and finance	Tracks aggregate market value (adjusted to eliminate capitalization changes, new listings, and delistings). The sum of individual market values divided by adjusted base market value multiplied by base value set at 50.00 on December 31, 1965.
NASDAQ 100	Includes major industry groups: computer hardware and software, retail, telecommunications, and biotechnology	Market-value weighted: sum of the capitalization of the component stocks divided by the base period value or real value accounting for inflationary effects.

Exhibit 1.15 (*Continued*)

Market index	Coverage	Equation
NASDAQ Composite	5000 domestic companies and non-US based common stocks	Market-value weighted: sum of the capitalization of the component stocks divided by the base period value or real value accounting for inflationary effects.
NASDAQ Financial 100	100 largest financial companies	Market-value weighted: sum of the capitalization of the component stocks divided by the base period value or real value accounting for inflationary effects.
NASDAQ Bank	All types of banks	Market-value weighted: sum of the capitalization of the component stocks divided by the base period value or real value accounting for inflationary effects.
NASDAQ Biotechnology	100+ companies engaged in biomedical research	Market-value weighted: sum of the capitalization of the component stocks divided by the base period value or real value accounting for inflationary effects.
NASDAQ Computer	600+ computer hardware and software companies	Market-value weighted: sum of the capitalization of the component stocks divided by the base period value or real value accounting for inflationary effects.
NASDAQ Insurance	100 insurance companies: life, health, property, etc…	Market-value weighted: sum of the capitalization of the component stocks divided by the base period value or real value accounting for inflationary effects.
NASDAQ Transportation	100+ railroads, trucking, etc…	Market-value weighted: sum of the capitalization of the component stocks divided by the base period value or real value accounting for inflationary effects.

Exhibit 1.15 (*Continued*)

Market index	Coverage	Equation
NASDAQ Telecommunications	170+ telecommunications companies	Market-value weighted: sum of the capitalization of the component stocks divided by the base period value or real value accounting for inflationary effects.
NASDAQ National Market Industrial	2000 agricultural, mining, construction, etc…	Market-value weighted: sum of the capitalization of the component stocks divided by the base period value or real value accounting for inflationary effects.
NASDAQ Industrial	3000 agricultural, mining, construction, etc…	Market-value weighted: sum of the capitalization of the component stocks divided by the base period value or real value accounting for inflationary effects.
S&P 500 Composite	–	Price performance and dividend yield.
S&P Midcap 400	Midsize company	–
S&P 100	(OEX) large company US stock market performance	Market capitalization-weighed index.
AMEX Composite	Any company	Aggregate market value relative to aggregate value: closing price times number of outstanding stocks. Not altered by stock splits, stock dividends, trading halts, or new listings.
Wilshire 5000 Equity	Performance of all US headquartered equity securities (7000 capitalization weighted security returns)	Closing price times outstanding of all stocks.
Wilshire Large Cap 750	Large stocks	Market capitalization-weighted portfolio.

Exhibit 1.15 *(Continued)*

Market index	Coverage	Equation
Wilshire Mid Cap 500	Mid-sized stocks	Cap-weighted: combination of 500 large and small stocks from 501st largest in Wilshire 5000 to the 1000th largest.
Wilshire Small Cap 1750	Small stocks	Cap-weighted: from 751–2500 by market capitalization.
Wilshire Micro Cap	Small stocks	Cap-weighted: bottom half of Wilshire 5000.
Wilshire Large Value	Large-cap stocks	Market cap weighted index from Wilshire Large Cap 750.
Wilshire Large Growth	Large-cap stocks	Market cap weighted index from Wilshire Large Cap 750.
Wilshire Mid Cap Value	Mid-cap stocks	Market cap weighted index from Wilshire Mid Cap 500.
Wilshire Mid Cap Growth	Mid-cap stocks	Market cap weighted index from Wilshire Mid Cap 500.
Wilshire Small Value	Small-cap stocks	Market cap weighted index from Wilshire Small Cap 1750.
Wilshire Small Growth	Small-cap stocks	Market cap weighted index from Wilshire Small Cap 1750.
Wilshire All Value	Measures all value stocks	Combination of all stocks in Wilshire Large Value and Wilshire Small Value.
Wilshire All Growth	All growth stocks	Combination of all stocks in Wilshire Large Growth and Wilshire Small Growth.
FORTUNE 500	500 biggest companies in US (in FORTUNE 500)	Market capitalization-weighted index.
FORTUNE e-50	50 companies in Internet sector	Closing price times number of outstanding stocks.

Exhibit 1.15 (*Continued*)

Market index	Coverage	Equation
Frank Russell 3000	3000 largest US companies based on total market capitalization	Capitalization-weighted index: (adjustments made for cross-ownership) capitalization of the component stocks divided by the base period value (set at 100.00 in 1979).
Frank Russell 1000	1000 largest companies in Russell 3000; top tier of domestic equity market, or companies with market value of greater than $300 million	Capitalization-weighted index: (adjustments made for cross-ownership) capitalization of the component stocks divided by the base period value (set at 100.00 in 1979).
Frank Russell Midcap	800 smallest companies in Russell 1000	Capitalization-weighted index: (adjustments made for cross-ownership) capitalization of the component stocks divided by the base period value (set at 100.00 in 1979).
Philadelphia Semiconductor	16 US stocks from design, distribution, manufacture, and sale of semiconductors	Price weighted index: benchmarked against the value at which it is originally set.
Morgan Stanley 35	Measures nine technology subsectors from computer service to semiconductor capital equipment	Equal-weighted index has been set to 200.00 as of close of trading on December 16, 1994. Rebalanced annually.

1.4 Types of Accounts

An investor typically opens with his or her broker either a cash account or a margin account. The cash account requires settlement of the fall value of the purchase or the delivery of securities in the case of a sale within three business days. Buying on margin means that one borrows a portion of the purchase price. The minimum cash currently required is 50%. The remaining 50% are effectively being borrowed from the broker at a rate tied to the prime rate.

The initial margin requirement is set by the Federal Reserve System (the Fed) under Regulation T. The margin is also set by the National Association of Securities Dealers (NASD), and by the brokerage firm. The initial maximum borrowing allowed against a position is set by the Fed. It is 50% of the value of the investment. The NASD sets the "maintenance" requirements, that is, the minimum required equity level in the margin account before a margin call is made by the broker and additional cash is deposited by the investor in her account. The intent here is for the investment firm to keep some "collateral" by the investor against his position and never allow him to "play" purely with borrowed money. A fall in the value of the investment below the amount borrowed jeopardizes the position of the investment house because the remaining collateral has a value in this case that will not cover the loan even if the entire investment is liquidated. The margin call will protect against such a possibility well before it happens.

Also, a securities firm may require more (never less) than 50% in margin for securities it deems highly volatile. This is to protect itself against a market move that negatively impacts the position of the investor.

Let us now offer an example. Assume that an investor purchases $30,000 worth of securities in her margin account. Her position at $t = 0$ (at the moment of purchase, zero time) is as follows:

cash (equity)	$15,000
borrowed funds	$15,000
total value of investment	$30,000

Assuming that at $t = 2$ (two days after the purchase) the market value of the portfolio falls to $16,000. The position of the investor is now as follows:

cash	$1000
borrowing (constant until the position is closed)	$15,000
total value of investment	$16,000

But, the NASD requires that the minimum margin does not fall below 25% of the original value of the position. That is, the customer's equity cannot fall below $7500 ($30,000 *25%). Therefore, the customer would receive a margin call for $6500 ($7500–$1000 (existing equity)).

Should the margin call not be met, the investment firm may liquidate an equivalent amount (almost always higher than the amount dictated by the 25%, bordering on the 30%) from the investor's holdings in the affected security. The investment firm may grant an extension to a client to meet the margin call.

The holder of the margin account must note that the extension is at the option of the firm that leverage works both ways. You double up on the upside if you are holding a long position. But, you may lose on the downside more than your initial cash commitment. The investment firm could also sell securities in your account without notice to you in order to settle an unanswered margin call. Margin accounts are therefore risky.

It must be pointed out further that certain transactions, like short sales, can only be executed in the margin account. Almost every brokerage firm requires additional documentation and confirmations for their trading of options and futures contracts in their accounts.

1.5 Types of Orders

Buy or sell orders differ in terms of the time limit, price limit, discretion of the broker handling the order, and nature of the position. All of these are fodder in the arsenal of Internet traders. There is no broker to guide them if they wish to receive the lowest commission costs. The sites of the discount brokers are very user-friendly in this regard.

Time limit orders are of two types: time-limited orders and good-'til-canceled orders (GTC). If not executed, a time-limited order expires at the end of the specified time period (usually a day). A GTC order is in effect unless cancelled by the investor.

The price limits available to the investor are as follows:

1. **Market order:** The "limit" here is set, in a way, by the market. The investor buys at the ask and sells at the bid. Every stock has a quoted bid and a quoted ask. The bid is always less than the ask. The difference between the bid and the ask is referred to as the spread. The investor could pay more than the observed ask price, however, as the market may have shifted by the time the order is executed. The ask price used for execution may be higher or lower than the one observed by the trader. Market orders are the quickest but not necessarily the cheapest way to buy or sell a security.
2. **Limit order:** The investor using a limit order specifies the maximum buy price or the minimum sale price at which the transaction will be consummated.
3. **Stop order:** A stop order is an order to buy or sell a security when a certain price is reached or passed. A stop order can be used on the sell or on the buy side. A stop order to sell is treated as a market order after the stop price is reached or passed if the stock is listed on the NYSE. However, a limit may be specified. Stop orders are used in order to preserve a level of profit in a security, to purchase a security as it begins a vigorous upward movement, or to protect the investor from loss.

   An investor who purchased a stock at 50 and watched it appreciate to 90 may wish to "lock in" at least 3–5 points if the stock begins to show weakness. This is done by placing a stop sell order at, say, 85. This order, however, does not guarantee a sale at 85, for the stock can fall substantially below 85 before the position of the investor is closed. Another disadvantage of a stop order emanates from the unpredictable nature of the stock market. The stock may fall below 86 causing the order to be executed, and the stock may then reverse course and rise to 100. The investor in this case would have missed a 10-point appreciation in the price of the stock.

   An investor who had just purchased a security that began to show weakness after the purchase date may wish to place a stop-loss (sell) order at below the current market price in order to limit the potential loss in the security. Similarly, an investor with a short position (a position intended to profit from a decline in securities price (see next section)) would place a stop-buy order at above currently prevailing prices to gain protection against an appreciation in the price of the underlying security that causes a loss in a short position.

4. **Discretionary order:** This type of order gives the broker discretion over when, at what price, and how an order is executed. The broker is liable if negligence is proved in the event a "good" opportunity in the market is missed. No investor should be encouraged to issue such an order as it is unwise as a long run proposition.

1.6 Types of Positions

Two positions in securities are available to the investor: a long position and a short position.

A long position represents actual ownership of the security regardless of whether personal funds, leverage, or both are used in its purchase. Profits are realized through appreciation in the price of the security. In derivative contracts, options and futures, a long position represents a commitment to buy (a call option) or to sell (a put option) the underlying security, but does in no way represent an actual position in the underling asset. The long position is nothing more than a commitment to do something in the case of derivatives.

A short position, on the other hand, involves a sale first, followed by a purchase at, it is hoped, a lower price. The anatomy of a short sale is illustrated in Exhibit 1.16. The process begins with a sale of a borrowed security from the investment broker, who ordinarily holds a substantial number of shares in street name and/or who has access to the desired security from other investment brokers. The securities must be borrowed as the settlement of the transaction (the delivery of shares and the payment by the buyer) must be done within three business days. But the trader is "short" (does not own the security). That is why the security is borrowed. The short position holder owes the shares to the broker and

Exhibit 1.16: The anatomy of a short sale.

ABC Corp. is selling at $100 per share, and you think it will go lower. You sell 100 shares short at $100.

Proceeds

= $10,000, less commission

You deposit 50% of the sale price, or $5000 in your margin account.

Your broker borrows 100 shares from another broker to make delivery to the buyer of your 100 shares, using the proceeds of $10,000 as collateral.

Enter a stop-loss order at 115. If the stock price rises against you, your loss is limited to $1500, since your broker will buy 100 shares at 115 to cover your short sale and close you out.

If the stock price drops, ride it down, shorting more stocks as deposits in your 50% margin account are freed. For example, if the stock drops to 50, you need only $2500 to maintain your deposit. The other $2500 is available to back another 100 shorted sales.

If the stock price drops, ride it down, shorting more stocks as deposits in your 50% margin account are freed. For example, if the stock drops to 50, you need only $2500 to maintain your deposit. The other $2500 is available to back another 100 shorted sales.

When you think that the stock has hit bottom, instruct your broker to cover by buying 100 shares and closing you out. If you sell at 50, your profit is $5000 less commissions.

Source: Taken from the October 26, 1981 issue of *Business Week* with special permission.

nothing more. Once he decides to cover the short position, that is, buy back the shares, he will deliver the purchased shares to the broker. This will constitute a full settlement of the "loan" outstanding. The short owns a certain number of shares to the broker, and not a certain sum of money.

The reader must keep in mind, however, that not every security can be sold short and not every country allows short positions in some securities or in any security. Listed securities in the US are all eligible, but only the more risk-averse short sellers are more likely to use some vehicle to limit their loss in case the price of the security rises instead of falls. One way to protect a short position is to use the stop-buy order discussed in the preceding section. Other ways to protect a short position are discussed in Chapter 8. The stop-buy order is placed at 15%, e.g., above the price at which the short sale was established and is usually reduced ("trail") as the stock price declines. After the stock price has fallen sufficiently, the short position is covered; that is, the stock is bought at the prevailing market price and is returned to the investment broker to settle the loan of shares. The investor could have elected to increase the size of his or her short position as the stock price moved in the right direction.

So, what is in it for the brokerage house to lend the stock to the holder of the short position?

- The commission revenue on the sell and on the buy side.
- The stocks held in street name do nothing for the revenue of the broker unless they are put to use. Lending them is one way to activate the shares. Since the trade is done in a margin account, the trader will then be borrowing money from the broker (up to 50 P/D of the value of the transaction). The broker will charge interest on the loan. The interest is a function of the risk profile of the investor. The riskiness of the position of the brokerage house is limited through marking to market. As the price of the stock rises, that is, the short is losing money, the broker asks the short to post more margin (pay more money). The money in the account at any point in time should cover the loss in the event the short decides to close his position.
- The net proceeds from the sale of the stock borrowed from the broker are not, typically, released to the short. They are held in the account of the short. The broker could use the money in the short accounts to earn income on the money through money market investments, typically overnight lending to other financial institutions.

The short position in the case of derivative contracts, one must note, translates into a commitment (creating an obligation on oneself by the short position holder to deliver something or to take delivery of something) opposite that of the long. No shares are being borrowed here. There is simply a contractual commitment to do something: to satisfy the long.

Three facts must be kept in mind with regard to short positions:

1. The security, if qualified, must be available to be borrowed. This is not usually a problem.

2. Short selling can only be effected on an "uptick"; that is, the price at which the short position is established must be a price that is higher than that on the preceding transaction. An order to sell short at 59 1/2 could not be transacted unless the 59 1/2 is an uptick, that is, the 59 1/2 follows, say, a trade at 59 1/4.
3. The short seller is liable for the dividends on the stocks borrowed.

As the above scenario makes clear, a short position is ordinarily established if an investor is bearish on the stock. An appreciation in the price of the stock after the short sale would produce a loss because the borrowed share would have to be replaced at a higher price. A "bad market" is, therefore, not an excuse to stay out of the stock market. In fact, there is no such thing as a bad market, there is only the wrong position in a market. Furthermore, short selling is not necessarily riskier than a long position. The probability of a decline in the price of a security could be significantly higher than that of an appreciation in its price at a certain point in time.

Short sales can also be used to lock in profits in a long position and to postpone the tax liability from one tax year to another. The former use is best illustrated with an example.

A trader with a long position established at $50 a share would have a book gain of $20 per share if the stock trades at $70. At $70, the trader may well decide to go short against the box (the box refers to the fact that actual shares are actually owned by the trader) as one form of protection if, e.g., the volatility in the price of the stock increases from its historical level.

In general, if an investor is convinced that the security is a good investment, but still concerned about its downside risk, the investor can use one of the following methods to buy varying levels of protection:

- Sell the stock and buy it later at a lower price. The danger here is that immediately after the sale, the stock may move vigorosly upward instead of falling in price.
- Place a stop-sell order. The advantages and the disadvantages of this type of order were discussed in the previous section.
- Buy a put option or sell a call option (see Chapter 8).
- Go short against the box, that is, establish a short position for the same number of shares held long.

The last method would require a short position at $70. The investor now has perfectly offsetting positions. Every $1 appreciation in the price of the stock yields profits of $1 per share in the long position and a simultaneous $1 loss in the short position. The reverse is true if the price of the stock falls by $1.

In the event of a price decline, the investor's costs of protection are the transactions costs incurred when the short position is established and when it is covered. These costs are likely to be lower than those resulting from depreciation in the price of the security. In the case of price appreciation, the investor would incur the same costs as above and would forego in addition the appreciation in the price of the security. The sooner the short position is covered, the smaller the foregone profit from a price appreciation will be.

Short selling, if wisely used, should prove to be a valuable tool in portfolio management. Short selling in conjunction with current or expected long positions has proved to be of great value to hedgers, spreaders, and arbitragers in the fixed securities and futures markets. This should become clearer from the chapters to follow.

1.7 Dates to Remember

Three dates are important in trading securities:

1. **Trade date:** The trade date is the date when the transaction is consummated.

"I hear things that go bump in the night. I think it's my investments hitting rock bottom."
GLASBERGEN
Copyright 2002 by Randy Glasbergen www.glasbergen.com

2. **Settlement date:** The settlement date refers to the date when the transaction is settled. For stocks and bonds, it is the third business day from the trade date.
3. **Ex-dividend date:** This is the date on which the investor buys a stock with our dividend. The recently declared dividend belongs to the seller of the stock. The ex-dividend date is the fourth business day prior to the record date (the date at which the actual ownership of the stock is confirmed by the corporation).

Open buy and sell stop orders and sell stop-limit orders are reduced by the value of the dividend on the ex-dividend date. Both the stop price and the limit price (if any) are reduced by the dividend.

1.8 Conclusion

No matter the investor's level of confidence in her choices, it is advisable to always remember that an ounce of care is better than a pound of cure. Beware of those promising you the moon. Beware of those who only speak of doom. Even the chairman of the Federal Reserve System is often wrong about the stock market. He warned us all in 1996 about irrational exuberance and the bubble it was creating in asset prices. The interpretation was that that bubble will burst soon. All the market did after that was to take off. No one is discounting his insights fully, but the market is calling its own tune and has been performing admirably, generally speaking. The lessons from the depression to some are that it was caused by asset price bubbles. There is no question they were a factor. The driving factors were fiscal and trade policies, and the unwise Fed policies.

An investor is best advised to recall the twelve golden rules of investing:

1. Never invest in anything you do not understand.
2. You cannot be right if the market is telling you you are wrong. The market is always right.
3. Do not just look at returns. Consider always the risk. In fact try to exaggerate the risk a bit before making the decision. There

Exhibit 1.17

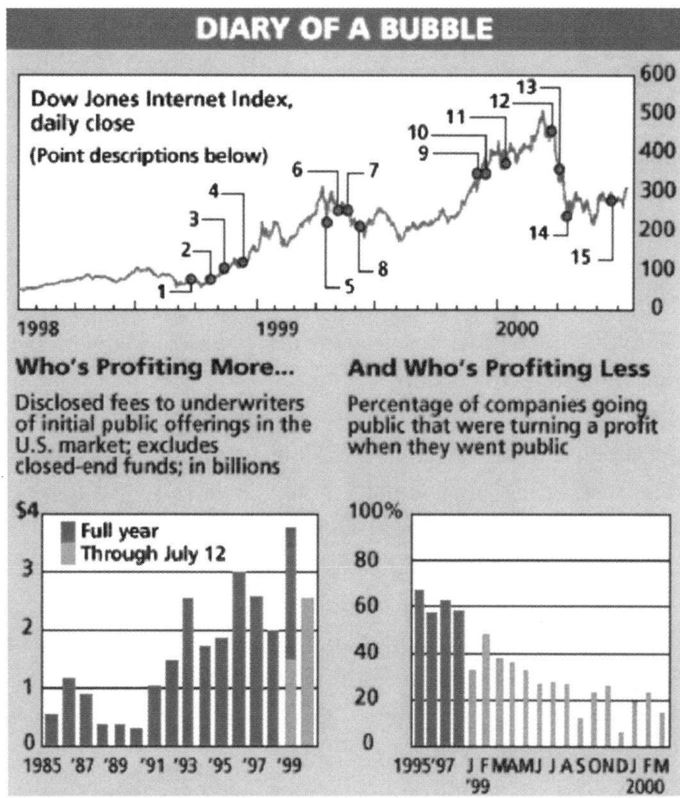

Source: WSJ Market Data Group; Thomson Financial Securities Data; Sanford C. Bernstein

1. eBay's IPO
2. Theglobe.com postpones its IPO because of market turmoil
3. Theglobe.com IPO sets then-record for first day price gain of 606%
4. Henry Blodget puts $400 price target on Amazon.com
5. E*Trade's new TV campaign begins
6. SEC chairman Arthur Levitt criticizes online brokers' ads
7. eToys' IPO
8. Drkoop.com goes public
9. FreeMarkets almost triples filing range on its IPO to $40–42
10. VA Linux IPO sets new record for first day price gain of 698%
11. AOL announces merger with Time Warner
12. Accountants question Drkoop.com's ability to remain "going concern"
13. Settlement talks collapse in Microsoft antitrust case
14. Higher-than-expected inflation number released
15. Lehman credit analyst questions Amazon's viability

are a lot of risks hidden in the income statements, the balance sheets and in their footnotes, and there are a lot of risks inherent in every sector of the US economy. Exhibit 1.17 should give you a reason to pause, "...between March 10 and May 23 (2000), Internet stocks as a group, valued at $1.4 trillion at their March peak, have lost 40% of that — erasing almost as much paper wealth as the 1987 crash." (*The Wall Street Journal*, July 14, 2000)

4. Run with a winning position. Get rid of losing ones.
5. Remember that no one has ever beaten the market consistently. Warren Buffet lost money in 1999 while the NASDAQ was setting an all time high.
6. If it sounds too good to be true, it invariably is.
7. Never invest before you figure out what your objectives are.
8. The market has always paid more for those who stuck with it in the long run than for those who tried to outsmart it.
9. What is perfect for your neighbor is not necessarily even good for you.
10. Remember that in the best of markets there are stocks making new lows. Do not try to rationalize every dog in your portfolio. Dogs do not become lions. Do not wait for this surprise, much as you desire it.
11. Keep your ear to the ground. Some new company with a better idea may be speeding by. Fortunes were made in the tech and the Internet areas. Fortunes were also lost.
12. Stay informed. Your broker does not know better. There is no virtue, nor profits in ignorance. The overwhelming evidence suggests that professional investment advisors do not earn their fees in extra profits in your portfolio. Have you wondered lately why indexed funds (funds whose fortunes are tied to one of the market indices) have become so popular.

Chapter 2

INVESTMENT PHILOSOPHIES AND TECHNIQUES

2.1 Introduction

Investors without an investment philosophy are like a ship without an anchor. They live on tips, hunches, dreams, and other professional and often not so professional opinions. This is not the foundation on which Warren Buffett made his fortune. His company, Berkshire Hathaway, which sells for about $70,000 per share, was built on identifying value companies and sticking with them through aggressive management. Some faulted Mr. Buffett for having missed the "ride of the Internet". Some argue that his uncommon wisdom was an example to be emulated. Philosophies come and go, but there are some philosophies that only get fine-tuned with time. This is the Buffett case.

There are as many investment philosophies as there are investors to formulate them, if not more. Some investors refuse to buy stocks in companies that manufacture arms or defense-related equipment, others refuse to buy stocks in unionized companies, still others insist on only buying stocks of unionized companies, some insist on low-priced securities, others on companies with few shares outstanding, and some investors insist on low price-to-earnings (P/E) shares or low price-to-book value (P/B) shares or on shares in new-frontier technology. These are but a few of the philosophies (biases) of investors. Their proponents are often confused and confusing.

This chapter focuses on the various philosophies and on the various venues for participating in the market.

2.2 The Fundamental School

The fundamental school concentrates on the determination of the "intrinsic" value of the security; that is, the present value of all net cash flows to be derived from the ownership of the security, mathematically:

$$MP_o^s = \sum_{l=1}^{n} \frac{D_i}{(1+K_e)^t} + \frac{MP_n^s}{(1+K_e)^n},$$

where MP_o^s = Current market price of a security.

MP_n^s = Selling price at time n.

D_t = Dividend at time t.

K_e = Investor's required rate of return.

The equation above shows that the present value of a stock (theoretically, its market value) is determined by the profits that are a proxy for dividends, discounted at a rate K_e over the investment horizon (n). This is but one formulation of a universal valuation principle: the market value of anything is the present value of all the quantifiable benefits received from it over the life of the investment. If an investor plans to hold a stock *ad infinitum*, she would earn only dividends from it. There are no capital gains if the stock is never sold. The present value of this benefit is the market value of the security.

The dividends in the stock price equation are a proxy for the earnings of the firm. The concentration by fundamental analyst on future earnings requires sorting of all variables that come to bear on the levels and growth rate of earnings-variables like:

1. Quality and depth of management.
2. Standing of the company relative to the industry in terms of the competitive position of its product line.
3. Degree of company participation in growth areas.
4. Strength of company balance sheet and its accounting policies.

5. The nature of the economic, human, and technological environment in which the company will be operating.
6. The industry environment and the industry characteristics.
7. Investor perception of the company and of its product.
8. Other factors to be covered in the next two chapters.

The higher the level of excitement about the company's position and prospects and the larger the company's participation in the "hot" areas (silicon chips, artificial hearts, genome research, computers that can talk or reason, etc.), the higher the multiple (the price/earnings ratio) the investor is willing to pay for the company's earnings.

The question in the context of these complex and detailed analyses is the following: can fundamental analysis be of any value if securities markets are efficient?

The answer is in the affirmative. Fundamental analysis is used in the following ways:

1. To determine whether a given security is underpriced or overpriced in relation to its intrinsic value. This value is not constant and changes when new information becomes available. A security is underpriced only in the opinion of the analyst; it is not underpriced as far as the market is concerned. The analyst's forecast should occasionally (not consistently) produce an above-average rate of return given that it is accurate, unique, and significantly different from the markets. As special opportunities are identified, arbitragers move in to capitalize on them and bring the market to equilibrium.
2. The collection and processing of data may be increasingly useful if economies of scale are present in the information market. Declining marginal cost of information, to the extent it exists, encourages the formation of larger research departments.
3. Security analysis is further justified as a tool in assessing risk of securities (total, systematic, and unsystematic risk) and of portfolios, and in evaluating ways to diversify risk. Portfolio theory has come a long way since it was introduced in the early 1950s by Harry Markowitz. Elaborate mathematical and statistical models are currently being employed in order to keep portfolios on the

efficient frontier; that is, in order to ensure that the highest rate of return is realized for a given level of risk or that the lowest risk is assumed for a given level of return.

4. Security analysis is very helpful as a tool to minimize transactions costs in all their forms. Taxes are very important considerations for many investors, as are commissions and other fees. The structuring of portfolios in such a way as to minimize tax liability and the cost of trade should substantially improve net returns on invested capital.
5. While there exists a large array of securities from which to choose, knowledge about the various characteristics of securities should be of considerable help in the attempt to match them with the needs and requirements of individual investors. Attitude toward risk, cash-flow requirement, personal biases (buy or do not buy defense issues, for example), tax considerations, and other matters are all very important in the selection of suitable securities.

   The risk profile of an individual should prove most important from an asset-selection standpoint. According to the prescriptions of the Capital Asset Pricing Model (CAPM), investors wishing to diversify their portfolios will hold the market portfolio that includes every security in the market. The distribution of funds among the securities should be in accordance with the value of each security in relation to the total value of all securities in the market. The only choice left to the investor according to the CAPM is the extent of risk he or she is willing to bear. This will determine the extent to which investors are willing to leverage themselves, or the extent to which they are willing to commit portions of their capital to risk-free government securities. As new information becomes available and as the investor's needs and attitudes shift, portfolios must be adjusted to reflect the changes. In fact, frequent reviews of a portfolio are the norms and the recommended course on Wall Street.

6. While efficiency may characterize the securities market (evidence to follow) in the long run, the market is not in a permanent state of equilibrium. Markets may drop or rise substantially in price for a

variety of reasons, such as (a) euphoria (panic) over an election of a president (sickness or death), (b) threats to the flow of oil supplies, (c) the recommendation of an investment advisor with a large following, (d) one major holder deciding to "dump" securities as a result of portfolio adjustments, and (e) for other reasons, some of which elude the most astute of market observers.

Those deviations from intrinsic value, while temporary, provide many opportunities for investors as the market moves back to equilibrium.

One additional comment worth making deals with the difference between available and observable data. It took some very astute auditors to uncover the scandal at Equity Funding Corporation. The auditors discovered in March 1973 that 66% of the insurance policies the company was holding were bogus policies. The stock fell 13 points by March 19, 1973. By March 27 the stack was trading at $14. Trading in the stock was suspended by the SEC on March 28, 1973. The company was later reorganized and started operations in October 1976 under the name Orion Corporation. There simply is no substitute for careful scrutiny of data. Similar issues were raised with many other companies recently, such as Toys "R" Us and even Microsoft. Some held, and some were proven wrong.

The fundamental school is split between those who believe in value investing and those who believe in growth. The promoters of value investing like Warren Buffet are looking for values under every financial rock: wonderful companies that have been systematically ignored or "undiscovered" by the market. Or companies that have staying power, strong balance sheets, strong earning growth, strong market penetration, and companies that have proven themselves over a long period of time as they answer a fundamental need in the market place.

The promoters of growth are focused, among other things, on relative growth (compared to the industry and to its past) in earnings, in sales, in free cash flows, in return on equity capital, in return on assets, in the cash bum ratio, and in how fast the stock price has been reflecting the growth prospects of the company. In their scenario, the market will assign the highest multiple to that company that has the highest and most sustainable growth rates.

The problem with the distinction across these two schools lies in the fact that it is one without much difference. The surest way to destroy value is to not grow. Growth is an essential ingredient for value creation and its long-term realization is most assuredly the certification of legitimacy and hence of value. The transmission mechanism is thus as follows: profits to cash flows to above average growth rates to higher stock prices to greater wealth for the shareholders.

So it is not growth vs. value, but growth and value, and if the stock market has not assigned enough value to high and sustainable growth rates, then the stock is undervalued and is an excellent investment opportunity. Those advocating value stocks tend to refer to old economy stocks or to cyclical stocks, There is no lasting value in industries on which the sun is setting, and certainly no value in companies looking on the west side of the cycle curve.

There are companies that most assuredly look for mispriced companies by the stock market and seek pricing inefficiencies between fair and current market value, and pricing inefficiencies between related securities. They are referred to as hedge funds. We discuss them below.

In conclusion, it can be said that an active pursuit of information coupled with active portfolio management are very likely to pay handsome dividends in the long run, whether the market is efficient or not, or whether value or growth dominate in the minds of some investors.

2.3 The Technical School

The technical school is at the opposite pole of the fundamental school. It asserts that market prices are not a random process: expected price changes are not independent of past price changes nor are distributions of rates of returns independent from past distributions. Market prices exhibit identifiable patterns that are bound to be repeated. The "art" lies in devising the proper techniques to identify trends, interpret them, and interpret any deviation from them.

The technical school places little if any emphasis on earnings, dividends, market share, size of order backlog, and other fundamental factors. The argument of the school is basically that too many factors come to bear in the evaluation of a stock. To sort these factors out,

Exhibit 2.1: Typical chart summarizing stock price movements.

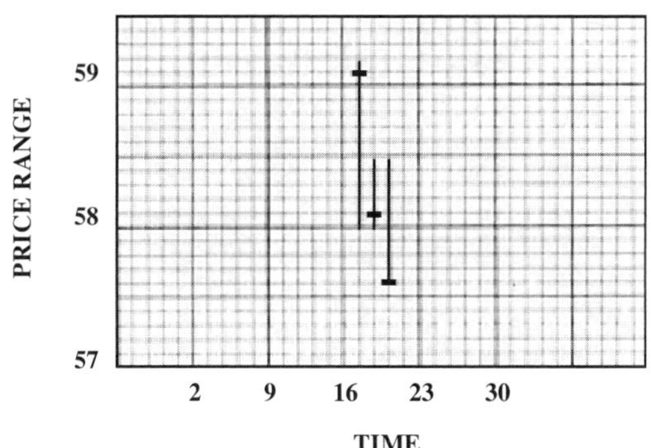

Source: Merrill Lynch Pierce Fenner & Smith, Inc.

identify the exact weight each has in the determination of the market value of a security, and gauge the time lag necessary for the impact of each factor to manifest itself are not practical if indeed possible consideration. What is important, the school argues, are supply and demand factors that are internal to the securities market. Investors should spend their valuable time trying to understand the "psychology" of the market; that is, they should grasp the determinants of supply and successive bars (Exhibit 2.1) from a "trend." Technical analysts do not concur with academic findings, that price movement is a series of random events. Trends may be up, down, or sideways, as shown in Exhibit 2.2.

Exhibit 2.2b shows an uptrend (suggesting a buy — a long position). The trend line is drawn under the prices. Exhibit 2.2a shows a downtrend (a sell or a short position). The trend line is drawn over the prices. The price movement from point B to point C, which fails to exceed the previous high at A, and the subsequent drop below B confirms a downtrend, technicians argue. Exhibit 2.2c shows a sideways trend, where stock prices are contained between two parallel horizontal lines. Here the trader must be very skillful to realize short-term gains. Picking tops and bottoms is much harder than following a distinct trend.

Trend channels are shown in Exhibit 2.3. These channels represent major thrusts in one direction characterized by minor price setbacks. The channel represents the development of a trend over a period of time. It

Exhibit 2.2: Successive bars showing (a) downtrend (b) uptrend (c) sideways trend.

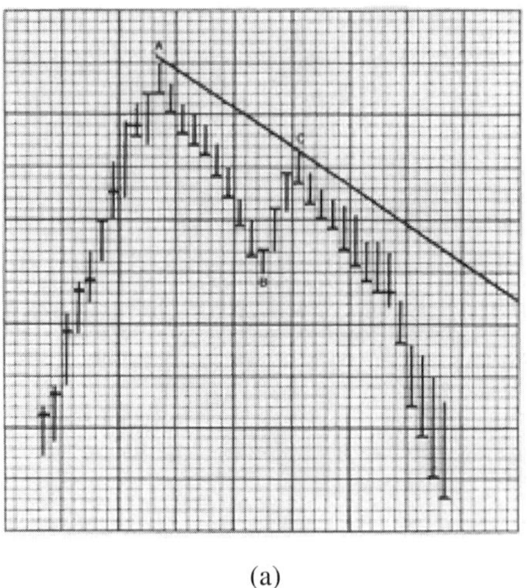

(a)

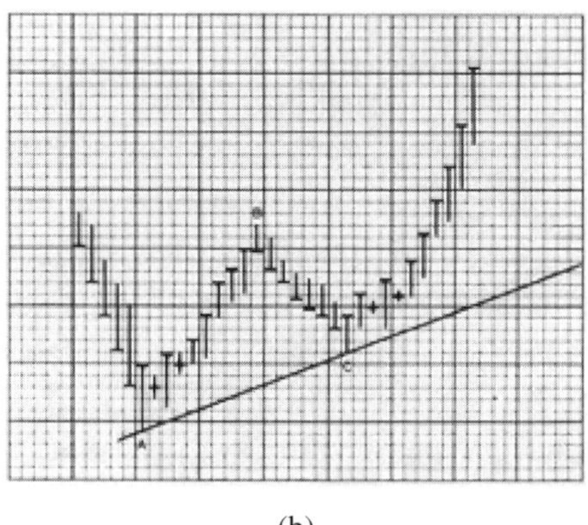

(b)

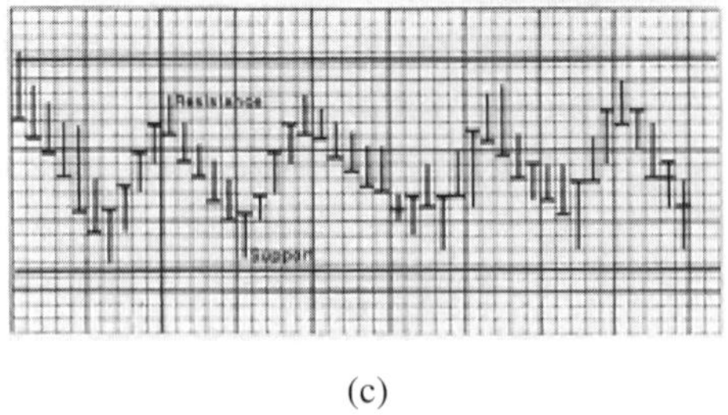

(c)

Source: Merrill Lynch Pierce Fenner & Smith, Inc.

Exhibit 2.3: Trend channels.

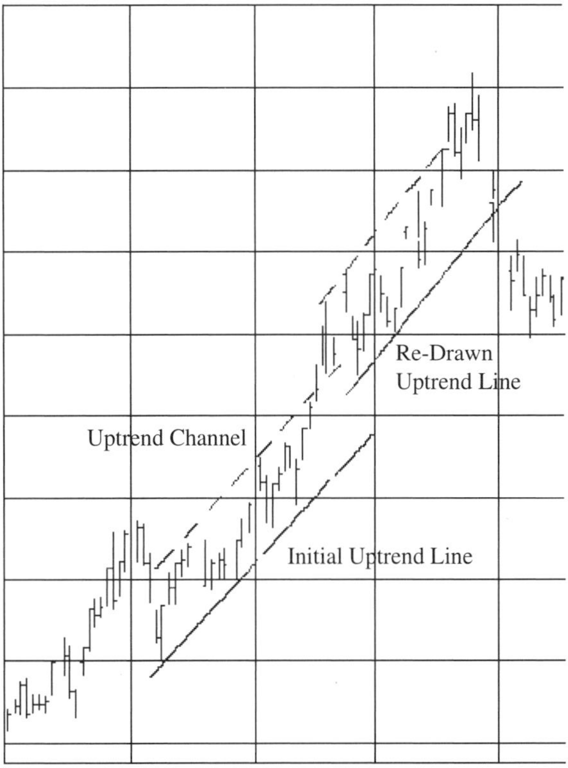

Source: Merrill Lynch Pierce Fenner & Smith, Inc.

is identified by drawing lines connecting high market prices and low market prices. The longer prices move within the channel, the stronger the trend is. A "breakout", a price advance or decline outside the boundaries of the channel, could signal a new direction in the price of the security. The price breakout below the channel in Exhibit 2.3 could signal a very bearish market (a sell or a short position) unless a countertrend quickly sets in. Traders usually wait until closing time after the breakout before they establish their positions. If the stock price at closing remains outside the channel, a long or a short position is established, depending on whether the closing price is above or below the channel. The stock may well establish a sideways trend for a period

Exhibit 2.4: Trend channels showing resistance and support levels.

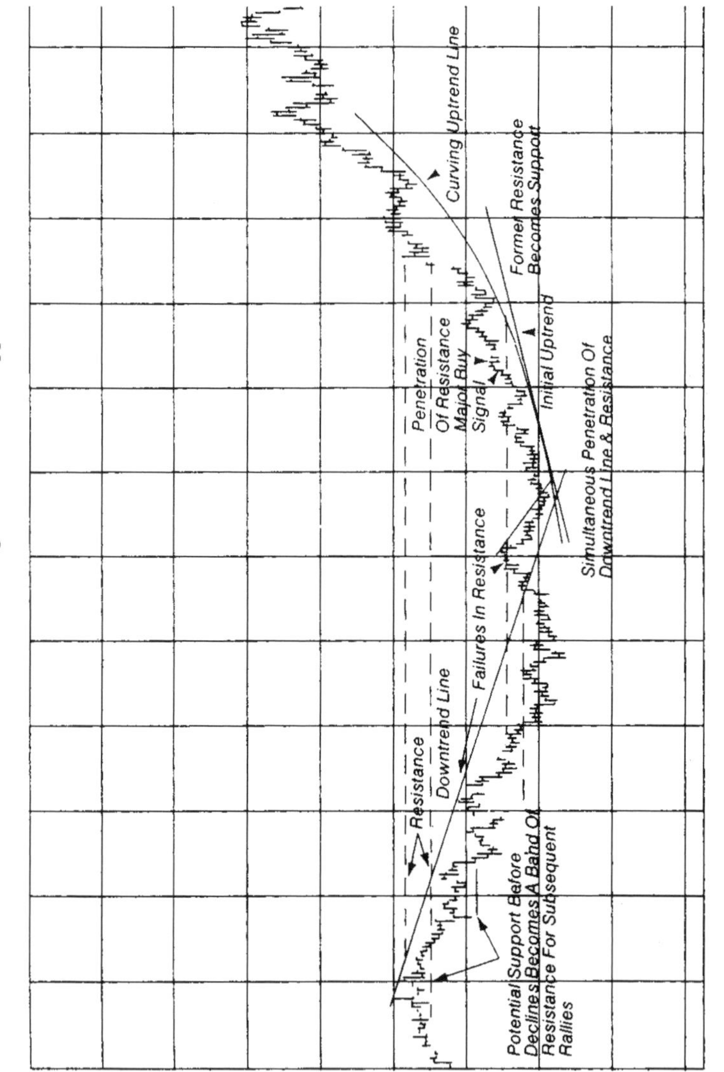

Source: Merrill Lynch Pierce Fenner & Smith, Inc.

of time before a clear upward or downward direction is established once again.

Technicians also believe that the market remembers resistance and support levels. Resistance represents price levels beyond which the market has failed to advance, and support represents price levels at which failing stock prices are arrested. Chartists usually identify several resistance and support levels, as Exhibit 2.4 indicates. A penetration of either level on a high volume is considered a strong indication of the direction of the market.

Several other formations are helpful, some technicians argue, in predicting the direction of the stock market. One hears descriptions such as "head and shoulders top", "head and shoulders bottom", "right triangle" or "coil top", "double tops", "double bottoms", "triple bottoms and tops", "flag", "symmetrical triangle", "V-bottom", "pennants", "ascending triangle", and so on. (See Exhibit 2.5). The art of chart reading is getting even more creative. We shall now discuss a few of the price formations.

The triangles and flags represent consolidations or corrective moves in market trends. A flag is a well-defined price movement contrary to the main trend. Ordinarily, stock prices break out of a flag and rejoin the main trend. A line drawn across the high prices of the corrective phase and another across the low prices form either an ascending or a descending triangle. The tip of the triangle represents the breakout point. Stock prices at this stage are expected to rejoin the main trend.

Double tops form an inverted W (M) represent a price high followed by a drop and then a rise to the previous high, indicating that price trends may be changing. Double bottoms are exactly the opposite, resembling a regular W with two equal price lows separated by a price rise. Double bottoms, and triple bottoms as well, are bullish indicators. Double and triple tops are bearish indicators.

The head-and-shoulder formations can be either top or bottom. In the "bottom" case, for example, a major market low is flanked on both sides (shoulders) by two higher lows. Cutting across the shoulders is some resistance level called the neckline. The breakdown of a bottom head-and-shoulder formation is a very bullish indication, as shown in

Exhibit 2.5: Various types of trend channels.

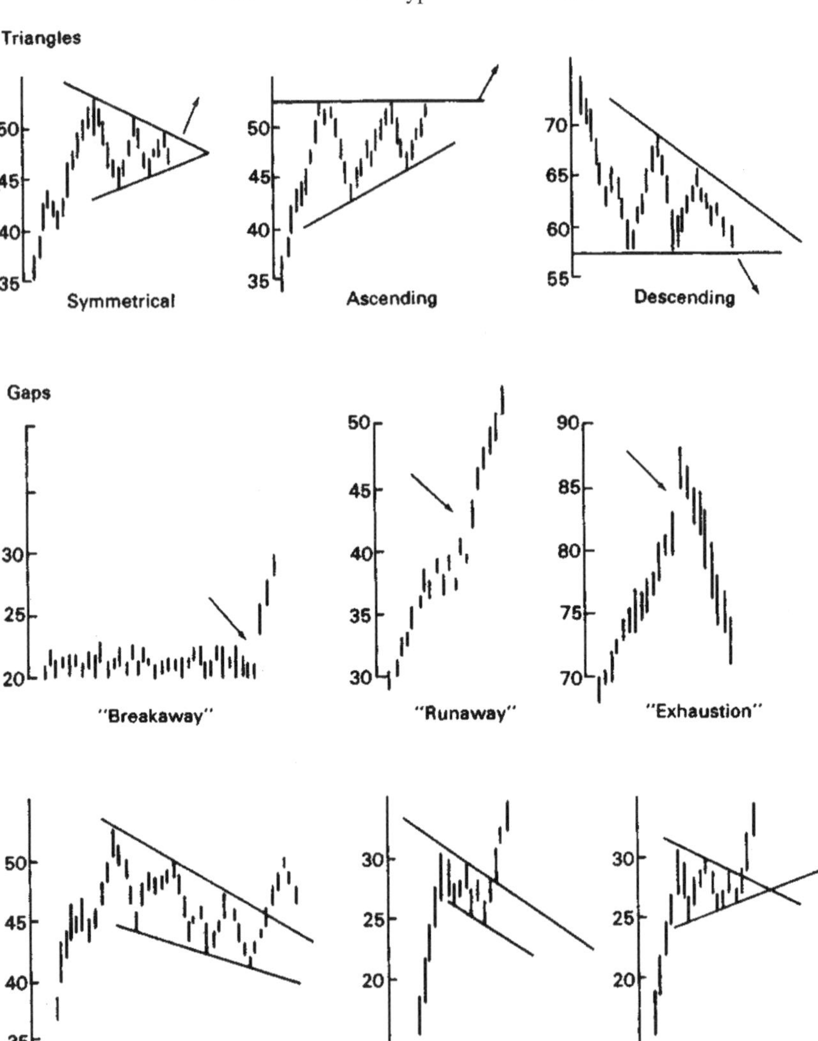

Source: Alan R Shaw: "Technical Analysis" in Summer N. Levine, ed., *Financial Analyst's Handbook* (Dow Jones-Irwin, Inc., Homewood, Ill., 1975).

Exhibit 2.5 (*Continued*)

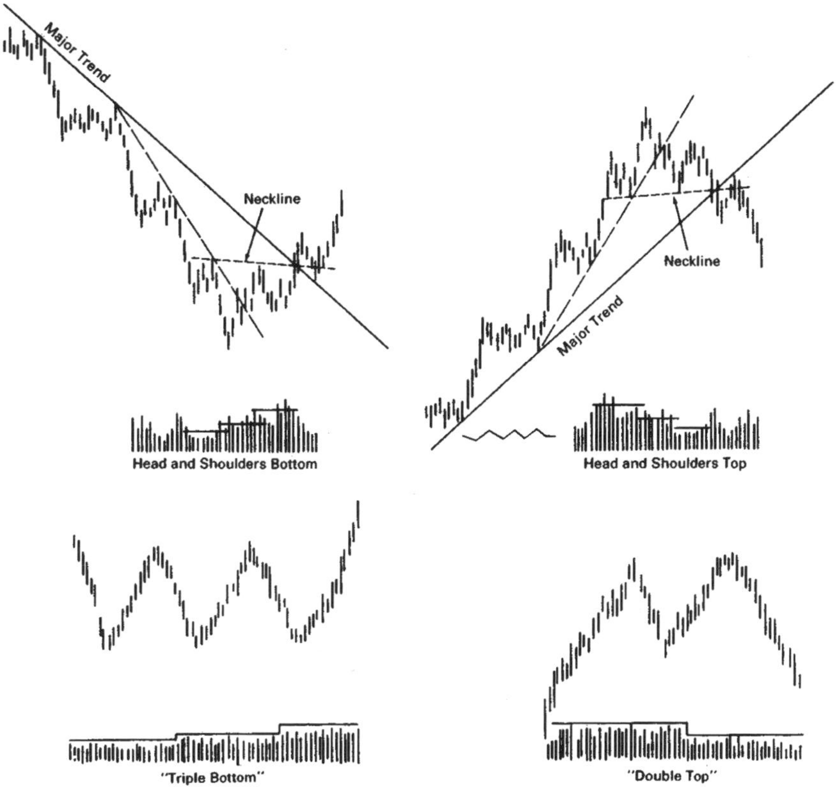

Exhibit 2.6. The breakdown of a top head-and-shoulder formation is a bearish signal.

The analysis of other formations is beyond the scope of this book. The interested reader should consult one of the many books on technical analysis.

Point-and-Figure Charts

The point-and-figure chart is an alternative to the bar chart in the representation of the trends in stock prices. This method of chart construction ignores small price changes and the time dimension and discounts the importance of volume. With respect to the former, the concern is more with

Exhibit 2.6: Head and shoulder formations.

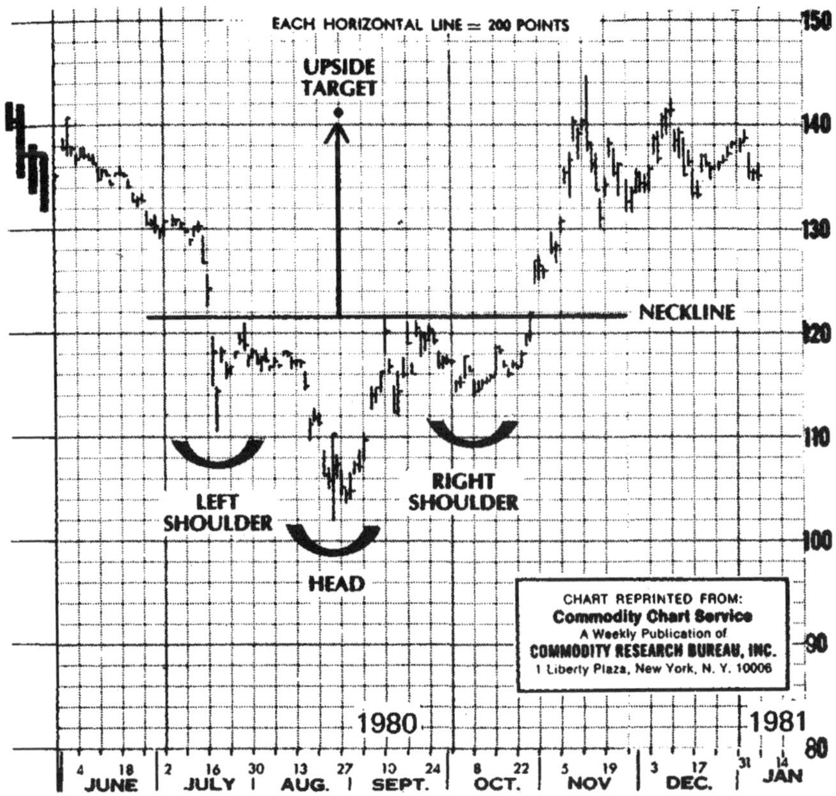

Source: Archer Commodities, Inc., Chicago

price movement over a broad time period as opposed to movement over subperiods; hence the small concern for calendar time. Point-and-figure charts are constructed merely to show the direction of price changes.

Point-and-figure charts are constructed in a series of columns once the required size of the price change has been decided. An entry is made in a new column when price reversals of the designated magnitude (regardless of the length of the period) occur. Consecutive positive price changes x each equal in size to the minimum required would be entered in a column like so: x. As soon as a price reversal of the minimum required level occurs, a new column is introduced. The chart now looks like so: x 0, where 0 marks a price decline, although it is not always

Exhibit 2.7: Point and figure chart pattern.

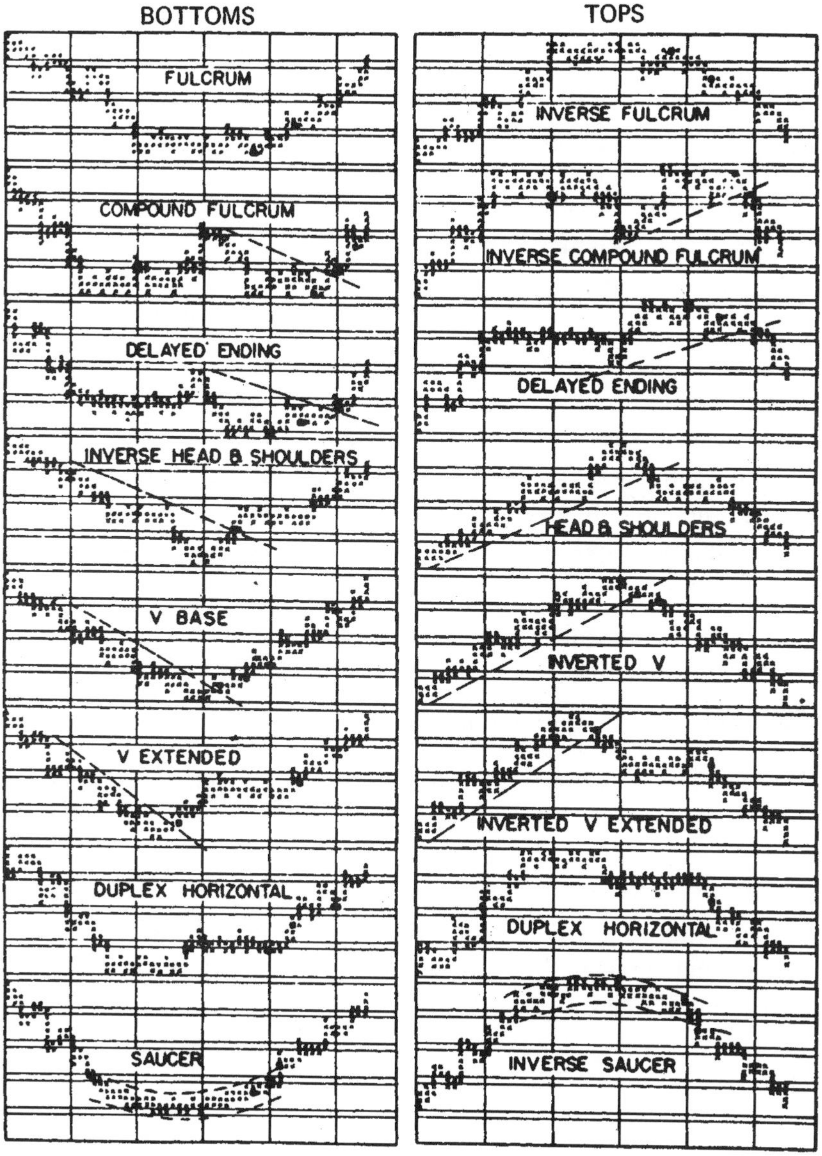

BOTTOMS

FULCRUM
COMPOUND FULCRUM
DELAYED ENDING
INVERSE HEAD & SHOULDERS
V BASE
V EXTENDED
DUPLEX HORIZONTAL
SAUCER

TOPS

INVERSE FULCRUM
INVERSE COMPOUND FULCRUM
DELAYED ENDING
HEAD & SHOULDERS
INVERTED V
INVERTED V EXTENDED
DUPLEX HORIZONTAL
INVERSE SAUCER

Source: Alan R Shaw: "Technical Analysis" in Summer N. Levine, ed., *Financial Analyst's Handbook* (Dow Jones-Irwin, Inc., Homewood, Ill., 1975).

used. The various forms that point-and-figure charts can assume are shown in Exhibit 2.7. A buy signal is usually generated when a new column of x's moves higher than the previous x column; a sell signal is generated when a new 0 column moves lower than the previous 0 column.

Other Market Barometers

There are as many barometers as there are inventive people to make them. Among these are the following:

The Dow Jones 20-Bond Average

When this bond average falls and the DJIA rises, a weakening stock market in the future is signaled because the yield on bonds becomes more and more attractive and investors would sell stocks to buy bonds. The opposite circumstances indicate a strengthening stock market.

Widening yield spreads between the bond market and the stock market are considered bearish. Investors may shift out of stocks for the higher yields.

Dow Jones Price/Earnings Ratio

The lower the Dow Jones Industrials P/E ratio in relation to its trend value, the more undervalued investors consider the stock market to be and the more bullish they are. The common wisdom is that the market "cannot go much lower" and an upward trend is inevitable. A low P/E translates into a high E/P — the (simplified) cost of equity — which reduces if not eliminates the attractiveness of financing corporate growth through equity financing.

Member Trading

Trading by members of the exchanges is carefully watched by market traders. Purchases by members are netted out from sales by members in order to get net sales (+ or –). Excessive high net sale positions indicate a weakening stock market; a stronger stock market is presumed if net sales positions indicate a weakening stock market; a stronger stock market is presumed if net sales are negative. Also carefully watched by the public and by the members are net short positions. Short positions established by the public in excess of 30% of total short positions are considered signs of excessive pessimism and indicate a bullish market. When covered, short positions lead to higher stock prices. Some have disputed this hypothesis. Joseph Seneca argues that an increase in short interest is a sign of weakness in the stock market.

Barron's Confidence Index

Barron's Confidence Index consists of the ratio of yields on Aaa bonds to the yield on Baa bonds. The maximum value the ratio can assume is one. The closer to one the ratio is, the more bullish the market, because investors are willing to accept lower yields on the riskier bonds. The lower the ratio is, the more bearish the indication. Investors are losing confidence in lower-quality issues and are requiring higher-risk premiums in order to hold the bonds. The record of this indicator is mixed.

Volume of Trade

High volume in a market trending upward indicates a strong rally. High volume in a market trending downward is an indication of a bearish market. That is why price movements must always be analyzed in conjunction with volume movements.

Advance/Decline Line

The advance/decline line, sometimes referred to as the overbought/oversold index, is the ratio of the number of shares advancing during a given period to that of shares declining. The higher the ratio, the more "overbought" the market is thought to be; the smaller the ratio, the more "oversold" the market is. The market is considered overbought if the ratio exceeds 1.25 and oversold if the ratio is lower than 0.75. Substantial and spontaneous movements in one direction or another

Exhibit 2.8: DJIA advance-decline line and DJIA breadth.

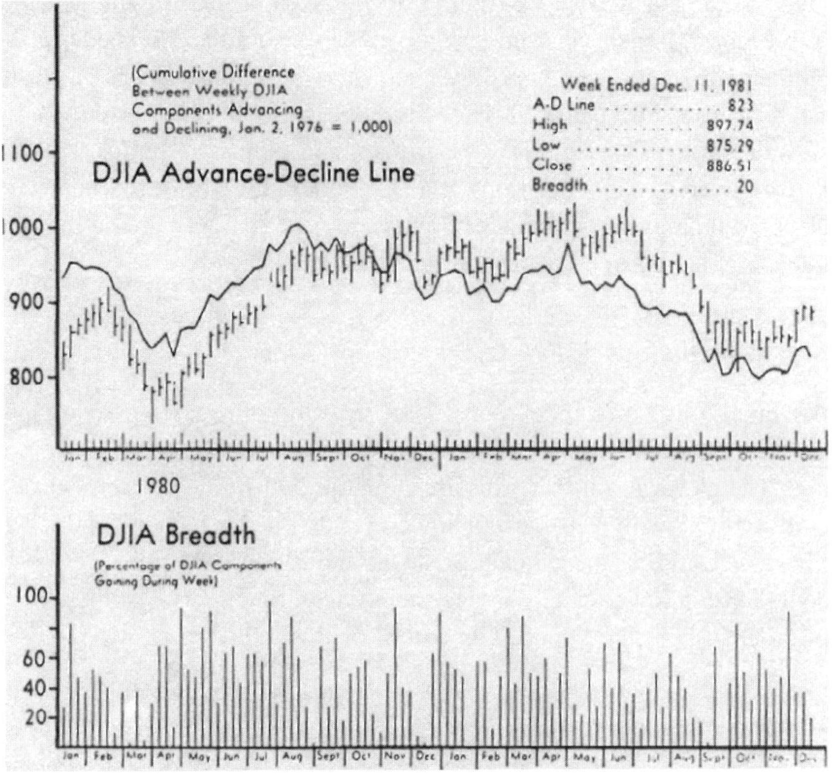

Source: *The Media General Financial Weekly*

indicate a very bullish (if up) or very bearish (if down) market. Some traders focus on the advance-decline line (instead of advance/decline) for the DJIA and on the DJIA breadth (percentage of DJIA components appreciating in value during a week) to gauge the direction of the market (Exhibit 2.8). A rising advance-decline and breadth is a bullish indication.

NYSE Active Stocks

The 20 most active shares (in terms of trading volume) are usually indicative of the "quality" of the rally or the seriousness of the decline.

If members of the most active list are traditionally good (blue-chip) securities, then the quality of the rise (in a bull market) is different from that if the list contains securities that are not identified with healthy, well-established companies. The latter case could be considered as excessive speculation auguring a declining market.

Moving Averages

Moving averages are utilized by securities traders as a mechanism for identifying trends and to help develop trading strategies.

The development of a moving average is quite simple. First, decide on the length (in days, weeks, or months, etc.) of the time period over which the moving average is to be calculated. Then, calculate the average price and proceed to calculate the next average by dropping the earliest observation and adding a new one. If this continues, a trend should become apparent, as is shown in Exhibit 2.9. The variation in the number of observations in the moving average allows chartists to reinforce their interpretation of price movements and to devise new trading strategies. Some chartists use the double moving average, which is the moving average of a moving average, and various levels of exponential smoothing to forecast stock prices.

Chartists use the averages depicted above in various ways. A sustained upward movement in all the averages is clearly bullish. A downward

Exhibit 2.9: An illustration of the 4-day, 9-day, and 18-day moving averages for the daily closing values for Dow Jones Industrial Average during a two-month period in 1999.

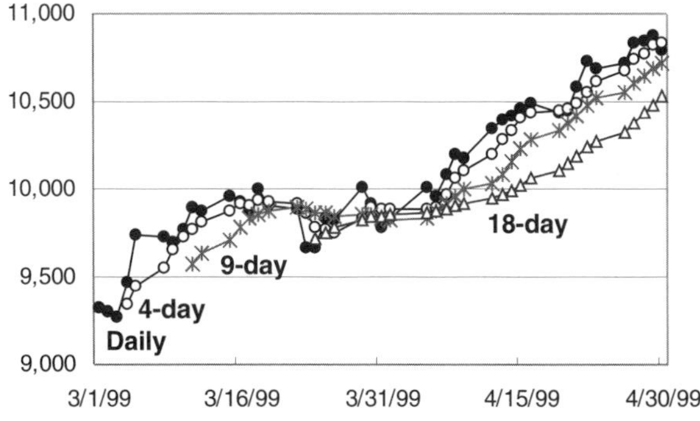

movement in all the averages is bearish. A 4-day moving average cutting across rising 9-day and 18-day moving averages is considered bearish; it is bullish if the 9-day and 18-day averages are trending downward.

Theory of Contrary Opinion

This theory attempts to capitalize on the hypothesis that there is an unwise stampede in the market toward conformity. When a substantial majority of "experts" (financial analysts) agree that the market is likely to improve, the trader should establish a short position, and a long position if the expectations are bearish. This should prove, it is argued, that the trader has not lost the capacity for critical thought.

What the above indicators suffer from, as a unit, is the conflicting-signal syndrome. What if two of these indicators say buy and the remainder say sell? How does one construct the weighting system that gives consistently correct signals? The answers to these complex questions have not been provided as yet.

In addition, professionals use predominantly the following valuation and sentiment indicators. According to *The Wall Street Journal*, these are:

Measuring Value

- Price/earnings ratio
  The S&P 500 is selling for 19.8 times the per-share earnings in the past year of the companies in the index. This is well above the postwar average P/E multiple of 13.5, but well below the high of 25.6 set in 1992.
  Bears say such high prices cannot last. Bulls argue this indicator is not too high for a period of low inflation.

- Price-to-book value
  Stocks are selling for a record high of 3.8 times the value of assets on companies' balance sheets. That is almost double the average price-to-book multiple since 1977. Bears see them as evidence investors are buying without locking the tires. Bulls say book

value is an accounting measure that is less relevant in a fast-evolving, technology-driven economy.

- Dividend yield
  Quarterly cash payouts by S&P 500 companies amount to a record low of 2.16% of stock prices. If S&P estimates for 1996 hold true, companies will pay out in dividends an all-time low of 35% of their profits this year. Bears see it as another sign of speculation, reflecting investors' willingness to pass up income for a chance at greater paper gains. Bulls say it simply shows investors want long-term returns, not short-term taxable gains.

- Yield ratio
  The ratio of the yield on the 30-year Treasury bond to the earnings yield on the S&P 500, which is the inverse of the P/E ratio, is 1.4 to 1. This ratio, used to compare returns on bonds and stocks, has been higher at the peak of only one other bull market, says Arnold Kaufman, editor of *S&P Outlook*. That was in August 1987 when the ratio rose to 2.2. Bears see this as incontrovertible proof that stock buyers are ignoring critical market conditions. Bulls say many investors have stopped seeing bonds as an alternative long-term investment.

Measuring Sentiment

- Bulls vs. bears
  A weekly survey of investment advisors by *Investors Intelligence* newsletter shows 29.5% are bearish, 48.4% are bullish and 22.1% are generally bullish but expect the market to drop soon. Bullishness has been increasing in recent weeks but is still below a three-year high set in February, the newsletter reports. This measure is viewed as a contrary indicator. Bearishness hit a 12-year high in late 1994, just before the current bull cycle began.

- Put-call ratio
  Investors often buy put options on stocks they think will fall and call options on stocks they think will rise. The ratio of the volume of puts to calls on the Chicago Board Options Exchange

is considered a contrary indicator. Analysts see a reading below 70% as a sell signal for stocks.

We now look at how to participate in the stock market once you have figured out your sentiment.

2.4 Venues for Participating in the Stock Market

One may participate in the stock market in various ways. The common way to participate directly is to buy the stock outright (directly) through a broker using direct contact or through the Internet. Many of the direct investments are done in retirement plans controlled by investors such as 401K plans. There were 230,000 such plans in 1998 with a total asset value of $828 billion. Indirect forms of participation are through insurance programs and employer pension fund programs. There were $1043 billion invested in private pension funds in the United States at the end of 1999.

The other ways are as follows:

1. Mutual Funds

   The mutual fund industry dates back to the 1920s. Mutual funds are also referred to as investment companies. By the 1960s they had attracted 40 million investors. By the end of 1999, $1077 billion dollars were invested in mutual funds. This strong record was eclipsed, however, by the money market fund where funds are invested in money market instruments such as T bills, etc. The total value of the money market funds at the end of 1999 was $1149 billion.

   A mutual fund is one that is "mutually" owned by a group of individuals each of whom may have too little money, too little time, too little expertise, or any combination of these to have a successful, fully diversified portfolio. The mutual fund is run by professional managers for the benefit of shareholders. One becomes a shareholder by buying into the fund. The price of admission: the price per share is the net asset value (NAV) of the fund at the end of a business day when the market is opened and when the order is placed prior to 4:00 p.m. EST. Should an investor be able to invest the typically required minimum of $1000, and should the NAV equal to $21, then the investor would become the owner of 47.62 shares in the fund. Yes, it is possible to own a fraction of a share in a mutual fund. Borrowing the money from a broker to make the investment is not possible. Mutual fund shares are not marginable. The investment made by the fund in each stock is referred to as its holding. The holdings put together are the portfolio of the fund. So the shareholder will actually be holding a fraction of the portfolio of the mutual fund, that is, a fraction of Intel, Microsoft, General Motors, etc., if they are actually owned by the fund. The fund is barred from committing more than 25% of their resources to securities issued by a single business firm. They must also distribute at least 90% of the net income derived from share ownership and from trades.

The fund we have been describing is an "open-end" mutual fund. Clearly this type of fund has a fluid capital structure, that is, the number of shares outstanding is not fixed. A closed-end fund on the other hand, is one that issues a fixed number of shares to investors. The outstanding shares have a market value determined by supply and demand on a given day. That price may well be below or above the NAV of the fund depending on the expectations of the investor with regard to the future of the fund's specific holdings. The total value of closed-end funds at the end of 1999 was $107.1 billion.

Country and industry-specific funds such as the China Fund and the Internet Fund are proliferating. These type of funds are allowing the investor to enter lucrative areas where he/she has no expertise, and where his resources and contacts may not allow him to get his share of an IPO when the stock is actually issued. Many of the country funds are closed-end funds.

The professional management that either open or closed-end funds provide is not free. There are annual administrative charges of about 1.0% on the actual amount invested regardless of the performance of the fund. An investor is well advised to check on the size of the management fee before committing himself to the fund. Those fees must be justifiable by the fund. Every mutual fund has a board of directors to look out for the interests of the shareholders. Their activities are regulated by the Securities and Exchange Commission (SEC) under the Investment Company Act of 1940. Full disclosure of information is required and it comes in the form of a prospectus that must be made available to the investor. Included in the prospectus are the investment objectives of the fund. They range from the very aggressive to the very sedate. A full range of objectives is often offered by fund management groups like the Vanguard Group or Fidelity. Many brokers allow investors to shift from one type of fund to another without paying fees or commissions. There are limits on the number of shifts, however. E*Trade and Charles Schwab lead in this regard in terms of the flexibility allowed to an investor.

The fees that funds charge are many, but are carefully monitored. No load funds do not charge a fee at the point of purchase or sale of the shares, but do charge fees for marketing, advertising and other operating expenses. These are called 12b-1 fees and must be less than 0.25% of the funds assets, otherwise, the fund will be considered a load fund.

Load funds charge either front or back-end loads. The front-end load is included in the public offering price and is limited by law to 8.5% of the initial investment. It is paid upon purchase. Back-end loads are paid when the shares are sold (redeemed). The fees are typically reduced as the holding period increases.

In addition to these loads, the broker may charge a fee to buy or sell fund shares.

The performance of these funds is monitored by numerous entities and reported widely. Lipper and Morningstar do an outstanding job in providing timely data and excellent performance measurement. The results of Lipper are reported in *The Wall Street Journal* as the condensed Exhibit 2.10 shows.

Exhibit 2.10: Mutual funds performance yardsticks.

HOW LIPPER INDEXES STACK UP

Investment Objective	May	Year To-Date	Total Return 1 Year	Annualized 3 Years	Annualized 5 Years
GENERAL STOCK FUNDS					
Large-Cap Core	-2.55%	-1.71%	-12.49%	19.46%	21.70%
Large-Cap Growth	-5.76	-5.98	21.05	23.36	25.84
Large-Cap Value	0.07	-0.89	3.06	14.02	18.46
Midcap Core	-4.11	2.33	28.77	17.64	19.22
Midcap Growth	-8.99	-9.73	45.88	25.72	23.26
Midcap Value	0.73	1.72	9.14	8.56	-13.31
Multicap Core	-3.48	-0.19	14.29	17.6	-20.49
Multicap Growth	-6.74	-2.30	33.86	26.58	25.19
Multicap Value	1.79	1.44	1.51	9.35	14.93
Small-Cap Core	-4.25	-0.25	20.16	10.5	14.70
Small-Cap Growth	-8.18	-5.11	51.30	20.23	20.36
Small-Cap Value	-0.85	2.07	2.78	4.73	10.78
Equity Income	1.51	-0.07	-1.50	10.14	14.84
S&P 500 Fund	-2.08	-2.96	10.35	20.12	23.47
SECTOR FUNDS					
Science & Technology	-12.07	-5.41	-79.53	44.75	35.23
Health/Biotech	1.81	10.78	26.62	19.94	22.66
Financial Services	5.88	2.20	-5.90	10.16	19.02
Natural Resources	9.67	21.42	30.91	11.02	15.07
Utility	-1.04	1.75	10.56	16.30	16.87
Real Estate	1.15	7.93	-3.23	0.56	N.A.
WORLD STOCK FUNDS					
International	-2.75	-8.35	23.77	11.97	19.48
Emerging Market	-5.32	-13.86	19.82	-5.28	0.85
European	-2.02	2.11	32.56	21.14	20.32
Global	-2.97	-3.59	23.86	15.53	16.32
Pacific (Excl. Japan)	-6.39	-14.78	27.57	-6.92	-2.36
Pacific	-8.31	-20.28	21.55	-0.94	1.52
MIXED EQUITY					
Balanced	-0.94	0.14	5.63	13.86	13.86
Global Flexible	-1.57	-2.10	13.33	12.89	12.89
FIXED INCOME					
General Bond	-0.59	0.58	1.05	4.69	6.31
General US Government	-0.12	1.98	1.22	4.78	4.94
General US Treasury	-0.33	5.22	2.18	6.21	3.61
Global Income	-0.06	-1.60	-1.69	1.89	4.38
GNMA	-0.33	2.09	2.45	5.19	5.67
High Yield Bond	-1.80	-3.72	-2.85	3.14	-6.59

BENCHMARKS FOR MUTUAL-FUND INVESTORS

Investment Objective	May	Year To-Date	Total Return 1 Year	Annualized 3 Years	Annualized 5 Years
DIJA (w/ divs.	-1.78	-7.93	1.13	14.66	20.92
S & P 500 (w/ divs.	-2.06	-2.82	10.48	-20.45	23.77

N.A. Not applicable   Note: Bond data preliminary through May 31

Source: *The Wall Street Journal*, June 5, 2000.

2. Hedge Funds

The 1990s saw the emergence and the incredible expansion of hedge funds. These funds were private partnerships for the privileged, super rich for all practical purposes. Paine Weber started a hedge fund that allowed entry for a minimum advance commitment of $250,000.

Initially the word hedge was supposed to imply that the investor will not have to be concerned about the direction of the market as the fund splits the investable funds between investments expected to rise in value and those expected to fall in value. The fund may have also hedged its exposure using immunization techniques or derivative assets.

Today hedge funds refer to any fund that is not a conventional investment fund buying bonds, equities and money market instruments. These funds include those using short sales, arbitrage, leverage to enhance returns, investing in out of favor securities or undervalued securities in the hope that the market will converge to their view of the world, and investing in the expectation that a company will be a takeover target. The arbitrage would typically involve finding unjustified differences between assets that have similar risk characteristics but are traded at different prices. The bet will be that the prices will revert to their normal relationship. So, the hedge fund has no typical risk/return profile these days and is unregulated compared with mutual funds. Their investment performance is more predictable as their strategies are not dependent exclusively on the current direction of the market. Their managers are compensated based on performance as well as fixed fees.

The size of these funds is shrinking as their biggest stars are pulling back after massive losses in the waning years of the twentieth century. By the third quarter of 1998, hedge funds had $400 billion under management. This has been falling ever since as opportunities kept shrinking, as investors began to realize that much of the returns were actually due to a rising stock market and not to extraordinary skills, and as the patience of investors to see their performance of 1994 repeated began to evaporate. The near bankruptcy experienced by Long Term Capital Management (LTCM) in September 1998 was a huge lesson for investors in the hedge funds market. Theirs was a story of big stars and big academics, including two Nobel Laureates, who were allowed to be excessively leveraged and who made huge bets on the stock market. These were later deemed to be threatening to the financial system and required a bailout strategy using the strong arm of the Federal Reserve Bank of New York. The company escaped the worst outcome: liquidation of its assets. It later straightened itself out and managed to pay its principals the outrageous sum of $50 million in bonuses in 1999.

The bailout of LTCM required a new commitment of $3.5 billion from the top investment banks in the United States. There were 14 investment banks involved altogether.

The problem with LTCM was very predictable. A major error or a major market turn would bring down any company if it is as leveraged. LTCM had about $2.2 billion in capital. It borrowed enough money to buy securities worth $90 billion. Some of these securities were used as collateral to make speculative bets representing $1.25 trillion. As the market began to move contrary to the expectations of the fund managers, disaster began to loom and the intervention of the Fed became necessary. No public money was used in the bailout, but the Fed played a major role treating LTCM as a "too big to fail" firm. The interesting thing was that LTCM would not have failed and the bailout was a way to prevent massive losses for the super rich who made up the clientele of LTCM. The involvement by the Fed was severely criticized in various circles.

The lessons from LTCM were not lost on the market. LTCM elected to pay back in June 1999 all the initial investors freeing them to do what they please with their money. Returning the money to the initial investors became the mode for many of these funds, which explains their shrinking asset base in 1999. By the end of 1998, there were 5830 hedge funds in the world managing $311 billion in assets. The rate of return on US hedge funds was 11.7% in 1998, while the average offshore hedge fund lost 1.5% in 1998. One must note, parenthetically, that the rate of return on the NASDAQ in 1998 was 35.4%.

3. Venture Capital and Private Equity

The venture capitalist has become the ultimate cornerstone in the development of free markets and in bringing the latest of ideas and technologies from the concept stage to the product stage. The venture capital industry grew by 150% only in 1999 to a record $48.3 billion. The Internet sector received the lion's share of these funds for a total of $31.9 billion. Every other industry sector experienced growth in funding from venture capitalists. The number of companies receiving venture capital in 1999 increased to 3649. This furious pace was expected to continue. In the third quarter of 2001, it fell 72% from the third quarter of 2000. Nothing is permanent. Venture capitalists are spread over the world. They range from boutiques to major investment houses in the United States and abroad. They are primarily responsible for the creation of the new economy in the United States and for sustaining our high economic growth.

Venture capital is risk capital invested in medium and small size companies in the form of equity or convertible bonds underwriting. The interest is in companies with high growth potential, and in taking an active part in management in order to achieve that potential. The primary objective is to realize capital gains. Venture capitalists typically have 3–5 years' horizon.

Venture capital is for investors who are risk takers and have high net-worth. The typical participation route is as a limited partner in a venture capital limited partnership. The general partners typically provide the management skills and the limited partners the vast majority of the risk capital.

Private equity companies (partnerships) are also for the same profile investor. They are also limited partnerships and range in size from a few millions to about $1 billion. The individual limited partners are referred to as angels.

Exhibit 2.11: Asset class private equity.

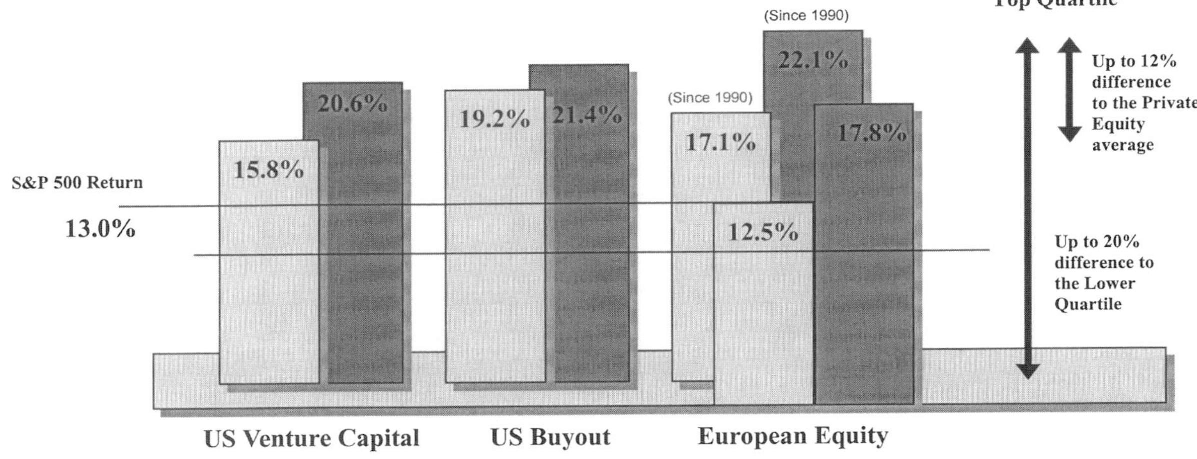

Source: Venture Capital IBR 1999, p. 237; Buyout IBR 1999, p. 143; European Private Equity IBR 1999, p. 168 (Returns 1984–1988)
Venture Economics: Yearly compounded performance S&P 500 1980–1997, no reinvestment of dividends
Bloomberg: Yearly compounded performance MSCI Europe 15 1984–1999, no reinvestment of dividends

Private Equity — An asset class in revolution

These firms have appeared on the investment scene only in the last ten years. They target privately owned companies and are interested in equity stakes. Their deals are privately negotiated and there is an active involvement in management. Typically the limited partners provide about 80% of the capital to the private equity firms.

The strong growth of this industry has spawned a new industry to cater to those desiring to liquidate their participation in private equity arrangements, and another that basically creates the equivalent of fund of funds where the money is raised from private investors and invested in a range of private equity funds. This allows for risk diversification for the limited investor.

The returns and the risks in absolute and comparative terms are shown in Exhibits 2.11 and 2.12. Both venture capital and private equity companies have outperformed the S&P 500 since 1990. The top quartile of private equity has vastly outperformed a holding of public equity as Exhibit 2.11 shows. This suggests that caveat emptor does in fact have a universal applicability and benefit.

Exhibit 2.13 shows that venture capital may well be the ideal way to participate in the growth of certain regions and certain countries in the world. China alone attracted $7.2 billion from foreign sources (65% of which are Asian, however) in 1998 alone. This level was easily exceeded in 2002.

Exhibit 2.12: Private equility — An asset class in evolution.

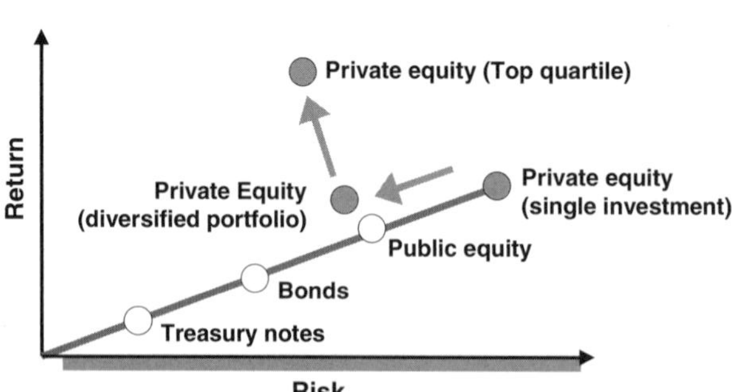

Exhibit 2.13: Comparison: VC China versus VC Asia.

	Total in billion US$	**Annual growth**	**% of GDP**	**% of FDI (fundraising)**	
VC China (PRC) 1998	7.2	+7%	0.75%	2%	65% from Asian sources
VC Asia 1998 (incl. PRC, excl. Japan)	33.6	+27%	1.31%	8.5%	

Source: Pacific Consult AG

Big companies in the services sector and in the investment sector are taking notice of the trends and the returns in venture and private capital and have shown increasing inclinations to enter the fray and provide for stiff competition. This could only increase the choices to investors, but there are only so many deals.

The Trading Forums

Never in human history have the financial markets done more to add wealth to investors. The United States needs very efficient financial markets to facilitate the flow of money to consuming and investment units. The United States consumes 25% of the world savings and needs, consequently, a financial network with a global reach in order to lubricate its industrial and governmental operations and allow the US citizen to at least maintain her standard of living. The financial markets thus constitute a vital link in the global economic system as Exhibit 2.14 shows. They provide a payment system for the exchange of goods and services, a mechanism for pooling funds, a mechanism for transferring economic resources across time and space and economic units, an avenue for the management of risk, a good signaling mechanism through the prices they generate, and a way to deal with differential information across market participants. In the performance of these functions the markets are merciless. Those who perform are rewarded and those that do not are penalized. Investors pay close attention to this basic reality as they watch for winners and losers in the market.

Exhibit 2.14: Types of markets in the global economic system.

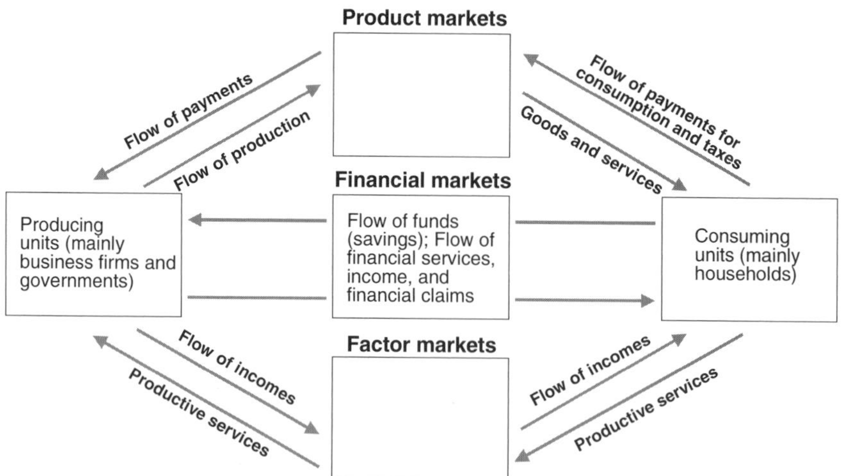

Source: Peter Rose: *Money and Capital Markets: Financial Institutions and Instruments in a Global Market Place* (Irwin McGraw-Hill, 1997).

The markets have become more efficient in an operational sense, allowing the investor to trade at ever lower prices; in an allocational sense, allowing funds to flow from those with surplus funds to the most efficient investor. In the process, the monitoring of fraud and manipulative practices has improved dramatically, as has the confidence in the financial markets. The latter is evidenced by the massive increase in the participation of individuals in the stock market. The markets have also become more efficient in an innovative sense as they have become more responsive to the changes in market forces, expectations and the dynamics of technology.

"Nothing succeeds like success," so said a wise man. The success of the stock market, especially in the last 16 years of strong performance, has been very impressive and very supportive for those who took the initiative and made their first investment. Their own successes translated into recommendations to their friends and their relatives and the market boom continued. This was fueled by the proliferation of business channels and the explosion of financial information over the Internet. This is

Exhibit 2.15: Percentage of times stocks have been positive.

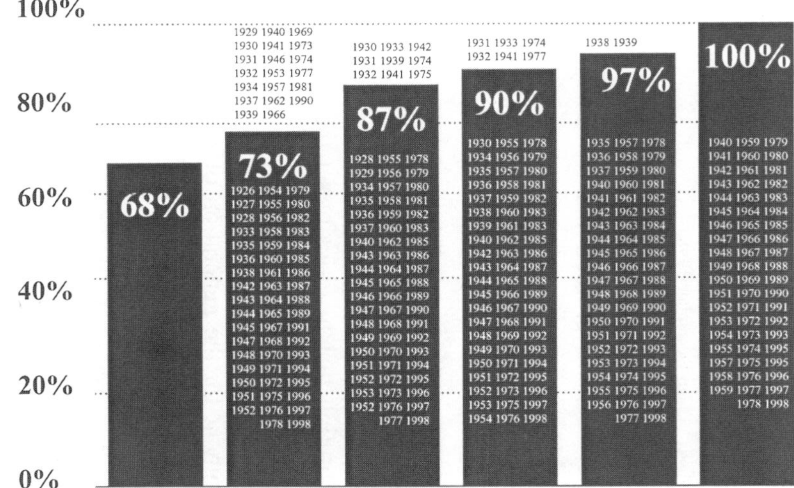

Source: Ibbotson Associates annualized returns of the S&P 500.

Estimates used of year end 1998 numbers. Past performance is not indicative of future results.

Exhibit 2.16: Outperformance of equities.

	Stock outperform	
	Bonds	**T bills**
1 year periods	65.5%	67.6%
3 year periods	73.5%	73.3%
5 year periods	77.6%	76.0%
10 year periods	81.9%	83.2%
20 year periods	98.2%	100.0%

Source: Ibbotson Associates. Based on rolling one year time periods beginning any month from 1926 to December 1998.

what is referred to as promotional efficiency: do things well and you promote even more efficiency and you broaden the appeal of the market.

The performance of the stock market will be examined in detail in the next chapter. Suffice it to point out here that anyone with a long run view has been rewarded by the market compared with other investments such as fixed income securities. Exhibit 2.15 and 2.16 show the promise of the stock market, especially when the investment horizon lengthens.

The institution that historically set the pace for the world financial markets is the New York Stock Exchange (NYSE). Its primary functions, like any other successful exchange, are to provide liquidity, to create the environment for the generation of fair (competitive) prices through the forces of supply and demand, and to transmit accurate information to the public on prices and trading volume.

The NYSE started over 200 years ago in front of the Trinity Church in East Manhattan where certificates in silver shipments were traded. This graduated into trading in government issued bonds followed by stocks in banks and then railroad companies.

The original form of trading was in the form of a single auction. Buyers were trying to out bid one another for the securities offered. In 1792, twenty-four men signed an agreement that created the NYSE. They started on 40 Wall Street and then moved to the current location of the NYSE. Stocks had to qualify in order to trade on the floor of the NYSE.

Those that did not traded outside "on the curb". The curb became known as the American Stock Exchange.

By 1842 the auction room was characterized by long tables at which each member occupied a seat. Thus, the reference is made to an exchange membership as a "seat". The number of seats is limited to 1366. The seat gives the owner the right to trade on the NYSE. The price of a seat is determined by supply and demand and was over $2 million in 2000. That same seat fetched only $220,000 in 1981. But despite the market weakness in 2001, the price appreciated to $2.3 million by January 2002.

The NYSE is governed by a board of directors made up of ten industry members and ten non-industry members. Its professional staff runs the operations and monitors all the activities of participating members and their agents.

The two most important individuals on the floor of the exchange are the specialist and the floor broker. The specialist is critical to the double auction system. Today's trading consist of a double auction system where buyers are competing with one another for the highest "bid" on a specific security, and where the sellers are competing on the other side for the best "offer" on a stock they are trying to sell. So buyers buy at the offer or the ask price (the best one available, and the NYSE guarantees that) and the sellers sell at the best available bid for their security assuming that a market order is in effect. The difference between the ask and the bid is called the spread. The specialist makes all of this work.

The specialist, so called because he specializes in the stock assigned to him by the NYSE, is best viewed as a traffic cop. The latter is charged with maintaining orderly streets, and the specialist is expected to maintain an orderly market. This duty could require him to buy or sell from his own account against the trends in the market. The intent here is not to reverse market trends, but rather to soften the fall or to temper the rise in stock prices. The specialist also works on the determination of an opening price (once the trading bell sounds) in a security when there is a substantial imbalance between supply and demand.

The specialist is an agent for the floor broker in limit orders. He electronically quotes and records current bids and offers and transmits them for the whole world to see and act on. The typical transaction in the market takes place directly between the individuals and the institutions trying to buy or sell securities. The specialist is a facilitator.

The floor broker, the commission broker specifically, buys and sells securities for the general public on behalf of the securities firm that employs him. The orders executed by the floor broker are sent electronically to the floor of the exchange by the registered representative (the stockbroker). The floor broker then shuttles these orders to that trading post specializing in that specific security that an investor wishes to buy or to sell. All the trades are executed quickly and efficiently and the exchange guarantees that the investor receives the best possible price.

While the NYSE provides for a physical location for the execution of orders, the NASDAQ Stock Market, the fastest growing stock market in the United States today, provides for a huge electronic network for the execution of orders. In 1994 total volume on the NASDAQ began to exceed that of the NYSE. The stocks listed on the NASDAQ turned in a stellar performance in 1999, up a whopping 85.59% for the year, continuing their fifth consecutive year of record gains. Also in 1999, and for the first time ever, two NASDAQ stocks: MSFT and Intel, became members of the DJIA.

The NASDAQ, also referred as the over-the-counter market, is a negotiated market made up of brokers and dealers connected by a sophisticated electronic network. The NASDAQ, which started in 1971, is the world's first electronic stock market. The trading information on the NASDAQ is simultaneously broadcast over 500,000 computers worldwide. Any stock would have a list of "market makers" who stand ready to buy the stock at their bid or to sell the stock at their ask. The bid and the ask observed by the investor on any given stock is the best available at that point in time (this is what is referred to as the "inside market") among all the market makers. When your stockbroker on the NASDAQ is acting as a "broker", he is representing you against a third party. In a market order, the order is placed through the broker whether orally or through the Internet. The order is then submitted and is executed at the best offer or bid price at the time it is entered in the computer. A limit order that is submitted, e.g., to buy at below the current ask price but above the prevailing bid price, would result in a new bid price that investors can observe the world over. The order will execute at the next sale by any other market participant. It will be the first in line as it is the highest bid.

NASDAQ also introduced another electronic trading system called OptiMark. This is a "wholesale market" where a trader indicates his interest in trading across range of price and size parameters. These orders are matched with other orders on the other side of the market.

The ease, the speed and the falling costs of execution have led to historic volumes on the NASDAQ. Volume for 1999 exceeded 276 billion shares, 35% above the 1998 level. The dollar value of all of these trades exceeded $11 trillion in 1999. Also contributing to the explosion of volume is the fact that NASDAQ has become a truly global market through many deals like the joint venture with SOFTBANK to create NASDAQ-Europe.

We now discuss Globex (used for derivative contracts) and Instinet for after-hour trades.

If you ever wondered what happens after the trading hours of the New York Stock Exchange (4:00 p.m. EST), trading continues using an alternative mechanism.

GLOBEX2, a unit of the Chicago Mercantile Exchange (CME), created the first international 24-hour electronically-based trading system. The system is primarily focused on trading a large array of those derivative contracts traded on the CME. The total number of contracts traded on GLOBEX2 in 1999 was 16.2 million, up 180% from the volume registered in its year of introduction, 1998.

Instinet is the world's largest agency brokerage firm with global trading capability in over forty markets. It was founded in 1969 and was acquired by Reuters in 1987. It trades in over 40 global markets and is a member of 19 exchanges in North America, Europe and Asia. As a pure agency broker, it maintains strict neutrality in all transactions. It acts merely as a transaction facilitator by offering its execution system. This is an integrated, electronic trading system on a 24-hour basis. It allows the client to execute orders on a continuous basis and often in numerous securities markets simultaneously. "Clients can communicate, negotiate, and trade electronically either directly with each other using Instinet's block brokerage service or can link to exchanges. Clients are able to enter orders on screen and trade with fund managers, broker/dealers, market makers and specialists around the world." All is done in complete anonymity and transparency. This explains why firms managing 90% of the institutional equity funds are Instinet members and why 20% of the NASDAQ volume and 170 million of all shares traded on a daily basis are done through Instinet. The market is, consequently, a wholesale market. On June 14, 2000, for example, of the 58 million shares of Cisco Systems traded on NASDAQ, 9.9 million, or 17.2%, were traded through Instinet.

In August 1999, Instinet signed an agreement allowing a retail customer of E*Trade, a discount broker house, to access its trading facilities for after-hour trading. The customer will be able to trade NASDAQ stocks as well as exchange-listed stocks. Online access for self-directed individual investors became a 24-hour reality. Instinet accounts for the largest after-hour order flow, which allows the investor using its services a wide possibility to have the order executed at a fair price.

There are other companies offering after-hour trading as well. They are referred to as electronic computer networks (ECN). Instinet is such an ECN. Its competitors include companies like Ready Book and Island. It also includes the Chicago Stock Exchange, which offers after-hour trading.

Despite these trading systems, the use of after-hour market trading is still limited and the transaction costs and spreads therein are still relatively high, but falling.

The Constant Reminders

It is often said, "If you did not die, did you not witness those that did?" The bulls, especially the baby boomers among them, having been running for the last 16 years, may have forgotten the Depression or even the 1987 crash. The predictors of doom are often in the media reminding all of us of the terrible days and of the fact that no market has ever gone permanently up, and that the downturn is around the corner.

There had been many scares in the stock market, the most recent of which was that of the week of April 10 which caused near panic in the US stock market and echoed strongly throughout Asia where huge losses were reported. During that week the market as measured by the Wilshire 5000 index (includes 7200 companies or nearly every publicly traded company with headquarters in the United States) lost $2 trillion. The DJIA lost 617.78 points on April 14, 2000 alone. Between April 11 and 14, 2000 the DJIA fell by 981.31 points or a fall of 8.7%. The NASDAQ did not do better. On April 17 the market roared back. The NASDAQ rose by the second highest percentage gain ever. The rise was not sustained. The NASDAQ was down 19.9% in 2001.

All the talk of a bear market that followed was clearly premature. Many likened the drop to the stock market crash of October 19, 1987 when the market fell by 508 points in a single day, its biggest daily percentage drop ever (22.6%). This marked the end of a bull market which saw the DJIA rise from 776.92 in August 1982 to a high of 2722.42 in August 1987. The effects on US portfolios and the stock markets of the rest of the world were devastating. Prior to that there were periods of major drops, but nothing like that in a single day. Between January 1973 and October 1974 the DJIA fell by 48.2%. Between November 1980 and August 1982 the DJIA fell by 27.1%. Any drop of more than 20% is considered a confirmation of a bear market.

The interesting thing about the recent crashes is that the markets have rebounded decidedly after the crashes. By September 1989, the average had regained all the value it had lost in the 1987 crash. Also after the April 2000 drop, the market recovered decidedly and it traded at around 10,800 by July 2000, well above the 10,305.77 level reached on April 14, 2000.

But, the seasoned investor remembers the Great Depression of 1929. It appears that policy makers have learned many lessons from the depression. In fact, the actions of the Federal Reserve System immediately after the October 19, 1987 crash indicate the robustness of the financial system. The Fed stepped in to provide liquidity to the stock market and was able to stabilize it as it prevented a huge number of bankruptcies. Even the percentage drop of the Great Crash is no longer possible as the NYSE has instituted a large number of measures to prevent its reoccurrence. The circuit breakers which ultimately permit the NYSE to shut down trading completely if the market falls by more than 3150 points are now in place and will be swiftly implemented if a crash is looming. The circuit breakers were introduced after the 1987 crash and have been revised a few times since. They work as follows. Should the DJIA fall by 200 points, all index arbitrage transactions will be regulated. Should the DJIA fall by 1050 points before 2:00 p.m., then trading is closed for one hour. Should it fall by 1050 points between 2:00 and 2:30 p.m., the market is then closed for one half hour. Should it fall by 1050 points after 2:30 p.m., trading will continue until the end. Should the DJIA fall by 2100 points before 1:00 p.m., then trading is shut down for two hours. Should this fall take place between 1:00 and 2:00 p.m., trading is halted for an hour. Should it occur after 2:00 p.m., then trading is halted for the rest of the day. Should the DJIA fall by 3150 points at any time, trading is halted and there will be no further trading for the day.

2.5 Conclusion

There is no substitute for having a core set of beliefs or investing with investment advisors that do. The market, no matter how it deviates from what is fair and accurate valuation, will ultimately come back to levels that are consistent with fundamental values. This reality has not in any way discouraged those who believe that they can guess every top and every bottom. It did not prevent an entire army of day traders from emerging. History will continue to generate an army of losers who refused to heed its lessons.

Chapter 3

THE PERFORMANCE HISTORY OF US EQUITY MARKETS

3.1 Introduction

This chapter surveys the performance history of the US stock market. It is an important component of our national fabric, and serves as a leading indicator[1] *of the nation's economic health. True, the economy does not stagger with every drop in the market, but a prolonged drop in the market affects the economy. Understanding the history of the stock market is also important if we are to glean any patterns from its performance that can help guide our investment goals, strategies and expectations.*

The history of the market is replete with surprises, melancholy, and great performances. Our evidence confirms that, in the long run and in most sub-periods of its history, no investment has surpassed the risk-adjusted rate of return yielded by the US stock market. The current travails (2001–2003) of the market are but a bump on the road to superior performance, therefore, that perhaps present the great buying opportunity that many may have missed during the market's 1990s high-flying performance.

Specifically, this chapter seeks answers to two questions:

- *What has the stock market's returns been like, in the 1990s and before, through history?*

- *Have these returns been worth chasing, in terms of the risks posed by inflation on one hand and the market's gyrations on the other?*

The idea here is to see if history can guide us about the returns we can expect, and the risks they entail, when we invest in stocks. Therefore, this chapter is divided into three sections that survey the market's history, starting with its present bear run in the first section, the bull run of 1990s in the second section, and the market's two-century history in the third section.

The goal, throughout this chapter, is to see whether the investors' success in the US equities market so far has been fortuitous or reflects the workings of some fundamental truths about the market's overall performance that cannot be dismissed as happenstance.

3.2 The Y2K[2] Strikes, with a Bear Market

This section surveys the ongoing "bear" phase of the US stock market's two-century history — a run that, having begun in early 2000, was more than two years long by mid-year 2002 and, though not the longest in the market's history, has already produced steep declines. The blue chip Dow[3] is poised for a rare three consecutive years of negative returns, if the second half of 2002 fails to offset the losses that have already occurred in the first half of the year. But then, over time, neither this nor any other index can move independent of the market and the economy. A closer look at this bear run of the market will thus help us focus on three issues: the returns that investors receive, the macroeconomic environment that makes these returns possible, and the demographics that set the priorities and time horizon for investments.

The Market and Its Sectors

Exhibit 3.1 traces the price performances of some of the broad US stock market indexes during this bear run. Note how precipitously all these indexes had fallen by mid-2002 from their early-2000 peaks, the technology-heavy NASDAQ Composite having lost the most. Despite transforming the global geopolitical arena dramatically, the terrorist events

Exhibit 3.1: The major US equity indexes have all dropped precipitously since they peaked in early-2000. Of these, the technology-heavy NASDAQ Composite has lost the most, and the blue chip Dow the least.

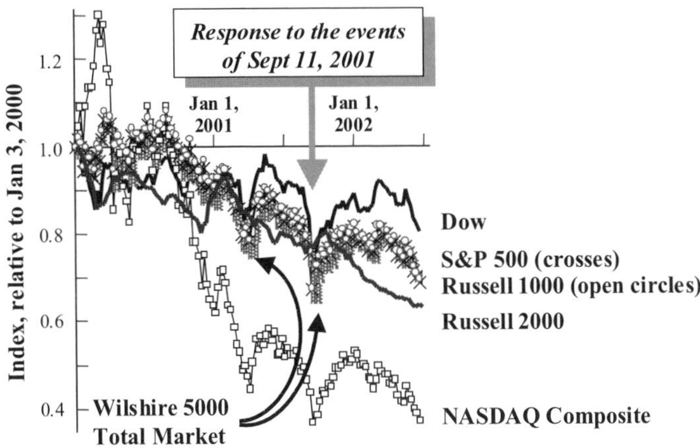

of September 11, 2001 appear to have had little lasting effect on this trend. Indeed, since the closure of the market for a few days in the immediate aftermath, all these indexes initially dropped precipitously, reaching new lows on September 21, but soon recovered and temporarily peaked by March–April 2002. That hardly lasted, however, as the market resumed its earlier, declining, trend that had begun two years earlier.

At the time of this writing in mid-year 2002, it remains to be seen if the market has already bottomed or is yet to establish the lowest levels in this bear run. The Dow seems poised to revisit the September 21, 2001 low of 8235.8 that it reached in response to the September 11, 2001 events, an end towards which the far broader S&P 500, Russell 1000 and Wilshire 5000 indexes appear to be galloping even faster.

Clearly, the chain of events that began with the preparations for the Y2K has been of greater consequence to the investors and the market than the events of September 11, 2001. That it was a bubble waiting to burst is evident from the fact that neither the Fed's aggressive interest-rate cuts in 2001, nor President Bush's $1.35 trillion tax cut, have yet been able to stem the market's slide. The market's woes began with the early-2000 implosion of the equity price bubble: the dotcoms heralded this collapse but the contagion soon spread to the technology sector before engulfing the entire market. The corporate and Wall Street excesses, seen in the scandals that have led to the fall of such one time titans as Enron, Anderson, WorldCom, Tyco, Adelphia, Quest, Bethlehem Steel, Global Crossings, Xerox, and the like, have sapped investors' confidence further. Add to these the looming bursts of possible bubbles in the foreign exchange and real estate markets, and a gloomier investment scene would be hard to picture.

Indeed, if you compare the midnight mass at St. Peter's Basilica on December 31, 999, with the passage of 1999 into 2000 a millennium later,[4] you would notice a striking similarity. Those present at that ancient event felt relieved when the world continued unaffected by the change in that year's digital code. Likewise, the equities market perhaps felt a similar relief when the dreaded Y2K bug failed to bite, an event that it celebrated by taking the prices of many stocks and their indexes to stratospheric heights. That jubilation was premature, however. Investors who saw in the nonoccurrence of a calamity the sign that the market's ascent would continue were betting on a trend that, having begun in the mid-late 1990s, was tiring itself out already. Most of those gains soon fizzled, therefore, as gravity inevitably reasserted itself in order to let the market eventually revert to its historic pattern of 10–12% average annual rise.

It is not that all the stocks have lost, or lost equally, since January 2000. The performances of some broad market and sector indexes, compared in Exhibit 3.2, clearly show that the indexes and sectors that had appreciated the most in the market's bull run have since lost the most. This may illustrate the market's tendency to revert to the mean. Of the broad market indexes, for instance, the Dow did not rise as much during 1995–1999 as the NASDAQ Composite and S&P 500 indexes. Not surprisingly, therefore, the latter two have led the decline since their 2000 peaks, not the Dow. Likewise, the AMEX Internet index was a top performer during 1995–1999, when it grew at a 52.64% annual rate, whereas the Philadelphia Gold and Silver index, which then fell at a −8.33% annual rate, was a leading laggard. But if we extend this period to the end of June 2002, then these rates change to 2.06% for the AMEX Internet index and −4.66% for Philadelphia Gold and Silver index. The former has obviously depreciated significantly since March 2000 whereas the latter has appreciated.

Exhibit 3.2: Comparing the price performances of selected broad market indexes and sector indexes since January 3, 2000. They are listed here in descending order of index appreciation for the period of January 3, 1995 through June 28, 2002.

Index	Index appreciation in the year...			Annualized growth from January 3, 1995 to...	
	2000	2001	2002*	June 28, 2002	December 31, 1999
Selected Broad Market Indexes					
Dow Jones Industrial Average	−6.17%	−7.10%	−7.76%	12.43%	24.53%
S&P 500	−10.14%	−3.04%	−13.78%	10.79%	26.19%
Whilshire 5000 Total Market	−11.85%	−12.06%	−12.46%	10.18%	24.98%
NASDAQ Composite	−39.29%	−21.05%	−24.89%	9.46%	40.49%
Russell 1000	−4.20%	1.03%	−5.29%	8.71%	15.34%
Selected Sector Indexes					
S&P Homebuilding	52.79%	31.95%	9.77%	18.56%	10.13%
NASDAQ Biotechnology	20.41%	−16.20%	−44.48%	16.55%	41.28%
Philadelphia Semiconductor	−18.16%	−9.44%	−24.44%	15.17%	38.80%
NASDAQ Financials	−27.91%	−2.09%	−10.20%	12.91%	31.43%
Dow Jones Transportation Average	−1.03%	−10.41%	3.42%	8.57%	15.11%
GSCI Energy	40.90%	−41.09%	31.18%	6.72%	8.38%
Dow Jones Utilities Average	45.45%	−28.68%	−6.82%	5.52%	9.13%
AMEX Internet	−51.24%	−47.81%	−44.74%	2.06%	52.64%
Philadelphia Gold and Silver	−24.36%	5.87%	34.89%	−4.66%	−8.33%

*Only the first one-half of the year, i.e., until June 28, 2002.

The alternative to using indexes to assess relative performances of the market's different segments during this bear run is to see the returns realized by the equity mutual funds. Exhibit 3.3 does so by comparing Morningstar's[5] statistics on the annualized trailing returns on diversified mutual funds. These data cover 5864 of the 7891 funds in Morningstar universe of mutual funds and account for \$2.3 trillion in assets, i.e., 83.4% of the total assets of all the mutual funds analyzed. Morningstar groups these funds into a 3×3 matrix along the dimensions of market capitalization[6] (large-caps: the largest 5% of 5000 plus equities by market capitalization; small-caps: the bottom 5%, and mid-caps the remaining equities) and investment objective (the growth stocks tend to have high price-to-earnings and price-to-book value ratios, and future growth prospects, compared to the smaller price-to-earnings (P/E) and price-to-book value (P/B) ratios but higher dividend yields of the value stocks).

Exhibit 3.3: Performance of equity mutual funds categorized by market capitalization and growth versus value criterion. The size of the block reflects net assets of the fund category, i.e., largest: \$774 billion, large \$499–554 billion, small \$93–143 billion, and smallest \$44–77 billion.

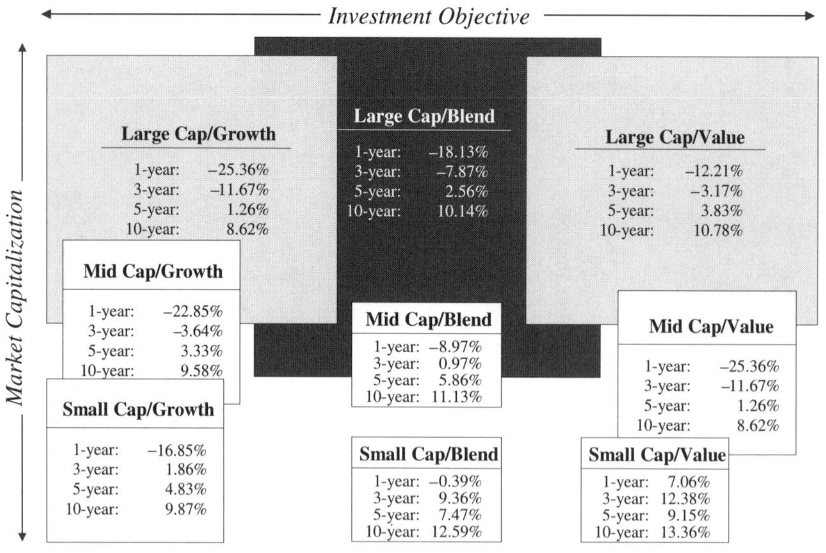

Source: http://screen.morningstar.com/quarterend/Q22002/QEFundCategoryReturns.html

These data offer an interesting insight. The small-cap value funds are best performers here, and the large-cap growth funds the worst, whether we look at the past one year record or ten. But, despite their apparent immunity to the market's bull versus bear states, small-cap value funds account for less than 3% of the total assets. Why this reluctance to embrace such stellar performers? The reason is volatility. Judging from the 1926–2001 statistics in Ibbotson Associates' 2001 yearbook,[7] for instance, the expected annual returns on small-company stocks range from −48.9% to 87.7% at a 95% confidence level, compared to the expected annual returns of 26.6% to 53% for the large-company stocks. Investing in the small stocks clearly involves a roller-coaster ride. As will be discussed in Chapter 5, this illustrates a simple fact, that investors demand higher returns on the equities that entail greater risks, forms the core of modern financial theory and is precisely what the Capital Asset Pricing Model (CAPM) is based on.

A "Buying" Opportunity!

The tendency of returns to revert to their long-term averages, seen so clearly in Exhibit 3.2, is at once a reassuring and yet worrisome aspect of the market's behavior during its current bear run. Though steep, the considerable drops suffered by the broad market indexes since their March 2000 peaks have only brought their average annualized growth rates closer to the historic rates. Take the S&P 500 index, for instance. Based on the data in Ibbotson Associates' 2001 yearbook, its total annual returns (i.e., capital appreciation and dividend reinvestment) during the 1926–2001 period have averaged 10.7% per year, over two-thirds of which came from capital appreciation and the rest from dividends. But these returns averaged a whopping 25.13% in the 5-year period from 1995 to 1999, so much so that, despite its 9.1% and 11.9% drops in 2000 and 2001, a $1000 investment in this index on January 3, 1995 still amounted to $2813.49 on December 31, 2001, and $2443.23 on July 1, 2002, the latter because of a 13.16% drop in the first half of 2002. This is the reassuring part. These drops have already brought the average total annual returns on this index for the last ten years to 11.43%, a figure that is considerably close to the historic mean. The worrisome

Exhibit 3.4: Total returns for 20-year trailing and forward holdings on the S&P 500 index show a strong negative correlation (= −0.59). The periods of stellar growth are likely to be followed, therefore, by those of mediocre to poor returns. The returns here are real, having been adjusted for inflation, and cover the entire 1871–2001 history of S&P 500 index.

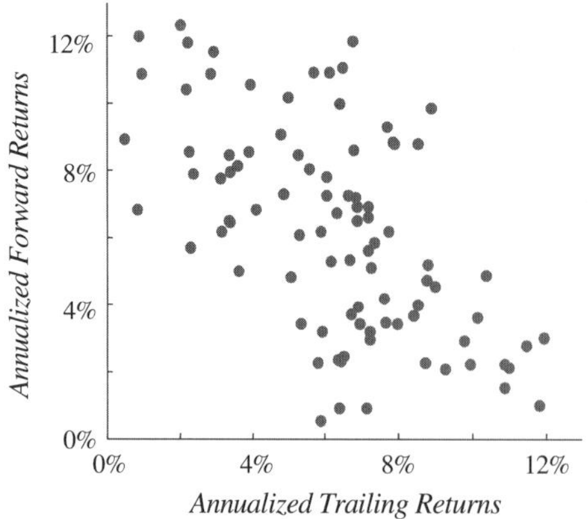

Source: http://www.globalfindata.com

part is the implicit possibility that the market's periods of stellar performance tend to be punctuated by those of sub-average returns.

Looking once again at the S&P 500 total return index, for instance, it can be seen in Exhibit 3.4 how strongly negative the correlation[8] of returns for the trailing (or past) and forward (or next) 20-year holding periods has been through the 1871–2001 history of the index.[9] This shows the market's strong tendency to revert to the mean. With such stellar returns in the 1990s, therefore, there is a good chance that the market will give substantially sub-average returns in the immediate future.

How low might these sub-average returns turn out to be? Exhibit 3.4 tells us that they are unlikely to be negative, if held for 20 years or longer — note the total absence of any negative returns here. Another guidance that this exhibit offers is the mean of these returns: they average to $6.26 \pm 0.52\%$ per year at the 95% confidence level. As will be shown later in this chapter, this is a stable estimate, and is statistically indistinguishable from the $6.59 \pm 3.23\%$ mean of annual returns, and $6.77 \pm 1.32\%$ mean annualized return for 5-year holdings, over the market's history.[10]

Compared to the 15–20% returns that the 1990s had deluded the investors into expecting from the market, even this average rate seems paltry, not to speak of returns inferior to this. But then, with the annual US inflation at 1.2%, 1-year US Treasury bill at 2.1%, 10-year Treasury securities at 4.86% and 30-year Fannie Mae, Ginnie Mae funds and corporate bond index at 6.4–7%, even a 5–7% annual rate of return over the long haul implies a decent enough premium[11] on the total return index.

The fear that future returns on the market may not match the historic average of 7% per year, adjusted for inflation, that Social Security Administration's Office of Chief Actuary assumes[12] for the next 75-year time horizon, has been central to the ongoing debate on the future of the Social Security program. This rate, based on Ibbotson Associates' yearbook and Jeremy Siegel's popular book[13] on investing in the stocks, is higher than what our analyses later in this chapter show. Our analyses yield rates higher than what the equilibrium future rate may turn out to be,[14] based on the Gordon growth model explained in Box 3.1, and the extrapolation of historic price, earnings and dividend data. But this is not an issue that defines whether equity investing would be healthier for or detrimental to the future of our social security

Box 3.1: The Gordon Growth Model

The Gordon growth model provides a simple way to value an equity as also the market. The price (P) here is the present value of the future cash stream. If this cash stream comes as dividend (D) that grows at the annual rate g, and r is the annual rate for discounting that future receipt to its present value, then,

$$P = \frac{D}{1+r} + \frac{D(1+g)}{(1+r)^2} + \frac{D(1+g)^2}{(1+r)^3} + \cdots$$

$$= \int_0^\infty De^{-(r-g)t}dt = \frac{D}{r-g},$$

because this cash flow can continue *ad infinitum*, the life-expectancy of a business, or of the market, being infinite.

Successful firms do not pay out all their earnings (E) in dividends, and plow the retained earnings back in order to finance growth. In the equilibrium state, or over the long term, the sustainable rate for g = ROE × RR, where ROE is the return on equity (= r), which is also called the *capitalization rate*, if market value = book value, and RR is the *retention rate* (= 1 – D/E). These mean that

$$P = \frac{D}{(r-g)} = \frac{E}{\text{ROE}} \quad \text{or} \quad \frac{P}{E} = \frac{1}{\text{ROE}}.$$

This also explains why the P/E ratio is so important, i.e., the larger the P/E ratio, the smaller the firm's return on its equity and the more stressed the firm's management.

system. Instead, as will be shown in the next chapter, our rationale here is that risk-adjusted returns on equities have been historically superior to those on fixed income instruments. We therefore set this issue aside, for now, and address two other questions that are more immediately related to this discussion of the market's current bear run: one, if a long-term investor can expect to retrieve the paper money lost in this bear run and two, if this is not the right time to invest.

Indeed, caught in the market's continued hemorrhage is the plight of the patient but hapless investor whose concern is no longer whether the boom era of dotcom millionaires will return but whether the wealth already lost can be retrieved, if ever. Consider, for instance, someone who invested in the market when the S&P 500 index peaked at 1527.46 on March 24, 2000 and has thus lost over one-third of that investment by June 28, 2002. How long might it take for such a person to recoup this loss? To answer this question, Exhibit 3.5 summarizes the time that the S&P 500 total return index has taken in the post-World War II period to recover from its 10% or deeper drops. Only real or inflation-adjusted returns are used here. Also, in order to compare realistically with the present situation, included here are only those of the market's troughs that coincided with the business cycle troughs.[15]

The growth in all these recovery phases has been rapid. Clearly, if this history is any guide as to what we can expect at the end of the

Exhibit 3.5: Recovery times and growth rates for the market's rebound from losses during economy-wide downturns in the post-World War II period.

Stock market trough	Associated business cycle trough	Market's drop from its last peak	Recovery time	The annualized growth rate during recovery
June 1949	October 1949	10.60%	3 months	44.82%
December 1957	April 1958	16.80%	7½ months	29.43%
June 1970	November 1970	38.70%	2½ years	19.58%
September 1974	March 1975	54.90%	8½ years	9.37%
March 1980	July 1980	31.60%	3 years	12.66%
July 1982	November 1982	32.60%	8 months	59.18%
October 1990	March 1991	20.20%	3½ months	59.18%
Current?	?	> 35.2% (?)	?	...

current bear run, then Exhibit 3.5 has answered the questions that we had posed earlier. One, even the "worst-case" scenario of investing in the market at its peak does not have to become a nightmare, so long as the time horizon for investment is long or the *patience capital* is not squandered, as would surely occur if one sells off at the market's bottom and thus lock in the losses. Two, whether or not the returns over the next decade or century will be as good as they have been in the past, the returns immediately at the end of this bear run are likely to be far from anemic — note that the slowest rates in Exhibit 3.5 are 9.37–12.66% per year! A downturn such as the one we now have is perhaps the type of buying opportunity that investors usually dream about. Incidentally, one need not be a computer wizard in order to estimate these rates. A crude estimate can be made from the *rule of 70*, an empirical formula an investor should always carry in the back of the head, i.e., the time a number would take to double in value is 70 divided by the rate of growth.

The *technical* concepts of moving averages and Bollinger bands provide a convenient tool to identify a "buying opportunity". Exhibit 3.6 illustrates this for the S&P 500 index. The index remained above its 20-month moving average through the first quarter of 2000 but has stayed below that level ever since. The first period usually exemplifies an overbought or overvalued market and the latter an oversold or

Exhibit 3.6: Technical analysis shows that the market has been "oversold" since November 2001 and has already tested its floor several times during the ongoing bear run.

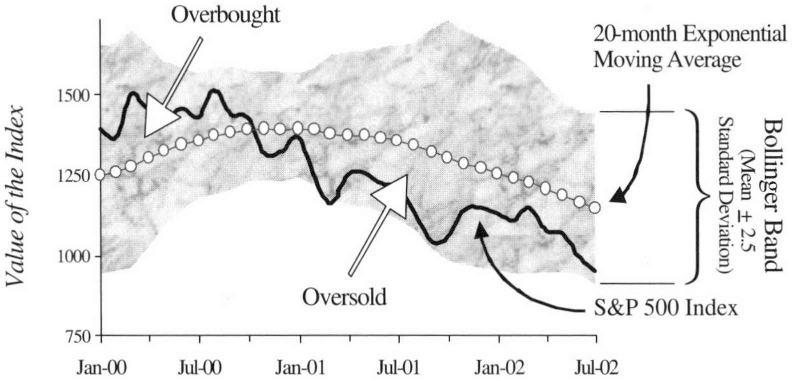

undervalued one. In such a *technical analysis*, the support for the market floor is identified at the lower end of the Bollinger band, set at *mean minus 2.5 times the standard deviation* (the band's upper end is set, likewise, at *mean plus 2.5 times the standard deviation*). As will become apparent when we discuss the properties of a normal distribution model in Section 3.4, this band contains almost 99% of the observations. Exhibit 3.6 thus shows that, by mid-year 2002, the market was already seeking its floor for the third time during its current bear run. Once it finds that bottom, the question would be whether it is *a bottom* or *THE bottom*. Being based on the current statistics, this *floor* is hardly inviolate, however. Rather, it is a dynamic number that adjusts itself continually to the evolving market fluctuations.

This search for the bottom of the market is where *technical* analysis meets *valuation* analysis, simply because an oversold market or equity is also an undervalued one. After all, it is not that the galloping overvaluation of the 1990s market had raised no alarms until the bubble eventually burst in early 2000. Recall, for instance, the Fed chairman Alan Greenspan's famous 1996 quote, "*irrational exuberance*". Of the predictions about where the market was headed then, the two most successful calls were made in the popular press using two valuation measures: the P/E (price-to-earnings) ratio[16] and Tobin's Q.[17] Exhibit 3.7 graphs the 20th century history of these ratios for the S&P 500 index. Notice how both the ratios were rising to their historic highs in the late 1990s.

Correct as these calls were, they have also exposed a problem with the valuation models. The P/E ratio did not peak with the market in early 2000, for instance, but in mid-year 2002 when the prices had already popped sharply. Why? Because earnings tumble when the overall economy shrinks, and if they drop faster than the prices then P/E ratio can only rise. How good a valuation measure would this ratio be, then, if it does not distinguish the market's rise from its fall? Add to this the fact that, as was mentioned in the endnote earlier, aggregate prices of the equities in S&P 500 index have risen faster than earnings, while the corresponding dividends have grown the slowest. The graph for the P/E ratio in this exhibit shows its deviations from the resulting trend, therefore, not the ratio itself. Likewise, as for Tobin's Q, seeking to

Exhibit 3.7: The top panel shows the variation of P/E ratio (as log deviations from the trend) and bottom panel shows that of Tobin's Q (as log deviations from the mean) for the S&P 500 index.

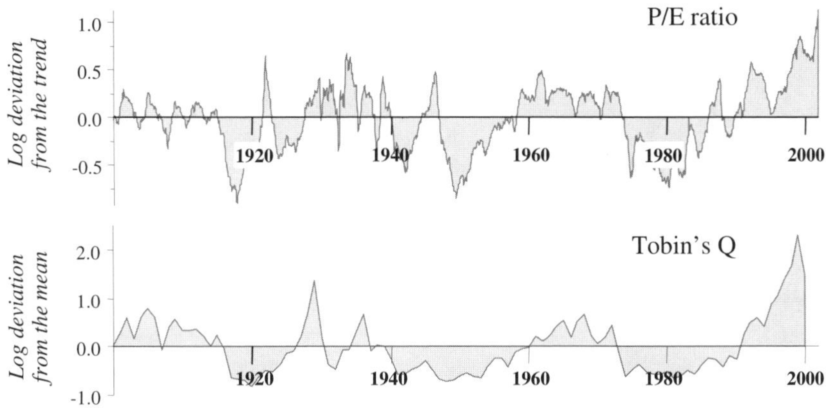

Sources: P/E ratios: http://aida.econ.yale.edu/~shiller/data/ie_data.htm
Tobin's Q: http://www.smithers.co.uk

identify its peaks as the harbingers of market's doom makes it hard to reconcile its lows during 1940–1960 with the June–October 1949 and December 1957–April 1958 market and business cycle troughs. Perhaps we could argue that this parameter is not as effective in a depressed economic environment as when the economic times are good. But that only begs the question whether a reliable measure should not work in all contingencies. A better alternative would then be to examine the macroeconomic environment under which the market functions.

The Macroeconomic and Demographic Factors

The determination by Business-Cycle Dating Committee of NBER (National Bureau of Economic Research), in November 2001, that the US economic activity had peaked in March 2001, also meant determining that the present recession had begun on that date. A recession is an economy wide slump that depresses employment, personal income, sales and industrial production. That the equity markets too would be depressed, then, is hardly a revelation. Thus, the market's present bear

Exhibit 3.8: As GDP was operating above its potential from 1998 through the first half of 2001, it is likely that an overheating economy could not have sustained the market's continued rise.

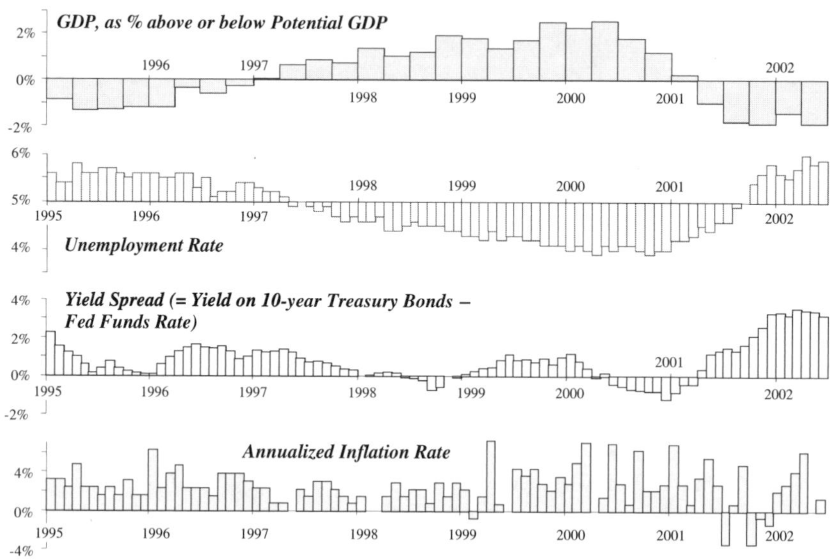

run merely reflects the fact that the GDP (Gross Domestic Product[18]) had three quarters of negative growth in 2001 and is yet to recover from the recession. This also explains the market's impressive growth in the late 1990s. As is evident from Exhibit 3.8, the GDP was operating above its potential from 1998 through 2000.

Of the macroeconomic indicators that are shown in Exhibit 3.8, yield spread (10-year treasury bonds less the federal funds) and GDP gap (i.e., potential GDP less actual GDP) are of immediate relevance to the market's performance. As will be shown in the next chapter, the former is a leading indicator of the stock market and the latter a lagging indicator. Clearly, while yield spread is not the concern that it was in 2000–2001, the GDP gap is. This is the reason why Exhibit 3.8 also shows unemployment and inflation rates.

Two other macroeconomic factors raise particular concerns, though. One, while personal income has been rising, consumer debt service burden has been rising faster than disposable personal income. As the

Exhibit 3.9: The consumer debt service payments have risen faster than disposable personal income, personal savings rates are about the lowest they have been in decades, and the corporate profitability is down.

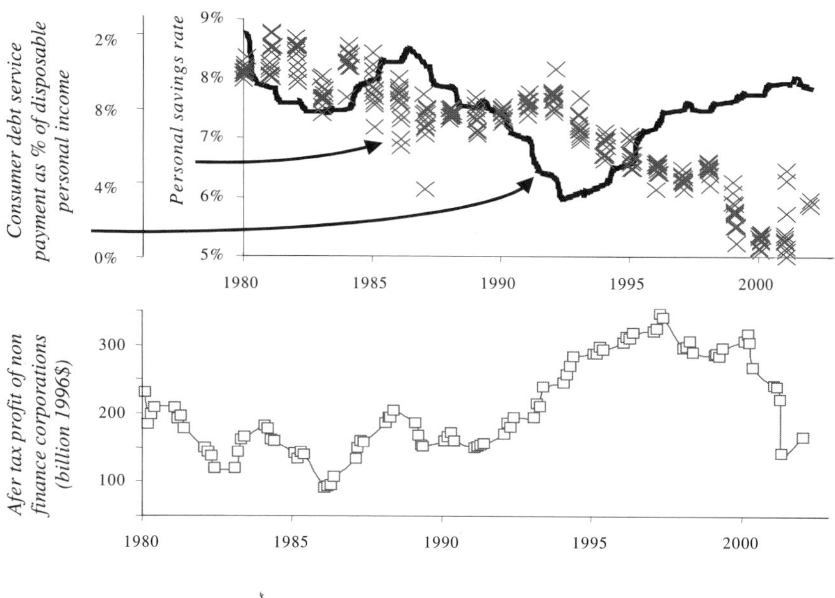

1990s growth was consumption driven, personal savings rate has steadily declined, from 8–8.5% of disposable personal income in 1990–1992 to −0.4–0% at times in 2000–2001, before climbing to 2.8–3.1% so far in 2002.

The top panel in Exhibit 3.9 summarizes these trends. To the extent that consumer spending has kept the economy resilient, any dampening of this debt-laden consumer's confidence can be deleterious to the economy's speedy recovery that the market now needs. Two, as shown in the bottom panel of Exhibit 3.9, after-tax corporate profitability is now back to the 1991–1992 levels. On the face of it, the rise in corporate profitability during 1995–1999 correlates well enough with the rise in P/E ratios (Exhibit 3.7) to make the exuberance seem quite rational.

Prices rise and fall faster than earnings, however, so exacerbating volatility in the earnings. Therefore, we now confront a situation where either the profits need to double in order to justify the current prices, depressed as they are, or prices need to fall still farther. Corporate America's debt burden[19] is the limiting condition here: it amounted to

60% of nonfinancial companies' net-worth at the start of 2002, when financial liabilities were 91% of the financial assets. But, unlike the situation the consumers face, corporate America's ratio of net interest payments to cash flow has declined, to about 25% in 2001, from a little under 40% in 1990–1991 and about 30% in 1981–1982.

With over one-half[20] of American households now participating in the stock market, one would ordinarily expect the market's woes to adversely affect the consumer's confidence and the economy. But part of the shock from the market's fall appears to have been cushioned by skyrocketing housing prices, and partly by retirement and pension plans contributions. This is because most of America's savings go to mortgage payments and retirement plans. As for the former, while the drop in interest rates has kept the payments low, the rise in housing prices has kept the perception of wealth high. On the retirement preparation front, much of the investment is through IRAs (individual retirement accounts), 401(k) and 403(b) retirement and annuity plans, and pension plans. Only about 42 million workers in private industry and state and local governments now depend on the defined benefit plans like those of CalPERS (California Public Employees' Retirement System) and General Motors (GM). Compared to this, the number of workers covered by the defined contribution plans has now risen to about 58 million. The bear market's toll on these plans has not been as heavy as the market's drop itself, thanks to their conservative management styles that force strict allocation ratios among stocks, bonds and real estate. But then, while their losses are insignificant compared to the 401(k) losses suffered by the Enron employees, they have hardly escaped unscathed.[21] The approximately $150 billion CalPERS, the nation's largest public pension plan, lost about 5% in 2001, for instance, and the assets of GM's $65 billion pension plan, the nation's largest corporate plan, dropped by about 5.7%. The pension plan assets of S&P 500 companies, net of obligations, are likely to be $200 billion in the red in 2002, however, compared to their 1999 surplus of almost $300 billion. Add to this the clamor to expense stock options, and we can see why the earnings picture may take a while to improve.

Bidding house prices up has not been the only result of the market's decline, however. Despite the fact that interest rates now are the lowest

Exhibit 3.10: Savings deposits have been attracting money since early 2000 in much the same way as the market did until its early 2000 peak.

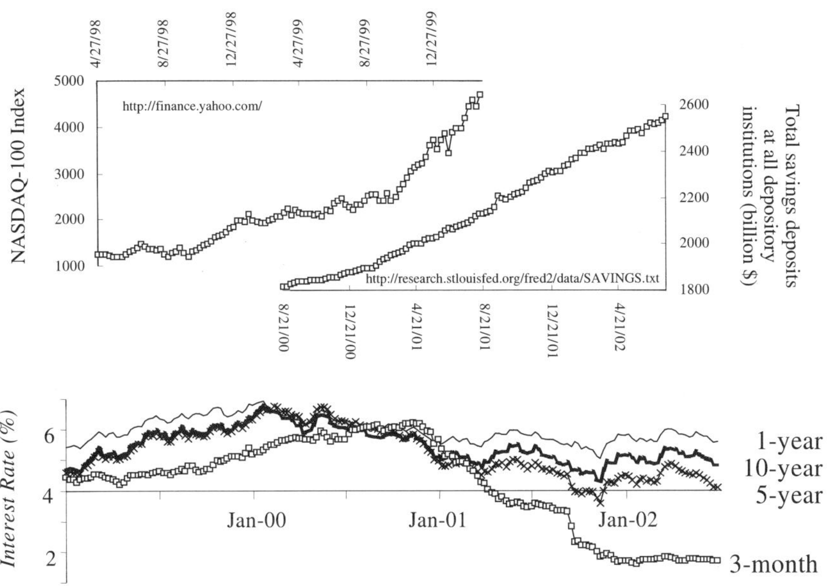

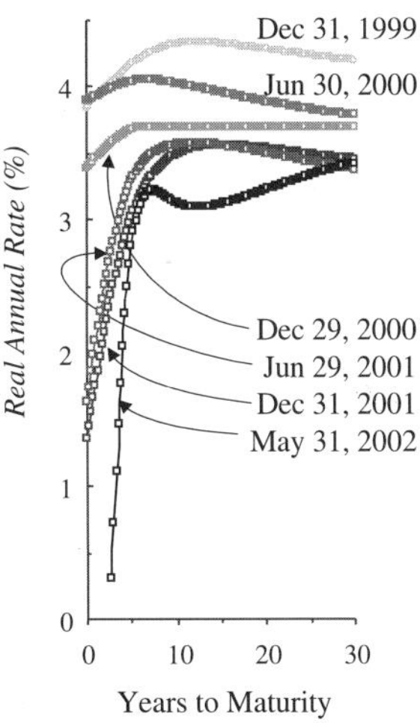

Exhibit 3.11: The top panel shows how interest rates have generally moved since January 1999. Notice how the 1-year rates have been generally the highest throughout this period, except for a brief interlude in late 2000 when the 3-month rates were the highest. As to blaming the Fed for engineering the yield-curve inversion, these data suggest that the Fed's tightening of rates in 2000, and the aggressive cuts in 2001 may well been reactive rather than proactive moves. The real yield curves on the right show that it was not until the second quarter of 2002 that we had a more normal looking yield curve.

Sources: (a) Interest rates: St. Louis Fed at http://research.stlouisfed.org/fred/data
(b) Yield curves: Professor J. Huston McCulloch's home-page at http://economics.sbs.ohio-state.edu/jhm/ts/ts.html

they have been in decades, money has continued flowing into the savings deposits. Exhibit 3.10 shows a 100-week graph for NASDAQ 100 leading to its early 2000 peak and the 100-week graph of total savings deposits in all institutions since that peak. Notice how eerily similar they seem, particularly when we look at the latter in the light of abysmal interest rates!

Interest rates have played a major role in the market's history since January 2000 (Exhibit 3.11). As measured through the rates on Treasury's 2–30 year bonds and 13-week bills in the secondary market, long-term interest rates generally declined throughout the year 2000, but the short-term rates continued rising until early November. Lenders usually demand, and receive, higher rates on long-term bonds, in compensation for letting the money remain tied up over the long haul, than on short-term debt instruments such as a 13-week or 3-month treasury bill or note. Since yields received on these instruments relate inversely to interest rates,[22] the yield curve usually slopes upwards, much like the May 31, 2002 yield curve in Exhibit 3.11 (bottom right panel). But notice in this exhibit how this yield curve remained inverted[23] through much of 2000–2001, with greater yields on 2–5 year bonds than on those with 10–30 year maturities. This ordinarily points to darker clouds of inflation and defaults on the horizon, when spiraling interest rates increase the demand for fixed-rate instruments like bonds, so raising their prices and lowering their yields. The Fed's recurrent rate hikes in 2000 had a salutary effect on the yield curve, but a more normal looking picture could not emerge until the second quarter of 2002, after a series of aggressive rate cuts in 2001.

The historically low interest rates have exacerbated the weakening of the dollar (Exhibit 3.12) which, having had an extraordinarily long bull run, was ripe for correction anyway. This compounds the market's woes, though, partly by encouraging foreign investors to take their profits and run and partly because the pressure to support the dollar adds to the Fed's need to raise the interest rates in order to stem inflation. An attractive alternative for the Fed is to raise the money supply, much like what had to be done in order to be ready for the Y2K. But that is what led to the drama of rising in interest rates in 2000 followed by cuts in 2001!

Exhibit 3.12: Though welcome news for exports, dollar's drop can translate into the flight of foreign investor.

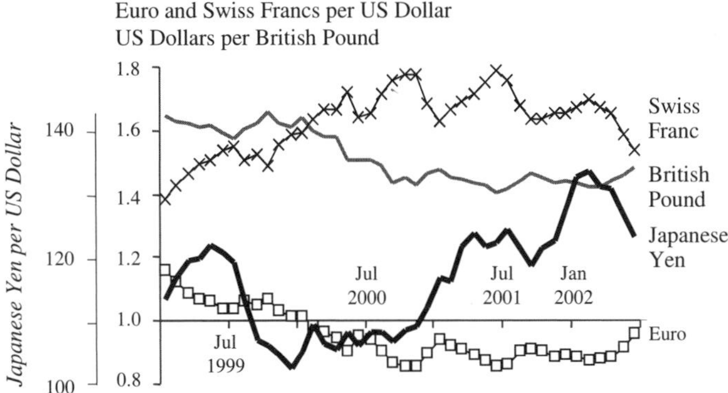

Why invest in the midst of such vexing uncertainties about the market, the economy and interest rates, one may well ask. But then, as logic and the past experience tell us loud and clear, the opportunities for investment abound in a depressed market, as at the present time. Besides, as we show in Chapter 5, ignoring the market instead of braving its gyrations is a costly option. This is because of three imperatives: life expectancy is rising worldwide, work life expectancy is falling, and the

---

expectancy gap for receiving full retirement benefits is rising. More and more of us should thus expect to spend longer years in retirement, and retire sooner than planned, but may have less and less to live on, if what most of us have budgeted for retirement income is to be the only source of income when we retire.

This look at the market's ongoing bear run illustrates the need to analyze the statistical structure of the market's performance history. Implicit in the statistics quoted here, for instance, is the fact that the stocks, large and small, give negative returns one-third of the time. While this certainly offers a better than even chance of positive returns, negative returns tend to come in seemingly interminable droves, of which the present bear run itself is an example, as do positive returns. Also, as is evident in Exhibit 3.4, holding a diversified portfolio tied to a broad market index for 20 years can still give returns that may not be any improvement over the relatively safe US Treasury bills and bonds. To learn whether such risks are indeed common, and if the probability of their recurrence can be lowered, we need to look at the statistical structure of real total returns. This is the task that the last section of this chapter will address, after we have looked at the market's 1990s bull run in the next section.

3.3 The Soaring 1990s

The capitulation since March 2000 can hardly mask the impressive growth of financial markets worldwide in the past decade. This apparent "peace dividend" at the end of the Cold War generated great euphoria and an unprecedented fascination with CNBC, the Motley Fool and 13,000 like sites on the Internet. Recall the clamor,[24] on the eve of the new millennium, for the DOW at 36,000 to 100,000 within the next 15–25 years. The market was truly a raging bull through much of the 1990s, particularly its latter half.

The Win-Win Game

In hindsight, it has become fashionable to label that bull run as hype. Some even called it "irrational exuberance". But it will take a long while, and a more pessimistic view of the future than investors have, before we can separate the speculative part of that growth from the fact that it was also propelled by a significant increase in economic productivity. What also remains true as yet is that, despite the incessant drops since March 2000, the cumulative gains of the past 10–15 years surpass most other similar intervals in the market's history. These gains were basically market wide, as can be seen in Exhibit 3.13, which compares the total returns (i.e., with reinvesting of dividends) data for selected indexes. Note that all posted significant gains through the 1990s, as the total returns in all these indexes multiplied three to four-fold between December 29, 1989, and January 2, 2000. Suppose you had invested $1000 in these indexes on the first trading day of 1990. As for NASDAQ 100 index, that investment would have grown almost seventeen-fold, to $16,887, at the opening of trade on January 2, 2000, before giving up over two-thirds of it so far in the current bear run.

Taken together with Exhibit 3.1, these data show why the market's continuous decline since March 2000 has not caused the crisis in investor confidence that one would have ordinarily expected. Had the market registered 10.7% annual total returns in nominal dollars, as it has averaged during 1926–2001 based on the Ibbotson Associates' 2001 yearbook, then a $1000 investment made in January 1990 would have only amounted to $2764 at the end of the decade. But the growth in the decade of the 1990s was so rapid that even the almost nonstop bleeding since March 2000 is yet to take away those gains. Also note that what

Exhibit 3.13: The growth of a $1000 investment made on opening of trade on January 2, 1990, the first trading day of the 1990s, at the close of trading on December 31, 1999.

Market index	Value of the investment	Cumulative total return	Annualized rate of return
Dow	$4674	367%	16.67%
NASDAQ 100	$16,887	1589%	32.66%
S&P 500	$5239	433%	18.21%
Wilshire 5000	$5453	445%	18.49%

Sources: http://finance.yahoo.com; http://www.globalfindata.com and http://www.fool.com

we hear in the daily press is the index, not the total returns on it. Many of the S&P 500 companies periodically pay dividends that most of the NASDAQ stocks do not. The loss in S&P 500 total return index during the current bear run is considerably less, and almost inconsequential to a long-term investor, therefore. The index itself lost 10.14% in 2000 and 13.04% in 2001, for instance, whereas the total returns on it suffered losses of 9.1% in 2000 and 11.9% in 2001. The $1000 investment of December 1989 in an S&P 500 portfolio would have thus become $3596 on June 28, 2002. Of course, your investment would not have dropped in the year 2000 at all, and would have instead gained over 40% in the year, had it been committed to a broad-based real estate index like the S&P Homebuilding Index (to compare with the results in Exhibit 3.13, this investment would have reached $2354 on January 2, 2000, and $3271 on October 31, 2000). These figures yield annualized growth rates of 8.94% and 11.56%, respectively, and are clearly paltry compared to the other rates here.

Investing is a matter of making choices between different stocks and their indices, and between diverse types of assets as stocks, bonds, real estate, currencies, precious metals, and the like. This requires understanding how the markets for these different asset types perform over time, individually and relative to one another, under diverse economic conditions. It is not that this requires a 20/20 vision of the future — those with foresight comparable to the hindsight might well be better off playing the lottery, after all! It is just that, as will be examined in the following pages, financial economics does indeed have over three centuries of history offered a broad, and reasonably reliable, road map to make these choices.

A look at Exhibit 3.14 clarifies this point further. It graphs the monthly data on selected indexes and shows that robust growth is the main reason why one-half of American households today are investors in the stock market. Notice how, despite the significantly higher appreciation of NASDAQ index than those of the other indices compared here, particularly since mid-1998, the gains to investors in a fund or portfolio indexed to the S&P 500 index were comparable, most of the time, to those by the NASDAQ Composite. This is also true of the Dow, although the data on this index are not shown here, and reflects

Exhibit 3.14: Overall, stock market has risen appreciably through the 1990s, although that of the technology heavy NASDAQ Composite has been most noted. The indices shown here are normalized at 1000 at the opening of trade on January 2, 1990.

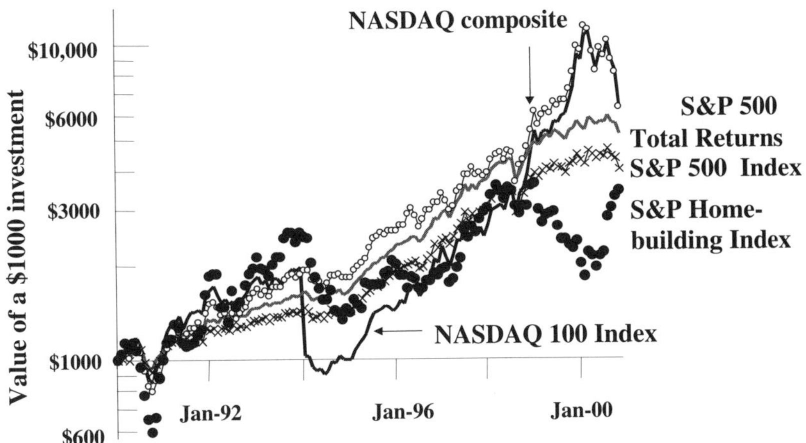

the fact that many of the S&P 500 and Dow companies pay dividends whereas most of the NASDAQ companies do not. Looking only at this pattern of growth, it is clear that this growth is exponential — when the vertical axis is scaled logarithmically as in Exhibit 3.14, the time-paths of all these indices are broadly linear.

This opens up a convenient way for computing the corresponding annual growth rates. Suppose P_0 is the initial price of any stock or asset, or the value of an index as in the present case, that rises to P_1 after one period. The return r on P_0, given by $r = (P_1 - P_0)/P_0$, can be then generalized as

$$
\begin{aligned}
P_1 &= (1 + r)\ P_0 \\
P_2 &= (1 + r)\ P_1 = (1 + r)^2\ P_0 \\
\cdots &\quad \cdots \quad\quad \cdots \\
P_T &= (1 + r)^T\ P_0 = P_0 \exp\ (rT), \qquad (3.1)
\end{aligned}
$$

after T periods, if r remains constant through the entire period. Here, "exp" denotes the exponential or Euler's constant (= 2.71828), and r has been taken to be such a small number that r^2 and higher power can be neglected.[25]

Equation (3.1) is the well-known compound interest formula that captures the time value of money. Simply stated, the value of money changes with time, depending on what use we put it to.[26] You could leave it under the pillow, for instance, or in a secured locker, and use it at a later date. The risk, then, lies in inflation that would eat into its value by the time the money is used. You could also deposit it in a bank at a fixed rate of interest, or buy a bond, a Treasury bill, or a certificate of deposit, or buy real estate or gold, for that matter. Still another alternative would be to use the money to either finance your own business or buy a share in another business. The goal, of course, is to find and maximize the real rate of return (i.e., the nominal yield adjusted for inflation).

A well-known example of how the "time value of money" works in practice is Peter Minuit's 1626 purchase of Manhattan Island for \$24. Taking the current value of this real estate as \$60 billion, the annual growth of such an initial investment would have to average 5.94% through these 375 years, as the computations in Box 3.2 show. This assumes a continuously compounding rate, however, whereas the rates computed in Exhibit 3.13 use the annual compounding formula $P_T = (1+r)^T P_0$. To compute the average value of r, we note from Equation (3.1) that

$$r = \ln\left(\frac{P_{T=1}}{P_0}\right) = \ln\left(\frac{P_{T+1}}{P_T}\right).$$

Box 3.2: The Time Value of Money

For Peter Minuit's purchase of the Manhattan Island for \$24 in 1626, a real estate whose current value is \$60 billion, say, we set P_0 = \$24, P_T = \$60 billion and T = 2000 − 1626 = 374 years in Equation (3.1).

Taking the logarithms of the two sides, we then have, for...

Annual compounding:

ln (60,000,000,000 ÷ 24)
 = 374 ln (1 + r)
or ln (1 + r) = 21.63956 ÷ 374
 = 0.05786
so that r = 5.96% per year.

Continuous compounding:

ln (60,000,000,000 ÷ 24) = 374 r
so that
r = 21.63956 ÷ 374
 = 0.05786
 = 5.79% per year

Thus, compounded continuously, the average rate $\tilde{r}$ over time horizon T is

$$\tilde{r} = \left(\frac{1}{T}\right)\ln\left(\frac{P_T}{P_0}\right). \tag{3.2}$$

As is evident in the last column in Exhibit 3.13, annualized growth rates for the investments that are compared here range from 16.67% (Dow) to 32.66% (NASDAQ 100). These rates are certainly impressive, particularly as the corresponding numbers have averaged 2.95% for inflation and 4.9% for the 3-month Treasury bills during this period. Also note that all these stock market indexes did better than the real estate-based Homebuilding Index by a wide margin. It is hardly surprising, then, that the 1990s saw the emergence of stocks as the preferred investment vehicle. This is corroborated by the comparison of house prices and Homebuilding Index in Exhibit 3.15. Note that, during the past 15 years, house prices nationwide have barely kept pace with the CPI whereas

Exhibit 3.15: Based on the data from OFHEO (the Office of Federal Housing Enterprise Oversight), HUD and the Census Bureau, real estate prices have barely kept pace with inflation. A real estate stock index like S&P Homebuilding Index has annually grown at three times this rate.

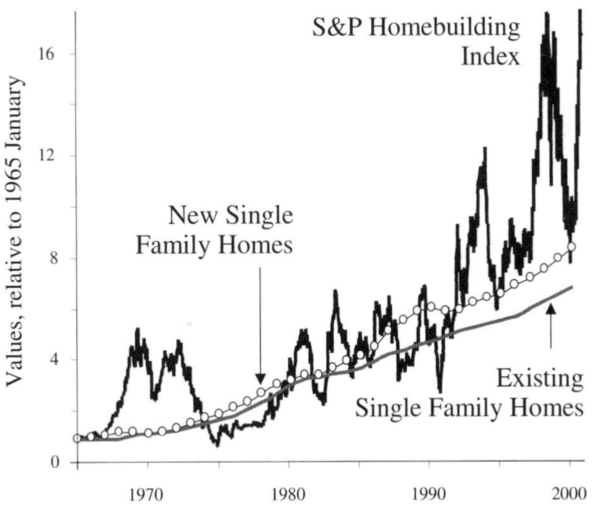

Source: http://www.ofheo.gov

the S&P Homebuilding Index has galloped rapidly. Apparently, stocks often do better than the underlying assets themselves.

The Tech Sector's Growth in Perspective

Perhaps the most noted feature of the market's performance in this bull run was first the spectacular rise of technology stocks, particularly the Internet sector comprising the stocks commonly labeled as the dotcoms, in the late 1990s and their rather precipitous decline in 2000. Exhibits 3.13 and 3.14, in which we saw the NASDAQ 100 index as having appreciated the most in the late 1990s, reflects this. But it is doubtful if the market's tumble in this first year of the new millennium was indeed engineered by the fall of the dotcoms. For instance, Exhibit 3.16 compares the AMEX Internet index (IIX) and the Semiconductor index (SOXX) of

Exhibit 3.16: The relative price performances of Internet, Semiconductor and NASDAQ indexes, all set at one in January 1996.

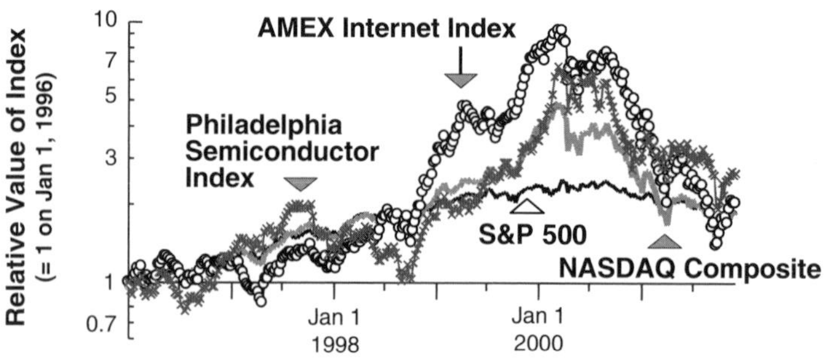

Exhibit 3.17: The market's growth accelerated in the 1990s.

Period	Years	Dow		S&P 500	
		Average annualized return	Cumulative total return	Average annualized return	Cumulative total return
1995–1999	5	20.12%	190.64%	24.08%	251.37%
1990–1999	10	17.73%	367.39%	19.20%	432.91%
1980–1999	20	17.10%	2442.73%	17.75%	2584.11%

the Philadelphia Stock Exchange with the NASDAQ Composite and S&P 500 indices. The much smaller (in terms of market capitalization) IIX and SOXX indices gained the most during market's upturn in 1999, and gave up those gains during the market's 2000–2002 downturn. But, despite this volatility, they were not particularly lower than the broader NASDAQ Composite and the S&P 500 indices than their relative levels in January 1996.

There is no disputing the fact that the market's growth in the 1990s was spectacular by all accounts, particularly in the second half of the decade. As the total returns data in Exhibit 3.17 for 5, 10 and 20-year holdings ending in 1999 show, the annualized returns are highest for 1995–1999, lower for 1990–1999 and lowest for 1980–1999. Even these "low" 1980–1999 annualized returns are appreciably superior to the 1926–2001 annual average of 10.7% mentioned earlier, however. The market moves in cycle and the 1995–1999 phase was clearly the culmination of a cycle that had already begun earlier.

Explaining what might have triggered this acceleration is difficult, however. The renowned Warren Buffett recently put forth a seductive idea,[27] for instance, that buying stocks is likely to work well when the

Exhibit 3.18: The market value of US stocks peaked at 190% of GNP in March 2000. Despite the drop since then, the ratio was 133% in October 2001, compared to 109% at the market's peak in September 1929.

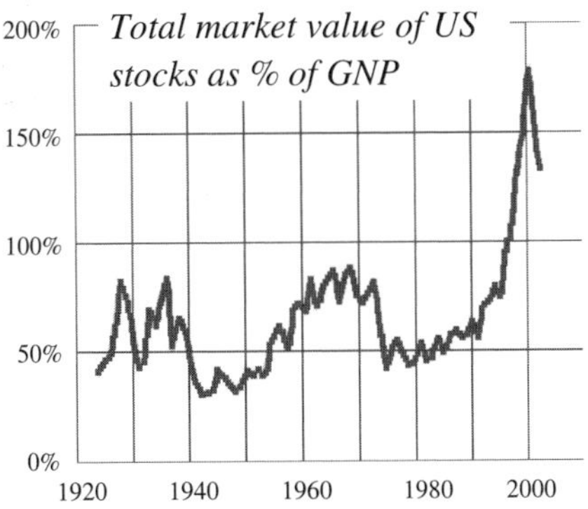

Source: Redrawn from the *Fortune Magazine* (December 10, 2001) article: "Warren Buffett on the Stock Market".

market value of publicly traded securities is within 70–80% of the GNP (Exhibit 3.18) (and rising). This would make a good working rule to spot the danger of market's imminent collapse, and matches the patterns in P/E ratio and Tobin's Q data that we saw in Exhibit 3.7, but making sense of a ratio in which the denominator is a cash flow number (GNP or GDP) and the numerator an asset (market value) is difficult. Mercifully, though, Exhibit 3.18 also tells us that the need for such an exercise does not arise every day.

The ratio of corporate profits to GDP presents a similar picture and is shown in Exhibit 3.19 where we graph after-tax corporate profits, adjusted for inventory valuation and capital consumption, as deviations from the mean (= 5.56% + 0.12% at 95% confidence level). Notice that the market's bull run in the 1990s, particularly towards the end of the decade, coincided with one of the best runs in corporate profitability. The last time corporate America's profits enjoyed a similar bull run was in the 1960s and, as will be shown in Section 3.3, the 1960s were indeed comparable to the 1990s in terms of real total returns on the market, notwithstanding the seemingly unsettling social upheavals of that era.

Exhibit 3.19: After-tax corporate profits, with adjustments for inventory valuation and capital consumption, relative to the GDP. The data presented here are deviations from the average.

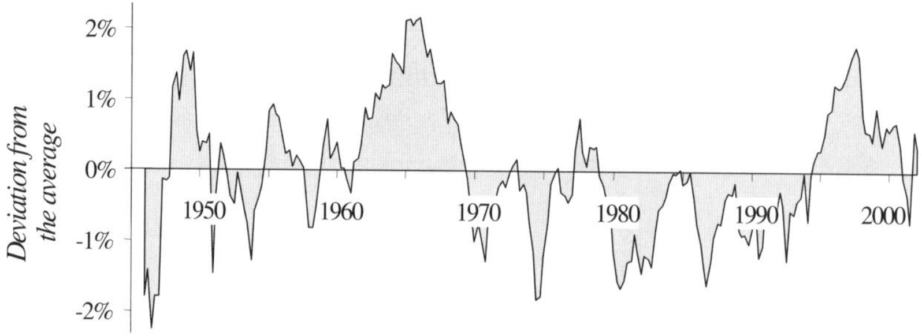

Apparently, expectations about the growth potential matter the most here. Returning briefly to the Gordon growth model of stock valuation that we introduced in the previous section, it is easy to see why expected growth (g) dominates the pricing (P) of a stock. This equation can be written as

$$P = \frac{D}{(r-g)} = \left(\frac{D}{r}\right)\left[1-\left(\frac{g}{r}\right)\right]^{-1}$$
$$= \underbrace{\left(\frac{D}{r}\right)}_{\text{No-growth component}} + \underbrace{\left(\frac{D}{r}\right)\left[\left(\frac{g}{r}\right)+\left(\frac{g}{r}\right)^2+\left(\frac{g}{r}\right)^3+\cdots\right]}_{\text{The present value of growth opportunities}}, \qquad (3.3)$$

based on Binomial series expansion,[28] because g is smaller than r, and (g/r) is positive but less than one. Looking at the right hand side of Equation (3.3), note that D/r is the equity price of a company that pays out all its earnings as dividends and therefore has no prospects of growth whereas the second factor is defined largely by the (g/r) ratio, i.e., the closer g is to r the closer (g/r) will be to one and the greater the number of terms that will need to be used. The multiplier $[(g/r) + (g/r)^2 + (g/r)^3 + \cdots]$ is therefore the reason why we are willing to pay higher prices for the shares of companies with better prospects of growth. It is called the present value of future growth opportunities. To understand its impact, note that if $(g/r) = 0.9$ then $P = 10 \times (D/r)$, if $(g/r) = 0.5$ then $P = 2 \times (D/r)$, and if $(g/r) = 0.1$ then $P = 1.11 \times (D/r)$.

In terms of the assumptions explained earlier, (g/r) in Equation (3.3) can be treated as the plowback ratio or retention rate and, as the examples of successful companies amply demonstrate, plowing part of their earnings back into the business is a strategy that businesses, particularly in dynamic sectors, commonly use in order to finance their growth. Indeed, we can do no better on this issue than reproduce from Buffett's above article his following quote of John Meynard Keynes:[29]

> "Well-managed industrial companies do not, as a rule, distribute to their shareholders the whole of their earned profits. In good years, if not in all years, they retain a part of their profits and put them back in the business. Thus there is *an element of compound interest* operating in favor of a sound industrial investment."

Interestingly, despite numerous fluctuations over time, this plowback or retention ratio has been generally increasing. Exhibit 3.20 illustrates this pattern for the average of S&P 500 companies since 1940. Notice how rapid this ratio spiraled in the mid-1990s. This rising trend in the

Exhibit 3.20: The average retention rate or plowback ratio for stocks in the S&P 500 index has been generally rising.

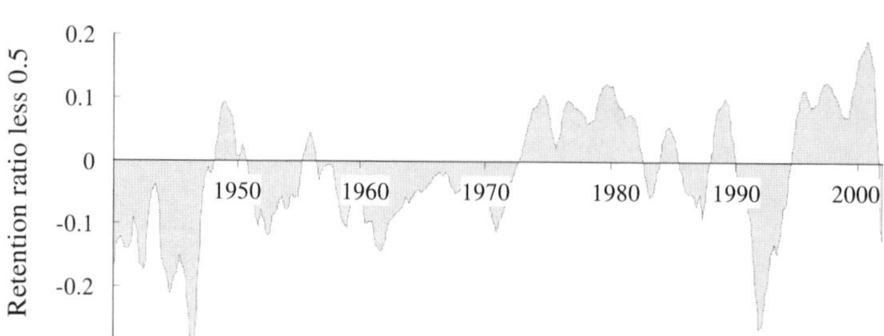

retention rate has been the subject of several recent studies, most notably by Eugene Fama and Kenneth French[30] whose detailed study documents an increasing reluctance of the companies to pay dividends.

The importance of retention rate is also borne out by the fact that, as mentioned earlier, dividends accounted for less than one-third of the 10.7% average annual total return on S&P 500 stocks during the 1926–2001 period. An increase in this rate implies a concomitant decrease in dividend payment or the payout ratio, and the data in Ibbotson Associates' 2001 yearbook also show that, over this 75-year history, the long-term decline in payout ratio has added about 2% per year to the returns on stocks. Could we, therefore, blame the increase in the retention rate for the market's spectacular price spiral in the 1990s? Perhaps only to some extent because the 1990s also witnessed an equally spectacular demographic shift on one hand and the dawn of the information technology based work life and virtual market place on the other.

Do Demographics Matter?

Demographics amply justify the optimism that the investors have about the US stock market's enduring capacity to give excellent returns. For instance, the Census Bureau's population estimates and projections identify 45–64 year-old — the stage in life when we tend to accumulate the most of our retirement focussed savings — as the fastest growing age-cohort of US population in this decade (Exhibit 3.21). Before we get excited about this, however, we should note that Census Bureau

Exhibit 3.21: The 45–64 year-olds are likely to be the fastest growing age-cohort in this decade, and 65 years and older in the following two decades, reflecting the fact that 75 million babies were born in the US between 1946 and 1964, i.e., the generation known as baby boomers.

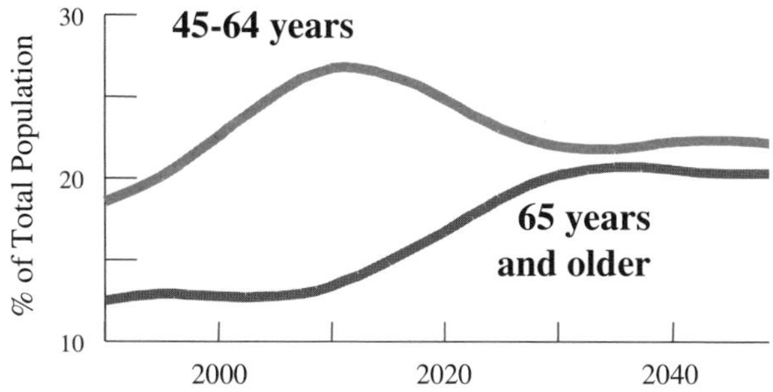

Source: US Census Bureau

projections also show a rapid rise of the 65-plus age-cohort in the immediately following decades, coupled with a concomitant fall in the 45–64 year cohort. Implicit in the assumption that retirement focussed savings of baby boomers will propel the stock market skywards in the immediate future, therefore, is the prospect of the market's imminent crash when this generation begins its post retirement selling or consumption. Spectacular as the market's recent growth has been, this raises the question whether the 1990s growth rates can be indeed sustained over a protracted period of time.

As can be seen in Exhibit 3.22, economic history amply attests to this assumption. The top panel graphs the S&P 500 total return index, set at one in January 1930, and the bottom panel shows changes in three demographic factors during this period: total US population and its 45–64 and 65-plus segments. Note how all the three periods of stock market's accelerated growth — mid-1930s, 1960s and 1990s — coincided with accelerations in the growth of the 45–64 cohorts. Therefore, arguing that Americans reach their peak earning and spending levels at 47, economists like Harvard's Harry Dent[31] even advocate investment strategies that focus completely on demographic trends.

The direct evidence of how this aging of baby boomers fueled the demand for stocks comes in the form of retirement savings accounts.

Exhibit 3.22: Demographics have clearly played an important role in shaping the history of the stock market. The top panel shows how the S&P 500 total returns index has appreciated since January 1930 and the bottom panel the annual changes in total population and in its 45–64 year and 65-plus segments. Notice how closely the market's appreciation matches the relative growth of 45–64 year segment.

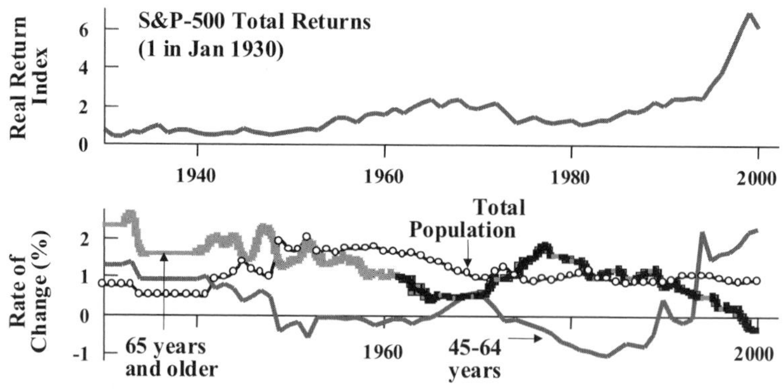

Exhibit 3.23: The ballooning of Americans' retirement assets in the 1990s.

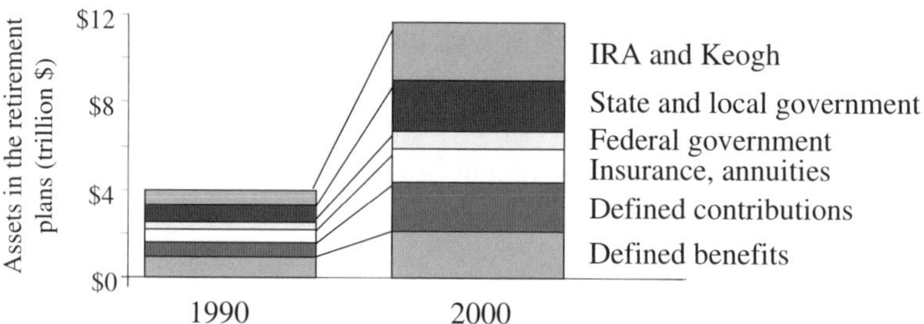

Source: Employee Benefit Research Institute

Exhibit 3.23 shows the different kinds of assets, and their worth, that Americans had in their retirement savings plans. Total assets in all these accounts amounted to almost $12 trillion in 2000, compared to a little under $4 trillion in 1990. This itself amounts to almost 11% annual growth in the demand for different kinds of investment assets. What compounded this demand is the fact that most of it came under the individual retirement and Keogh accounts, with an annualized growth rate of over 14%, and defined contribution plans, which include 401(k)s and 403(b)s and had an annualized growth rate of over 12%. Significant proportions of both these types of accounts, IRAs and the defined contribution plans, tend to be invested in stocks. Earlier we saw how the market's 2000–2002 meltdown has adversely affected many of these accounts (many Enron employees have lost all their nest eggs, for instance). Here we can see the demand side of this equation! True, part of this growth was fueled by ballooning stock prices. But it also brought in new money into the market.

The High-Flying High-Techs

The rapid growth of the stock market in the waning years of the twentieth century has coincided not only with a rapid growth of the 45–64 year age-cohort but also with an equally impressive growth of the technology sector of US equities market. The result has been the rise of such wealth-builder stocks like EMC, Microsoft, Dell and the like. Exhibit 3.24 shows what an investment of $1000 in such technology stocks, made on the day each began trading on the exchange, would have grown to by

Exhibit 3.24: What an initial investment of $1000 in selected high-flying equities, made on the first trading day of each stock, would have grown to by June 30, 2000, in nominal dollars. Stocks are identified here with the ticker symbols given in Exhibit 3.25.

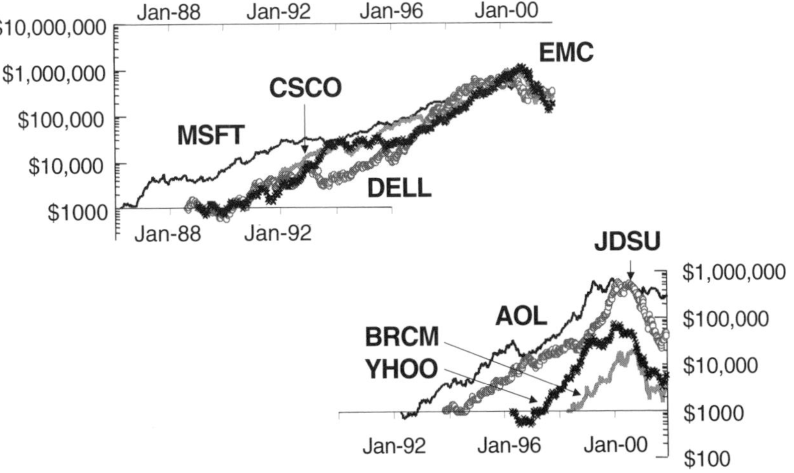

Exhibit 3.25: Statistics on the high-flying wealth-builders graphed in Exhibit 3.24

		$1000 invested on	...would, on December 31, 1999, have become	...at the annualized growth rate of	Value of the investment on June 28, 2002
Microsoft	MSFT	March 14, 1986	$668,760	47.17%	$308,870
Dell Computers	DELL	August 17, 1988	$576,270	55.88%	$295,370
EMC Corporation	EMC	December 16, 1988	$582,360	57.67%	$80,490
CISCO Systems	CSCO	March 26, 1990	$656,370	66.53%	$170,960
America Online	AOL	March 19, 1992	$606,960	82.27%	$117,680
JDS Uniphase	JDSU	November 16, 1993	$312,860	93.81%	$10,360
Yahoo	YHOO	April 12, 1996	$78,670	117.66%	$5370
Broadcom	BRCM	April 21, 1998	$10,160	138.83%	$1310

June 30, 2000. This is only a sampling of the high-flying issues that have glamorized the stock market in general and its technology sector in particular. As is apparent from some of the statistics summarized in Exhibit 3.25, these have, until the tech sector's meltdown during 2000–2001, been the outstanding millionaire-makers since the market's October 1987 crash.

The market's 2000–2002 correction has taken some glamour off these wealth-builders. The wisdom of listing Yahoo and Broadcom here too could perhaps be questioned, despite our disclaimer that this is not an exhaustive list. But then, even with their recent declines, it is surprising to see how well these stocks have held their own since their inception. All these companies are young, in the technology sector, and have been the market leaders in their niches. But, as Exhibit 3.24 shows, the average annually compounding growth rate tends to flatten with the company's age.

The success of the equities of these companies masks the striking failures of a large numbers of other companies, however. The spectacular rise of "dotcom" stocks in the late 1990s, and their catastrophic fall after the first quarter of 2000, clearly illustrates this. The product life

Exhibit 3.26: The five stages in a product's life cycle are development, introduction, growth, maturity and decline. The first two of them effectively collapse into one for investing purposes other than venture capital, because that is when the revenues from sales rise but the profits are yet to catch up. The risk here is that of the promise of prospective profits from growth not materializing in time for the firm's survival.

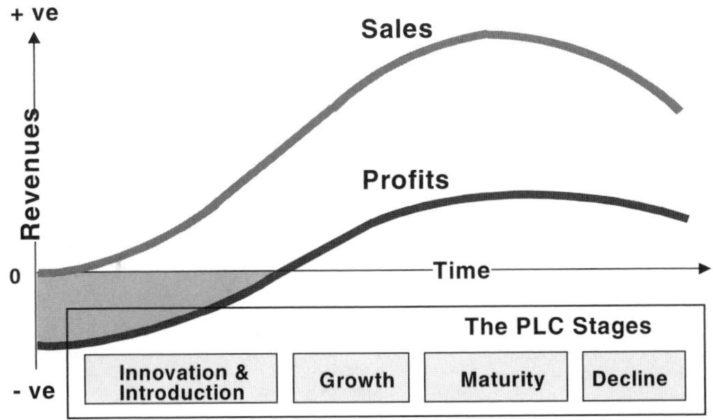

cycle (PLC) theory[32] helps us understand the underlying economic rationale. As Exhibit 3.26 explains, growth is most rapid, on this picture, in the second stage of the product life cycle. The technology sector in today's market is mostly at the innovation, introduction and growth stages of this cycle when the sales are yet to build up and profits are negative. Pricing a mature business in the more established or traditional sectors of the economy is less prone to uncertainties than pricing the prospective superstars of new technology that dominate the NASDAQ indices.[33]

Stocks of companies and businesses in a growing sector of the economy are likely to gyrate faster with the economy than those in the other sectors. But, in addition to this consequence of the PLC concept, two other criteria are equally germane to understanding why some companies and businesses succeed while others do not. One is the concept of *strategic intent*. The companies that have risen to global leadership began, according to this concept,[34] with ambitions that bore no proportion to their resources and capabilities, and succeeded through strategic intent, by setting the goals that greatly exceeded their grasp and marshaled the will and the resources to achieve those goals. Note, however, that in the extremely dynamic industries like the technology sector, strategic intent soon begins to either lead or lag strategic action. Divergences such as these produce *strategic dissonance*[35] that necessitates the reformulation of strategic intent.

The other concept is that of the *competitive advantage*. As argued by Michael Porter[36] in the context of nations, but also relevant to businesses in today's technology-induced and intricately globalized market place,

---

Stocks, bonds, IRA, 401(k) ... it's all too risky and complicated! Our retirement package is a 25-year supply of arthritis cream, denture adhesive, and adult diapers."

www.glasbergen.com

Exhibit 3.27: The determinants of national competitive advantage, according to Michael Porter.

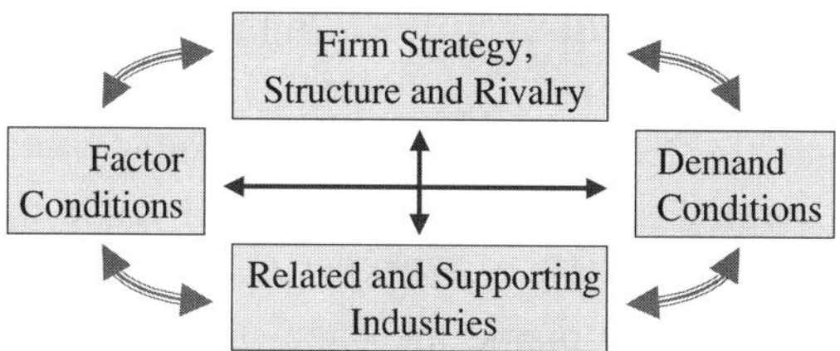

businesses today are those that learn to meander through the determinants of competitive advantage shown in Exhibit 3.27 above.

These are the issues that lead to the question of valuations — a subject that we will explore in depth in Chapter 6. For now, therefore, it should suffice to assert that we view the market's recent turbulence more as the opportunity for future growth than as the prospect of imminent disaster. This reinforces the message that was abundantly clear from data in Exhibit 3.5 earlier.

We now look for further confirmation using the longer data sets on stock performance.

3.4 The Long-Term History of US Stock Markets

The Early History

Let us now examine if the stock markets have generally performed as well in the past as they did in the 1990s. The problem is that, treating the stocks as reliable investment vehicles, as we now do, is a rather recent phenomenon. Common stocks have carried the stigma of speculation through much of history. This was the view held by such acknowledged stalwarts of the 1930s like Lawrence Chamberlain[37] who preferred bonds over stocks and Benjamin Graham whose advocacy of careful selection over holding a broad portfolio of diversified common stocks is now known as *value investing*. The market's rather wild gyrations, and most notably the infamous crash of October 1929, undoubtedly shaped these views. Note that, even though the crash did make the common stocks inexpensive enough to become attractive for value investing, it would be another 25 years before Dow reclaimed the pre-crash peak of 381.2 that it had reached on September 3, 1929. In the book *Security Analysis*,[38] Benjamin Graham and David Dodd were particularly harsh on Edgar Smith[39] for helping unleash the bull market mania of the 1920s. Smith had argued for owning a diversified portfolio of common stocks as the recipe for wealth accumulation. But Smith is not the person whom posterity would eventually blame the most for this. Instead, that credit is commonly accorded to John Raskob, albeit unjustly as will be noted elsewhere later. He had claimed, in an interview published in the Summer 1929 issue of the *Ladies' Home Journal*, that good common stocks bought for $15 every month for 20 years would grow into a portfolio worth $80,000. But the markets were on such a roll in the 1920s that the great Irving Fisher, a noted authority on the strategies[40] for successful investing in a rising market, had proclaimed barely a fortnight before the crash of 1929 that stock prices had reached *a permanently high plateau*!

This vigorous questioning of any claimed superiority of stocks over bonds as reliable instruments for long-term investment could not withstand the test of time, however. But, before comparing the historic performances of these two asset classes, let us first examine how well the stocks themselves have performed over time. Speculative gains are unlikely to be sustained over time, after all, based on the law of averages. It would be unrealistic, therefore, to expect a speculative market to have given any consistently positive returns over an adequately protracted period.

Exhibit 3.28 looks at the 200-year history of the US stock market, therefore. Now, exchange traded funds or indexes, e.g., spider (SPY) for the S&P 500 index, diamonds (DIA) for the Dow, QQQ for NASDAQ 100 etc., are rather new. The oldest of them, the SPY, debuted on the AMEX (American Stock Exchange) only on January 29, 1993. Nonetheless, if a unit trust investment like SPY was available for $1 on January 1, 1802, it would have, as shown in Exhibit 3.28, grown to about $630 at the end of 2000, if all the dividends had been used up in personal consumption. Based on Equation (3.1), this yields a paltry annual return of 3.29%! But, deferring the immediate gratification by plowing back

Exhibit 3.28: Top panel shows the growth of a $1 investment in the stock market made in January 1802, middle panel the monthly change in total return index, and bottom panel the total annual return, and its components, in annually rolling bands for 10-year averaging of the annual data. The data used here are freely available in the public domain, e.g.,

- Monthly data for 1871–1968, including the Cowles Commission reconstruction of a capitalization-weighted index of NYSE stocks are available at the NBER (National Bureau of Economic Research) macrohistory site http://www.nber.org/databases/macrohistory
- Monthly total return data for S&P 500 Composite Index since January 1970 can be retrieved from the website of Federal Reserve Board's Saint Louis branch at http://www.stls.frb.org/fred/data/business/trsp500
- Yahoo financial pages (http://finance.yahoo.com) and trial access at Global Financial Data website (http://www.globalfindata.com) also allow free access to these and related financial and economic time series data.

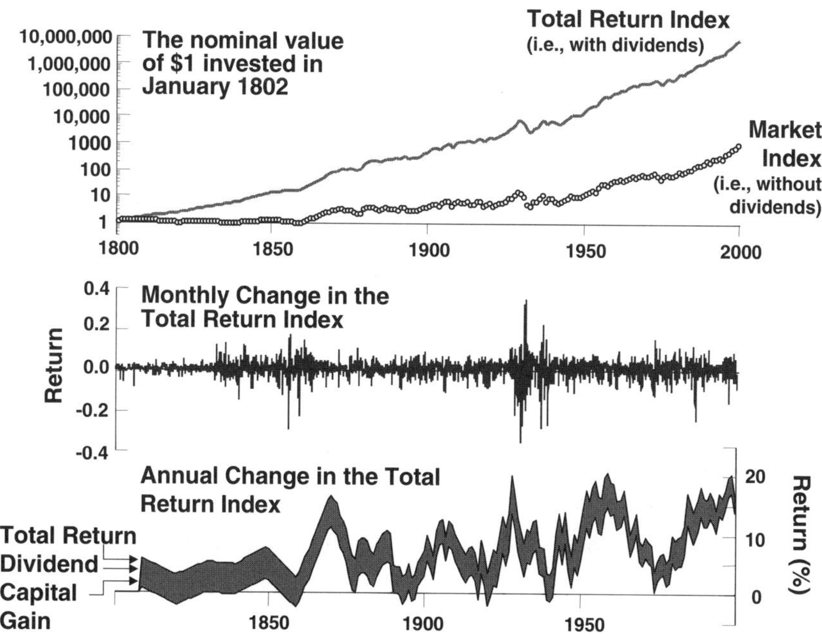

these dividends into that investment portfolio, instead of using them up upon receipt, would have raised this investment to $6.78 million at the end of 2000. The annual returns now average to a respectable and robust rate of 8.22% over this 199-year period. Peter Minuit's successors would have certainly found even the broad equities market equally attractive, nay, an even better, investment opportunity than Manhattan Island! Was such an opportunity indeed available then? It certainly was, as can be seen from the history of the Dutch and British stock markets that extend back farther into the past.

Dividends Made the Difference

These results clearly show, as was first established by Ibbotson and Sinquefield[41] for 1926–1975 and in Jeremy Seigel's[42] update of the reconstruction of the US stock market index for 1802–1870 by William Schwert,[43] that stocks offer robust returns in the long run. Dividends have contributed substantially to this staggering difference between the index values and total returns. This is because capital gains from price appreciation are not the only payoffs from owning a common stock. More often than not, the total return r received from such an investment comes partly from capital gain and partly from dividend, i.e.,

$$\begin{aligned} \text{return } r &= \text{capital gain} + \text{dividend yield} \\ &= \frac{(p_{t+1} - p_t)}{p_t} + \frac{\text{Div}_{t+1}}{p_t} = \frac{(p_{t+1} - p_t) + D_{t+1}}{P_t} . \end{aligned} \tag{3.4}$$

Here, p_t is the security's price at time t, p_{t+1} at time $t+1$, and D_{t+1} is the dividend received.

Since a stock's price is almost as likely to rise as fall, a proposition that flows directly from the *efficient market hypothesis* examined in Chapter 5, capital gains are likely to be positive as often as negative. This particularly holds when we consider daily returns only. Dividends are positive, however, and equal zero at worst because the firms that pay dividends to the shareholders do so by choice, not by obligation.[44] Dividends add to the capital gains, therefore, and cushion the effects of any losses that may occur.

Exhibit 3.29: Price, dividends and earnings on the S&P 500 stocks normalized for their values in January 1871.

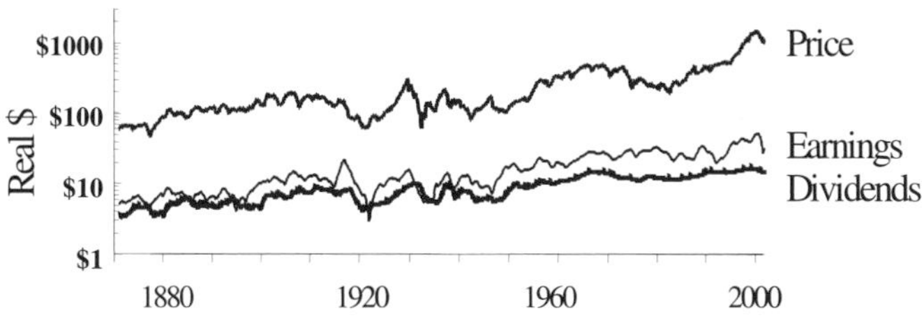

Source: http://aida.econ.yale.edu/~shiller/data/ie_data6.xls

Box 3.3: The Emperor, the Chess-Inventor, and the Power of Compounding

So enamored was the Emperor with chess, it is said, that he called the game's inventor and asked him to name his own reward. "Only one grain of rice, Your Majesty, ..." said the inventor, "...for first square on the board, two grains for the second, and so on, doubling the quantity at each step."

All the world's rice would not have been enough. With 64 such squares on the board, the final tally comes to $(2)^{63} = 9.22 \times 10^{18}$ grains of rice which, for the 65 milligrams traditional measure of a grain, amounts to 599.5 billion metric tons of rice. Even in 1999, the world produced only 596.5 million tons of rice!

A misperception that often crops up even in the otherwise well-informed circles is that dividends have declined in value. They have not, as can be seen in Exhibit 3.29 which traces the history of price, earnings and dividends for the S&P 500 index since January 1871. It is just that the growth in dividends has not kept pace with the growth in price, particularly in the 1990s.

The results in Exhibit 3.28 also display the effect of compounding — an effect that, as is apparent from the example of chessboard in Box 3.3, is indeed a powerful one. Notice how significantly this effect has amplified the cushion that an automatic reinvestment of dividends provides to an investment in the stock market. Thanks to these dividends, as can be seen in the bottom panel in this exhibit, the total returns have never been negative when we look at the 10-year averages of these data. Monitoring the hourly, daily, weekly or monthly performance of the market, as is apparent in the middle panel in Exhibit 3.28 that graphs the monthly returns, creates a noisy picture that masks such broad trends. Hence the recourse to a 10-year averaging.

These results ignore the effects of inflation, however, as they are given in nominal dollars. But \$1 fetched far more in 1802 than now — based on the consumer price index, \$1 in January 1802 had the same purchasing power as \$10.32 in December 2000. Thus, our nominal wealth of \$6.78 million at the end of 2000, to which the \$1 investment of Janaury 1802 grew, had the same purchasing power in 2000 that \$656,911 had in 1802. Therefore, a realistic comparison across these two centuries requires adjusting the dollar figures in Exhibit 3.28 for this change in the dollar's worth over time. The top panel in Exhibit 3.30 accomplishes this by recasting the results of Exhibit 3.28 in real dollars. It also graphs how the consumer price index has changed during this period.

This adjustment is made in the following way. Suppose $(X_n)_{\text{nominal}}$ is what the initial amount $(X_0)_{\text{nominal}}$ has grown to in n periods at the rate of r_{nominal} per period and that, during this period, inflation has raised the corresponding initial cost $(C_0)_{\text{nominal}}$ to $(C_n)_{\text{nominal}}$ at the rate $r_{\text{inflation}}$ per period. It then follows from Equation (3.4) that,

$$\begin{aligned}(X_n)_{\text{real}} &= \frac{(X_n)_{\text{nominal}}}{(C_n)_{\text{nominal}}} = \frac{(X_0)_{\text{nominal}}\,(1+r_{\text{nominal}})^n}{(C_0)_{\text{nominal}}\,(1+r_{\text{inflation}})^n} \\ &= (X_0)_{\text{real}}\,(1+r_{\text{real}})^n,\end{aligned} \tag{3.5a}$$

where $1 + r_{\text{real}} = (1 + r_{\text{nominal}})/(1 + r_{\text{inflation}})$.

Likewise, for the continuous time approximation $X_n = X_0 \exp(r^T)$ in terms of Equation (3.1), we have

$$\begin{aligned}(X_n)_{\text{real}} &= \frac{(X_0)_{\text{nominal}}\exp(r_{\text{nominal}}\,T)}{(C_0)_{\text{nominal}}\exp(r_{\text{inflation}}\,T)} \\ &= (X_0)_{\text{real}}\exp[(r_{\text{nominal}} - r_{\text{inflation}})\,T] \\ &= (X_0)_{\text{real}}\exp(r_{\text{real}}\,T),\end{aligned} \tag{3.5b}$$

where $r_{\text{real}} = r_{\text{nominal}} - r_{\text{inflation}}$.

Exhibit 3.30: The growth, in real dollars, of $1 investment in the stock market on January 1, 1802. The graph for the consumer price index is also shown here. As in Exhibit 3.28, the returns shown in the bottom panel are computed in annually rolling bands for 10-year averaging of annual data.

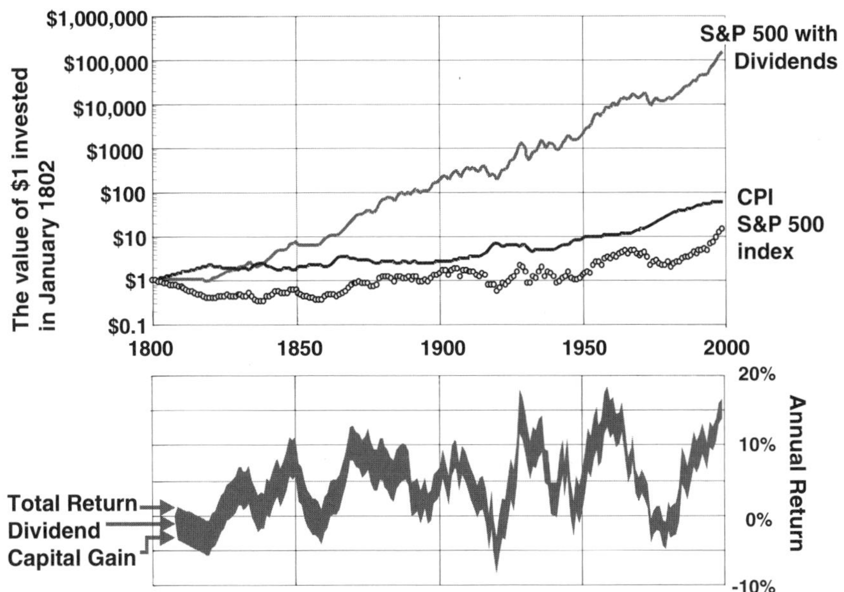

With this correction for inflation, the logarithmically scaled market index of Exhibit 3.30 is far more linear than the corresponding unadjusted data in Exhibit 3.28. Notice how the graph for the consumer price index (CPI) in Exhibit 3.30 remained almost flat through much of the nineteenth century but shows a faster rise through the twentieth century, particularly since the 1950s. Inflation, on the other hand, was the major scourge of the nineteenth century, a period that witnessed an overall deflationary trend as well.[45] This adjustment has had the effect of increasing the slope of the nineteenth century segment of market index in Exhibit 3.28, while flattening its twentieth century segment.

This adjustment also has a dramatic effect on our earlier inference, made from bottom panel of Exhibit 3.28, that the 10-year averaged total annual returns have never been negative. Those data also pointed to an overall rising trend until the present. But the corresponding

Exhibit 3.31: US economy in the twentieth century has experienced three periods of major stress — mid-late 1920s, late 1940s, and the 1970s.

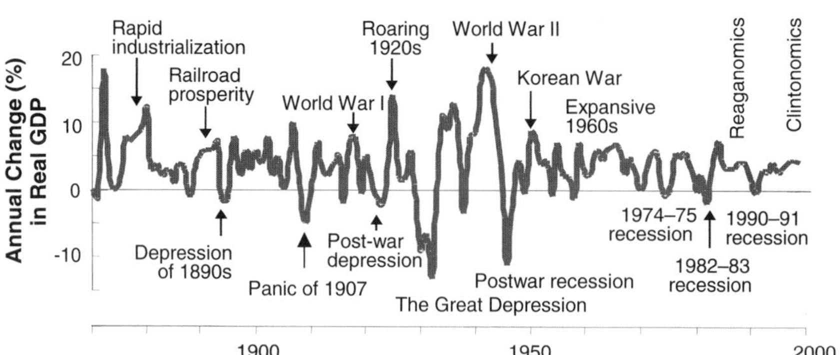

Source: Updated from *Macroeconomics* by Baumol and Blinder.[46]

inflation-adjusted data in Exhibit 3.30 contradict both these inferences. Instead, they show that, within the twentieth century, the market gave conspicuously negative real returns in the 1920s and 1970s, and rather abysmal total returns in late 1940s. This raises the scary possibility that the sluggish returns that the investors have received so far in this new millennium may well signify a repeat of the 1920s, 1940s and the 1970s. But then, as can be seen from Exhibit 3.31, these were economically stressful times for the nation at large. The market could have hardly remained immune to such macroeconomic constraints. Even the most pessimistic amongst us would not identify the present macroeconomic scene as anything comparable to those hard times.

Are the Returns Really Gaussian?

How reasonably can we extrapolate the market's pattern of past performance into the future, so that the investor can have some idea of what returns to expect? To answer this, we need to first ascertain if there are any patterns to these returns. Interestingly, a curiosity of the market's historic performance has been that, irrespective of whether we track the market continually during trading on the exchange floor or through its daily, weekly, monthly, quarterly or yearly closings, changes in the stock prices and index values fluctuate randomly. This is consistent with a basic observation in nature, known as Brownian motion,[47] and is the domain of probability theory and statistics. Much like all the other aspects of modern life, therefore estimation and use of mean, standard deviation and the related methods and techniques of statistical analysis have become integral to modern financial analysis.

Now, a sequence of empirical observations is taken to be randomly distributed if these observations occur independently of each other, and unpredictably so, and the statistical structure of the series remains unchanged no matter how often we replicate the experiment generating these observations. The data with these properties of independent, identical distribution (i.i.d.) often conform to the bell-shaped curve of normal[48] or Gaussian distribution. Take stock market returns $r_1, r_2, \ldots, r_n$, with $r_n = \ln (P_n/P_{n-1})$ from Equations (3.2) and (3.4), i.e., $P_n = (P_n + \mathrm{Div}_n)$, over n consecutive intervals. Their geometric mean $\tilde{r}$ is computed as

$$\tilde{r} = \left(\frac{1}{n}\right)\sum_{i=1}^{n} r_i = \left(\frac{1}{n}\right)\sum_{i=1}^{n} \ln\left(\frac{P_i}{P_{i-1}}\right). \tag{3.6a}$$

Much like the preferred path of particles in the Brownian motion, this mean value is where the individual values of returns tend to cluster, defining the central tendency.[49] Standard deviation (s) is the measure of how tight or dispersed this cluster is. It is the square root of variance (s^2) where the latter is estimated as

$$s^2 = \frac{1}{n-1}\sum_{i=1}^{n}(r_i - \tilde{r})^2 = \frac{1}{n-1}\sum_{i=1}^{n} r_i^2 - \frac{n}{n-1}\tilde{r}^2. \tag{3.6b}$$

Obviously, the tighter the cluster the smaller the values of $(r_i - \tilde{r})$ will be, and smaller, therefore, will be the variance and the standard deviation, and vice versa. As for the changes in either stock prices or indices, standard deviation (s) is a measure of volatility: the large values of standard deviation indicate large volatility.[50] This is true irrespective of whether the data follow normal or any other distribution. Following Tchebysheff's theorem that, given a number $k \geq 1$ and a set of n data $r_1, r_2, \ldots, r_n$, at least $[1 - (1/k^2)]$ data are within k standard deviations from the mean, at least 75% of the data should be within two standard

Exhibit 3.32: Normal distribution curve is symmetric about the mean, where it peaks, and tapers off to zero on either side, i.e., at $\pm\infty$. Note the standardization of returns in the horizontal axis by conversion into z-scale, where $z = (r_I - \tilde{r})/s$. As a practical application of this, note that the region to the left of $z = -1.645$ covers 5% of the normal curve's total area, and the region to the right the remaining 95%.

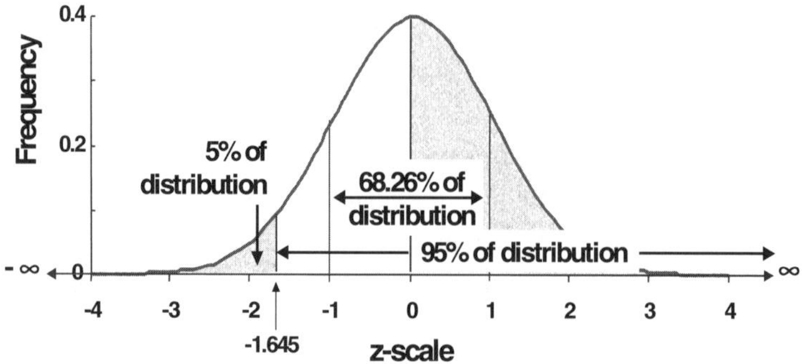

deviations from the mean, and almost 90% within three standard deviations. For normal distribution, 68.26% of the data lie within one standard deviation from the mean, 95.44% of the data lie within two standard deviations from the mean, and 99% of the data lie within 2.575 standard deviations from the mean. Recall our earlier discussion of normal distribution model in the context of Bollinger bands. We had then defined the band at 2.5 standard deviations from the mean. That was only for simplicity: actually, we would need to define the band within 2.326 standard deviations from the mean if we set the limit at exactly 98% and at 2.575 standard deviations, as mentioned above, in the case of 99%. Exhibit 3.32 displays a typical normal distribution curve.

The use of "geometric mean" rests on the approximation derived earlier in the context of Equation (3.1). If we compute the return (r) as the price change per period, i.e.,

$$r_n = \frac{(P_n - P_{n-1})}{P_n}, \tag{3.7}$$

and not as $r_n = \ln (P_n/P_{n-1})$, the result would be arithmetic mean.

Practical, conceptual and analytical reasons make geometric mean the preferred measure for the financial time series analysis. Suppose that a stock, trading at \$100 on day one, falls by 10% on day two and then rises by 10% on day three. Before you imagine that these rates give the stock's price as \$100 at the end of day three, think again: a 10% drop from \$100 means a day two price of \$90 which, raised by 10%, gives the day three price of \$99. Thus, at the end of day three, this stock has actually lost 1% of its day one price. For these data, the geometric mean $(= -0.10536 + 0.09531 = -0.01005)$ shows a 1.005% loss, so reflecting the reality better, than the formula for arithmetic mean $(= -0.1 + 0.1 = 0)$ which gives the mean return for this period as zero. Also, as shown in Exhibit 3.32, a normal distribution curve tapers off to zero at $\pm\infty$, whereas, in reality, the most that the price can drop to is 0, not $-\infty$. As to the other extreme of $+\infty$, would sane persons not reject the prospects of returns rising to $+\infty$, not a theoretical impossibility, as "wishful"? This implausibility to reach the extremes of $\pm\infty$ denies the arithmetic model the conceptual basis for using the normal distribution curve. This poses no problem to the geometric model, in which $r = \ln (P_n/P_{n-1}) \rightarrow -\infty$ as $(P_n/P_{n-1}) \rightarrow 0$ and $r \rightarrow +\infty$ when the prices rise exponentially. As discussed in the following section, this also enables the estimation of multi-period returns and risks by way of time-aggregation. A word of caution, though. Our use of the geometric mean rests on Equation (3.1), it applies only to the time-series data and would produce erroneous estimates if it is used for spatial data. Strictly speaking, the geometric mean of n data is the nth root of their product. Suppose you had a portfolio of two stocks and both were priced at \$100 at a given point in time. The mean price then is \$100, irrespective of whether you compute the arithmetic mean $[= (100 + 100) \div 2 = 100]$ or the geometric mean $[= \sqrt{(100 \times 100)} = 100]$. Suppose one of these stocks slid to \$90 at the next point in time, while the other rose to \$110, and you wish to compute the mean stock price in your portfolio now. The arithmetic mean will give you the accurate value of \$100 $[= (90 + 110) \div 2]$ whereas the geometric mean gives this value as \$99.7 $[= \sqrt{(90 \times 110)}]$!

Exhibit 3.33 shows the frequency histograms for the real monthly data for total returns on whole market index, i.e., for the 1802–2000 real or inflation adjusted total returns data presented in Exhibit 3.30. Note how these histograms display a symmetric distribution, much like the normal distribution model in Exhibit 3.23, with a pronounced peak

Exhibit 3.33: Histograms for total monthly returns on the US whole market index for the real 1802–2000 data of Exhibit 3.30. These returns have been computed using the geometric model here. The dark-shaded region corresponds to negative returns.

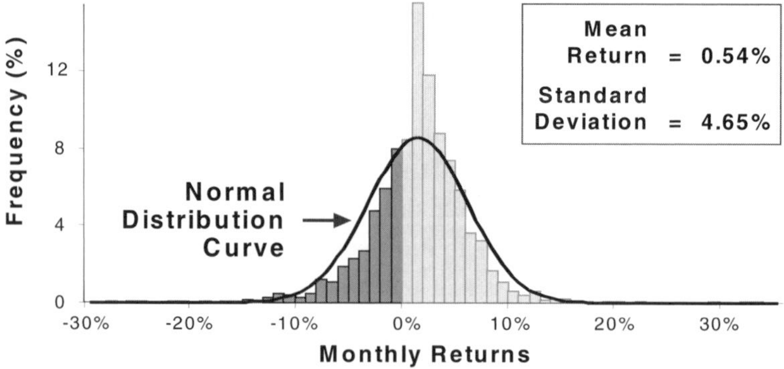

at the mean and diminution away from it. The problem is that, compared to the normal distribution curve drawn for the mean (= 0.54%) and standard deviation (= 4.65%) values of the observed data shown in this exhibit, these histograms have an excessively strong peak and extended tails. This raises the question whether our observed real monthly returns indeed follow the normal distribution model. The advantages of being able to describe the empirical data by a standard statistical model are obvious, however. For instance, it enables us to draw expectations of the market's likely performance, and thus formulate suitable strategies to hedge against the market's gyrations. The validity of a normal distribution model also means that the price next minute, next hour, or next day, should be independent of its current and past levels.[51] This cannot happen, of course, unless we assume that the price at any given point in time essentially reflects all the information needed to determine it. Curious as it may sound, this is the crux of the *efficient market hypothesis*, i.e., a financial economist does not define the market's efficiency in terms of how perfectly neat and tidy it is in following a pre-determined or predictable price path! Rather, the efficiency of a market is defined by how well it absorbs and reflects in price all the relevant information.

Applying the normal distribution model to market returns has been a matter of considerable critical concern in financial economics, therefore, ever since Maurice Kendall[52] first used it to formally describe the behavior of stock and commodity prices over time, arguing that that their random changes seem evenly distributed about the mean. Applying this model would certainly make it easier for the investors to draw rational expectations. The problem is that these data generally show volatility clustering and fat tails[53] of the kind seen in Exhibit 3.33, no matter what returns are used and how they are analyzed. The question, therefore, is whether the observed returns are indeed normally distributed.

Two statistical measures can help us answer the question as to how valid the assumption of normal distribution is for any given empirical data: skewness (S_k) and kurtosis (K_u). The first, S_k, measures how symmetric the observed distribution is and the other, kurtosis (K_u), measures if it is either too flat or too peaked relative to the theoretical curve. In terms of the nomenclature used in Equations (3.6a) and (3.6b), these two measures are estimated using Equations (3.8a) and (3.8b).

$$S_k = \frac{n}{(n-1)(n-2)} \sum_{i=1}^{n} \left(\frac{r_i - \tilde{r}}{s} \right)^3, \tag{3.8a}$$

and

$$K_u = \frac{n(n+1)}{(n-1)(n-2)(n-3)} \sum_{i=1}^{n} \left(\frac{r_i - \tilde{r}}{s} \right)^4. \tag{3.8b}$$

As shown in Exhibit 3.34, $S_k > 0$ or positive if the distribution is right-skewed, $S_k < 0$ or negative when the distribution is left-skewed, and $S_k = 0$ when the distribution is symmetric about the mean, as would occur for normal distribution. As for kurtosis, $K_u = 3$ for normal distribution. Therefore, $K_u > 3$ if the distribution is strongly peaked (leptokurtic) relative to a normal distribution, and $K_u < 3$ if the distribution is flatter (platykurtic) than normal distribution. These statistics for our 1802–2000 total monthly returns data are summarized in Exhibit 3.35.

Clearly, our monthly returns data of Exhibit 3.33 are leptokurtic and mildly left-skewed. Of these, the latter (i.e., skewness) value in Exhibit 3.35 is too small to be statistically significant, however. This is consistent with Peiro's[54] analyses of daily returns of several international

Exhibit 3.34: Skewness (top) and kurtosis (bottom) of distribution.

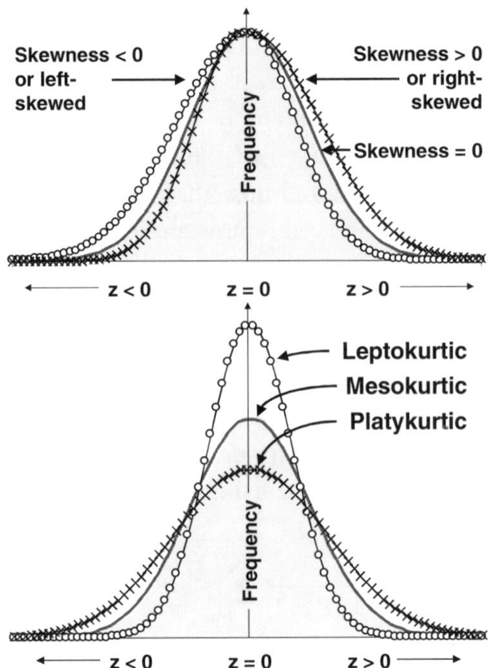

Exhibit 3.35: The characteristics of the normal distribution model as applied to 1802–2000 real monthly total returns of Exhibit 3.33.

Mean = 0.54%
Standard Deviation = 4.65%
Skewness = −0.44
Kurtosis = 6.66

stock markets and spot exchange rates that failed to find statistically significant asymmetries in most of the series. Skewness is hardly irrelevant, however, for it matters[55] greatly in day-to-day trading and investment decisions, and in pricing the options and evaluating their volatility, the details of which are discussed in our subsequent chapter on hedging and options. For our present focus on long-term investing, though, the results in Exhibit 3.35 make skewness an unlikely candidate for further exploration. Curiously, this applies to kurtosis as well. True, a high kurtosis ($\gg 3$) connotes as significant a deviation from the normal distribution model as a low kurtosis ($\ll 3$) does. But then, by implying a very high cluster of values within a rather narrow range, the former also assures the long-term investor of a higher probability that the realized return will not stray too far from the expected return.

The problem in using normal distribution model for our data on real monthly returns is also brought out, graphically, in the Q–Q plot[56] in Exhibit 3.36. It compares standardized values (or z-scales) of observed cumulative distribution with the corresponding normal distribution. These two data sets diverge appreciably beyond two standard deviations from the mean (i.e., for $z > \pm 2$). Had the observed data been normally distributed, all these values would have plotted on the 45°-Line. As 95.44% of the area under the normal curve falls within two standard deviations from the mean, this suggests that we can have 95% confidence in the estimation of the mean and its dispersion but cannot use a normal distribution model to estimate the extreme values.

Exhibit 3.36: The Q–Q plot graphically compares the standardized values of observed distribution of real monthly returns for the 1802–2000 period with the corresponding standardized normal distribution. Significant deviations from 45°-Line are clearly seen at the extremes.

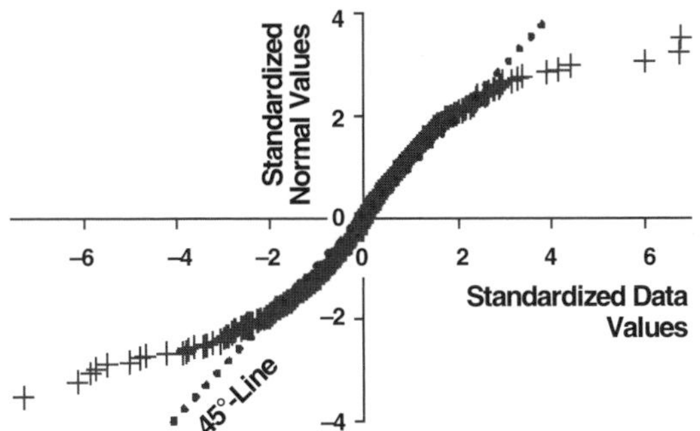

This has led to such alternatives[57] to the normal distribution model to describe stock market returns as the discrete mixtures of normal distributions, Student's t distribution, ascribing fat tails to jump processes, and the like. A typical investor tends to be in the market for the long haul, however, and seldom enters the market on a daily, weekly or monthly basis. What if we consider annual returns, then, instead of monthly returns? As shown in Exhibit 3.37, the histograms of observed returns now show a better fit to the normal distribution model than was the case with the monthly returns. Notice the appreciable drop in kurtosis. The Q–Q graph for these annual data, shown in Exhibit 3.38, too suggests a better fit to normal distribution model than what the monthly data show.

Should we really sacrifice the convenience of a normal or Gaussian distribution, then, in order to estimate the expected returns and volatility?

Exhibit 3.37: Annual returns computed for the US whole market total return index match the normal distribution curve more closely. As in Exhibit 3.33, these returns have been computed using the geometric model and dark-shaded region corresponds to negative returns.

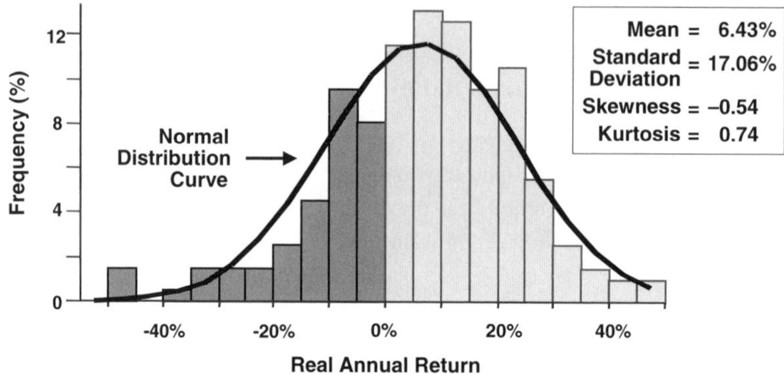

Exhibit 3.38: This Q–Q plot graphically compares standardized values of observed distribution of real annual returns for the 1802–2000 period with the corresponding standard normal distribution. Note how greatly subdued the deviation from 45°-Line is, when compared to that seen in Exhibit 3.36.

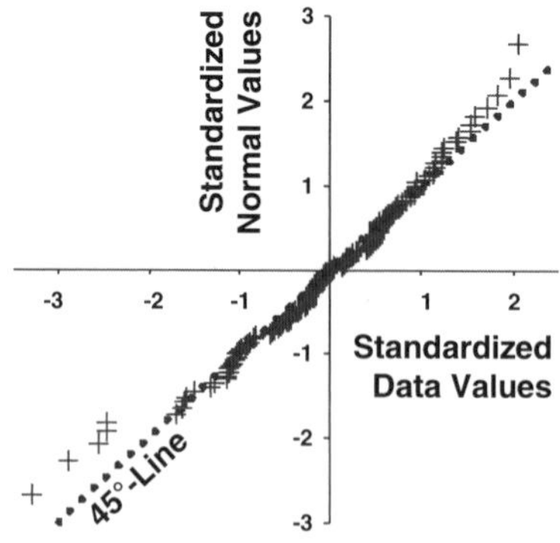

Obviously not, judging from the results in Exhibit 3.39 in which selected features of the observed monthly and annual total returns data are compared with those expected by assuming that they fit the Gaussian model.

Exhibit 3.39: Selected statistical features of the observed monthly and annual total returns compared to what would be expected by fitting the normal distribution model.

	Probability computed from the observations		Probability expected from the normal distribution model
	Annual returns	**Monthly returns**	
Returns within one standard deviation of the mean	0.73	0.78	0.68
Returns within two standard deviations of the mean	0.94	0.95	0.95
Probability of a 10% or greater loss in a month	–	0.02	0.01: monthly data 0.02: annual data
Probability of a 10% or greater loss in a year	0.14	–	0.15: monthly data 0.17: annual data

This assertion of the validity of a normal distribution model would be reasonable, therefore, so long as we avoid seeking statistical inferences using the extreme values. The obvious concern here is the left tail simply because complaints about greater forward jumps are unlikely. This is because of the need to assess the "Value-at-Risk" (VaR),[58] a robust and effective statistical measure for financial risk management that uses the first 1–5% of a cumulative normal density function when the "at risk" value of a portfolio is estimated from the historic data. Exhibit 3.40 illustrates this by comparing the left tails of empirical and theoretical cumulative density functions in Exhibit 3.33.

Consider, for instance, a portfolio worth W (= \$100,000, say) that is wholly invested in a broad market index like S&P 500, Russell 3000 or Wilshire 5000. The historic estimates in Exhibit 3.33 then give a 5%

Exhibit 3.40: Comparing the left tails of theoretical and empirical data of Exhibit 3.33. The vertical axis has logarithmic scaling so as to emphasize the divergence of empirical data from theoretical model. The shaded region denotes probabilities of 0.05 and less.

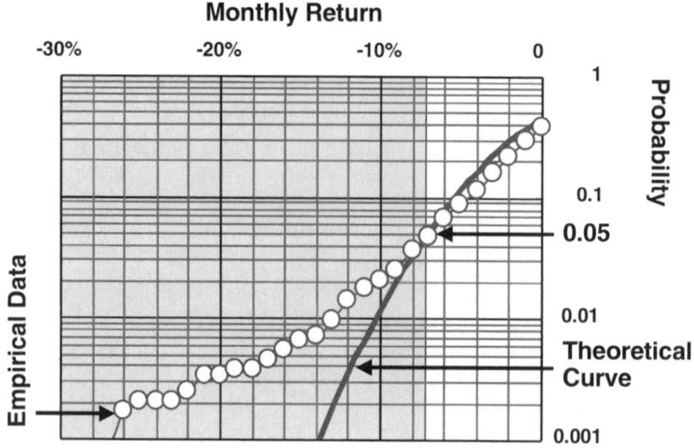
Monthly Return
-30%
-20%
-10%
0
1
0.1
0.05
0.01
0.001
Probability
Theoretical Curve
Empirical Data

chance that this portfolio will suffer a loss of \$7110 or more in a given month. The computation is as follows.

$$(\tilde{r} - 1.645s) \times W = (0.54 - 1.645 \times 4.65)\% \times \$100{,}000 = \$7110.$$

But then, as 96.27% of the area of our empirical distribution lies to the right of $r = -7.11\%$ $(= \tilde{r} - 1.645s)$, the actual data suggest that this

---

"The sports car and sailboat are investments for my retirement. I'm using them to attract a younger woman who can support me in my old age."
FINANCIAL PLANNING SERVICES
GLASBERGEN

risk is slightly less. In other words, our above estimate of $7110 for the value-at-risk carries a probability of 0.0373 or a 3.73% chance, not 5%, if we use the cumulative distribution of total monthly returns for the whole market in real or inflation-adjusted numbers.

3.5 Lessons from History

Our use of the market's history from 1802–2000 in making these deductions has advantages as well as disadvantages. The advantage lies in the fact that a long history such as this means the inclusion of all the periods of turbulence as also euphoria that resulted from forces beyond the market's control. This lends considerable confidence in projecting into the future the statistical inferences drawn from the observed data. The disadvantage is that 200 years is too unrealistically long a period for any investor's time horizon.

Exhibit 3.41 graphs in decadal segments the statistics on real geometric returns through the market's 1802–2000 history. The top panel in this exhibit shows the mean values, and the bottom panel the corresponding standard deviations.

Three inferences follow from these graphs:

- Neither the decades of high returns have persisted, nor those of low returns. Instead, decadal returns tend to revert to the historic mean.

Exhibit 3.41: Mean returns (top panel) and standard deviation values (bottom panel) computed in decadal segments for the total return index of Exhibit 3.30.

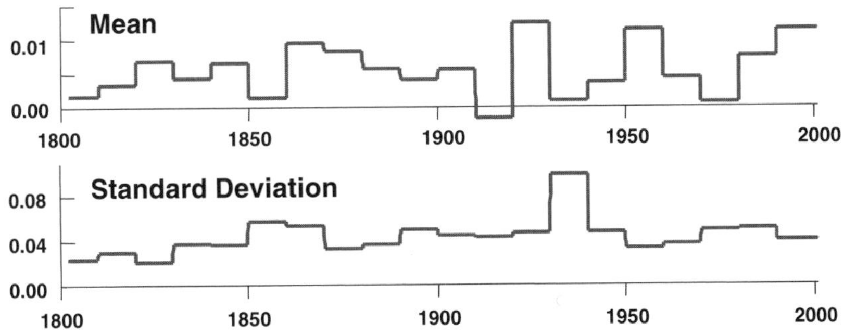

- The returns in 1920s and 1950s were just as good as in the 1990s, with the best returns by far in the 1920s.
- The 1930s were the times of extraordinary volatility.

Taken together, these inferences suggest that the rather high returns in the 1990s were hardly exceptional. They also suggest that the returns of the 1990s may not be sustainable in the long run, unless the earnings grow even faster.

Time alone can tell if this means that this first decade of the new millennium will turn out to be the same as the decade of the 1930s, when low returns but high volatility followed the preceding decade's high returns and moderate volatility. What history can tell us in this respect is this: compared to high to moderate volatility at such times of low returns as the 1860s, 1910s, 1930s and 1970s, such periods of high returns as the 1920s, 1950s and 1990s generally experienced moderate to low volatility. We would need to watch out for high volatility in this first decade of the 2000s, therefore, if the market's growth in the 1990s is to be compared with its growth in the 1920s. Such a caution will not be warranted, however, if we compare the 1990s with the 1950s. This is because, while decadal mean returns in the 1920s and 1950s were comparable and the following decades had depressed mean returns, volatility in the 1960s was comparable to the 1802–2000 average but that in the 1930s was the highest in the market's history.

Exhibit 3.42 explores further the question whether the market's growth in the 1990s was indeed without parallel or matched its performance at other points in its past. We do this by examining how the market's 1990s performance record correlates with the other segments of its history. The top panel shows the linear correlation coefficients (ρ),[59] computed in successive 158-month segments ending in December 2000, between the 1990s (November 1987–December 2000) record and the market's 1802–2000 history. We have used November 1987–December 2000 for the 1990s, and not January 1990–December 1999, for two reasons. As for the beginning of this bull run, November 1987 was when the whole-market total return index dipped to its lowest value, in real dollars, after the infamous October 1987 crash. As for the

Exhibit 3.42: Correlating the market's 158-month long November 1987–December 2000 record with consecutive 158-month segments ending in December 2000. Graphed in the top panel are linear correlation coefficients for the total return index and in the bottom panel the monthly total returns.

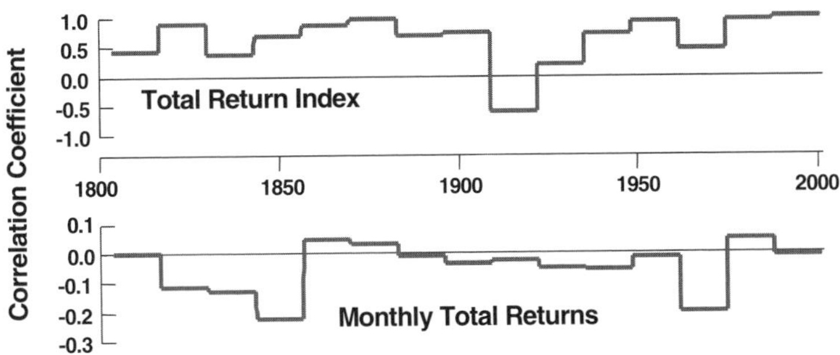

other end, we have used December 2000 for completeness. In any case, while the bull run of the 1990s seems to have ended in March 2000, it is hardly clear, as yet, if the present bear run is only a pause or that bull run is really gone for good. The bottom panel in this exhibit graphs the correlation coefficients for the corresponding monthly total returns.

Except for a foray into negative territory during November 1908–December 1921 ($\rho = -0.60$), correlation coefficients for total return index are positive for the rest of this 1803–2000 history. This is only to be expected, however, because the total return index in Exhibit 3.30 shows a generally rising trend. But, other than with itself, the November 1987–December 2000 record of total return index correlates 90% or better with only three of the intervals shown in Exhibit 3.30: May 1869–June 1882 ($\rho = 0.97$), May 1948–June 1961 ($\rho = 0.93$) and September 1974–October 1987 ($\rho = 0.95$). This record also includes $\rho > 0.90$ from September 1915 through August 1930, but that is not seen in Exhibit 3.42 because of our choice of the display parameters. As for the bottom panel in this exhibit, not one of the intervals shows a statistically significant correlation coefficient. What makes this comforting is that this is precisely what we would expect if, as we assumed earlier in this section, the returns are indeed i.i.d.

Judging from the results in Exhibit 3.42, the 1990s were not the only times when the market grew appreciably. However much this finding

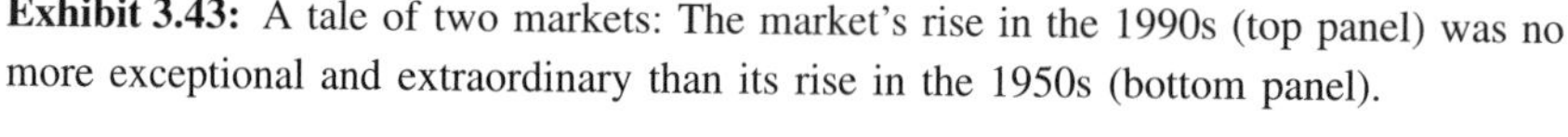

Exhibit 3.43: A tale of two markets: The market's rise in the 1990s (top panel) was no more exceptional and extraordinary than its rise in the 1950s (bottom panel).

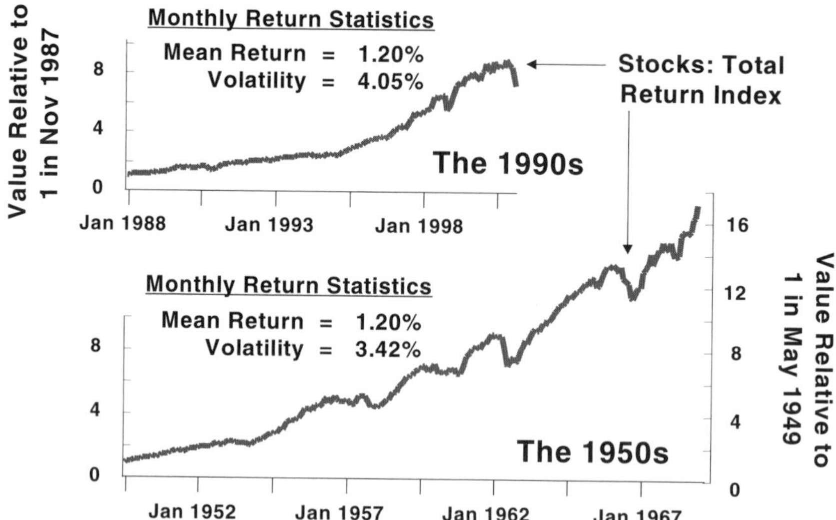

may dampen the proclaiming of uniqueness for real returns in the 1990s, it does not eliminate the fact that the market grew rapidly in the 1990s. Monthly returns during this period were appreciably higher (= 1.20%), and volatility ($s = 4.05\%$) during this period was somewhat subdued compared to the market's historic average. But, with identical mean monthly returns of 1.20% but a significantly lower volatility, the 1950s hold a far more stellar record, however. Thus, as can be seen in Exhibit 3.43 where we compare the history of market's performance in these two periods, the market's growth in the 1990s was no more exceptional or extraordinary than that in the 1950s.

Exhibit 3.44 summarizes the monthly and annual statistics on real total returns on the market since 1802. Of the statistical measures given here, the coefficient of variation is the only one that has not been explained so far. It is the ratio of standard deviation to mean and describes the variability of data by a single number, i.e.,

$$\text{coefficient of variation[60]} = \frac{\text{standard deviation}}{\text{mean}}. \tag{3.9}$$

Exhibit 3.44: Statistical summary of real total returns on the US stock market since 1802. Returns are estimated as the geometric mean, as explained in the text, and volatility is measured as standard deviation.

Period beginning January …ending December	**1802–2000**	**1802–1899**	**1900–1999**	**1802–1870**	**1871–1925**	**1926–1970**	**1971–2000**
Monthly Data (Annualized):							
Mean return	6.48%	6.36%	6.72%	6.12%	6.00%	6.96%	6.96%
Volatility	16.11%	13.82%	18.05%	13.68%	14.51%	20.75%	16.18%
Coefficient of variation	2.49	2.17	2.69	2.24	2.42	2.98	2.32
Skewness	−0.44	−0.36	−0.46	−0.45	−0.35	−0.32	−0.83
Kurtosis	6.66	5.4	6.41	7.5	0.87	6.92	3.47
Annual Data:							
Mean return	6.43%	6.40%	6.46%	6.14%	6.05%	6.95%	6.80%
Volatility	17.06%	13.98%	19.66%	14.85%	15.68%	21.32%	17.23%
Coefficient of variation	2.65	2.18	3.04	2.42	2.59	3.07	2.53
Skewness	−0.54	−0.28	−0.61	−0.33	−0.25	−0.56	−1.25
Kurtosis	0.74	1.35	0.19	1.49	0.23	0.2	1.32

The choice of intervals here is only in order to conform to what has now become the convention in stock market research. It carries no significance in terms of the statistical structure of returns.

The following three inferences now emerge:

- The market has delivered remarkably consistent 6%-plus total annual returns, in real or inflation-adjusted terms, ever since 1802 when this history begins.
- The market has performed better in the twentieth century than in the nineteenth century, on a month-to-month as well as year-to-year basis, although this superiority extracted the toll of greater volatility.
- The past 30 years have not been exceptional to the market's history; they have given about the same returns as the rest of the twentieth century, but with a somewhat lower volatility.

Obviously, over time, the market's growth has been truly exceptional. Two questions then arise: (a) exceptional compared to what? and (b) over how long a period of time? These are the questions that we will explore in the chapter that follows.

3.6 Conclusion

This chapter has confirmed conclusively that the stock market, while risky to be sure, affords the opportunity to realize consistently high rates

---

"I retire on Friday and I haven't saved a dime. Here's your chance to become a legend!"

of returns, even when adjusted for risk and for inflation. The investor's horizon must be longer than 20 years for the comfort level to rise substantially.

Endnotes

[1] The business cycle indicators are as follows:

Leading indicators: Interest rate spread (10-year Treasury less Fed Funds); M2 money supply; average weekly hours (manufacturing); manufacturer's new orders of consumer goods and materials; stock prices (500 common stocks, i.e., S&P 500); vendor performance (slower deliveries diffusion index); average weekly initial claims for unemployment insurance; index of consumer expectations; building permits for new private housing units; manufacturer's new orders for non-defense capital goods.

Coincident indicators: Employees on nonagricultural payrolls; personal income less transfer payments; industrial production; manufacturing and trade sales.

Lagging indicators: Average prime rate; consumer installment credit to personal income ratio; change in consumer price index for services; inventories to sales ratio for manufacturing and trade; commercial and industrial loans; change in labor cost per unit of output (manufacturing); average duration of unemployment.

Source: The Conference Board's Business Cycles Indicators at http://www.globalindicators.org/GeneralInfo/bci4.pdf

[2] Y2K stands for year 2000 and is the acronym for the much feared glitch that would have paralyzed the built-in clocks in most of the world's computers had they failed to recognize the new century because their calendars identify a year by its last two digits, e.g., 00 for 2000 is indistinguishable from 00 for 1900, 01 for 2001 is indistinguishable from 01 for 1901, and so on.

[3] As discussed in Chapter 1, Dow, short for the *Dow Jones Industrial Average*, is the best known of all stock market indices and was created by Charles Dow in 1885 when he first began publishing an index of ten railroad and two industrial stocks. This price-weighted average now comprises 30 stocks. The most important and best diversified benchmark of the overall US stock market is the Standard & Poor's S&P 500 index. It is a capitalization or market-value weighted index of 500 of the largest US corporations and is effectively

the continuation of what Alfred Cowles began in 1939 when he constructed back to 1871 a value-weighted index of all stocks that then traded on the New York Stock Exchange (NYSE). In its present form, the S&P 500 index was inaugurated on March 4, 1957. The 500 corporations that then comprised this index accounted for nine-tenths of the value of all NYSE stocks. It now accounts for about three-quarters of the value of all publicly-traded stocks in the US. The Russell 1000 index is more representative of the large capitalization firms, with over 85% of the total value of equities, while Russell 2000 index accounts for another 10%. NASDAQ (National Association of Security Dealers Automated Quotation System) is an electronic trading system that now accounts for over 4000 securities, compared to about 2700 common stocks that trade on the NYSE and about 1000 that trade on the AMEX (American Stock Exchange). The most comprehensive, though not the most tracked index of securities traded in the US is Wilshire 5000 — an index of almost 7500 stocks valued at about $10 trillion. Russell 3000 is the next, but S&P 500 is most popular. Further details on all these averages and indices were provided in the previous chapter.

[4] These two dates are 1000 years and 13 days apart. Pope Gregorius XIII proclaimed the Gregorian calendar to replace the Julian calendar the day after October 4, 1582. This was to solve the problem that vernal equinox, traditionally fixed to March 21 since the first official council of the Christian Churches in 325 AD, was slipping by a day every 130 years during Julian calendar's reign from 325 AD to 1582 AD. Unlike the 365.25-day long Julian year, the shorter Gregorian calendar (= 365.2425 days per year, because it only allows a century year to be a leap year once every 400 years) reduces this slippage of vernal equinox to one day in 4000 years.

[5] Morningstar is perhaps the best research and analysis firm there is for tracking the performance of mutual funds.

[6] The market capitalization of a firm is computed by multiplying the price of a firm's share with the number of its shares outstanding.

[7] Ibbotson Associates: *Stocks, Bonds, Bills and Inflation Yearbook, 2001*. Jeremy Seigel's popular book, *Stocks for the Long Run* (McGraw-Hill, 2000), too presents an excellent analysis of the historic returns on US stocks and their comparison with other investment alternatives.

[8] The inflation-adjusted total annual returns for S&P 500 index (downloaded from Global Finance Data at http://www.globalfindata.com) for 1871–2001 have an annualized mean of 6.26% for 20-year holdings numbering 111, the corresponding standard deviation value being 2.84%. The linear regression

analysis of these trailing and forward 20-year holdings gives the following equation:

annualized returns for forward = A − B × annualized returns for trailing,
20-year holdings 20-year holdings

where A = 0.1055 ± 0.0062 and B = 0.6965 ± 0.0891.

Thus, if future returns could be predicted from this equation and the annual returns of 4.7–12.3% for the trailing 20-year holdings ending in 1991–2001, then the total annual returns for such holdings ending in 2002–2010 could well range from 4.9% to 11.2%.

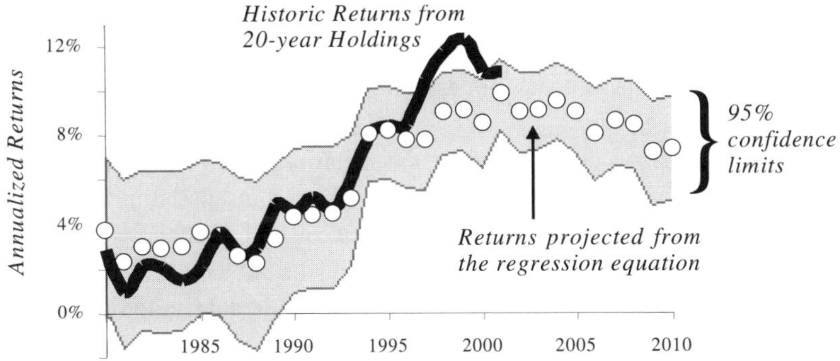

Lacking any cause-effect relationship, such regression analyses as this carry little predictive power, however. If this or any other similar technical analysis could indeed predict the future returns then we should either have some smart chartists who would consistently beat the market over a protracted period of time, or have all the technical analysts performing poorly *en masse* because if they all are privy to the same information and are adept in the same strategies then they would all move together and at the same time. Neither of these is true, in reality, and the market has a strong element of randomness in returns. As will be discussed in Chapter 5, this is essentially what the efficient market hypothesis is all about, particularly the weak form of the hypothesis.

It is not that one can never get lucky, get out of a declining market in time and get into a winning market. This is called "beating the market" because the annual returns from the success of such a strategy would greatly exceed the average returns from the market. But, other than such legendary figures as Peter Lynch and Warren Buffet, it is hard to name an investor or a financial manager who has managed to outperform the market consistently for a decade or two. Also, even these two legends have had their odd years.

To further illustrate the limitations of this strategy, note that our analysis too underestimates the annual total returns for 20-year holdings ending in 1995–2001 at 7.78–9.87%, compared to the realized returns of 8.43–12.30%! It captures the trend rather well, though. One lesson is clear from this exercise, nonetheless: excellent performance in the past hardly guarantees excellent returns in the future.

[9] This corroborates the analyses of price-earnings (P/E), price-dividends (P/D) and price-book value (P/B) ratios (e.g., John Cochrane: "Where is the Market Going? Uncertain Facts and Novel Theories", *Economic Perspectives*, vol. 21, 1997; John Campbell and Robert Shiller: "Valuation Ratios and the Long-Run Stock Market Outlook", *Journal of Portfolio Management*, vol. 24, pp. 11–26, 1998) which show that decades of high stock prices, normalized for earnings, dividends and/or book values, tend to be followed by decades of poor appreciation in stock prices, with corresponding poor returns to the investors.

[10] The holding horizon does not affect the mean return, nor it should. It only lowers volatility. This follows from the fact that, as discussed in Section 3.3, when individual returns are indeed independent and identically distributed, the mean return for n-period holdings would be $n \times$ the mean return for single period holdings whereas the volatility or standard deviation for n-period holdings would be $\sqrt{n} \times$ mean return for single period holdings. The statistics summarized below on annualized total returns on S&P 500 index, computed using inflation-adjusted data for different holding horizons covering the 1871–2001 period, amply corroborate this.

Holding time (years)	1	5	10	15	20	30
Number of holdings	130	126	121	116	111	101
Annualized mean	6.59%	6.77%	6.58%	6.40%	6.26%	6.17%
Standard deviation	18.79%	7.55%	4.80%	3.83%	2.84%	1.57%

Clearly, the longer the holding-horizon the smaller the volatility — stocks *are* for the long run!

[11] The problem boils down to estimating the "equity risk" premium, the extra returns on stocks that investors need to receive, over and above the safer fixed income investments like government bills and bonds, in compensation for taking the risks imposed by market's fluctuations. This premium has fluctuated widely over time, as we show later in this chapter. While some researchers (e.g., Robert Arnott and Ronald Ryan: "The Death of the Risk

Premium: Consequences of the 1990s", *Journal of Portfolio Management*, Spring 2001) argue that it is currently zero, the consensus estimates range from 2% to 13% (Ivo Welch: "Views of Financial Economists on the Equity Premium and Other Issues", *Journal of Business*, vol. 73, pp. 501–537, 2000).

[12] The Social Security Administration assumes a 7% average annual return on stocks (e.g., the 2001 *Annual Report of the Board of Trustees of the Federal Old-Age and Survivors Insurance and Disability Insurance Trust Funds* available at the Social Security Administration website at http://www.ssa.gov).

For a comprehensive critique of this assumption, see the paper by Peter Diamond: "What Stock Market Returns to Expect for the Future?", *Social Security Bulletin*, vol. 63, pp. 38–52, 2000. This paper can also be downloaded from http://www.ssa.gov/policy/pubs/SSB/v63n2y2000/diamond.html

[13] Jeremy Siegel: *Stocks for the Long Run* (McGraw-Hill, 2000).

[14] This anticipates what will be explored further in Chapter 6. Suppose we start with the Gordon growth equation for equity price valuation, i.e.,

$$P = \frac{D}{(r-g)},$$

where P = price, D = dividend, r = discount rate and g = dividend growth rate.

This is the well known Gordon growth formula for equity valuation that was first reported by J.B. Williams (*The Theory of Investment Value*, Harvard University Press, 1938) and popularized, in the recent times, by M.J. Gordon and E. Shapiro ("Capital Equipment Analysis: The Required Rate of Profit", *Management Science*, vol. 3, pp. 102–110, 1956).

The 1871–2001 history of S&P 500 index is sufficiently long to let us now make two simplifying assumptions:

(a) r = ROE (or the return on equity), an assumption that implies that market and book values are identical, i.e., the market is neither undervalued nor overvalued.

(b) g = ROE × RR (or the retention rate $(E - D)/E$, where E = earnings), i.e., g denotes the sustainable rate of growth.

In that case, $(r - g)$ = ROE × (1 − RR) = ROE × D/E, so that

$$P = \frac{E}{\text{ROE}} \quad \text{or} \quad \frac{E}{P} = \text{ROE}.$$

Thus, E/P ratio directly tells us what returns to expect on equity investments. The assumptions (a) and (b) above demand, of course, that we look for secular trends in P and E in order to secure a reasonable estimate the long-term ROE.

Turning now to the historic data, fitting exponential trend lines to the real monthly price and earnings data on S&P 500 index companies gives the following two regression equations

$$P = 64.824 \exp(0.0156\, T) \quad \text{and} \quad E = 5.1981 \exp(0.0144\, T),$$

where T is counted in years since 1871.

As the data tabulated alongside show, these two empirical equations enable the estimates of what P/E ratio and ROE values should be expected in the future, if we assume that the historic trend continues. Taking the ROE estimated here as the expected return on equities, then, it is unrealistic to set either 1871–2001 or 1926–2001 estimates of real total returns on the stocks as the expected returns for the 2002–2076 period.

	P/E	ROE
1871	12.47	8.02%
1926	13.32	7.51%
2001	14.58	6.86%
2076	15.95	6.27%

[15] The business cycle troughs here are those identified by the National Bureau of Economic Research (NBER). While these troughs are the periods of severe economy-wide contractions, the NBER looks for declines in total output, income, employment, and trade, and does not define a contraction in terms of two consecutive quarters of decline in real GDP (gross domestic product). Not all stock market troughs coincide with the business cycle trough, e.g., the largest decline in the market's recent history, the 29% decline in mid-late 1987, was not associated with any business cycle trough, for instance. The NBER has already identified the market's current drop with an economy-wide slowdown, however.

[16] Robert Shiller: *Irrational Exuberance* (Princeton University Press, 2000); and the papers by John Cochrane (1997) and John Campbell and Robert Shiller (1997) referenced in Endnote 8 earlier.

[17] Named after its author, the Nobel Laureate James Tobin ("A General Equilibrium Approach to Monetary Theory", *Journal of Money, Credits and Banking*, vol. 1, pp. 15–29, 1969), Tobin's Q is the ratio of market value of assets (debt and equity) to their current replacement cost. Andrew Smithers and Stephen Wright (*Valuing Wall Street: Protecting Wealth in Turbulent Markets*, McGraw-Hill, 2000) used this ratio, graphed in Exhibit 3.7 using the data downloaded from Smithers' website, to argue that the market was getting dangerously overpriced.

[18] Gross domestic product is the sum of all goods and services produced within the country.

[19] *Business Week*, May 20, 2002.

[20] As many as 49% of the American households owned stocks in 2000, either directly in their portfolios or by way of options, mutual funds or retirement plans, whereas only 4% of American households held stocks in 1952, when President Eisenhower was inaugurated.

[21] David Henry, David Welch, Michael Arndt and Amy Barrett: "The New Pinch from Pensions", *Business Week*, August 5, 2002; James Flanigan: "Nest Eggs Cushioned from Market's Drop", *Los Angeles Times*, July 26, 2002.

[22] Bonds are debt instruments and usually have a face value of $1000 in the US. The way they work is this. On January 3, 2001, the quote on a 3-year Treasury note with 11 7/8% coupon and November 15, 2003 maturity was $118.567. For the buyer, such a bond would generate a cash inflow of $118.75 on November 15, 2001, $118.75 on November 15, 2002, and $1118.75 (= face value + coupon) on November 15, 2003, for a total of $1356.25 during the life of the bond. For the buyer who has paid $1185.67 at the time of the purchase, this cash stream amounts to an overall 4.843% rate of return. This rate of return is the bond's "yield" to maturity. When the bond was originally issued, perhaps as a 20-year bond on November 15, 1983 when the long-term interest rates were 11–12%, that original buyer must have paid $1000 for it and would have, had the bond been held to maturity, received a yield of 11.875%. But, as rates have fallen since then, the present buyer has to pay a premium so that the price paid reflects the current rate at which that original cash flow, promised at the time the bond was issued, is received.

[23] The price of the bond rises, and its yield declines, when interest rates fall and the opposite occurs when interest rates rise. For bonds with coupons exceeding the current rates, you thus pay a premium or a higher price, as in this case. Likewise, if the coupons were below the current rate, then the bond will sell at a discount (i.e., the buyer will pay a price below the bond's face value) to raise the yield to current rate. For example, the quote on January 3, 2001 on a 3-year Treasury note with 4¼% coupon and November 15, 2003 maturity was $98.099. The buyer of this bond would thus pay $980.99 to receive $42.50 on November 15, 2001, $42.50 on November 15, 2002 and $1042.50 on November 15, 2003, for a yield of 4.983%. Evidently, a bond is a fixed income instrument, with yield that equals the coupon rate, only for a buyer who holds it to maturity. For notes, bills and bonds issued by the US Treasury, the risk of default is generally considered nonexistent. Relatively risky parties, e.g., other governments, corporations etc., have to pay higher coupons to

reflect this risk that the buyer of the bond must assume. Likewise, the longer the bond's time to maturity the longer the bond's holder must weather the risk of interest rate fluctuations, risk of default, etc., and the more that holder must be compensated for assuming such risks. Long-term bonds are more sensitive to interest rate changes than short-term notes, therefore, and long-term interest rates are generally higher than the short-term rates.

24 James Glassman and Kevin Hassell: *Dow 36000: The New Strategy for Profiting from the Coming Rise in the Stock Market* (Times Books, 1999). See also David Elias: *Dow 40000: Strategies for Profiting from the Greatest Bull Market in History* (McGraw-Hill, 1999)

25 This is because, taking the logarithms of two sides of the first part of Equation (3.1), we have

$$\ln\left(\frac{P_T}{P_0}\right) = T\ln(1+r) \approx rT\,,$$

when we use the Taylor series expansion of ln $(1 + r)$, i.e.,

$$\ln(1+r) = \sum_{k=1}^{\infty}(-1)^{k+1}\frac{r^k}{k} = r - \frac{1}{2}r^2 + \frac{1}{3}r^3 - \frac{1}{4}r^4 + \cdots \approx r\,,$$

because, when r is very small, the terms with r^2 and higher powers of r can be neglected altogether. This series is named after the English mathematician Brook Taylor (1685–1731).

The rule of 70 is a simplified version of this. For instance, using this equation to estimate the time T that P_0 will take to double in value (i.e., $P_T = 2P_0$), we have ln (2) = 0.6931 = rT. This means that T = 69.31 years ≈ 70 years if r = 0.01 or 1% per year. Likewise, if r = 0.02 or 2% per year, then T = 34.66 or 35 years, T ≈ 23 years if r = 0.03 or 3%, and so on. Some researchers prefer using the *rule of 72*, instead; 70 admittedly sounds a more round number than 72 but requires a greater degree of approximation than 72.

26 The concept of "value", intuitively so easy to understand, has proven to be almost intractable to define quantitatively. St. Thomas Aquinas defined "just" value as divinely ordained, and the "just" rate of interest — our basic premise, today, for determining the cost of money — as zero. This is also the view enshrined in the world of Islam where the charging or paying of interest is essentially a sinful act. Indeed, for much of the history, the view towards the time value of money has been somewhat ambivalent. Recall the famous advice, "neither a borrower nor a lender be", of Polonius in Shakespeare's Hamlet, for instance. Modern economic theory has provided a more reasoned attitude

towards cost, profit and value. Such early economists as Adam Smith (1723–1790) and David Ricardo (1772–1823) distinguished between price as "value in exchange" from value as "value in use". But this led to the "water-diamond" paradox — water has much value in use but little value in exchange, for instance, whereas the converse is true of diamond — until Alfred Marshall (1842–1924) showed "price" as the point at which supply and demand are in equilibrium. Profit is the difference, then, between this price of a commodity, or service, and the cost of producing it. But this still left the concept of "value" undefined, except identifying it as the benefit perceived by the buyer in the supply-demand transaction. Since cost of production already includes the costs of labor and materials, it is this profit that then amounts to the returns received on the capital invested. Of course, if this capital came from sources other than the entrepreneur, then the cost of capital, or the time value of money, would be the part of this profit that needs to be apportioned to the investor.

[27] Interview with Carol Loomis: "Warren Buffett on the Stock Market", *Fortune Magazine*, December 10, 2001. This article is accessible at http://www.fortune.com/indexw.jhtml?channel=article.jhtml&doc_id=205324

[28] Returning to Endnote 14, note that the factor $1/(r-g)$ in the Gordon growth equation can be expanded using the Binomial series

$$(a+x)^n = a^n + n\,a^{n-1}\,x + \left\{\frac{n(n-1)}{2!}\right\} a^{n-2}\,x^2 + \left\{\frac{n(n-1)(n-2)}{3!}\right\} a^{n-3}\,x^3 + \cdots.$$

Thus, setting $a = r$, $x = -g$ and $n = -1$, and noting that, as $g < r$, $0 < (g/r) < 1$, we have

$$\begin{aligned} P = \frac{D}{(r-g)} &= D \times \left[\left(\frac{1}{r}\right) + \left(\frac{g}{r^2}\right) + \left(\frac{g^2}{r^3}\right) + \left(\frac{g^3}{r^4}\right) + \cdots\right] \\ &= \left(\frac{D}{r}\right) \times \left[1 + \left(\frac{g}{r}\right) + \left(\frac{g}{r}\right)^2 + \left(\frac{g}{r}\right)^3 + \cdots\right] \\ &= \frac{D}{r} + \left(\frac{D}{r}\right) \times \left[\left(\frac{g}{r}\right) + \left(\frac{g}{r}\right)^2 + \left(\frac{g}{r}\right)^3 + \cdots\right]. \end{aligned}$$

[29] This passage comes from the review by Keynes of the book *Common Stocks as Long Term Investments* by Edgar Lawrence Smith (Macmillan, New York, 1925).

[30] E.F. Fama and K.R. French: "Disappearing Dividends: Changing Firm Characteristics or Lower Propensity to Pay", *Journal of Financial Economics*, vol. 60, pp. 3–43, 2001.

[31] In his bestseller, *The Great Boom Ahead* (Hyperion Press, 1994), Dent shows how well US economic growth and stock market have matched the birth rates by 47-year lag. See also Michael Weiss: "The Demographic Investor", *American Demographics*, December 2000.

[32] R. Vernon: "International Investments and International Trade in the Product Life Cycle", *Quarterly Journal of Economics*, pp. 190–207, May 1966; George D. Day: "The Product Life Cycle: Analysis and Applications Issues", *Journal of Marketing*, pp. 60–67, Fall 1981.

[33] That strategic overkill can turn investing in "growth" sector into a financial nightmare is demonstrated by the disappointing results from BCG's (Boston Consultancy Group) "stars" of the 1970s and 1980s. This idea, based on the PLC theory, advocated using excess revenues from the mature segment of a business (the "cash cow") to feed the growing segment (the "star"). But the star may then end up attracting investment so beyond its capacity as to make the initial projection of growth into profitability completely moot.

[34] Gary Hamel and C.K. Prahalad: "Strategic Intent", *Harvard Business Review* (May/June, 1989) and *Competing for the Future* (Harvard Business School Press, 1994).

[35] Robert Burgelman and Andrew Grove: "Strategic Dissonance", *California Management Review* (Winter, 1996).

[36] Michael E. Porter: "The Competitive Advantage of Nations", *Harvard Business Review* (March/April, 1990).

[37] Lawrence Chamberlain and William Hay: *Investment and Speculations* (Henry Holt, New York, 1931).

[38] Benjamin Graham and David Dodd: *Security Analysis* (McGraw-Hill, New York, 1940).

[39] Edgar Smith: *Common Stocks as Long-Term Investments* (Macmillan, New York, 1925).

[40] Irving Fisher: *How to Invest When Prices are Rising* (G. Lynn Sumner & Co., Scranton, PA, 1912).

[41] Roger Ibbotson and Rex Sinquefield: "Stocks, Bonds, Bills, and Inflation: Year-by-Year Historical Returns", *Journal of Business*, vol. 49, pp. 11–43, 1976.

[42] Jeremy Siegel: "The Equity Premium Stock: Stock and Bond Returns Since 1802", *Financial Analysts Journal*, January/February 1992; also Jeremy Siegel: *Stocks for the Long Run* (McGraw-Hill, 2000).

[43] G. William Schwert: "Indexes of the United States Stock Prices from 1802 to 1987", *Journal of Business*, vol. 63, pp. 399–426, 1990.

[44] This only applies to the common stocks, however, and not to the preferred stocks.

[45] The reason why the CPI graph fails to reflect the fluctuations is that CPI presents an integrated picture of inflation. Suppose inflation averaged 5% one year and −5% the next year. Starting with the value of one at the beginning of this period, then, CPI will be 1.05 at the end of the first year and 0.9975 at the end of the second year. Note how subdued these fluctuations are than our +5% and −5% swings in the inflation rate.

[46] William Baumol and Alan Blinder: *Macroeconomics: Principles and Policy* (Dryden, 2000).

[47] In 1827, the English botanist Robert Brown (1773–1858) first found microscopic pollen grains jiggling constantly along a preferred path when they were suspended in water, as if they had come back to life even after they had been stored for a long time. We now know that this erratic motion occurs in a colloidal suspension of tiny particles through incessant bombardment by molecules of the dispersion medium, i.e., gravity takes over, and the particles settle down, when this motion and the suspension are broken. In 1905, Albert Einstein developed and integrated the mathematics of this explanation into kinetic theory to win the Nobel Prize in Physics. The preferred path of Brown's microscopic pollen grains leads to a basic observation in modern probability theory and statistics: that samples from a large number of independent observations from the same distribution tend to form the bell shaped curve of normal distribution, a tendency that improves with the number of observations.

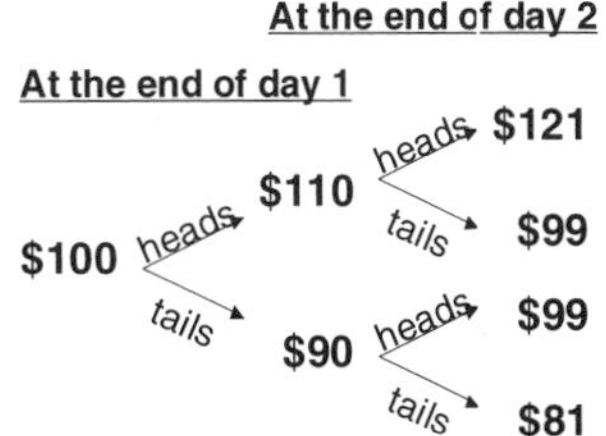

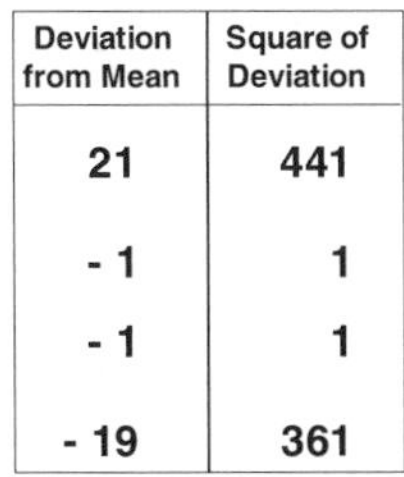

Deviation from Mean	Square of Deviation
21	441
- 1	1
- 1	1
- 19	361

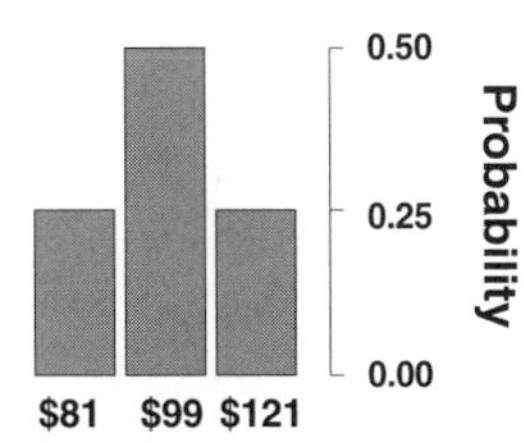

[48] Normal distribution is also called Gaussian, after Karl F. Gauss (1777–1855) who observed this pattern while studying celestial mechanics. It was Sir Francis Galton (1822–1911) who first called it "normal" and used it extensively in his work in eugenics, mainly to show that many of our intellectual and physical traits are passed from one generation to another. The above example shows

how normal distribution applies to our context. Suppose that you start with a \$100 investment in the stock market and that the extent of your gain or loss is determined by the flip of a coin at the end of the day: heads you gain 10%, tails you lose 10%. We will assume, of course, that the coin is a fair one so that each outcome is equally likely. At the end of end of day one, you will thus end up with either \$110 or \$90, depending on whether the coin flipped heads or tails. Likewise, there is 25% chance or a 0.25 probability that you end day two with either \$81 or \$121 and 50% chance that you end the day with \$99. Thus, as shown, a bell-shaped curve has started forming already in merely two days of trading! For these data, the mean (r) at the end of day two is 100, from Equation (3.5a), while the corresponding standard deviation (s) value is $\sqrt{(804/3)} = \sqrt{(268)} = 16.37$.

[49] Median (defined as the value such that it is less than one-half of the values and greater than the other half) and mode (the value that occurs most frequently) are the other two measures of central tendency. Because of its symmetry, a normal distribution has the same mean, median and mode.

[50] To be specific, mean ($\tilde{r}$), variance (s^2) and standard deviation (s) defined here are sample estimators of the corresponding population characteristics — μ, σ^2 and σ, respectively.

[51] Hence the i.i.d. (independent, identically distributed) assumption made earlier in this section.

[52] Maurice G. Kendall: "The Analysis of Economic Time-Series. Part I. Prices", *Journal of the Royal Statistical Society*, vol. 96, pp. 11–25, 1953.

[53] Donncheol Kim and Stanley Kon: "Alternative Models for the Conditional Heteroscedasticity of Stock Returns", *Journal of Business*, vol. 67, pp. 563–598, 1994. See also Stanley Kon: "Models of Stock Returns — A Comparison", *Journal of Finance*, vol. 39, pp. 147–165, 1984.

[54] Amado Peiró: "Skewness in Financial Returns", *Journal of Banking and Finance*, vol. 23, pp. 847–862, 1999.

[55] C.R. Harvey and A. Siddique: "Autoregressive Conditional Skewness", *Journal of Financial and Quantitative Analysis*, vol. 34, pp. 465–488, 1999. See also F.D. Arditti and H. Levy: "Portfolio Efficiency Analysis in Three Moments: The Multi-Period Case", *Journal of Finance*, vol. 30, pp. 797–809, 1975; M. Brennan: "The Pricing of Contingent Claims in Discrete Time Models", *Journal of Finance*, vol. 34, pp. 53–68, 1979.

[56] Richard Devor, Tsong-How Chang and John Sutherland: *Statistical Quality Design and Control: Contemporary Concepts and Methods* (Prentice Hall, 1992).

[57] Nassim Taleb: *Dynamic Hedging — Managing Vanilla and Exotic Options* (John Wiley, 1997). See also David Hsieh: "Nonlinear Dynamics in Financial Markets — Evidence and Implications", *Financial Analysts Journal*, vol. 51, pp. 55–62, 1995; James Hamilton: "A Quasi-Bayesian Approach to Estimating Parameters for Mixtures of Normal Distributions", *Journal of Business and Economic Statistics*, vol. 9, pp. 27–39, 1991; C.A. Ball and W.N. Torous: "A Simplified Jump Process for Common Stock Returns", *Journal of Financial and Quantitative Analysis*, vol. 18, pp. 53-61, 1983; R.C. Blattberg and N.J. Gonedes: "A Comparison of the Stable and Student Distribution as Statistical Models for Stock Prices", *Journal of Business*, vol. 47, pp. 247–280, 1974; P. Boothe and D. Glassman: "The Statistical Distribution of Exchange Rates", *Journal of International Economics*, vol. 22, pp. 297–319, 1987.

[58] Phillippe Jorion: *Value at Risk: The New Benchmark for Controlling Market Risk* (Irwin, Chicago, 1997).

Phillippe Jorion and Sarkis Khoury: *Financial Risk Management: Domestic and International Dimensions* (Blackwell, Cambridge, MA, 1996).

[60] Suppose we have n number of observations of any two variables, X and Y, and wish to quantitatively ascertain how closely they vary with one another. We would then compute their linear coefficient of correlation (ρ) statistic as follows:

$$\rho = \frac{[n\sum XY - \sum X \cdot \sum Y]}{[\{n\sum X^2 - (\sum X)^2\}\{n\sum Y^2 - (\sum Y)^2\}]^{1/2}}$$

Here, Σ denotes summation of the entire data. Also known as Pearson's correlation coefficient, and computed assuming that this relationship is linear, this statistic (ρ) varies from a minimum of –1, denoting an inverse relationship, to a maximum of +1, denoting a direct relationship, while $\rho = 0$ denotes a lack of any relationship. Note that this is a purely statistical measure that connotes no causal relationship whatever.

[60] As will be shown in the following chapter, the customary practice in finance literature is to use the reciprocal of this, called the Sharpe ratio, after adjusting mean return for the risk by deducting from it the "risk-free" rate (usually the rate on 3-month Treasury bills).

Chapter 4

US STOCK MARKET PERFORMANCE RELATIVE TO OTHER INSTRUMENTS AND MARKETS

4.1 Introduction

This chapter compares the performance history of the US stock market with those of other stock markets worldwide and with other investment instruments such as bonds, commodities and the real estate. After all, if history is to help guide our investment goals, strategies and expectations, then, much like the need to understand the history of the US equities market, we need to know if the performance of US equities is unique to the US, or can be generalized to other equity markets.

This chapter examines how, when adjusted for risks, do the returns on the US stock market compare with those on other assets and markets. The chapter is divided into three sections. The first two sections apply the insights gained from the last chapter to the other investment alternatives: the first section looks at the relative attractions of fixed income instruments and commodities vis-à-vis the US stock market and the second section examines the performance of non-US financial markets and the macroeconomic factors. The last section then assesses these data conjunctively with the lessons drawn in the preceding chapter.

The goal here is to see whether the investors' success in the US equities markets so far has been fortuitous or reflects the workings of some fundamental truths about the markets' overall performance that cannot be dismissed as happenstance.

4.2 Bonds and Other Investment Alternatives

The Resurgence of the Bond Market

One way to combat the risk associated with the stocks, so apparent in the preceding discussions, is to seek safer investment alternatives. Using the common stocks as investment instruments is a relatively recent practice, after all. Such fixed-income instruments as government and corporate bonds and tangible assets like precious metals and real estate, and cash, have been traditionally popular alternatives. Besides, US financial markets are not the only alternatives available to investors, more so in today's globally interconnected marketplace. In this section, therefore, we examine how the first of these alternatives, bonds and commodities, have fared relative to the US stock markets.

Take the fixed-income investment instruments — bonds and bond funds. As shown in Exhibit 4.1, the average annual returns on taxable bonds in the year 2000 amounted to 6.3%, and 10.1% on the tax-free bonds. These figures contrast sharply with the −10.1% return for the year on S&P 500 index (−9.2% with the dividends) and −6.2% return on the Dow Jones Industrial Average (−4.7% in total returns). This contrast is particularly striking because, all through the twentieth century, real annual returns on 3-month Treasury bills had averaged 1.2%, with a standard deviation of 4.8%. The corresponding figures for long-term Treasury bonds, with ten years and longer maturities, were 1.6% and 8.3%, respectively. Clearly, there were times in the last century when these bills and bonds gave negative real returns! Much like 2000, though, 1994 too was a good year for the bond market, and not so good a year for the stock market.

Bonds[1] are fixed income instruments because they carry predetermined rates of interest (or coupons) that last the life of the individual securities. Changes in interest rates from time to time subject the prices of these

Exhibit 4.1: Y2K breathed new life into the bond market.

	Average annual total return*	
	2000	**1996–2000**
Long Government	14.1%	5.7%
Muni. National Long	11.1%	4.9%
Intermediate Government	10.8%	5.7%
Long (General)	9.6%	5.5%
Intermediate (General)	9.5%	5.5%
Emerging Market Bond	9.0%	10.2%
Short (General)	7.8%	5.5%
Short Government	7.5%	5.4%
Ultrashort	6.0%	5.4%
International Bond	3.0%	4.3%
Multisector	0.8%	4.7%
Convertibles	0.0%	13.3%
High Yield	−8.1%	4.1%
All Tax-Free	10.1%	4.8%
All Taxable	6.3%	5.7%

*Appreciation plus reinvestment of dividends and capital gains before taxes

Source: *Business Week*, February 5, 2001.

instruments to market fluctuations, however. Their annual yields vary, therefore, when they change hands, as they do in the large secondary market. During 2000, interest rates rose in the first half of the year and started falling in the second half. It would hardly seem surprising, in this volatile milieu, that the safer bonds were those with larger yields. Note that the returns on long and intermediate-term bonds in 2000 were not only the highest but were also often more than double the corresponding average annual yields for 1996–2000. Compared to these, returns on the international bonds were poorer than during 1996–2000, multi-sector and convertible bonds gave near-zero returns, and the high yield or junk bonds actually gave negative returns, much like stocks.

The US debt market is sizeable. As estimated by the Bond Market Association, it stood at $15.8 trillion, as of December 31, 2000. Exhibit 4.2 gives the breakdown of this market. The Treasuries and the corporate

Exhibit 4.2: As of December 31, 2000, outstanding public and private debt in the US stood at $15.8 trillion. Treasuries, with $3 trillion, and corporate bonds, with $3.4 trillion, together accounted for over two-fifths of it.

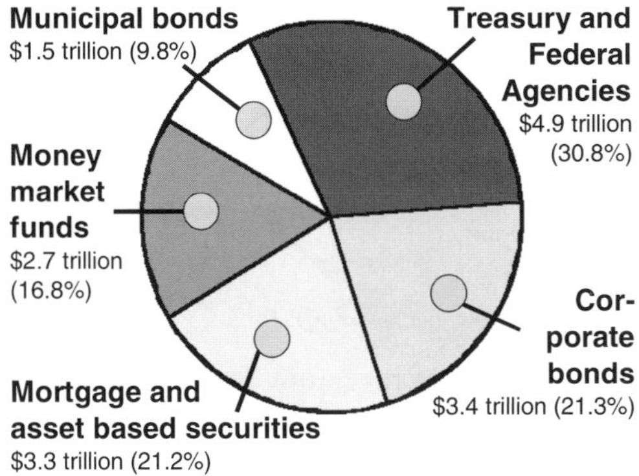

Source: The Bond Market Association

bonds, totaling about $3 trillion and $3.4 trillion in 2000, respectively, accounted for over two-fifths of the market. Overall, though, new issue activity was lower in 2000, than in 1999. As the Treasury Department continued reducing borrowing and paying down the outstanding debt, the supply of Treasury securities in 2000 was down by $492.8 billion from its peak value of $3.46 trillion in 1996. Measured relative to GDP, the Treasury Department's total marketable debt is now at its lowest level since 1992, when it stood at $2.75 trillion. Indeed, it can be seen in Exhibit 4.3 where we graph the total outstanding public and private debt in the US since 1985, the growth of debt owed by Treasury and the Federal Agencies[2] has been steadily decelerating since 1995. All of this reversed direction after September 11, 2001.

The issuance of corporate debt, mortgage and asset-based securities, and money market instruments like commercial paper, large time deposits, bankers' acceptances, etc., has accelerated since 1995, however. With the rise in federal budget surplus that the Congressional Budget Office estimated to total over $5.6 trillion over the next decade, there was a real fear that the supply of the Treasuries could fall substantially farther. That would have raised the demand for corporate bonds as individuals and pension funds rely on the long-term Treasuries to plan

Exhibit 4.3: After accelerating in the early 1990s, the growth in total outstanding debt of the Treasury Department and Federal Agencies started slowing down in 1995, but with no discernible effect on the other sectors of the debt market.

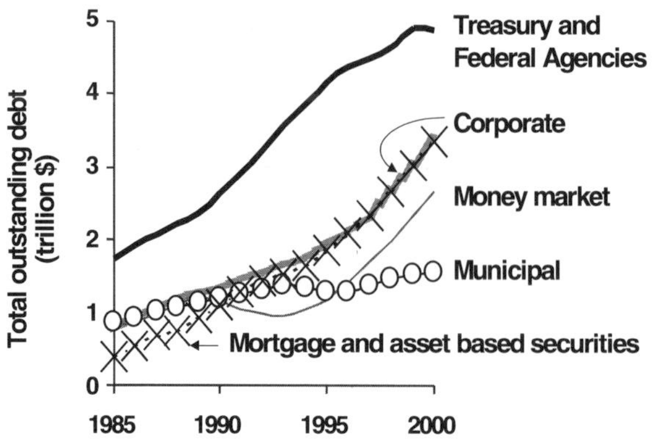

Exhibit 4.4: A reduced supply means increase in price.

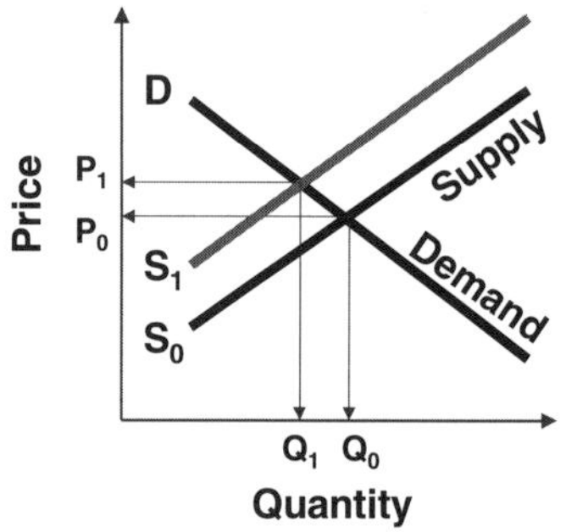

and schedule annuity payments. As Treasuries carry no risk of default, whereas corporate bonds do, a good issue at this juncture would be to explore whether this would drive long-term investors from bonds to the stocks, even though the problem of disappearing Treasuries has now receded with the return of deficit financing.

Following the Marshallian supply-demand curve, it is easy to see why reduction in long-term debt issuance would make these instruments pricey. Suppose that the market is in equilibrium at a given point in time, when the supply matches demand. With the notations used in Exhibit 4.4, for instance, this equilibrium quantity is Q_0, and the corresponding equilibrium price is P_0. Suppose that the supply schedule now shifts from S_0 to S_1 while the demand schedule remains unchanged. Obviously, this will lower quantity to Q_1 but raise the price to P_1.

Does the observational evidence corroborate this contention? Exhibit 4.5 shows the changes in yield curves for government and

Exhibit 4.5: The yield curves for the corporate bonds slope upwards, conforming to the lenders' expectation of higher yields for the longer maturities. When compared to 1999, this slope became steeper in 2000. The problem for the Treasuries has been rather complex. As was discussed earlier in the context of Exhibit 3.11, the Treasury yield curve got totally inverted in 2000, although it now seems to be reverting to its normal pattern.

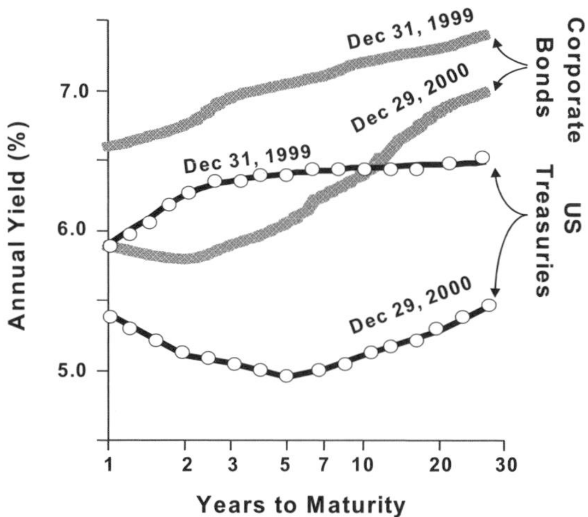

corporate bonds during the year 2000. Note the substantial rise in yield differential between intermediate-term (3–5 years) and long-term (≥ 10 years) bonds in both cases. This is perplexing. After all, the pricier a bond gets the lower the yield should be. Based on Exhibit 4.5, the demand for intermediate-term bonds surged the most in 2000.

Bond Pricing, Yield and Inflation

Bonds issued in the US usually have a face value (also called *par* or *maturity* value) of \$1000 and pay typically semiannual coupons,[3] although bonds with annual payments and zero coupons (i.e., no coupon payments) also exist. The pricing of such an instrument requires computing the present value (PV) of future cash flow. This can be formulated as:

$$\begin{aligned}\text{price} &= \text{present value}\\ &= \frac{\text{face value}}{(1+r_{\text{period}})^n} + \sum_{i=1}^{n} \frac{\text{coupon}}{(1+r_{\text{period}})^i}.\end{aligned} \tag{4.1a}$$

In this equation, which basically restates Equation (3.1) as $P_0 = P_n/(1 + r_{\text{period}})^n$ for n number of coupon payments and the interest rate per period as r_{period}, the first part discounts the face value to the present date while the second part is the n period annuity formula[4] given by

$$\sum_{i=1}^{n} \frac{\text{coupon}}{(1+r_{\text{period}})^i} = \text{PV}_{\text{annuity}} = \frac{\text{coupon}}{r_{\text{period}}}\left\{1 - \frac{1}{(1+r_{\text{period}})^n}\right\}. \tag{4.1b}$$

For the initial buyer holding the bond to maturity, the coupon value per unit price is the yield on the bond that is unaffected by the fluctuations in r_{period}, the market-determined discount rate, save for comparing the returns on other similar assets. But, for a buyer in the secondary market where the previous holder has already received some coupons, r_{period} is the yield to maturity[5] that amounts to the internal rate of return on the investment and varies with time. Thus, pricing a bond in the secondary market is a two-stage process: cash flow is first discounted to the date of the first coupon payment after the settlement, and this value is then discounted to the settlement date. If N is number of days from the last coupon date to the next and M the number of days to the next coupon from the date of settlement, then the entire right hand side of Equation (4.1a) needs to be discounted by the factor $(1 + r_{\text{period}})^{M/N}$. Thus, the complete equation for a bond's price is

$$\text{price} = \frac{1}{(1 + r_{\text{period}})^{M/N}} \left[\frac{\text{face value}}{(1 + r_{\text{period}})^n} + \frac{\text{coupon}}{r_{\text{period}}} \left\{ 1 - \frac{1}{(1 + r_{\text{period}})^n} \right\} \right]. \tag{4.1c}$$

It is clear from this equation how the price of a bond and the yield on it vary with the market rate of interest and the time to maturity. As for the interest rate, the bond's yield to maturity r_{period} changes such that a bond whose coupon exceeds r_{period} will sell at a premium, in order to adjust its yield to the current rate. Conversely, a bond whose coupon rate is less than r_{period} will sell at a discount, whereas the bond whose coupon rate equals r_{period} will sell at par. As for the time to bond's maturity, note in Equation (4.1c) that the larger the value of n the more a change in r_{period} will affect the discount factor $(1 + r_{\text{period}})^n$. This makes long-term bonds far more sensitive to the fluctuations in market rate of interest than short-term bonds. Suppose r_{period} changes by half a percentage point, say from a 5.5% annual rate to 5%. Then the discount factor $1/(1 + r_{\text{period}})^n$ will change by 2.48%, from 0.765 to 0.784, if n = five years, by 4.96%, from 0.585 to 0.614, if n = ten years, and by 9.9%, from 0.343 to 0.377, if n = 20 years. The bond prices drop as interest rates rise, and the prices rise as interest rates fall, of course. But notice how these changes are the most for the 25-year bond here, and the least for the 5-year bond. Also, all bonds are priced on par when interest rate is the same as the coupon, sell at a premium when the coupon exceeds the interest rate, and sell at a discount when market interest rates exceed the coupon.

This makes it natural to expect the rates on long-term bonds to exceed those on bonds with shorter terms. But Exhibit 4.6, where we graph the yields on 3-month Treasury bills and long-term government bonds ($\geq$ ten year maturity) since January 1952, shows that this has held only generally, not invariably. Treasury yields are clearly seen to have moved with inflation here, particularly since 1980, but there have also been

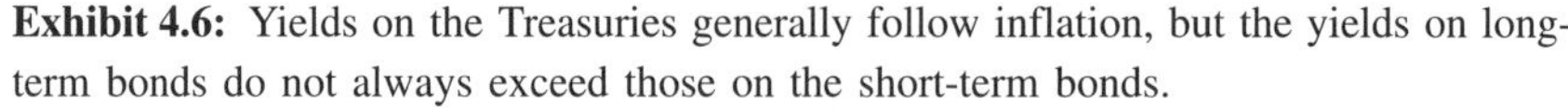

Exhibit 4.6: Yields on the Treasuries generally follow inflation, but the yields on long-term bonds do not always exceed those on the short-term bonds.

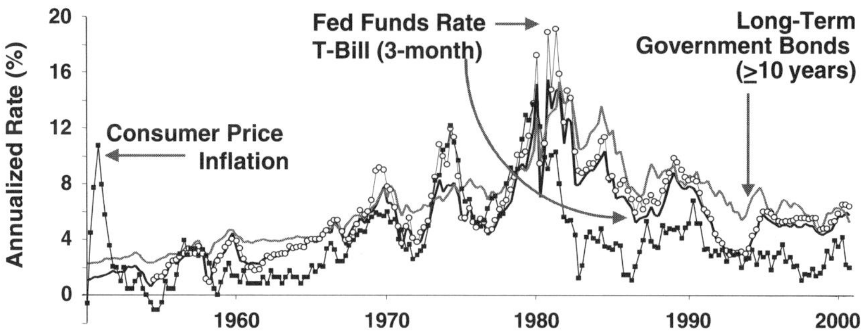

Exhibit 4.7: The two-century history of bond yields, Fed discount rate and inflation. Until 1980, the yields or interest rates tracked inflation only vaguely, at best.

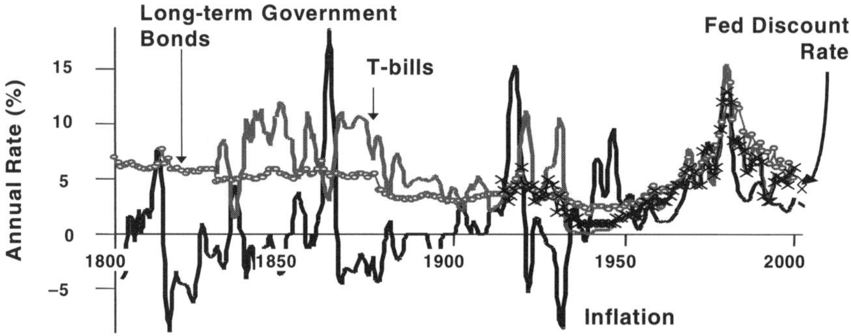

times when yields on Treasury bills exceeded the yields on long-term bonds.

Now, while combating inflation by way of discount rates is the avowed task of a central bank[6] as the Fed in the US, accomplishing it is seldom practicable. What renders it seemingly intractable is the fact that central banks seek to adjust interest rates in anticipation of inflation whereas questions about the magnitude of inflation can only be settled after inflation has already occurred. Nonetheless, the Fed has done an excellent job of adjusting the monetary policy to moderate inflation ever since assuming, in 1980, the sole responsibility for combating inflation in the US. This comes out explicitly in Exhibit 4.7 where the time line of Exhibit 4.6 is extended back to 1800. The movements in interest rate and inflation were largely uncorrelated and occurred erratically relative to one another until 1980. This is the crux of *the Taylor rule*,[7] an empirical relation that first described the Fed Funds Rate during 1987–1992 as a function of realized (π_T) and target (π^*) inflation rates and the output gap Y, i.e.,

$$\text{Fed Funds Rate} = r + \frac{1}{2}(3\pi_T - \pi^*) + \frac{1}{2}Y\,. \tag{4.2}$$

Here π_T, the realized inflation, is the average GDP deflator for the preceding four quarters, r is the equilibrium real Fed Funds Rate (or the natural rate consistent with full employment), and Y, the output gap, is measured in percentages as

$$\text{output gap} = 100 \times \frac{\text{real GDP} - \text{potential GDP}}{\text{potential GDP}}\,.$$

With target inflation rate at 2%, annualized rate of change in GDP deflator for 2000 as 2.3%, and the output gap[8] as 2.4% for the fourth quarter of 2000, this gives the Fed Funds Rate as 2% + 1/2(6.9% – 2%) + 1/2(2.4%) = 5.65% if r = 2%. Compared to this, the Fed Funds Rate stood at 5.98% at the end of 2000. With inflation well above the target rate, a positive output gap since the second quarter of 1997, and an unemployment rate below 5% since May 1997, one can understand why, throughout the year 2000, the Fed had a bias towards tightening. But, based on the Taylor rule, the Fed Funds Rate was high throughout that year when it averaged a 6.24% annual rate. This rule thus offers a simple explanation for what went wrong with the stock market in 2000: the Fed raised the rates earlier in the year, instead of either cutting them or leaving them alone, so upsetting the market's projections of future earnings and growth. But then, equally cogent arguments can be made that the Fed's not raising the rates earlier allowed the bubble to build up in the first place. Both views thus give the Fed the role that Adam Smith had assigned to the *invisible hand*. In reality, perhaps the best that the Fed can do is to react to the prevalent market conditions, as Laffer[9] has argued, and the statistical tests[10] show that the Fed has done so rather well, so far.

The History of Returns on Bonds

How has the bond market performed over time? This can be gauged from Exhibit 4.8 in which we summarize the statistics on real annual returns on different kinds of bonds in the 1802–2000 period, and for its different sub-periods. This is analogous to the stock market data of Exhibit 3.44.

The results summarized in Exhibit 4.8, and their comparison with the results on stock market returns in Exhibit 3.44, lead to the following inferences:

- Though always positive, the time-averaged real returns on bonds have fluctuated significantly over time, e.g., they were substantially poorer during 1926–1970 than in the preceding and the following periods.
- Much like the case with stocks, seeking better returns on bonds requires accepting greater volatility. The comparison of Treasury

Exhibit 4.8: Statistics on real annual returns on Treasuries and corporate bonds since 1802 and for the sub-periods for which the corresponding returns on stocks are summarized in Exhibit 3.44.

Period beginning January … ending December	**1802* –2000**	**1802* –1899**	**1900 –1999**	**1802* –1870**	**1871 –1925**	**1926 –1970**	**1971 –2000**
Treasury Bills							
Mean return	3.20%	5.40%	1.20%	5.10%	4.20%	0.50%	1.70%
Volatility	6.00%	6.70%	4.80%	7.70%	5.30%	4.90%	2.20%
Coefficient of variation	1.88	1.24	4.00	1.51	1.26	9.80	1.29
Treasury Bonds							
Mean return	3.30%	5.00%	1.60%	4.80%	3.30%	1.10%	3.20%
Volatility	8.00%	7.40%	8.30%	8.30%	6.90%	5.90%	11.20%
Coefficient of variation	2.42	1.48	5.19	1.73	2.09	5.36	3.50
Corporate Bonds							
Mean return	3.80%	7.10%	2.30%	5.40%	4.80%	1.70%	4.10%
Volatility	7.80%	6.70%	7.90%	10.30%	7.30%	5.80%	9.90%
Coefficient of variation	2.05	0.94	3.43	1.91	1.52	3.41	2.41

*Our data on the returns on corporate bonds only begin in 1857.

and corporate bonds presents a confounding picture in this respect. Note that, through most of the period sampled here, the Treasury bonds seem to have been no more appealing than corporate bonds, particularly when we consider the variability of returns or the coefficient of variation.

- Despite an apparently inverse relationship between bond and stock returns (e.g., 1926–1970 was the worst period in bonds' performance history but the best period in the stocks' performance history), their overall correlation is weakly positive, not inverse.

Why did the bonds perform so poorly during the 1926–1971 period? An equally important question is why investors settled for such paltry returns when they could have done so much better in the stock market? The answer to both these questions lies in one word, demand. After all, inflation was as much the scourge of the twentieth century as it was of the nineteenth century and could not, therefore, have made this difference. But it was in the twentieth century when the two most severe recessions of the past two centuries occurred — first in the late 1920s and early 1930s and then immediately after World War II (Exhibit 3.31). We should also add here the twentieth century stock market's high volatility trough (Exhibit 3.44), including the crash of 1929, and the patriotic fervor that the bonds issued for war preparations were able to tap into. It is easy to understand why the demand for bonds was so high. The greater the demand, the higher prices are likely to be, and the lower the returns are.

Turning to our second observation, that long-term government bonds have given persistently poorer returns but have greater volatility compared to similar corporate bonds. Corporate bonds have greater risk of default over comparable Treasuries and therefore carry higher discount rates. The reason for lower volatility of yields on corporate bonds then lies in the call provisions that bonds often carry. Callable Treasuries have not been issued since 1985, but corporate debt usually lets the issuer call the bond prematurely at a predetermined price. The sensitivity of long-term bonds to interest rate fluctuations means that there are times when the market price of a bond matches or exceeds the call price. At such times, the issuer is clearly better off calling the bond.[11] This caps the upper limit for a bond's price volatility at its call price.

Our third inference relates to the relative performances of the bonds and stock markets. It is easy to see by comparing Exhibits 3.44 and 4.8 that the returns on these two sets of investment instruments are inversely related. Compare two periods, 1871–1925 and 1926–1970, for instance. Real annual returns on stocks were nearly 1% higher during 1926–1970, than during 1871–1925, while those on the Treasuries and corporate bonds were 2.2–3.7% lower during 1926–1970 than during 1871–1925. Interestingly, though, while this improvement in the stocks' performance came with a price tag of about 50% increase in annual volatility, the volatility of bills and bonds did not drop in the same proportion as the drop in their returns. Clearly, investors did not abandon bills and bonds during 1926–1970. The overall correlation of these returns, in Exhibit 4.9, shows a weakly positive pattern.[12]

An important difference between the returns on stocks versus those on bonds must be clarified at this juncture. As has been noted before

Exhibit 4.9: Historic returns (1871–2000) on stocks and fixed income securities are correlated weakly at best. If returns were the only consideration, then bonds are expected to do better than stocks when the market is depressed, and vice versa. But then, as bonds promise fixed returns, they have significantly lower volatility and therefore comprise a significant proportion of many investment portfolios, particularly of those with limited time-horizon and risk-tolerance.

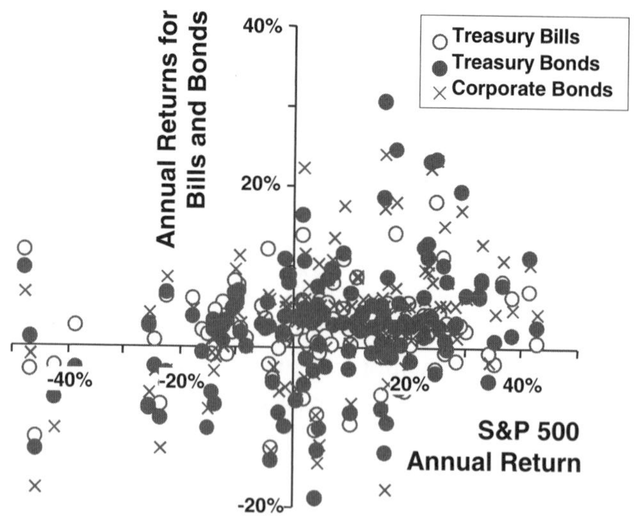

and will be explored further later in this chapter, the tendency for stock returns to revert to the long-term mean, called mean reversion, gives us the ability to reduce the effect of their volatility on the individual portfolio by lengthening the time horizon. This is because the mean return over N number of holding periods is merely N times the return per period but the volatility over this holding horizon is $\sqrt{N}$ times the per period volatility or standard deviation. The fixed income instruments like Treasuries and corporate bonds offer no such advantage. Their yields depend on the interest rates. Seeking to identify any specific statistical distribution model in the data on interest rate changes is an exercise in futility. Thus, as Siegel[13] has argued, the mean reversion property of stock returns contrasts with the mean aversion property of fixed income instruments.

It is not surprising, therefore, to find in Exhibit 4.10 that the real total return index for stocks has grown continuously whereas the index for bonds has stayed flat through much of the twentieth century. Exhibits 4.8 and 4.10 also show that 1970s reverted the 1926–1970 pattern of returns on bonds back to the situation that existed before. Thus examined, the high returns on bonds in 2000, noted at the beginning of this section, appears to be as much the continuation of a trend that

Exhibit 4.10: Comparing the growth of $100, in real terms, invested in 1850 in the bills and bonds (Treasury bills and corporate bonds) *vis-à-vis* the stock market.

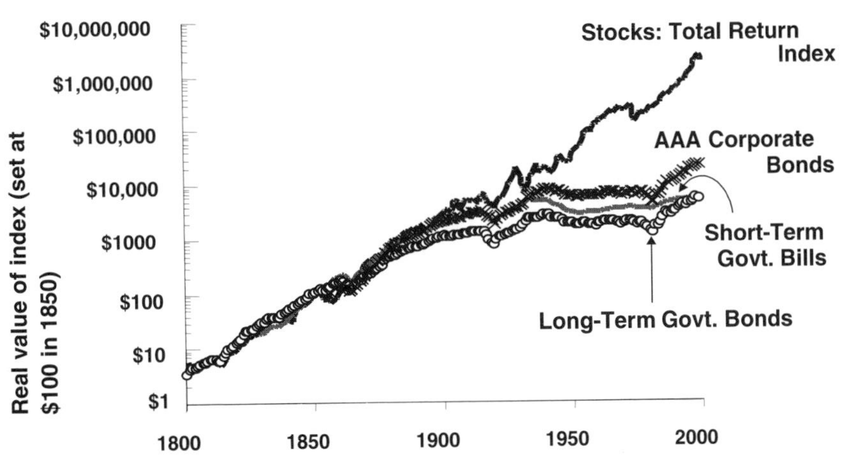

began in the 1970s as the reflection of the fact that bonds often do better during periods when the stocks underperform. We must caution, at this juncture, that our comparison of total return indexes for stocks and bonds in Exhibit 4.10 only serves the limited purpose of graphically evaluating the relative performance of stocks. It would be perfectly fine to infer from Exhibit 4.10 that a $10,000 investment in whole market total return index in January 1982 would have grown almost eight-fold, in real terms, to $79,400 on December 31, 2000. In nominal dollars, this averages to an annually compounded nominal rate of 12.6%. But this exhibit is not designed to tell you what you would get for investing the same $10,000 in the other instruments. Bonds are fixed income instruments, after all, so that what you get out of a bond depends on what you buy, when you buy and what you paid. For instance, the yields in September 1981 were 14.14% for long-term government bonds and 15.49% for Aaa corporate bonds. As for the Baa corporate bonds, the yields peaked at 17.18% in February 1982. A Treasury or corporate bond with 20 years or longer maturity would have thus been a better investment in 1981–1982 than the stock market.

Two of the results in Exhibits 4.8 and 4.10 merit special mention at this juncture. The first of these is the fact that the Treasury bills seem to have become particularly "risk-free" since the 1970s. Harry Markowitz[14] was the first to coin the phrase "risk-free" for Treasury bills because of the small standard deviation of the yields on these instruments. As was shown in Exhibit 4.6, the smallest standard deviation that the yields on Treasury bills show for any of the sub-periods examined here was during 1971–2000. The second is the recent surge in bond returns, particularly since the 1980s. For the 1981–2000 period, the nominal yields on Treasury bonds have averaged 7.1% per year, with a standard deviation of 11.2%, and the corresponding numbers for corporate bonds are 7.7% and 8.4%, respectively. Compared to the Treasuries, corporate bonds thus offer slightly superior mean returns at appreciably lower volatility. This suggests that a universe without the long-term Treasury bonds would have hardly become as unwelcome a situation as was feared until the recent return to the deficit financing of federal budget. Its effect on portfolio selection would have been largely inconsequential.[15]

The returns on stocks have historically exceeded those on bonds, by an amount called *equity risk premium*, reflecting their greater risks of loss. But this amount has changed over time. A particularly hot issue in financial research[16] has therefore been to understand what factors affect the investors' apparent aversion to the risk of owning stocks, seen in the high stock returns in the second and the third quarters of the 20th century when bond yields were low. Interestingly, the comparison of Exhibits 3.44 and 4.6 tells us that this premium is low during the times of comparable returns on stocks and bonds (e.g., both were moderate to low during 1871–1926 period and have been high since 1961–1971) and high when the stock returns have been high but bond returns depressed (e.g., during the 1926–1981 period). Exhibit 4.11 summarizes these phases in the market's history based on Dr. Bryan Taylor's analysis of the 30-year holding data (http://www.globalfindata.com).

Not surprisingly, therefore, the results of the Federal Reserve Board's triennial Consumer Finance Surveys, summarized in Exhibit 4.12, show that bonds occupy a decreasing proportion of the average American family's total financial assets. Stocks possibly account for a larger

Exhibit 4.11: The history of equity risk premium for 30-year holding periods since 1871.

	Holding period	*Annualized return on*		*Equity risk premium*	*Average inflation rate*
		Stocks	*Bonds*		
	1871–1901	6.64%	4.37%	2.18%	−0.36%
Moderate stock returns &	1881–1911	5.85%	3.24%	2.53%	0.60%
moderate bond returns =	1891–1921	5.88%	3.27%	2.53%	2.89%
moderate risk premium	1901–1931	5.26%	3.42%	1.77%	2.18%
	1911–1941	5.23%	3.95%	1.23%	1.64%
High stock returns &	1921–1951	9.47%	3.38%	5.90%	1.43%
moderate bond returns =	1931–1961	12.89%	2.68%	9.96%	2.43%
moderate risk premium	1941–1971	13.34%	2.56%	10.51%	3.30%
	1951–1981	9.91%	3.06%	6.64%	4.31%
High stock & bond returns =	1961–1991	10.26%	7.45%	2.61%	5.22%
moderate risk premium	1971–2001	12.25%	8.71%	3.26%	4.98%

Exhibit 4.12: The results of Fed's triennial Consumer Finance Survey[17] show that bonds comprise a steadily smaller slice of the financial assets of an average American family.

Type of financial asset	1989	1992	1995	1998	2001
Transaction accounts	19.1%	17.5%	14.0%	11.4%	11.5%
Certificates of deposit	10.2%	8.0%	5.7%	4.3%	3.1%
Savings bonds	1.5%	1.1%	1.3%	0.7%	0.7%
Bonds	10.2%	8.4%	6.3%	4.3%	4.6%
Stocks	15.0%	16.5%	15.7%	22.7%	21.6%
Mutual funds (excluding money market funds)	5.3%	7.7%	12.7%	12.5%	12.2%
Retirement accounts	21.5%	25.7%	27.9%	27.5%	28.4%
Cash value of life insurance	6.0%	5.9%	7.2%	6.4%	5.3%
Other managed assets	6.6%	5.4%	5.9%	8.6%	10.6%
Others	4.8%	3.8%	3.4%	1.7%	1.9%
Financial assets as share of total assets	30.4%	31.6%	36.7%	40.7%	42.0%

Exhibit 4.13: Net new cash flow to mutual funds during 1985–2000.

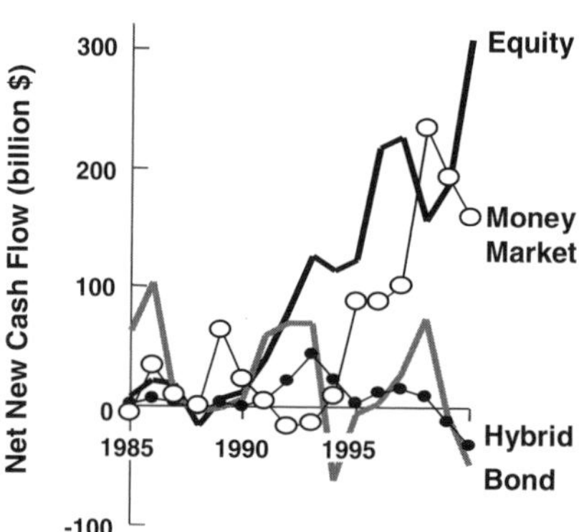

Source: Investment Company Institute

proportion than is seen in Exhibit 4.12. This is because stock funds account for 55–60% of the mutual fund holdings, based on the statistics from Investment Company Institute[18] (Exhibit 4.13). Of the $388 billion net new cash flow to the mutual funds in 2000, for instance, $309 billion came into the equity funds and the bond funds suffered a net cash outflow of $48 billion. The market's ongoing problems since March 2000 have drastically amended this picture, though.

The Other Investment Alternatives

If bonds are poor investment alternatives to the stocks, as has been amply demonstrated in the preceding pages, other traditional investment instruments such as precious metals (e.g., gold and silver) and commodities have actually been even worse.

Take the case of gold. Much like bonds and real estate, gold and the related stocks and bonds have given excellent returns during stock market's downturns (Exhibit 4.14). The fascination with gold dates back 6000 years, however. Stories about gold rush in California and Montana earlier in the history of the US, in the Amazon rain forest in recent times, and similar adventures have filled pages after pages in the history books. Pioneering men and women have risked their lives and often broken the law in pursuit of gold. During the middle ages, nations undertook vast expeditions in its quest. As for the role of gold in the history of the world of finance and investments in the past two hundred years, 1816 is the first important date to note. That is when the British government first circulated the gold sovereign as its primary monetary

Exhibit 4.14: The top ten best performing stock mutual funds of 2002.

	% Annual return through December 27, 2002			
	1 year	**3 years**	**5 years**	**10 years**
Van Eck International Investors Gold A	94.0	22.1	7.3	4.7
Tocqueville Gold	85.8	26.8		
American Century Global Gold Investor	77.4	21.9	8.9	3.9
Evergreen Precious Metals A	75.0	24.4		
USAA Precious Metals & Minerals	68.9	24.3	15.2	6.7
Scudder Gold & Precious Metals S	68.0	21.2	9.9	7.8
Fidelity Select Gold	67.2	20.4	11.2	7.7
Prudent Bear	64.4	32.2	2.2	
Rydex Venture 100	46.9			
Oppenheimer Gold & Special Minerals A	44.3	14.2	11.0	6.3

unit. The United States was to pass the US Coinage Act later, in 1873, which tied the dollar to gold. Thus began the age of the gold standard. By 1879, the price of gold was fixed at $20.67 an ounce. Between 1879 and 1933, the price of gold remained set at $20 an ounce, and was $35 an ounce between 1933 and 1971. The role of gold as an official international currency effectively ended in 1971, however, when President Richard Nixon suspended the dollar's convertibility into gold.

Over the long-term horizon of 20 years or more, gold is no longer as popularly used for investment, therefore, as it once was. This is because the price of gold largely depends on income levels, inflation rate and on the rates of return on alternative investment opportunities. The following result[19] of a regression analysis amply exemplify this:

$$Y = -751.37 - 2.89X_1 - 0.31X_2 + 0.33X_3 + 0.006X_4 + 679.80X_5. \quad (4.3)$$

Here Y = Price of a troy ounce of gold.

X_1 = Real interest rate = T-bill rate minus the rate of inflation lagged by one period to reflect expectations.

X_2 = Rate of return on the S&P 500 composite index, used as a proxy for return on alternative investments.

X_3 = Real income in the US, used as a measure of investable funds.

X_4 = Average monthly foreign exchange holdings of major official participants in the gold market.

X_5 = Monthly US consumer price index, used to test the hypothesis that gold is a hedge vehicle against inflation.

Note the negative coefficients of both, real interest rate (X_1) and rate of return on the stock market (X_2), in the above equation. These suggest that the price of gold rises when the rates drop, and vice versa, as has indeed been the case during the opening years of this new millennium.

That gold is at best an investment alternative to equities during times of stress or inflation is brought out in Exhibit 4.15. Note that, despite the recent upsurge in price, the gold indexes are barely as pricey as yet as in 1996. Clearly, had you invested here in 1996, the chances are that you are yet to recover that initial investment.

Investments in other minerals, oil and agricultural commodities would have hardly fared better in the long run. This can be seen in Exhibit 4.16.

Exhibit 4.15: The past 20-year history of Dow Jones Spot Index (top panel) and Philadelphia Gold Index (bottom panel) shows that, despite the recent upsurge, gold has yet to return to its 1995–1996 price level.

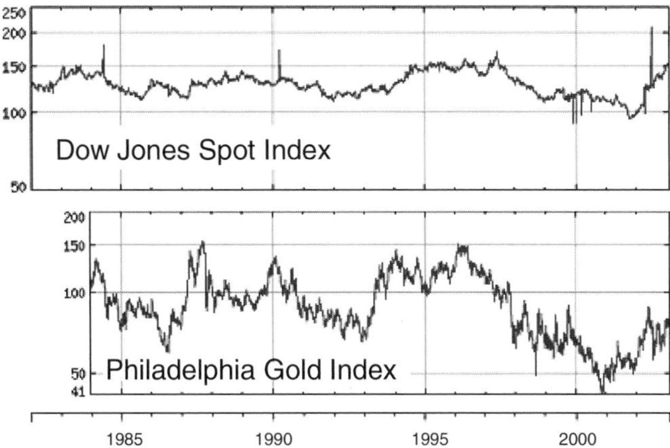

Exhibit 4.16: The commodity prices have largely remained flat. Of the panels on the left, the top panel shows long-run inflation-adjusted world prices of selected nonferrous metals (aluminum, copper, tin and zinc) and the bottom panel shows the history of world oil prices, in constant 1996 dollars, since 1869 (source: www.wtrg.com). The panel on the right shows the price history of selected food/farm items (source: www.ace.uiuc.edu/FarmIncome/lowprices.pdf).

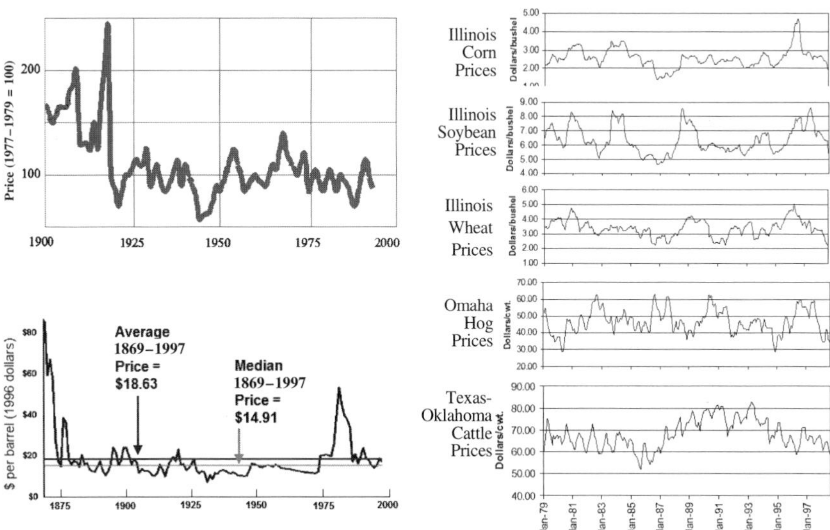

Here the top panel graphs the twentieth century history of world prices of four nonferrous metals (aluminum, copper, tin and zinc), the middle panel shows the history of oil prices, and the bottom panel shows price histories of selected food items and agricultural commodities. Note how these prices have largely fluctuated about flat levels.

How about the pattern over the last two centuries that we are interested in examining? Suppose you had two investments of $1 each in gold and the total market index in 1801. As Exhibit 4.17 shows, compared to about $440,000 in real dollars that this initial investment in the stock market would have grown to in 2000, an investment in gold would have barely kept its value after adjustment for inflation. This is also what would have been the case with oil (petroleum) whereas a similar passive investment in silver and soybean would have lost in value.

How about investing in the real estate? As we saw in Exhibit 3.15, compared to buying a home as we are often prone to, buying into a real estate based stock index like the S&P Homebuilding Index often proves to be a better investment choice. Recall, for instance, Peter Minuit's $24 purchase of Manhattan Island in 1626. It proved to be an excellent investment, of course, but still fetched less than 6% per year in nominal dollars. That real estate investing too gives good returns through an

Exhibit 4.17: Comparing the growth of a $1 invested in the commodities with that in the stock market.

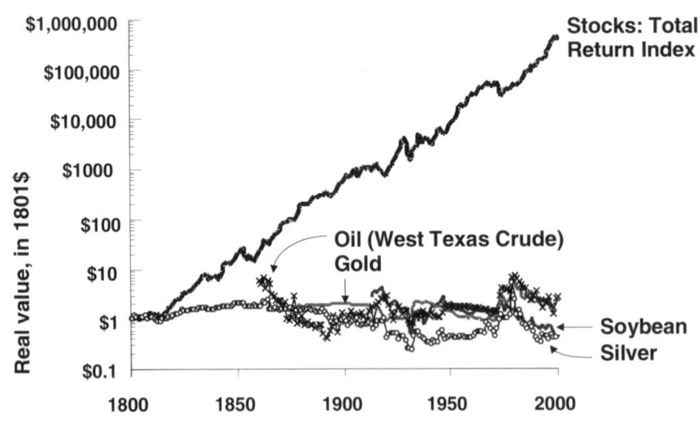

index or an index-tracking fund is corroborated by the results summarized in Exhibit 4.18. Compared in this exhibit are total return index for REITs (Real Estate Investment Trusts) with that of our familiar S&P 500 index. Note how well the REIT index[20] has moved. The annualized statistics computed from monthly returns data for the December 1971–August 2001 period show comparable rates of returns and volatility for the two datasets. Strictly speaking, though, the wisdom of seeking in the REITs an effective alternative to the S&P 500 index makes little sense: the REIT index offers 1.34% less in annual returns than the S&P 500 total return index, with about the same volatility which makes its coefficient of variation slightly larger. But its total returns have a correlation coefficient of 0.55 with those of the S&P 500 index. As will become clear when we discuss portfolio theory in the next chapter, this makes

Exhibit 4.18: REITs have given the best returns, in the long run, compared to the other real estate investment alternatives, largely because of their need to distribute all earnings as dividends. Return statistics tabulated below are annualized from monthly data for the period of December 1971 to August 2001.

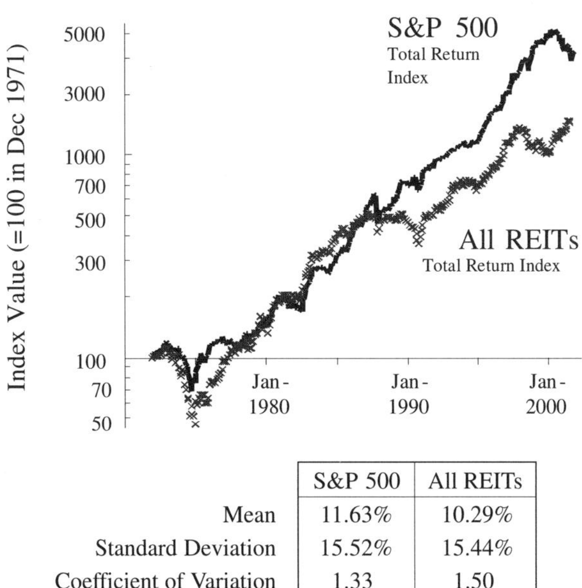

	S&P 500	All REITs
Mean	11.63%	10.29%
Standard Deviation	15.52%	15.44%
Coefficient of Variation	1.33	1.50

Source: http://www.nareit.com

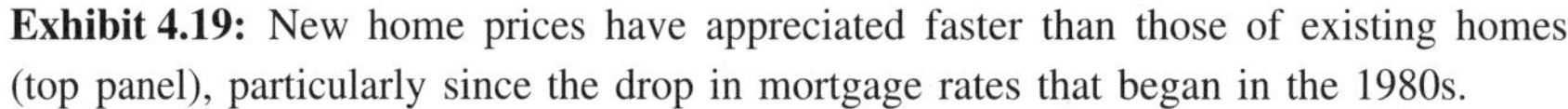

Exhibit 4.19: New home prices have appreciated faster than those of existing homes (top panel), particularly since the drop in mortgage rates that began in the 1980s.

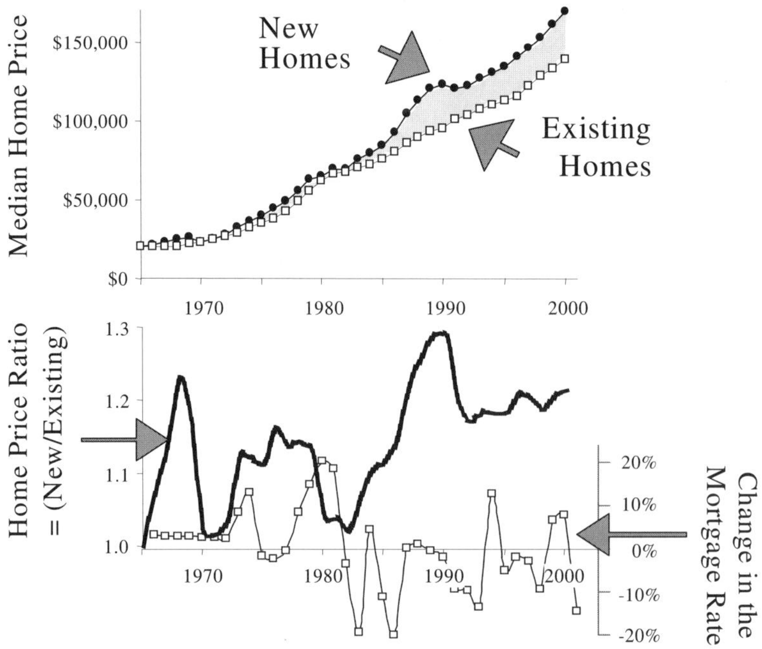

the REIT index ideally suited for diversifying your investment portfolio for a higher return at a lower risk.

As for the housing market itself, Exhibit 4.19 shows the median new home prices of Exhibit 3.15 together with their relative median prices (i.e., the prices of new homes relative to those of existing homes) and the changes in mortgage rates. This highlights a troubling aspect of home pricing. Note that new home prices have appreciated faster than those of existing homes, particularly since the fall in mortgage rates that began in the 1980s. Clearly, the real gains from interest rate drops did not really go to the buyers.

The above arguments should not make investment in housing seem an exercise in futility. First, adjusted for inflation, home prices nationwide have retained their value. Second, interest payments on the home mortgage carry its own tax advantages. Third, the joy of living in your own home is something hard to price. Investment opportunities too abound here. For instance, buying a house in California's Silicon Valley, say even in 1990, would have certainly given far superior returns in ten years than what the overall stock market has done in the soaring 1990s.

Likewise, the surge in the oil prices in the 1970s and early 1980s and in the precious metals prices in the late 1970s and early 1980s appear as tiny blips in Exhibit 4.18. But recall the chaotic effect they had on the global economy. As for the US economy, their impact is clearly seen in the interest rate data. Fortunes have been made oftentimes, and lost many more times, through such spurts. Rather than seeking such windfalls to build fortunes, Exhibit 4.18 only shows how the stock market could have helped accomplish the same goals through investment in any of the "wealth-builders". For instance, for an average investor interested in investing only in the real estate market, the stock market offers such varied choices as the S&P Homebuilding Index (Exhibit 3.15) and the real estate investment trusts. You could likewise focus on other specific sectors, either in the S&P or in the NASDAQ indices, for metals, energy or the like, if a specific sector rather than the broad market is what you are looking for. The reason why we have focused on the broad market is that it encompasses all these sectors. Thus, a passive investor benefits from the periodic rises in individual sectors while softening the declines that individual sectors experience from time to time. Such declines seldom occur in all the sectors at the same time. While this admittedly slows down the march towards prosperity, it also leaves much less to the vagaries of chance.

"You invested $100 a week ago and we are not rich yet. I thought you knew how to use a computer!"
© 2000 Randy Glasbergen
www.glasbergen.com

4.3 Global Comparisons and Macroeconomic Factors

The UK Stock and Bond Markets

History has amply demonstrated the superiority, over time, of stock market returns over the returns that are available from such other investment tools as bonds and commodities. We now examine if this has been unique to the US market or is true of the stock markets in general. Two other issues finally arise, and are also examined here: how the market's performance relates to that of the economy at large and what the investors can and should now look forward to.

Perhaps the most notable long-term history to look at, in this context, would be the performance of the British stock market. Exhibit 4.20 below does precisely that: it shows that £1 invested in August 1694 would have grown to £193.8 million in December 2000, after dropping from its August 2000 peak of £203.2 million. This corresponds to an average monthly compounding rate of 0.52%, or an annualized rate of 6.22%. Though slightly slower than the US stock market's 8.22% annual growth

Exhibit 4.20: The history of long-term performance of the overall British stock market.

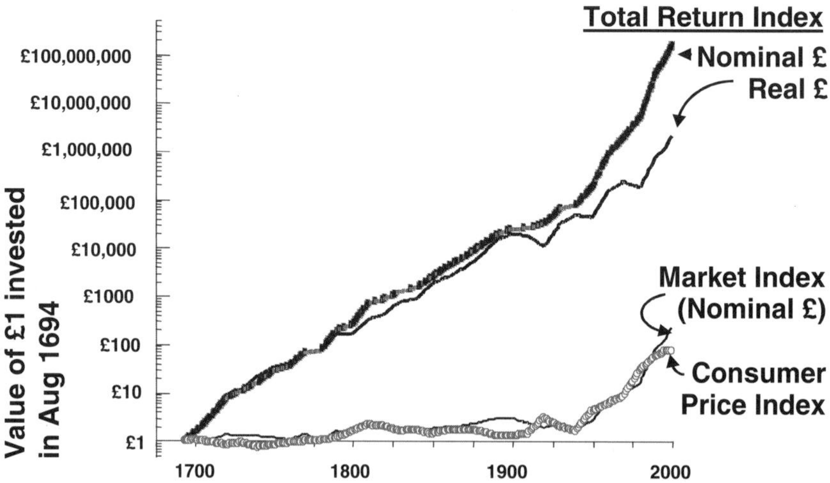

Source: http://www.globalfindata.com

rate since 1802, this performance has been registered over a considerably longer, actually more than a century, period. It is also superior to the annually compounding rate of 5.96% that we estimated for Peter Minuit's purchase of the Manhattan Island! This further corroborates our earlier inference, that investments in the stock market indeed yield robust returns over time. Exhibit 4.20 also shows that the corresponding market index, as opposed to the total return index, would have barely kept pace with inflation. The reinvestment of dividends clearly made the difference here, in much the same way as we found for the US market.

Examining the nominal returns over a protracted interval, in excess of three centuries, makes little sense, however, because inflation rates are unlikely to have remained the same throughout. Indeed, as the British consumer price index in Exhibit 4.20 shows, price changes there particularly accelerated since the 1930s. Thus, a sizeable proportion of the acceleration in nominal total return index since 1930 can be directly ascribed to price inflation. The result of adjusting for inflation, also presented in this exhibit, shows that the £1 investment of August 1694 in the total return index grew to £2.85 million at the end of 2000, at the average annually compounding rate of 4.85%. Notice also, in Exhibit 4.20, how the nominal and real values of total return index have diverged particularly in the twentieth century. But the fact that the consumer price index in the UK was largely flat through the eighteenth and nineteenth centuries does not mean that the British economy experienced placid conditions during this period. Rather, these were the times when the economy experienced periodic bursts of inflation, deflation as well as stagflation. As consumer price index presents a cumulative picture, it tends to obscure this volatility.

Has the UK fixed-income market performed as spectacularly relative to the stock market, over time, as the US stock market has? Judging from Exhibit 4.21, where we compare the inflation-adjusted total return indexes for the UK stock market and the British government's short-term bills and long-term bonds, shows the history since the 1930s. The stock market dominated. Total return index for long-term government bonds would have grown over 11,000-fold between 1700 and 2000 after adjusting for inflation, for instance, but would have still been about 1/250th of that of the stock market. As for the short-term government bills, our time series begins only in 1800 and, since then, the real total return index for these instruments has grown a little over 100-fold. If we set these three indexes at one on January 1800, as is done in Exhibit 4.21, then the stock market index rises to 15,880, whereas the corresponding numbers for the other indexes are 148 for the government bonds index and 107.7 for the government bills index. The British data thus corroborate our earlier findings from the US data that, over time, stocks vastly outperform the short-terms bills and long-term bonds.

Exhibit 4.21: Much like the performance of the US stock market, real total returns on the British stock market have greatly exceeded the returns of government bills and bonds. This has been particularly true since the later half of the twentieth century. All the indices here have been set at one in January 1800.

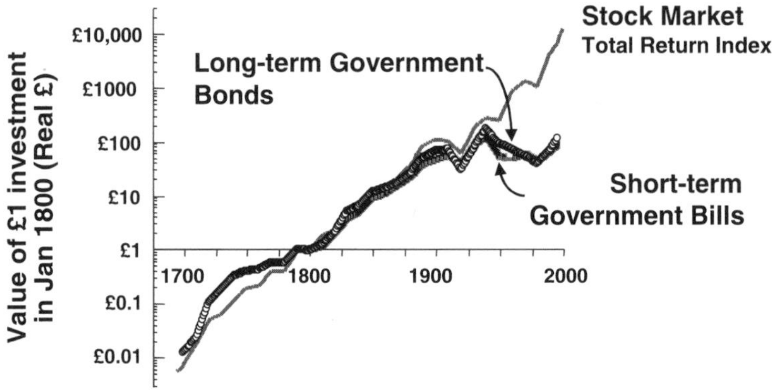

Exhibit 4.22: Compared to any other time in history, bonds performed better than stocks in the UK in the 19th century, when they also had a remarkably low volatility.

		1694–2000	1700–1799	1800–1899	1900–1999
Stocks, Total	Mean Return	4.85%	4.60%	4.76%	4.97%
Return Index	Volatility	12.21%	10.89%	6.91%	15.33%
Short-term	Mean Return	2.28%	—	3.85%	0.65%
Govt. Bills	Volatility	3.88%	—	1.59%	4.80%
Long-term	Mean Return	3.08%	4.34%	4.23%	0.58%
Govt. Bonds	Volatility	4.85%	4.42%	2.22%	6.18%

This superiority of long-term performance of stocks over bonds is hardly as categorical as it may seem, however. Exhibit 4.22 compares the statistics on real annual returns on stocks, bills and bonds for the entire 1694–2000 period as also for the individual centuries. These statistics parallel those for the US financial markets that we have discussed earlier, in the contexts of Exhibit 3.44. Notice how poorly the short-term government bills and long-term government bonds fared, through most the twentieth century, in both the markets, the UK and the US. The two markets also gave comparable returns on these kinds of investment instruments in the 19th century. Judging from the data in Exhibit 4.22, British government bills and bonds proved to be decidedly superior investment instruments in the nineteenth century, than the UK stock market. Notice how low the volatility on their returns was during that period.

One can well understand why the British bond market has survived through the twentieth century, despite its abysmal returns. As was discussed earlier, in the case of the US stock market, the experience of the 1929 stock market crash kept many American investors in the bond market. Since this crash was global, it is not surprising that the same fear also kept the British government bills and bonds popular with investors. But that raises the question of how the British stock market survived the eighteenth and nineteenth centuries, when its returns were comparable to the bonds but the volatility of these returns was so much greater.

The answer to this puzzle perhaps lies in the lingering memory of the "South Sea Bubble"[21] of 1720. Basically, it started with the London-based South Sea Company's plan to assume British national debt in exchange for the interest on that debt and for monopoly trading rights to the South Seas. It was a bold move, and would have perhaps worked, had Spain not already controlled these trading rights! Despite this assumption of additional

Box 4.1: The South Sea Bubble

How goes the Stock, becomes the gen'ral Cry.
Rather than fail we'll at Nine Hundred Buy.
Instead of Scandal, how goes Stock's the Tone.
Ev'n Wit and Beauty are quite useless grown.
No ships unload, no Looms at Work we see.
But all are swallow' by the damn'd South Sea.

Alexander Pope
(1688–1744)

national debt, and the fact that Britain's 1718 peace with Spain brought no new rights or agreements that would raise the company's profits, the company's share price spiraled from £128 on January 1, 1720 to £1050 on June 24 that year. They finally crashed down to £128 in December 1720. Box 4.1 quotes the words of the poet and essayist Alexander Pope on this episode. Included amongst those who paid dearly for the experience was Sir Isaac Newton, the famous scientist and the master of the Royal mint. He first made 100% profit by selling his £7000 stock in April but then reentered the market at the top and lost £20,000. "I can calculate the motions of the heavenly bodies," he said, "But not the madness of people."

Some Other Stock Markets Worldwide

The performance of other stock markets has been equally robust and impressive. Exhibit 4.23 compares the real total return indices for Japan, Germany and the World (MSCI: Morgan Stanley Capital International) with those for the US and the UK. Notice how all of them show appreciable acceleration in the second half of the twentieth century. This phenomenon has apparently not been limited to the US and UK markets alone. Also note how impressive the performance of Germany and Japan,

Exhibit 4.23: An international comparison of the real total returns on the US and other selected stock markets.

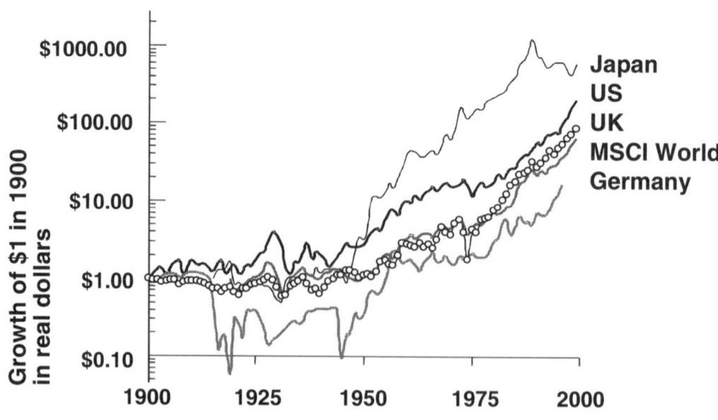

Source: http://www.globalfindata.com

so totally devastated during World War II, has been. Interestingly, most of the growth in Japan's total return index came in the immediate aftermath of World War II. At the time of its official launch on May 16, 1949, the Nikkei 225 index opened at 176.21. This was about the same as the value of 175.2 that the Dow closed at on the previous trading day. At the close of trading on December 29, 2000, the Nikkei was 13,785.69 when the Dow was 10,787.99. But the Nikkei has been declining since closing at its peak of 38,916 on December 29, 1989 whereas the Dow reached its peak closing value of 11,287.10 on April 11, 2000. Clearly, despite its continuing downward spiral, the Nikkei has done better than the Dow, when we consider its 50-plus years of performance, and did exceptionally better than the Dow when it reached its peak. Note also that the exchange rate was ¥360 per $1 in 1949 but was less than one-third as much, at ¥114.50 per $1 on December 29, 2000.

The data in Exhibit 4.23 highlight a basic challenge that investors and financial managers face continuously, particularly in this era of the globalization of trade, commerce, supply and production. One, it makes a powerful case for diversifying equity investments internationally. That can help cushion a market's downtrend if the asset price movements in two markets do not synchronize. But globalization has set in the trend towards increasing convergence, rather than divergence, of the markets. Exhibit 4.24 illustrates this by presenting the correlation coefficients among monthly returns of 18 major stock markets, after converting them to the US dollar, for two 10-year periods, 1977–1986 and 1987–1996. Note that the correlation coefficients for 1987–1996 are generally higher than those for 1977–1986. As a result, the average values of these correlation coefficients are 0.34 for 1977–1986 and 0.46 for 1987–1996. The progress towards the convergence of Europe's economy that culminated in the launch of Europe's new currency, the euro, on January 1, 1999, has only helped further this convergence. For instance, the correlation coefficient for daily returns on French and German stock market indexes reached 0.78 during the one-year period ending July 21, 1999. Likewise, for this one-year period, the correlation coefficient for daily returns on Frankfurt's DAX and London's FTSE indexes stood at 0.70. Curiously though, judging from the results of a recent study,[22] the international equity market correlation appears to increase in bear

Exhibit 4.24: Correlation coefficients amongst the monthly returns of selected major stock markets in the MSCI (Morgan Stanley Capital International) index. Shaded regions pertain to the 1987–1996 period, unshaded regions to the 1977–1986 period.

		AU	AS	BE	CA	DE	FR	GE	HK	IT	JA	NE	NO	SI	SP	SW	SZ	UK	US
Australia	AU		**0.25**	**0.43**	**0.65**	**0.14**	**0.43**	**0.33**	**0.62**	**0.23**	**0.25**	**0.49**	**0.51**	**0.68**	**0.50**	**0.49**	**0.38**	**0.60**	**0.56**
Austria	AS	0.09		**0.35**	**0.22**	**0.26**	**0.42**	**0.62**	**0.34**	**0.36**	**0.14**	**0.44**	**0.36**	**0.40**	**0.39**	**0.34**	**0.45**	**0.38**	**0.18**
Belgium	BE	0.23	0.52		**0.52**	**0.32**	**0.71**	**0.63**	**0.49**	**0.35**	**0.41**	**0.65**	**0.50**	**0.54**	**0.52**	**0.45**	**0.53**	**0.56**	**0.56**
Canada	CA	0.55	0.18	0.27		**0.19**	**0.46**	**0.35**	**0.65**	**0.34**	**0.29**	**0.60**	**0.49**	**0.63**	**0.46**	**0.42**	**0.43**	**0.59**	**0.77**
Denmark	DE	0.28	0.31	0.46	0.27		**0.42**	**0.40**	**0.16**	**0.36**	**0.42**	**0.38**	**27.00**	**0.26**	**0.43**	**0.25**	**0.32**	**0.38**	**0.18**
France	FR	0.27	0.49	0.58	0.36	0.30		**0.68**	**0.42**	**0.40**	**0.42**	**0.65**	**0.45**	**0.47**	**0.53**	**0.43**	**0.54**	**0.59**	**0.55**
Germany	GE	0.24	0.62	0.60	0.25	0.47	0.54		**0.38**	**0.49**	**0.25**	**0.67**	**0.47**	**0.45**	**0.50**	**0.49**	**0.57**	**0.52**	**0.42**
Hong Kong	HK	0.31	0.19	0.22	0.22	0.22	0.19	0.29		**0.25**	**0.19**	**0.55**	**0.38**	**0.78**	**0.52**	**0.45**	**0.38**	**0.58**	**0.61**
Italy	IT	0.23	0.21	0.35	0.30	0.31	0.43	0.28	0.33		**0.41**	**0.33**	**0.35**	**0.36**	**0.44**	**0.43**	**0.28**	**0.33**	**0.23**
Japan	JA	0.25	0.28	0.44	0.20	0.30	0.42	0.43	0.27	0.40		**0.36**	**0.26**	**0.37**	**0.47**	**0.45**	**0.39**	**0.45**	**0.26**
Netherlands	NL	0.33	0.43	0.58	0.52	0.48	0.52	0.64	0.42	0.33	0.40		**0.55**	**0.59**	**0.52**	**0.52**	**0.60**	**0.74**	**0.65**
Norway	NO	0.41	0.26	0.47	0.46	0.37	0.45	0.34	0.30	0.19	0.11	0.52		**0.52**	**0.50**	**0.57**	**0.45**	**0.58**	**0.52**
Singapore	SI	0.30	0.03	0.20	0.26	0.23	0.07	0.12	0.37	0.09	0.14	0.26	0.22		**0.58**	**0.54**	**0.48**	**0.66**	**0.66**
Spain	SP	0.25	0.26	0.29	0.22	0.22	0.33	0.30	0.19	0.38	0.39	0.29	0.15	0.04		**0.62**	**0.49**	**0.59**	**0.53**
Sweden	SW	0.29	0.24	0.33	0.29	0.40	0.25	0.30	0.28	0.26	0.31	0.39	0.31	0.20	0.28		**0.54**	**0.60**	**0.50**
Switzerland	SZ	0.36	0.56	0.63	0.42	0.52	0.56	0.77	0.32	0.30	0.42	0.68	0.48	0.20	0.25	0.41		**0.59**	**0.47**
United Kingdom	UK	0.44	0.27	0.46	0.54	0.38	0.49	0.43	0.32	0.36	0.31	0.59	0.40	0.24	0.33	0.30	0.51		**0.67**
United States	US	0.35	0.09	0.27	0.66	0.26	0.37	0.24	0.13	0.24	0.16	0.51	0.38	0.31	0.15	0.32	0.38	0.40	

Source: David Eiteman, Arthur Stonehill and Michael Moffett: *Multinational Business Finance* (Addison-Wesley, 1998).

markets, not in bull markets. This finding is of particular significance because, as we will examine in the following chapter, diversifying amongst assets with poorly to negative correlated returns is a desirable risk-reduction strategy.

Two, as exchange rates hardly remain fixed over time, their volatility presents arbitrage opportunities in the short-run but an investment dilemma in the long-run. Using the figures given above, for instance, the Nikkei would seem to have offered a better opportunity to an American investor than the Dow has offered to the Japanese investor. That would be a rather simplistic inference, however. Based on the results of their recent study on the performance of global stock markets in the twentieth century, for instance, Jorion and Goetzmann[23] have shown that longevity or survivorship of a market significantly contributes to that market's overall performance over time. Their results, summarized in Exhibit 4.25, show that US equities have given the best annual returns since 1920, arguably because the US has proven to be the most successful capitalist system in the world. Reflecting this, foreign participation in US equities and bond markets has only been rising, not declining, over time.

As we noted earlier in the context of the American (Exhibits 3.28 and 3.30) as also the British (Exhibit 4.21) stock markets, dividends have contributed significantly to the total returns. But dividends have been generally declining. As for the US market, this is evident in

Exhibit 4.25: The performance of global stock indexes (1921–1996), as reported by Jorion and Goetzmann. Ending wealth here is December 1996 value of $1 invested in December 1920. The Global Index includes the US.

	US Index	Global Index	Non-US Index
Nominal Return in US $			
Return	8.04%	7.76%	7.28%
Volatility	16.19%	12.14%	12.08%
Ending Wealth	211.2	171.2	146.2
Real Annual Return			
Return	5.48%	4.59%	3.84%
Volatility	15.83%	11.05%	9.96%
Ending Wealth	27.3	21.9	13.1

Exhibit 4.26, in which we summarize the payout and plowback ratios for the S&P 500 index. Suppose that, we denote a firm's earnings per share by E, and its dividends by D. Then,

$$\text{payout ratio} = \frac{\text{dividend paid } (D)}{\text{total earnings } (E)} \quad \text{and}$$

$$\text{plowback ratio} = \frac{\text{retained earnings } (E - D)}{\text{total earnings}} = 1 - \text{payout ratio}. \qquad (4.4)$$

Note that the overall pattern in Exhibit 4.26 is one of a progressive decline in the average payout ratio and a concomitant rise in the average plowback ratio. An increase in the plowback ratio means that the firms are retaining increasingly larger proportions of their earnings to finance future growth. Likewise, a decrease in the payout ratio means that the investors are accepting increasing proportions of their returns through capital appreciation. If this translates into growth then the firms would be certainly justified, and the investors satisfied, with this practice. This is most plausibly the case in what the rising trend in average annual return data, also shown in Exhibit 4.26, suggests.

It matters little, in perfect capital markets, whether investor receives the returns by way of capital gains alone or partly through capital gains and partly through dividends. After all, as we saw earlier, the pricing of

Exhibit 4.26: Average payout and plowback ratios, and the annual returns, for the firms comprising the S&P 500 index. The data presented here are annual averages of 10-year data, shown in annually rolling bands.

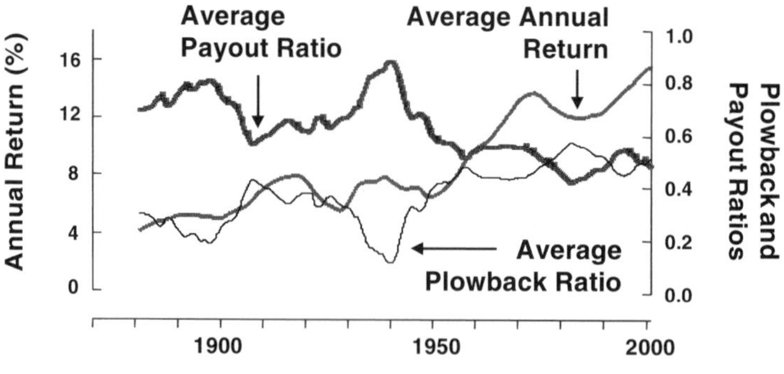

Source: http://aida.econ.yale.edu/~shiller/data/ie_data.htm

a firm's share involves both dividends as well as the part of the earnings that a firm retains in order to finance its future growth. The firms like IBM and AT&T pay quarterly dividends, for instance, whereas Microsoft does not. This is the famous MM postulate, so named after Miller and Modigliani who first argued, in their classic 1961 paper,[24] that a firm's dividend policy would have no relevance in a universe free of taxes, transaction costs, and other market imperfections. But the fact that the payout ratio has steadily declined over the 130-year life of the S&P 500 index, so readily apparent in Exhibit 4.26, suggests that market imperfections exist aplenty. Several reasons have contributed to this decline. Earlier, particularly until the Tax Reform Act of 1986, individuals were taxed more favorably on the capital gains than on dividends. Many firms therefore transmuted dividends into capital gains.[25] Also, as we mentioned in Section 3.1, Fama and French[26] have recently explored the issue of disappearing dividends by examining if this reflects changing firm characteristics or the firms' increasing reluctance to pay dividends. Their statistics show that only 20.8% of the firms paid cash dividends in 1999, compared to 66.5% who did so in 1978. Part of the reason, they argue, is that the newer listings of publicly traded firms increasingly include firms that are often unlikely to pay dividends — small firms with low profitability but strong growth opportunities. While this can account for almost one-half of the decline in the payout ratio, an equally important reason, according to this study, is that the perceived benefits of dividends may well have declined with time. Even the traditional dividend-paying type firms (e.g., large and profitable firms with fewer investments) have become increasingly less likely to pay dividends.

The evidence from global equity markets corroborates this. Of the 39 countries examined in the Jorion and Goetzmann study mentioned earlier, the equity indexes of 11 countries with continuous histories extending back to the 1920s showed a 5.09% average annual growth due to dividends whereas, when all the countries are considered, this average drops to 3.11%. Clearly, firms in the newer markets pay lower dividends. As older economies are also likely to have more mature firms, and the more mature a firm the fewer its avenues for growth, this also raises the possibility that shareholders of such firms demand and secure the payout, to the extent the law can help them do so, because of the fear that plowback may encourage wasteful squandering by the management. A recent study[27] has thus found that the firms in countries where law is more lenient towards the management tend to pay smaller dividends than those where the laws are less relaxed.

4.4 Reducing Risk Through Dollar-Cost-Averaging and Long-Term Investing

Slow and Steady Wins the Race!

The lesson to learn from the history of US and global stock markets is rather harsh, therefore. The dividends that have as yet been the main reason why returns on the stock market have been so robust may now become truly irrelevant. This may well be because, with investments coming in more from individuals and mutual funds than from the traditional sources like investment banks, we are perhaps approaching what Miller and Modigliani visualized as the perfect markets! This may have been further enhanced by the most recent (May 2003) US tax reduction law which targeted dividends.

Such a prospective universe of non-dividend paying stocks is likely to be volatile. Capital gains are not always positive, after all, as has become all too apparent in these first few years of the new millennium. As dividends can be either zero or positive, they cap the downside of capital gains that result from the market's gyrations.

From the perspective of investing, on the other hand, the problem of price volatility has a simple solution — dollar cost averaging. The idea here, first proposed by Wilford Eiteman and Frank Smith[28] almost half a century ago, is that if you invest a certain amount periodically — whether once a month, fortnightly or weekly — the number of shares your fixed amount will buy will be less when the market is up but more when it is down. In the process, then, you have captured the average.

Exhibit 4.27 illustrates this. This exhibit shows the growth by early 2000 of two investments, both in monthly installments of $100 in real 1970 dollars, if both the investments began at the end of 1970 and one was made in the S&P 500 index and the other in the NASDAQ composite index. The S&P 500 index, a proxy for the overall stock market, includes

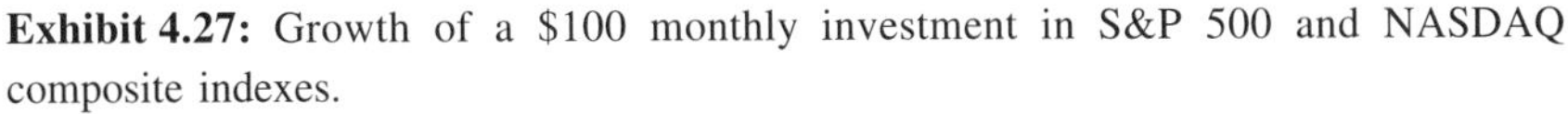

Exhibit 4.27: Growth of a $100 monthly investment in S&P 500 and NASDAQ composite indexes.

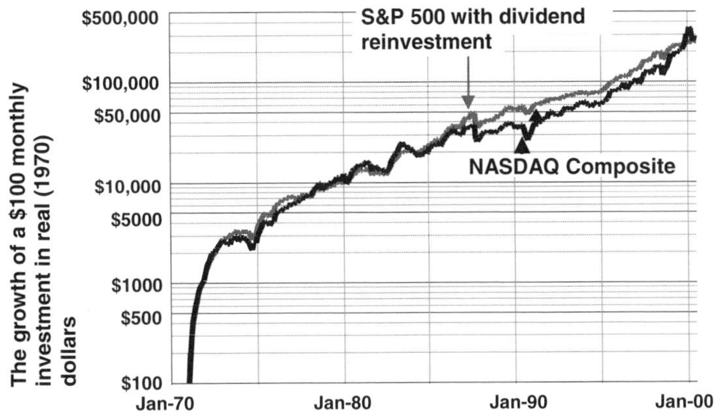

a large proportion of dividend-paying companies whereas the technology-weighted NASDAQ mostly comprises firms that pay little or no dividends. Thirty years later, the two investments would have still reached about the same value in real dollars, although the route taken by NASDAQ would have been somewhat jagged. This is because, as mentioned earlier, dividends have the effect of reducing the negative effect of volatility in prices.

The adverse effect of volatility is also greatly diminished when we hold the stock for an adequately long period. One way to estimate what length of time would be really "adequate" here is look at past returns. Exhibit 4.28 shows the annualized real total returns on the total market index for ten, 20 and 30-year holding periods through the past two centuries. Note how the volatility (standard deviation) as also variability (coefficient of variation) of the returns gets greatly reduced as when we extend the holding period. Note also that at no time in the 20th century has a 20-year or longer holding period ever produced negative returns. Based on these results, it is clear that the market's normal price fluctuations would have themselves insured your investment against losses during these past two centuries if you had held on for at least 20 years.

The characteristics of normal distribution, discussed in Section 3.4 earlier, offer an alternative way to estimate what duration would be

Exhibit 4.28: Over the past two centuries, no 20-year or longer holding period has produced negative total returns (real). Indeed, the longer the holding period the smaller the volatility and variability of returns.

Holding Period	*10 years*	*20 years*	*30 years*
Return	6.45%	6.44%	6.38%
Volatility	4.17%	2.44%	1.51%
Variability	0.65	0.38	0.24

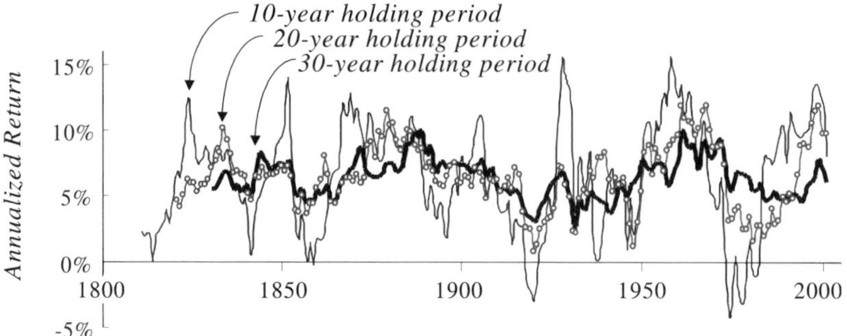

adequate. Suppose we define the holding period as the minimum number of years that an investment in the given equities market needs to be held, with dividends continually reinvested and based on the historic performance, in order to ensure with 95% confidence that the investment will retain its value. This holding period can now be estimated from the market's historic returns and volatility. Take the returns on the US market, for instance. With an annual mean return of 6.43% in real dollars, and a standard deviation of 17.06%, the negative returns have z-values less than 0.3769 (= 6.43 ÷ 17.06). As 14.67% of the normal curve lies between $z = 0$ and $z = 0.3769$, this gives a 35.33% chance that the real total returns in any given year will be negative.

Clearly, the smaller the standard deviation relative to the mean, a task that requires our extending the holding period (e.g., Exhibit 4.28), the smaller will be the probability of negative returns. To this end, the following two properties of our statistical distribution become appropriate:

1. Cumulative return over n periods is merely n times the average single period return,[29] i.e.,

$$\tilde{r}_{n\text{-period}} = n \times \tilde{r}_{1\text{-period}} \text{ or } \tilde{r}_{\text{annual}} = 12 \times \tilde{r}_{\text{monthly}}.$$

2. Volatility or standard deviation over n periods[30] is the single period standard deviation times square root of n, i.e.,

$$s_{n\text{-period}} = (\sqrt{n})\, s_{1\text{-period}} \text{ or } s_{\text{annual}} = (\sqrt{12})\, s_{\text{monthly}}.$$

Now, for normal distribution, 95% of the values lie to the right of z = mean − 1.645 × standard deviation (Exhibit 4.26). Combining this with (1) and (2) above, we thus find that there will be 95% chance of being able to avoid negative return in a given year if we seek the value $\tilde{r}_{n\text{-period}}$ such that

$$\tilde{r}_{n\text{-period}} = 1.645 \times s_{n\text{-period}}, \tag{4.5a}$$

or

$$n \times \tilde{r}_{1\text{-period}} = 1.645 \times (\sqrt{n})\, s_{1\text{-period}}. \tag{4.5b}$$

Hence

$$n = \left(\frac{1.645 \times s_{1\text{-period}}}{\tilde{r}_{1\text{-period}}} \right)^2. \tag{4.5c}$$

For the US data, plugging in the values $\tilde{r}_{1\text{-period}} = \tilde{r}_{1\text{-year}} = 6.43\%$ and $s_{1\text{-period}} = s_{1\text{-year}} = 17.06\%$ in Equation (4.5c), we obtain the value $n = 19.05$ years for our holding horizon. How reasonable is this estimate? After all, the assumption of normal distribution for the stock market returns is itself an approximation, as we discussed earlier in the context of Exhibits 3.33 and 3.37. Exhibit 4.29 therefore graphs, for different holding periods, the mean returns, the corresponding bands at one standard deviation level, and minimum and maximum values of annual returns for each holding period. Note that no negative annual returns occur for any 20-year or longer holding periods.

This match between the estimates made from the normal distribution based Equation (4.5c) and the empirical data in Exhibit 4.29 amply attests

Exhibit 4.29: Based on 1802–2000 performance of the US stock market, the cumulative real returns are essentially positive for all the values of holding period ≥ 20 years.

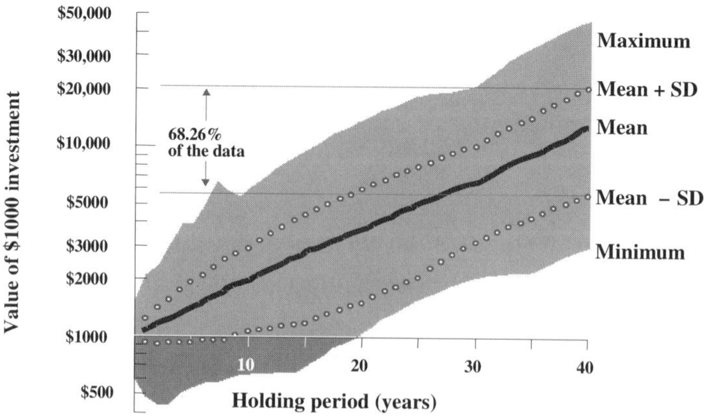

Exhibit 4.30: The real value of a $1000 initial investment for 20- and 40-year holding periods.

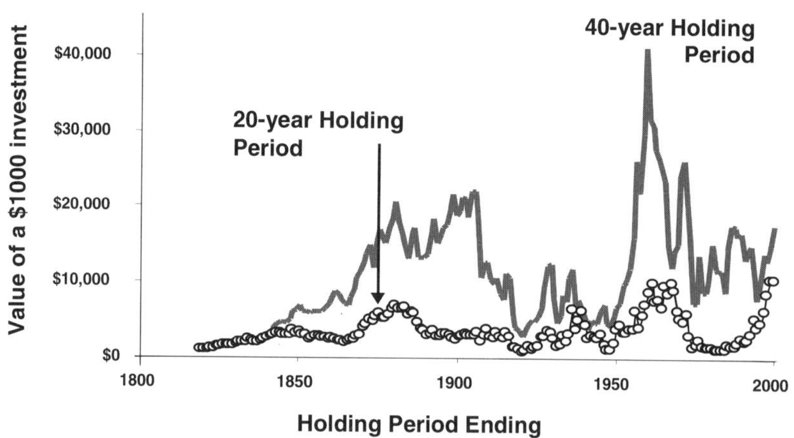

to the robustness of normal distribution model for long-term returns. The reader may also recall here our inference, drawn in the context of Exhibit 3.4, that the real returns for 20-year and longer periods have been always positive.

We can also look at the historic data by directly computing the path of wealth from the historic record. As shown in Exhibit 4.30, this path is more impressive for the 40-year holding period than when the holding period is one-half as long. This is only to be expected. After all, as the *rule of 70* tells us, a 7% real annual growth rate makes the 40-year cumulative return four times the 20-year return, not double! The advantage that Exhibit 4.29 has over the computations based on Equation (4.5c) and Exhibit 4.27 is that it shows how the gains from investing in the US stock market have varied since 1802. The narrow spikes in Exhibit 4.30 show that investors who got out of the market in 1958–1959 after holding steady for a 40-year period received the best returns that the US total return index has offered in its entire history!

Exhibit 4.31 extends this analysis to the international arena, by looking at the statistics for inflation-adjusted annual returns on some of the stock markets worldwide with long survival histories. Though not an exhaustive

Exhibit 4.31: The statistics on real total annual returns for selected stock markets worldwide. The last column shows the "holding horizon", defined as the time needed to ensure, at the 95% level of confidence, that real cumulative returns are positive.

Market	*Period annual return*	*Real*	*Volatility*	*Holding horizon (years)*
US	1802–2000	6.43%	17.06%	19.05
UK	1694–2000	4.85%	12.21%	17.15
Japan	1921–2000*	7.23%	18.95%	18.59
Germany	1924–2000*	7.24%	22.30%	25.67
Sweden	1921–2000	5.60%	16.65%	23.92
France**	1921–2000	7.76%	25.50%	29.22
Netherlands**	1921–2000	5.85%	16.50%	21.53
Portugal**	1930–2000*	11.61%	29.49%	17.46
Canada**	1921–2000	6.88%	18.17%	18.87
Austria**	1925–2000	7.22%	21.49%	23.97
Belgium	1921–2000	5.77%	21.80%	38.63
Denmark**	1926–2000	6.10%	14.36%	15
Switzerland	1926–2000	4.35%	14.73%	31.24

*Denote interruptions, e.g., Germany from August 1944 to December 1949; Portugal from May 1974 to February 1977; Japan from June 1944 to March 1949.
**Real returns computed in the US dollars.

Source: The Jorion and Goetzmann study

list, it is representative enough of the stock markets worldwide in general and gives us an idea of how positive their long run returns have been, no matter what the socioeconomic history. Also given in this exhibit are the values of the "holding period". The pattern reveal by the data is: the greater the volatility, and the smaller the return, the longer the holding horizon needs to be.

Is It Really the Economy, Stupid?

The cyclicity evident in Exhibits 4.28 and 4.30 reflect the long-term cyclicity seen in the annual return data in Exhibits 3.28 and 3.30. The source of these fluctuations is hard to identify, however. Earlier, in the context of Exhibit 3.31, we had noted that capital markets can hardly remain immune to macroeconomic constraints. After all, markets perform well for the investors when the firms are not only profitable but increasingly so. But this demands that economy grow exponentially. The question is whether that is really possible, and the economy can really grow continually, without occasional foray into the negative territory. So far, and at the macro level, the evidence from overall growth of the US economy has been supportive of this possibility. This can be seen in Exhibit 4.32 where we compare the US Gross Domestic Product (GDP),[31] in chained 1996 dollars, with the CPI-adjusted S&P 500 total return index, for the entire twentieth century. For ease of comparison, the two datasets have been normalized at one on January 1, 1900. The GDP data for 1900–1928 are from Angus Maddison's compendium[32] on the world economy, and the subsequent data are from the US Department of Commerce.

As the quote from Professor Tobin in Box 4.2 explains, GDP — the total domestic output of all goods and services — is a simple but elegant measure of the nation's economic well-being that guides planning as much for the government as for the corporations. The stock market is a leading indicator of the economy, after all. Comparing the growth of GDP and the stock market as in Exhibit 4.32, it would seem as if the stock market has indeed fueled the growth of the GDP.

As Exhibit 4.33 shows, fluctuations in the stock prices occur far more frequently than the changes in GDP. Not all the downturns in the

Exhibit 4.32: Throughout the 20th century, US stock market has grown faster than the nation's GDP. Both these datasets have been adjusted for inflation and are set at one on January 1, 1900.

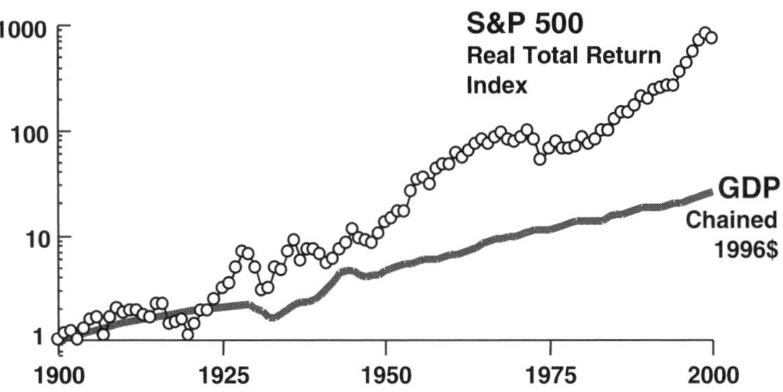

Box 4.2: Why GDP Matters?

GDP! The right concept of economy-wide output, accurately measured. The US and the world rely on it to tell where we are in the business cycle and to estimate long-run growth. It is the centerpiece of an elaborate and indispensable system of social accounting, the national income and product accounts. This is surely the single innovative achievement of the Commerce Department in the 20th century. I was fortunate to become an economist in the 1930s when Kuznets, Nathan, Gilbert, and Jaszi were creating this most important set of economic time series. In economic theory, macroeconomics was just beginning at the same time. Complementarily, these two innovations deserve much credit for the improved performance of the economy in the second half of the century.

James Tobin
Nobel Laureate and Yale University Professor Emeritus of Economics
(http://www.bea.doc.gov/bea/aw/0100od/maintext.htm)

market translate into corresponding drops in GDP, nor do all the market's upturns herald rises in GDP. The most notable example of this is the market's 29% drop on October 19, 1987. It produced a –23% real total return for the month of October 1987, while GDP rose by 1.74% in that quarter. As Professor Paul Samuelson, a Nobel Laureate in Economics,

Exhibit 4.33: The annual data for the 1947–2000 period, graphed in quarterly intervals, show far more frequent dips in the total returns on stock market than in the GDP changes.

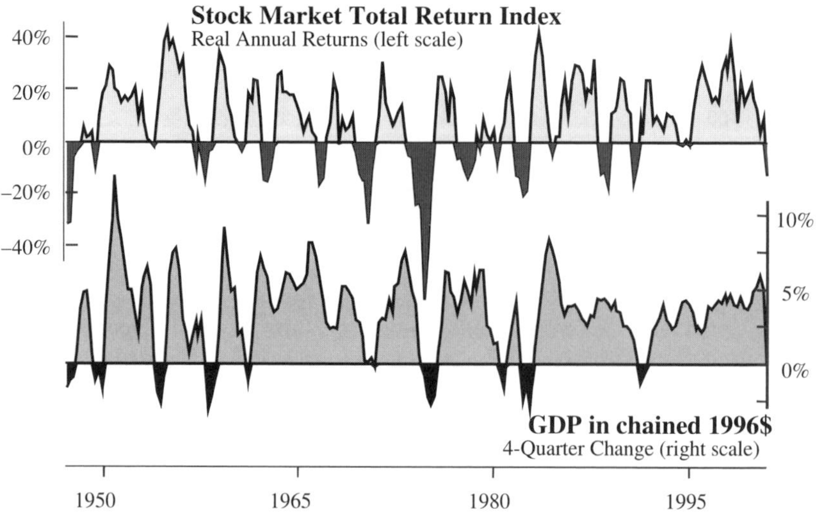

quipped in a *Newsweek* magazine article[33] 35 years ago, the stock market has accurately "*predicted nine out of the last five recessions*"! This is particularly explicit in Exhibit 4.33 where annual data on real total returns on the market during 1947–2000 are compared with the corresponding data on GDP changes. As can be seen here, real total returns on the overall stock market dropped by 10% or more on 12 occasions since January 1947, but GDP depreciated on only ten of these occasions.

Perhaps one should examine other factors that can predict GDP growth and how they might help predict the stock market's overall behavior. The results of a recent study by John Stock and Mark Watson[34] are instructive here. It examined the performance of different predictor signals over time, only to find that the signals such as these work more effectively in hindsight than in foresight, i.e., the signals that have worked well in the past do rather poorly in the future. Exhibit 4.34 compares the performances of three of the signals examined by these authors. As can be seen here, the yield spread on short-term and long-term Treasuries improved the GDP growth forecasts by an average of 52%

Exhibit 4.34: The effect of selected indicators on the accuracy of the GDP growth forecasts.

Indicator	1971–1984	1985–1999
Stock prices	10%	−12%
Yield spread on the corporate versus government bonds	44%	−88%
Yield spread on the short-term versus long-term Treasuries	52%	−59%

Source: The study by James Stock and Mark Watson

during 1971–1984 but almost wrecked these forecasts during the next 15-year period! Perhaps this reflects the dynamics of the economy — the successful indicators of the past lose their predictive power when economic policy absorbs their signals as the economy evolves.

Does this make predicting business cycle's ups and downs from those of the stock market a futile exercise? Certainly not, as is quite obvious from a closer look at Exhibit 4.34. Investors are more immediately concerned with the market's, and not the economy's, prospective performance. Their interest[35] in the GDP is oblique at best, particularly in the short run, based on the premise that the market is more likely to do better when the economy is rising than when it is declining. Exhibit 4.33 merits a closer examination, therefore, because it is unreasonable to expect a direct correlation between the two variables presented here if the change in one of them (the stock market) can be a leading indicator of the change in the other (the GDP). A direct correlation would make the stock market a "coincident", not a leading or lagging, indicator of economy's direction. The question, therefore, is the time by which the change in the market either lags or leads that of GDP. Exhibit 4.35 presents the results of this analysis.

Note how scattered the graph in the left panel of Exhibit 4.35 is! Clearly, with a statistically insignificant correlation coefficient (ρ) value of 0.25 (left panel), changes in the S&P 500 total return index and the GDP show no discernible relation whatever. But, on lagging the GDP data by two quarters relative to the stock market data, their correlation

Exhibit 4.35: Correlation analyses of the graph in Exhibit 4.33. The "same-time" S&P and GDP changes are poorly correlated (left panel) but their relationship improves significantly when GDP time-series lags the S&P time-series by two quarters (right panel).

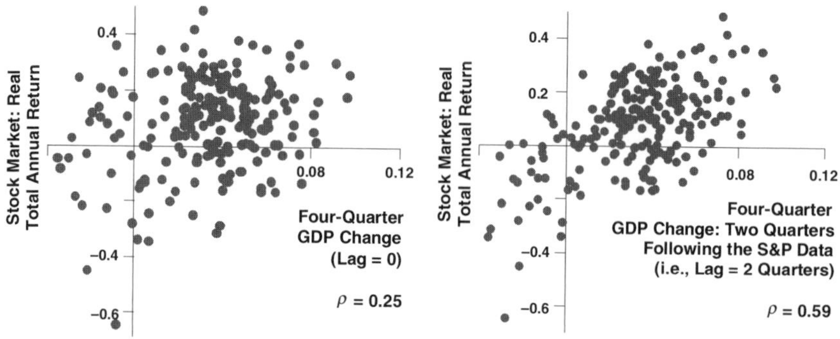

dramatically improves, to a statistically significant $\rho = 0.59$ (right panel). This makes the stock market an effective leading indicator of the nation's economic output by two quarters.

While stock prices are likely indicators of the economy, the converse is not necessarily true. We therefore compare the pattern of changes in stock prices with two other variables, yield spread (= yields on long-term treasury bonds less the Fed Funds Rate) and GDP gap (= real GDP less potential GDP), for the 1954–2000 period, in Exhibit 4.36. It presents the correlograms for changes in the S&P 500 total return index (labeled ΔSP here), for different quarterly lags, with these two variables. The variables that correlate for positive lags would then be the leading indicators for the stock market, while those that correlate best for the negative lags would be lagging indicators. For instance, yield spread has the highest positive correlation with market changes with a lag of two quarters. This makes the yield spread a leading indicator of the market by two quarters. Likewise, the correlation of ΔSP and GDP gap is positive at a −3 quarters lag, and negative at a lag of three quarters. Obviously, the more real GDP is above its potential, the more negative the GDP gap and the greater the danger signal for the market.

Though statistically significant at a 95% confidence level, these correlations do not cover adequate variability in the stock market to be

Exhibit 4.36: For the 1954–2000 period, yield spread with two-quarter lag and GDP gap with three-quarter lag have been the leading and lagging indicators for annual changes in the S&P 500 real total return index, respectively.

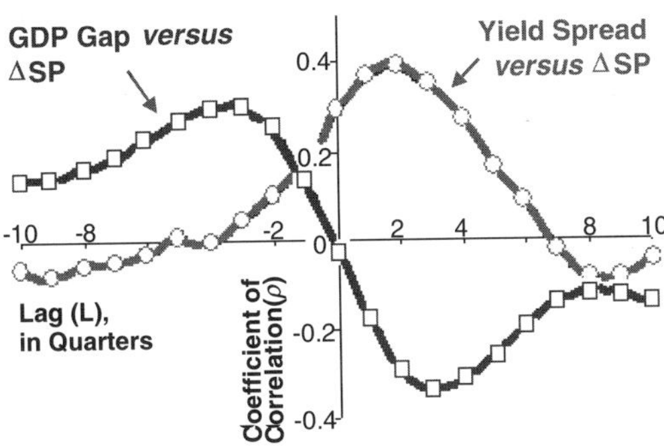

the strong predictors of the market that we as investors would like to see. For instance, multiple regression analysis shows that yield spreads and GDP gaps together explain only one-fifth of observed variability in stock market returns. Nonetheless, this analysis shows that investors are well advised to continually monitor the changes in yield spread and GDP gap.

The remaining issue deals with the lessons that could be learned from the experience of other countries with regard to the effect of the stock market on the economy. Let us take the case of Japan. Exhibit 4.37 updates *The Economist* magazine's 1999 comparison of the 1991–1999 performance of the US stock market with the 1921–1932 and the 1981–1992 performance of Japan's Nikkei index. Apart from updating the data, the only difference here is that we have used the S&P 500 index, and not the Dow index used by *The Economist* magazine. But the Dow mirrors the S&P 500 index so closely that the inferences one can draw from Exhibit 4.37 should not diverge significantly from what *The Economist* magazine concluded. The problem with this picture is that, as was noted in Exhibit 3.42 earlier, the best correlation that US market's 1990s history of total return index in real dollars shows is with its 1950s history, and not with its history in the 1920s and early 1930s.

The market's bear run since March 2000 makes the analysis of *The Economist* magazine seem quite prophetic. Japan's growth in the 1980s

Exhibit 4.37: History appears to support the fear that the ongoing turmoil in the stock market may well obliterate the US economy's sterling gains of the 1990s.

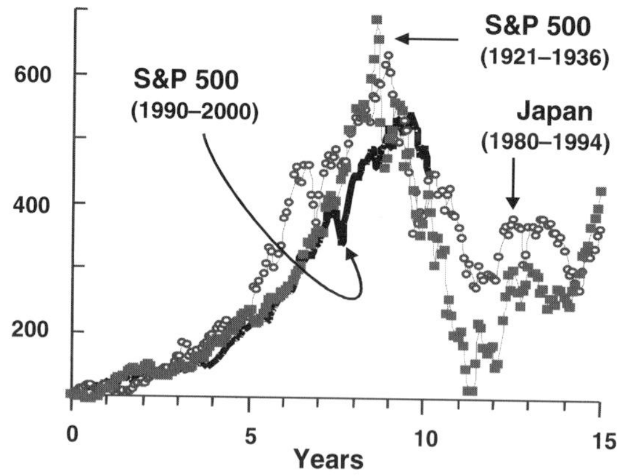

Source: "Bonfire of the Insanities", *The Economist*, September 25, 1999.

was associated with that in business productivity and resulted from a pronounced investment boom. With the current slowdown in business investment in the US, particularly in information technology, the US appears to be following an eerily similar path. Also, as Japan's bust since the 1990s has covered the stock market as well as real estate, one should wonder if America's housing bubble is next. The lesson clearly is that, as America's boom in the 1990s came mainly from the productivity growth brought about by investment in technology, the sooner the current dip in these investments reverses the better off the economy is likely to be. But then, investment in technology is often the last to recover after a trough in the business cycle. And, based on the data in Exhibit 3.8, we may not have reached the trough in this business cycle as yet. As to the US housing market, the correlation of house prices with income growth substantially weakens the evidence of any bubble.

An intense pessimism about the immediate future of the stock market is one extreme lesson that one can perhaps draw from these discussions. This is the message in such recent bestsellers as *Irrational Exuberance* by Robert Schiller and *Valuing Wall Street* by Andrew Smithers and

Stephen Wright. The opposite extreme of unbridled exuberance is painted in bestsellers like *Dow 36000: The New Strategy for Profiting from the Coming Rise in the Stock Market* by James Glassman and Kevin Hassell, *Dow 40000: Strategies for Profiting from the Greatest Bull Market in History* by David Elias, and *Dow 100000: Fact or Fiction* by Charles Kadlec and Ralph Acampora, on the other hand.

Our narrative shows that the truth perhaps lies somewhere in the middle. Take, for instance, the statistics on real annual returns summarized in Exhibits 3.44 and 4.28. Let us assume that the market's 1981–2000 performance is hard to repeat, and that the real returns during 1971–2010 will be the same as the returns during 1802–2001. In that case, with the geometric model discussed earlier, the 1802–2001 and 1981–2001 average annual returns as 6.33% and 8.58%, respectively, and the time-aggregation property discussed in the context of Equations (4.5a)–(4.5c), we can write

$$\begin{aligned} \ln(P_{2030}/P_{2002}) &= \ln(P_{2030}/P_{1981}) - \ln(P_{2001}/P_{1981}) \\ &= 50 \times 6.33\% - 21 \times 8.58\% = 29 \times 4.70\% . \end{aligned} \tag{4.6}$$

With equal justification, we could use the 1971–2001 average annual returns of 6.32% here, of course. Equation (4.6) would then give the estimate of expected average returns during 2002–2010 (or 2002–2020 or 2002–2030) about the same as that during 1971–2001. Recall our estimate of 4.9–11.2%, in Section 3.1, for the expected average annual total returns (real) on the S&P 500 index during 2002–2010.

This suggests that the average growth rate in the next 29–30 years may well turn out to be slower than the historic annual average of 6.3–6.5% in real dollars. But, adding an annual 3% for inflation, this also suggests that, in nominal dollars, there is no reason why the Dow, say 8500 in mid-year 2002, may not reach about 15,000 in 2010 and approach 40,000 in 2020, assuming the historic rates hold. This sailing may not turn out to be a smooth one, however.

In crunching the above numbers, we have only considered the mean returns and have ignored their volatility. A measure in financial statistics that captures this is the Sharpe ratio. It shows the risk-adjusted performance of equities by normalizing the excess returns on equities in relation to short-term bonds (or the market-determined interest or inflation rate) for the fluctuations in the former, i.e.,

$$\text{Sharpe ratio} = (\tilde{r}_{\text{equities}} - r_f)/s_{\text{equities}}\ , \tag{4.7}$$

where r_f is the "risk-free" rate computed for the short-term bonds, s_{equities} is the standard deviation for equities, and $\tilde{r}_{\text{equities}}$ the corresponding average return on equities. Exhibit 4.38 shows how the Sharpe ratio for the US market, computed here in annually rolling 30-year segments, has varied through the past 150 years. Note that the overall risk-adjusted performance of the US stock market, which peaked in the 1960s, has now remained positive for more than a century.

What lessons from the market's performance history can be gleaned from this analysis? Exhibit 4.39 answers this question by comparing the mean, standard deviation and Sharpe ratio statistics for the real annual returns on stocks and bonds over the 1871–2001 period. For the stock market, these data have been annualized from 20-year holdings and have been computed using real annual data in annually rolling bands. The bond statistics are for 10-year Treasuries and have been computed from 20 annual data taken in annually rolling bands. Notice how these data point to an emerging convergence of stocks and bonds. Historically bond yields have been far less volatile than stock returns, even in the early 1940s when their yields briefly approached those of the stocks. But bond volatility is already close to that of the stocks, although their returns

Exhibit 4.38: Changes in US market's Sharpe ratio, computed in annually rolling bands of 30-year segments.

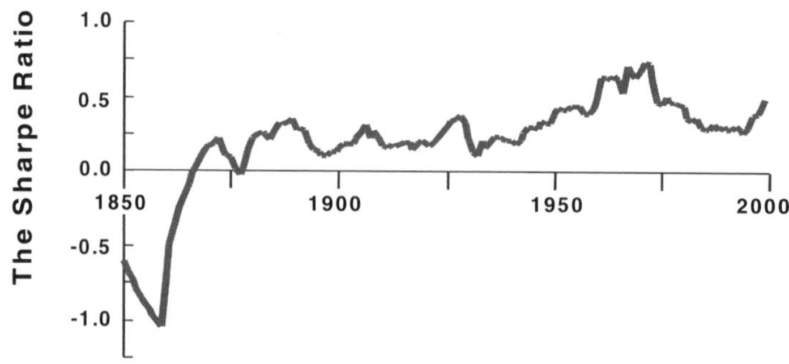

Exhibit 4.39: The comparison of statistics of annual returns on stocks (S&P 500) and bonds (10-year Treasuries), computed for real annual data in annually rolling bands, shows that the stock returns have always surpassed yields on bonds but the two now have similar volatility. Their "modified" Sharpe ratios[36] point to a possible resurgence in the demand for bonds, though.

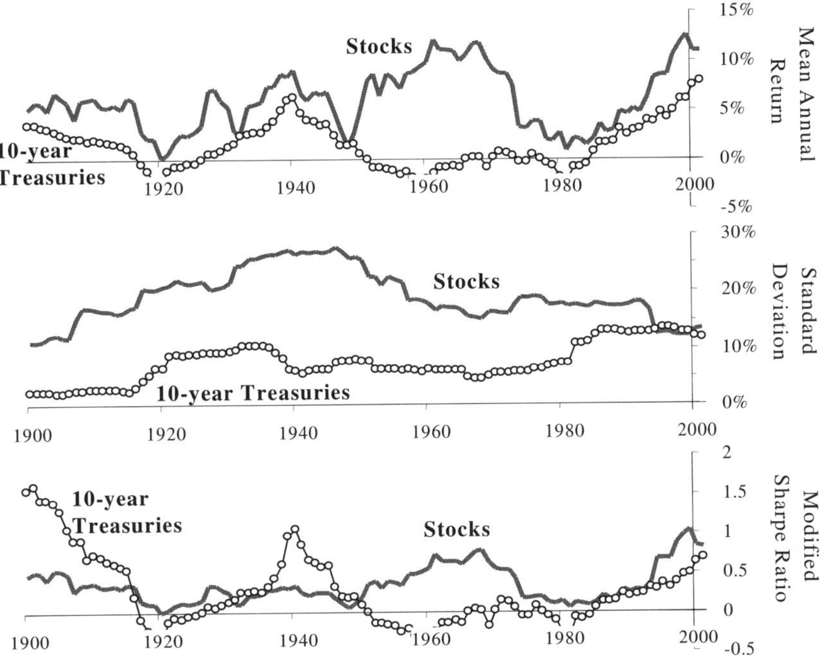

are yet to match. Perhaps we may soon have bonds in the same basket as the stocks and not as their alternatives!

The Return of Positive Returns

As for investments, the market's troughs provide buying opportunities. After all, if the cooling of the market points to that of the economy at large, then the market is also likely to anticipate the economy's rise as well. Exhibit 4.40 thus examines the returns an investor would have received from buying at the market's troughs and holding (1) to the business cycle troughs and (2) for one year. Note how impressive the

Exhibit 4.40: Real total returns from buying at the stock market troughs.

Stock market trough	Business cycle trough	Returns by holding from stock market trough to business cycle trough		Returns for 1-year holding from stock market trough
		Return	Period	
July 1945	October 1945	14.89%	3 months	27.74%
May 1947	...	...	...	5.71%
June 1949	October 1949	14.99%	4 months	34.44%
August 1953	May 1954	25.56%	9 months	31.61%
February 1957	...	...	...	–4.42%
December 1957	April 1958	8.03%	4 months	29.75%
October 1960	February 1961	19.27%	4 months	25.71%
June 1962	...	...	...	27.63%
September 1966	...	...	...	23.67%
June 1970	November 1970	17.72%	5 months	33.45%
September 1974	March 1975	26.68%	6 months	30.26%
October 1978	...	...	...	15.97%
March 1980	July 80	17.46%	4 months	22.43%
July 1982	November 1982	28.18%	4 months	51.08%
July 1984	...	...	...	25.86%
November 1987	...	...	...	19.09%
October 1990	March 1991	23.84%	5 months	28.06%
June 1994	...	...	...	16.15%
August 1998	...	...	...	31.77%
September 1999	...	...	...	18.01%

real total returns would have really been, overall! Barring one exception, they all are positive and greatly exceed the market's average returns. Clearly, the market's downturns are the buying opportunities that we should covet, no matter whether they presage the economy's slowdown or not. For instance, the investors who braved into the market in November 1987 and stayed in it for one year, despite the October 1987 crash, received an impressive 19.1% return in real or inflation-adjusted dollars. The challenge is to be able to identify the troughs.

Thus, as the writer Art Buchwald points out in a skit reproduced in Box 4.3 here, investors are what the market is now apparently waiting

Box 4.3: Tom, Dick and Harry, the Economy Misses You

Art Buchwald

People talk about a recession the way they do about the weather. And like the weather, no one can do anything about it.

Frederick Hollcomb is an expert on recession and predicts the confidence of the man in the street.

"No one likes a recession. Even Al Greenspan hates them. But if you are going to have one, you might as well have it now than later."

I said, "Is it true that recession is caused by the level of consumer confidence? The lower the confidence, the more the chance there is of the boat sinking?" Hollcomb replied, "There is something to that. The consumer can make or break the economy. For eight years confidence was high and recessions were unthinkable. Tom, Dick and Harry were spending money willy-nilly and not concerned about the tomorrow.

"Then something happened — Tom first, then Dick, and then Harry, the people who set the confidence tables, started hoarding money instead of spending it. Tom said he was cutting back because there was a talk of layoffs at his firm. Dick stopped going to boat shows because he didn't want to add any luxuries to his lifestyle. Harry lost half his money when he got into an ugly divorce lawsuit with his wife.

"All sorts of solutions to avoid the recession problem were advanced. Bank interest rates were cut. Tax relief was offered, and department stores cut another 50% off most items in their stores.

"The big question was would Tom start spending again, and the second question was would Dick take any credit on his MasterCard after he decided he didn't want any more debt? Harry was hardly getting by after paying $1500 a month in alimony: he told his lawyer, 'How can we have consumer confidence when my ex-wife takes all my money?'

"By this time, Wall Street got into the act and said, 'Our stocks are not going to make any money if nobody buys anything.'"

"What is the solution?"

"Another fed interest rate cut."

"Will that bring Tom, Dick and Harry back into the economy?"

"If it doesn't, Orville Redenbacher will go broke and Amazon is going to cry uncle." So that's where we stand right now. I tried to talk to Tom, Dick and Harry to get their side of it, but they wouldn't answer my calls.

(*Los Angeles Times*
March 8, 2001)

for! When might that happen? A plausible scenario is this. The *value investors* are usually the ones to herald the end of a bear market but, macabre as it may seem, the fair value for them often implies a 20–25% discount on what would be commonly identified as the fair value. Unfortunately, though, the mid-year 2002 market is priced at about its fair value, as will be seen in the next two chapters. It will need to wait a while longer, therefore, to become attractive to such investors.

4.5 Conclusion

Our examination of the history of the US stock market in the last two chapters has shown that the market has, over time and over any given 30-year segment in its almost 200-year long history, always outperformed the other investment vehicles like Treasury bills and bonds, corporate bonds, commodities and the real estate. A nineteenth century investor would have justifiably considered these other investment vehicles as equally attractive alternatives for wealth preservation. But the situation through the twentieth century has been vastly different. During the 1802–1899 period, real annual returns on the market exceeded those on the long-term government bonds by barely 1.4%, but were almost 1% less than those on corporate bonds. During 1900–1999, on the other hand, the market's real or inflation-adjusted excess returns over these two instruments averaged 4–5% per year! This is also true of the commodities and the real estate markets.

"For online investors, our new keyboard has four extra buttons: BUY, SELL, PANIC, and BRAG!"

The data from other markets worldwide paint an identical picture. In the UK, for instance, real annual returns on long-term government bonds were 0.26–0.53% less than those on the stocks during 1700–1899, but 4.39% less during 1900–1999. The stock markets in Germany, Japan, Canada, France and Austria have performed even better than the US stock market during the twentieth century.

To an investor, these factors alone should make the stock market the preferred, nay, the only, choice. Add to this the fact that investment itself is no longer a matter of choice. We are living longer but also have to retire sooner, and the age at which full retirement benefits can become available is receding farther into the future. Therefore, investing is now needed as much for creating wealth as for preserving it, and investing in the stocks satisfies both these needs simultaneously.

The stock market is a volatile place, of course. It is for this reason that we suggest stocks as wealth-preservers and wealth-builders over the long haul. How long a haul should that be? We find a 20-year holding horizon to be adequate. Indeed, apart from the fact that this is what the statistical structure of the annual returns data suggests, there has been no 20-year or longer period in the history of the US stock market when the cumulative real returns have been negative. Now that the market has taken a rather prolonged pause, and has started the new millennium on a rather depressed note, the picture that we have drawn may seem irrationally exuberant, particularly to the investors who entered the market towards the waning years of the long bull market of the 1990s. But then, what else to call it if not the best buying opportunity that has taken a long time to come?

Endnotes

[1] F.J. Fabozzi and T.D. Fabozzi: *Handbook of Fixed Income Securities* (Irwin, 1995).

[2] Federal Home Loan Bank System, Freddie Mac, Fannie Mae, Sallie Mae, Farm Credit System, Tennessee Valley Authority.

[3] A coupon is basically the interest payment on the bond and is called so because, in order to receive the payment, the holder of the bond usually needs to clip it off and mail it to the bond's issuer. Take a Treasury bill

carrying 15.75% coupon rate and maturing in November 2001, for instance. For semiannual payments, buying this \$1000 bond in January 2001 means receiving two \$78.75 coupons, one in May 2001 and the other in November 2001, when the \$1000 face value of the bond too will be redeemed. The price that this bond will sell for is the present value (PV) of this cash flow, or the value of this cash stream discounted to the present and, for a 4.86% effective annual yield, was quoted at \$108.21 (per \$100) on January 12, 2001. The bond was thus selling at a premium because its coupon exceeded the current interest rate.

[4] The PV of an annuity can be easily computed as the difference between two perpetuities. Take two perpetuities, X and Y, with the present values of PV_X and PV_Y and both having the same coupon, say C. The n-period annuity with this cash stream of C per period is then $\mathrm{PV}_X - \mathrm{PV}_Y$. Since a perpetuity (e.g., a consol in the UK and Canada or a preferred stock in the US) offers a never-ending stream of level cash flow, we have

$$\mathrm{PV}_X = \frac{C}{r_{\text{period}}} \quad \text{and} \quad \mathrm{PV}_Y = \frac{C}{r_{\text{period}}(1+r_{\text{period}})^n}.$$

This is because, by writing

$$\mathrm{PV}_X = \frac{C}{(1+r_{\text{period}})} + \frac{C}{(1+r_{\text{period}})^2} + \frac{C}{(1+r_{\text{period}})^3} + \cdots,$$

so that

$$(1+r_{\text{period}})\,\mathrm{PV}_X = C + \frac{C}{(1+r_{\text{period}})} + \frac{C}{(1+r_{\text{period}})^2} + \cdots,$$

we obtain

$$(1+r_{\text{period}})\,\mathrm{PV}_X - \mathrm{PV}_Y = r_{\text{period}}\,\mathrm{PV}_X = C\,.$$

We then have $\mathrm{PV}_X = (1 + r_{\text{period}})^n\ \mathrm{PV}_Y$ because the payments on our perpetuity Y begin period n after those on X.

[5] The yield to maturity (YTM) of a bond is basically its internal rate of return (IRR). By definition, IRR is the rate of return that makes the net present value (NPV) of an investment equal zero, NPV being the present value of the cash stream net of investment. For instance, suppose an initial investment of C_0 generates a cash stream C_1, C_2 and C_3 in the manner shown here. For this investment, we have

$$\text{NPV} = -C_0 + \frac{C_1}{1+r} + \frac{C_2}{(1+r)^2} + \frac{C_3}{(1+r)^3},$$

Time	0	1	2	3
Cash Flow	$-C_0$	C_1	C_2	C_3
Discount Rate		r	r	r

and IRR would be the value of r for which NPV = 0.

[6] In the US, the legislated goal of monetary policy that defines the Fed's task is to keep the economy growing at a moderate pace while keeping inflation low.

[7] John Taylor: "Discretion versus Policy Rules in Practice", *Carnegie-Rochester Conference Series on Public Policy*, vol. 39, pp. 195–214, 1993. See also John B. Taylor: "A Historical Analysis of Monetary Policy Rules", in *Monetary Policy Rules* (Ed. John B. Taylor) (University of Chicago Press, 1999), pp. 319–347.

[8] For the fourth quarter of 2000, real GDP was \$9394.2 billion, in chained 1996 dollars, when the potential GDP, according to the Congressional Budget Office, was \$9171.3 billion.

[9] Arthur Laffer has recently argued ("So You Thought the Fed Set Interest Rates?", *The Wall Street Journal*, March 22, 2001) that, rather than setting the rates, the Fed merely adjusts the discount rates to the prevailing 3-month T-Bill rates.

[10] Although widely used by the central banks (e.g., "Monetary Policy, Made to Measure", *The Economist*, p. 60, August 10, 1996), some economists find the source of the Fed's success in combating US inflation since 1980 in aggressively seeking to prevent inflation, not in John Taylor's premise of responding to inflation. For instance, R.L. Hetzel ("The Taylor Rule: Is it a Useful Guide to Understanding Monetary Policy?", *Federal Reserve Bank of Richmond Economic Quarterly*, vol. 86, pp. 1–33, 2000) has reported a significantly improved correlation coefficient, from 0.66 for November 1965–July 1979 to 0.81 for August 1979–July 1987 and 0.91 for August 1987–May 1999, from regression analysis of empirical data and Taylor rule predictions, suggesting that the Fed action in setting the interest rates is becoming increasingly timely.

[11] M.J. Brennan and E.S. Schwartz: "Saving Bonds, Retractable Bonds, and Callable Bonds", *Journal of Financial Economics*, vol. 5, pp. 67–88, 1977.

[12] Edwin Elton, Martin Gruber, Deepak Agrawal and Christopher Mann ("Explaining the Rate Spread on Corporate Bonds", *Journal of Finance*, vol. 56, pp. 247–277, 1998) have argued that, rather than merely the expected default, the premium should be considered.

[13] Jeremy Siegel: "Are Stocks Still Right For the Long RUN?" *Mckenna Lecture Series, St. Vincent College* (http://www.facweb.stvincent.edu/Academics/cepe/Articles/Siegel.html, accessed on July 7, 2002).

[14] In his seminal paper "Portfolio Selection" (*Journal of Finance*, vol. 7, pp. 77–91, 1952), Harry Markowitz was the first to explain how the standard deviation of returns is a direct measure of volatility. He further argued that risk reduction requires selecting such assets in a portfolio that do not move together, or correlate inversely, in other words.

[15] Antulio N. Bomfim: "Optimal Portfolio Allocation in a World Without Treasury Securities", *Finance & Economics Discussion Series*, No. 2001–2011, Federal Reserve Board.

[16] See, for instance, the article by R. Mehra and E.C. Prescott ("The Equity Risk Premium: A Puzzle", *Journal of Monetary Economics*, vol. 15, pp. 145–161, 1985), who first raised this problem. Recent studies (e.g., I. Welch: "Views of Financial Economists on the Equity Premium and Other Issues", *Journal of Business*, vol. 73, pp. 501–537, 2000; and R. Arnott and R. Ryan: "The Death of the Risk Premium: Consequences of the 1990s", *Journal of Portfolio Management*, Spring 2001) estimate the equity premium at 0–13%.

[17] Ana M. Aizcorbe, Arthur B. Kennickell and Kevin B. Moore: "Recent Changes in US Family Finances: Results from the 1998 and 2001 Survey of Consumer Finances", *Federal Reserve Board Bulletin*, vol. 89, pp. 1–32, 2003.
For details of 1998 and earlier surveys, see Arthur B. Kennickell, Martha Starr-McCluer and Brian J. Surette: "Recent Changes in US Family Finances: Results from the 1998 Survey of Consumer Finances", *Federal Reserve Board Bulletin*, vol. 86, pp. 1–29, 2000.

[18] URL: http://www.ici.org

[19] Sarkis J. Khoury: *Investment Management: Theory and Application* (Macmillan, New York, 1983).

[20] These data are from the NAREIT (National Association of Real Estate Investment Trusts) website (www.nareit.com) and from the press release of May 29, 2001, that reported the results of Ibbotson Associates' analysis.

[21] Charles P. Mackay: *Memoirs of Extraordinary Popular Delusions and Madness of Crowds* (Bentley, 1941); Charles P. Kindleberger: *Manias, Panics, and Crashes: A History of Financial Crises* (John Wiley, 2000); P.M. Garber: *Famous First Bubbles: The Fundamentals of Early Manias* (MIT Press, 2000).

[22] François Longin and Bruno Solnik: "Extreme Correlation of International Equity Markets", *Journal of Finance*, vol. 56, pp. 649–676, 1998.

[23] Philippe Jorion and William Goetzmann: "Global Stock Markets in the Twentieth Century", *Journal of Finance*, vol. 54, pp. 953–980, 1999.

[24] M.H. Miller and F. Modigliani: "Dividend Policy, Growth and the Valuation of Shares", *Journal of Business*, vol. 34, pp. 411–433, 1961.

[25] M.H. Miller and M. Scholes: "Dividends and Taxes: Some Empirical Evidence", *Journal of Political Economy*, vol. 90, pp. 1118–1141, 1982. See also D.F. Bradford and R.H. Gordon: "Taxation and the Stock Market Valuation of Capital Gains and Dividends", *Journal of Public Economics*, vol. 14, pp. 109–136, 1980; and M.H. Miller: "Behavioral Rationality in Finance: The Case of Dividends", *Journal of Business*, vol. 59, pp. S451–S468, 1986.

[26] E.F. Fama and K.R. French: "Disappearing Dividends: Changing Firm Characteristics or Lower Propensity to Pay", *Journal of Financial Economics*, vol. 60, pp. 3–43, 2001.

[27] R. La Porta, F. Lopez-de-Silanes, A. Shleifer and R. Vishny: "Agency Problems and Dividend Policies around the World", *Journal of Finance*, vol. 55, pp. 1–34, 2000.

[28] Wilford Eiteman and Frank Smith: *Common Stock Values and Yields* (University of Michigan Press, 1953). Also see Lawrence Fisher and James Lorie: "Rates of Return on Investment in Common Stocks", *Journal of Business*, vol. 37, pp. 1–21, 1964.

[29] This is a major advantage of time aggregation and follows from our preference, discussed in Section 3.3, for the geometric mean. For instance, if $r_{t=2}$ is the total return for two-period holding, then it follows from Equation (3.2) that $r_{t=2} = \ln (P_{t=2}/P_{t=0}) = \ln (P_{t=2}/P_{t=1}) + \ln (P_{t=1}/P_{t=0}) = r_{t=1} + r_{t=0}$.

[30] Basically, the variance $\text{var}_{t=2}$ for our two-period return follows the same linearity as our two-period return $r_{t=2}$ if we assume that the returns are normally distributed, i.e., $\text{var}_{t=2} = \text{var}_{t=1} + \text{var}_{t=0}$. As standard deviation is the square root of variance, annualizing the standard deviation from monthly data requires multiplying the latter by $\sqrt{12}$.

[31] At its simplest, GDP is computed from its expenditure identity as GDP = C + I + G + (X − M) where C = Personal Consumption, I = Investment, G = Government Purchases, X = Exports, and M = Imports.

[32] Angus Maddison: *Monitoring the World Economy, 1820–1992* (OECD, Paris, 1995).

[33] Paul Samuelson: "Science and Stocks", *Newsweek*, p. 92, September 19, 1966.

[34] John Stock and Mark Watson: "Macroeconomic Forecasting Using Diffusion Indexes", *Journal of Business and Economic Statistics* (forthcoming). The paper is available at http://www.wws.princeton.edu/~mwatson/publi.html

[35] Following are amongst the numerous research papers that discuss the various facets of this interesting topic:
Eugene Fama: "Stock Returns, Real Activity, Inflation, and Money", *American Economic Review*, vol. 71, pp. 545–565, 1981.
G. Kaul: "Stock Returns and Inflation: The Role of the Monetary Sector", *Journal of Financial Economics*, vol. 18, pp. 253–276, 1987.
Campbell Harvey: "Forecasts of Economic Growth from the Bond and Stock Markets", *Financial Analysts Journal*, vol. 47, pp. 38–45, 1989.
Jeremy Siegel: "Does it Pay Stock Investors to Forecast the Business Cycle?", *Journal of Portfolio Management*, vol. 18, pp. 27–34, 1991.

[36] This ratio is called "modified" in this exhibit because, for the real or inflation-adjusted data used here, $r_{f=0}$ in Equation (4.7).

Chapter 5

BALANCING RISKS AND RETURNS: THREE THEORETICAL INSIGHTS

5.1 Introduction

This chapter looks at the three basic ideas about balancing the investment returns that we seek against the risks — portfolio diversification, correlation of asset returns, and random fluctuations in stock returns — that have become the foundations of modern finance theory.

The chapter is divided into three sections. The first section examines the Markowitz efficiency frontier and portfolio, the merits of global diversification, and the implications of portfolio diversification for the individual investor. The central idea in modern finance theory seeks to construct a portfolio of financial assets so that the returns to the investor are maximized for given risk levels. The second section looks at the Capital Asset Pricing Model, which relates the riskiness of an asset to its returns, the limitations of this model, and the alternatives to it, such as the Arbitrage Pricing Theory. The third section examines what has now emerged as the most controversial aspect of modern financial theory; whether the markets are indeed informationally efficient or inefficient, and the implications of this debate to the investor.

As we show here, indexing and dollar cost averaging make sense to a passive investor, irrespective of whether the market is informationally efficient or not.

5.2 Portfolio Diversification

Why Diversify?

Remember your mother's admonishment, "Don't put all your eggs in one basket!" This is what diversification is all about. The historical evidence examined in the previous chapter clearly points to the superior performance of the equities market, on the whole and in the long run, over the other investment instruments like bonds, commodities and real estate, in nominal as well as in real terms. But the fact that we focused on the whole market, and showed that these returns follow the normal distribution model reasonably well, also suggests that there are equities whose returns have surpassed our whole market mean statistics[1] for long periods. The "high-fliers" equities have produced returns superior to the market average, for instance (Section 4.2). Their volatility can be often

Exhibit 5.1: Higher returns involve higher risks, as this graph of risk versus returns for the Dow and its components shows. These returns are in nominal terms, i.e., unadjusted for inflation, and include dividends. They cover the January 1995–December 1999 period, and have been annualized from the monthly data.

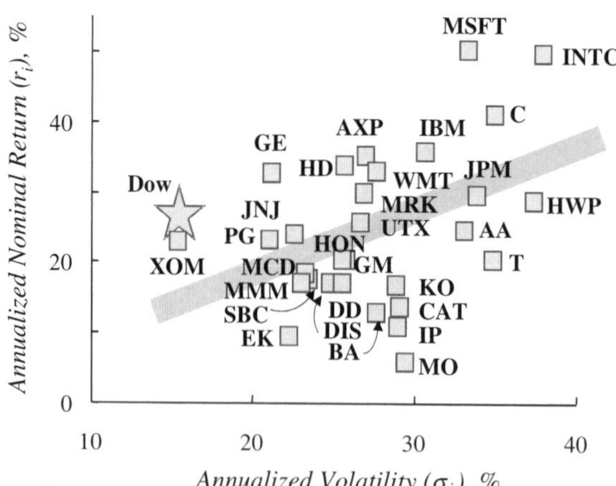

unnerving however. Indeed, a basic axiom of the market is that the *greater the volatility, the greater will the return be*. Exhibit 5.1 illustrates this graphically by comparing the annualized returns and volatility for Dow Jones Industrial Average and its components for the 1980–2000 period. Notice the direct overall relation between risk (volatility) and return here, i.e., the larger the return the greater the volatility.

Two factors are particularly noticeable here: (a) the higher the risk the greater the return, and (b) the volatility of a portfolio (the Dow) is far less than the volatility of its components. As for (a), while a large volatility itself does not guarantee a large return, this direct relation between risk and return is well supported by the market's overall history. Based on the CRSP[2] database at the University of Chicago, for instance, the average annual return on small-company stocks during 1926–1998 was 17.4%, with a standard deviation of 33.8%. The annual returns for large-company stocks averaged 13.2%, with a standard deviation of 20.3%, during the same period. The market volatility has not stayed the same through its history, as discussed in the preceding chapter. A direct relation between returns and volatility has persisted throughout history, nonetheless. But this does not mean that an investor seeking to maximize returns needs to helplessly resign to the prospects of a bumpy ride through the market's swings. Rather, a savvy investor would exploit the fact that the volatility of an index or a portfolio is less than the average of the volatility of its individual components. We see in Exhibit 5.1 that the return on the Dow has been far less volatile than the returns its components.

Markowitz and Portfolio Diversification

Harry Markowitz[3] was the first to show exactly how a portfolio of suitably chosen stocks can reduce volatility to the level that an investor can be comfortable with, but without having to sacrifice the returns significantly. His basic idea was simple and straightforward. Aside from the random fluctuations, prices of individual securities also reflect the risks that are specific to the particular company, industry and the market. While market risk would affect all securities, albeit to varying degrees, industry or sector risk would affect only the companies in that sector and company risk would be specific to the individual company. Combining two or more assets with uncorrelated variability thus means diversifying the company risk away, and diversifying the industry or sector risk as well if these equities represent different industries or sectors.

To understand this, let us consider a portfolio of two stocks, X and Y, and suppose that the proportion of total wealth invested in stock X is w_x and that in stock Y is w_y, i.e., $w_x + w_y = 1$ or $w_y = (1 - w_x)$. Let the historic average returns be r_x and r_y for these two stocks and the corresponding standard deviation (the designated measure of volatility or risk) values σ_x and σ_y. Let us also accept the continued validity of a normal distribution and expect this historic pattern to continue into the future. If we denote the expected returns by $E(r_x)$ and $E(r_y)$ for the two stocks, respectively, then the expected return on this portfolio, $E(r_p)$, is

$$\begin{aligned} E(r_p) &= w_x\ E(r_x) + w_y\ E(r_y) \\ &= w_x\ E(r_x) + (1 - w_x)\ E(r_y). \end{aligned} \tag{5.1a}$$

Therefore, the return on a portfolio is the weighted sum of returns on its component securities.

Computing the portfolio's variance is not as straightforward a matter, however. With σ_x^2 and σ_y^2 as the individual variances of the returns of our two stocks, the portfolio variance, σ_p^2, is

$$\begin{aligned} \sigma_p^2 &= w_x^2\sigma_x^2 + w_y^2\sigma_y^2 + 2w_x w_y \sigma_{xy} \\ &= w_x^2\sigma_x^2 + w_y^2\sigma_y^2 + 2w_x w_y \rho_{xy}\sigma_x\sigma_y. \end{aligned} \tag{5.1b}$$

Here, $\sigma_{xy} = \rho_{xy}\sigma_x\sigma_y$ is the covariance of X and Y, and ρ_{xy} their coefficient of correlation. This coefficient tends to -1 if the two stocks move in opposite directions, $+1$ if they move exactly in tandem and 0 if they are uncorrelated altogether, i.e., $-1 \leq \rho_{xy} \leq +1$. It then follows from Equation (5.1b) that $\sigma_p \leq (w_x\sigma_x + w_y\sigma_y)$, i.e., the volatility of a portfolio comprising any two stocks is always smaller than the weighted sum of the stocks' individual volatilities.[4]

We can eliminate portfolio volatility altogether,[5] by combining two stocks X and Y such that $\rho_{xy} = -1$, and setting $w_x = \sigma_y/(\sigma_x + \sigma_x)$. That dream may not be worth chasing, however, as two stocks with $\rho_{xy} \approx -1$ are even harder to find than those with $\rho_{xy} \approx +1$, particularly if both have a history of giving better returns than the market. Besides, the variability of returns, whether for the whole market or for individual stocks, hardly ever stays steady for long.

Practical examples of how volatility is reduced when an investment portfolio comprises two or more stocks are not hard to find. Take Microsoft (MSFT) and Home Depot (HD), two of the Dow high-fliers, for instance. Based on monthly returns over a 15-year period, from April 1, 1986 to March 31, 2001, the geometric annual returns have averaged 37.71% for Microsoft, with a standard deviation of 40.92%, and the corresponding numbers for Home Depot are 32.07% and 32.01%, respectively. While these returns are certainly impressive, their volatility is rather high (Exhibit 5.2), and must have given their investors many anxious moments and sleepless nights. The weak but positive correlation (Exhibit 5.3) of their returns, with the correlation coefficient of 0.39, is apparently fortuitous. The period covered here includes the entire bull run of the market, from the crash of 1987 to the bear market of 2000–2001. These two stocks have been amongst the top performers of this period.

Exhibit 5.2: The monthly price changes (left) and corresponding statistical distribution (right) for Microsoft (MSFT) and Home Depot (HD) common stocks. The portfolio shown here is the minimum-variance portfolio computed from Equation (5.1b).

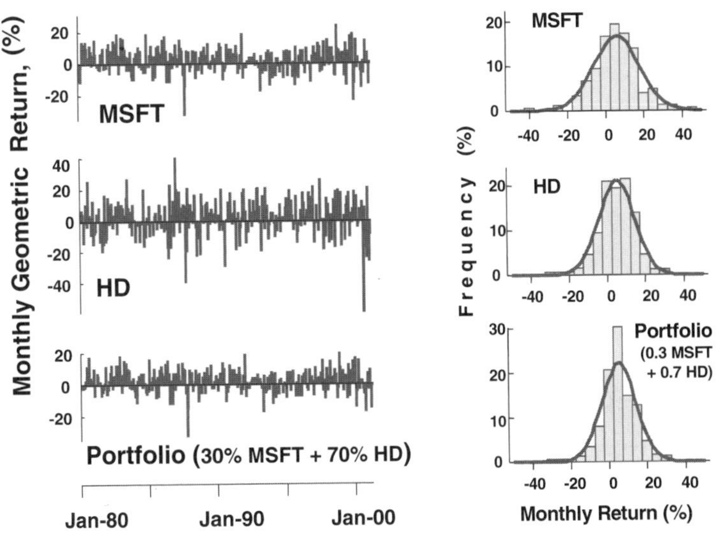

Exhibit 5.3: The monthly geometric returns for Microsoft (MSFT) and Home Depot (HD) stocks are weakly, but positively, correlated. Their coefficient of correlation is 0.3896. The April 1986–March 2001 period has generally been one of rising prices, however, and may well account for this correlation.

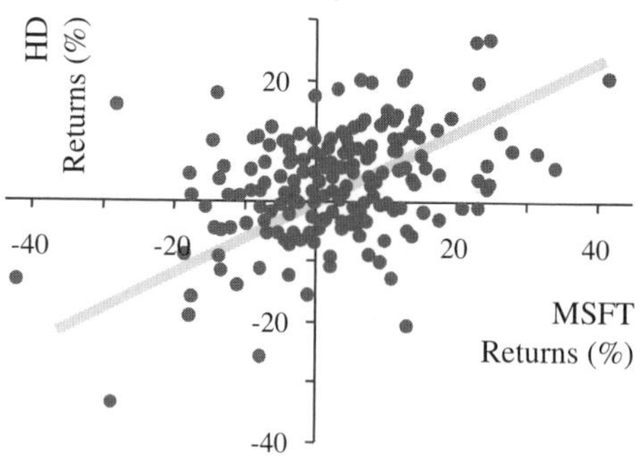

Setting Microsoft as stock X and Home Depot as stock Y,[6] we thus have r_x = 37.71%, σ_x = 40.92%, r_y = 32.07%, σ_y = 32.01% and ρ_{xy} = 0.3896. These numbers can be now plugged into Equations (5.1a) and (5.1b), to estimate the expected returns and corresponding variances for portfolios with varying proportions w_x and w_y of the two stocks. Suppose, for instance, that we wish to estimate $E(r_p)$ and σ_p^2 for a portfolio with 30% Microsoft and 70% Home Depot stocks. Then, w_x = 0.3 and w_y = 0.7, so that Equations (5.1a) and (5.1b) yield

$$\begin{aligned} E(r_p) &= 0.3 \times 0.3771 + 0.7 \times 0.3207 \\ &= 0.3376 = 33.76\%, \end{aligned} \tag{5.2a}$$

and

$$\begin{aligned} \sigma_p^2 &= (0.3)^2 \times (0.4092)^2 + (0.7)^2 \times (0.3201)^2 \\ &\quad + 2 \times 0.3 \times 0.7 \times 0.3896 \times 0.4092 \times 0.3201 \\ &= 0.01507 + 0.05021 + 0.02143 \\ &= 0.08671, \end{aligned} \tag{5.2b}$$

so that $\sigma_p = \sqrt{0.08671} = 0.2945 = 29.45\%$.

To understand what benefits this accomplishes, recall that a typical characteristic of the normal distribution curve of Exhibit 3.32 is that a little over two-thirds (68.26%) of the data would be within one standard deviation from the mean. Using this model, the annual returns on a 100% Microsoft portfolio would have 68.26% chance of ranging from a low of −3.21% to a whopping 78.63% whereas a 100% Home Depot portfolio would give between 0.06% to 64.08% annual returns at this probability level. The corresponding numbers for our portfolio of 30% Microsoft and 70% Home Depot stocks are 4.31% and 63.21%. Clearly, we have sacrificed some gains and have reduced the risk substantially.

What we have just calculated is not for the minimum-variance portfolio. The results of these computations for different values of w_x and w_y are graphed in Exhibit 5.4. It shows that a portfolio comprising 25% in Microsoft stocks and 75% in Home Depot stocks would have indeed had the minimum variance here. Note that, in terms of returns, every combination of the two stocks here is superior to investing 100% in Home Depot and all combinations with ≤50% in Microsoft carry either the same or less risk than 100% Home Depot. Indeed, if you were to settle for the same risk as the Home Depot, then investing 50% in Home Depot and 50% in Microsoft would have given you superior returns than carrying only the Home Depot stocks. Also, any combination of the two stocks with more than 50% but less than 100% in Home

Exhibit 5.4: Based on monthly return statistics for the past 15 years, we use Equation (5.1b) to find minimum-variance portfolio for Microsoft (MSFT) and Home Depot (HD) stocks at 25% MSFT and 75% HD.

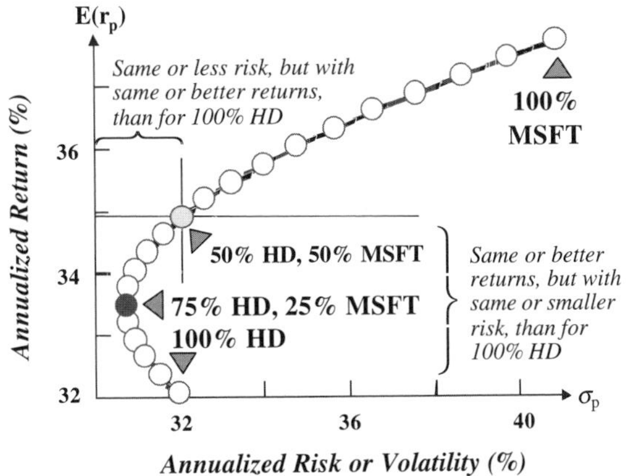

Exhibit 5.5: In nominal dollars, a $1000 investment made at the opening of trade on April 1, 1986 would have grown, by March 31, 2001, to $286,000 in the case of Microsoft, $123,000 in the case of Home Depot, and $172,000 for the minimum-variance portfolio computed here.

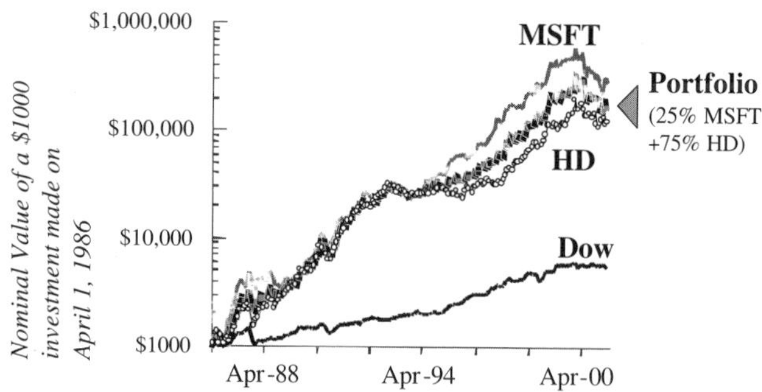

Depot would have given you better returns at lower risk than if you had owned only the Home Depot stocks in the portfolio.

For comparison, Exhibit 5.5 shows the growth, in nominal dollars by March 31, 2001, of a $1000 investment of April 1, 1986, for Microsoft, Home Depot, our minimum-variance portfolio and the Dow. With a perfect hindsight, one would have picked Microsoft, of course. But, considering that even the best investor is still human, this example clearly shows that diversification is the way to go.

This idea, that a judicious combination of uncorrelated or poorly correlated stocks greatly lowers the variance of a portfolio while enhancing its return, is what portfolio management is mainly about. Suppose we have any number N of stocks that we wish to combine in a portfolio. We then need to extend Equations (5.1a) and (5.1b) from two to the N stock case, to find their relative proportions, w_1, w_2, …, w_N, and the expected portfolio return $E(r_p)$ and variance σ_p^2, e.g.,

$$E(r_p) = \sum_{i=1}^{N} w_i \, E(r_i), \tag{5.3a}$$

and

$$\sigma_p^2 = \sum_{i=1}^{N} w_i^2 \sigma_i^2 + 2 \sum_{i=1}^{N-1} \sum_{j=i+1}^{N} w_i w_j \rho_{ij} \sigma_i \sigma_j \, . \tag{5.3b}$$

Exhibit 5.6: The $N \times N$ matrix to find the variance of an N-stock portfolio. The diagonal boxes contain the variance terms ($w_i^2\sigma_i^2$) while off-diagonal boxes contain the covariance terms ($w_i w_j \sigma_{ij}$).

Stock

Stock	1	2	3	4			N
1	$w_1^2\sigma_1^2$	$w_1w_2\sigma_{12}$	$w_1w_3\sigma_{13}$	$w_1w_4\sigma_{14}$			$w_1w_N\sigma_{1N}$
2	$w_2w_1\sigma_{21}$	$w_2^2\sigma_2^2$	$w_2w_3\sigma_{23}$	$w_2w_4\sigma_{24}$			$w_2w_N\sigma_{2N}$
3	$w_3w_1\sigma_{31}$	$w_3w_2\sigma_{32}$	$w_3^2\sigma_3^2$	$w_3w_4\sigma_{34}$			$w_3w_N\sigma_{3N}$
4	$w_4w_1\sigma_{41}$	$w_4w_2\sigma_{42}$	$w_4w_3\sigma_{43}$	$w_4^2\sigma_4^2$			$w_4w_N\sigma_{4N}$
N	$w_Nw_1\sigma_{N1}$	$w_Nw_2\sigma_{N2}$	$w_Nw_3\sigma_{N3}$	$w_Nw_4\sigma_{N4}$			$w_N^2\sigma_N^2$

Intimidating though this computational horror may seem, the general scheme here is simple and straightforward, and is illustrated in Exhibit 5.6. The diagonal boxes in this $N \times N$ matrix contain the variance terms $w_i^2\sigma_i^2$, and the off-diagonal boxes the covariance terms $w_i w_j \sigma_{ij}$ ($= w_i w_j \rho_{ij} \sigma_i \sigma_j$). Suppose, for simplicity, that we invest equally in all the N stocks in this portfolio. Then $w_1 = w_2 = \cdots = w_N = 1/N$. The N diagonal boxes then add up to $N \times (1/N)^2 \times$ average variance and the $(N^2 - N)$ off-diagonal boxes will add up to $(N^2 - N) \times (1/N)^2 \times$ average covariance. This gives

$$\text{Portfolio variance} = \frac{1}{N} \times \text{average variance} + \left(1 - \frac{1}{N}\right) \times \text{average covariance}. \qquad (5.4a)$$

As $N \to \infty$, $(1/N) \to 0$, and the variance term here vanishes. Thus, for large values of N,

$$\text{Portfolio variance} = \text{average covariance} \qquad (5.4b)$$

The result summarized in Equation (5.4b) has an important implication. It shows that the variance of a portfolio asymptotically approaches the average covariance of returns on stocks comprising the portfolio, no matter how many additional stocks we add to it. There is a practical limit, however, to the number of stocks that one can add to a portfolio. Take three indexes for instance: the Wilshire Total Market Index comprises over 97% of the entire US equities market, in terms of market capitalization, whereas the S&P 500 index comprises the stocks of the 500 largest US businesses, and the Dow comprises only 30. As the volatilities of these three indexes are largely comparable, it is clear that the average covariance of the market never vanishes. We can decompose the risk associated with security price changes into two principal components (Exhibit 5.7). Diversification can only eliminate what is commonly called the "unique risk" (the unsystematic risk). This is also known as diversifiable risk because it can be diversified away by adding uncorrelated stocks to a portfolio and is specific either to a single company or to a group of them. The other component of risk, known as the "market risk" or systematic risk, is immune to diversification and comes from the market or economy-wide forces.

Is there a size limit, then, for the number of stocks in a well-diversified portfolio? The fact that Dow's 30 stocks mimic the S&P 500 so well, the latter itself being a good proxy for the Wilshire 5000 and the whole

Exhibit 5.7: Investors in the stock market face two kinds of risk: unique risk tends to be company specific, and can be diversified away, whereas market risk arises from economy-wide forces and is immune to portfolio diversification.

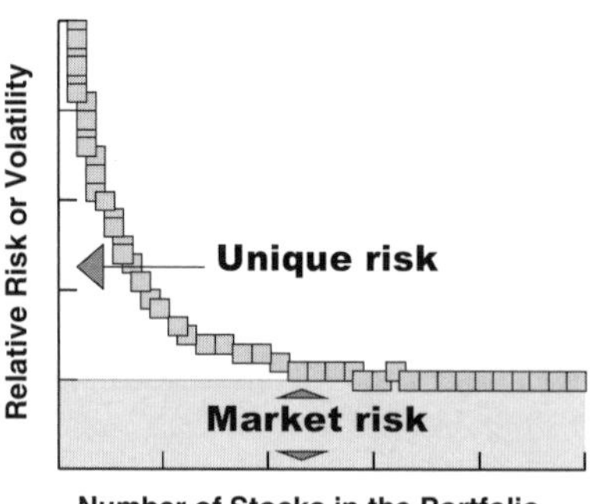

Exhibit 5.8: Total monthly returns on the Dow compared to those on the S&P 500. Despite the rather wide scatter, the relation between the two sets of data here is markedly direct, with a correlation coefficient of 0.78.

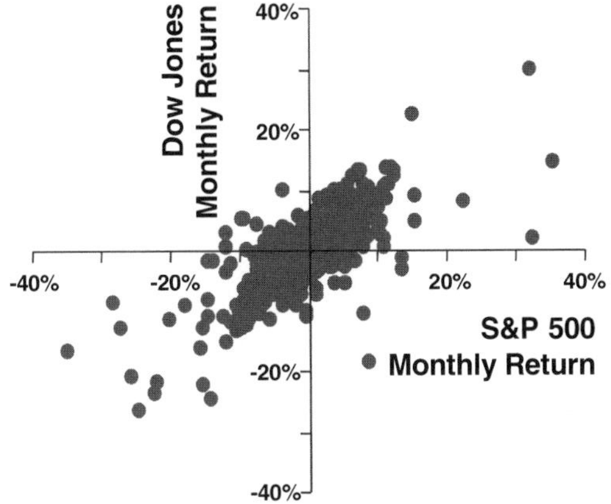

Exhibit 5.9: Fama argued that the standard deviation or volatility of a portfolio changes little after about 25 stocks, and that most of the drop in volatility occurs before 10–15 stocks. This suggests that unique risk can be effectively diversified away by carefully selecting a portfolio of 15–25 stocks. International diversification offers an even more efficient way to eliminate unique risk than domestic diversification.

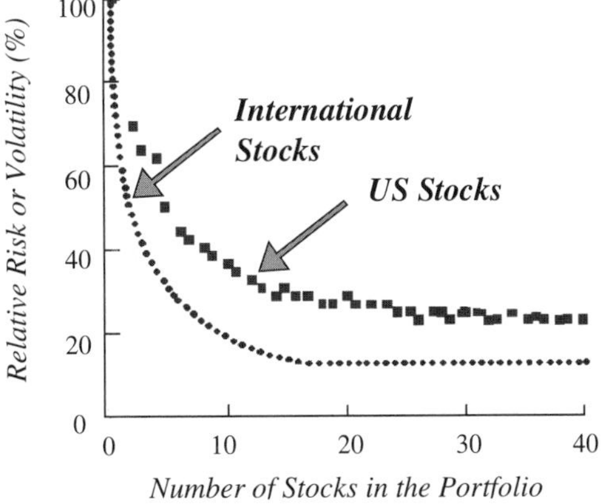

market, suggests that 30 may well be a good enough number. This is illustrated in Exhibit 5.8 where we compare the total monthly returns on the Dow and the S&P 500 indexes. The period covered here extends from January 1897 through December 2000. The two sets of returns show a direct relationship, with a correlation coefficient of 0.78. This compares reasonably well with the correlation coefficient of 0.75 for the returns on the Dow versus the Wilshire 5000.

In one of the earliest studies to systematically examine this issue, Fama[7] showed that the volatility of a portfolio drops substantially on the introduction of the first few stocks and practically flattens after about 25 stocks. This result, reproduced in Exhibit 5.9, suggests that unique risk is effectively diversified away when we use a carefully crafted portfolio of 15–25 stocks. Statman[8] has argued that effective diversification does not really require representing the entire market in a portfolio, as a portfolio of no more than about 30 stocks can suffice.

Seeking Diversification Globally

If selecting a few US domestic stocks can help diversify a portfolio, so reducing its risk without sacrificing the returns, then international diversification should achieve similar results with even greater efficiency. This was the rationale for Solnik's[9] study, the results of which are included in Exhibit 5.10 as "international stocks". This study found that a portfolio of 5–6 international stocks has the same volatility that a comparable combination of 15 or so domestic (US) stocks would have. This is mainly because systematic risk for a portfolio of domestic stocks is more than double that of the international portfolio. Recent research[10] suggests that a market portfolio of all the world's endowments would also contribute to societal welfare.

Now, diversifying domestically means seeking a representative selection across all the principal market sectors. International diversification then implies diversification not only across different countries and their markets but also across the principal sectors of those markets. It is not surprising, therefore, that unique risk is far more effectively diversified away when we construct an international portfolio than when the portfolio is purely domestic. Domestic factors do not disappear in an internationally

Exhibit 5.10: The average coefficients of variation of regression of factors show that domestic factors explain almost one-half (46%) of the variations in stock returns worldwide, and more than one-half (55%) of those in the United States.[11]

	Single-factor tests				Joint test of all four factors
	World	Industrial	Currency	Domestic	
Switzerland	0.18	0.17	0.00	0.38	0.39
Germany	0.08	0.10	0.00	0.41	0.42
Australia	0.24	0.26	0.01	0.72	0.72
Belgium	0.07	0.08	0.00	0.42	0.43
Canada	0.27	0.24	0.07	0.45	0.48
Spain	0.22	0.03	0.00	0.45	0.45
United States	0.26	0.47	0.01	0.35	0.55
France	0.13	0.08	0.01	0.45	0.60
United Kingdom	0.20	0.17	0.01	0.53	0.55
Hong Kong	0.06	0.25	0.17	0.79	0.81
Italy	0.05	0.03	0.00	0.35	0.35
Japan	0.06	0.16	0.01	0.26	0.33
Norway	0.17	0.28	0.00	0.84	0.85
Netherlands	0.12	0.07	0.01	0.34	0.31
Singapore	0.16	0.15	0.02	0.32	0.33
Sweden	0.19	0.06	0.01	0.42	0.43
All countries	0.18	0.23	0.01	0.42	0.46

diversified portfolio, however. Instead, as is clearly brought out in Exhibit 5.10 in which we reproduce Solnik's summarization of the results of a factor regression study on the relative importance of world, industrial, currency and domestic factors in explaining the stock returns, domestic factors do matter greatly.

An interesting feature of the data in Exhibit 5.10 is that they show the currency factor to have the least impact of the four factors considered here. Otherwise, basically, exchange rates vary[12] with interest and inflation rates, by way of International Fisher Effect (Exhibit 5.11), balance of trade and foreign direct investments.

Two empirical evidences will suffice to explain this. As shown in Exhibit 5.12(a), countries with higher interest rates in a given year tend to have higher inflation rates in the following year and, as shown in

Exhibit 5.11: How the domestic interest (denoted by $r_¥$ and $r_\$$, for Japan and the US, respectively) and inflation ($i_¥$ and $i_\$$) rates affect the spot ($S_{¥\$}$) and forward ($f_{¥\$}$) foreign exchange rates.

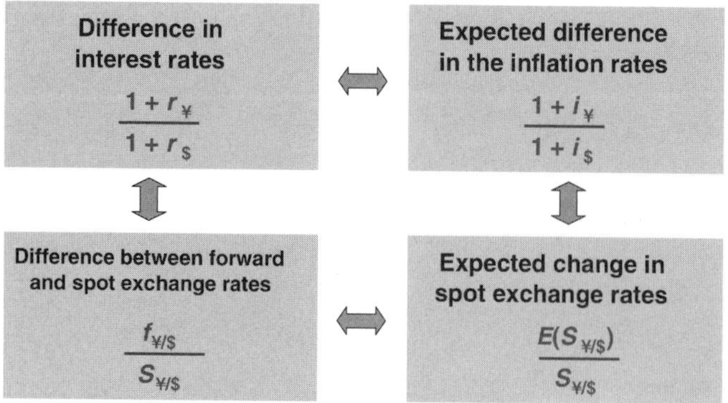

Source: Richard Brealey, Stewart Myers and Alan Marcus: *Fundamentals of Corporate Finance* (Irwin McGraw-Hill, 1999).

Exhibit 5.12: (a) Countries with higher interest rates one year tend to have higher inflation rates next year (left). (b) Countries with high inflation rates tend to see their currencies depreciate (right).

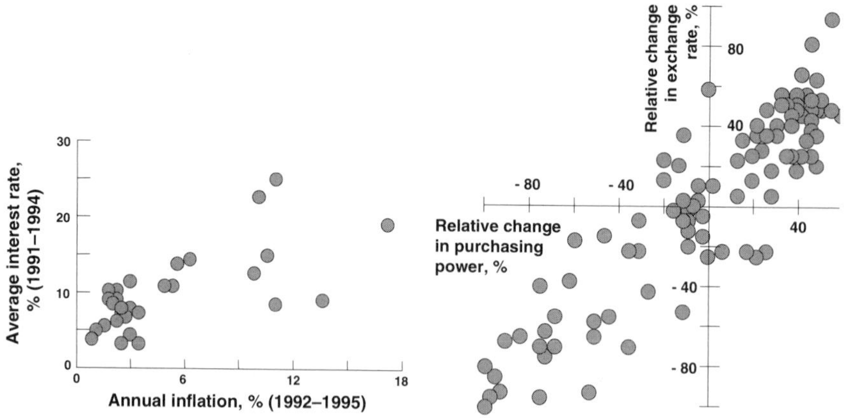

Source: Richard Brealey, Stewart Myers and Alan Marcus: *Fundamentals of Corporate Finance* (Irwin McGraw-Hill, 1999).

Exhibit 5.12(b), the countries with higher inflation rates tend to see their currencies depreciate compared to appreciation of the currencies of countries with lower inflation rates.

With rapid globalization, deregulation and privatization since the 1990s, country barriers are gradually falling, however. Indeed, today's world is an increasingly tripartite one (Exhibit 5.13) comprising North America, Europe and Asia. In constructing a globally diversified portfolio, the industry factors are therefore becoming increasingly important,[13] instead of the country factors. This calls for a sector rather than a country approach to portfolio diversification. This has several advantages.[14] As for the investment universe itself, for instance, companies are increasingly hard to classify within a country and can be better compared with their peers in a cross-country approach. Same selection criteria for investment

Exhibit 5.13: "Global" increasingly implies a tripartite world in which Japan is no longer the sole Asian representative. Indeed, there is not a single country or region that dominates global merchandise production, trade and commerce. This may well signify the past, however, particularly as the impacts of China and India on the world's merchandise production and hi-tech industry, respectively, are hard to gauge as yet.

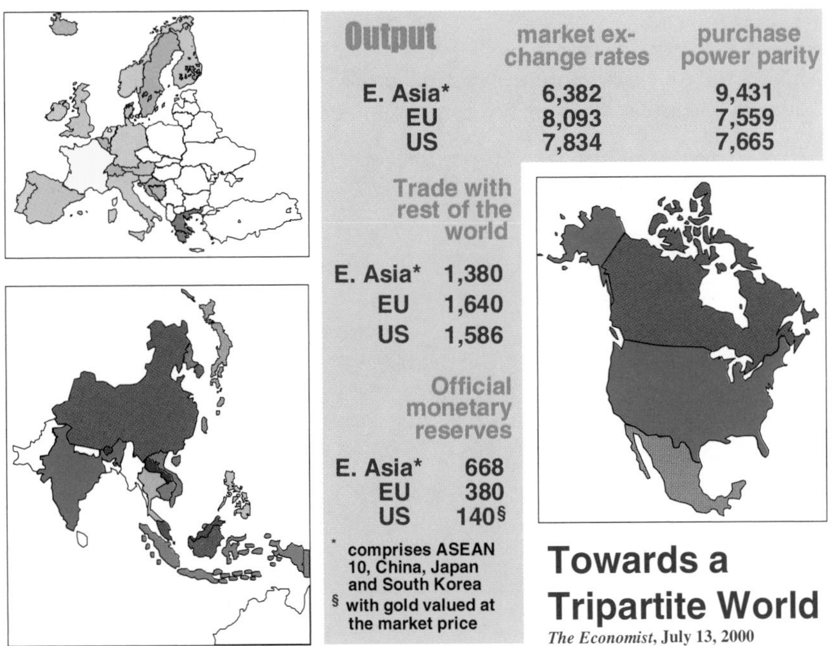

analysis applies within a sector, even when we compare the companies in these sectors across the countries, whereas, were we to focus on a country-by-country analysis then we would need to use a sector-dependent multiplicity of selection criteria for each country. Focus on the sectors also helps us emphasize growth industries, in terms of the investment style that, in the country approach, depends on the country's economic structure. The sector approach also delegates the allocation of capital to company's management, thus making asset the allocation more efficient. This does not, of course, mean that the sector approach has no pitfalls. Nations are sovereign entities, after all, and all politics is essentially local. Sector diversification, for example, does not eliminate currency risk, considered the scourge and the opportunity in international investment. Different accounting principles and practices exacerbate the problems in cross-country comparison of businesses, even when they are in the same sector, as do customs and cultural factors. Information asymmetry remains a problem and investors still prefer to invest in their own country and currency. Exhibit 5.14, taken from MSCI-World Index, presents one example of the weights for individual country and sectors in implementing such an approach.

Exhibit 5.14: An example of the sector and country factors in the sector approach for creating an internationally diversified portfolio.

Industry	World	US	Europe	Japan	Pacific
Energy	6.1%	3.0%	3.0%	0.1%	0.0%
Materials	3.7%	1.4%	1.4%	0.6%	0.2%
Industrials	10.3%	5.8%	2.4%	1.8%	0.3%
Consumer: (a) Discretionary	14.4%	7.6%	3.4%	3.1%	0.3%
(b) Staples	7.2%	3.9%	2.7%	0.5%	0.1%
Health Care	12.1%	7.6%	3.7%	0.7%	0.0%
Financials	21.2%	9.2%	8.7%	1.9%	1.4%
Information Technology	13.1%	9.3%	2.2%	1.6%	0.0%
Telecommunications	8.0%	3.6%	3.7%	0.5%	0.2%
Utilities	4.1%	2.2%	1.4%	0.4%	0.1%
Total	100.0%	53.6%	32.5%	11.1%	2.8%

Source: Fabrice Vallat

Note that, however diversified a portfolio is at any given point in time, it needs to be continually monitored and modified. For instance, the data for the 1962–1997 period suggest[15] that the volatility of individual stocks has increased in recent years while the correlation among stock returns has fallen steadily. As for portfolio diversification, this has two implications: (a) the number of stocks needed to eliminate unique risk has been rising, and (b) portfolio volatility has increased even after this risk has been eliminated. If you thought that international diversification could come to your rescue, think again. Another recent study[16] has found higher correlation between international equities in bear markets, than in the bull markets. Needless to stress, such a co-movement of equities during the bear markets when the risk of loss is only likely to rise, robs portfolio diversification of its principal attraction as a risk-reduction strategy.

Diversification and the Individual Investor

Our discussions so far have focused on minimizing the variance. But the risk-return profile of a portfolio of stocks is determined as much by the market as by the investor. The market determines the expected return and volatility, $E(r_p)$ and σ_p^2, for instance, and the investor selects the acceptable combination of risk and return by distributing the wealth between the selected securities. Stocks are not necessarily the only game in town here, after all. More often than not, three alternatives are typically available — stocks, bonds and money market instruments, for instance. Nor is the choice between domestic and international markets limited to stocks. Exhibit 5.15 shows the risk/return trade-off for an internationally diversified portfolio of bonds. This example, taken from Solnik,[17] uses 1971–1994 data and shows that a US bond investor would have been better off including foreign bonds in the portfolio. Indeed, reducing the US bond content from 100% (point A) to 70% (point B) would have reduced volatility the most. What is more, this bond portfolio would have been no more volatile than the 100% US bond portfolio, but with vastly improved returns, had it comprised 50% US and 50% foreign bonds (point C).

Exhibit 5.15: An internationally diversified portfolio of bonds, based on 1971–1994 data, shows that a US investor would have been better off adding some foreign bonds to the portfolio.

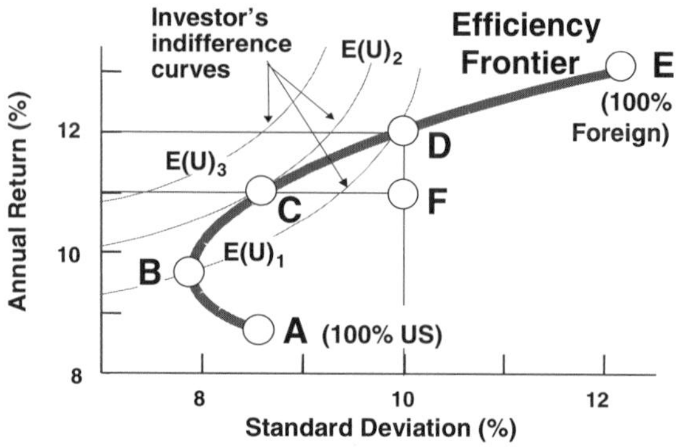

The points A–E in Exhibit 5.15 are located on a curve that defines all conceivable combinations of the US and foreign bonds here. This curve, or a similar curve in Exhibit 5.4, defines the efficiency frontier — the locus of points where the investor receives the highest rate of return for a given level of risk and assumes the lowest possible risk for a given level of return. Compare any of the points A–E in this exhibit with F. For the same level of risk as F, point D gives a better return here whereas, for the same level of return as F, point C assumes a far smaller risk.

Minimizing the variance (point B in Exhibit 5.15 or the point in Exhibit 5.4 for 75% HD and 25% MSFT) is not the only choice available to an investor, however. Any point on the efficiency frontier could be appropriate. The exact point on the efficiency frontier where the investor decides to be is determined by that individual's utility curve — this curve represents his or her level of satisfaction with the risk and the return on the investment.

The logic behind the utility or indifference curves $E(U)_1$–$E(U)_3$ in Exhibit 5.15, with utility (or wealth W) increasing from $E(U)_1$ to $E(U)_3$, is simple. The investor can choose any combination of $E(r_p)$ and σ_p on the efficiency frontier for the indifference curve tangential to it, e.g., $E(U)_2$ in this exhibit. Hence their designation as indifference curves.

The shape of these curves suggests that there is a certain level of substitution between $E(r_p)$ and σ_p. The utility function that is often used in these studies, and the one used here, is a quadratic function[18] of the type

$$E(U) = a + b\, r_p + c(r_p^2 + \sigma_p^2), \tag{5.5}$$

where a, b and c are constant such that $b > 0$, $c < 0$ and $(b + 2c) > 0$ for all the relevant values of W.

The indifference curves implied by this utility function have positive slopes, i.e., $(\partial\sigma_p^2/\partial_p) = -(b + 2cr_p)/c > 0$ and $(\partial^2\sigma_p^2/\partial r_p^2) < 0$ at any point along the curve. The marginal rate of substitution (MRS), the rate[19] at which an individual is willing to trade one good for another while remaining equally well off (this is what the absolute value of the slope of indifference curve actually is), diminishes here as σ_p^2 is progressively higher for higher r_p. While this is the assumption that economists usually make in such studies, this suggests that aversion to risk increases with wealth. The proportion of wealth invested in risky securities should decrease, in that case, as the amount of wealth increases. But this has been a contentious issue.[20]

Consider the results of the Fed's triennial Consumer Finance Survey, the most recent of which was conducted in 2001,[21] for instance. As shown in Exhibit 5.16, these data show that wealthier families are more exposed to stocks than the less wealthy families. The proportion of families holding certificates of deposit, where the risk of default is almost nonexistent for up to \$100,000 thanks to FDIC (Federal Deposit Insurance Corporation) insurance, appears to move slowest with family wealth, however. Perhaps this suggests that families invest in the stock market only after they have exhausted the other avenues. After all, this survey also revealed that 58% of the total assets of all families in 2001 were held in nonfinancial instruments, mostly in residential and nonresidential properties and equities. As for stock holdings, though, we should note that mutual fund and retirement accounts tend to be dominated by stocks and that, between 1998 and 2001, the relative proportion of those holding financial assets gained slightly, at the expense of nonfinancial holdings. Curiously, if we group certificates of deposit and bonds as low risk

Exhibit 5.16: As the results of Federal Reserve Board's 2001 Consumer Finance Survey show, exposure to stock market rises with family wealth. But the proportion of families investing in stocks versus bonds seems to have remained independent of family wealth.

Classification based on personal income ⇒	Poorest quintile	20–39.9%	40–59.9%	60–79.9%	80–89.9%	Richest 10%
% of families in the income groups holding the assets:						
Certificates of deposit	10.0%	14.7%	17.4%	16.0%	18.3%	22.0%
Bonds (also savings bonds)	3.8%	11.0%	15.6%	28.1%	34.2%	42.4%
Stocks	3.8%	11.2%	16.4%	26.2%	37.0%	60.6%
Mutual funds	3.6%	9.5%	15.7%	20.6%	29.0%	48.8%
Retirement accounts	13.2%	33.3%	52.8%	75.7%	83.7%	88.3%
Insurance	13.8%	24.7%	25.6%	35.7%	38.6%	41.8%
Other managed accounts	2.2%	3.3%	5.4%	8.5%	10.7%	16.7%
Median family holdings of financial assets:						
Certificates of deposit	$10,000	$14,000	$13,000	$15,000	$13,000	$25,000
Bonds (also savings bonds)	$1000	$600	$10,500	$41,000	$51,000	$90,700
Stocks	$7500	$10,000	$7000	$17,000	$20,000	$50,000
Mutual funds	$21,000	$24,000	$24,000	$30,000	$28,000	$87,500
Retirement accounts	$4500	$8000	$13,600	$30,000	$55,000	$130,000
Insurance	$3600	$6200	$7000	$12,000	$10,000	$24,000
Other managed accounts	$24,200	$36,000	$70,000	$60,000	$70,000	$112,000

Exhibit 5.16 (*Continued*)

Classification based on personal income ⇒	**Poorest quintile**	**20–39.9%**	**40–59.9%**	**60–79.9%**	**80–89.9%**	**Richest 10%**
Median family holdings of selected nonfinancial assets:						
Vehicle	$3000	$8400	$12,600	$17,600	$22,700	$30,000
Residential and nonresidential property, including residential equity	$122,500	$185,000	$175,000	$249,500	$283,500	$646,200
Business equity	$56,300	$35,000	$61,700	$62,500	$100,000	$268,300
Other nonfinancial assets	$6000	$6000	$10,000	$10,000	$20,000	$50,000
Median family debt:						
Residential and nonresidential property	$28,000	$70,000	$94,900	$107,500	$122,200	$211,000
Other debts	$13,300	$23,400	$42,800	$83,500	$126,900	$293,600

Source: *Federal Reserve Bulletin*, January 2003.

assets, and group stocks with the presumably equity dominated mutual funds and retirement accounts as the relatively risky assets, then the ratio median family holdings in these risky to low risk asset groups is actually higher for the poorer 40% of families than for the richest 10%. These data hardly support the proposition that the propensity for bearing financial risks increases with family wealth.

A more compelling reason[22] why most researchers prefer using the quadratic utility function, however, is that it is completely specified by its mean and variance regardless of whether the underlying statistical distribution is normal or otherwise. It is positively related to the expected wealth and negatively to the risk in securing that wealth.

Returning to Exhibit 5.15, we can now see why point C is where on the efficiency frontier our savvy investor would choose to be. It is the only point at which an indifference curve, $E(U)_2$ in this case, is tangential to the efficiency frontier and is, therefore, an optimal point at which utility is maximized for an efficient combination of return and risk.

The applicability and relevance of modern portfolio theory need not be limited to the supposedly esoteric world of high finance. Examples abound of how profitably its rationale can be applied in a miscellany of diverse areas like production diversification and product line diversification. Box 5.1 presents an early example of this type. Japan's Keiretsu system, or General Electric's diverse holdings for that matter, too illustrate portfolio diversification.[23]

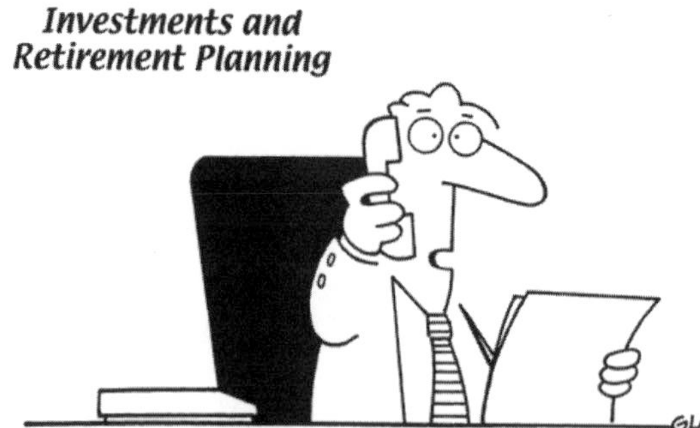

Okay, this time we'll try it your way: 3% in stocks, 2% in bonds and 95% in lottery tickets."

Box 5.1: Product Diversification at the Automobile Dealerships

In an article published in the *Journal of Marketing* (Spring 1980), T. Marx ("The Economics of Single- and Multiple-Line Retail Automobile Dealerships") presents an interesting application of the Markowitz efficiency frontier for product line diversification by automobile dealerships. Single-line dealerships, he argued, minimize the capital investment in sales, staff training, service facilities, and inventories, but raises the risk of public unacceptability. Despite the economic disadvantage of having to forgo these advantages of single-line dealerships, it is this risk that has motivated multiple-line dealerships. By the early 1980s, for instance, one-half of the thirty thousand and odd automobile dealerships had multiple lines. Using the correlation between various product lines in a region is an effective way to identify products for a multiple-line dealership in that region, this study argues. This idea makes immediate sense to the students of portfolio theory, particularly when we look at the correlation matrix, shown below, for the total US domestic car sales during 1970–1987. Extending the argument put forth by Marx, one can also see in this correlation matrix an important factor behind Chrysler's acquisition of American Motors, Plymouth and Dodge.

	Amer. Motors	Plymouth	Dodge	Chrysler	Ford	Mercury	Lincoln	Buick	Cadillac	Chevy	Olds
Plymouth	0.79	–	–	–	–	–	–	–	–	–	–
Dodge	0.61	0.91	–	–	–	–	–	–	–	–	–
Chrysler	−0.39	−0.36	−0.00	–	–	–	–	–	–	–	–
Ford	0.71	0.90	0.94	−0.10	–	–	–	–	–	–	–
Mercury	−0.33	−0.22	0.17	0.70	0.16	–	–	–	–	–	–
Lincoln	−0.35	−0.28	0.10	0.78	0.11	0.91	–	–	–	–	–
Buick	−0.57	−0.50	−0.22	0.58	−0.36	0.65	0.53	–	–	–	–
Cadillac	−0.23	−0.27	0.07	0.70	0.09	0.89	0.88	0.64	–	–	–
Chevy	0.60	0.67	0.70	−0.19	0.86	0.26	0.16	−0.22	0.25	–	–
Oldsmobile	−0.62	−0.59	−0.25	0.73	−0.35	0.80	0.77	0.89	0.81	−0.17	–
Pontiac	−0.15	0.13	0.48	0.52	0.44	0.84	0.78	0.49	0.72	0.53	0.63

5.3 The Asset Pricing Model and Theory

Capital Asset Pricing Model (CAPM)

It is thus clear that, in designing a suitable portfolio of risky assets like stocks, determining an optimal combination of returns and risk represents only a partial analysis. Completing it requires looking at the investor's own risk/reward tradeoffs and matching them with the available market opportunities. This Markowitz model is built on the following assumptions:

- Investors focus on the expected rate of return and on the volatility of a security.
- Investors prefer higher expected returns at lower expected risk, and therefore wish to hold efficient portfolios: those yielding maximum expected returns for the given level of risk, or the minimum level of risk for a given level of expected return.
- Investors agree on the probability distribution of rates of return on securities. This ensures a unique efficiency frontier.

The investor in a Markowitz world proceeds systematically in selecting securities that are less than perfectly correlated. The construction of the efficiency frontier is not based on a random selection of securities. Where along this efficiency frontier an investor chooses to be is determined by his or her own utility function. For one investor, for instance, point C in Exhibit 5.15 is the optimum point. Another investor, with different preferences, may prefer another point on the same efficiency frontier. There is no unique combination of risky securities that all investors should prefer, therefore. Instead, each investor may allocate his or her wealth differently among the risky securities, albeit on the same efficiency frontier. That is why Markowitz could not derive a general equilibrium asset-pricing model. The model could only describe the tradeoff between return and risk in the market for securities and in the mind of the individual investor.

The development of the Capital Asset Pricing Model (CAPM) began with the work of William Sharpe[24] and John Lintner.[25] Sharpe introduced the concept of risk-free asset in the analysis, whose effects now reverberate throughout the world of investment and capital management. The CAPM adds the following assumptions to those in the Markowitz model:

- There is equilibrium in the security markets (this equilibrium is only partial, the effects of the securities markets on the production sector was ignored, for example, and is a characteristic of the pure exchange economy).

- Investments are divisible, i.e., any size of investment is feasible.
- There is a risk-free asset, with a risk-free rate, at which the investors can borrow or lend.
- Transaction costs or taxes are ignored.
- The *ex ante* expectations about the market as a whole are homogenous and all investors agree on the distribution of rates of return (i.e., this translates into the idea, explored in the next section, that the market is efficient).
- Investors are risk-averse and maximize the mean-variance utility functions. They maximize one-period expected-utility-of-wealth and the length of the period (the investment horizon) is identical for all investors.

To derive the Sharpe model, we start by decomposing the portfolio, with expected return $E(r_p)$ and volatility σ_p as before, into its market and risk-free components: the market component of risky securities accounts for the proportion w_m of the investor's wealth while the remaining proportion w_f (= 1 − w_m) of the investment is risk-free. Let the expected return and volatility for this risky component be $E(r_m)$ and σ_m, and those for the risk-free component be $E(r_f)$ and σ_f, respectively. By definition, then, this risk-free component is characterized by $\sigma_f^2 = 0$.

Exhibit 5.17: Annualized return and risk statistics for selected financial assets for 1926–2000. Here, return is computed as geometric monthly mean return times 12, the corresponding standard deviation (= monthly standard deviation times √12) being the measure of risk.

	Return		Standard Deviation
	Nominal	Real	
Large Company Stocks (S&P 500)	13.0%	9.7%	20.2%
Small Company Stocks	17.3%	13.8%	33.4%
Corporate Bonds	6.0%	3.0%	8.7%
Government Bonds	5.7%	2.7%	9.4%
Treasury Bills	3.9%	0.8%	3.2%

Source: Ibbotson Associates 2001 Yearbook, *Stocks, Bonds, Bills, and Inflation.*

Where would the investor find such an asset? For this we turn to Exhibit 5.17. It summarizes the return and risk statistics for selected financial assets for the 1926–1999 period from the CRSP database. Notice how the risk term effectively disappears from the statistics for Treasury bills if inflation is factored in. Here, the standard deviation for Treasury bills, which translates into their risk or volatility, is barely two-thirds of that of inflation for this period whereas the mean return for these bills exceeds the inflation rate. An investment in these assets will retain its value, therefore, carrying little risk of loss.

Plugging the above nomenclature in Equations (5.3a) and (5.3b), we then find[26] that, for our portfolio

$$E(r_p) = r_f + \frac{[E(r_m) - r_f]}{\sigma_m}\sigma_p \,. \tag{5.6a}$$

The graph of $E(r_p)$ versus σ_p is called the capital market line whose slope, $[E(r_m) - r_f]/\sigma_m$, is the Sharpe ratio that we discussed earlier, in Section 4.4 and Exhibit 4.38. It serves as a measure of the market's risk-adjusted performance. The capital market line defined by Equation (5.6a) is shown as line AMB in Exhibit 5.18. As point M here, with the coordinates $[E(r_m), \sigma_m]$ as the market portfolio, a risk-averse investor would choose a point between A and M on this line, depending on the degree of aversion to risk, whereas a risk-taker might even borrow at the risk

Exhibit 5.18: Investing in a portfolio of risky and risk-free assets means being on the capital market line AMB. The curve XMY here describes the efficient set of risky assets.

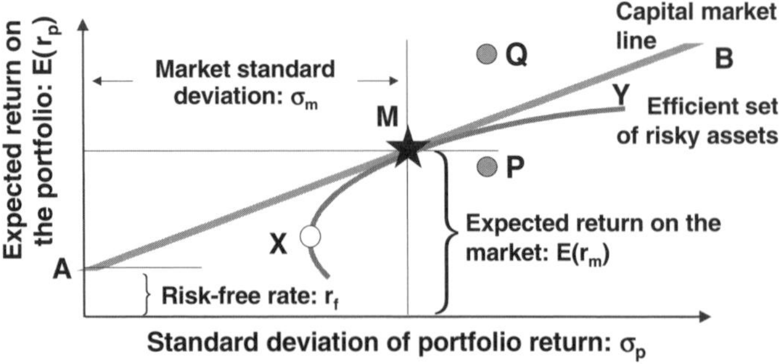

free rate to invest in M and therefore choose to be anywhere between M and B or beyond.

This construct has simplified the investor's choice to one of deciding between the weights in M, the market portfolio, and r_f, so limiting the flexibility allowed by individual preferences. As for the risky assets themselves, the curve XMY describes their efficient set, as this curve is the Markowitz efficiency frontier described in the preceding section. Notice that point M is at the tangency of the efficiency frontier and the capital market line. This is the *separation principle* in financial economics. Rather than having to qualitatively evaluate the levels of utility and risk aversion, it decomposes the investment decision into two. The investor first finds the efficient set of risky assets (i.e., curve XMY) using the relevant return, variance and covariance statistics, and then adds risk-free assets to it depending on the desired location on the capital market line.

Let us now look at two points, P and Q, in Exhibit 5.18 and suppose that they represent return and risk on any two portfolios. By construction, both have the same variance or standard deviation but different returns, that for Q being greater than that for P. As P is located below the capital market line here, it has clearly underperformed the market. After all, the market portfolio M not only has a return that exceeds the return for P but also has a standard deviation that is less than the standard deviation for P. Our portfolio Q presents the opposite picture. Notice that it lies above the capital market line. Thus, even though its standard deviation exceeds that of the market returns, its returns exceed the market returns by a proportionately wider margin.

Equation 5.6(a) and Exhibit 5.18 thus provide us with a direct mean to evaluate the performance of mutual funds. Exhibit 5.19 illustrates this with a practical example. Here we compare the load-adjusted 5-year average returns on the top mutual fund performers under different categories, e.g., US stock funds (large, mid-cap and small growth, value and blend and the specialty funds like those in communications, financials, health, natural resources, precious metals, real estate, technology and utilities), international stock funds (world stock, diversified emerging markets), bond funds (high-yield, intermediate-term, international, government, multi-sector, short-term) and hybrid funds (domestic and international). Since some mutual funds are "load-funds" while others are "no load" funds, our use of load-adjusted returns creates a level playing field for comparison. Our capital market line has been constructed hereby joining plots for market return (annualized total return on the S&P 500 index) and 90-day Treasury bill rates. The funds that plot about or above the capital market line here are clearly the market performers and over-performers while those that plot below this line are the underperformers. The past five years have hardly been the best time for precious metals. It is not surprising to find the best-performing specialty fund in this sector, Vanguard Gold and Precious Metals (VGPMX), as the worst of all funds in our select list of funds in Exhibit 5.19! Notice, also, that the best performing real estate fund, Delaware Pooled Real Estate Investor Trust (DPRIX), has only performed at or about the market index.

The universe of mutual funds is huge, of course, and has been the subject of innumerable examinations since Jensen's[27] classic study. Jensen found it possible to distinguish consistently good managers from the persistently bad ones but, overall, these studies suggest that the gains by

Exhibit 5.19: A sampling of the top mutual fund performers in different categories, as of August 2, 2001, based on the past five years' returns. WMICX, the Wasatch Micro Cap fund has had the highest load-adjusted annual return while FSELX, the Fidelity Select Electronics fund, has had the highest volatility. DPRIX, Delaware Pooled Real Estate Investment Trust, topped the real estate category.

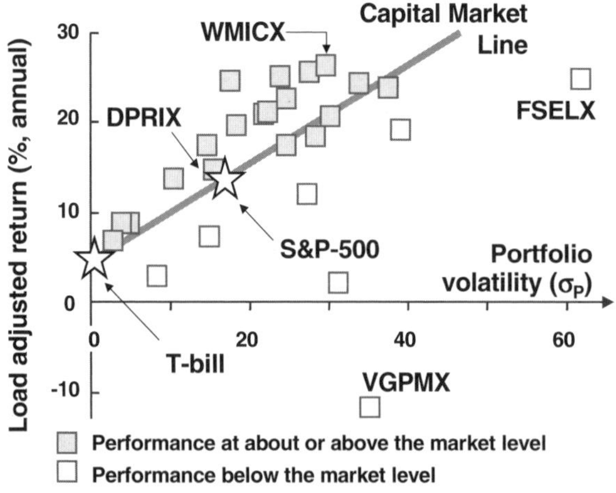

professional fund managers generally cover the portfolio management expenses. A discussion of these and related matters would be tangential here, however. Our purpose is to show, with the help of Exhibit 5.19, how easy William Sharpe's seminal work had made it for an individual investor to track the performance of mutual funds or portfolios that he or she may have invested in.

We had, in Exhibit 5.18, defined point M as representing the market portfolio. But the securities markets price individual securities, not the portfolios or indexes comprising them. For instance, the value of the Dow at any given point in time depends on what its component stocks are priced at, not vice versa. We need, therefore, to be able to find how the return and the variance of individual securities in a portfolio are related.

CAPM for Measuring Performance

To compute the expected return $E(r_i)$ on *i*th security in the market portfolio, we note, in Exhibit 5.18, the tangency of capital market line AMB to the efficient set XMY at M and, therefore, equate the slope $[E(r_m) - r_f]/\sigma_m$ of capital market line with that of the efficient set at this point. This yields[28] the following basic statement of the Capital Asset Pricing Model (CAPM):

$$E(r_i) = {}_f + [E(r_m) - r_f] \times \beta_i, \tag{5.6b}$$

where $\beta_i = \rho_{im} (\sigma_i/\sigma_m)$ is the measure of the extent to which our *i*th security's rate of return moves with that of the market. It is also the measure of systematic or non-diversifiable risk, the component of risk that cannot be eliminated through portfolio diversification. The entire second term on the right hand side of this equation, $[E(r_m) - r_f] \times \beta_i$, is the *risk premium* on our *i*th security with systematic risk equal to β_i.

Equation (5.6a) defines the linear relationship between risk and return by stating that the rate of return from a security comprises (a) the risk-free rate and (b) the adjusted risk premium. The first of these compensates for the time value of money while the second is that security's β (beta) times the market risk premium. For the whole market, $\rho_{im} = 1$

and $\beta_m = \rho_{im}\ (\sigma_i/\sigma_m) = \rho_{im}\ (\sigma_m/\sigma_m) = 1$. In practice, β is the sensitivity of an equity's risk premium to the changes in market risk premium, or the slope of the *security market line*. This is because Equation (5.6b) can be written as

$$\beta_i = \frac{E(r_i) - r_f}{E(r_m) - r_f} = \frac{\text{Risk premium on the security}}{\text{Risk premium on the market}}. \tag{5.6c}$$

By way of illustration, Exhibit 5.20 compares the performances of four stocks for the April 1986–March 2001 period. With the highest β of all the stocks compared here, Microsoft (MSFT) has also given the best returns. The returns on General Motors (GM) and Proctor & Gamble (PG) stocks have been poorer in comparison, but their β values are also appreciably smaller.

Exhibit 5.20 is a variant of one of the classic empirical tests supporting the CAPM — that study, by Fama and MacBeth,[29] demonstrated a positive relation between average return and beta. It also illustrates a common method for estimating beta. If, based on Equation (5.6c), we regress the observed risk premium $[E(r_i) - r_f]$ for a security or portfolio against the market risk premium $[E(r_m) - r_f]$, then β_i is the slope of the resulting linear regression equation. The straight line from such a regression would have an intercept as well, say α, at $[E(r_m) - r_f] = 0$. We deliberately set it at zero when computing the data presented in Exhibit 5.20 in order to conform to Equation (5.6c). Jensen[30] introduced α as a performance measure and showed that mutual funds that outperformed the market had statistically significant positive α and those with statistically significant negative α consistently underperformed the market. It is therefore called Jensen's α.

As for the market, the S&P 500 index usually serves as an excellent proxy whereas, as for the risk-free rate, the rate on 3-month Treasury bills is the most commonly used proxy. The alternative is to find a zero-beta security or portfolio whose expected return, $E(r_z)$, bears no correlation with the market return (i.e., $\rho_{mz} = 0$). Equation (5.6b) would then modify[31] to

$$E(r_i) = E(r_z) + [E(r_m) - E(r_z)] \times \beta_i\ . \tag{5.6d}$$

Exhibit 5.20: The beta (β) of a stock or a portfolio can be seen as its sensitivity to the market risk premium. Thus, Microsoft's β of 1.46 means that a 1% change in the market risk premium changes the risk premium on Microsoft by 1.46%. The relatively low β stocks like General Motors (GM) and Proctor & Gamble (PG) are less volatile. But, as the data tabulated below show, the higher the beta the greater will be the returns.

	Annual return	Annual risk
MSFT	50.17%	33.27%
HD	33.74%	25.72%
PG	23.25%	21.15%
GM	20.47	25.82%

Note: Standard deviation is the measure of risk.

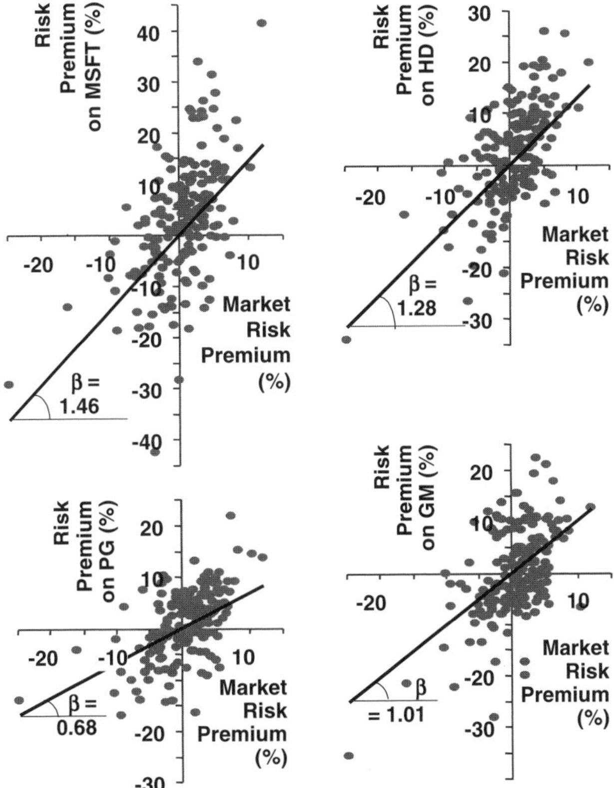

An updated version of the other classic empirical test[32] of CAPM is presented in Exhibit 5.21 where we compare average annual returns on the five asset classes of Exhibit 5.17, covering the 1926–1999 period, with their CAPM-derived values shown as the capital market line. Notice how well the theory matches the observed data!

Exhibit 5.21: Average annual returns for five asset classes of Exhibit 5.17 graphed against their β values. Also shown is the capital market line derived from Equation (5.6b).

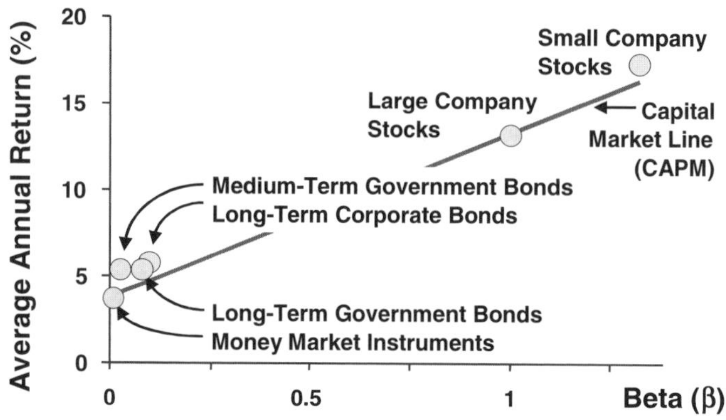

Exhibit 5.22: The January 1995–December 1999 monthly data show that most of the Dow components performed better than or on par with the market (open symbols) than underperformed (solid symbols). Star denotes the S&P 500 index and the market line is based on Equation (5.6b).

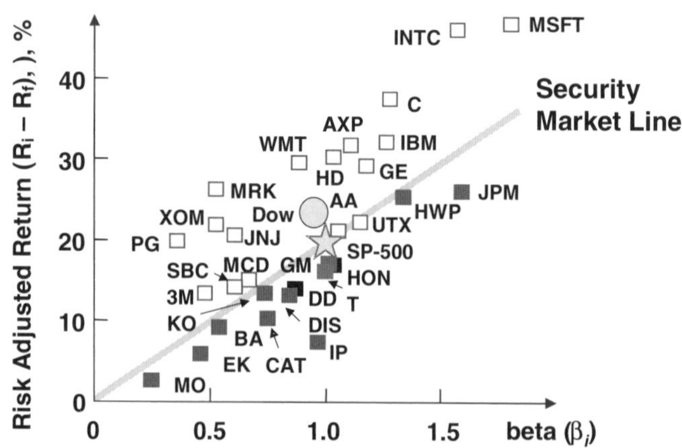

As security prices fluctuate, so do the corresponding returns and betas. Rather than using the CAPM as a deterministic predictor of market behavior, therefore, we need to use it as a broad stochastic guide to the market. As graphed in Exhibit 5.22, fitting Equation (5.6b) to the 1995–2000 data shows that more of the Dow components performed either better than or the same as the broad market, as represented by the S&P 500 index, than underperform it. Despite this scatter of data, however, the pattern seen here is what the CAPM tells us to expect, i.e., the greater the beta the higher the returns and the risk premiums.

The Dow is an excellent portfolio, of course, and the fact that some of the Dow components may plot below the CAPM's security market line during some periods does not necessarily render them rejectable. As for the Dow's merits as a portfolio, Exhibit 5.23 shows how two of the CAPM-based measures have varied through the history of this index. One of these, the Sharpe ratio, was mentioned earlier in Equation (4.7) and graphed for the overall US equities market in Exhibit 4.38. It measures the risk premium that an investor receives in terms of the portfolio risk borne. Treynor ratio is the other measure. Defined as

$$\text{Treynor ratio} = \frac{[E(r_m) - r_f]}{\beta_i}, \tag{5.7}$$

it measures the risk premium in terms of beta, or the portfolio's systematic risk. These two ratios give similar results if the portfolio is well-diversified such that only the systematic risk remains. A poorly diversified

Exhibit 5.23: Dow's Sharpe and Treynor ratios through the twentieth century have moved in tandem, suggesting that it is a well-diversified portfolio. These ratios have been computed in annually rolling bands of 30-year segments here, using Equations (4.7) and (5.7).

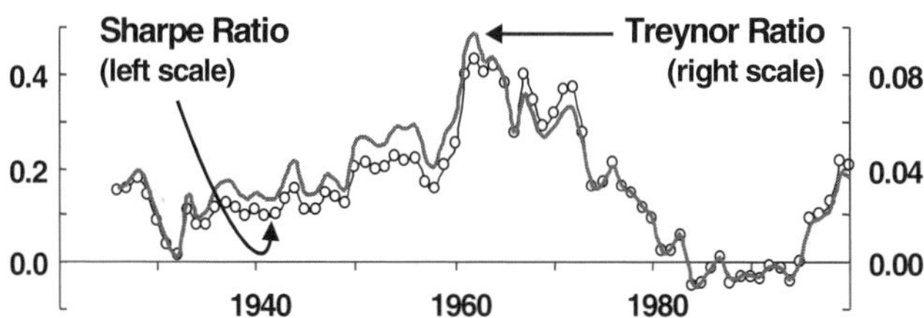

portfolio, on the other hand, would have a smaller Sharpe ratio but a larger Treynor ratio. Note how closely together the two ratios for the Dow have moved in Exhibit 5.23. This justifies our claim that Dow is a well-diversified portfolio.

CAPM's Problems and Limitations

Coming now to the second issue raised above, while it is easy to gauge a security's or portfolio's performance relative to the CAPM's market line, the question of retaining or ejecting underperformers from the portfolio rests on the reliability and consistency of beta as a valid measure of risk. For instance, Exhibit 5.23 shows that investors received better equity premium[33] in the 1950s through 1970s than in the 1980s and early 1990s. Indeed, as the market's return and risk statistics have varied over time (e.g., Exhibits 3.33 and 3.36), so has the risk premium. But what poses a problem for the CAPM is the fact that there have been protracted periods in history when beta has been a poor measure of the risk premium. Exhibit 5.24 summarizes the results of Fischer Black's famous study[34] that showed, for the 1931–1991 data, returns below the market line from high beta securities and returns above this line for the low beta securities. Indeed, the data for the 1966–1991 segment of this study showed statistically comparable returns, about the same as the whole market portfolio, across all beta levels.

The results such as those in Exhibit 5.24 are particularly bothersome because, as we saw in Exhibit 5.21, small company stocks have historically higher betas and returns than the large company stocks. Apparently, and contradicting the CAPM premise, beta alone cannot explain why the expected returns differ. Banz[35] was one of the first to show that returns are better explained by a firm's size, measured in terms of the market valuation of its equity, than by CAPM's beta. Fama and French[36] have found a firm's price to book ratio to be an even better indicator of the returns on its stock than size.

The validity of beta as a measure of risk has thus become a contentious issue for the academics as well as the practitioners. The seeds of the controversy were planted by Roll who argued that, for a theory that

Exhibit 5.24: In a study of 1931–1991 NYSE stock returns, Fischer Black found a general rise in risk premium with β, as the CAPM predicts. The returns across differrent levels of β did not lie on the market line, however. The numbers here denote a β-based grouping of the stocks. Also, for 1966–1991, risk premiums were about the same across all β levels.

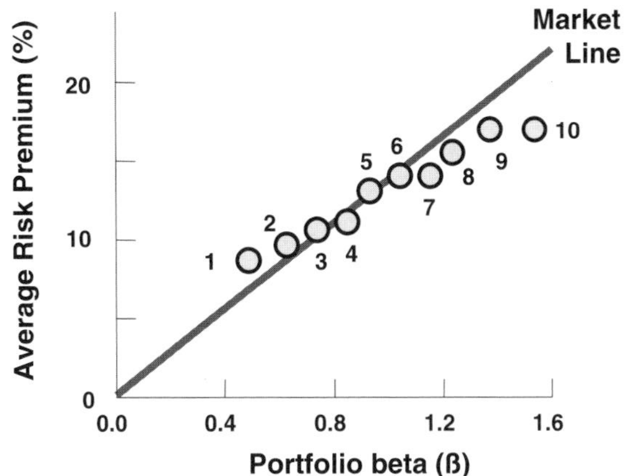

acquired its reputation on the claim of easy testability, the CAPM has never been correctly and unambiguously tested and "there is practically no possibility that such a test can be accomplished in the future".[37]

That the beta of a security itself changes over time was documented by Sharpe himself, one of the principals of what can be now called the SLB (Sharpe–Lintner–Black) one-beta CAPM, in a paper coauthored[38] with Cooper. They estimated betas of securities in the CRSP database for 60-month rates of return for each year from 1931 to 1967, by first ranking and dividing them into ten risk classes and then repeating this procedure for each year. In some cases, almost two-thirds of the securities did not remain in the same risk class, thus pointing to a significant instability of beta. Beta is now known[39] to vary over the business cycle and Jagannathan and Wang[40] have sought to resuscitate the CAPM by advocating that we use more than one beta. They incorporate Mayers'[41] human capital concept in measuring return on aggregate wealth and use time-varying beta and risk premium instead of a single beta over the market's entire history. Pursuing a similar strategy, Breeden[42] and

Exhibit 5.25: Consumption CAPM defines risk as the uncertainty stocks impose on investor's consumption of wealth, compared to the standard CAPM in which risk is the uncertainty that stocks bring to investor's wealth.

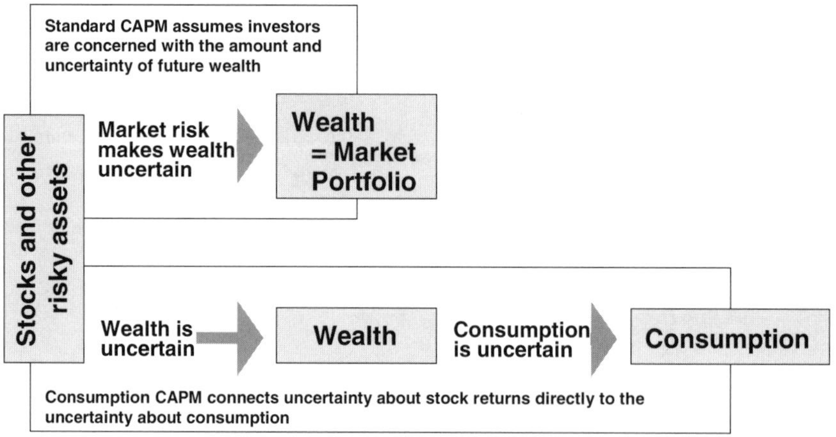

Source: Richard Brealey and Stewart Myers: *Principles of Corporate Finance* (McGraw-Hill, Irwin, 2003).

his associates advocate measuring a security's risk by its sensitivity to changes in investors' consumption. Exhibit 5.25 schematically explains this consumption CAPM and shows how it contrasts with the conventional CAPM.

The Arbitrage Pricing Theory

Arbitrage pricing theory (APT)[43] offers an alternative to the CAPM. Unlike the CAPM's one factor model, that the tradeoff between risk and return is the investors' only choice, APT envisions a multi-factor scenario. An arbitrage situation is one that involves no commitment in capital and yields a positive rate of return. For it to work effectively, capital markets must be perfectly competitive, and the investors must be rational (i.e., prefer more wealth to less wealth).

To derive the basic expression for the APT, let us start by decomposing the expected return on a stock, $E(r)$, into its supposedly known macroeconomic sources or "factors" and the ubiquitous "noise", i.e.,

$$E(r) = a + \sum_{i=1}^{n} \beta_i \times r_{\text{factor } i} + \text{noise}\,. \tag{5.8a}$$

The factors 1, 2, 3, ..., *n* could be interest rates, energy prices and the like, and β_i the sensitivity of *i*th security's return to the corresponding factor. Roll and Ross[44] identify five distinct sources of systematic, non-diversifiable risk for a well diversified portfolio — investor confidence, interest rates, business cycle, long-term inflation and short-term inflation — that together explain about 25% of the price fluctuations of an individual company's common stock. At the level of an individual company, most of the price volatility comes from such company specific risk factors as production, marketing and management risks. A large diversified portfolio of equities, with at least 40 individual companies and not heavily concentrated in any particular one according to these authors, retains only a very small exposure to these company-specific, idiosyncratic risks but possesses a large amount of exposure to the non-diversifiable common factors (Exhibit 5.26). Also, as the portfolio's sensitivity to these macroeconomic risk factors is directly proportional to the aggregate of the individual companies in the portfolio, different weightings of the universe of individual companies produce portfolios with varying risk sensitivities.

Exhibit 5.26: The sources of volatility for individual companies (left) and large and well-diversified portfolios (right).

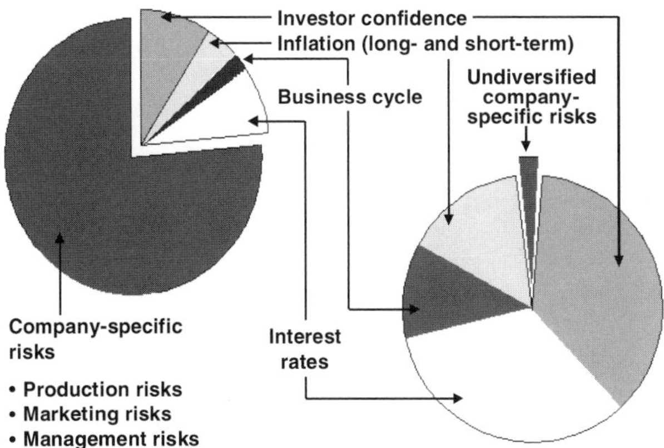

Source: Roll & Ross Asset Management (http://www.rollross.com)

Based on Equation (5.8a), the expected risk premium can be expressed as:

$$E(r) - r_f = \sum_{i=1}^{n} \beta_i \times (r_{\text{factor } i} - r_f) . \tag{5.8b}$$

The idea here is that (a) each source of systematic risk has its own risk and reward and (b) not all these sources or factors carry the same reward/risk ratio at all time. For each $\beta_i \times (r_{\text{factor } i} - r_f)$ in Equation (5.8b), therefore, we can construct a suitable portfolio and then monitor, and suitably adjust, each portfolio's risk exposure. For instance, if the sensitivity to each of the factors is zero, then it can be seen by plugging in $\beta_i = 0$ in Equation (5.8b) that we have essentially a risk-free portfolio. Its expected return would be $E(r) = r_f$, the risk-free rate. Note that any other situation, with $E(r) \neq r_f$, offers arbitrage profit here. If $E(r) > r_f$, you would buy into the portfolio after borrowing at r_f whereas, if $E(r) < r_f$, then you would profit by selling the portfolio to buy the Treasury bills. As against this, constructing a diversified portfolio that is sensitive

Exhibit 5.27: Estimating the risk premium by arbitrage pricing theory.

Factor	**Measured by**	**Factor risk (β)**	**Expected risk premium ($r_{\text{factor}} - r_f$)**	**Factor risk × risk premium $\beta \times (r_{\text{factor}} - r_f)$**
Yield spread	Return on long-term government bonds less that on the Treasury bills	5.10%	1.04	5.30%
Interest rate	Change in Treasury bill return	−0.61%	−2.25	1.37%
Exchange rate	Change in the value of the US dollar against a basket of currencies	−0.59%	0.70	−0.41%
Real GNP	Change in the forecast of real GNP	0.49%	0.17	0.08%
Inflation	Change in forecast of inflation	−0.83%	−0.18	0.15%
Market	...	3.36%	0.32	2.04%

to the desired factor would give a risk premium proportional to the corresponding sensitivity β_i.

The case study of nine New York utilities, reported by Elton *et al.*[45] and discussed by Brearley and Myers[46] is an excellent illustration of the APT in practice. Exhibit 5.27 summarizes their basic data and computations.

The first two columns show the factors that these authors identified as the ones most likely to affect the prices of utility stocks in the portfolio and their measures. The sixth factor, called market, was not a direct measure but was included, instead, to account for the portion of the return that could not be explained by the other five factors. Estimates of factor risk and risk premium were made using the empirical evidence for the 1978–1990 period and are given in the next two columns whereas the numbers in the last column are merely the products of the preceding two columns. Adding up these numbers in the last column, as suggested by Equation (5.8b), the expected risk premium for this portfolio works out to 8.53%. This means that, with a 1-year Treasury bill rate at about 7% in December 1990, the last year covered in this study, the expected return on the portfolio would be 15.53% (= 7% + 8.53%).

The APT certainly captures the market's reality far more effectively than CAPM's one-size-fits-all strategy can. Also, by allowing for multiple sources of risk, it enables constructing the portfolios suited for specific needs. But identifying the factors and their relative importance is a task replete with uncertainties. Generally, for instance, macroeconomic factors

“Our online investments are growing too slowly. We need to get a faster computer!”

such as surprises in inflation, GNP and investor confidence and shifts in the yield curve explain the changes in security returns reasonably well. But if they really do as good a job of explaining the market's gyrations as is needed for the APT to work, then we must already have the means to predict the market! The fact of the matter is that we do not even know if these are indeed the "true" factors that we need. Add to this two other problems that we need to contend with. One, adding the number of betas only means compounding the problems we already have with the one-beta case of CAPM. If time-varying betas and risk premiums are what we need to make the CAPM work, then having to seek a multitude of betas for the same time horizon is unlikely to solve the problem. Two, arbitrage pricing implies the prospects of securing profits without having to commit the capital, and this is accomplished here by constructing zero-beta portfolios. But then, in the stochastic universe of mean-variance optimization that CAPM and APT inhabit, where is the guarantee that the arbitrage *pricing* of a zero-beta expected return will indeed end up as the arbitrage *price* of a zero risk premium, once we have introduced such a miscellany of statistical variables?

5.4 The Efficient Market Hypothesis and its Implications

The Random Walk of Returns

The extensive use of statistics in our narrative so far makes it hard to imagine that it is only in the past five decades or so that statistical analysis has become an indispensable tool in financial economics. Indeed, when Maurice Kendall[47] claimed in 1953 that stock prices follow a random walk, little did he realize that he was pioneering an altogether new era in financial economics. It is not that Kendall was the first ever to have recognized this, however. That distinction should rightfully go to Louis Bachelier except that (despite anticipating by five years Einstein's seminal work on Brownian motion) Bachelier's study[48] had largely remained unkown until Kendall's claim that the daily changes in stock prices are as likely to be positive as negative. As a matter of fact, it was

Bachelier, and not Kendall, who had first conceived the concepts of lognormal distributions[49] and geometric mean for the stock price returns that we have discussed in Section 3.4. Nor was the *Journal of the Royal Statistical Society, London* the first to let statistics muddle its way into economics, by giving Kendall the forum for such thoughts and analyses. That distinction goes to the *Journal of the American Statistical Association*, in whose pages Halbrook Working[50] had first talked of the random behavior of commodity prices almost two decades earlier. Kendall's was a pioneering effort, nonetheless, for the avalanche of studies that followed his work eventually led to Eugene Fama's[51] formulation of the *efficient market hypothesis*.

What does market efficiency mean and why should it arouse any investor concern or interest? Fama defined an efficient market as one

> "where there are large numbers of rational, profit-maximizers actively competing, with each trying to predict future market values of individual securities, and where important current information is almost freely available to all participants",

so that, on average, "competition will cause the full effects of new information on intrinsic values to be reflected "instantaneously" in actual prices". But then, if stock prices indeed adjusted to all the available information as rapidly as this definition demands, then all stocks should be correctly priced nearly at all times. It would then become pointless to seek any overperformers that could be added to a portfolio and identify the underperformers that need to be dumped from it. As we discussed in the context of Exhibit 5.22, not all stocks justify their price all the time.

The question as to what market efficiency is all about boils down, therefore, to what kind of "information" is reflected in stock prices and when. This has produced the following three forms of efficient market hypothesis[52] of which Fama's above definition is for the strong form:

Weak form: The market price of a security reflects the information contained in that security's price history. For an investor, seeking superior returns entails turning to the fundamental analysis[53] (discussed in the next section), therefore, in order to retrieve the information that will eventually get impounded in the market price.

Semi strong form: Market prices not only reflect the past prices but also rapidly adjust to all publicly available information. Seeking superior returns then necessitates anticipating the market's response to news or announcements on earnings, dividends, stock-splits, mergers, and the like.

Strong form: The market price reflects all information that could conceivably be used to determine the "true" value of a stock. As a hyper-efficient market such as this will always price securities fairly, or at their true worth, the quest for superior returns here would rely on the technical analysis[54] that we discuss in the following chapter of past trends and patterns, if at all.

All these definitions start with the same basic observation, that stock prices fluctuate randomly. Even the weak form denies the presence of any patterns in stock prices. A look at Exhibit 5.28 will explain what this really means. Two datasets are compared here for the period of one year, or 250 trading days: the S&P 500 index and a sequence of random numbers. For the S&P 500 index, this exhibit shows the daily closing numbers from May 3, 2000 to April 30, 2001. The sequence of random

Exhibit 5.28: The pattern of daily price changes for the S&P 500 index for a one-year period (May 3, 2000–April 30, 2001) appears closely mimicked by the random numbers generated with normal distribution (for annual mean = 0% and annual standard deviation = 15.81%).

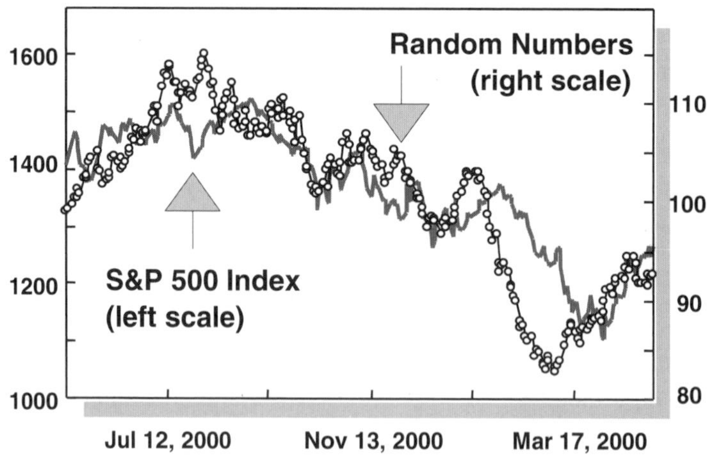

numbers has been generated here for a normal distribution with annual mean = 0 and annual standard deviation = $\sqrt{250}$ = 15.81%. These numbers correspond to daily return = 0% and daily volatility[55] = 1%. Notice how hard it would be, without labeling them, to tell one graph from the other.

From "Compass Rose" to Chaos and Fractals

A random walk implies a lack of memory. Thus, if today's price carries no memory of past prices, then the price tomorrow is unlikely to be determined by the price today. This is precisely what an efficient market is. Here, a firm's stock is priced at the level commensurate with that firm's intrinsic worth, in the long run. The challenge is to determine if one can benefit from short-term fluctuations in stock prices, by "buying low and selling high", say. The problem is that the converse is equally likely. As Samuelson argued,[56] asset prices respond to the unanticipated component of news by fluctuating randomly through time. Based on the CAPM, the only trend would then be for either the price to adjust to the level of these fluctuations or for fluctuations to adjust to the price, or both, so that the equity's risk premium is its beta times the market risk premium. This is an empirically testable postulate. All that we need to do is compare a security's price on any given day with the corresponding price on the following day or any subsequent day.

Exhibit 5.29 presents such a scatter diagram for IBM's daily price changes since January 2, 1962, compared to the following day. Had a pattern in the price changes existed here, it would have been reflected in the trend and correlation. Suppose, for instance, that the change in tomorrow's price followed that of today. We should then find an upward sloping linear trend with a positive correlation. What if prices fell the next day, to compensate for the rise today, or vice versa? That would show up here as a downward sloping linear trend and a negative correlation. What we find here, instead, is the total lack of any trend and a correlation coefficient of 0.017 that is not significantly non-zero. The only inference that would be consistent with this picture would be that the price changes here are completely random. This exhibit shows only the data for IBM. But that is only by way of illustration. One can

Exhibit 5.29: This graph, comparing one day's change in IBM's stock price with that next day from January 2, 1962, to December 29, 1999, lacks a distinct pattern, and the correlation coefficient of 0.017 carries no statistical significance. The "compass rose" pattern is intriguing, however, even if it only reflects the fact that stock prices change in discrete jumps.

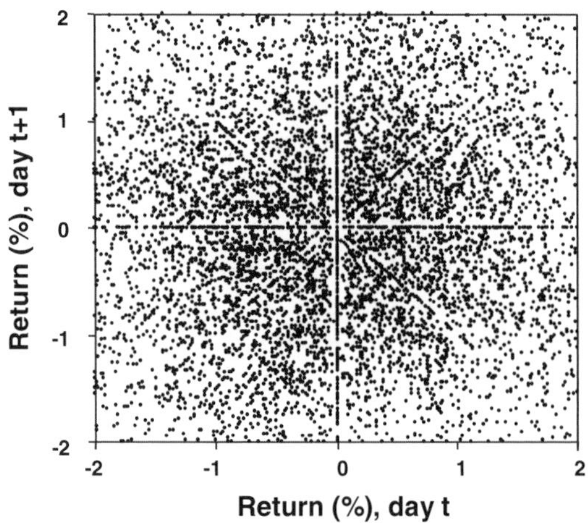

choose any other security, or an index for that matter, and the results would be no different.

A peculiarity is seen in Exhibit 5.29, in the form of evenly spaced lines radiating from the origin with the thickest lines pointing in the major directions of a compass. The lines at 90° are most readily visible here, followed by those at 45°. Crack and Ledoit,[57] who first detected it, dubbed it the "*compass rose*" pattern and ascribed it to the discrete nature of stock prices which restricts the returns to a limited number of values. While they found no predictive use of this pattern, it merits our immediate attention because of its following implications for estimation and predictability:

- This pattern is most commonly seen for the "high-growth" or "glamour" stocks that investors often prefer. It appears clearly, according to Crack and Ledoit, if (a) daily stock price changes are small relative to the price level, and occur in discrete jumps of a small number of ticks, while (b) the stock price itself varies over a rather wide range. Subsequent research[58] shows that these price changes need not really be small.

- This pattern can perhaps be used for improving stock return forecasts, according to Chen,[59] whereas Kwämer and Runde[60] argued that it adversely affects the statistical testing of deviations from i.i.d. The former result is of interest to most investors, fund managers and annuity providers while the latter should interest option traders and the employees in high growth firms who increasingly receive significant proportions of their wages in stock options. Recall our discussion that a normal distribution model is used for analyzing stock returns because these returns are independent and identically distributed.

Contrasted with this caution is the recent argument of Amilon and Byström,[61] that the constraints Chen, Kwämer and Runde have imposed on their models are too unrealistic to yield economically meaningful statistical inferences. The question whether the compass pattern can be used to identify the "glamour stocks" that we all seek must therefore remain open, as yet.

The question, therefore, is if the empirical data indeed depart significantly enough from the random walk pattern to jeopardize our use of the normal distribution based statistical measures. This brings us to the world of chaos and fractals and their implications to the financial markets.[62] The problem basically lies in fitting the normal distribution to the empirical data on stock returns. Recall our finding, in the preceding chapter, that annual returns fit the normal distribution model better than the monthly returns. But this finding creates a curious problem. Note that the normal or Gaussian model describes a continuous distribution, not a discrete one. Therefore, if a normal distribution is indeed the correct model, then monthly returns should not describe a poorer fit than the annual returns. Instead, the monthly returns are found to be far too strongly peaked but fat tailed than the normal curve.

A probability density function that mimics this situation better than normal distribution is a Cauchy density.[63] Its characteristic function $g(x)$ is

$$g(x) = \frac{1}{\pi(1+x^2)} \quad \text{for } -\infty < x < +\infty . \tag{5.9}$$

Exhibit 5.30: Compared to the Gaussian or normal curve, Cauchy curve mimics better a high peaked but fat tailed distribution like the monthly geometric returns in Exhibit 3.33. The normal curve here has mean = 0 and standard deviation = 1. Thus, x here corresponds to z in Exhibit 3.32. Shaded regions show where the two curves differ.

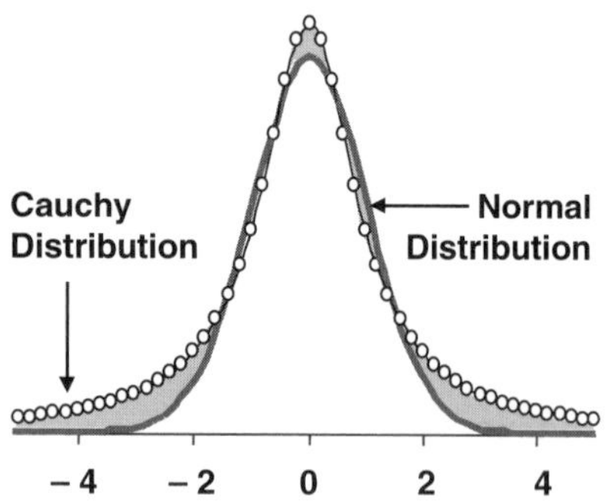

Here, x is the variable whose statistical distribution we are trying to examine. Obviously, $g(x)$ is symmetric about $x = 0$ where it has its highest value, and tapers off to zero as $x \to +\infty$. As can be seen in Exhibit 5.30 where we compare the normal and Cauchy curves, a major peculiarity of the latter is that it is far more strongly peaked and fat tailed than the normal curve.

It requires no great imagination, therefore, to see in the Cauchy curve the panacea to our problem in seeking to realistically mimic our high peaked but fat tailed monthly geometric returns that the normal curve matches poorly. Benoit Mandelbrot,[64] amongst whose disciples was Eugene Fama, was perhaps the first to appreciate this reality of the statistical distribution of stock returns.

Then why not use a Cauchy curve, instead of the normal curve, to analyze stock returns? The simple answer is convenience. Based purely on the statistical structure, it is quite likely that the distribution of stock market returns is non-Gaussian. Note that Fama[65] had himself started with the exploration of non-Gaussian probabilities for price distributions. Suppose the invisible hand that Adam Smith invoked sets the just price for a security and, while we all have a fair idea of what it might be, we do not know what it actually is. In that case, as the meteorologist Lorenz[66] discovered when he rounded off the input numbers in his iteration equations, even deterministic equations produce chaotic results if the equations are nonlinear. Perhaps this is what that great mathematician Henri Poincaré had in mind when he concluded, at the dawn of the twentieth century, that "*small differences in the initial conditions produce very great ones in the final phenomena*". Likewise, it is plausible that, in reality, our nonlinear, geometric, price changes keep looping about an elusive Lorenz attractor and can be better mapped, therefore, by the Cauchy curve. Exhibit 5.31 graphically displays this behavior of a single-point Lorentz attractor.

Clearly, had fitting a curve to the empirical data been our primary goal, then we have erred grievously by using the normal curve. But our goal is to seek the broad patterns that can guide our investment strategies. Using the simple but well-defined lognormal distribution certainly enables this. As is readily apparent in Exhibit 3.30, the resulting discrepancy is marginal when we limit ourselves to 95% of the probability curve. This is also suggested by a recent study[67] of the returns on US (S&P 500), UK (FTSE 100), German (DAX) and Japanese (Nikkei 225) stock markets, which showed nonlinearity in the time of returns

Exhibit 5.31: Notice how, in this picture of chaos, a dynamic system like a Lorenz system changes over time in 3-D space, with the path or trajectory looping around and around a central attractor, but never intersects itself.

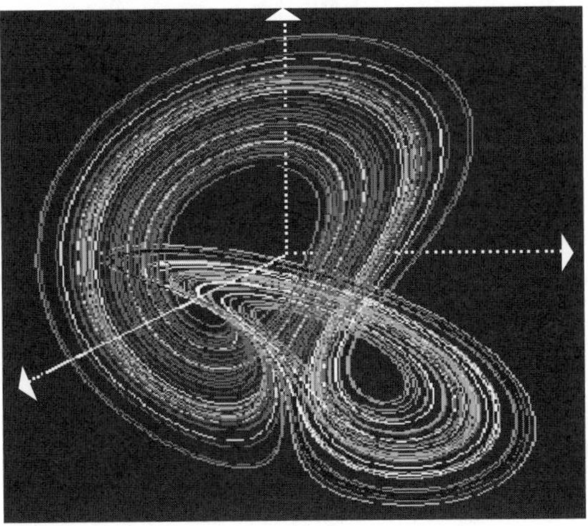

Source: Dr. J. Orlin Grabbe's homepage at http://www.aci.net/kalliste/chaos1.htm

but no evidence of chaos. But then, there is no reason why an aggregation of chaotic processes may not turn out to be nonchaotic.[68]

The random walk premise[69] of efficient market hypothesis has often led to the notion that selecting stocks is a skill-less task that is best left to chance. Nothing could be farther from the truth, however. What the "randomness" in statistical distribution[70] of price changes, whether normal or lognormal, actually implies here is that the prices randomly drift about an overall trend. History amply testifies to the fact that, as for the broad market, this overall trend itself is an exponential one. How else would you have an inflation-adjusted annual rate of return that has never dipped below 6% over any 30-year period through the history of the US stock market?

The question whether investment professionals can significantly outperform the random throw of darts is indeed one that an irreverent, but nonetheless significant experiment *The Wall Street Journal* has

Box 5.2: *The Wall Street Journal's* "Dartboard Portfolio" Experiment[*]

Investment Dartboard was born at *The Wall Street Journal* in 1988, when the Dow stood at just over 2100, mainly responding to Burton Malkiel's following explanation[**] of **efficient market theory**.

"*Taken in its logical extreme*," the theory suggests "*that a blind folded monkey throwing darts at a newspaper's financial pages could select a portfolio that would do just as well as one carefully selected by experts.*"

To test this idea, the journal pitted four investment professionals each month, in a series of one-month contests that it later extended to six months, against the forces of chance as exercised by four journal staffers tossing the darts. The results after 100 six-month contests strongly favor the pros. What is particularly reassuring, however, is the fact that the dart throwers outperformed the Treasury bills but not the market!

Average investment performance in 100 six-month contests, January 1, 1990 to September 30, 1998

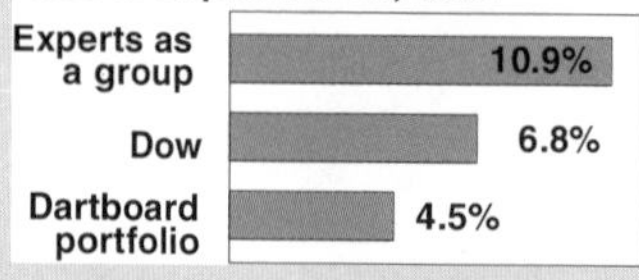

[*]Georgette Jasen: "A Brief History of Our Contest", *The Wall Street Journal*, October 7, 1998.
[**]Burton Malkiel: *A Random Walk Down Wall Street* (W.W. Norton, June 2000).

explored at length. Box 5.2 summarizes its results. Note that the data presented here do not debunk the dart-throwing strategy altogether. Racking up a 4.5% annual rate of return is somewhat superior to the yield on Treasury bills, as a matter of fact. But then, this was a period of substantial market, though not exceptional, growth.

Some Empirical Tests of Market Efficiency

Overall, the basic premise of the efficient market hypothesis, that asset prices fluctuate randomly over time, is a reasonably workable idea. True, above average returns in a given period — a day, a week or a month — sometimes follow similar returns in the preceding period.[71] But then, the predictive power of these patterns is rather weak, and stock returns often display mean reversion over a 3–5 year horizon.[72]

An early evidence that security prices reflect the market's immediate absorption of relevant news came from the work of Arthur Keown and John Pinkerton.[73] As summarized in Exhibit 5.32, this study found that

Exhibit 5.32: While impending mergers and acquisitions are poorly held secrets, and may give the insiders some excess returns, most of the jump in price occurs on the day of announcement.

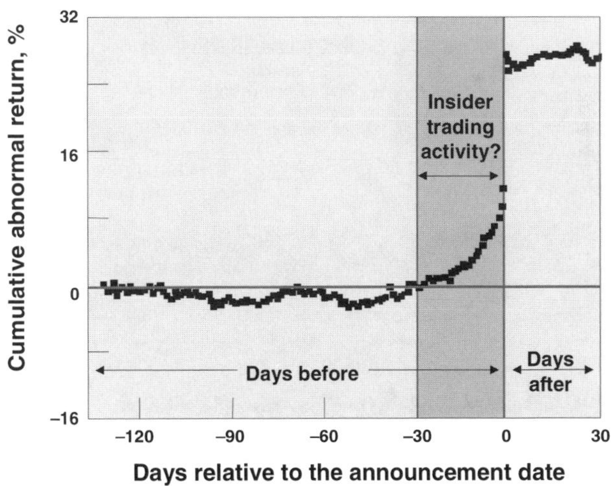

Source: Arthur Keown and John Pinkerton

the stock price of the target company jumps up immediately at the announcement that it is being taken over or bought out but the subsequent days bring no change in this price. There is an upward shift in price in the days immediately preceding the announcement, however, pointing to a gradual leakage of information to insiders. This is consistent with the efficient market hypothesis because most of the jump in price occurs on the day of the announcement, and no significant change occurs later, i.e., once made public, the information is absorbed fully and immediately. What about the acquiring firms? Their stocks generally fall,[74] by about 10% on average, over a 5-year post-merger period.

The merger of America Online and Time Warner is a case in point. At the time the merger was announced (January 10, 2000), America Online was the nation's largest Internet service provider, with over 20 million subscribers and about \$163 billion in market capitalization. Time Warner was then the biggest name in the world of traditional media and was valued at about \$100 billion. The effect of this announcement on their share prices was marginal, if at all. Exhibit 5.33 graphs these price paths

Exhibit 5.33: The merger announcement of America Online and Time Warner did little to arrest the falling trend in America Online's price and may have only given a temporary boost to Time Warner's price, if at all. The top panel here shows the prices and the bottom panel their daily changes.

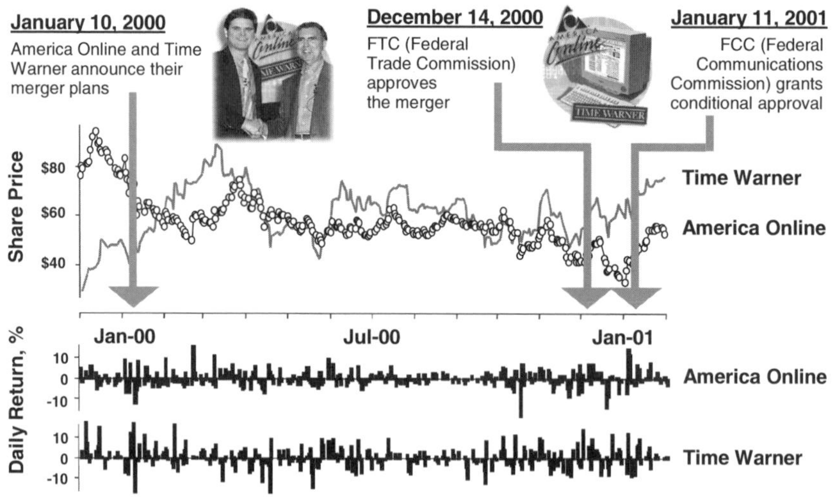

from December 1, 1999 to January 31, 2001, a period that covers the initial announcement as well as the FTC (Federal Trade Commission) and FCC (Federal Communications Commission) approvals about a year later. These data show no conspicuous effect of the merger on prices of Time Warner shares, which have fluctuated between $42.5 and $76.05 in this period (we have used the Time Warner Trading Company (TWTC) shares as the proxy for Time Warner shares). As for America Online, the trend throughout has been one of a continuous decline in share prices. The broad market itself has been rather flat, or in the trading range, in this period and the S&P 500 index has fluctuated between 1265 and 1527.

Now, the fact that the markets are efficient does not really make it impossible, over time, to log a better performance than the market. Take the example of Warren Buffet, for instance. As shown in Exhibit 5.34, his Berkshire Hathaway fund has consistently beaten the S&P 500 index. Of the three investments compared here, a $7455 investment on January 1, 1990, would have grown to $28,305 in the S&P 500 index, $37,653 in Fidelity's Magellan fund, and $68,000 in Buffet's Berkshire Hathaway

Exhibit 5.34: The managers and funds that have beaten the market consistently for ten years or longer are hard to find. Here are two of the notable exceptions: Warren Buffet's Berkshire Hathaway fund and Fidelity's Magellan fund.

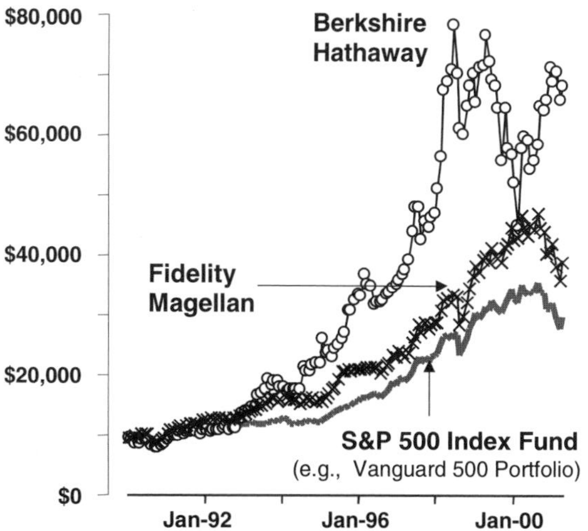

fund.[75] Why this odd investment amount of $7455? This is what the shares of Berkshire Hathaway were priced at on January 1, 1990.

Though not uncommon altogether, cases such as these are rather rare. But, even here, the record is not altogether unchequered. For instance, if you had bought a Berkshire Hathaway share (BRK.a) at its all time high of $83,330 a certificate in June 1998 then, not counting the appreciation in book value, you would have lost 18% on it by April 2001. Comparable investments would have had you up by 13% in the S&P 500 index and 17.4% in Fidelity Magellan.

Overall, though, if you expect that professional fund managers with active hands-on management of their funds would get you better returns than what you would receive by passively investing in an index, think again. Mutual funds are often the best examples of active portfolio management. Thus, if active management indeed works, then their average performance should be superior to that of the market index. But innumerable studies of the vast US mutual fund industry have consistently demonstrated[76] their chronic underperformance. Even when performance has been better, and a fund has "beaten the market" so to speak, the excess return over the market has mostly gone into the fund's management expenses, and seldom into the investor's pockets.

Strategies (e.g., *Dogs of Dow, Fabulous Five*) and effects (e.g., *the January effect*) that often help beat the market also exist, and are discussed in Chapter 7. To the supporters of the efficient market hypothesis, such market "anomalies"[77] only cause satisfaction, not disappointment, however. The fact that they are anomalies reaffirms the notion that, despite periodic exuberance (in either direction), the market always returns to the fundamentals of fairly pricing the equities based on what they are truly worth.

The Efficient Market's Irrational Exuberance

A problematic issue for the efficient market hypothesis is that of market bubbles and crashes. Indeed, it is hard to imagine how they could recur if the markets indeed absorbed information efficiently over time so that equities were priced at levels commensurate with their economic fundamentals. No price misalignments would then occur, producing the speculative bubble that a subsequent market crash would correct. Bubbles (e.g., Holland's Tulipmania or Great Britain's South Sea Bubble) and crashes (e.g., the end of these bubbles, the crashes of 1792, 1929 and 1987 in the US) do occur, however. Take the October 1987 crash, for instance. The first nine months of that year saw a bubble, with 33% appreciation of the S&P 500 index, and this trend got dramatically reversed by the middle of October. Most of the fall occurred in one day, on October 19, when the index fell by 22%, but this was after a 9% decline in the preceding week. The Dow lost 508 points that day, and the overall US stock market lost about $500 billion. There were signs that could, in retrospect, have forewarned of the disaster almost a week in advance. Three of them[79] particularly stand out — the announcement of one of the largest merchandise trade deficits in the history of the US, the possible elimination by the US Congress of the tax benefits of leveraged buyouts, and the likelihood of the Fed raising the discount rate.

These problems could not have directly affected markets outside the US, however. But, as can be seen in Exhibit 5.35, the stock markets crashed worldwide. The US stock market had the most capitalization of all equity markets worldwide, and accounted for a larger share of the global markets then. Its turmoil is unlikely to have left the other markets unaffected. This global crash was perhaps the domino effect, therefore. But that still begs the question as to why the market, if it is indeed so efficient that equities stay priced about their fundamental worth over time, allowed prices to rise so high, speculatively, that they would have to come crashing down when the bubble burst. And, if the crash did not drag stock prices down to the levels well below their intrinsic value, then we also need to explain how the market recovered so rapidly. Had you invested $10,000 in the S&P 500 index at the market's pre-crash peak in August 1987, then the crash would have left you almost $3000 poorer in November 1987 but, exactly two years later, in July 1989, your investment would have grown to $11,240, in nominal dollars! Chances are that you would have blissfully slept through what Wall Street calls "Black Monday" of October 19, 1987, without ever noticing that the market had experienced a severe crash. Patience does pay, indeed!

Stock prices often stray from their intrinsic worth or the fundamental value for extended periods of time. As we clearly saw from our

Exhibit 5.35: The crash of October 1987 was not limited to the Wall Street, as can be seen from the drops suffered by the stock market indexes worldwide.[78]

	Local currency	US dollars
Australia	−41.8%	−44.9%
Austria	−11.4%	−5.8%
Belgium	−23.2%	−18.9%
Canada	−22.5%	−22.9%
Denmark	−12.5%	−7.3%
France	−22.9%	−19.5%
Germany	−22.3%	−17.1%
Hong Kong	−45.8%	−45.8%
Ireland	−29.1%	−25.4%
Italy	−16.3%	−12.9%
Japan	−12.8%	−7.7%
Malaysia	−39.8%	−39.3%
Mexico	−35.0%	−37.6%
Netherlands	−23.3%	−18.1%
New Zealand	−29.3%	−36.0%
Norway	−30.5%	−28.8%
Singapore	−42.2%	−41.6%
South Africa	−23.9%	−29.0%
Spain	−27.7%	−23.1%
Sweden	−21.8%	−18.6%
Switzerland	−26.1%	−20.8%
UK	−26.4%	−22.1%
US	−21.6%	−21.6%

examination of the market's history, the trend for most of the time has been one of appreciation. This translates into increasing returns, and makes the stocks pricier, so that the returns must eventually drop and trigger a concomitant fall or "correction" in the price. The pricier a stock gets the greater will be its price earnings (P/E) ratio, which would drop when the price gets corrected. This, as can be seen in Exhibit 5.36 where we compare the 10-year averages of annualized returns and P/E ratios for the S&P 500 index, gives the market the kind of cyclicity that we first saw in Chapter 3.

Note the lagged, not coincident, cyclicities in market returns and P/E ratios in Exhibit 5.36. Overall, high P/E ratios here coincide with the onset of declining returns and low P/E ratios portend rising returns, as Campbell and Shiller[80] have reported. This is also reminiscent of the negative correlation of annualized returns for trailing and forward 20-year holdings that we saw in Chapter 3. The problem is that the cyclicities so pronounced in the two time series in Exhibit 5.36 match approximately at best. As Exhibit 5.37 shows, their correlation improves when, rather than the P/E ratio, we use deviations from the long-term trend in P/E ratios that we discussed earlier. But even this improvement (coefficient of correlation = 0.58) is not strong enough to make the P/E a reliable gauge for the likely market returns.

Exhibit 5.36: The presence of similar but lagged cyclicities in the graphs of real returns on the S&P 500 index and the corresponding P/E ratios suggests that a self-correcting mechanism is built into the market. Monthly data for the S&P 500 index have been used here. The returns here are annualized total returns (real) for 10-year holdings and are shown here in monthly rolling bands.

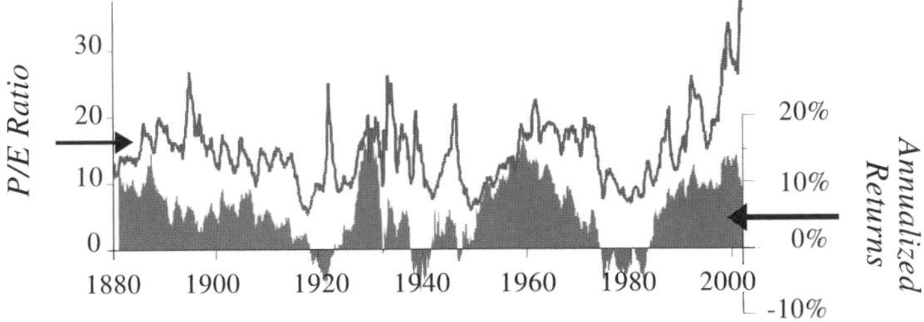

Exhibit 5.37: P/E ratios correlate well with annualized returns (left panel), and this correlation improves when we use the deviations of monthly P/E ratios from the long-term trend (right panel).

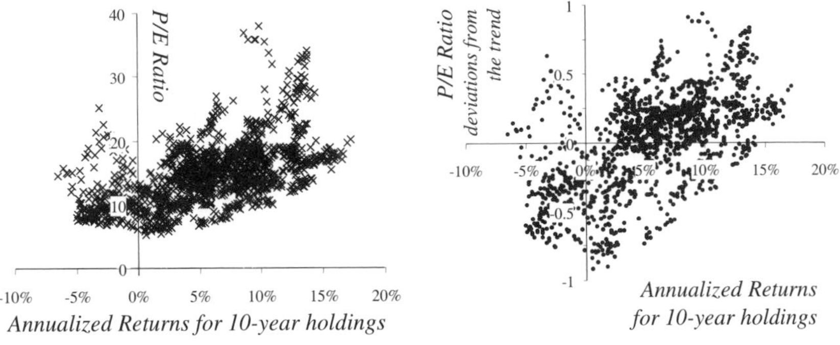

It is hard, nonetheless, to label as random fluctuations the cyclicities in the P/E ratio and annualized returns data seen in Exhibit 5.36. In terms of real prices, for instance, the January 1960–December 1979 period averaged a 1.63% annual drop (standard deviation = 15.39%), compared to an average annual rise of 8.62% (standard deviation = 13.76%) during January 1980–December 1999.

Is there a fundamental explanation for such rapid changes in prices over protracted periods. We revisit the Gordon growth model, in Box 5.3, to seek an answer. Note that, compared to the steady growth (g) and discount rate (r) model in Box 3.1, where $(r - g)$ is constant, a rising $(r - g)$ scenario translates into a steep drop in the price (P). By the same token, a falling $(r - g)$ environment has the opposite effect of a runaway price spiral. To find what could have produced such swings in $(r - g)$, we only need to look at Exhibit 4.7. Notice how steeply interest rates generally rose in the 1960s and 1970s, and how they have been falling since the early 1980s. Thus, as Exhibit 5.36 shows, 1960–1979 was a period of declining P/E ratios and returns, whereas 1980–1999 witnessed rising P/E ratios and returns.

Misalignments such as these between the asset fundamentals and their market values are hardly limited to the stock markets, however. They particularly afflict the foreign exchange market. In the case of the stock markets, Summers has argued[81] that, for most of the times, the market's misalignments either gradually build up or unwind. The asset prices deviate appreciably from the fundamentals during these times, therefore, even if the daily price fluctuations reflect the market's immediate response to the relevant new information and mimic the random walk. The reversion to the mean, in this picture, takes 3–5 years, as mentioned before.

Likewise, as for the foreign exchange rates, we would ordinarily expect that future spot rates in an efficient, risk-neutral market, would converge towards the present forward rates. Suppose the euro, the common currency of 12 of the European Union members, has a spot ($s_{\text{euro/\$}}$) rate of 1.18 euro/$ and 1-year forward rate ($f_{\text{euro/\$}}$) of 1.191 euro/$, suggesting the euro's likely fall against the US dollar. It will therefore attract those buyers and traders who agree with the implicit rate of the euro's fall, or expect that the euro may fall farther. But those traders who expect the euro to rise would prefer to wait for a better rate in the

Box 5.3: Gordon Growth Model and the Logic of Irrational Exuberance

Real prices rose barely (= 0.36% per year) during 1970–1979 but rose 8.13% annually during 1980–1999. Let us examine if the Gordon growth model can explain why. The analytical expression derived in Box 3.1 for price (P) as the present value of future cash stream, i.e., $P = D/(r - g)$, where D denotes dividends, r the discount rate and g the divident growth rate, can be rewritten as

$$r = \left(\frac{D}{P}\right) + g. \qquad \text{(i)}$$

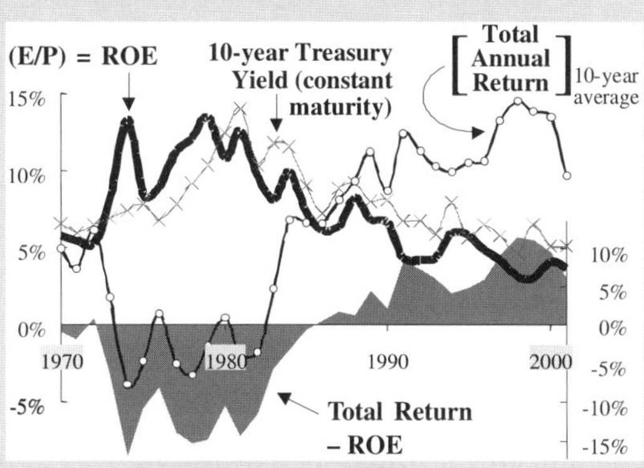

If we treat g as the growth in price G_P (= $\Delta P/P$, say) then r is the total return. Also, as was seen in Box 3.1, if book value = market value then r becomes the return on equity (ROE), so that, if g is the *sustainable growth rate*, i.e., g = ROE × (1 − D/E), then Equation (i) can be written as

$$r = \text{ROE} = \frac{E}{P}. \qquad \text{(ii)}$$

The exhibit above compares these two rates — total returns from Equation (i) and ROE from Equation (ii) — with the 10-year Treasury yields, for the January 1970–December 2001 period, and also shows the spread (= Total Return − ROE) of these returns. We have computed $g = G_P$ for Equation (i) as annualized price changes for 10-year holdings, in order to reduce the fluctuations that make visualization difficult without adding much more to information. The 1970–2000 interest rate cycle clearly affected stock prices dramatically. Note that:

- The spread has been positive since the mid-1980s, with the 10-year Treasury yields marking the mean of the two rates, perhaps as the decline in interest rates started taking effect.
- Total returns were greatly subdued in the preceding period of rising interest rates, and the ROE remained appreciably higher and generally exceeded the 10-year Treasury yields, so producing a negative spread of returns.

As high prices should lower both the estimates of r, this difference can be ascribed directly to the term g in Equation (i) which we have computed here as G_P (= $\Delta P/P$).

This reflects the fact that future cash streams acquire greater weight in a falling interest rate environment (e.g., during 1982–1999), as can be gauged from the Gordon growth equation itself. The cash receipts that are to come farther into the future count for increasingly less in present values when interest rates are rising (e.g., during 1970–1982). It can be argued, therefore, that price changes can be explained by changes in interest rates and by changing expectations of future growth. Obviously, exuberance is not necessarily irrational. This also shows how efficient the market is in incorporating the secular changes in interest rate regime.

spot market, so drying the supply of the currencies. The resulting supply-demand equilibrium for the two currencies for forward trading would justify formulating the rule

$$\frac{f_{\text{euro/\$}}}{s_{\text{euro/\$}}} = \frac{E(s_{\text{euro/\$}})}{s_{\text{euro/\$}}}, \tag{5.10}$$

where $E(s_{\text{euro/\$}})$ denotes spot exchange rate expected at the time corresponding to the forward rate $f_{\text{euro/\$}}$. This states the *expectations theory* of exchange rates,[82] that *forward rate equals expected future spot exchange rates*, and ensures that returns expected on interest-bearing assets in the two currencies are equal. The empirical evidence paints the opposite picture,[83] however, because spot exchange rates tend to diverge from, not converge to, the initial value of the forward rate.

Overall, the foreign exchange market also shows the fluctuations that broadly mimic a normal distribution. This is clearly brought out in Exhibit 5.38. The distribution of daily changes in the US dollar price of ECU, precursor currency to the euro, for the January 1, 1997–December 31, 1998 period is shown in the top panel here. The bottom panel shows the corresponding distribution of daily changes in the US dollar price of a euro for the January 1, 1999–March 20, 2001 period.

Much like those in the equities markets, misalignments in the foreign exchange markets too must eventually disappear, as they do, after persisting for protracted periods comparable to the equities markets[84] though. This is not to claim, of course, that we know the economic fundamentals[85] that presumably govern the equilibrium levels that rates in the foreign exchange market would eventually settle to.

Exhibit 5.38: Price changes in the foreign exchange market too show random fluctuations that, much like the stock returns, reasonably mimic the normal distribution model.

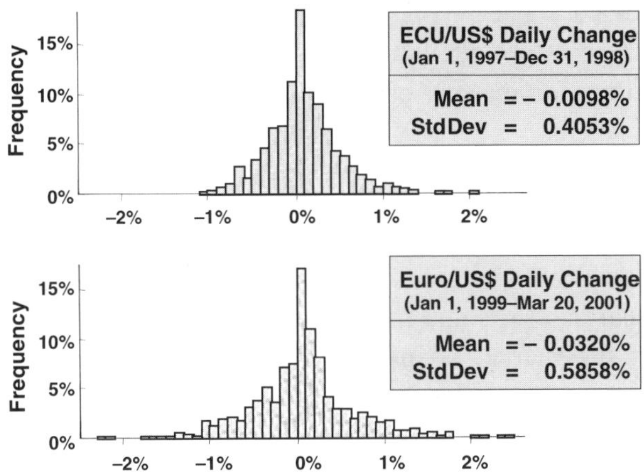

Market Efficiency and the Investor's Choices

Some scholars advocate either discarding the efficient market hypothesis altogether, whether for the equities market or for the foreign exchange market, or modify it so drastically that it can no longer help understand the market behavior. De Jong *et al.*[86] trace this problem to the fact that agents who trade in the asset markets are of two types: the "noise traders" who operate by reacting to the market hype or noise,[87] while the "rational traders" operate based on careful analysis of the market fundamentals, price patterns or charts, and the statistical structure. Whether it is due to the noise, or due to inherent limitations of the efficient market hypothesis, there is a rising clamor for behavioral finance[88] and against the random walk model, the bedrock of the efficient market hypothesis. Two questions therefore arise: (a) does it really matter whether the market is efficient or not? and (b) what is an investor to make of these academic debates about market efficiency?

The best answer to the first question comes from Goetzmann,[89] who identifies the following benefits of an efficient market:

- Price in an efficient market will not stray too far from the true economic price if you allow arbitrageurs to exploit deviations. This will avoid sudden, nasty crashes in the future.

- An efficient market increases liquidity, because people believe that the price incorporates all public information, and are therefore less concerned about paying too high a price.
- Arbitrageurs provide liquidity to investors who need to sell or buy securities for reasons other than betting on changes in expected returns.

The answer to the second question is given in Box 5.4. It reproduces the six lessons of the efficient market hypothesis that Brearly and Myers[90] consider crucial for corporate financial management but are equally valid for individual investors and investment managers.

What if the market is informationally inefficient?[91] That poses a paradox, as Grossman[92] has argued. If stock prices reflect all the necessary information then there is no incentive to acquire information. Why would anyone either seek or process the information that the market could share, then, and if no one has sought to gather information then how can prices reflect that nonexistent information?

Box 5.4: Six Lessons of Market Efficiency

υ **Market has no memory.**
It is therefore futile to try capturing the market's recurrent cycles of upturns and downturns.

ϖ **Trust the market prices.**
Trying to outwit the market can be a risky proposition, therefore.

ω **The market's assessment of a firm's securities holds important clues about the firm's prospects.**

ξ **There are no financial illusions.**
Investors are only concerned with the firm's cash flows and the part of it that they are entitled to.

ψ **The do-it-yourself alternative.**
Whether it is about mergers, or debt-versus-equility financing, investors are unlikely to pay others for what they can replicate themselves.

ζ **Seen one stock, seen them all.**
Investors buy stocks for their risk-reward characteristics, not for any other attributes.

Obviously, there are two dimensions to the informational efficiency that need to be considered in formulating a suitable investment strategy, or sets of them. One is the market's informational efficiency; and the other is the informational efficiency of investors who may be either well informed, or moderately informed, or poorly informed. A good case can be then made for investment by indexing if the market is efficient. Since prices in such a market reflect all available information, their changes will occur randomly. Passively investing in an index or a mutual fund, such as a Vanguard 500 portfolio that tracks the performance of the S&P 500 index or a fund indexed to the total market, would then make eminent sense. One could have ridden with the NASDAQ 100, for instance, by buying into the "cube" (QQQ) as was mentioned in the previous chapter.

The virtues of passive investing do not stop at the threshold of an efficient market, however. Every year, no more than one-third of active investors perform either at or above the market's level, and two-thirds underperform. Therefore, as Steven Thorley[93] has argued, "if market prices are not efficient and investing is a matter of talent, then the investors in the underperforming majority will tend to be the same from year to year". If all the investors started indexing as a matter of routine, on the other hand, then a proportionately larger number of them will obviously start performing at the level of the market, so doubling the proportion of market performers and overperformers. This would certainly be an improvement, overall. As passive investing involves no information costs, gross and net returns are the same as the market's, no matter whether the market is informationally efficient or not.

This is shown in Exhibit 5.39 where we conceptually examine the investor's returns using two variables: market's informational efficiency and the investor's use of that information. By using the cost of information as zero, we have integrated our *information quotient* dimension, i.e., whether or not the investor uses the information, with the active versus passive style of investing. Here, a "poorly-informed" investor is merely one who is not extracting and incorporating information into her decision making.

How does active investing fare in this picture? The acquisition and use of information is not a costless exercise but the information above

Exhibit 5.39: Net returns on investment are defined by the market's informational efficiency and the investor's information quotient.[95]

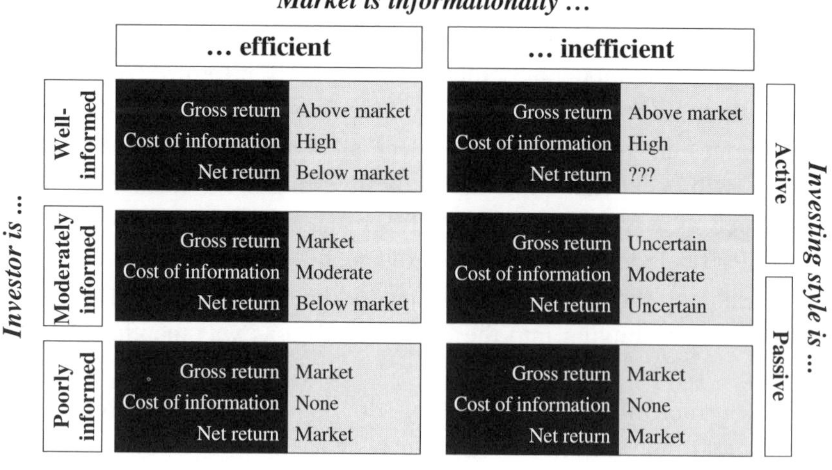

and beyond what is already impounded in the price is hard to find if the market is efficient. By definition, such a market also precludes the possibility of above-market returns. This leaves us with gross returns at the market rate or, taking the cost of information out, a sub-market rate for net returns. As Sharpe[94] has argued, in an efficient market "before costs, the return on the average actively managed dollar will equal the return on the average passively managed dollar" so that "after costs, the return on the average actively managed dollar will be less than the return on the average passively managed dollar".

On the other hand, if the market is inefficient, or weakly efficient at best, then looking at the prices and their history alone will do little good. Now there is a real possibility of identifying a Microsoft or an AOL in the offing. But this also means saying good bye to no-load mutual funds, selecting stocks from the universe of 7000 and odd offerings, and timing when to buy and when to sell. There is also room now for designing and using suitable hedging strategies. The potential for rich rewards is tremendous, therefore, but so is the risk of total loss. The gross returns are as likely to exceed the cost of information in the process, as to be dwarfed by it, leaving the net returns open to question.

Box 5.5: Beating the Market with the Dogs of Dow

Looking for ways to beat the market? Try the "Dogs of Dow",[§] or "Fabulous Five", its junior variant. These strategies combine the growth potential of undervalued stocks with the strength of the 30 of the best known and most successful companies in the world, the components of the Dow Jones Industrial Average. The chart and the graph below show their impressive 1971–2000 performance statistics.

Return statistics for 1971–2000	**Fabulous Five**	**Dogs of Dow**	**Dow**	**S&P 500**
Return	20.70%	17.87%	14.29%	14.32%
Volatility	18.69%	15.45%	16.23%	16.32%
Correlation*	0.62	0.77	0.95	1
Beta*	0.71	0.72	0.94	1
Sharpe ratio	0.75	0.73	0.47	0.47
Treynor ratio	0.20	0.16	0.08	0.08

*Measured against S&P 500

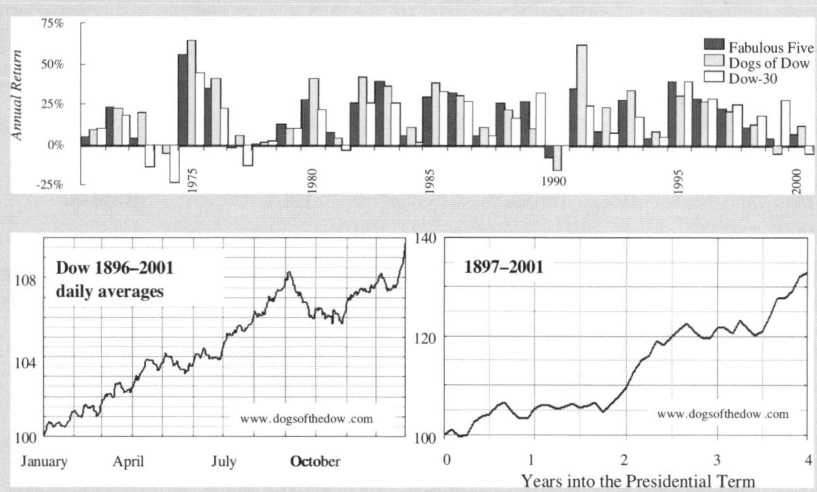

How to play these strategies? For the "Dogs of Dow", select 2nd through 11th of the least priced Dow stocks with the highest yields (2nd to 6th for the "Fabulous Five"), preferably at the bottom of the fall decline, and sell towards the top of the summer rally. For better results, we could try the latter 2–2½ years of the Presidential term,

[§]Michael O'Higgins & John Downes: *Beating the Dow* (Harper-Collins, 1991).

although the question whether it would work in this new millennium remains to be answered!

Based on these 1896–2001 averaged data, you could certainly improve your yield by selling Dow at the peak of the summer rally in late August–early September and buying back at the fall bottom in late October–early November. The cycle seems to have shifted about a month back in the 1990s, however.

Recent research,[96] as also the examples presented above, do point to significant gains from active investing, however. Indeed, there is no reason why an informationally efficient market should preclude the success of simplified strategies that can beat the market. Take the example of the "Dogs of Dow" strategy, or its cousin the "Fabulous Five", for instance. As shown in Box 5.5, their 1971–2000 performances have certainly surpassed that of the market by a significant margin. A normal distribution of returns provides room for above average as also sub-average performances, after all. It is not as if we are looking at a statistical distribution with a finite mean but no variance although such a distribution does exist, as an extreme of the Pareto–Levy family of distributions[97] to which a normal distribution model belongs. But we would then have to also contend with the other, scary, extreme with no mean and an infinite variance. Mercifully, though, such a situation does not really arise here, particularly as the market beating strategies like "Dogs of Dow" do not call for staying with the same stock year after year. Besides, these strategies may not have above market returns if we consider their risk-adjusted returns, transaction costs and tax implications[98] and also note that a company like Microsoft that paid no dividend until recently would have been an outcast from such lists during the period of its most spectacular growth!

5.5 The Insights from Insights — Concluding Remarks

This chapter has examined diversification across stocks, investment vehicles, sectors of the economy and the national markets. It reaffirmed the indispensability of diversification as a stabilization tool and a mechanism for dealing with the cyclicity and unpredictability of the market.

Basic to the three insights discussed here — portfolio diversification or the Markowitz model, the risk-return correlation models of asset prices, CAPM and APT, and the efficient market hypothesis based on a Gaussian distribution of returns — is the assumption that returns are symmetrically distributed. The simplicity and elegance of this assumption certainly makes generalizations possible, but extracts a major cost in that it ignores skewness and kurtosis in the data. While the latter is actually a desired property of the returns, as we have discussed in Chapter 3, the former is not. What would be the point in investing, for instance, if the returns were not biased towards the positive, or displayed skewness? But, if the returns were indeed skewed, then what accuracy can be placed on the assumption of a symmetric distribution of returns?

Since returns show lognormal distribution, Leland's[99] suggestion that we replace CAPM's portfolio beta ($\beta_p = \sigma_{pm}/\sigma_m^2$) by a modified risk measure B_p, offers an interesting solution to this problem. This risk measure B_p can be written as

$$B_p = \frac{[\text{covariance}\{\mu_p - (1+\mu_m)^{-b}\}]}{[\text{variance}\{\mu_m - (1+\mu_m)^{-b}\}]}, \tag{5.11a}$$

compared to the CAPM portfolio beta

$$\beta_p = \frac{[\text{covariance}\,\{\mu_p - (1+\mu_m)\}]}{[\text{variance}\,\{\mu_m - (1+\mu_m)\}]}. \tag{5.11b}$$

Here, μ_p and μ_m denote the mean returns on the portfolio and the market, respectively, coefficient $\beta = (\mu_m - r_f)/\sigma_m^2$ is the *market price* of risk, and σ_m^2 is the variance of market returns. As $B_p \to \beta_p$ to a first order approximation, when volatilities are small, neglecting the deviations from symmetric model affects long time horizon more adversely than short time horizons. The irony is that active management is better equipped to deal with such problems than passive management, although the latter may need it more than the former!

Clearly, this chapter's detailed look at the market efficiency debate, and the implications that it has on investors' choices and strategies, affirms that investment in research intended to beat the market has dubious results, but could not conclude that ignorance may prove to be a bliss.

Endnotes

[1] This is because a typical normal distribution is symmetric about the mean, with about one-half of the values on one side of the mean and the remaining on the other side. As was explained through Exhibit 3.34, the fit to this distribution can be gauged from low skewness and kurtosis values, although these higher moments (third and fourth, respectively, mean and standard deviation being the first and the second) themselves are not used for describing the normal distribution model.

[2] The CRSP (Center for Research on Security Prices, University of Chicago) database and its annual updates are available in the Yearbook "*Stocks, Bonds, Bills, and Inflation*" published by Ibbotson Associates, Inc., Chicago.

[3] Harry M. Markowitz: "Portfolio Selection", *Journal of Finance*, vol. 7, pp. 77–91, 1952. Also see Harry M. Markowitz: *Portfolio Selection: Efficient Diversification of Investments*, 2nd Edition (Blackwell Pub., 1991).

[4] Specifically, based on Equation (5.1b), $\sigma_p^2 \rightarrow (w_x \sigma_x + w_y \sigma_y)^2$ as $\rho_{xy} \rightarrow +1$, $\sigma_p^2 \rightarrow (w_x^2\sigma_x^2 + w_y^2\sigma_y^2)$ as $\rho_{xy} \rightarrow 0$ and $\sigma_p^2 \rightarrow (w_x\sigma_x - w_y\sigma_y)^2$ as $\rho_{xy} \rightarrow -1$.

[5] At $\rho_{xy} = -1$, $\sigma_p^2 = 0$, the condition we need for zero volatility, if $w_x\ \sigma_x = w_y\ \sigma_y = (1 - w_x)\ \sigma_y$ or $w_x = \sigma_y/(\sigma_x + \sigma_y)$.

[6] This is arbitrary as using Home Depot for stock *X* and Microsoft for stock *Y* would make no difference whatever.

[7] Eugene F. Fama: *Foundations of Finance* (Basic Books, New York, 1976).

[8] Meir Statman: "How Many Stocks Make a Diversified Portfolio?", *Journal of Financial and Quantitative Analysis*, vol. 22, pp. 353–364, 1987.

[9] B. Solnik: "Why Not Diversify Internationally Rather than Domestically", *Financial Analysts Journal*, July 1976.

[10] Stefano G. Athanasoulis and Robert J. Shiller: "The Significance of the Market Portfolio", *The Review of Financial Studies*, vol. 13, pp. 301–329, 2000.

[11] Bruno Solnik: *International Investments* (Addison-Wesley, 1996).

[12] Some of the other outstanding recent books on the complexities of international finance, investing and related issues are:

David Eitman, Arthur Stonehill and Michael Moffett: *Multinational Business Finance* (Addison-Wesley, 1998);

J. Orlin Grabbe: *International Financial Markets* (Prentice-Hall, 1996);

Paul Krugman and Maurice Obstfeld: *International Economics — Theory and Practice* (Addison-Wesley, 2000);

Maurice Obstfeld and Kenneth Rogoff: *Foundations of International Macroeconomics* (MIT Press, 1996);

Michael Porter: *The Competitive Advantage of Nations* (Free Press, 1998);

Jagdish Bhagwati: *A Stream of Windows: Unsettling Reflections on Trade, Immigration, and Democracy* (MIT Press, 1999).

13 Stefano Cavaglia, Christopher Brightman and Michael Aked: "The Increasing Importance of Industry Factors", *Financial Analysts Journal*, vol. 56, pp. 41–54, 2000.

14 Fabrice Vallat: "Investment Strategy by Business Sectors", *Global Investors Forum 2001*, Montreux, May 9–11, 2001.

15 John Y. Campbell, Martin Lettau, Burton G. Malkiel and Yexiao Xu: "Have Individual Stocks Become More Volatile? An Empirical Study of Idiosyncratic Risk", *Journal of Finance*, vol. 56, pp. 1–43, 2001.

16 François Longin and Bruno Solnik, "Extreme Correlation of International Equity Markets", *Journal of Finance*, vol. 56, pp. 649–676, 2000.

17 Bruno Solnik: *International Investments* (Addision-Wesley, Reading, MA, 1996).

18 G.V. Bierwag and M.A. Grove: "Indifference Curves in Asset Analysis", *Economic Journal*, pp. 337–373, June 1966. See also J. Hirshleifer: "The Investment Decision under Uncertainty: Choice Theoretic Approaches", *Quarterly Journal of Economics*, vol. 79, pp. 509–536, 1965 and M.J. Machina: "Choice under Uncertainty: Problems Solved and Unsolved", *Journal of Economic Perspectives*, pp. 121–154, Summer 1987.

19 See, for instance, Walter Nicholson: *Microeconomic Theory, Basic Principles and Extensions* (Dryden, 1992).

20 Irwin Friend and Marshall Blume: "The Demand for Risky Assets", *American Economic Review*, pp. 900–922, December 1975. See also R.A. Cohn, R.W.G. Lewellen, R.C. Lease and G.G. Schlarbaum: "Individual Investor Risk Aversion and Investor Portfolio Composition", *Journal of Finance*, May 1975.

21 Ana M. Aizorba, Arthur B. Kennickell and Kevin B. Moore: "Recent Changes in US Family Finances", *Federal Reserve Bulletin*, vol. 89, pp. 1–32, 2003.

22 Sarkis J. Khoury: *Investment Management, Theory and Application* (Macmillan, New York, 1983).

23 Markowitz portfolio optimization is basically a problem in quadratic programming. Basically, the idea here is to compute the proportion w_i of portfolio

to be invested in the *i*th asset so as to maximize the return $E(r_p)$ given by Equation (5.3a) and minimize the risk or variance σ_p^2 given by Equation (5.3b). Following are some of the websites that provide practical demonstrations of how it is computed:

www-fp.mcs.anl.gov/otc/Guide/CaseStudies/port
www.solver.com/invcenter.htm
www.princeton.edu/~rvdb/307/lectures/lec21.pdf

[24] William Sharpe: "Capital Asset Prices: A Theory of Market Equilibrium under Conditions of Risk", *Journal of Finance*, vol. 19, pp. 425–442, 1964.

[25] John Lintner: "The Valuation of Risky Assets and the Selection of Risky Investments in Stock Portfolios and Capital Budgets", *Review of Economics and Statistics*, vol. 47, pp. 13–37, 1965. See also John Lintner: "Security Prices, Risk and Maximal Gains from Diversification", *Journal of Finance*, vol. 20, pp. 587–615, 1965.

[26] The derivation of Equation (5.6a) is as follows. For the nomenclature used here, Equations (5.3a) and (5.3b) can be rewritten as

$$E(r_p) = w_m\, E(r_m) + w_r\, E(r_f),$$

and

$$\sigma_p^2 = w_m^2\, \sigma_m^2 + w_f^2\, \sigma_f^2 + 2 w_m w_f\, \rho_{mf}\, \sigma_m\, \sigma_f = w_m^2 \sigma_m^2,$$

assuming that $\sigma_f = 0$.

This yields $w_m = \sigma_p/\sigma_m$. As $(w_m + w_f) = 1$, this means that $w_f = 1 - (\sigma_p/\sigma_m)$, so that, writing risk-free rate $E(r_f) = r_f$, we have

$$E(r_p) = \left(\frac{\sigma_p}{\sigma_m}\right) E(r_m) + \left[1 - \frac{\sigma_p}{\sigma_m}\right] r_f\,.$$

Equation (5.6a) now follows from rearrangement of the terms in this equation.

[27] M.C. Jensen: "The Performance of Mutual Funds in the Period 1945–1964", *Journal of Finance*, vol. 23, pp. 389–416, 1968. Some of the recent studies include:

Darryll Hendricks, Jayendu Patel and Richard Zeckhauser: "Hot Hands in Mutual Funds: Short-Run Persistence of Relative Performance, 1974–1988", *Journal of Finance*, vol. 48, pp. 93–130, 1993.

Burton Malkiel: "Returns from Investing in Equity Mutual Funds 1971 to 1991", *Journal of Finance*, vol. 50, pp. 549–572, 1995.

Mark Grinblatt and Sheridan Titman: "The Persistence of Mutual Fund Performance", *Journal of Finance*, vol. 47, pp. 1977–1984, 1992.

Mark Carhart: "On Persistence in Mutual Fund Performance", *Journal of Finance*, vol. 52, pp. 57–82, 1997.

Russ Wermers: "Mutual Fund Performance — An Empirical Decomposition into Stock-Picking Talent, Style, Transaction Costs, and Expenses", *Journal of Finance*, vol. 55, pp. 1655–1703, 2000.

28 The slope of the efficient set is $\partial E(r_p)/\partial\sigma_p = [\partial E(r_p)/\partial w_i]/[\partial\sigma_p/\partial w_i]$.

Now, if w_i is the proportion of the market portfolio invested in security i, then

(a) $E(r_p) = w_i E(r_i) + (1 - w_i)E(r_m)$ and

(b) $\sigma_p^2 = w_i^2\sigma_i^2 + (1 - w_i)^2\sigma_m^2 + 2w_i(1 - w_i)\rho_{im}\sigma_i\sigma_m$.

We now differentiate $E(r_p)$ and σ_p^2 with respect to w_i and note that, in reality, $w_i = 0$ because our ith security could not exist outside the portfolio M if it is indeed the market portfolio. This gives

$$\frac{\partial E(r_p)}{\partial\sigma_p} = \left[\frac{\sigma_m}{(\sigma_m - \sigma_m^2)}\right] \times [E(r_i) - E(r_m)]\,,$$

which must be equated with the slope $[E(r_m) - r_f]/\sigma_m$ of Equation (5.6a) at M, i.e.,

$$\left[\frac{\sigma_m}{(\sigma_{im} - \sigma_m^2)}\right] \times [E(r_i) - E(r_m)] = \frac{[E(r_m) - r_f]}{\sigma_m}.$$

On cross-multiplying and rearranging the terms, this gives Equation (5.6b).

29 Eugene Fama and James MacBeth: "Risk, Return and Equilibrium: Empirical Tests", *Journal of Political Economy*, vol. 81, pp. 607–636, 1973.

30 Michael Jensen: "The Performance of Mutual Funds in the Period 1945–1965", *Journal of Finance*, vol. 35, pp. 389–416, 1968.

31 Fischer Black: "Beta and Return", *Journal of Portfolio Management*, vol. 20, pp. 8–18, 1993.

32 Fischer Black, Michael Jensen and Myron Scholes: "The Capital Asset Pricing Model: Some Empirical Tests" in *Studies in the Theory of Capital Markets* (Ed. Michael Jensen), pp. 79–121, 1972.

33 For a detailed discussion about the equity risk premium, see Bradford Cornell's recent book, *The Equity Risk Premium: The Long-Run Future of the Stock Market* (John Wiley, 1999).

[34] Fischer Black: "Beta and Return", *Journal of Portfolio Management*, vol. 20, pp. 8–18, 1993.

[35] Rolf W. Banz: "The Relationship Between Return and Market Value of Common Stocks", *Journal of Financial Economics*, vol. 9, pp. 3–18, 1981.

[36] G. Fama and K. French: "The Cross-Section of Expected Stock Returns", *Journal of Finance*, vol. 47, pp. 427–465, 1992.

[37] Richard Roll: "A Critique of the Asset Pricing Theory's Tests", *Journal of Financial Economics*, vol. 4, pp. 129–176, 1977. See also Richard Roll: "Ambiguity When Performance is Measured by the Securities Market Line", *Journal of Finance*, vol. 33, pp. 1051–1069, 1978.

[38] W.F. Sharpe and G.M. Cooper: "Risk-Return Classes of New York Stock Exchange Common Stocks, 1931–1967", *Financial Analysts Journal*, vol. 28, pp. 46–54, 1972.

[39] Campbell Harvey: "Time-Varying Conditional Covariances in Tests of Asset Pricing Models", *Journal of Financial Economics*, vol. 24, pp. 289–317, 1989. See also Wayne Ferson and Campbell Harvey: "The Variation of Economic Risk Premiums", *Journal of Political Economy*, vol. 99, pp. 385–415, 1991.

[40] Ravi Jagannathan and Zhenyu Wang: "The Conditional CAPM and the Cross-Section of Expected Returns", *Journal of Finance*, vol. 51, pp. 3–53, 1996.

[41] David Mayers: "Nonmarketable Assets and Capital Market Equilibrium Under Uncertainty" in *Studies in the Theory of Capital Markets* (Ed. Michael Jensen), pp. 223–248 (Praeger, 1972).

[42] D.T. Breeden, M.R. Gibbons and R.H. Litzenberger: "Empirical Tests of the Consumption-Oriented CAPM", *Journal of Finance*, vol. 44, pp. 231–262, 1989.

[43] Stephen Ross: "The Arbitrage Theory of Capital Asset Pricing", *Journal of Economic Theory*, vol. 13, pp. 341–360, 1976.

[44] Richard Roll and Stephen Ross: "An Empirical Investigation of the Arbitrage Pricing Theory", *Journal of Finance*, vol. 35, pp. 1073–1103, 1980. See also E. Burmeister, R. Roll and S. Ross: "A Practitioner's Guide to Arbitrage Pricing Theory" in *A Practitioner's Guide to Factor Models* (The Research Foundation of Chartered Financial Analysts, Charlottesville, VA, 1994).

[45] E. Elton, M. Gruber and J. Mei: "Cost of Capital Using Arbitrage Pricing Theory: A Case Study of Nine New York Utilities", *Financial Markets, Institutions, and Investments*, vol. 3, pp. 46–73, 1994.

[46] Richard Brealey and Stewart Myers: *Principles of Corporate Finance* (McGraw-Hill, Irwin, 2003).

[47] M.G. Kendall: "The Analysis of Economic Time-Series, Part I. Prices", *Journal of the Royal Statistical Society*, vol. 96, pp. 11–25, 1953.

[48] L. Bachelier: *Theorie de a Speculation* (Gauthier-Villars, Paris, 1900). It would be 64 years before this classic book first appeared in English translation, in *The Random Character of Stock Market Prices* (Ed. P.H. Cootner) pp. 17–78 (MIT Press, 1964).

[49] Lognormal distribution is the normal distribution of logarithmically transformed data, as in Exhibits 3.33 and 3.37 where we have fitted normal distribution curves to the geometric monthly and annual data, respectively. Interested readers may find the book by J. Aitchison and J.A.C. Brown (*The Lognormal Distribution*, Cambridge University Press, 1957) to give perhaps the most exhaustive exposition of this distribution.

[50] H. Working: "A Random Difference Series for Use in the Analysis of Time Series", *Journal of the American Statistical Association*, vol. 29, pp. 11–24, 1934.

[51] E.F. Fama: "Random Walks in Stock Market Prices", *Financial Analysts Journal*, p. 4, September–October 1965. See also E.F. Fama, L. Fisher, M. Jensen and R. Roll: "The Adjustment of Stock Prices to New Information", *International Economic Review*, vol. 10, pp. 1–21, 1969 and E.F. Fama: "Efficient Capital Markets: II", *Journal of Finance*, vol. 46, pp. 1575–1617, 1991.

[52] Eugene Fama: "Efficient Capital Markets: A Review of Theory and Empirical Work", *Journal of Finance*, vol. 25, pp. 383–417, 1970. See also R.A. Brearly and S.C. Myers: *Principles of Corporate Finance* (McGraw-Hill, Irwin, 2003).

[53] Fundamental analysis, discussed in the following section, seeks to identify undervalued and overvalued securities by analyzing such fundamental information as earnings, asset values, business prospects, and the like.

[54] As discussed in the chapter that follows, technical analysis charts the historic price path to identify the patterns that would indicate its future course, e.g., MACD (moving average convergence-divergence), momentum etc.

[55] With standard deviation σ_{daily} for the daily data as 0.01, the annualized (= 250 days) standard deviation $\sigma_{\text{annual}} = \sigma_{\text{daily}} \times \sqrt{250} = 0.01 \times \sqrt{250} = 0.1581$ or 15.81%.

[56] Paul Samuelson: "Proof that Properly Anticipated Prices Fluctuate Randomly", *Industrial Management Review*, vol. 6, pp. 41–49, 1965.

[57] T. Crack and O. Ledoit: "Robust Structure Without Predictibility: The "Compass Rose" Pattern of the Stock Market", *Journal of Finance*, vol. 51, pp. 751–762, 1996.

[58] G. Szpiro: "Tick Size, the Compass Rose and Market Nanostructure", *Journal of Banking and Finance*, vol. 22, pp. 1559–1569, 1998.

[59] A.S. Chen: "The Square Compass Rose: The Evidence from Taiwan", *Journal of Multinational Financial Management*, vol. 7, pp. 127–144, 1997.

[60] W. Kwämer and R. Runde: "Chaos and the Compass Rose", *Economic Letters*, vol. 54, pp. 113–118, 1997.

[61] H. Amilon and H.N.E. Byström: "The Compass Rose Pattern of the Stock Market: How Does it Affect Parameter Estimates, and Statistical Tests?", Working Paper 2000:18, Department of Economics, Lund University, Sweden.

[62] J. Orlin Grabbe's 7-part essay, "Chaos and Fractals in Financial Markets", available at his home page located at http://www.aci.net/kalliste/homepage.html, provides a fascinating introduction to this otherwise complex topic. See also:

Jess Benhabib: *Cycles and Chaos in Economic Equilibrium* (Princeton Univ. Press, 1992);

Paul A. Glendinning: *Stability, Instability and Chaos* (Cambridge Univ. Press, 1994);

David A. Hsieh: "Chaos and Nonlinear Dynamics: Applications to Financial Markets", *Journal of Finance*, vol. 46, pp. 1839–1877, 1991.

[63] William Feller: *An Introduction to Probability Theory and Its Applications*, Vol. I (John Wiley, New York, 1968).

[64] Benoit Mandelbrot: "The Variation of Certain Speculative Stock Prices", *Journal of Business*, vol. 36, pp. 394–419, 1963.

[65] E.F. Fama: "Mandelbrot and the Stable Paretian Hypothesis", *Journal of Business*, vol. 36, pp. 420–429, 1963.

[66] E.N. Lorenz: "Deterministic Non-Periodic Flow", *Journal of Atmospheric Sciences*, vol. 20, pp. 130–141, 1963.

[67] Abhay Abhyankar, Laurence Copeland and Woon Wong: "Uncovering Nonlinear Structure in Real-Time Stock Market Indexes: The S&P 500, The FAX, the Nikkei 225 and the FTSE 100", *Journal of Business and Economic Statistics*, vol. 15, pp. 1–14, 1997.

[68] M. Atchison and M. White: "Disappearing Evidence of Chaos in Security Returns: A Simulation", *Quarterly Journal of Business and Economics*, vol. 35, pp. 21–37, 1996.

[69] The fact that variances and betas have varied over time makes using the random walk model, which demands stationarity, a gross approximation. A better alternative is to use the less restrictive martingale model. In this case, $r_t + 1 = r_t + \varepsilon_t$, where ε_t is the martingale difference. See, for instance, Stephen LeRoy: "Efficient Capital Markets and Martingales", *Journal of Economic Literature*, vol. 27, pp. 1583–1621, 1989.

[70] Svetlozar Rachev and Stefan Mittnik: *Stable Paretian Models in Finance* (John Wiley, 2000).

[71] J.Y. Campbell, A.W. Lo and A.C. MacKinlay: *The Econometrics of Financial Markets* (Princeton University Press, Princeton, NJ, 1997).

[72] J.M. Poterba and L.H. Summers: "Mean Reversion in Stock Returns: Evidence and Implications", *Journal of Financial Economics*, vol. 22, pp. 27–59, 1988. See also E.F. Fama and K. French: "Permanent and Temporary Components of Stock Prices", *Journal of Political Economy*, vol. 96, pp. 246–273, 1988.

[73] Arthur Keown and John Pinkerton: "Merger Announcements and Insider Trading Activity", *Journal of Finance*, vol. 36, pp. 855–869, 1981.

[74] A. Agrawal, J.F. Jaffe and G. Mandelker: "The Post-Merger Performance of Acquiring Firms: A Re-Examination of an Anomaly", *Journal of Finance*, vol. 47, pp. 1605–1621, 1992.

[75] Indeed, had you put $10,000 in Berkshire Hathaway when Buffett bought control of it in 1965, you would have been worth $49.5 million in April 2001 whereas that investment in the S&P 500 would have brought your net worth to a measly $505,000 by this date!

[76] This has been one of the most researched areas in empirical finance and all the studies have generally come out with the same finding, a chronic under-performance of mutual funds as a group. One of the earliest studies was by M.C. Jensen: "The Performance of Mutual Funds in the Period 1945–1964", *Journal of Finance*, vol. 23, pp. 389–416, 1968. Subsequent studies include:

M. Grinblatt and S. Titman: "The Persistence of Mutual Fund Performance", *Journal of Finance*, vol. 47, pp. 1977–1984, 1992;

D. Hendricks, J. Patel and R. Zackhauser: "Hot Hands in Mutual Funds: Short-Run Persistence of Performance, 1974–1978", *Journal of Finance*, vol. 48, pp. 93–130, 1993;

E.J. Elton, M.J. Gruber, S. Das and M. Hlavka: "Efficiency and Costly Information: A Reinterpretation of Evidence from Managed Portfolios", *Review of Financial Studies*, vol. 6, pp. 1–21, 1993;

R.A. Ippolito: "Efficiency with Costly Information: A Study of Mutual Fund Performance, 1965–1984", *Quarterly Journal of Finance*, vol. 104, pp. 1–23, 1989;

J. Lakonishok, A. Shleifer and R. Vishny: "Contrarian Investment, Extrapolation and Risk", *Journal of Finance*, vol. 49, pp. 1541–1578, 1994;

C. Lee and S. Rahman: "Market Timing, Selectivity and Mutual Fund Performance: An Empirical Investigation", *Journal of Business*, vol. 63, pp. 261–278, 1990;

S. Brown and W. Goetzmann: "Performance Persistence", *Journal of Finance*, vol. 50, pp. 679–698, 1995.

[77] Ray Ball ("Anomalies in Relationships between Securities' Yields and Yield-Surrogates", *Journal of Financial Economics*, vol. 6, pp. 103–126, 1978) was the first to use this phrase to describe departures from the efficient market behavior.

[78] Richard Roll: "The International Crash of October 1987", in *Black Monday and the Future of Financial Markets* (Ed. R. Kamphis), p. 37 (Irwin, 1989).

[79] Kenneth French: "Crash-Testing the Efficient Market Hypothesis", *NBER Macroeconomics Annual*, No. 3, pp. 277–285, 1988.

[80] John Campbell and Robert Shiller: "Valuation Ratios and the Long Run Stock Market Outlook", *Journal of Portfolio Management*, vol. 24, pp. 11–26, 1998.

[81] Lawrence Summers: "Does the Stock Market Rationally Reflect Fundamental Values?", *Journal of Finance*, vol. 41, pp. 591–601, 1986.

[82] Bruno Solnik: *International Investments* (Addison-Wesley, 1996). See also Paul Krugman and Maurice Obstfeld: *International Economics: Theory and Policy* (Addison-Wesley, 2000).

[83] L.P. Hansen and R.J. Hodrick: "Forward Exchange Rates as Optimal Predictors of Future Spot Rates: An Econometric Analysis", *Journal of Political Economy*, vol. 88, pp. 829–853, 1980. See also C. Goodhard: "The Foreign Exchange Market: A Random Walk with a Dragging Anchor", *Economica*, vol. 55, pp. 437–460, 1988; K.A. Froot and J.A. Frankel: "Forward Discount Bias: Is It An Exchange Risk Premium?", *Quarterly Journal of Economics*, vol. 53, pp. 139–161, 1989; J.A. Frankel and M. Chinn: "Exchange Rate Expectations and the Risk Premium: Tests for a Cross-Section of 17 Currencies", *NBER Working Paper* No. 3806, 1991; C.M. Engel: "The Forward Discount Anomaly and the Risk Premium: A Survey of Recent Evidence", *NBER Working Paper* No. 5312, 1995.

[84] K.A. Froot and K. Rogoff: "Perspectives on PPP and Long-Run Real Exchange Rates" in *Handbook of International Economics* (Ed. G. Grossman and K. Rogoff), vol. III, pp. 1647–1688 (Elsevier, 1995).

[85] R.A. Meese and K. Rogoff: "Empirical Exchange Rate Models of the Seventies: Do They Fit Out of Sample?", *Journal of International Economics*, vol. 14, pp. 3–24, 1983; see also R. MacDonald and M.P. Taylor: "The Monetary Approach to the Exchange Rate: Rational Expectations, Long-Run Equilibrium and Forecasting", *IMF Staff Papers* 40, pp. 89–107, 1993.

[86] J. Bradford De Long, J.A. Shleifer, L. Summers and R. Waldman: "Noise Trader Risk in Financial Markets", *Journal of Political Economy*, vol. 98, pp. 703–738, 1990.

[87] This is the so called CNBC or CNN effect: Notice how the stocks mentioned favorably on CNBC or CNN spike temporarily, but then revert to their usual level soon after.

[88] Andrei Shleifer: *Inefficient Markets: An Introduction to Behavioral Finance* (Oxford Univ. Press, 2000). See also Gary Belsky and Thomas Gilovich: *Why Smart People Make Big Money Mistakes — And How to Correct Them, Lessons from the New Science of Behavioral Economics* (Simon and Schuster, 1999); Andrew Lo and Archie Mackinlay: *A Non-Random Walk Down Wall Street* (Princeton Univ. Press, 1999); Robert Haugen: *The New Finance: The Case Against Efficient Markets* (Prentice-Hall, 1999); Robert Haugen: *The Inefficient Stock Market: What Pays Off and Why* (Prentice-Hall, 1998); Richard Thaler: *Winner's Curse* (Princeton Univ. Press, 1994).

[89] William Goetzmann: *An Introduction to Investment Theory* (http://viking.som.yale.edu/will/finman540/classnotes/class8.html)

[90] Richard Brearly and Stewart Myers: *Principles of Corporate Finance* (McGraw-Hill, 1996)

[91] Andrei Shleifer: *Inefficient Markets — An Introduction to Behavioral Finance* (Oxford Univ. Press, 2000). See also Robert Haugen: *New Finance — The Case Against Efficient Markets* (Prentice-Hall, 1995).

[92] Sanford Grossman: "On the Efficiency of Competitive Stock Markets Where Traders Have Diverse Information", *Journal of Finance*, vol. 31, pp. 573–585, 1976. See also:

Sanford Grossman and Joseph Stiglitz: "On the Impossibility of Informationally Efficient Markets", *American Economic Review*, vol. 70, pp. 393–408, 1980.

George Yu: "Information Revelation and Aggregation in Financial Markets" in *Financial Markets, Institutions and Instruments*, pp. 29–54 (Blackwell, 1993).

[93] Steven Thorley: "The Inefficient Market Argument for Passive Investing" (http://marriotschool.byu.edu/emp/srt/passive.html)

[94] William Sharpe: "The Arithmetic of Active Management", *Financial Analysts Journal*, vol. 47, pp. 7–9, 1991.

[95] Adapted from Klaus Schredelseker: "On the Value of Information in Financial Markets — A Simulation Approach", privately released study.

[96] Russ Wermers: "Mutual Fund Performance — An Empirical Decomposition into Stock-Picking Talent, Style, Transaction Costs. and Expenses", *Journal of Finance*, vol. 55, pp. 1655–1703, 2000.

[97] Nassim Taleb: *Dynamic Hedging — Managing Vanilla and Exotic Options* (John Wiley, 1997). See also W. Feller: *An Introduction to Probability Theory and Its Application*, Vols. I and II (Wiley, 1971).

[98] Grant McQueen, Kay Shields and Steven Thorley: "Does the Dow-10 Investment Strategy Beat the Dow Statistically and Economically?", *Financial Analysts Journal*, vol. 53, pp. 66–72, July/August 1997. See also Grant McQueen and Steven Thorley: "Mining Fool's Gold", *Financial Analysts Journal*, vol. 55, pp. 61–72, March/April 1999.

[99] Hayne E. Leland: "Beyond Mean-Variance: Performance Measurement in a Nonsymmetric World", *Financial Analysts Journal*, vol. 55, pp. 27–36, January/February 1999.

Leland shows that this risk measure B_p is given by

$$B_p = \frac{\text{covariance}[\mu_p - (1+\mu_m)^{-b}]}{\text{variance}[\mu_m - (1+\mu_m)^{-b}]}$$
$$= [\exp(\mu_p - \mu_m + 5.0\sigma_p^2 - 0.5\sigma_m^2)]\,\frac{\exp(-b\sigma_m) - 1}{\exp(-b\sigma_m^2) - 1}\,.$$

Here, μ_p and μm denote the mean returns on the portfolio and the market, respectively, while σ_p and σ_m denote the corresponding variances and σ_{pm} the covariance of portfolio and market index returns, and the coefficient b is the market price of risk that amounts, in continuous time, to $b = (\mu_m - r_f)/\sigma_m^2$. As the CAPM beta, β_p, is given by

$$\beta_p = [\exp(\mu_p - \mu_m + 0.5\sigma_p^2 - 0.5\sigma_m^2)\,\frac{\exp(\sigma_{pm}) - 1}{\exp(\sigma_m^2) - 1}\,,$$

the first-order Taylor series expansion $[\exp(x) = 1 + x]$ yields

$$\frac{B_p}{\beta_p} = \frac{[\exp(-b\sigma_{pm}) - 1]/[\exp(\sigma_{pm}) - 1]}{[\exp(-b\sigma_m^2) - 1]/[\exp(\sigma_m^2) - 1]} = \frac{(-b\sigma_{pm})\sigma_m^2}{(-b\sigma_m^2)\sigma_{pm}} \approx 1\,.$$

Thus, for small volatilities or short time horizons, $B_p \rightarrow \beta_p$, so that CAPM's mismatches have no adverse effects on the portfolio, as in the case of portfolio managers, but the differences between theory and reality can be substantial when the time horizon is long, as in the case of the long-term investors!

Chapter 6

EQUITY VALUATION

6.1 Introduction

This chapter examines the theory and the performance of models that can help us value the equities, the firms and the market at large. The chapter is divided into four sections.

The first section deals with valuation by the market multiples and finance ratios and examines how price-to-earnings (P/E), price-to-book value (P/B), price-to-sales revenues (P/S) and price-to-cash flow (P/CF) ratios can help us in valuing equity. This is followed, in the second section, by an examination of valuation by cash flow analysis. We look at both, discounted cash flow as well as free cash flow, methods and, for the latter, the practicalities of how they can be used for valuing equities as well as firms. The third section deals with such other valuation strategies as the economic-value-added (EVA) concept and valuation by call options that have been found to be particularly applicable to the nascent firms that, lacking any established positive cash flows and earnings as yet, defy valuation by the more traditional methods.

The fourth and final section puts these ideas together and seeks to extend them to the valuation of the market as a whole and then discusses how the valuation of equity can relate to its price performance in the market.

6.2 Valuation by Multiples and Ratios

The Valuation Models

Equity valuation has indeed been the undercurrent of our discussions so far. In an efficient market, we would expect the price of an undervalued security to rise to the level commensurate with its true economic value. Likewise, when we use the CAPM to identify an underperforming security or portfolio as one with a risk premium below the market risk premium when adjusted for risk, what we basically mean is that its market price is above its true economic value.

Take, for instance, the CAPM graph for the Dow companies shown in Exhibit 5.22. Of these companies, the ones whose risk-adjusted returns plot above the CAPM's security market line have clearly performed better than the market, while those that plot on this line have performed as

Exhibit 6.1: Using CAPM for relative valuation of the Dow companies.

	Annual Return*	
	Actual ($\bar{r}$)	Expected $E(r)$
Overperformer [$\bar{r} > E(r)$]		
American Express (AXP)	26.99%	25.15%
Citigroup (C)	40.95%	28.46%
Exxon Mobil (XOM)	25.30%	13.84%
General Electric (GE)	32.64%	26.51%
Home Depot (HD)	33.74%	23.78%
Intel (INTC)	49.56%	34.12%
Internat. Bus Machices (IBM)	35.60%	28.27%
Johnson & Johnson (JNJ)	23.95%	15.40%
McDonalds (MCD)	18.46%	16.57%
Merck (MRK)	29.77%	13.84%
Minn. Mining & Manuf. (MMM)	16.90%	12.86%
Microsoft (MSFT)	50.17%	38.60%
Proctor & Gamble (PG)	23.25%	10.52%
SBC Communications (SBC)	17.69%	15.40%
Wall Mart (WMT)	32.91%	20.86%

	Annual Return*	
	Actual ($\bar{r}$)	Expected $E(r)$
Average performer [$\bar{r} \approx E(r)$]		
Alcoa (AA)	24.55%	26.51%
Hewlett-Packard (HWP)	28.86%	29.63%
United Techno. (UTX)	25.63%	25.93%
Underperformer [$\bar{r} < E(r)$]		
Boeing (BA)	12.75%	14.03%
Caterpillar (CAT)	13.70%	18.13%
Coca Cola (KO)	16.81%	17.93%
Eastman Kodak (EK)	9.40%	12.47%
General Motors (GM)	20.47%	23.39%
Honeywell (HON)	20.42%	23.59%
J.P. Morgan (JPM)	29.58%	34.51%
Phillip Morris (MO)	6.00%	8.38%
Walt Disney (DIS)	16.96%	20.08%

*Actual returns are annualized from 5-year (January 1995–December 1999) monthly returns, expected returns are from CAPM.

well as the market and the remaining have performed poorly. Exhibit 6.1 compares the actual returns on these stocks with the returns expected of them based on the CAPM. We could perhaps identify these overperformers as undervalued, the fairperformers as fairly valued and the underperformers as overvalued. But then, while consistent with the efficient market hypothesis, that returns be received in proportion to the risks taken, it hardly tells us what the exact price should be. Nor does it tell us whether these underperformers will continue to remain so. They may well become overperformers, instead, in order to accomplish mean reversion over the long term.

The valuation of a common stock[1] requires consideration, much like any capital asset, of the net benefits that can be derived from owning it. Unfortunately, the full net benefits and their duration are not specified at the time of purchase. Neither do the corporations have to pay dividends on common stocks, nor do the common stocks always appreciate in price, despite all the wishes and prayers of the holders. The task of valuing a stock or the underlying business thus entails gauging the prospective benefits of ownership that the investor is likely to realize in the future. As Exhibit 6.2 shows, there are several ways to accomplish this task.[2]

Exhibit 6.2: The equity valuation models.

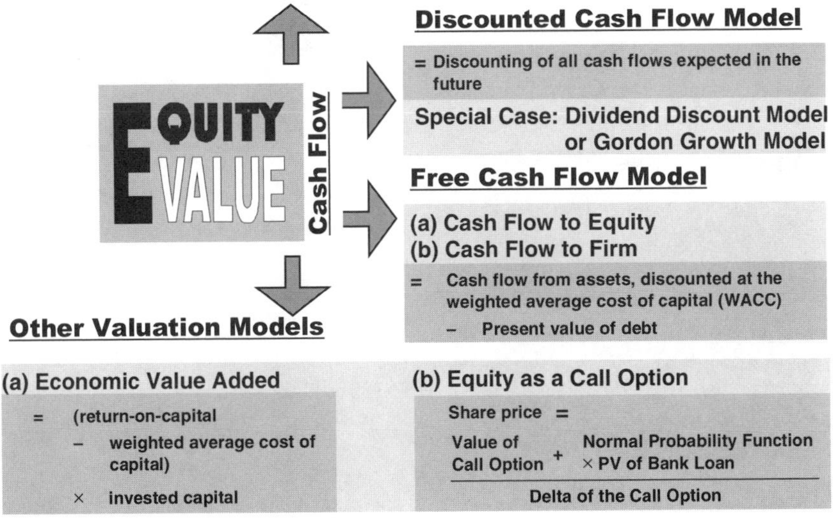

EQUITY VALUE

Cash Flow

Discounted Cash Flow Model

= Discounting of all cash flows expected in the future

Special Case: Dividend Discount Model or Gordon Growth Model

Free Cash Flow Model

(a) Cash Flow to Equity
(b) Cash Flow to Firm

= Cash flow from assets, discounted at the weighted average cost of capital (WACC)
− Present value of debt

Other Valuation Models

(a) Economic Value Added

= (return-on-capital
− weighted average cost of capital)
× invested capital

(b) Equity as a Call Option

Share price =

$$\frac{\text{Value of Call Option} + \text{Normal Probability Function} \times \text{PV of Bank Loan}}{\text{Delta of the Call Option}}$$

Valuation by the Market Multiples

Perhaps the simplest and the best known of these is the use of such market multiples as price-to-earnings (P/E), price-to-book value (P/B), price-to-sales revenues (P/S) and price-to-cash flow (P/CF) ratios. Recall the use of P/E ratio in a series of commercials for the discount brokerage giant, Charles Schwab, for instance (Box 6.1).

The idea here is that a company would average the same price-to-earnings and the like valuation ratios[3] as the peers in its industry. Let E_X denote the earnings, per share, of a company X, the price P_X of whose shares we wish to estimate and $(\mathrm{P/E})_{\mathrm{average}}$ the average price-to-earnings ratio of the industry that this company belongs to. In that case,

$$P_X = E_X \times (\mathrm{P/E})_{\mathrm{average}}, \qquad (6.1)$$

i.e., we have implicitly assumed that $(P_X/E_X) = (\mathrm{P/E})_{\mathrm{average}}$.

Box 6.1: The Duchess and the P/E ratio

A recent commercial for Charles Schwab shows a little girl listening to Sarah Ferguson, the Duchess of York. She will grow up into a beautiful young lady, predicts the Duchess, and will be swept off her feet by a prince on a white stallion, whisked away to a beautiful

castle, and given everything her heart desires, "for ever and ever".

"Of course, if it doesn't work out, you'll need to understand the dfference between a P/E ratio and a dividend yield, a growth versus value strategy...", cautions the Duchess.

P/E ratio is the most commonly understood and popularly cited measure of valuation.

The problem, then, is to determine what average value to use for the selected multiple and how. Two alternatives are available for this purpose:

- Identify the multiple and use as its average estimate the sector or industry average that can be freely obtained from such popular sites as yahoo.com, multexinvestor.com, quicken.com, morningstar.com, cnbc.com, and the like.
- Identify the multiple and the factors that govern its variation, quantitatively relate the multiple and these governing factors, and then use this relationship and the values of these factors for the equity under consideration to derive the average value of the multiple that would be relevant to that equity's valuation.

By way of illustration,[4] let us consider the examples of Microsoft (MSFT), United Technologies (UTX) and Eastman Kodak (EK), each representing one of the three performance-based groups in Exhibit 6.1. The details of estimating the share prices for these three companies are summarized in Exhibit 6.3. Here, panel (a) summarizes the relevant per share data for these three companies, panel (b) the corresponding valuation ratios, and panel (c) the share prices computed using these data. For instance, panel (a) shows that Microsoft Corporation's past twelve months' earnings are $1.81 per share, and panel (b) shows the average P/E ratio of 43.20 for its industry in this period. Multiplying the two numbers then gives the estimate of $78.19 as Microsoft's share price. This is given in panel (c).

Two advantages of using the ratios, instead of using CAPM to separate the overperformers from the underperformers and hoping that either the former will continue the same way or the latter will reverse their past pattern, are immediately obvious in panel (c), Exhibit 6.3. One, we now have some numbers for the prices, which can help us identify the underpriced stocks that we may wish to acquire. For instance, the results in Exhibit 6.3 show that, on average, Eastman Kodak is correctly priced whereas Microsoft is slightly underpriced and United Technologies is way underpriced. Two, instead of CAPM's bland look at an equity's price performance, we have now looked at factors like earnings, book value, sale revenues and cash flow that actually facilitate that performance. In the process, we have also incorporated the fact that

Exhibit 6.3: An example of valuation by the market multiples (data as of July 2001).

(a) Some basic, per share data for the three companies.

	Microsoft	United Technologies	Eastman Kodak
Earnings (ttm)	$1.81	$3.68	$4.16
Book value (mrq)	$9.01	$15.74	$11.47
Sales revenues (ttm)	$4.43	$52.96	$46.07
Cash flow (ttm)	$1.95	$5.53	$7.21
Recent share price	$68.80	$73.50	$48.85

ttm: trailing twelve months
mrq: most recent quarter

(b) Valuation ratios for the three companies in panel (a) and the corresponding ratios for the respective industries and the whole market (S&P 500).

Ratio	Microsoft		United Technologies		Eastman Kodak		S&P 500
	Company	Industry	Company	Industry	Company	Industry	
price-to-earnings	37.99	43.2	19.97	34.7	11.75	11.7	28.18
price-to-book	7.64	8.76	4.67	8.47	4.26	4.14	6.09
price-to-sales	15.52	12	1.39	3.33	1.06	1.03	4.02
price-to-cash flow	35.28	36.72	13.29	21.82	6.77	6.67	20.91

(c) Share prices computed using the market multiples in panel (b) and Equation (6.1), e.g., for Microsoft, $P = \$1.81 \times 43.20 = \$78.19$ from company earnings and the industry P/E.

	Microsoft	United Technologies	Eastman Kodak
Estimated from the			
price-to-earnings ratio	$78.19	$127.70	$48.67
price-to-book value ratio	$78.93	$133.18	$47.69
price-to-sales ratio	$53.16	$176.36	$47.45
price-to-cash flow ratio	$71.60	$120.66	$48.09

all the industry sectors of the market do not grow at the same rate over time. Eastman Kodak no longer appears as unattractive a "buy" as it did in Exhibit 6.1, nor does Microsoft appear as attractive a "buy" now as the data in that exhibit made it seem.

If we divide a firm's price-to-book value (P/B) ratio by the corresponding price-to-earnings (P/E) ratio, then we get another popular valuation tool, the firm's ROE (return-on-equity), i.e.,

$$\begin{aligned}\frac{\text{price-to-book value (P/B) ratio}}{\text{price-to-earnings (P/E) ratio}} &= \frac{\text{price/book value per share}}{\text{price/earnings per share}}\\ &= \frac{\text{earnings per share}}{\text{book value per share}}\\ &= \frac{\text{earnings available for common stock}}{\text{total equity}}.\end{aligned} \tag{6.2a}$$

Therefore,

$$\frac{\text{price-to-book value (P/B) ratio}}{\text{price-to-earnings (P/E) ratio}} = \text{Return-to-equity (ROE)}.$$

Though strictly an accounting number that basically measures a firm's profitability or managerial effectiveness, investors often use ROE as an equity selection criterion. The problem is that high rates of growth in earnings often translate into faster appreciation in share prices, so raising the ROE. For an investor buying the share of a high ROE firm, then, the question is whether a good firm invariably makes an equally good stock and, more often than not, the answer is in the negative. What exacerbates this problem is the fact that ROE rises with the debt-equity ratio so long as returns on the firm's investments exceed the interest on its debt. This is because,

$$\begin{aligned}\text{return-on-equity (ROE)} &= \frac{\text{earnings available for common stock}}{\text{total equity}}\\ &= \frac{\text{net income}}{\text{total assets}} \times \frac{\text{total assets}}{\text{total equity}}\\ &= \begin{matrix}\text{return-on-}\\ \text{assets (ROA)}\end{matrix} \times \begin{matrix}\text{equity}\\ \text{multiplier}\end{matrix},\end{aligned} \tag{6.2b}$$

where

$$\text{equity multiplier} = \frac{\text{total equity} + \text{total liability}}{\text{total equity}}$$
$$= 1 + \frac{\text{total debt} + \text{other liabilities}}{\text{total equity}}$$
$$= 1 + \text{debt ratio} + \frac{\text{other liabilities}}{\text{total equity}}.$$

Obviously, if debt is large, then the larger the debt the greater the liability-equity ratio will be, and so will the equity multiplier and the ROE, even if the return-on-assets (ROA) remains the same. Thus, as can be seen in Exhibit 6.4 where we compare these statistics for the three companies examined in Exhibit 6.3, the greater a firm's debt-to-equity ratio the greater the equity multiplier by which its ROE rises over the ROA.[5]

The alternate, more quantitative, approach to equity valuation by the market multiples requires:

- Identifying the principal factors or primary variables that govern the changes in a multiple.
- Establishing their precise relationship, say, by using multiple regression analysis.
- Estimating what the value of the multiple should be, based on this relationship, for the current values of these principal factors or primary variables.

Exhibit 6.4: Profitability and liquidity ratios for the companies compared in Exhibit 6.3.

	Microsoft		United Tech.		Eastman Kodak		S&P 500
	Company	Industry	Company	Industry	Company	Industry	
return-on-assets‡	24.86	15.13	6.38	4.49	7.28	7.1	8.33
return-on-equity‡	35.09	27.82	22.27	25.22	26.62	25.88	22.16
debt-equity ratio§	0.00	0.08	0.60	3.04	1.18	1.18	0.99

‡5-year average

§the most recent quarter

- Examining how this value compares with the current value of that multiple.

Take Damodaran's[6] approach to P/E estimation, for instance. It is based on the premise that the P/E ratio is affected most by the expected growth in earnings, the payout ratio and the CAPM-based beta of an equity and therefore uses these measures as independent variables, and P/E ratio as the dependent variable. In July 2001, his website[7] gave the following multiple regression equation for the dependence of P/E ratio on estimated corporate earnings growth over the next five years, current payout ratio, and beta for the past five years:

$$(\mathrm{P/E})_{\text{regression}} = 145.32 \times \begin{bmatrix} \text{expected earnings growth} \\ \text{for the next 5 years} \end{bmatrix} + 3.2 \times \begin{bmatrix} \text{payout ratio} \\ \text{(most recent year)} \end{bmatrix} + 2.37 \times \text{beta}, \qquad (6.3a)$$

when the regression line is forced through the origin, i.e., intercept = 0. This is because a P/E ratio can hardly exist if the other fundamentals vanish.

We can now use the following version of Equation (6.1) for the valuation of our stock X:

$$P_X = E_X \times (\mathrm{P/E})_{\text{regression}}. \qquad (6.3b)$$

Exhibit 6.5 illustrates the use of this strategy to value the three stocks — Microsoft, United Technologies and Eastman Kodak — that we examined earlier in this section. Except for United Technologies, these estimates are of about the same order as in Exhibit 6.3. Even for United Technologies, an earnings growth at the sector average rate of 20% will raise the estimate of its $(\mathrm{P/E})_{\text{regression}}$ to 32.48, and its price to \$119.54, or about the same as in Exhibit 6.3. This is because, as can be seen in Equation (6.3a), the estimation of $(\mathrm{P/E})_{\text{regression}}$ is far more sensitive to the rate of expected growth in earnings than to the other two independent variables here.

Damodaran also reports the results of similar multiple regression analyses for the other equity multiples used in Exhibit 6.3. The data for

Exhibit 6.5: Equity valuation by $(P/E)_{regression}$ method.

	Microsoft	United Technologies		Eastman Kodak
Expected earnings growth*	25%	15%	20%	6%
Payout ratio	0%	21.70%	21.70%	42.12%
Beta	1.8	1.15	1.15	0.46
$(P/E)_{regression}$ based on Equation (6.3a)	40.6	25.22	32.48	11.16
Earnings (annual, last twelve months)	$1.81	$3.68	$3.68	$4.16
Price, estimated from Equation (6.3b)	$73.48	$92.80	$111.54	$46.41

*The values used here are the analysts' estimates.

two of them are reproduced below, mainly in order to complete the picture and to show that an analytically rigorous and data-adaptive alternative to our simplified use of market multiples does indeed exist.

$$(P/B)_{regression} = 4.97 \times \begin{bmatrix} \text{return on} \\ \text{equity} \end{bmatrix} - 0.05 \times \begin{bmatrix} \text{payout} \\ \text{ratio} \end{bmatrix} + 0.85 \times \text{beta} + 8.97 \times \begin{bmatrix} \text{expected growth} \\ \text{in earnings} \end{bmatrix}, \qquad (6.3c)$$

and

$$(P/S)_{regression} = 16.17 \times \text{margin} - 0.59 \times \begin{bmatrix} \text{payout} \\ \text{ratio} \end{bmatrix} - 0.44 \times \text{beta} + 7.60 \times \begin{bmatrix} \text{expected growth} \\ \text{in earnings} \end{bmatrix}. \qquad (6.3d)$$

Another aspect of the predictive power of financial ratio analysis was demonstrated in William Beaver's pioneering comparison[8] of selected financial ratios of 79 firms that failed with an equal number of firms that remained solvent. As can be seen from Exhibit 6.6, which summarizes the main results of this study, Beaver found that the businesses that failed carried an unmanageable debt burden, relative to cash flow and assets, and lower returns on sales and assets. The results of this study, replicated in several similar studies since it was first reported thirty-five years ago,

Exhibit 6.6: Beaver's classic study identified large debt, in terms of cash flow and assets, and lower returns on sales and assets as the guaranteed recipes for business failure.

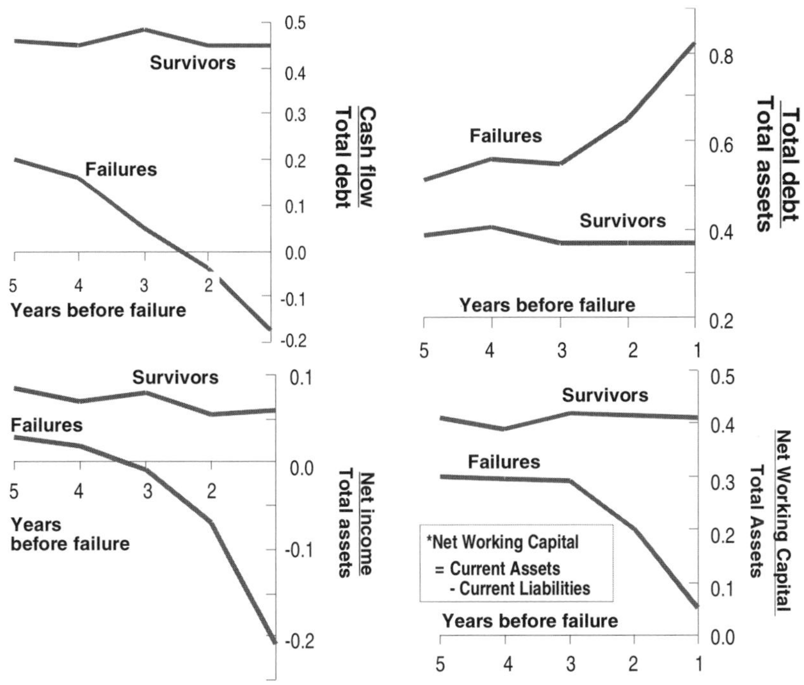

brought out the following signs of failing businesses at least three years before they actually failed:

- Dwindling to negative cash flow and net income, relative to total debt.
- Dwindling net working capital, relative to total assets.
- Total debt approaching total assets.

Interestingly, these are precisely the reasons why the once booming dot.coms of the late 1990s would disappear almost 35 years to the date. Some lessons are clearly never learned, despite the considerable advances that have been made since Beaver's study, particularly in using the quantitative models to predict business failures by combining several financial ratios. For instance, take the pioneering quantitative model of Altman,[9] and its modification by Dambolena and Khoury[10] who added to

Altman's multiple discriminant analysis model the volatility of ratios prior to business failure. By way of illustration, the Dambolena–Khoury model computes the z-score of a firm, a measure of its survival prospects, as

$$\begin{aligned} z = 1.189 - 8.436 \times \frac{\text{net profit}}{\text{sales}} + 18.850 \times \frac{\text{net profit}}{\text{total assets}} \\ + 1.955 \times \frac{\text{fixed assets}}{\text{net worth}} + 0.739 \times \frac{\text{funded debt}}{\text{net working capital}} \\ - 4.921 \times \frac{\text{total debt}}{\text{total assets}} - 1.588 \times \frac{\text{inventory standard deviation}}{\text{net working capital}} \\ - 6.330 \times \frac{\text{fixed assets' standard deviation}}{\text{net worth}}. \end{aligned} \tag{6.4}$$

The idea here is that, as Altman had initially pointed out, a low value of z is deleterious to a firm's health. Specifically, in Altman's initial model,

- If $z < 1.8$, the firm will fail.
- If $1.8 < z < 3$, the firm will not likely fail.
- If $z > 3$, the firm will not fail.

"... and that's why you need to raise my allowance!"
SPENDING = GROWTH
GROWTH = JOBS
JOBS = SECURITY
SECURITY = HAPPINESS
GLASBERGEN

Integrating and analyzing the financial ratios has been a much studied area of firm valuation, of course, particularly because investment firms need to constantly monitor if the businesses that they have invested in are likely to survive. Recent corporate problems such as those related to the bankruptcies of Enron and WorldCom have emphasized the importance of this analysis further. Our above discussion only provides a sample of this rather complex area, therefore, and seeks mainly to help the investors understand how diverse factors can be incorporated into making intelligent choices of stocks for their portfolios. Interested readers may wish to browse a book like that by Foster[11] for a detailed exploration of this issue.

6.3 Valuation by Cash Flow Analysis

Compared to the market multiples and financial ratios, though, cash flow analyses have offered, over time, far more powerful and versatile tools for equity valuation. In the ultimate analysis, the survival of a firm depends on the cash flow that it can continue to generate, after all. Likewise, as for the investor, the value that the equity of a firm carries depends primarily on the cash flow that the assets promise to generate. Two alternatives are available here: (a) discounted cash flow models and (b) free cash flow models.

The Discounted Cash Flow Model

This method is typically used for valuing the companies that pay dividends. In general, the holder of a common stock expects to receive net benefits as dividends and/or capital gains. Although neither of these can be predictable with certainty, least of all the latter, investors do form reasonable expectations that can be quantified. Simply stated, the present value of these expected benefits is a stock's intrinsic value. Given efficient equity markets, this intrinsic value should equal the stock's market price. We can therefore write Equation (3.4) as

$$P_0 = \frac{[D_1 + E(P_1)]}{(1 + k_e)}, \tag{6.5a}$$

where P_0 is stock's price at time = 0, $E(P_1)$ the expected price after one period, D_1 is the dividend payment in this period and k_e is the cost of equity to the firm or the required rate of return on the stock that prevents its market value from falling. Suppose the stock is to be held for n number of periods. If the cost of equity per period, k_e, remains constant, then we have

$$P_0 = \sum_{t=1}^{n} \frac{D_t}{(1+k_e)^t} + \frac{E(P_n)}{(1+k_e)^n} \approx \sum_{t=1}^{\infty} \frac{D_t}{(1+k_e)^t}, \tag{6.5b}$$

when $n \rightarrow \infty$, i.e., the stock is held over the expected infinite length of a corporation's life.

Thus, in this discounted cash flow (DCF) formula for the present value of a stock, the price in any period is obtained by discounting to that period dividends and capital gains received in the subsequent period. Notice how the term containing $E(P_n)$ in Equation (6.5b) vanishes for an infinitely long time horizon because $(1 + k_e)^n \rightarrow \infty$ and $1/(1 + k_e)^n \rightarrow 0$ as $n \rightarrow \infty$. In effect, therefore, we are pricing the stock in Equation (6.5b) solely by discounting the future dividend stream to its present value. This method of pricing a common stock is therefore known as the dividend discount model.

Predicting the future values of D_t is not an easy task, however, and verges on the impossibility. Some simplifications can be sought, nonetheless. At its simplest, for instance, let us assume that a constant dividend is being paid out every year, starting next year, i.e., $D_t = D_1$. In that case,

$$P_0 = \frac{D_1}{k_e}, \tag{6.5c}$$

because this is the case of a simple perpetuity.[12]

Suppose D_t is not a fixed amount but grows, instead, at the constant rate g every year, i.e.,

$D_{t+1} = (1 + g) \times D_t$,
$D_{t+2} = (1 + g) \times D_{t+1} = (1 + g)^2 \times D_t$ and so on.

Equation (6.5c) then modifies[13] to

$$P_0 = \frac{D}{(k_e - g)}. \tag{6.5d}$$

Recall that we have earlier used this model in Box 3.1, where an alternative method of deriving this equation was presented.

This constant growth dividend discount model is the well-known Gordon growth model, having been popularized by Myron Gordon[14] in the late 1950s. Although widely used in practice, using Equation (6.5d) is hardly as problem-free as its simple appearance suggests, as we saw in Box 5.3. A more complete form of it is derived in Box 6.2. This still shows valuation to be a speculative exercise, however, because we now need to fix the holding period for the stock that we seek to value!

Box 6.2: The Correct Form of Gordon Growth Equation

Suppose that, at some starting point $t = 0$, dividend $D = D_0$ and price $P = P_0$, and that the firm sets its dividend policy as payout ratio $= p = D_0/P_0$. Let us also suppose that these dividends are to grow at a steady rate of g per period into the foreseeable future, i.e.,

$$D = D_0 \exp(g_t) = pP_0 \exp(g_t).$$

Now, as for the firm's price P, we can write its rate of change per period as

$$\begin{aligned}\frac{dP}{dt} &= rP - D = rP - D_0 \exp(gt) \\ &= rP - pP_0 \exp(gt),\end{aligned}$$

where r is the return per period, or the market capitalization rate.

Treating this equation as a linear first order differential equation in P gives its solution as

$$P = \frac{P_0}{r - g}\left[(r - g - p)\exp(rt) + p\exp(gt)\right].$$

This should be the correct expression for the dividend discount model for constant payout ratio, dividend growth and capitalization rate.

Several reasons add to the uncertainties in this valuation approach. First of all, for instance, using Equation (6.5d) makes sense only so long as $k_e > g$ because $(k_e - g) \to 0$ as g approaches k_e, driving P_0 to infinity. Likewise, Equation (6.5d) is of little use for valuing a firm that does not pay dividends unless dividend is a proxy for earnings. How about the relatively mature firms that have slow growth rates and pay dividends regularly (i.e., the so-called "income" stocks)? Uncertainties abound there as well, thanks to the simple fact that, however well informed, the data on future rates of dividends (D_t), returns (k_e) or the cost of equity, and growth (g) that we need here are largely matters of speculation. Above all, as we saw in Box 5.3, Equation (6.5d) fails when $(k_e - g)$ is not a constant. Likewise, its more complete version in Box 6.2 fails when we note that it was derived by assuming that the payout ratio is constant. This is not the case, in reality, as has been discussed earlier.

Despite these limitations, this simple method of valuation often works reasonably well for relatively mature companies, as the following example of United Technologies Corporation (NYSE: UTX) demonstrates. One of the 30 companies that comprise the "Blue Chip" Dow Jones Industrial index, UTX is a conglomerate comprising four principal operating segments — Otis (elevators and escalators), Carrier (heating, ventilating and air conditioning systems), Pratt and Whitney (aircraft engines and space propulsion) and Flight Systems (helicopters, propeller and electrical systems). As we saw earlier, its risk adjusted return plots exactly on the security market line. With the β value of 1.15, the company has consistently given investors returns superior to the market. Not surprisingly, therefore, a $10,000 investment in UTX in January, 1970, would be worth $1.32 million in May, 2001, assuming an automatic reinvestment of dividends, compared to $460,000 in the S&P 500 total return index (Exhibit 6.7).

Now, we need three estimates in order to use Equation (6.5d) to price UTX: its dividend next year (D_1), cost of equity (k_e) and the growth rate (g). Analysts[15] expected a dividend of $0.90 for 2001, based on the company's estimated EPS (earnings per share) value of $4.07 that year, and assuming that its year 2000 payout ratio[16] of 21.70% were to

Exhibit 6.7: \$10,000 invested in the United Technologies (UTX) in January 1970 would have grown to \$1.32 billion by the end of May 2001, compared to \$460,000 in the case of S&P 500 total return index.

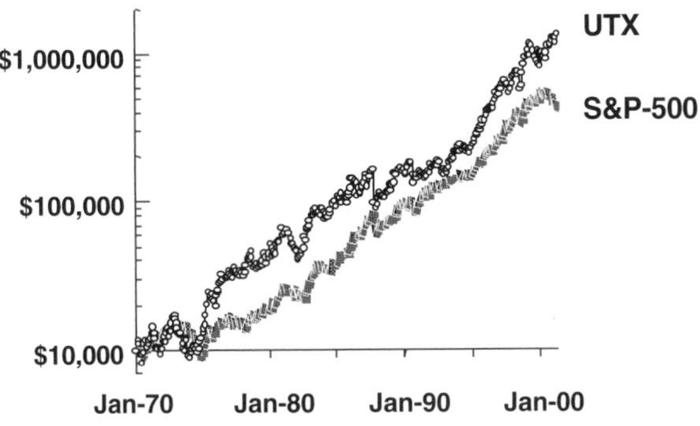

continue. This was a reasonable estimate because UTX is a financially healthy company with a total debt/equity ratio (= 0.60) that was far less than the average of 2.99 for its sector and the S&P 500 companies (= 0.97), that has not been extravagant in its dividend payments. As for k_e, let us use the estimate of ~11% from the CAPM, based on (a) the UTX beta of 1.15 for the past 60 months, (b) the 6.06% real annual rate we estimated earlier for the market's long-term growth, and (c) a long-term annual inflation (or risk-free) rate of 4.0%. We can thus write

$$\begin{aligned} k_e &= r_i = r_f + \beta \times (r_m - r_i) \\ &= 4.0\% + 1.15 \times 6.06\% = 10.97\% . \end{aligned} \tag{6.6a}$$

As for the remaining number, g, *the sustainable growth rate* is given by

$$g = \text{plowback ratio} \times \text{return on equity (ROE)} . \tag{6.6b}$$

For UTX, plowback ratio is 78.30% (= 1 – payout ratio = 1 – 21.70%) and the return on equity (ROE) = 22.27%. By plugging these numbers into Equation (6.6b), we obtain g = 17.44%. This is the maximum sustainable rate based on the recent history, however, and not necessarily the rate that is likely to be sustained over the infinite time horizon that

Equation (6.5d) is based on. Note that, while its ROE has averaged 22.27% during 1996–2000, UTX has only managed a dividend growth rate of 9.99% through this period. This is not really surprising because, as we discussed in the previous chapter, recent years have witnessed a marked propensity for the firms to either not pay dividends at all or reduce these payments. As dividends tend to be sticky in that firms seldom lower their historic payout ratios, the best way to lower dividend payments is to reduce their rate of growth. These make assuming a continuation of the past five years average of g = 9.99% into the foreseeable a far more realistic proposition, therefore, than using g = 17.44%. Given these numbers, Equation (6.5d) yields the estimate of share price for UTX as

$$P_0 = \frac{D_1}{(k_e - g)} = \frac{\$0.90}{(10.97\% - 9.99\%)} = \$91.84\,. \tag{6.6c}$$

Notice how close this estimate is to our earlier estimate in Exhibit 6.5. For comparison, in July 2001, the Morningstar business appraisal for UTX was $91.62 (June 20, 2001), Quicken's valuation was $101.26 and, based on estimates by 14 financial analysts, Yahoo Finance cited a 12-month target price of $85–95 for UTX!

Applying this valuation method to Eastman Kodak, its beta of 0.46 (Exhibit 6.5) corresponds to k_e = 6.79%, from Equation (6.6a). Its dividend has grown at the same annual rate of 1.92% for the past five years as the average for its industry. Thus, taking g = 1.92% for this company, and noting that its dividend payment for the year 2001 was at $1.76, Equation (6.5d) yields the estimate for Eastman Kodak's shares as $36.14. Of all the valuation methods that we have tried as yet, this is by far the lowest estimate for Eastman Kodak shares.

Apart from the derivation in Box 6.2, one can think of several modifications or innovations to Equation (6.5d) that can broaden its applicability. For instance, we could use current year's dividend (D_0) instead of next year's estimate D_1, by writing $D_1 = D_0 \times (1 + g)$, and then divide both sides by the current year's earnings per share (E_0). This yields

$$\frac{P_0}{E_0} = \left(\frac{D_0}{E_0}\right) \times \frac{1+g}{k_e - g}, \tag{6.7a}$$

where (P_0/E_0) is our familiar P/E ratio and (D_0/E_0) is the payout ratio. For the above values of k_e, g and the payout ratio, this gives P/E ratios of 21.52 for UTX and 8.81 for EK. For the earnings data given earlier, these correspond to the share prices of \$79.19 for United Technologies and \$36.65 for Eastman Kodak.

The Free Cash Flow Model

Notice that we have, in using these variations of the Gordon growth or dividend discount models, been unable to value a company like Microsoft that has paid no dividends until recently. Two added limitations of these models must already be apparent. The dividend based models are not only hard to apply when a company pays no dividend but also when growth exceeds the cost of capital, simply because the price estimate remains positive only so long as k_e exceeds g and shoots through the ceiling when g approaches k_e! Likewise, how would we use a market multiple like the P/E ratio to value a firm that is yet to turn in positive earnings?

One solution lies in using cash flow instead of dividends. This is because, irrespective of whether a company pays dividends or not, its cash flow affects its solvency and growth potential. There are two kinds of cash flow[17] measurements, in the main: simple cash flow and free cash flow. What is the difference? The simple cash flow is literally the cash that flows through the company's account and is otherwise known as EBITDA, for earnings before interest, taxes, depreciation and amortization. It is also roughly estimated by adding net profits after taxes to depreciation. This measure is best used when we wish to value companies with considerable capital expenditure upfront, or with significant amortization burdens. Huge depreciation and amortization changes often mask a firm's ability to generate cash, as does the tax rate if it changes drastically from one year to another, so impacting the current and future earnings. Free cash flow, on the other hand, is a measure of what a firm can pay as dividends, even when it does not. Not all the earnings go to equity, after all, so that a firm's cash flow will be positive even if its cash flow to equity is negative. Depreciation is not a cash flow to equity, for instance, and only affects a firm's cash flow for tax purposes. Note, also, that net cash flow to equity is net of debt related expenses as well. A narrow view even holds that dividends and stock buybacks comprise the only cash flow to equity.

Free cash flow analysis thus enables two kinds of valuation models:

- Equity valuation is based on free cash flow to equity (FCFE): only the cash that flows to equity is considered here.
- Firm valuation is based on the free cash flow to the firm (FCFF): this uses all the free cash flow to the firm, including the cash flow generated from capital raised in the debt market, which must be excluded in the case of equity valuation.

These two types of free cash flow are computed as follows:

$$\begin{aligned}\begin{matrix}\text{free cash flow}\\ \text{to firm (FCFF)}\end{matrix} = \; & \text{earnings before interest and taxes (EBIT)} \\ & \times (1 - \text{tax rate}) \\ & - (\text{capital expenditure} - \text{depreciation}) \\ & - \text{change in working capital}\,,\end{aligned} \tag{6.8a}$$

and

$$\begin{matrix}\text{free cash flow}\\ \text{to equity (FCFE)}\end{matrix} = \begin{matrix}\text{free cash flow to firm (FCFE)}\\ - \text{debt} \times (1 - \text{tax rate})\,.\end{matrix}$$

For purposes of equity valuation, if we expect the firm to grow steadily at rate g into the foreseeable future, then, analogous to Equation (6.5d), its valuation equation can now be written as follows:

$$P_0 \approx \frac{\text{FCFE}_1}{k_e - g}\,. \tag{6.8b}$$

Likewise, as for valuing the firm, the form analogous to Equation (6.5b) is

$$\text{value of the firm } (V) \approx \sum_{t=1}^{\infty} \frac{\text{FCFF}_t}{(1+k_{\text{wacc}})^t}, \tag{6.8c}$$

where k_{wacc}, the weighted average cost of capital, is computed as

$$k_{\text{wacc}} = k_e \times \frac{\text{equity}}{\text{debt} + \text{equity}} + r_{\text{debt}} \times (1 - \text{tax rate}) \times \frac{\text{debt}}{\text{debt} + \text{equity}},$$

with r_{debt} as the average rate on the firm's debt.

Estimating cash flow to the firm over its infinitely long life is hardly a practical proposition, of course. This requires using a multi-period approach, with different growth rates for different phases. The simplest of them is the two-period model. In this case, we would:

- Use the appropriate version of Equation (6.8) for the initial period of relatively robust growth, say for n number of years.
- Assume a steady growth forever, at the same rate as the market, for the subsequent period and discount it to the present.

Equation (6.8c) thus modifies to:

$$\begin{array}{c} \text{value of the} \\ \text{firm } (V) \end{array} \approx \underbrace{\sum_{t=1}^{n} \frac{\text{FCFF}_t}{(1+k_e)^t}}_{\substack{\uparrow \\ \text{The initial high} \\ \text{growth period,} \\ \text{usually ten years}}} + \underbrace{\frac{\text{FCFF}_n}{(k_{\text{wacc}} - g_n)(1+k_e)^n}}_{\substack{\uparrow \\ \text{The subsequent} \\ \text{period of stable} \\ \text{growth forever}}}. \tag{6.8d}$$

What should be this growth rate g_n? The common practice is to use the 5% long-term nominal growth rate in the US. As nominal growth rate of the world economy is also about the same, this rate is almost a "universal" for any mature or stable firm nominal growth. Obviously, if we are dealing with a firm that is already in this stable growth mode, then we need to simply set $n = 0$ in Equation (6.8d). Only its second part will then remain, reducing it to the same form as Equation (6.8b), so long as we replace FCFE_1 by FCFF_1. Stable growth firms tend to be of average risk (i.e., beta = 1) and highly leveraged, pay high dividends, have low net capital expenditure, and earn about the same return on capital (ROC)[18] as k_{wacc}, the weighted average cost of capital. In contrast, the high growth firms tend to be of above average risk, pay little or no dividends, have high net capital expenditure, carry little or no debt, and earn excess return (i.e., high ROC). Such patterns are hard to sustain over a protracted period of time, however. Oftentimes, the valuation of such firms and their equities is carried out using a three-stage model. The common practice in this case is to assume an initial period of high growth, followed by a transition period when the high growth rate declines to the stable growth rate, and finally, the stable growth phase of keeping up with the market forever. Usually, the larger the firm the shorter its high growth phase is likely to last, but the higher the current growth rate the longer this growth period may last. Add to this the business strategies, the size and nature of the knowledge capital of the firm, barriers to entry and differential advantages. The stronger the firm is in these respects, the longer the high growth period is likely to last.

Equations (6.8c) and (6.8d) are far more versatile than they seem in that they can be conveniently used for equity valuation as well. Just subtract the market value of debt from the value of the firm thus derived and divide the resulting figure by the number of shares outstanding to get the price per share.

We are now adequately equipped to use cash flow analysis for valuing Microsoft. With 5.38 billion shares outstanding, the mid-year 2001 share price of $68.80 gives Microsoft the market capitalization of $370 billion. For fiscal year ended June 30, 2001, Microsoft had income of $7.35 billion on revenue of $25.3 billion, compared to the fiscal 2000 income of $9.42 billion on revenue of $22.96 billion. This drop includes $2.62 billion investment losses, however, and reflects the general market conditions that have already persisted for more than a year now. Before the June 30, 2001 report, the company's trailing twelve months EBITDA was $12.2 billion, with $10.1 billion available to common. But Microsoft's free cash flow is vastly different from the reported net income. Much like most of the high growth companies, particularly in the technology sector, virtually all Microsoft employees receive stock options. To offset the dilution effect of the options, the company spends a large portion of net income on buying back the shares. The result of these and related expenses is that Microsoft's price-to-free-cash ratio was at 27.27 in June 2001 (or \$2.57 per share), compared to its price-to-cash flow ratio of 35.28. Otherwise, a totally debt-free business like Microsoft should receive the same return on assets as on equity.

We now need to estimate the rate at which this cash flow will grow in the foreseeable future and the rate at which this cash stream is to be discounted to the present. Microsoft's earnings have averaged an impressive 35% annual growth during 1995–2000. This high growth rate and Microsoft's singular domination of the market favor a prolonged period of high growth. The problem is that it may already be too large to continue being the innovator that it once was. Indeed, the resulting barrier to competitors' entry was the crux of the government's case against Microsoft. Recall the coincidence, albeit an eerie one, that the technology sector's currently continuing slump began, almost to the day, with Judge Jackson's ruling against Microsoft. The hands that were invisible to Adam Smith truly work in mysterious ways!

For our valuation exercise, these factors favor using a multi-period model. Let us, for simplicity, use a two-period model by assuming the continuation of the present growth rate until 2010 and a stable phase thereafter. For the rate in this high growth phase, we could assume the same value as the past five years' ROE (= 22.77%), by using a plowback ratio of one. But this rate is excessive, particularly as the PC (personal computer) market is fast approaching saturation. To err on the cautious side, therefore, let us use the consensus estimate of 15% that analysts usually cite for the future growth in Microsoft's earnings. As for the discount rate, Microsoft's beta of 1.8 gives the estimate of 14.8%, i.e., about the same as this 15% growth rate.

The value for stable phase, or the terminal value, is the second part of Equation (6.8d) and is even easier to compute. Let us assume that Microsoft will enter this phase in 2010, after which its stock will move perfectly with the market. Let us also assume, for simplicity, that Microsoft's present capital structure (i.e., debt ratio = 0) will remain unchanged. Therefore, for beta = 1, we now have k_e = 10% for this

Exhibit 6.8: Valuing the Microsoft shares by free cash flow analysis.

Assumptions:

(a) The present high growth phase will continue, despite the ongoing economy-wide slump, until 2010 after which growth will stabilize at the broad market rate. Microsoft's present capital structure will remain unchanged (i.e., no debts and dividends) throughout.

(b) During the growth phase (2001–2010), per share FCFE grows at the annual rates of 10–15%. Let the cost of equity, for discounting to the present value, be the same. Thus, the 2001 PV of each year's FCFE will then be the same as in 2001.

(c) During the stable phase (i.e., after 2010), the 2010 per share FCFE grows annually at the 5% nominal rate of overall economy. The cost of equity is the same as the historic 10% rate of the overall market, and is discounted from 2010 to 2001 at the 10–15% rate of growth, as assumed.

per share data	FCFE for the growth rate of			PV of FCFE
	15%	**12.50%**	**10%**	
(a) the 2001–2010 growth phase				
2001	$2.57	$2.57	$2.57	$2.57
2002	$2.96	$2.89	$2.83	$2.57
2003	$3.40	$3.25	$3.11	$2.57
2004	$3.91	$3.66	$3.42	$2.57
2005	$4.49	$4.12	$3.76	$2.57
2006	$5.17	$4.63	$4.14	$2.57
2007	$5.94	$5.21	$4.55	$2.57
2008	$6.84	$5.86	$5.01	$2.57
2009	$7.86	$6.59	$5.51	$2.57
2010	$9.04	$7.42	$6.06	$2.57
			SUM of the 2001 PVs =	$25.70
(b) the post-2010 stable phase				
PV in 2010	$180.82	$148.37	$121.20	
PV in 2001	$51.40	$51.40	$51.40	

Result:

Tabulated above are the computations based on these assumptions. As DCF method treats share value as the present value of future cash flow, all that we now need to do is add the two PVs, i.e.,

Microsoft's current share price = Sum of the PVs of annual FCFEs during the growth phase + the PV of the FCFEs to be received during the stable phase = $25.70 + $51.40 = $77.10

phase and assume $g = 5\%$, the historic nominal growth rate for the economy. As for discounting to the present value, we will use the same discount rate as in the 2001–2010 phase.

Exhibit 6.8 summarizes the resulting numbers and computations. For the two-stage model used here, the 2001–2010 yearly PVs (present values) for free cash flow add up to \$25.70 while the 2010 terminal value for post-2010 steady growth performance has the 2001 value of \$51.40. We would thus price the Microsoft shares at \$77.10 by adding these two numbers. Note that it makes no difference as to what rate is assumed for the growth phase, so long as we use the same rate for discounting to compute the PV.

What if Microsoft did not grow at its 1995–2000 above-the-market rate and grew at the market rate instead? We would then ignore the first part of the computation in Exhibit 6.8 and use the estimate of 2001 terminal value (= \$51.40 = \$2.57/{0.10 – 0.05}) for Microsoft's current share price. Can this be a practical proposition? Quite plausibly, particularly as it does not necessarily imply consigning a star performer of recent years, and one of the world's leading companies, to the status of a laggard. The looming prospects of economic slowdown in the US and elsewhere can accomplish that. Obviously, at the 52-week low of \$40.25 on December 21, 2000, Microsoft shares offered the "buy" opportunity that value investors are unlikely to receive for a long time. Thus, despite the market's prolonged bear run, the Microsoft share prices have held remarkably steady above that level.

"Our books are balanced. 50% of our numbers are real and 50% are made up."

6.4 Other Valuation Models

Valuing Nascent Enterprises

As our example of valuing the Microsoft shares amply demonstrates, cash flow analysis offers a reasonable tool to value the firms and their equities, irrespective of whether they pay dividends or not. There is one situation where it may not work as easily, and requires deft projections, however: when the cash flow is negative. This is usually the case with the yet-to-be-profitable start up companies. Take the case of Amazon.com, the online retailer that started selling books in 1995 and generated revenues of $511,000, based on the 2001 first quarter estimates of $700 million, and was expected in mid-2001 to end up with $3.4 billion in revenues for 2001. This averages to a better than four-fold rise each year since inception. As shown in Exhibit 6.9, however, the company was yet to turn profitable although, guessing from the continuation of the trend, it seemed poised to turn that corner soon.

This is reflected well in the market's valuation of Amazon whose stock, which grew from $1.50 a share in 1995 to $113 at the peak of

Exhibit 6.9: Amazon.com, the online retailer, has grown dramatically since it began selling books in 1995. The company has yet to turn in profits, however, although that situation seems poised to reverse, judging from the trend graphed here.

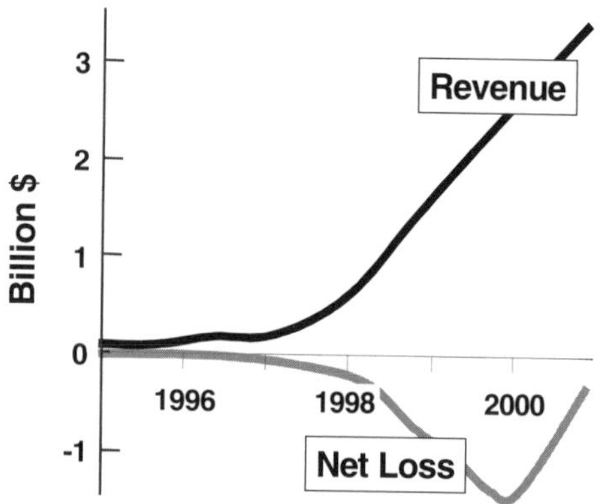

Source: David Streitfeld, "Long Amazon.com Tale Still Written in Red Ink", *Los Angeles Times*, July 21, 2001, pp. A1 and 17.

the dot.com bubble, hovered around \$16 in June 2001, after having dropped to \$8.10 at its 52-week low on April 4, 2001. Thus, the question to examine is whether Amazon.com is a nascent Microsoft, Dell or AOL or one more dot.com dream that has gone awry.

Two valuation strategies particularly commend themselves in this context: (a) the EVA (economic-value-added) method, and (b) valuation by options.

Valuation by the EVA concept

In essence, a valuation based on the EVA (economic-value-added)[19] concept is an analytical approach. The idea here is that, to add economic value, the firm must receive a greater return on the invested capital than what that capital itself costs. We can therefore define EVA as:

$$\underset{\substack{\text{economic-}\\\text{value-added}}}{\underset{\uparrow}{\text{EVA}}} = (\underset{\substack{\text{return-on-}\\\text{capital}}}{\underset{\uparrow}{\text{ROC}}} - \underset{\substack{\text{weighted average}\\\text{cost of capital}}}{\underset{\uparrow}{\text{WACC}}}) \times \text{invested capital}. \tag{6.9a}$$

As Amazon's ROC remains negative as yet, and WACC is a positive number, Equation (6.9a) is not directly applicable to the task at hand, that of valuing Amazon. The alternative approach that we will try, instead, is as follows[20]:

- Determine Amazon's current operation value (COV) by assuming that the company is at the stage where it earns the normal operating margin of 10%, and has become profitable, compared to its five-year average operating margin of about –30%.
- The now known COV and the market value (MV) allow us to estimate the future growth value (FGV), using the following relation:

$$\begin{matrix}\text{market}\\\text{value (MV)}\end{matrix} = \begin{matrix}\text{current operation}\\\text{value (COV)}\end{matrix} + \begin{matrix}\text{future growth}\\\text{value (FGV)}\end{matrix} \tag{6.9b}$$

- Examine how practicable and sustainable this future growth value indeed is.

Now, with 359.2 million shares outstanding, Amazon's June 2001 stock price of $16.49 translated into a market value of $5.92 billion. For 2001 sales revenues of $3.2 billion, a 10% operating margin meant a NOPAT (net operating income after taxes) value of $320 million, because Amazon had no tax liability as yet. What would this amount grow to in ten years? This requires estimating the discount rate or the cost of the capital that Amazon will need so as to generate these earnings. Amazon has a high beta (= 3.23). Its cost of equity is very high, therefore, and amounts to 23.8% for the numbers we have been using here. Suppose that the cost of debt is 7% and that Amazon settles for the debt/equity ratio = 1. This capital structure is similar to the overall market's long-term debt/asset ratio and implies a 20.4% weighted average cost of capital (k_{wacc}) for Amazon. The corresponding estimate of COV = NOPAT/k_{wacc} (= $320 million/0.204) is $1.57 billion, or $4.37 per share. This should also be the price of an Amazon stock if the company stops growing after reaching the point where its operating margin is 10%, instead of the present –30%.

What kind of growth does Amazon need in order to justify its mid-2001 share price of $16.49? We determine this by turning to Equation (6.9b). Note that, on subtracting our estimate of COV = $1.57 billion from MV = $5.92 billion, we obtain the future growth value (FGV) of $4.35 billion. Clearly, for our estimate of NOPAT = $320 million to grow to FGV = $4.35 billion in ten years' time, Amazon's revenues will need to grow at about 26% per year. Is this rate sustainable? The graph in Exhibit 6.9 suggests that it is, as does Amazon's performance record. Its 5-year sales growth has been almost 460%. The fact that this is faster than the 381.63% growth in capital spending during this period is certainly a promising sign. But then, Amazon's 5-year average ROA is –58.53%, the corresponding ROI (return-on-investment) and ROE values being –103.9% and –246.02%, respectively. Note that these are measures of management effectiveness. While certainly reassuring, the estimate of value remains an imprecise exercise, however.

Equity Valuation by Call Options

That continued rapid growth in revenue is the key to Amazon's survival is also the message from the options model of equity valuation. As

Exhibit 6.10: Tabulated on the left are the July 20, 2001 quotes for selected call and put options on Amazon, with expiration in January 2002. The two cartoons are the profit-loss diagrams for holders of call and put options. Notice how a call option helps you hedge in a rising market, a put option in a falling market.

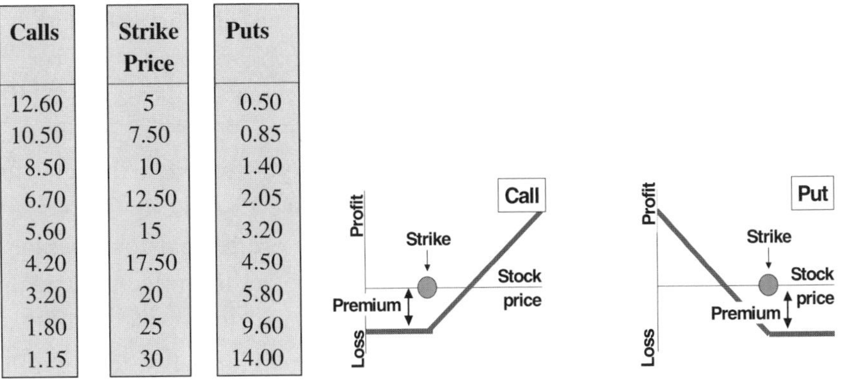

Calls	Strike Price	Puts
12.60	5	0.50
10.50	7.50	0.85
8.50	10	1.40
6.70	12.50	2.05
5.60	15	3.20
4.20	17.50	4.50
3.20	20	5.80
1.80	25	9.60
1.15	30	14.00

discussed in Chapter 8, an option gives the holder the *right* to buy or sell a stock at a specified strike or exercise price on or before a set expiration date. A call option gives the holder the right to buy, a put option the right to sell. By way of illustration, Exhibit 6.10 shows the July 2001 prices of selected puts and calls on Amazon for January 2002 expiration and different strike prices. These data are for the close of trading on July 20, 2001, when Amazon shares closed at $16.98. Note that the call option becomes more valuable the more the stock price rises above the options strike price whereas the opposite holds for the put option. With the stock trading at $16.98, for instance, the call option for $5 strike is trading at $12.60 whereas that for $30 strike is trading at $1.15. Here, all the call options with strike prices below the stock price are said to be in the money, as are all the put options whose strike prices exceed the stock price. Suppose you bought a $5 call option in April 2001, when stock was trading at about $8.50, and paid $3 for this option. Clearly, your bet was for a rise in the stock's price before your option expired. As this is what has happened, your call option is already worth more than four times what you had paid for, and you might be well advised to pocket your profits by selling it. What if you had then bought a put option for the same strike price, instead, paying $2 for it. Your bet then was for a further fall in the stock's price. As the opposite has happened since then, and your option is now worth one quarter of what you had invested, you are better off holding on to it and let it expire worthless if its price does not rise to your level of satisfaction.

Now that we have your attention, we hasten to add that speculations of this type are not the main reason why the options market thrives.[21] To give an example, suppose you bought Amazon stocks at the April 2001 low of \$8.10, then you would have also bought yourself the insurance against fall in the stock's price if you had also bought an adequate amount of put options. Indeed, as we discuss in Chapter 8, call options serve a myriad of purposes. They are bought for leverage, to limit trading risk and/or release cash, to protect the principal and/or short positions, for psychological sustenance, and to fix the security's price for a later-day purchase. Likewise, put options are bought for leverage, to protect long positions and/or book profits, for limited-risk trading and for psychological sustenance. We will return to these fascinating issues in Chapter 8, but must now turn to the reason why we got on to this discussion on options — mainly to explain how we can use options for equity valuation.

As we saw in Exhibit 6.10, the price of an option depends on the price of the underlying security. How the two are related is precisely what the famous Black–Scholes formula[22] is all about. It gives the value of a call option as

$$\text{value of the call option} = \underset{\substack{\uparrow \\ \text{option's} \\ \text{delta}}}{N(d_1)} \times \underset{\substack{\uparrow \\ \text{share} \\ \text{price}}}{S} - \underset{\substack{\uparrow \\ \text{PV of a} \\ \text{bank loan}}}{N(d_2) \times e^{-rT} X} . \qquad (6.10)$$

Here, X = Option's strike price.

S = Price of the underlying security.

$N(d)$ = Cumulative normal probability density function.[23]

$d_1 = \frac{\ln(S/X) + rT}{\sigma\sqrt{T}} + \frac{1}{2}\sigma\sqrt{T}$.

$d_2 = d_1 - \sigma\sqrt{T}$.

T = Option's time to maturity.

σ = Volatility of the asset price.

We can use Equation (6.10), and value Amazon.com and its equity as a call option, by noting that while Amazon's equity is actually a deficit as yet, *sensu stricto*, the most that the equity investors in this or any other publicly traded firm can lose is their investment. This is because of the principle of limited exposure. The reason why this issue arises here is because we are going to value Amazon's assets and debts and apply the residual to the equity. After all, much like a call option where the payoff exists only when the stock price (S) exceeds the strike price (X), the equity holders receive only the residual from the firm's liquidation proceeds (V) that remains after meeting the demands of other financial claim holders (D). This makes it reasonable to use the value of the call option as the proxy for the value of the firm.

In terms of Equation (6.10), we therefore set, for Amazon.com

S = Value of the underlying asset = \$3.2 bill in 2001 (\$4.0 bill in 2002).
X = Face value of outstanding debt = \$2.2 bill in 2001 (\$2.5 bill in 2002).
T = Life of the option = duration of Amazon's debt = 5 years, say.
r = Risk-free rate = Treasury bond corresponding to option-life = 5%.
σ = Volatility of underlying asset = Standard deviation of Amazon stock price.

To compute the last of these numbers, note that Amazon's year 2000 asset/debt ratio (\$2.25 billion/\$2.08 billion) is about the same as the above projections for 2001 and 2002. Computing σ for an asset/debt ratio of 1.2 would be a reasonable generalization, therefore. With $\sigma_{\text{debt}} = 0.12$, the annualized volatility of returns on Amazon's stock price $\sigma_{\text{amazon}} = 0.95$, and the correlation of their changes $\rho_{\text{amazon-debt}} = 0.25$, the volatility of Amazon's assets works out[24] to $\sigma = 0.54$, so that the other numbers that we need are

$$d_1 = 0.9874 \qquad d_2 = -0.22$$
$$N(d_1) = 0.8383 \qquad N(d_2) = 0.4129\,.$$

Thus,

$$\begin{aligned}\text{value of the call option on Amazon} &= 0.8383 \times \$3.2\text{ billion} - 0.4129 \times 0.7047 \times \$2.2\text{ billion} \\ &= \$2.04\text{ billion}\end{aligned}$$

For 359.2 million shares outstanding, this firm value implies a per share price of \$5.69 which, though superior to the \$4.37 share value that we derived earlier using the EVA concept, is still a far cry from the current share price of about \$16. What if we incorporate growth by looking at our above projections for the year 2002? In that case the firm valuation works out to \$2.63 billion which, for the same number of stocks outstanding as now, means a price of \$7.31 per share. This is certainly an impressive return, with 28.5% price appreciation in one year, but still suggests that Amazon shares will remain overvalued for several years even if the present price does not change. Indeed, even if we ignore the debt term here altogether by assuming that $T \rightarrow \infty$ in Equation (6.10), we obtain a price of \$9.34 for Amazon's shares. Mathematically, though, this is a monstrosity because the $N(d_1)$ term in Equation (6.10) is indeterminate if T is set at ∞!

The use of real options for managerial decision making has proven to be a major improvement over the conventional NPV (net present value) analysis.[25] High growth companies have numerous options for growth, for instance, all of which add to the present value of a firm even though they are not necessarily amenable to valuation by the traditional methods. However inadvertently, though, this method unfortunately got used more for rationalizing[26] the hypervaluation of Internet stocks during the bull market's extraordinary run-up in the late 1990s, than for predicting prices.

What do the traditional valuation models say about Amazon's price? The company's negative earnings and negetive equity leave us with price-to-sales ratio as the only multiple that we can use here. The problem is that Amazon.com is a business that has neither a peer nor a history. If we treat it as a bookseller then, for the \$69 per share of sales that Barnes & Noble generated for its July 2001 share price of \$36.28, we should price Amazon's shares at almost one-eight as much. But a brick-and-mortar business like Barnes & Noble has to invest far more than Amazon to generate the same revenue run rate.[27] What if we treat Amazon as the prospective Wal-Mart of the web? With almost \$200 billion in sales, and 4.5 billion shares outstanding, Wal-Mart has five times as much in sales revenues per share as Amazon does. Thus, valued relative to Wal-Mart's July 2001 share price of \$53.10, Amazon's shares should be priced at about \$10.

We could also use the price-to-cash flow multiple here, of course. But Amazon's difficult cash flow situation suggests that rather than using the cash flow data for a single year or an average as in the method of multiples, we perform the cash flow analysis in its entirety. This is shown in Exhibit 6.11. Several simplifying assumptions have been made here.[28]

Exhibit 6.11: The valuation of Amazon.com by free cash flow analysis.

Operating margin		Renenue growth (%)	Revenue (bill $)	EBIT (1-Tax) (mill $)	PV (mill $)
1995*	–6%	…	…	…	…
1996*	–10%	19,500	0.1	–10	…
1997*	–35%	100	0.2	–70	…
1998*	–33%	200	0.6	–200	…
1999*	–47%	185	1.7	–800	…
2000*	–54%	53	2.6	–1400	…
2001*	–7%	31	3.4	–234	–234
2002*	–5%	20	4.1	–204	–170
2003+	–3%	18	4.8	–144	–100
2004#	–1%	16	5.6	–56	–32
2005#	1%	15	6.4	42	20
2006#	3%	13	7.3	141	57
2007#	5%	12	8.1	263	88
2008#	7%	11	9.0	408	114
2009#	9%	10	9.8	575	134
2010#	10%	5	10.3	671	284

*Tax rate = 0%, +Tax rate = 15%, #Tax rate = 35%

For the data given here,

$\Sigma PV_{2001-2010}$ = \$0.16 billion

$\Sigma PV_{2010 \to \infty}$ = \$5.69 billion

Present value of free cash flow to the firm (ΣFCFF)

= \$5.85 billion

∴ ΣFCFE = \$(5.85 – 2.20) billion

= \$3.65 billion

Number of shares = 360 million

∴ Share price = \$11.14

But, if ΣFCFE = ΣFCFF, then share price = \$16.25

Source: Aswath Damodaran's Excel worksheet

We have used a two-stage growth model. We start with a growth rate of 20% in 2002, lower it by 10% each year until 2009, and then keep it fixed at 5% from 2010 in perpetuity. The operating margin, estimated at −7% in 2001, is assumed to turn positive in 2005, exactly a decade after the company started operating.

As Amazon is a "virtual" as opposed to a brick-and-mortar business, depreciation and amortization numbers are unlikely to be significant and are therefore ignored here. We have assumed a 20% cost of equity during 2001–2010 and 10% thereafter. Finally, if we take ΣFCFF = ΣFCFE by ignoring debt and the cost of employee options, then we obtain a \$16.25 share price. But each \$1 billion in present value of this burden knocks \$2.75 off the share price. As uncertainties are ubiquitous in these computations, a slight tweaking of the estimated growth rates can easily solve this problem, if these costs are not factored into the operating margin. Just raise the growth rate, by lowering the 2002 estimated growth rate of 20% by 6%, and not 10%, each year until 2009. Then ΣFCFF = \$6.81 billion while ΣFCFE would remain effectively unchanged if the debt burden is about \$1 billion, to support a \$16.25 share price. Otherwise, for \$2.2 billion as the present value of this burden, $\Sigma FCFE_{2001}$ = \$3.65 billion which implies a \$10.14 share price.

Both these possibilities, either factoring these costs into operating margins or assuming higher revenue growth rates, are realistic. Actually, the growth rates we have assumed here may turn out to be excessively cautious. What is not clear is whether Amazon can sustain[29] the cash flow that it needs in order to have these operating margins and generate these revenues.

Overall, Amazon.com is a good company, with an innovative, conceptually powerful and seductively simple business plan. Its revenue growth has been impressive (its sales grew 16% in the 2001 second quarter, for instance, with an 18% drop in the marketing costs) and it is already a gorilla in its market segment: the B2C segment of e-business (Exhibit 6.12).

As shown in Exhibit 6.12, Internet-based businesses can be broadly grouped, therefore, as B2B (business-to-business: e.g., I2 Technologies), B2C (business-to-consumer: e.g., Amazon.com, Priceline.com), and C2C (consumer-to-consumer: e.g., e-Bay). This reflects the fact that, in terms

Exhibit 6.12: The business-customer matrix in e-business. Here, Amazon is a pioneer and already a leader in the B2C sector.

	Business	Consumer
Business	B2B	B2C
Consumer	B2C	C2C

of business applications, the Internet is only a facilitator, and not an end in itself.

The entire e-business sector of the market is still in its infancy, however. These dismal valuations seem more likely, therefore, to capture the angst of growth than predict the future of Amazon.com and the like businesses. It is still too soon to tell what kind of future a "virtual" business with no brick-and-mortar presence and based on pure Internet play can indeed have. Internet empowers the individual, in the main. Perhaps some indications of what lies ahead are already implicit in the

continuing high valuations of a C2C e-business like e-Bay *vis-à-vis* the problems that plague a B2B gorilla like I2 Technologies (NASDAQ: ITWO) and B2C businesses like Amazon.com and Priceline.com (NASDAQ: PCLN). For the B2B and B2C sectors, perhaps the Internet can be no more than just another business tool, and not the basis for a stand alone operation. If this is true then it is likely some may argue that, instead of surviving independently, Amazon will be gobbled by AOL-Time Warner or a like company with a formidable presence on the web, i.e., if AOL can first resolve its ongoing problems!

6.5 Putting It All Together, Analytically

Four Questions

This chapter and the preceding chapter have focused on the lessons from financial economics as they apply to investment decisions. We have seen that success in financial investments is hardly a matter of luck alone. Reasoned judgement also matters,[30] perhaps a great deal more, particularly as we now possess an incredible array of quantitative tools and empirical wisdom to aid that judgement. Nonetheless, there are quite a few areas where much work remains to be done although, in the final analysis, it often boils down to what you basically believe in. Take the case of equity and firm valuations discussed in this chapter, for instance. We faced many uncertainties in the valuation of established firms in relatively mature industries and, yet, had an impressive array of strategies whose results are comparable. But seeking to assign value to an upcoming firm in a growing sector of the economy, where investing is likely to offer the best prospects for gain, turns valuation almost into an art!

A savvy investor may well ask, therefore, "Where do we go from here?" This deceptively simple question raises the following issues:

- How about the market's valuation itself? The issue to be examined is whether "correct" valuation is in fact possible.
- How reliable is a valuation indicator such as the P/E ratio in terms of future stock market performance?

- What implications do all of these have in terms of market efficiency and the development of a profitable investment strategy?
- How does global diversification influence the above results?

From Valuation to Performance

Three issues need to be tackled before we can proceed any further in these discussions. First, many readers may either not have the patience to perform the valuation analyses themselves or may find it too daunting an exercise to be left to the lay person. Second, we need to know how reliably such valuations can help us distinguish the overvalued equities from the undervalued ones. And three, how good a guide to the future it can be, i.e., do the undervalued equities indeed overperform the overvalued ones or are they undervalued for good reasons?

The first of these need not pose a problem, however, thanks to the miscellany of excellent sites on the Internet. By way of illustration, Exhibit 6.13 reproduces ValuePro's cash flow analysis of Microsoft Corporation that can be freely accessed at the site www.valuepro.net where you will find intrinsic valuation as well as cash flow analysis. This also updates the cash flow based valuation of Microsoft in Exhibit 6.8. The difference between the two estimates, $77.10 in Exhibit 6.8 versus $54.17 in Exhibit 6.13 is quite substantial. But times have changed too, rather drastically. ValuePro's DCF valuation of Microsoft Corporation shares in July 2001 was $65.37, for instance, compared to the appraisals at $47.24 and $38.65, respectively, by Quicken (www.quicken.com) and Morningstar (www.morningstar.com). Our estimates in Exhibit 6.3 ranged from $53.16 to $78.93! How can this be??

The valuation techniques used by ValuePro, Quicken and Morningstar are different, and many other equally reputed websites use still different techniques. For instance, the valuation at ValuePro is based on discounted free cash flow analysis whereas the intrinsic valuation at Quicken is "a hypothetical value that is based on the sum of a company's future earnings". The complete valuation at Quicken also includes (a) growth trends, (b) financial health, (c) management performance, and (d) market multiples. Morningstar, on the other hand, emphasizes not only the

Exhibit 6.13: Valuation of Microsoft by cash flow analysis at the site www.valuepro.net.

Period	Revenues	NOP	Adj. taxes	NOPAT	Invest.	Depreciation	Change in investment	Change in working capital	FCFF	Discount factor	Discounted FCFF
1	$31,201.50	$18,552.41	$6215.06	$12,337.35	$1360.39	$1893.93	–$533.54	$278.54	$12,592.35	0.92	$11,584.96
2	$34,321.65	$20,407.65	$6836.56	$13,571.09	$1496.42	$2083.32	–$586.90	$306.40	$13,851.59	0.84	$11,635.34
3	$37,753.82	$22,448.42	$7250.22	$14,928.20	$1646.07	$2291.66	–$645.59	$337.04	$15,236.75	0.77	$11,732.30
4	$41,529.20	$24,693.26	$8272.24	$16,421.02	$1810.67	$2520.82	–$710.15	$370.74	$16,760.43	0.71	$11,899.91
5	$45,682.12	$27,162.59	$9099.47	$18,063.12	$1991.74	$2772.90	–$781.16	$407.82	$18,436.46	0.65	$11,983.70
6	$50,250.33	$29,878.85	$10,009.41	$19,869.44	$2190.91	$3050.20	–$859.29	$448.60	$20,280.13	0.60	$12,168.08
7	$55,275.36	$32,866.73	$11,010.35	$21,856.38	$2410.01	$3355.21	–$945.20	$493.46	$22,308.12	0.55	$12,269.47
8	$60,802.90	$36,153.40	$12,111.39	$24,042.01	$2651.01	$3690.74	–$1039.73	$542.80	$24,538.94	0.50	$12,269.47
9	$66,883.19	$39,768.74	$13,322.53	$26,446.21	$2916.11	$4059.81	–$1143.70	$597.08	$26,992.73	0.46	$12,416.70
10	$73,571.50	$43,745.61	$14,654.78	$29,090.83	$3207.72	$4465.79	–$1258.07	$656.79	$29,692.11	0.42	$12,470.69

Note: These figures are in million $.

Discounted Excess Return Period FCFF = $120.43 billion
Discounted Corporate Residual Value = $136.71 billion
Short-Term Assets = $47.83 billion
Total Corporate Value = $304.96 billion

Number of shares outstanding = $5.42 billion

Total Corporate Value = $304.96 billion
Less Debt = $0.00
Less Preferred Stock = $0.00
Less Short-Term Liabilities = $11.64 billion
Short Value to Common Equity = $293.32 billion
Intrinsic Stock Value = $54.17

Source: ValuePro 2002 General Pro Forma Screen for MSFT at www.valuepro.net/cgi-v/valuate.pl

Exhibit 6.14: The world's top ten most valuable brands.

	Brand value (billion $)		
	2002	**2001**	**2000**
Coca-Cola	69.64	68.95	72.54
Microsoft	64.09	65.07	70.20
IBM	51.19	52.75	53.18
GE	41.31	42.40	38.13
Intel	30.86	34.67	39.05
Nokia	29.97	35.04	39.05
Disney	29.26	32.59	33.55
McDonald's	26.38	25.29	27.86
Marlboro	24.15	22.05	21.20
Mercedes	21.01	21.73	20.00

Source: *Business Week*, August 6, 2001 and August 5, 2002.

business prospects of the particular firm but also those of the sector, the industry, and the economy at large.

For an investor seeking less uncertainty, therefore, an effective strategy would be to start with the "no-growth" valuation from cash flow analysis, as if the company has already reached the stable phase. To this estimate (the benchmark), e.g., the share value of $51.40 for Microsoft in Exhibit 6.8, we can then add or subtract appropriate amounts for the different attributes.

Take Microsoft's brand value, for instance. Brands, as a matter of fact, expose a major limitation of the established valuation strategies. Valuations based on cash flows and ratios alone miss out on the value of intangible assets like brands or knowledge assets. Being a well known entity, the name "Microsoft" itself must surely be worth something. Why would businesses spend billions of dollars in advertising their names and services if a recognizable name carried no value? Microsoft's brand value itself is now estimated (perhaps quite inexactly) at $64.1 billion (Exhibit 6.14). We should therefore add $11.87 per share (i.e., $64.1 billion ÷ 5.4 billion shares) to our valuations of $51.40 (Exhibit 6.8) to $78.93 (Exhibit 6.3) for the Microsoft shares if we are to price them fairly.

Exhibit 6.15: A comparison of the performance of selected valuation strategies for the valuation of Dow companies.

Company	Ticket symbol	Mid-year 2002 data					Mid-year 2001 data				Valuation as a performance indicator			
		Price on August 21, 2002	Intrinsic valuation		12-month target at Yahoo Finance		Price on July 31, 2001	Intrinsic valuation		Morning-star business appraisal	1-year price change	Valupro	Quicken	Morningstar
			at Valuepro	at Quicken	Range	Mean		at Valuepro	at Quicken					
Aluminum Co. of America	AA	$26.87	$37.01	$9.67	$35–$53	$42.93	$39.06	$84.32	$36.30	$40.63	−31.21%	−53.68%	7.60%	−3.86%
American Express	AXP	$37.34	$55.45	$21.38	$33–$46	$36.90	$38.06	$8.00	$37.62	$48.58	−1.89%	375.75%	1.17%	−21.66%
AT & T	T	$12.22	−$32.10	—	$10–$23	$14.95	$20.05	—	—	$14.27	−39.05%	—	—	40.50%
Boeing	BA	$37.13	$101.94	$51.90	$40–$80	$52.67	$56.67	$213.43	$99.21	$71.80	−34.48%	−73.45%	−42.88%	−21.07%
Caterpillar	CAT	$44.85	$28.30	$3.19	$45–$66	$55.47	$53.00	$32.43	$28.63	$52.95	−15.38%	63.43%	85.12%	0.09%
Citigroup	C	$34.00	$83.94	$55.35	$42–$60	$50.61	$49.35	$105.12	$55.37	$65.75	−31.10%	−53.05%	−10.87%	−24.94%
Coca Cola	KO	$52.70	$43.83	$34.04	$51–$70	$61.40	$44.98	$36.01	$29.88	$35.95	17.16%	24.91	50.54	25.12%
Disney	DIS	$16.83	$18.96	$4.29	$14–$28	$21.28	$26.47	$8.29	—	$17.88	−36.42%	219.30%	—	48.04%
DuPont	DD	$41.12	$22.44	$99.23	$34–$57	$47.00	$43.21	$37.52	$13.95	$36.94	−4.84%	15.17%	209.75%	16.97%
Eastman Kodak	EK	$31.48	$20.28	$6.90	$27–$40	$32.00	$44.14	$63.81	$41.84	$61.73	−28.68%	−30.83%	5.50%	28.50%
ExxonMobil	XOM	$36.15	$43.19	$41.52	$30–$50	$40.14	$42.13	$68.69	$48.12	$33.92	−14.19%	−38.67%	−12.45%	24.20%
General Electric	GE	$32.25	$39.66	$23.85	$36–$50	$40.79	$43.80	$45.91	$34.87	$36.41	−26.37%	−4.60%	25.61%	20.30%
General Motors	GM	$47.92	−$121.69	$0.00	$45–$84	$64.18	$62.95	$150.93	—	$59.98	−23.88%	−58.29%	—	4.95%
Hewlett-Packard Co.	HPQ	$14.70	$21.53	$4.69	$18–$32	$22.08	$25.68	$37.49	$26.68	$22.61	−42.76%	−31.50%	−3.75%	13.58%
Home Depot	HD	$33.53	$30.16	$53.85	$31–$65	$44.33	$49.21	$20.07	$50.56	$38.96	−31.86%	145.19%	−2.67%	26.31%
Honeywell	HON	$30.35	$36.34	$12.85	$33–$50	$42.50	$36.80	$58.33	$15.24	$40.11	−17.53%	−36.91%	141.47%	−8.25%
Intel	INTC	$17.96	$6.34	$9.53	$18–$40	$28.00	$29.42	$27.09	$30.34	$14.69	−38.95%	8.60%	−3.03%	100.27%
International Bus. Machines	IBM	$80.40	$85.66	$61.28	$70–$120	$94.46	$104.89	$120.14	$107.15	$108.65	−23.35%	−12.69%	−2.11%	−3.46%
International Paper	IP	$37.91	$10.85	—	$31–$62	$48.43	$39.21	$87.92	—	$29.62	−3.32%	−55.40%	—	32.38%
Johnson & Johnson	JNJ	$54.82	$75.77	$52.13	$46–$75	$61.67	$52.70	$60.26	$45.76	$51.67	4.02%	−12.55%	15.17%	1.99%
McDonalds	MCD	$23.97	$21.96	$17.38	$26–$40	$32.00	$29.30	$27.54	$24.83	$27.69	−18.19%	6.93%	18.00%	5.81%
Merck	MRK	$50.43	$69.04	$56.41	$36–$72	$53.18	$64.99	$77.85	$65.24	$68.24	−22.40%	−16.52%	−0.38%	−4.76%
Microsoft	MSFT	$52.22	$54.17	$41.57	$45–$89	$66.29	$67.48	$65.37	$47.24	$38.65	−22.61%	3.23%	42.85%	74.59%
Minnesota Metals & Manuf.	MMM	$126.95	$85.93	$85.03	$100–$160	$131.56	$110.36	$103.70	$85.68	$94.36	15.03%	6.42%	28.80%	16.96%
JP Morgan	JPM	$24.60	−$31.97	$0.28	$27½–$45	$36.82	$150.62	$335.32	$42.91	$56.14	−83.67%	−55.08%	251.01%	168.29%
Phillip Morris	MO	$50.95	$107.38	$85.73	$43–$70	$59.43	$44.68	$114.18	$88.12	$75.68	14.03%	−60.87%	−49.30%	−40.96%
Proctor & Gamble	PG	$89.96	$76.80	$59.21	$88–$110	$97.89	$70.00	$63.37	$51.62	$59.34	28.51%	10.46%	35.61%	17.96%
SBC Comm.	SBC	$29.24	$37.32	$26.39	$25–$65	$34.66	$43.38	$53.05	$45.74	$42.13	−32.60%	−18.23%	−5.16%	2.97%
United Technologies	UTX	$61.30	$121.04	$99.26	$60–$90	$75.13	$73.77	$114.77	$102.46	$92.68	−16.90%	−35.72%	−28.00%	−20.40%
WalMart	WMT	$54.39	$30.05	$38.27	$49–$70	$62.35	$55.10	$30.23	$36.00	$39.47	−1.29%	82.27%	53.06%	39.60%

Note: These valuation data have been taken from the websites of ValuePro (www.valuepro.net), Quicken (www.quicken.com), Yahoo (www.yahoo.com) and Morningstar (www.morningstar.com). In the last three columns, negative numbers imply the identification that a stock price is undervalued.

The effect of incorporating the brand value is particularly dramatic on the valuation numbers of a company like Amazon. Recall that our exercises in the preceding section priced its shares at $4.37 to $10. But this did not include any price tag for the name Amazon.com itself. In the case of Amazon, therefore, our valuation should include its 2002 brand value of $3.2 billion, based on the data in *Business Week* magazine referenced above. For about 360 million shares outstanding, this amounts to a hefty $8.89 a share. Brand value is fickle and this valuation verges on the arbitrary. Be ready, therefore, for large year-to-year swings.

This brings us to the other two issues that were raised earlier in this section, viz., what information to glean from valuation and what purpose gets served in the process. Exhibit 6.15 should help us tackle both these questions. It compares the mid-year 2001 and mid-year 2002 price and valuation data for the 30 Dow components. The data summarized in this exhibit come from ValuePro (www.valuepro.net), Quicken (www.quicken.com), Morningstar (www.morningstar.com) and Yahoo Finance (finance.yahoo.com) websites, while the last four columns in this exhibit compare how well these measures have performed over the past one-year period. This is not to evaluate the excellent public service being performed by these sites, however, but only to maximize our use of the data that they are providing so generously.

The last three columns in this exhibit use these numbers to identify the companies that were overvalued in mid-year 2001, and the ones that were undervalued, by comparing these valuation data with the July 31, 2001 closing prices. They have been computed as the percentage points by which these prices were above or below the corresponding valuation numbers. Thus, the positive numbers here denote overvalued or over-priced companies and negative numbers the undervalued or under-priced ones. On regressing these valuation numbers against the corresponding prices, we find that valuation based mainly on cash flow analysis (i.e., the ValuePro data) correlated best (correlation coefficient $R = 0.74$), and intrinsic value estimates (i.e., the Quicken data) the least ($R = 0.48$), with the then current prices. These statistics are summarized in Exhibit 6.16 below.

With a sampling that is at once thoroughly biased and yet most representative, comprising perhaps the world's most watched and best

Exhibit 6.16: Correlation matrixes for valuation (left panel) and relative valuation or undervalued versus overvalued (right panel) data of Exhibit 6.15 corroborate the fact that there are no cut-and-dried measures to identify overvalued *vis-à-vis* undervalued stocks. The 2002 data are shown in parentheses, and for 2001 data outside them.

	Prices	**ValuePro**	**Quicken**
ValuePro	0.74 (0.45)		
Quicken	0.48 (0.61)	0.47 (0.68)	
Morningstar	0.67 (—)	0.48 (—)	0.87 (—)

ValuePro	**Quicken**
–0.02 (–0.50)	
0.01 (—)	0.57 (—)

analyzed companies, finding broad agreements on the prices of these equities and their valuations by different methods is hardly a surprising result. It only suggests that these prices were broadly consistent with cash flow and business prospects. But the correlation data in Exhibit 6.16 also reveal poor agreements between the results of different valuation methods. Quicken and Morningstar valuations match each other better, and poorly with the DCF valuations (ValuePro). The ValuePro and Quicken valuations correlate better for the 2002 prices, and the Quicken valuations seem to like the 2002 market prices better than the 2001 prices. Curiously, this improved agreement has had the opposite effect on relative valuation or the identification of whether a certain company is overvalued or undervalued. The correlation coefficient for relative valuations from ValuePro and Quicken numbers, almost zero for 2001 prices, actually became −0.5 in 2002!

In terms of our issue number two, viz., what information an investor can glean from a valuation exercise, the data in the last three columns of Exhibit 6.15 illustrate how undervalued firms can be distinguished from the overvalued ones. But they also show that this identification is hardly categorical — just because one method identifies any equity as overpriced or underpriced does not mean that other methods would do the same.

This brings us to issue number three, viz., to see what investment advantage does this information offer. Common sense tells us that we stand to gain the most by buying low and selling high. Helping an investor in selecting undervalued and properly valued stocks should thus be the obvious and most immediate advantage of a valuation exercise.

Exhibit 6.17: The correlation matrix for 1-year price changes and Dow valuations in Exhibit 6.15.

	Price changes	ValuePro	Quicken
ValuePro	0.14		
Quicken	−0.22	−0.02	
Morningstar	−0.47	0.01	0.57

The question, then, is whether today's overpriced stock is going to be tomorrow's overperformer or that its days of superior performance are behind it. Let us start with the premise that, on comparing future price performance against current valuation, we would expect overpriced stocks to underperform the underpriced ones. True, 2001 has continued to be bad for the market at large, the Dow itself having lost 20.4% in value and 15.4% in total returns. But then, one year is often the most we have to reevaluate the investment strategy and portfolio. Exhibit 6.17 thus summarizes the correlation coefficients for price performance and relative valuation data of Exhibit 6.15, to help us evaluate the performance of our Dow valuations.

Here, the correlation between performance and cash flow ($R = 0.14$) and intrinsic valuation (−0.22) models is poor. Perhaps this is because prices have generally moved in the same direction, downwards (e.g., 25 of these 30 have fallen), though in varying degrees. This is not a surprising result, therefore. Business valuation data (i.e., relative valuations from Morningstar data) show a stronger negative correlation ($R = -0.47$) of performance and overvaluation, however, and have thus been the best of the three valuations in indicating future price movements. Business appraisal looks at managerial efficiency as well as the broad market and macroeconomic factors, and not only the cash flow. This emphasizes the investor's need to also scan a company's survival and growth prospects.

Two inferences can be drawn from this appraisal: (a) cash flow is a reasonably reliable basis for valuation, at least for the large cap companies examined here, and (b) business appraisal provides a reasonable gauge of future price performance. Though important, valuation forms only a part of the arsenal that successful investing requires. The Warren

Buffett way,[31] for instance, is to focus not only on the financial factors but also on managerial efficiency and effectiveness. The questions in Exhibit 6.18, culled from the Quicken website, illustrate this.

The concept of EVA (economic-value-added) presented in Equation (6.9a) provides a possible way to quantify this, together with the concept of sustainable growth rate given in Equation (6.7b). The *financial strategy matrix* of Hawawini and Viallet[32] (Exhibit 6.19) illustrates this integration and can also be used as an investing tool. The horizontal axis here measures a firm's capacity to finance growth, and is the amount

Exhibit 6.18: Successful investors focus on managerial efficiency and effectiveness as the keys to a stock's market performance.

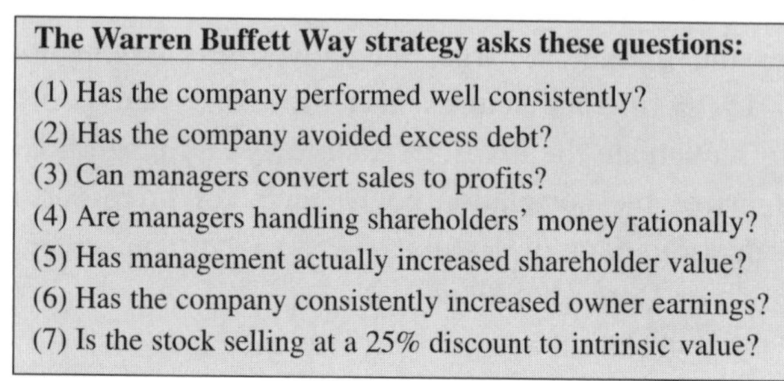

The Warren Buffett Way strategy asks these questions:

(1) Has the company performed well consistently?
(2) Has the company avoided excess debt?
(3) Can managers convert sales to profits?
(4) Are managers handling shareholders' money rationally?
(5) Has management actually increased shareholder value?
(6) Has the company consistently increased owner earnings?
(7) Is the stock selling at a 25% discount to intrinsic value?

Source: http://www.quicken.com

Exhibit 6.19: The financial strategy matrix of Hawawini and Viallet.

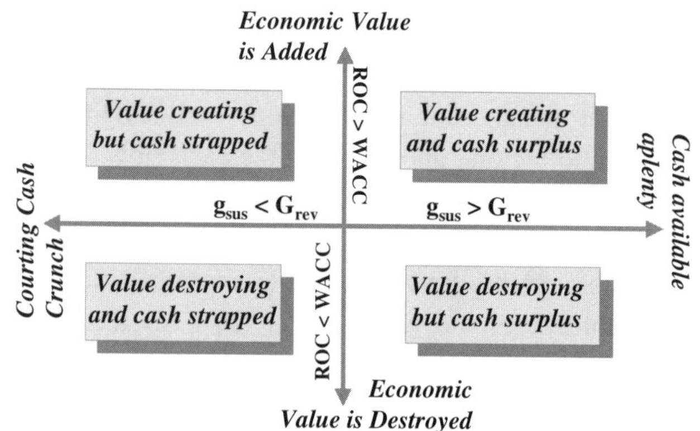

by which its sustainable growth rate (g) exceeds the growth rate for revenues (G_{rev}), i.e.,

$$\begin{matrix}\text{firm's capacity to} \\ \text{finance growth}\end{matrix} = \begin{matrix}\text{sustainable} \\ \text{growth rate } (g)\end{matrix} - \begin{matrix}\text{growth in} \\ \text{revenues } (G_{\text{rev}})\end{matrix}. \quad (6.11\text{a})$$

Note that Equation (6.7b) was an approximation for sustainable growth rate (g), its complete form being as follows[33]:

$$\begin{matrix}\text{firm's sustainable} \\ \text{growth in sales } (g)\end{matrix} = \frac{\text{return-on- equity} \times \text{retained earnings}}{1 - \text{return-on- equity} \times \text{retained earnings}}. \quad (6.11\text{b})$$

This number denotes the maximum growth in revenues that a firm can sustain without having to change its operating (i.e., operating profit margin and capital turnover) and/or financing (i.e., the debt-to-equity and dividend-payout ratios) policies.

The vertical axis here is the firm's ability to add economic value. It basically denotes the operating profit generated by the firm's net assets and net of the taxes, and the dollar cost of capital that financed these assets. As given in Equation (6.9a), it is computed as

$$\begin{matrix}\text{economic-} \\ \text{value-added}\end{matrix} = \left[\begin{matrix}\text{return on} \\ \text{capital}\end{matrix} - \begin{matrix}\text{weighted average} \\ \text{cost of capital}\end{matrix}\right] \times \begin{matrix}\text{invested} \\ \text{capital}\end{matrix}. \quad (6.11\text{c})$$

Here,

$$\begin{matrix}\text{return on capital} \\ \text{(ROC)}\end{matrix} = \begin{matrix}\text{operating} \\ \text{profit margin}\end{matrix} \times \begin{matrix}\text{net asset} \\ \text{turnover}\end{matrix}$$

and

$$\begin{matrix}\text{weighted average cost} \\ \text{of capital (WACC)}\end{matrix} = \begin{matrix}\text{aftertax} \\ \text{cost of debt}\end{matrix} \times \begin{matrix}\text{\% debt} \\ \text{financing}\end{matrix} + \begin{matrix}\text{cost of} \\ \text{equity}\end{matrix} \times \begin{matrix}\text{\% equity} \\ \text{financing}\end{matrix}.$$

The truth here is obvious: economic value is added only if returns on invested capital exceed the costs incurred in generating that capital.

Based on their financial strategy mix, the firms can be thus placed in one of the four quadrants in Exhibit 6.19. The ideal position is that of a *cash-rich* ($g > G_{rev}$) *value-creator* (ROC > WACC) (i.e., top right corner in the exhibit), whereas the *cash-strapped* ($g < G_{rev}$) *value-usurper* (ROC < WACC) (i.e., bottom left corner) is the worst placed. The other two — the *cash-strapped* ($g < G_{rev}$) *value-creator* (ROC > WACC) (top left) and the *cash-rich* ($g > G_{rev}$) *value-usurper* (ROC < WACC) (bottom right) — occupy intermediate positions between the two extremes.

How do our blue chip Dow components fare on this matrix? Exhibit 6.20 provides the answer. Note that all these companies are amongst America's best-known and most successful companies. Not surprisingly, therefore, they are mostly value-creators. In terms of their cash availability for growth, though, there is a wide scatter. At one extreme, we have the cash surplus companies like Coca-Cola and IBM, for instance, whereas, at the other extreme, we had the cash-deficit companies like Disney, Home Depot and Honeywell in 2001 and Eastman Kodak at the pack of a larger list in 2002. Perhaps we can now understand why a stock-picking genius like Warren Buffet would rather own Coca-Cola than Microsoft!

Exhibit 6.20: These two graphs show how the Dow components fare on the financial strategy matrix of Exhibit 6.19. The graph on the left is based on mid-year 2001 data, and the one on the right on mid-year 2002 data.

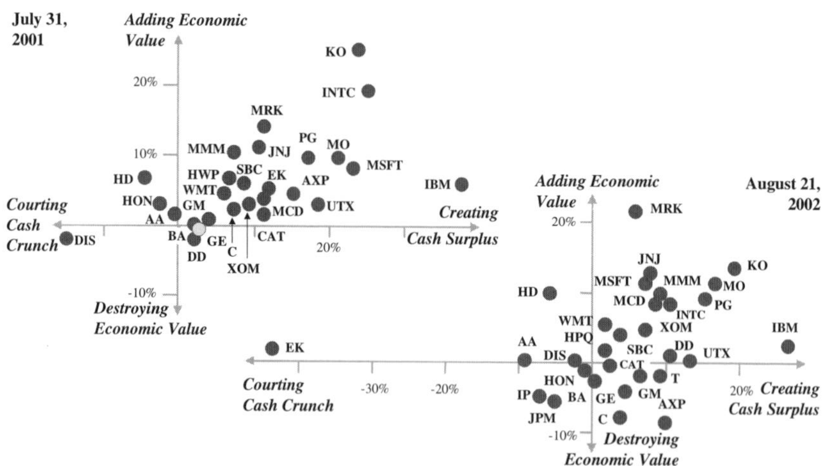

How well does this matrix predict future returns? To test this the same way as we tested the performance of the other models in Exhibit 6.17, we ran a multiple regression analysis of the two 2001 variables in Exhibit 6.19 against the 1-year price changes shown in Exhibit 6.15. That initial regression carried a multiple $R = 0.51$ which improved to 0.53 when we regressed price changes against the ratios $G = G_{\text{rev}}/g$ and R_{cost} = ROC/WACC as independent variables, instead of the differences given by Equations (6.11a) and (6.11c). The improvement was dramatic when we added one of the sets of valuation numbers in Exhibit 6.15 as an independent variable. The resulting regression equation, given below for Morningstar numbers, has a multiple R of 0.722 (the returns here are relative to the Dow index):

$$\begin{matrix}2001-2002 \text{ return relative} \\ \text{to Dow index}\end{matrix} = \begin{matrix}-0.078 + 0.107 R_{\text{cost}} \\ -0.054 G + 0.065 V_{\text{morningstar}}\end{matrix}. \quad (6.11\text{d})$$

Here $G = (G_{\text{rev}}/g)$ and R_{cost} = (ROC/WACC), as stated above, while $V_{\text{morningstar}}$ denotes the Morningstar relative valuation in the last column in Exhibit 6.15.

Exhibit 6.21 graphs the observed price changes against the corresponding values computed from Equation (6.11d). Notice how well the two sets of data match. Valuation numbers alone clearly provide an insufficient gauge of the returns that investors care about. Based on Equation (6.11d), they need to be augmented with the cost (R_{cost}) and growth (G) ratios defined above, although the coefficient for the G term in Equation (6.11d) is rather weak. This importance of ROC, enshrined in our cost ratio R_{cost}, brings to mind the assertion that Graham and Dodd made almost half a century ago in the book that has come to be known as the Bible of security analysis. They were amongst the first to argue that the "best gauge of the success of an enterprise is the percentage earned on invested capital".[34]

How would an investor scan all the miscellany of factors that affect a firm's prospective performance in the market? A good starting point would be to exploit the opportunities that the Internet offers. Instead of being overwhelmed by the valuation formulae, why not visit the different websites that offer to value a stock? Valuepro.net and quicken.com perform cash flow analyses, for instance. Morningstar also provides a

Exhibit 6.21: The 2001–2002 total returns of Dow companies relative to the Dow index (horizontal axis) are mimicked closely by the model returns (vertical axis) computed from Equation (6.11d). This model is based on multiple regression analysis of the two variables in Exhibit 6.19 together with the Morningstar valuation data of Exhibit 6.15 and carries a multiple R of 0.72.

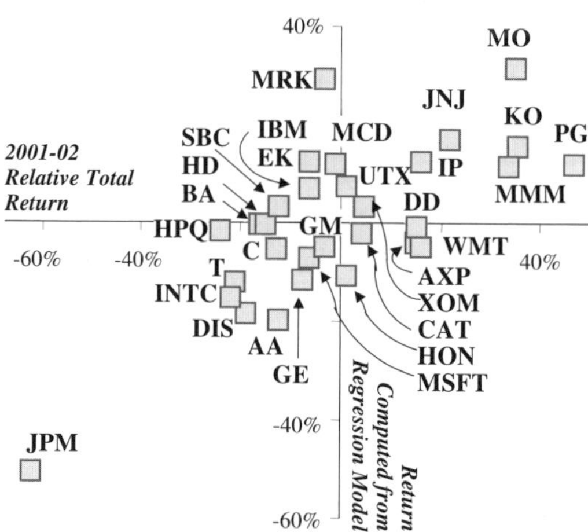

rating sheet that you can customize, as Exhibit 6.22 illustrates (we have added the dividend yield data) for the Dow components. You have thus saved the energy that you need to make the judgment call based, for instance, on the cost (R_{cost}) and growth (G) ratios that are identified here. These are an imperfect refuge, however.

Fundamental Valuation and Trading Signals

The wide dispersion of valuation numbers raises two issues. One, it helps us understand why stock prices tend to be so volatile. Two, it makes us wonder if, and to what extent, we can use the valuation numbers as trading signals.

The \$49.71–73.68 range of Microsoft share prices during 2001 hardly seems outrageous, after all, if we compare it with the \$51.40–78.93 range of our own valuation of these shares based on the mid-year 2001 data. This wide range of valuation numbers gets even wider when we include the data in Exhibit 6.15. Likewise, the valuation numbers for

Exhibit 6.22: The Morningstar valuation criterion and end-July 2002 ratings for Dow components (you can multiply these ratings with any factor that you decide).

Company	Ticker symbol	Dividend yeild	Morningstar criterion and ratings (0 = Lowest, 10 = Highest)								
			Growth	Profitability	Financial	Below 52-week high	Low P/E	Low PEG*	5-year EPS growth*	Net margin	Total score
Aluminum Co. of America	AA	2.33%	9	6	7	8	3	7	7	3	50
American Express	AXP	0.88%	4	7	8	3	5	6	6	7	46
AT & T	T	1.34%	2	6	8	10	0	1	6	1	34
Boeing	BA	1.80%	8	5	4	6	1	10	9	2	45
Caterpillar	CAT	3.16%	5	6	3	5	6	5	6	4	40
Citigroup	C	2.01%	6	6	8	7	9	10	8	0	54
Coca Cola	KO	1.55%	8	10	8	2	2	1	5	9	45
Disney	DIS	1.28%	5	6	7	9	10	2	5	4	48
DuPont	DD	3.44%	4	10	10	4	10	3	3	10	54
Eastman Kodak	EK	5.95%	4	4	4	8	0	5	1	2	28
ExxonMobil	XOM	2.54%	4	8	10	3	7	2	2	5	41
General Electric	GE	2.23%	9	5	4	5	6	8	9	8	54
General Motors	GM	4.26%	5	3	3	7	9	7	1	2	37
Hewlett-Packard Co.	HPQ	2.21%	10	1	1	7	7	10	1	1	38
Home Depot	HD	0.66%	10	10	10	9	7	9	10	4	69
Honeywell	HON	2.45%	5	6	8	5	2	8	7	3	44
Intel	INTC	0.42%	5	8	10	10	1	4	10	6	54
International Bus. Machines	IBM	0.74%	7	8	5	8	5	4	4	5	46
International Paper	IP	2.66%	5	1	1	3	0	0	0	1	11
Johnson & Johnson	JNJ	1.49%	7	8	8	2	4	5	7	9	50
McDonalds	MCD	0.92%	7	8	6	4	6	6	2	7	46
Merck	MRK	2.84%	9	10	7	6	8	6	3	9	58
Microsoft	MSFT	0.00%	8	10	10	6	3	4	9	10	60
Minnesota Metals & Manuf.	MMM	1.93%	5	10	10	1	4	3	5	8	46
JP Morgan	JPM	5.12%	3	1	5	7	5	0	0	0	21
Philip Morris	MO	4.49%	10	10	5	1	9	9	4	7	55
Proctor & Gamble	PG	1.82%	6	8	6	1	2	2	3	6	34
SBC Comm.	SBC	3.90%	1	8	7	9	8	8	2	8	51
United Technologies	UTX	1.57%	9	8	8	4	8	9	8	6	60
WalMart	WMT	0.56%	10	8	6	2	3	3	8	3	43

*projected

Box 6.3: Price Fluctuations and the Theory of Rational Expectations

Efficient market hypothesis is an extension of the theory of rational expectations that was first postulated by John Muth* in 1961. Let us use the Marshallian demand curve and apply Muth's original proposition, that all economic parameters are known and that no other random factors affect the supply-demand relationships. Suppose the price P_t of Q_t^S equities available for trade at time t is given by the equation

$$P_t = \alpha_S + \beta_S Q_t^S ,$$

where α_S and β_S are the known economic parameters. Let the investors' (or buyers') demand function for Q_t^B of these equities at an expected price $E(P_t)$ be defined by the equation

$$E(P_t) = \alpha_B - \beta_B Q_t^B .$$

Here α_B and β_B are the known economic parameters. And $E(P_t)$ is based on some precise valuation models say. The equilibrium price P^* and quantity Q^* can be then estimated as

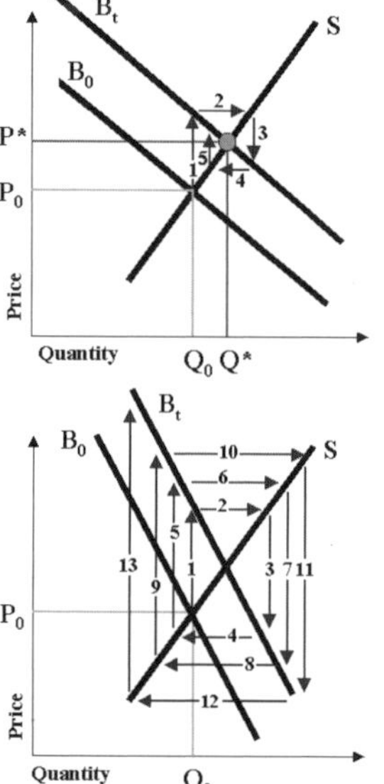

$$P^* = E(P_t) = P_t = \frac{(\alpha_B \beta_S + \alpha_S \beta_B)}{(\beta_B + \beta_S)} \quad \text{and}$$

$$Q^* = Q_t^B = Q_t^S = \frac{(\alpha_B - \alpha_S)}{(\beta_B + \beta_S)} .$$

Random fluctuations can still occur, despite the model's original premise, depending on how $E(P_t)$ is determined. For instance, P_t itself can be a random variable of the form $Q_t^B = f(P_t \mid I_{t-1})$ where I_{t-1} denotes the information available at time $t - 1$. Suppose $E(P_t) = P_{t-1}$, i.e., yesterday's closing price today's expected price. In that case, the equilibrium price P^* is reached through a price-quantity "*cobweb*" of the kind shown in the top panel in the exhibit here. Notice that, as demand rises from schedule B_0 to B_t, the original price P_0 at quantity Q_0 is pushed up (path 1), so raising the quantity by bringing more sellers into the market (path 2) but lowering the price (path 3). The process would continue (e.g., paths 4 and 5) and eventually settle at P^* and Q^*. This mimics the price fluctuations so typical of the equity markets.

As the bottom panel in this exhibit shows, the opposite behavior is also possible in this model, with prices explosively spinning out of control. The only diffrence between the two panels is in terms of the slope of the demand function. Theoretically, it follows§ from the assumption

$$E(P_t) = P_{t-1} = f(P_{t-1}, P_{t-2}, \ldots, P_{t-n}) \quad \text{that} \quad P_t = (P_0 - P^*)\left(-\frac{\beta_S}{\beta_B}\right)^t + P^* .$$

Here, P_t approaches P^* only if $(-\beta_S/\beta_B) < 1$. Price oscillations occur when this condition is satisfied. When it is not, the result would be the explosive price-spiral seen in the bottom panel here.

While the observed data do show the kind of oscillatory price behavior modeled in the top panel here, and the observed mean reverting property of market prices suggests that the equilibrium is often established over a long period of time, it is doubtful if the market's behavior in the 1990s can be modeled by the bottom panel in this exhibit. Interestingly, though, if such price-patterns exist then they should also show up in volatility. On comparing the Sharpe ratio of returns on the market with that of the long-term Treasuries, on the other hand, we find that the volatility of the latter has been rising while that of the former has been falling. The rising volatility of Treasuries is easy to understand within the CAPM framework, as their yields too have been improving. The results in the bottom panel of the exhibit here do hold a lesson against the advocacy of central bank's direct meddling into the stock market behavior, however. Note that the interest rates are modulated directly by the Fed's policies, although the equation whether the Fed acts on its own or merely responds to the market conditions remains hard to settle.

---

*John Muth: "Rational Expectations and the Theory of Price Movements", *Econometrica*, pp. 315–335, July/August, 1961. See also T. Sargent & N. Wallace: "Rational Expectations and the Theory of Economic Policy", *Journal of Monetary Economics*, pp. 169–183, April, 1976.
§Walter Nicholson: *Macroeconomic Theory* (Dryden, 1996).

United Technologies (UTX) computed in the preceding pages range from \$92.68 to \$176.36, compared to the 2001 fluctuation in UTX share prices from a low of \$41.02 to the high of \$85.65.

Theory too points to the problems inherent in reaching a *fair* price. The efficient market hypothesis follows from the economic theory of rational expectations in which, as Box 6.3 explains, a slight change in the investor demand function can force price oscillations and even run-away spirals. The tendency of market returns to revert to their long-term mean makes it hard to model even the worst bubbles through such spirals.

The quest, therefore, continues for a signal, or signals, that can guide our trading activity. After all, a signal that can warn us about an impending fall is just as good as the one that portends an imminent rise. The former can help us preserve the gains that the latter can help us realize. One way to look for such signals is to look at the overall economy. After all, the growth of the overall economy has emerged as a necessary precondition for the market's ongoing bear run to end, and yield-spreads and GDP gap seem to hold usable clues to the market's likely trend. But, as we saw in Chapter 4, such signals have become poorer predictor's of the macroeconomic trends than they once were. The problem becomes more complex for the market's valuation because of the added uncertainties associated, as we saw earlier in this section, with equity valuation. But logic also tells us that, if identifying the *fair* price is so uncertain, then there must be extended periods of over- and under-valuation of equities and the market as a whole. This is precisely what makes it so important to examine the success of recent calls[35] — popularized in the bestsellers by Messrs. Shiller, Smithers and Wright for instance — that labeled the 1998 and 1999 US stock markets as overvalued. Let us, therefore, turn to the P/E ratios and the Q statistic, to see if their success in identifying the market's overvaluation in the late 1990s indeed implies the presence of a predictive power that we have failed to see as yet.

Exhibit 6.23 tests the possibility of market timing based on the P/E ratio. The idea here is to enter the market when this ratio is low, and exit when it is high. Let us use the market's own statistics to identify how high is really *high*, and how low is really *low*? Suppose that the annual closing P/E ratios over the 1871–2001 history of S&P 500 index are normally distributed. We would then select any bottom percentile of this distribution to identify the *lows* and the corresponding top percentile to identify the *highs* by selecting, for normal distribution, any of the following cut-off points:

- Mean $\pm$ 1.283 $\times$ standard deviation, for the 10th–90th percentile range.
- Mean $\pm$ 0.675 $\times$ standard deviation, for the 25th–75th percentile range.

Exhibit 6.23: Total annual returns (real) for 10-year holdings on using the market's P/E ratio to make the buy and sell decisions. For comparison, the average return for all the 10-year holdings, numbering 121, in the real 1871–2001 total return index for S&P 500 (annual data) that we have used here is 6.38%, with a standard deviation of 4.90%.

	Real total returns per year for those...	
	...who sold at the P/E signal after having held for ten years	**...who bought at the P/E signal and sold after holding for ten years**
High P/E		
(a) Top 10%	10.49%	9.34%
(b) Top 25%	8.90%	5.72%
(c) Top 33%	9.03%	3.83%
Low P/E		
(a) Bottom 10%	0.23%	12.05%
(b) Bottom 25%	2.24%	10.23%
(c) Bottom 33%	3.05%	9.17%

- Mean $\pm$ 0.440 $\times$ standard deviation, for the 33rd–67th percentile range.

For the 15.07 average (standard deviation = 5.09) of P/E ratios in our database, these cut-off points are as given in Exhibit 6.23. As this exhibit shows, the best returns were obtained by those who bought when the P/E was below its bottom 10th percentile and sold after holding for ten years, whereas selling at this P/E naturally gave the worst returns. For the 6.38% mean of all the 121 annual returns in our database and the corresponding standard deviation of 4.90%, Exhibit 6.23 shows that above average returns have always accrued to the investments that were

1. Made at the *low* P/Es and held for ten years.
2. Sold at the *high* P/Es after having been held for ten years.

This is irrespective of how these lows and highs are defined, i.e., whether the cut-off points are at 10% or 25% or 33%. The other predictable pattern seen here is that selling at the low P/E is not a good idea at all.

We need not have carried out all this detailed analysis to reach this conclusion, of course. Common sense itself would identify selling at a low P/E either a desperate action or an exercise in poor judgement.

As for buying at the high P/Es, though, the results in Exhibit 6.23 are mixed. How about the investors who had bought at the top 10th percentile of these P/Es and sold after holding for ten years? Based on the results in this exhibit, their annual returns were superior to those who either did the same with the bottom one-third of the P/Es or sold at either the top one-third or the top quartile of the P/Es.

Using the high P/E ratios for a divesting strategy may have a dubious value, therefore. Indeed, other than seeking to gain the most by vigorously investing every time the P/E ratio falls precipitously, it is hard to formulate an all weather strategy of market timing that can give consistently superior returns over a reasonably protracted investment horizon. The fate of the Q statistic is hardly much different. This is because, as we saw in Chapter 3, the signals from the two indicators are broadly similar.

Exhibit 6.24 explores this by comparing these data for the history of S&P 500 index with the corresponding real total returns for 10-year holdings and real price changes (or capital gains) for the same holdings. The top panel in this exhibit compares these time series data. The P/E and Q data here are those used in Exhibit 3.7 earlier, i.e., rather than looking at the data, we are looking at their logarithmic deviations from the mean. Notice how differently these signals have moved over time. Neither the P/E ratio nor the Q statistic would have helped us pick the peak of the bull market of late 1950s to early 1960s, for instance, because both these statistics were hovering about their averages then. The bottom panels in Exhibit 6.24 compare the corresponding power spectra. This is a convenient way to identify the dominant cyclicities in any time series, and is particularly appropriate here because all the four datasets in the top panel of this exhibit have pronounced cyclicities. Notice that all the four spectra show a dominant peak at the 4th harmonic. Since we have used 128 annual data here, this corresponds to a 32-year cycle (i.e., four cycles in 128 years). But this is the only significant harmonic that is common to all these spectra. The spectra for P/E ratio and Q statistic also display a subordinate peak at 128-year cyclicity that the

Exhibit 6.24: Comparing the P/E ratios and Q statistic with annualized price changes and total returns for 10-year holdings. P/E ratio and Q data here are the same as in Exhibit 3.7, and are shown as log deviations from their respective mean values. The top panel displays the time series data while the two bottom panels present the corresponding power spectra obtained by the Fourier analyses of annual time series data from the top panel. The spectra have been computed by first detrending each data series, by the simple expedience of subtracting the average, and then adding zeros to make each time series 128 years long. The numbers for the harmonics shown in the power spectra here therefore mean the number of cycles in 128 years.

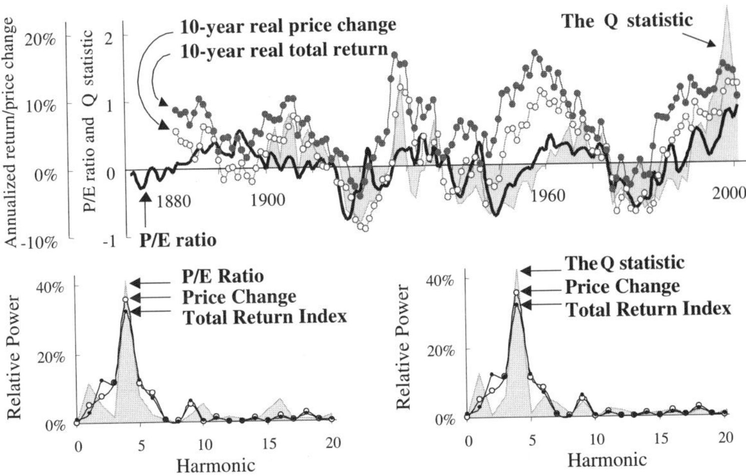

returns and price change data lack. As this analysis only seeks a spectral comparison of the four time series data, and not their spectral decomposition to identify the sources of the component harmonics, it would suffice to note here that spectral analysis also discourages the use of P/E ratio and Q data for investment timing decisions.

Apparently, while the P/E ratio and the Q statistic have provided 100% success in identifying the overvaluation of the 1990s market, the historical data examined here fail to identify them as the indicators for devising a reliable market timing based investment strategy.

The best that can be concluded, therefore, is that a low decile P/E is a good buying signal.

Does this mean that valuation offers no advantage to an investor? Of course not, as we saw in Equation (6.11d). Indeed, the general experience has been that value stocks have given 4% or better in annual returns than the so-called growth stocks. As is evident from Exhibit 6.25, where we graph the growth of $100 invested in the *value* versus *growth* segments of the US (top left) and world (top right) indexes and compare the corresponding annual return statistics (bottom panel), the value stocks have generally performed better than the growth stocks. The US data show higher annualized returns for growth stocks, particularly since January 1988, and thus seem the exception to this pattern. This is only superficial, however. Note that the value segment of the US stocks has lower average-to-standard deviation ratios than the growth segment. By definition, value stocks have higher book-to-market value ratios than the growth stocks. Valuation matters, therefore, as we have shown in

Exhibit 6.25: The top panels show how a $100 investment would have gained, in nominal dollars, in the value and growth segments of market indexes, during the December 1974–July 2001 period. Bottom panel summarizes the corresponding return statistics. The data compared here are the MSCI (Morgan Stanley Capital International) indexes.

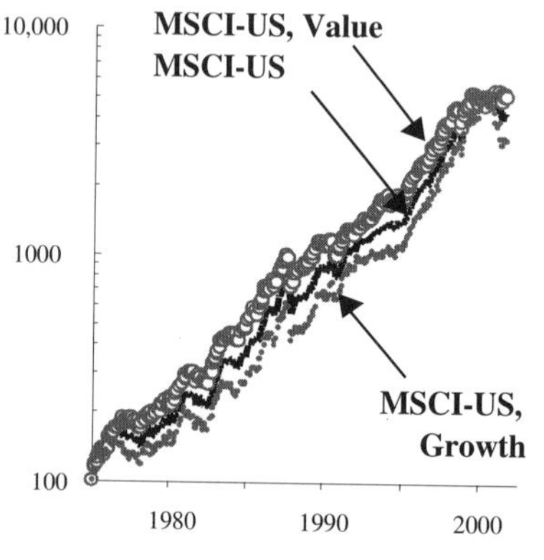

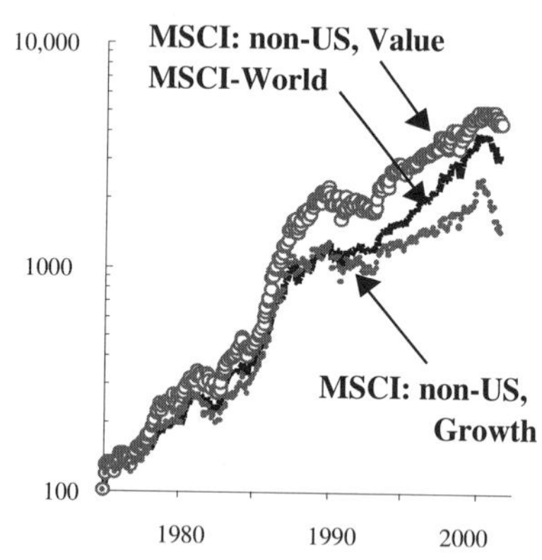

	Jan 1975–Dec 1987		Jan 1988–Jul 2001		Jan 1975–Jul 2001	
	Retun	St. Dev.	Retun	St. Dev.	Retun	St. Dev.
World	16.80%	14.27%	9.14%	14.19%	10.02%	14.22%
US	13.73%	16.32%	14.37%	13.87%	16.61%	15.66%
Non-US, Value	20.85%	15.91%	7.84%	16.31%	7.07%	14.37%
Non-US, Growth	17.35%	17.51%	3.14%	17.70%	2.15%	16.40%
US, Value	15.63%	15.39%	13.88%	13.11%	15.97%	14.54%
US, Growth	11.61%	18.06%	14.48%	16.59%	16.46%	19.53%

Equation (6.11d), but by way of book-to-market value ratio rather than the P/E ratio. This relation between return and market value is not new. It was first pointed out by Rolf Banz[36] in 1981 and has since been the subject of an extensive study by Fama and French.[37]

The question, then, is one of being able to formulate a simple and inexpensive investment strategy to benefit from this finding. In this context, an interesting result comes from Haugen's argument[38] that, instead of giving better returns to the investors who take greater risks, the market compensates those investors who reduce their risk. Apparently, fortune does not favor the brave! Haugen makes his point by constructing a minimum variance portfolio from S&P 500 stocks from monthly returns two years to the date, then adjust the portfolio every quarter, and compare the resulting returns with those of a similar maximum variance portfolio. Part of his results for NYSE stocks over the 1928–1992 period are shown in Exhibit 6.26, along with those in Bilson's[39] extension of this study to the global market place. Rather than making a persuasive case to discard the efficient market hypothesis, what these results show is that we can realize better returns on our investment dollars if we design and use a minimum variance portfolio instead of staying with the total market index.

One way to formulate a simple and inexpensive investment strategy would thus be to combine the merits of Exhibits 6.25 and 6.26, by designing a portfolio of domestic and international value stocks. Exhibit 6.27 summarizes the results of such a strategy, from the perspectives of the US as well as Japanese investors. The reason for selecting these two examples is obvious. The US stock markets have performed very well, particularly in recent years when they have effectively led the world's

Exhibit 6.26: Haugen's results for the NYSE stocks, and Bilson's matching results for international portfolio, show that the index is not a minimum variance portfolio.

	NYSE (1928–1992)		**International**	
	Minimum variance	**Index**	**Minimum variance**	**Index**
Average	10.80%	9.80%	19.26%	14.91%
St. Dev.	17.90%	20.20%	13.06%	13.27%
Ratio	0.60	0.49	1.47	1.12

Exhibit 6.27: Tabulated below are the statistics of domestic and foreign value and growth stocks, from the perspectives of US and Japanese investors, as computed from the MSCI indexes. Shown alongside are the corresponding minimum variance portfolios.

	For US investor			***For Japanese investor***		
	Return	Standard deviation	Sharpe ratio	Return	Standard deviation	Sharpe ratio
All Domestic Stocks	14.06%	15.10%	0.49%	7.29%	20.64%	0.18%
All Domestic Stocks, Value	14.73%	14.25%	0.56%	10.34%	19.94%	0.34%
All Foreign Stocks, Value	14.20%	16.20%	0.46%	11.23%	15.67%	0.29%

	For US investor	***For Japanese investor***
Proportion		
(a) Domestic Stocks	65%	35%
(b) Rest-of-World Stocks	35%	65%
Return	14.55%	11.47%
Standard Deviation	13.16%	14.10%
Sharpe Ratio	0.60	0.52

stock markets, whereas the Japanese market has been a laggard. Thus, if a strategy works well in these two extreme situations, then there is a good case to be made for its wider applicability elsewhere. This is indeed the case here. Note that, by constructing the minimum variance portfolios of domestic and foreign value stocks, US investors are just as better off as the Japanese investors, even though the performances of their respective domestic stock markets have been so dissimilar.

Towards a Fair Model of Market Valuation

This brings us back to the pressing question of market valuation that we had raised at the beginning of this section. Note that, despite its limitations, the P/E ratio gives a good indication of whether the market overall, or an equity individually, can be considered overvalued or not. After all, as we saw in Box 3.1, P/E is the reciprocal of ROE (return on equity) when market value and book value are comparable. As this condition translates into Q = 1, it is not surprising to find (e.g., Exhibit 6.24) that Q and P/E parallel one another. Indeed, a popular way to look at whether this ratio is high or not has been to find, as in the studies[40] by Heaton and Lucas and Diamond, the growth rates in the Gordon growth model that would justify the market's current price. The Heaton and Lucas study suggests that, compared to the past century's average growth rate (g) of 1.4% and P/E ratio of 14, a real annual stock return of 7% in the future would require an expected annual growth rate of 4.9% if the market's P/E ratio averages 24. This is a tall order and demands the P/E ratio to fall.

To examine what can facilitate this fall, consider a firm that pays out all its earnings as dividends. Next year's dividend, D_1, would thus be the same as next year's earnings E_1. Equations (3.3) and (6.5d) then give

$$\frac{P_0}{E} = \frac{1}{(k_e - g)} = \frac{1}{k_e} + \text{PVGO}\,, \tag{6.12a}$$

where

$$\text{PVGO} = \frac{g}{k_e \times (k_e - g)}\,,$$

is the present value of future growth opportunities and P_0 is the current price. To derive this expression for PVGO, just note that this factor in Equation (3.3) is a geometric series so that, for the nomenclature used here,

$$\left[\left(\frac{g}{k_e}\right) + \left(\frac{g}{k_e}\right)^2 + \left(\frac{g}{k_e}\right)^3 + \cdots\right] = \frac{g}{(k_e - g)}\,. \tag{6.12b}$$

For the P/E ratio to fall, then, we need a rise in k_e or a drop in PVGO or a drop in price. This raises several possibilities:

- Price could drop significantly if a sizeable proportion of stockholders either decides or needs to liquidate, e.g., during a market crash, when the retiring baby boomers start withdrawing from their

401(k)s and IRAs, say towards 2010, or a flight of the foreign capital that has been pouring into the US market.

- The discount rate, or the cost of equity, could rise if the equity premium rises or the interest rates rise, say bringing the 1970s back.
- The growth rate could decline either because the economy runs out of steam or because the US productivity may well be past its prime already,[41] or the US economy starts to mimic the ways of a mature economy as that of Western Europe.

Interesting as these possibilities are, they all require a reversal of the long-term trend, however. As can be seen in Exhibit 6.28, for instance, the reciprocal of P_0/E ratio, called the capitalization rate, has broadly followed the ups and downs in the long-term bond rates since 1960. Also notice how the spread between this rate and the 10-year Treasury bills has been negative since the early 1980s. Recall how this spread effectively compliments that in Box 3.1 between the total return on the market and the market's return on equity (ROE). A declining interest rate environment is generally good for stocks and, as we saw in Box 3.1, the US stock market's boom since the early 1980s amply testifies to this fact.

Exhibit 6.28: Changes in the capitalization rate (E/P_0) for S&P 500 index since January 1960 have generally followed those in the interest rates. This rate has also been persistently below the 10-year Treasury bills rates since 1980.

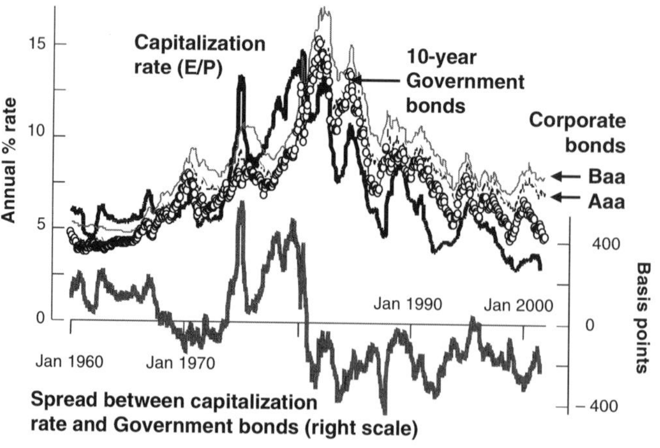

Interest rates can only come down so much, however. The current 1.75% Fed Funds rate has a lot less room to fall, after all, than in January 1981 when it stood at 19.08%. It may already be in the negative territory if we factor the inflation rate in. Once again, therefore, we face the perennial need to precariously balance[42] high growth with low inflation. Such thinking can be wise if it saves us from reverting to the inflationary spiral of the late 1970s and early 1980s but is not a meaningful proposition, as a long-term strategy, short of seeking to violate the economic fundamentals. For instance, Exhibit 6.29 shows how well Okun's law, proposed by the economist Arthur Okun[43] as a linear relation between the rises in unemployment and drops in GDP, has held over time. As a rough rule of thumb, this law suggests a 2–3% growth in output for each percentage point drop in the unemployment rate. The regression analysis of 1940–2001 data in this exhibit suggests that the effect may be stronger still. With the unemployment rate barely 1% above what economists generally take to be its natural level in the US, and the GDP barely 2% below its potential in the second quarter of 2002, clearly there is not much room before the economy starts overheating.

Exhibit 6.29: These data for the 1940–2001 period amply testify to the validity of Okun's law that the GDP drops when unemployment rate rises. The correlation coefficient here is –0.88. If we exclude the isolated point that represents 1946 (2% unemployment rise, 12% GDP drop), and use per capita GDP, then this coefficient rises to an even more significant value of –0.91!

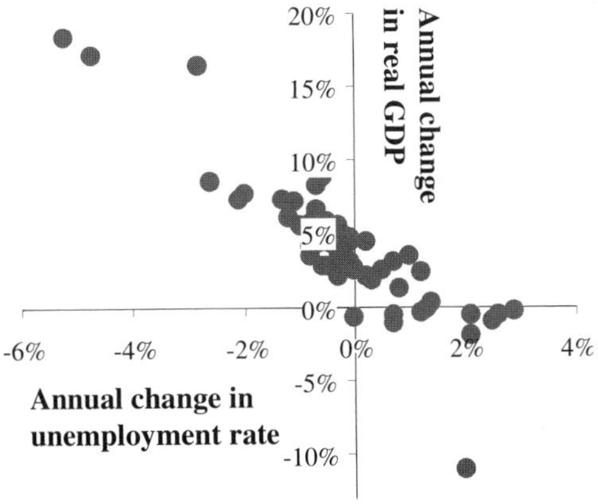

Exhibit 6.30: These 1929–2001 real annual data show that changes in the GDP tend to have a direct effect on the changes in corporate earnings.

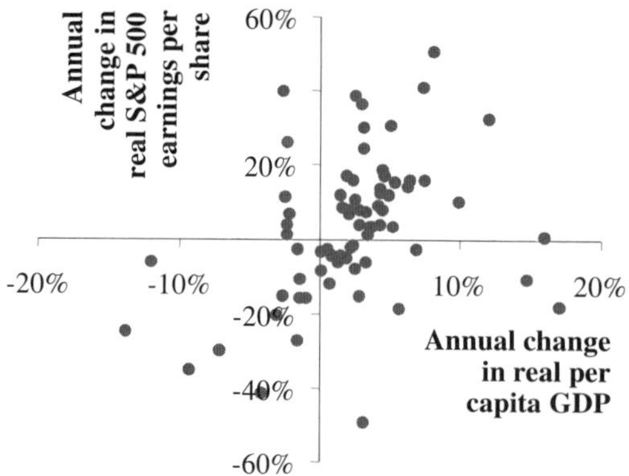

The market's sensitivity to the overall economy is often masked, as we saw in Chapter 3, by the fact that it fluctuates far more frequently than the economy does. This tendency is clearly brought out in Exhibit 6.30, where we compare the annual changes in real per capita GDP with those in the real earnings per share of S&P 500 companies for the 1929–2001 period. The two display a direct relationship, overall, though not in the same crisp and clear-cut manner as seen between the changes in unemployment rate and GDP in Exhibit 6.29. Despite the scatter, Exhibit 6.30 suggests that each 1% change in the GDP can bring about up to 4% or greater change in corporate earnings. The multiplier effect of GDP on the market thus has the same magnitude as that of the unemployment rate on GDP.

This is a hopeful picture because the economy, performing below its potential in mid-year 2002, clearly has room to grow. The question now is whether the market has. What if it has yet to correct itself to its appropriate level? And, if so, to what level? These questions are hard to answer with any modicum of certainty, because they call for the market's valuation whereas, as we have seen earlier in this chapter, even single equities are hard to value precisely. If we go by the historic P/E-based Campbell–Shiller model, then the August 21, 2002 closing price of 949.36 and year 2002 "reported" earnings estimate of $34.11 made the

S&P 500 index grossly overpriced. These numbers give the index a P/E ratio of 27.8, which is way above its historic average of 15. Even the 2002 year-end operating earnings estimate of $44.70 gives the index a P/E ratio of 21.2 which, though better than the August earnings estimate, makes the index pricey at its 949.36 value. Thus measured, the mid-year 2002 market is far from being underpriced. Much like the "Dogs of Dow" strategy that we discussed in Box 5.5, though, this is a backward looking measure because it ignores the fact that technology stocks that now make up almost one-fifth of the S&P 500 index usually have high growth and high P/Es. A decade ago, when its P/E was at about its historic average, the index was dominated by the low P/E sectors like automobiles, oil and other cyclicals, and was weighted barely two-fifths as much in the technology sector as it now is.

An alternative to this is the Fed model, so christened by Dr. Edward Yardeni[44] who gleaned it from the Fed chairman Alan Greenspan's August 1997 report to the Congress. It identifies fair value P/E as the reciprocal of the yield on 10-year Treasury bonds and thus considers the index overpriced if the bond yield exceeds the S&P 500 earnings yield. For 10-year bond yield at 4.228% on August 21, 2002, the resulting fair value P/E is 23.65. Thus, based on the $44.70 operating earnings estimate for 2002, the S&P 500 index would be fairly valued at 1057.16 whereas, if we use the $34.11 reported earnings estimate, then the fair

Exhibit 6.31: The real (solid line) versus computed (open circles) values of the S&P 500 index, the latter based on Equation (3.22) whose coefficients were obtained, as discussed in the text, by multiple regression analysis of 1900–2001 annual data.

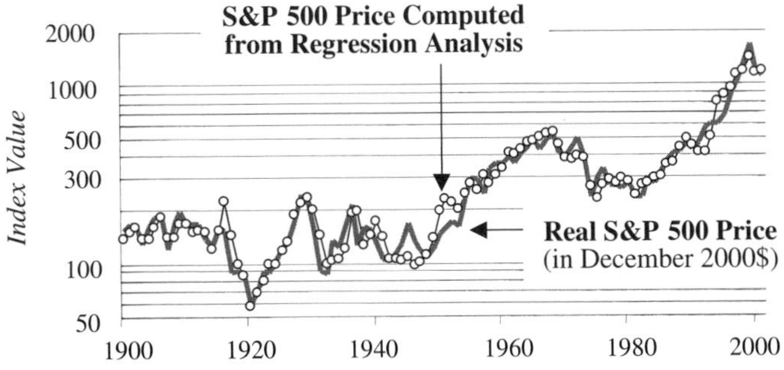

value would be about 20% less. You decide if this makes the index pricey at its 949.36 August 21, 2002 closing value.

A recent regression[45] analysis at the San Francisco Fed examined the 1926–2001 S&P 500 P/E ratios against the yields on long-term government bonds and volatilities of monthly stock and bond returns over the preceding 20 years. The resulting 2002 closing value of 876 for the index is only slightly above its mid-2002 dip. This too suggests that, at 949.36, the market can hardly be considered undervalued. Our extension of this model by adding retention rate and annual stock returns, and using annual instead of monthly data, gives an astounding result. As shown in Exhibit 6.31, our computed values match the index very closely over the 1900–2001 period, with multiple R at 0.8774 and R^2 = 0.76999. It thus explains 77% of the variance. Equation (6.13) is the result.

$$P_{\text{S\&P 500}} = 17.5314 \times E \times \exp\left[\frac{0.0015}{r_{\text{10-yr}}} - 0.987\, RR + 7.0477\, \tilde{r}_{\text{S\&P}} - 3.5734\, \sigma_{\text{S\&P}} + 5.0167\, \sigma_{r_{\text{10-yr}}}\right]. \tag{6.13}$$

Where

E = Average annual earnings (real) for the S&P 500 index.
$r_{\text{10-yr}}$ = Average annual yield on the 10-year Treasuries.
RR = Retention ratio = $(E - D)/E$ for the S&P 500 index.
$\tilde{r}_{\text{S\&P}}$ = Average annual total returns (real) on the S&P 500 index, computed from the preceding 20 years of annual data.
$\sigma_{\text{S\&P}}$ = Standard deviation of annual total returns on S&P 500 index, computed for preceding 20 years of annual data.
$\sigma_{r_{\text{10-yr}}}$ = Standard deviation of annual yields on 10-year Treasuries over the preceding 20 years.

Based as they are on the 20-year averaging of annual data, our $\tilde{r}_{\text{S\&P}}$, $\sigma_{\text{S\&P}}$ and $\sigma_{r_{\text{10-yr}}}$ statistics do not change drastically from one year to another, although, as we have shown earlier, they do contain significant long-terms trends. For annual estimates, therefore, Equation (6.13)

Exhibit 6.32: Estimates of 2002 closing values for the S&P 500 index using Equation (6.13).

With the 2002 earnings per share for S&P 500 as...	...Equation (6.13) gives the 2002 closing value of the S&P 500 index as...	
	Expected value	**Range at 95% confidence level**
\$35	856	829–882
\$40	978	948–1009
\$45	1100	1066–1135
\$50	1223	1185–1261

suggests that the index value is most sensitive to corporate earnings (E) and 10-year Treasury yields ($r_{10\text{-yr}}$). For instance, if $r_{10\text{-yr}} = 5.5\%$ this year, then, with $r_{S\&P} = 10.5\%$, $\sigma_{S\&P} = 13.5\%$ and $\sigma_{r_{10-\text{yr}}} = 11.5\%$, Exhibit 6.32 shows that the 2002 closing values for the S&P 500 index should range from 856 to 1223, based on Equation (6.13), for the corresponding EPS (earnings per share) estimates of \$35 to \$50. For $E = \$36.34$, the number used in the San Francisco Fed estimate of 876, Equation (6.13) gives the index a 2002 closing value of 889. Instead, if the earnings turn out to be \$44.70, then the index should be 1090. For comparison, the index closed at 1148 in 2000 when the earnings per share were \$50!

However desirable it may be, fitting an equation to the data does not necessarily translate into predictability. As Lord Kelvin,[46] the renowned 19th century mathematician and physicist, once noted, fitting a physical phenomenon to a random function implies admitting that you do not understand the mechanism. Be that as it may, note that the fit in Exhibit 6.31 clearly demonstrates the market's efficient response to corporate earnings, to the expectations of the economy's future (as captured in the Treasury yields and their volatility), and to its own history of long-term performance, in terms of returns and risks.

Another issue concerns the rationality of the investor and takes us back, therefore, to the entire debate on the efficient market hypothesis.

The fact that we are able to model the market's 1871–2001 history of performance in terms of corporate earnings, retention rate and the risk-return trade off between stocks and bonds itself makes it hard to call either the investor or the market crazy. This also explains the property of mean reversion, as a matter of fact, as the work of the slowest of the innumerable feedback loops, as part of a built-in servo-mechanism so to speak, through which the market absorbs information. The efficient market hypothesis is not sacrosanct, of course, and must be discarded if it fails to describe the data. But the alternatives are far worse and scary. Look back at the Exhibits 3.7 and 6.24, for instance, and you will discover that P/E and Q are the correct valuation measures then the market is either overvalued or undervalued, most of the time, and never fairly valued! Even the statistical criterion for average P/E that we used in Exhibit 6.23 show that, for the P/E signal to be correct, the market can be correctly valued two-thirds of the time at the most (i.e., buying at high P/E should give substantially sub-average returns).

Exhibit 4.39 showed a convergence of risk-adjusted returns on stocks and government bonds, particularly when we looked at their Sharpe ratios. Historically bond yields have been far less volatile than the stock returns, as we saw in Chapter 4. With bond volatility rapidly closing in on that of the stocks, although their returns are yet to match, perhaps we may soon have bonds in the same basket as stocks and not as their alternatives. That may take a while to show up clearly in the data,

FINANCIAL SERVICES
"I can't stop your investments from going down the toilet, but I know a guy who can sell you a nicer toilet."
GLASBERGEN
Copyright 2002 by Randy Glasbergen.
www.glasbergen.com

however, particularly in the form of increasing correlations between the stock and bond returns. In terms of the portfolio theory discussed in this chapter, this augurs ill for the strategies that use the past 75-year record to allocate between the stocks and bonds to suit an individual investor's utility preference. In such an emerging universe, bonds will look like today's income stocks, with more dividends than capital gains, while stocks in general will move towards today's growth stocks, but both with comparable volatilities that nonetheless reflect the CAPM-style risk-reward profile. An opposite scenario is equally likely. What if the long-term growth rate of the economy slowed down a little? That would drive the dividend non-payers like Microsoft into a rarity, then. The legendary Warren Buffett's recent description of a stock as a "disguised bond"[47] may have been a great deal more prophetic in this respect, than is readily apparent!

6.6 Concluding Remarks

We have, in this chapter, examined the different valuation models, their practical applications, and the implications they have for the individual investor.

No matter the efficiency level of the stock market, one must still have a solid benchmark. We document here the fact that the results of valuation would depend very much on the model being used, leaving the typical investor in somewhat of a quandary, to say the least, as to whether a stock is overvalued or undervalued.

It is pertinent to note in this context the recent debacle of the Long Term Capital Management group. It had made wrong bets on valuation, despite the impressive brainpower, at its disposal, that included two Nobel laureates. The best that could be said is that, on occasion, we can distinguish overvaluation from undervaluation, and can, therefore, make some reasonable guesses as to the general direction of the expected price movement. But determining the level to which the price will move, or the level that could be called the correct price, is an elusive task. The analysts at Goldman Sachs kept defending the business model of e-Toys even as it was being buried into the ground. Their leading "experts" simply would not give up on the company, even after it had piled an incredibly high mountain of debt, after it botched up on the deliveries, and after Amazon.com beat it handily in terms of the total price of toys delivered to the customer.

This chapter has further examined the merits of fundamental analysis, specifically the P/E ratio, and has looked at the "Dogs of Dow" strategy of beating the market. Our conclusion is that they can succeed in exploiting the market inefficiencies, if at all, only if the investor is well-informed and constantly vigilant. For the majority of us, therefore, it might be a better idea to simply follow the market, hold on for the long term, and tide over its ups and downs by dollar-cost-averaging.[48]

With all the talk about price bubbles, one is hard pressed to understand what assets are being priced. With knowledge assets accounting for as much as 80% of the total assets of some companies, an analyst needs to understand the exact relationship between knowledge assets and knowledge structures, and the value of the firm. We need to further identify value creators and the relationship between them and market value. The research in this area is still in its infancy, but is growing at an exponential rate.

In essence, there is no substitute for diligence, a dynamic approach to portfolio management, and for the wisdom, "if it sounds too good to be true, it often is".

Endnotes

[1] A common stock is evidence of ownership in a corporate entity. It can be a

- Class A common stock: It is issued to the public, ordinarily pays dividends, and carries full voting rights.
- Class B common stock: It is "bought" by the organizers of the corporation and does not pay dividends until the earning power of the corporation is proven.
- Founder's share: It resembles a class B common stock, except that it carries sole voting rights and guarantees that the control of the corporation remains in the hands of the founders.

[2] Following are some of the finance texts that specifically focus on valuation, of which this section of our treatment draws heavily on Damodaran's book and its excellent website:

Bradford Cornell: *Corporate Valuation* (Irwin, 1993).

Aswath Damodaran: *Damodaran on Valuation* (John Wiley, 1994).

Tom Copeland, Tim Koller and Jack Murrin: *Valuation* (John Wiley, 1995).

Simon Benninga and Oded Sarig: *Corporate Finance: A Valuation Approach* (McGraw-Hill, 1997).

[3] Following are amongst the most commonly used of these ratios:

$$\text{price-to-earning (P/E) ratio} = \frac{\text{stock price (P)}}{\text{earnings per share (E)}}$$

$$\text{price-to-book value (P/B) ratio} = \frac{\text{stock price (P)}}{\text{book value per share (B)}}$$

This ratio is also called the market-to-book ratio.

$$\text{price-to-sales (P/S) ratio} = \frac{\text{stock price (P)}}{\text{sales revenues per share (S)}}$$

$$\text{price-to-cash value (P/CF) ratio} = \frac{\text{stock price (P)}}{\text{cash flow per share (CF)}}$$

[4] These numbers can be freely downloaded from such financial websites as Yahoo (finance.yahoo.com), Morningstar (www.morningstar.com), Quicken (www.quicken.com) and CNBC (www.cnbc.com).

[5] The following three factors need to be borne in mind when examining these data for purposes of equity valuation:

- It is tempting to assume that ROE = ROA for a debt-free firm like Microsoft. This is not really true, however, because total assets = total liabilities (= debt + other liabilities) + shareholders' equity.
  For Microsoft, debt = 0 but other liabilities (e.g., accounts payable, accrued compensation, income taxes, unearned revenues, etc.) work out to about 25% of its total stockholders' equity, making its equity multiplier ≈ 1.25 and ROE $\approx$ 1.25 ROA.
- Debt is often integral to a firm's capital structure, and carries tax advantages, but the leverage ratios vary widely from firm to firm. This makes it appropriate to adjust a firm's net income for this tax shield of debt, by subtracting this tax shield (= tax rate × interest payment) from net income, so that all firms seem 100% equity financed.
- As employee compensation packages, particularly in the high-tech sector, increasingly include options and such awards carry hidden costs, the net

income of a firm with such costs needs to be adjusted in order to reflect this.

[6] Aswath Damodaran's homepage (www.stern.nyu.edu/~adamodar/New_Home_Page/) has an impressive collection of files explaining the numerous quantitative strategies for valuation, interactive Excel files for selecting the appropriate valuation strategy and performing valuations, and frequently updated downloadable data.

[7] http://www.stern.nyu.edu/~adamodar/New_Home_Page/datafileMReg97.html

[8] William Beaver: "Financial Ratios and Predictors of Failure", Empirical Research in Accounting: Selected Studies, supplement to *Journal of Accounting Research*, vol. 12, pp. 77–111, 1966.

[9] E.I. Altman: "Financial Ratios, Discriminant Analysis and the Prediction of Corporate Bankruptcy", *Journal of Finance*, vol. 23, pp. 589–609, 1968. See also E.I. Altman, R.B. Haldeman and P. Narayana: "Zeta Analysis: A New Model to Identify Bankrupcy Risk of Corporations", *Journal of Banking and Finance*, vol. 3, pp. 29–54, 1977.

[10] I. Dambolena and S. Khoury: "Ratio Stability and Corporate Failure", *Journal of Finance*, vol. 35, pp. 1017–1026, 1980.

[11] G. Foster: *Financial Statement Analysis* (Prentice-Hall, 1986).

[12] In this case,

$$P_0 = \frac{D_1}{1+k_e} + \frac{D_1}{(1+k_e)^2} + \frac{D_1}{(1+k_e)^3} + \cdots,$$

or

$$(1+k_e)P_0 = D_1 + \frac{D_1}{1+k_e} + \frac{D_1}{(1+k_e)^2} + \frac{D_1}{(1+k_e)^3} + \cdots,$$

so that, by subtracting the first line from the second, we have

$$k_e\, P_0 = D_1,$$

or

$$P_0 = \frac{D_1}{k_e}.$$

[13] We now have

$$P_0 = \frac{D_1}{1+k_e} + \frac{D_1(1+g)}{(1+k_e)^2} + \frac{D_1(1+g)^2}{(1+k_e)^3} + \cdots,$$

or

$$\frac{1+k_e}{1+g}P_0 = \frac{D_1}{1+g} + \frac{D_1}{1+k_e} + \frac{D_1(1+g)}{(1+k_e)^2} + \frac{D_1(1+g)^2}{(1+k_e)^3} + \cdots,$$

so that, by subtracting the first line from the second, we have

$$(ke - g)\,P_0 = D_1,$$

or

$$P_0 = \frac{D_1}{(k_e - g)}.$$

[14] Myron Gordon: *Finance, Investment and Macroeconomics* (Elgar, 1994). See also M.J. Gordon: "Dividends, Earnings, and Stock Prices", *Review of Economics and Statistics*, pp. 99–150, May 1959; M.J. Gordon and E. Shapiro: "Capital Equipment Analysis: The Required Rate of Profit", *Management Science*, vol. 3, pp. 102–110, 1956.

[15] These numbers can be freely retrieved from the financial websites such as Yahoo (finance.yahoo.com), Morningstar (www.morningstar.com), Quicken (www.quicken.com), CNBC (www.cnbc.com) and the like.

[16] Payout ratio = Dividend/EPS (for UTX, the last 12 months' payout ratio is 21.70%, compared to the industry and sector-wide rate of 42.93% and the market average of 26.11%).

[17] The dividend discount model discussed above presents discounted cash flow analysis in its simplest form.

[18] Return-on-capital (ROC) = [EBIT × (1 − tax rate)]/book value of capital.

[19] James McTaggart, Peter Kontes and Michael Mankins: *The Value Imperative* (The Free Press, 1994). Alfred Rappaport: *Creating Shareholder Value* (The Free Press, 1998); Bennet Stuart: *The Quest for Value* (HarperCollins, 1991, 1998).

[20] What follows is an updated adaptation of the *BusinessWeek* magazine's cover story, "Valuing an Internet Stock" published in its December 14, 1998 issue.

[21] Sarkis Khoury: *Speculative Markets* (Macmillan, 1984)

[22] Fischer Black and Myron Scholes: "The Pricing of Options and Corporate Liabilities", *Journal of Political Economy*, vol. 81, pp. 637–654, 1973. The original work by Black and Scholes applied mainly to the European options, which differ from the American options in that the former can be exercised only at date of expiration whereas the latter can be exercised at any time on

or before expiration. R.C. Merton ("Theory of Rational Option Pricing", *Bell Journal of Economics and Management Science*, vol. 4, pp. 141–183, 1973) extended the Black and Scholes model to American options on the stocks that do not pay dividends.

[23] $N(d)$ is the probability for a normally distributed random variable ξ to have a value less than or equal to d.

[24] For the numbers given here, $\sigma^2 = 0.55^2 \times 0.92^2 + 0.45^2 \times 0.12^2 + 2 \times 0.55 \times 0.45 \times 0.25 \times 0.95 \times 0.12 = 0.29$

[25] Richard Brealey and Stewart Myers: *Principles of Corporate Finance* (McGraw-Hill/Irwin, 2003). See also:

M. Amram and N. Kulatilaka: *Real Options: Managing Strategic Investment in An Uncertain World* (Harvard Business School Press, 1999).

L. Trigeorgis: *Real Options: Managerial Flexibility and Strategy in Resource Allocations* (MIT Press, 1996).

A. Dixit and R. Pindyck: *Investment Under Uncertainty* (Princeton Univ. Press, 1994).

[26] Margaret Popper: "Another Way of Valuing Dot.Coms, Sort Of", *Business Week*, December 31, 1999.

[27] Michael Mauboussin and Bob Hiller: "Rational Exuberance?", *Credit Suisse First Boston Equity Research*, January 26, 1999.

[28] Damodaran's homepage (www.sterns.nyu.edu/~adamodar/New_Home_Page) also has a working paper and an Excel worksheet with a detailed free cash flow analysis for Amazon.

[29] Ravi Suria, Wai Tung and Peter Kim: "Revisiting Amazon's Liquidity Issues", *Lehman Brothers Global Equity Research*, February 5, 2001.

[30] Mark Kritzman: *Puzzles of Finance — Six Practical Problems and Their Remarkable Solutions* (John Wiley, 2000).

[31] Robert Hagstrom: *The Warren Buffett Way: Investment Strategies of the World's Greatest Investor* (with preface by Peter Lynch) (John Wiley, 1994).

[32] Gabriel Hawawini and Claude Viallet: *Finance for Executives — Managing for Value Creation* (South-Western College Publishing, 1999).

[33] R.C. Higgins: "Sustainable Growth Under Inflation", *Financial Management*, Autumn, 1981.

[34] B. Graham, D.L. Dodd and S. Cottle: *Security Analysis — Principles and Techniques* (McGraw-Hill, 1962).

[35] Robert Shiller: *Irrational Exuberance* (Princeton Univ. Press, 2000).

John Campbell and Robert Shiller: "Valuation Ratios and the Long-Run Stock Market Outlook: An Update", *NBER Working Paper* No. 8221, 2001.

Andrew Smithers and Stephen Wright: *Valuing Wall Street* (McGraw-Hill, 2000).

Unlike the above P/E based studies of Shiller, and Campbell and Shiller, Smithers and Wright base their arguments on Tobin's Q, a valuation measure proposed by James Tobin ("A General Equilibrium Approach to Monetary Theory", *Journal of Money, Credit and Banking*, vol. 1, pp. 15–29, 1969). It is defined as

$$\text{Tobin's Q} = \frac{\text{market value of a firm's assets}}{\text{estimated cost of replacing these assets}} = \frac{n \times P + L}{K}$$

or equivalently as $\frac{n \times P}{K - L}$ as Smithers and Wright have shown.

Here, P is price, n the number of shares, L the market value of corporate liabilities and K the corporate assets.

Oliver Blanchard: "Movements in the Equity Premium", *Brookings Papers on Economic Activity*, No. 2, pp. 75–118, 1993.

John Campbell and Robert Shiller: "The Dividend-Price Ratio and Expectations of Future Dividends and Discount Factors", *Review of Financial Studies*, vol. 1, pp. 195–228, 1988.

[36] Rolf Banz: "The Relationship between Return and Market Values of Common Stock", *Journal of Financial Economics*, vol. 9, pp. 3–18, 1981.

[37] E.F. Fama and K.R. French: "The Cross-Section of Expected Stock Returns", *Journal of Financial Economics*, vol. 47, pp. 427–465, 1992. Their updated data can be accessed at http://www.mba.tuck.dartmouth.edu/pages/faculty/ken.french/data_library.

[38] Robert Haugen: *The Inefficient Stock Market* (Prentice-Hall, 1998). See also Robert Haugen: *The New Finance: The Case Against Efficient Markets* (Prentice-Hall, 1995), and Robert Haugen and Nardin Bader: "Commonality in the Determinants of Expected Stock Returns", *Journal of Financial Economics*, vol. 41, pp. 401–439, 1996.

[39] John F.O. Bilson: "Haugen's Heroes: Risk and Return in Global Equity Markets" (http://www.stuart.iit.edu/workingpapers/haugen/)

[40] John Heaton and Deborah Lucas: "Stock Prices and Fundamentals" in *NBER Macroeconomics Annual 1999* (Ed. Ben Bernanke and Julio Rotemberg), pp. 213–241, 1999. Recall similar calculations by Peter Diamond ("What Stock Market Returns to Expect for the Future?", *Social Security Bulletin*, vol. 63, pp. 38–52, 2000) that were mentioned in Chapter 3.

[41] Robert Gordon: "US Economic Growth Since 1870: One Big Wave", *American Economic Review*, vol. 89, pp. 123–128, 1999.

[42] Two essays by the noted economist, Paul Krugman, one in *The Economist* ("Stable Prices and Fast Growth: Just Say NO", 1996) and the other in the *Harvard Business Review* ("How Fast Can The US Economy Grow", July/August 1997) provide excellent and easy-to-read explanation of why the zero inflation and rapid growth propositions must be treated as mutually exclusive.

[43] Arthur M. Okun: "Potential GNP: Its Measurement and Significance", *Proceedings of the Business and Economics Section*, pp. 98–103, American Statistical Association, 1962.

[44] The assertion, that we have deciphered the Fed's code, was made by Dr. Ed Yardeni, then a Deutsche Bank economist and now with the Prudential Securities, based on the Federal Reserve chairman, Alan Greenspan's Monetary Policy Report to the Congress at his July 22, 1997 Humphrey–Hawkins testimony (www.federalreserve.gov/boarddocs/hh/1997/july ReportSection2.htm).

[45] This study, using the regression model proposed by Clifford Asness ("Stocks Versus Bonds: Explaining the Equity Risk Premium", *Financial Analysts Journal*, vol. 56, pp. 96–113, 2000) has been reported by Kevin Lansing ("Searching for Value in the US Stock Market", *Economic Letter, Federal Reserve Bank of San Francisco*, no. 2002-16, May 24, 2002).

[46] Lord William Thomson Kelvin (1824–1907) contributed to many branches of physics but is to be particularly remembered for his work on the laws of thermodynamics. The first of these laws states that energy is always conserved, in a closed system, either as mechanical energy or as heat energy, or both. The second law, which can be stated either as heat tends to flow from hot to a cold place or as entropy of the universe either remains constant or increases, but never decreases (the term entropy describes the unavailability of energy), basically means that there is no free lunch. Kelvin argued, for instance, that the key issue in interpreting the second law of thermodynamics was the explanation of irreversible processes. He noted that, as entropy always increased, the universe would eventually reach a state of uniform temperature and maximum entropy. There would then be no way to convert the heat energy of the universe into useful mechanical work. He called it the "Heat Death" of the universe. Kelvin also developed the *absolute temperature scale* (the 0°K or absolute zero temperature on this scale equals –273.15°C, or –523.67°F if one insists on measuring temperature only in degrees Fahrenheit). Kelvin was also noted for his hubris, and often fatuous remarks, however.

[47] Carol Loomis: "Warren Buffett on the Stock Market", *Fortune Magazine*, December 10, 2000. (http://www.fortune.com/indexw.jhtml?channel=artcol.jhtml&doc_id=205324).

Incidentally, while our presentation only raises the possibility of similar returns on stocks and bonds, working on the cyclicity in stock returns similar to those we have presented and discussed in Chapter 3, Michael Alexander (*Stock Cycles: Why Stocks Won't Beat Money Markets Over the Next Twenty Years*, iUniverse.com, 2000) even argues for extremely poor stock market returns in the future.

[48] If you invest a fixed dollar amount every month, or every week if you will, then you end up buying more of your target index or stock if its price is down and less of it if its price is up. This is called dollar-cost-averaging because, over time, you have managed to average your costs.

Chapter 7

HOW TO SELECT STOCKS: CAPITALIZING ON INEFFICIENCIES?

7.1 Introduction

As we have shown, based on the Capital Asset Pricing Model and the efficient market hypothesis, every investor should buy the market portfolio like S&P 100 or 500 index and follow a passive buy and hold strategy. Nevertheless, financial markets may not be always efficient and many investors often do not hold the market portfolio. Some even believe that they can consistently, or on the average, beat the market. The number of technical analysts, of books on fundamental analysis, of day traders, and of articles and seminars on active trading strategies, continue to multiply. This chapter focuses on predictability and possible inefficiencies in the stock market. It discusses popular approaches to selecting stocks with higher returns and reviews a number of asset pricing anomalies that have the potential to generate above normal investment outcomes.

7.2 Are Stock Returns Predictable?

To select a good portfolio of stocks to beat the market, one must be able to possess some ability for predicting future stock returns.

Economists and practitioners have identified quite a number of variables and methodologies that may predict future stock returns.

Return Predictability — Seasonalities

Empirical financial studies have revealed a number of seasonal anomalies of asset returns. For instance, French[1] and Gibbons and Hess[2] reported that Monday returns are on average lower than the weekly average, by about 20 basis points. Jaffe and Westerfield[3] also found seasonals in foreign stock markets, although the lowest returns are on Tuesdays for Japan and Australia.

Among the many explanations for Monday seasonals that have been proposed, the most convincing is that negative information is typically held for release after market close on Fridays. Indeed, Penman[4] found that firms with unexpected good news tend to deliver the news on or before the date expected, while firms with bad news tend to delay disclosing their results. If the timing of information release is not systematically recognized by the market, low Monday returns can be explained by a bias towards negative information release by firms over the weekend.

Of course, due to heavy transactions costs, it is difficult to take advantage of the Monday seasonal by buying at week beginnings and selling on Fridays. However, if, for instance, some investors decide to purchase shares, they would be better off avoiding buying on Fridays, assuming that the Monday effects were real.

The "January Effect"

The most prominent seasonal is the so-called January effect. It was revealed by Rozeff and Kinney[5] and has been reviewed by many others. Stock returns, especially for small-cap stocks, appear on average higher in January than in other months. This effect has received a lot of attention because of the magnitude of returns. For instance, Fama[6] found that the S&P 500 index earned an average return of 3.2% in January during 1982–1990, but only 1.2% per month in other months.

Exhibit 7.1: Global persistence of the January effect is amply displayed in this graph of monthly differences between the returns on small-cap and large-cap stocks, worldwide, for the 1962–1989 period.

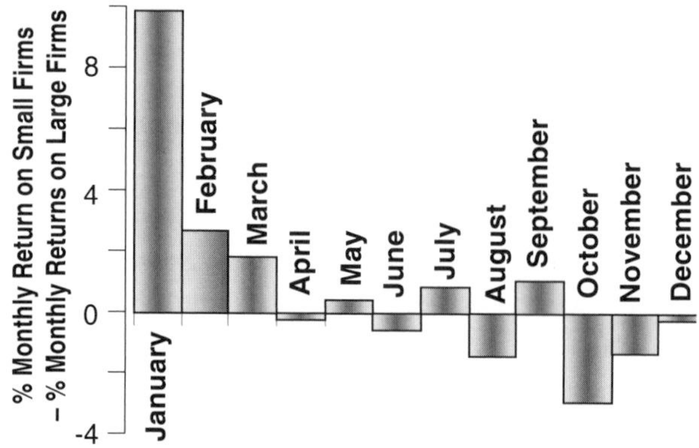

Exhibit 7.1, taken from the Hawawini and Keim paper,[7] shows that small firms worldwide tend to yield significantly higher returns in January, and lower returns late in the year, compared to the large firms. Not surprisingly, therefore, this has produced a simple mantra for small-stock investing: buy in December, sell in January. Indeed, based on this graph, a straightforward rule of thumb would be to switchover from a large-cap index to a small-cap index in October and revert to that large-cap index in January. This would simultaneously offer two benefits. While diversification attendant to indexing would lower the "unique risk" greatly, this switchover would maximize the gains from the two indices.

On the face of it, it would seem that nothing could go wrong with such a mechanical rule on the market's predictability. But then, if the market is indeed efficient then it would be strange if, having discovered this pattern, rational investors do not flock to the small-cap stocks in October, so raising their prices, and sell them off three months later and thus depress their prices in January. This is what may well have happened because, as can be seen in Exhibit 7.2, this effect appears to have been on the vanishing trail. The measure of this effect used in this exhibit is the difference between January returns on firms in the bottom two deciles of market capitalization in the CRSP (Center for Research on Security Prices at University of Chicago) database and the S&P 500

Exhibit 7.2: The January effect has been shrinking, and almost disappeared in the 1990s.

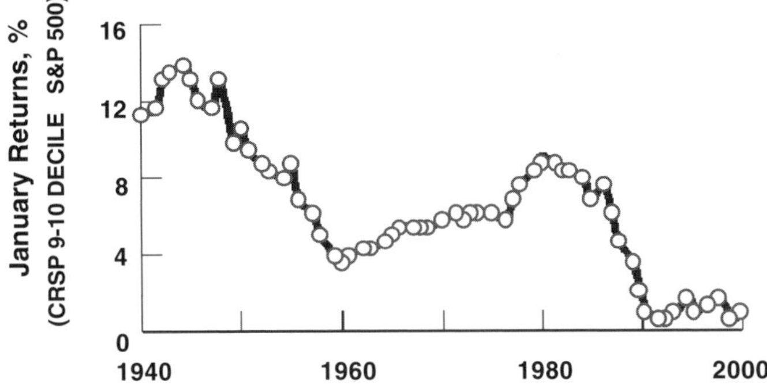

index. Interested readers can readily track these data by comparing Dimension Group's DFA US 9–10 Small Company Fund, DFSCX, with DFA US Large Company Fund, DFLCX.

This leads to an interesting corollary. If small stocks indeed fare better than large stocks in January, and poorer later in the year, then it apparently points to the failure of small stocks to sustain their January lead through the rest of the year. The converse appears to have been true, however. Exhibit 7.3 graphs the January returns on small-cap indexes (Russell 2000 and DFA US 9–10) and the NASDAQ Composite relative to S&P 500 against the corresponding rest-of-the-year relative returns. While the data do show considerable scatter, the correlation here is positive.

Thus, in the years when small-caps have led S&P 500 in January, they have sustained that lead through the rest of the year and, in the years when they have fared poorly relatively to S&P 500, they have been unable to do much better in the rest of the year. Overall, small-caps have outperformed the large-caps through most of the US stock market history, of course. Their outperforming the large-caps should not surprise us, therefore, except that the January effect, if true, would mean that most of this out-performance comes very early in the year. Taken together with Exhibit 7.2, Exhibit 7.3 discourages any practical application of the January effect. After all, for the January effect to be valid, the high relative performance of small stocks in January, and subsequent underperformance, means their failure to sustain the January

Exhibit 7.3: The returns on small-cap indices relative to the S&P 500 index in January can indicate their relative performance in the rest of the year, i.e., if they have done better in January then they are likely to continue that pattern for the rest of the year. Not many NASDAQ firms could qualify as small-cap, at least until the NASDAQ's precipitous fall in 2000. In the aggregate though, and despite the overlaps, market capitalization of S&P 500 firms greatly exceeds that of the NASDAQ firms.

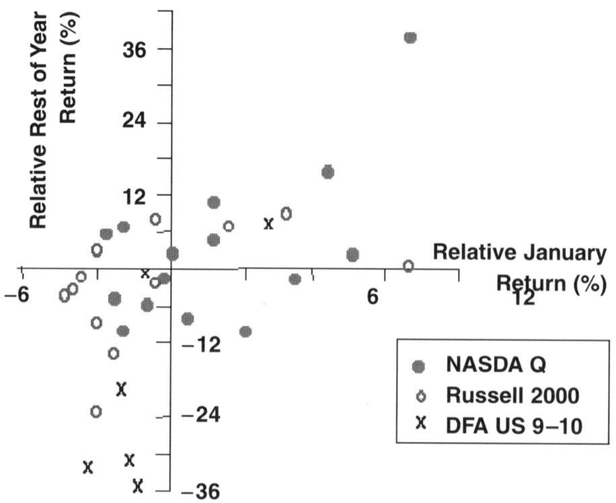

lead. Exhibit 7.3 suggests, on the other hand, that the converse may well have been true.

Various explanations have been proposed for the January effect. The most popular is the tax-loss hypothesis. When realized capital gains are taxed, investors have an incentive to realize losses by year-ends, by selling stocks that have decreased in value, and to delay realizing capital gains. December should thus be a month losers are sold to shield income from taxation. The evidence on tax-loss selling, however, is mixed. Schultz[8] found no January effect from 1900 to 1917, when there was no significant income tax, but Jones, Pearce, and Wilson[9] found the opposite results in a longer sample period.

Return Predictability — Ratio Analysis

Financial analysts and researchers have long recognized that certain information from companies' financial statements, such as dividend-yields and price earnings ratios are useful predictors. Consider a stock that pays a dividend at each period of time. The intrinsic value of this stock equals in principle the present value of expected future dividends. Assume that the required discount rate for the stock is r per period. Then the dividend discount model (DDM) indicates

$$P_0 = \frac{D_1}{1+r} + \frac{D_2}{(1+r)^2} + \frac{D_3}{(1+r)^3} + \cdots,$$

where P_0 denotes the intrinsic value of the stock at time 0 and D_i stands for the dividend (expectedly) to be paid in period i. If one further assumes that dividends grow at a constant speed g, one obtains

$$P_0 = \frac{D_1}{r-g}.$$

As we have seen earlier, the above formula is called the constant-growth dividend discount model (DDM) with an infinite life. (r must, of course, be greater than g).

Obviously, a high dividend-yield (D/P) implies a low valuation of the stock, *ceteris paribus*. Campbell,[10] Campbell and Shiller,[11] and Fama and French[12] all found that dividend yields predict future stock returns. That is, a high dividend-yield often implies high average stock returns in the future. For this reason, some researchers suggest to buy stocks with high dividend yields.

The problem with dividend-yields as a predictor for stock returns is that dividend-yields do not fully reflect the cash flows of firms: the yields depend closely on company's dividend payout policies. In the long run, dividend payout policies may vary significantly. For instance, the evidence suggests that many firms have lowered their dividend payout ratios in order to pursue more growth opportunities and reduce tax burdens.

Price-to-earnings (P/E) ratios can avoid the above problems with dividend yields. Traditionally, investors have looked at P/E ratios based on the previous 12 months' profits, known as trailing earnings. Today, though, investors commonly cite P/E ratios based on the consensus analysts' forecast of the next 12 months' profits, or forward earnings.

The rationale for this change is that forward P/E is a better reflection of a stock's future value — and that, after all, is what you are buying when you invest in stocks. But be careful: all projections involve guesswork and analysts frequently err on the high side when making earnings forecasts.

Assume that a company's plowback ratio (one minus dividend payout-ratio) is b and its current earnings are E_1. One obtains the current dividend of the company as $D_1 = (1 - b) \times E_1$. Furthermore, one can obtain that the growth rate of the company (dividends and earnings) will be $g = b \times \text{ROE}$, where ROE stands for the company's return on equity. The constant-growth DDM implies

$$\frac{P_0}{E_1} = \frac{1-b}{r-g} = \frac{1-b}{r-b\times \text{ROE}}.$$

It is easy to verify that the P/E ratio increases with ROE. This makes sense, because high-ROE projects give the company good opportunities for growth. Usually, investors call high P/E stocks growth stocks and low P/E stocks value stocks. Obviously, to be reasonably valued, a stock's P/E should be consistent with its ROE, or in general, the growth potential. A stock with an unjustifiable high P/E may signal an over-valuation and a low average return in the long run. In 1998 and 1999, many Internet stocks possessed amazingly high P/E ratios that were hard to justify with even very optimistic assumptions about growth. As a result, many of these stocks lost 80 percent or more of their values in 2000 and early 2001.

In a recent book, *Irrational Exuberance*, Shiller[13] claimed that a stock market downturn would be inevitable when the P/E of the market index is too high compared with the historical norm. There is no doubt that P/E ratios have the power to predict long-term stock returns, that is, a correction will be unavoidable if the P/E is too high or too low. But when? So far even Wall Street pros have not been very successful in timing the market based on P/E ratios. Shiller, no newcomer to the bubble theory of the stock market, briefed Fed chairman Alan Greenspan about high P/E ratios (Exhibit 7.4) two days before that 1996 speech of "irrational exuberance". The stock market, however, kept running up until the middle of the year 2000.

Exhibit 7.4: The P/E ratio of the S&P 500 index has fluctuated about 14 when we consider the entire history of the market (1871–2000) but has had an appreciably higher average of 24 through the 1990s.

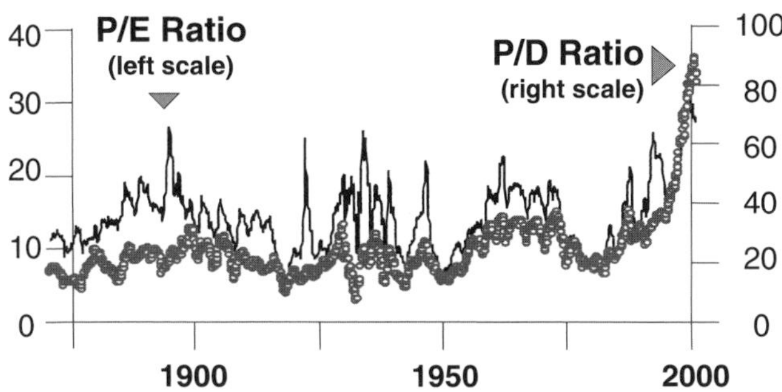

In the preceding chapter, we have already discussed, at length, the overall market's P/E ratios and the implications of this on the "irrational exuberance" hypothesis. We have also discussed there how this ratio can be used for valuing the individual equities and have examined its limitations. What makes this issue relevant in this chapter, nonetheless, is the fact that this multiple can be also used for selecting individual stocks. Since high growth rates in earnings should imply a high P/E, *ceteris paribus*, sometimes investors use the so-called PEG (price/earnings/growth) ratio, instead of P/E, in their security analyses. The PEG ratio is calculated by taking the P/E ratio based on forward earnings and dividing by the projected growth rate. Stocks with a PEG ratio of less than one (meaning that they are trading at less than their projected growth rate) are generally said to be cheap, while a PEG ratio of 1.5 or higher indicates a stock that may be overpriced. For stocks that pay a substantial dividend, the PEGY ratio — which is the P/E divided by the projected growth rate and the dividend yield — may be an even better measure than the PEG alone. Keep in mind, though, that both the PEG and PEGY ratios are highly speculative measures, as they are based on projections and no one can really foretell the future. For some companies, such as high-tech startups, whose earnings are negative, price-to-sales ratios are sometimes used in stock selections.

It is interesting to mention that financial researchers have found that the price-to-book (P/B) ratio, defined as a stock's market price divided

Exhibit 7.5: The market-to-book value effect (NYSE stocks, 1967–1987).

Decile	Compound annual return (%)	Standard deviation (%)	Ending index value ($)
1 (lowest)	16.0	17.1	22.6
2	17.1	21.5	27.6
3	15.7	21.1	17.8
4	12.8	20.3	12.6
5	11.1	19.7	9.1
6	9.8	17.7	7.1
7	10.9	19.1	8.8
8	9.3	20.6	6.5
9	7.9	17.4	5.0
10 (highest)	7.8	17.6	4.8

Source: Ibbotson Associates (1991)

by its book value, also predicts future stock returns. Fama and French[14] showed that low P/B ratios are associated with high-expected returns with the US data. Chan, Hamao, and Lakonishok[15] obtained similar results for Japan.

Exhibit 7.5 shows the estimated relation between P/B ratios and average stock returns during 1967–1987 in the US. NYSE stocks are sorted into deciles according to their P/B ratios. Stocks with low P/B ratios had substantially higher returns than stocks with otherwise high P/B ratios. For each dollar invested in 1966, firms in the lowest deciles would have grown to $22.6 in 1987, whereas firms in the highest decile would have grown to only $4.8.

Some researchers have also proposed to use the so-called Q value to judge the relative valuation of stocks and to forecast future stock returns. The Q in question is a ratio developed by economist James Tobin. It relates the stock market value of quoted companies to the replacement cost of their assets. If Q is above one, it is cheaper to buy assets directly than to buy stock market companies; the reverse applies if it is below one.

Few analysts will doubt that Q has in the past been a very good guide to stock market valuation — when Q is above or below its average level, the chances are strong that share prices will fall (or rise) until it

Exhibit 7.6: History of Tobin's Q ratio through the twentieth century.

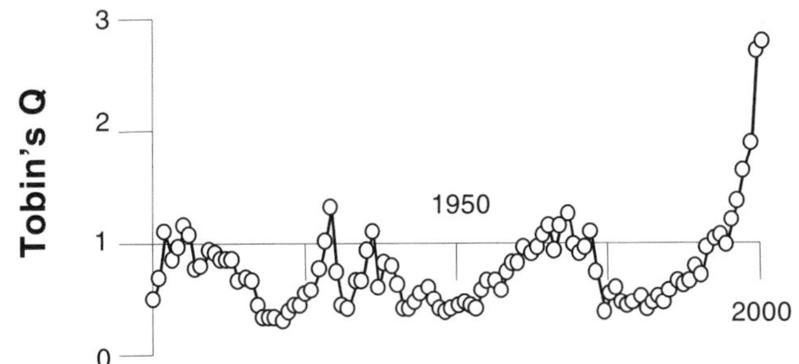

is back in line. The question is if the Q ratio always works in predicting the direction of the stock market.

Smithers and Wright[16] argue that Q can be an extremely useful indicator about whether the stock market is reasonably valued, although it cannot predict short-term market movements. Exhibit 7.6 indicates that the stock market has looked overvalued in terms of Q for a long time in the 1990s but has kept rising, until a downturn in the stock market, especially the NASDAQ market, happened after March 2000.

The Fama and French results, and those of Chan, Hamao and Lakonishok confirm the relevance of P/E ratios in predicting stock market trends. The results reported in Exhibit 6.23 show, however, that the P/E ratio is a good indicator for buying decision when it is in the bottom decile, but not necessarily a good selling signal when it is at the top decile.

Return Predictability — Past Returns

Using past returns to forecast future returns has been popular among both economists and practitioners. Early studies mainly address the question of whether asset prices are random walks. The simplest version of the random walk hypothesis is the independently and identically distributed (i.i.d.) increments case in which the dynamics of a variable are given by the following equation

$$x_{t+1} = \mu + x_t + \varepsilon_{t+1}, \quad \varepsilon_{t+1} \sim \text{i.i.d. } (0, \sigma^2),$$

where μ is the expected change in x, or drift, i.i.d. $(0, \sigma^2)$ denotes an independent and identical distribution with mean 0 and variance σ^2. The popular form of the random walk hypothesis on asset prices asserts that the natural logarithm of asset prices follows a random walk with normally distributed increments.

The empirical studies so far have in general rejected the random walk hypothesis. Lo and MacKinlay,[17] for instance, found weekly autocorrelations of stock returns ranging from 0.09 to 0.30. Fama and French[18] and Poterba and Summers,[19] however, found that long-term autocorrelations of stock returns are negative. That is, stock prices contain a transitory component that slowly dies away with time. More specifically, Fama and French decomposed the logarithm of the stock price p_t into two components, a permanent component q_t that follows a random walk, and a temporary component z_t that is mean-reverting, such that

$$p_t = q_t + z_t \,,$$
$$q_t = \mu + q_{t-1} + \varepsilon_t \,, \quad \varepsilon_t \sim \text{i.i.d.}\, N(0, \sigma_\varepsilon^2)\,,$$
$$z_t = \phi z_{t-1} + \eta_t \,, \quad 0 < \phi < 1, \quad \eta_t \sim \text{i.i.d.}\, N(0, \sigma_\eta^2)\,.$$

DeBondt and Thaler[20] and Chopra, Lakonishok, and Ritter[21] provided further evidence on long-term mean-reversal specified in the above model. In particular, DeBondt and Thaler found that when stock returns are ranked on three- to five-year past returns, past winners tend to be future losers and vice versa.

There is, however, good reason to be weary of inferences on long-horizon returns. Perhaps the most obvious concern is the small sample size. For example, Poterba and Summers' analysis[22] was based on US stock returns during 1926–1985. From 1926–1985, there are only 12 non-overlapping five-year returns. While overlapping returns do provide some incremental information, the results in Boudoukh and Richardson[23] and Richardson and Stock[24] suggest that this increment is modest at best and misleading at worst.

If the mean-reversion of stock prices in the long-run is real, one may use a long-term contrarian strategy to enhance his/her long-term investment performance. That is, buy stocks that have performed poorly in the past several years (say five years) and hold them for another several years, while sell stocks whose prices have gone up quickly in the past several years from one's long-term portfolio.

Recent financial studies have shifted from documenting the predictability of stock returns to constructing various trading strategies to taking advantage of predictable variations in asset returns. One of the most popular trading strategies discussed in academia and followed by practitioners is the so-called momentum strategy, investigated by Jagadeesh and Titman,[25] among the others.

Return Predictability — Momentum

Momentum is a terminology borrowed from physics. Simply speaking, in physics, it means that a moving object in acceleration or with force will not revert its moving direction instantaneously. A momentum strategy in financial investments, sometimes also called a relative strength strategy, suggests buying stocks that have been recent market winners and selling stocks that have been recent losers. Put it in another way, this strategy believes that winners (stocks have had above average returns) in the recent past will be most likely to keep being winners in the near future, and that past losers will be most likely future losers.

Using the US equity return data, Jagadeesh and Titman[26] show that stock returns are positively autocorrelated at horizons from one month to about one year. Similar evidence for international stocks is also reported in Rouwenhorst.[27] Jagadeesh and Titman[28] reported that buying stocks with high returns over the previous 3–12 months and selling stocks with poor returns over the same period earn profits of about one percent per month. More recently, Lesmond, Schill, and Zhou[29] provided some new evidence on the profitability of momentum strategies. Some of their results are reported in Exhibit 7.7. It shows that if one ignores trading costs, returns on buying past winners and selling past losers are very significant.

The momentum strategies and long-term reversals are based on own-autocorrelations of individuals stocks and market indexes, that is, the future returns on a stock (or market index) are statistically related to its past returns. The history shows that stock returns are also cross-autocorrelated, namely, some stocks lead other stocks in price movements.

Exhibit 7.7: Momentum strategy holding period returns and portfolio characteristics. The sample is composed of all NYSE, AMEX, and NASDAQ stocks listed on CRSP from January 1980 to December 1998. Firms are classified into three portfolios based on the respective breakpoint percentiles of performance during past six months. Here "W" stands for past winners, "L" stands for past losers and "M" stands for past middle-performers. For "10–90" breakpoints, W is the top 10% performers, L is bottom 10% performers, and M is middle 80% performers, respectively. For "30–70" breakpoints, W is the top 30% performers, L is bottom 30% performers, and M is middle 40% performers, respectively. Within the three portfolios, firms are initially equally weighted and held for six months. The portfolio beta is estimated from the CAPM model with the CRSP value-weighted portfolio return as the market portfolio return. Beta estimates are obtained for each portfolio over the 228 months of the sample period. The mean share price is estimated using the stock price at the end of the formation period and weighing each holding period equally. The mean market cap is estimated identically to the mean share price using the market price and shares outstanding at the end of the formation period. Standard errors are reported in parentheses.

	10–90 Breakpoints				**30–70 Breakpoints**			
	L	M	W	W–L	L	M	W	W–L
Semi-annual portfolio returns								
Mean	0.0435–0.04	0.0804–0.025	0.094–0.032	0.0505–0.027	0.0552–0.033	0.085–0.023	0.0917–0.027	0.0366–0.017
Minimum	−0.406	−0.249	−0.289	−0.518	−0.331	−0.231	−0.258	−0.261
Maximum	0.696	0.477	0.6	0.393	0.557	0.415	0.538	0.187
Portfolio characteristics								
Portfolio beta	1.11–0.09	0.97–0.04	1.25–0.05		1.04–0.06	0.93–0.03	1.11–0.04	
Mean share price	5.34–0.39	19.81–0.62	19.88–3.48		9.56–0.73	21.34–0.88	23.2–1.21	
Mean market cap ($ millions)	169.2–20.5	747.8–64.6	379.5–82.2		309.4–24.4	878.6–81.8	695.3–93.9	
Proportion of stocks traded on the NYSE	0.102	0.298	0.166		0.182	0.333	0.259	

More specifically, Lo and MacKinlay,[30] for instance, found that larger capitalization stocks tend to lead and smaller-capitalization stocks lag. They also observed that positive cross-effects imply that certain contrarian investment strategies could be profitable. Different from momentum strategies that follow the general market direction, contrarian strategies are contrary to the general market direction by advocating selling winners and buying losers.

To see how positive cross-effects provide a channel through which contrarian strategies can be profitable, suppose the market consists of two stocks, A and B, such that A's returns lead B's. If A's return is higher than the market today, a contrarian sells it and buys B. But if A and B are positively cross-autocorrelated, a higher return for A today implies a higher return for B tomorrow on average, and thus the contrarian will have profited from his long position in B on average. This example suggests that a contrarian investment strategy will be profitable even if each security's return is unpredictable using past returns of that security alone.

At a first glance, Jegadeesh and Titman's momentum strategy seems contradictory to Lo and MacKinlay's contrarian strategy. These seemingly contradictory results indicate the high complexity of the financial world. As a matter of fact, momentum strategies and contrarian strategies can coexist and can both be profitable, if used appropriately. The major reason behind the co-existence of both profitable momentum strategies and profitable contrarian strategies is that own and cross auto-correlations of stock returns vary substantially with time horizons and across stocks. For instance, over three-month to six-month horizons, we often see price continuations, but when we consider 3-year to 5-year horizons, we typically see asset price reversals.

Jegadeesh and Titman's momentum portfolios are formed based on returns in the past three-months to one-year, in terms of own auto-correlations of asset returns; whereas Lo and MacKinlay's contrarian strategies are based on lead-lag relations of weekly stock returns. The lead-lag relations do not exist among all stocks, for all kinds of news. McQueen, Pinegar and Thorley[31] found that the lead-lag relations exist only in the following form: small stocks lag large stocks in response to good news, but not to bad news.

In practical trading practice, one can obtain momentum information online from, for example, Yahoo!Finance (finance.yahoo.com), www.sixer.com, and www.tradetrek.com.

Return Predictability — Recent Revisions in Estimated Earnings

The recent history of Wall Street revisions of estimated earnings of a stock can sometimes provides useful information to predict future returns. A stock whose earnings estimates have been revised upwardly usually produce positive abnormal returns. In contrast, a stock whose earnings estimates have been revised downwardly are often associated with lower future returns. This is possibly because the analysts revise their earnings estimates in a gradual manner. That is, a revision in estimated earnings may signal further revisions in earnings estimates in the same direction.

Return Predictability — Firm Size

The central prediction of the Capital Asset Pricing Model (CAPM) is that the market portfolio of invested wealth is mean-variance efficient. The efficiency of the market portfolio implies that: (1) expected returns on securities are a positive linear function of their market betas (the slope in the regression of a security's return on the market's return), (2) market betas suffice to describe the cross-section of expected returns. Banz[32] reported a significant empirical relationship between the return and the total market value of New York Stock Exchange common stocks. Historically, the common stock of small firms had, on average, substantially higher risk-adjusted returns than the common stock of large firms. This "size effect" provides evidence that the CAPM is miss-specified. Fama and French[33] also found that size, together with book-to-market equity, provides a simple and powerful characterization of the cross-section of average stock returns for the 1963–1990 period. Further, when the tests allow for variation in beta that is unrelated to size, the relation between market beta and average return is flat, even when beta is the only explanatory variable.

Exhibit 7.8 presents the annual rates of return on five asset classes for the period of 1926–1996. "Large stocks" in the table refers to Standard

Exhibit 7.8: Rates of return, 1926–1996.

Year	Small stocks	Large stocks	Long-term T-bond	Intermediate-term T-bond	T-bills	Inflation
1926	−8.91	12.21	4.54	4.96	3.19	−1.12
1927	32.23	35.99	8.11	3.34	3.12	−2.26
1928	45.02	39.29	−0.93	0.96	3.21	−1.16
1929	−50.81	−7.66	4.41	5.89	4.74	0.58
1930	−45.69	−25.90	6.22	5.51	2.35	−6.40
1931	−49.17	−45.56	−5.31	−5.81	0.96	−9.32
1932	10.95	−9.14	11.89	8.44	1.16	−10.27
1933	187.82	54.56	1.03	0.35	0.07	0.76
1934	25.13	−2.32	10.15	9.00	0.60	1.52
1935	68.44	45.67	4.98	7.01	−1.59	2.99
1936	84.47	33.55	6.52	3.77	−0.95	1.45
1937	−52.71	−36.03	0.43	1.56	0.35	2.86
1938	24.69	29.42	5.25	5.64	0.09	−2.78
1939	−0.10	−1.06	5.90	4.52	0.02	0.00
1940	−11.81	−9.65	6.54	2.03	0.00	0.71
1941	−13.08	−11.20	0.99	−0.59	0.06	9.93
1942	51.01	20.80	5.39	1.81	0.26	9.03
1943	99.79	26.54	4.87	2.78	0.35	2.96
1944	60.53	20.96	3.59	1.98	−0.07	2.30
1945	82.24	36.11	6.84	3.60	0.33	2.25
1946	−12.80	−9.26	0.15	0.69	0.37	18.13
1947	−3.09	4.88	−1.19	0.32	0.50	8.84
1948	−6.15	5.29	3.07	2.21	0.81	2.99
1949	21.56	18.24	6.03	2.22	1.10	−2.07
1950	45.48	32.68	−0.96	0.25	1.20	5.93
1951	9.41	23.47	−1.95	0.36	1.49	6.00
1952	6.36	18.91	1.93	1.63	1.66	0.75
1953	−5.68	−1.74	3.83	3.63	1.82	0.75
1954	65.13	52.55	4.88	1.73	0.86	−0.74
1955	21.84	31.44	−1.34	−0.52	1.57	0.37
1956	3.82	6.45	−5.12	−0.90	2.46	2.99
1957	−15.03	−11.14	9.46	7.84	3.14	2.90

Exhibit 7.8: (*Continued*)

Year	Small stocks	Large stocks	Long-term T-bond	Intermediate-term T-bond	T-bills	Inflation
1958	70.63	43.78	−3.71	−1.29	1.54	1.76
1959	17.82	12.95	−3.55	−1.26	2.95	1.73
1960	−5.16	0.19	13.78	11.98	2.66	1.36
1961	30.48	27.63	0.19	2.23	2.13	0.67
1962	−16.41	−8.79	6.81	7.38	2.72	1.33
1963	12.20	22.63	−0.49	1.79	3.12	1.64
1964	18.75	16.67	4.51	4.45	3.54	0.97
1965	36.67	12.50	−0.27	1.27	3.94	1.92
1966	−8.08	−10.25	3.70	5.14	4.77	3.46
1967	103.39	24.11	−7.41	0.16	4.24	3.04
1968	50.61	11.00	−1.20	2.48	5.24	4.72
1969	−32.27	−8.33	−6.52	−2.10	6.59	6.20
1970	−16.54	4.10	12.69	13.93	6.50	5.57
1971	18.44	14.17	17.47	8.71	4.34	3.27
1972	−0.62	19.14	5.55	3.80	3.81	3.41
1973	−40.54	−14.75	1.40	2.90	6.91	8.71
1974	−29.74	−26.40	5.53	6.03	7.93	12.34
1975	69.54	37.26	8.50	6.79	5.80	6.94
1976	54.81	23.98	11.07	14.20	5.06	4.86
1977	22.02	−7.26	0.90	1.12	5.10	6.70
1978	22.29	6.50	−4.16	0.32	7.15	9.02
1979	43.99	18.77	9.02	4.29	10.45	13.29
1980	35.34	32.48	13.17	0.83	11.57	12.52
1981	7.79	−4.98	3.61	6.09	14.95	8.92
1982	27.44	22.09	6.52	33.39	10.71	3.83
1983	34.49	22.37	−0.53	5.44	8.85	3.79
1984	−14.02	6.46	15.29	14.46	10.02	3.95
1985	28.21	32.00	32.68	23.65	7.83	3.80
1986	3.40	18.40	23.96	17.22	6.18	1.10
1987	−13.95	5.34	−2.65	1.68	5.50	4.43
1988	21.72	16.86	8.40	6.63	6.44	4.42
1989	8.37	31.34	19.49	14.82	8.32	4.65

Exhibit 7.8: (*Continued*)

Year	Small stocks	Large stocks	Long-term T-bond	Intermediate-term T-bond	T-bills	Inflation
1990	−27.08	−3.20	7.13	9.05	7.86	6.11
1991	50.24	30.66	18.39	16.67	5.65	3.06
1992	27.84	7.71	7.79	7.25	3.54	2.90
1993	20.30	9.87	15.48	12.02	2.97	2.75
1994	−3.34	1.29	−7.18	−4.42	3.91	2.67
1995	33.21	37.71	31.67	18.07	5.58	2.54
1996	16.50	23.00	0.10	2.70	5.20	3.32
Average	19.02	12.50	5.31	5.16	3.76	3.22
Standard deviation	40.44	20.39	7.96	6.47	3.35	4.54
Minimum	−52.71	−45.56	−7.41	−5.81	−1.59	−10.27
Maximum	187.82	54.56	32.68	33.39	14.95	18.13

& Poor's market-value-weighted portfolio of 500 US common stocks with the largest market capitalization. "Small stocks" represents the value-weighted portfolio of the lowest capitalization quintile. Since 1982, this portfolio has included smaller stocks traded on the AMEX and NASDAQ markets as well. The portfolio contains approximately 2000 stocks with an average market cap of $100 million. On average, small stocks provided an annual return of about 19% during 1926–1996; while the average annual return to large stocks is only 12.5%. Of course, returns of small stocks are more volatile (that is, with higher standard deviations), but a substantial portion of their standard deviations can be diversified.

Return Predictability — Neglected Firms

Arbel and Strebel[34] considered an additional influence beyond size — attention or neglect. They measured attention in terms of the number of analysts who regularly follow a stock and applied the neglected-firm notion across size classes. They confirmed the small firm effect but also found a neglected-firm effect caused by the lack of information and limited institutional interest. Beard and Sias,[35] however, found no evidence of a neglected-firm premium after controlling for market capitalization size.

Return Predictability — Insider Trading

It is believed that insiders possess superior information and can exploit this information to outperform the market. Therefore, mimicking the trading of insiders can be profitable.

Givoly and Palmon,[36] among others, show that insider trading yields abnormally high returns. While the abnormal profits associated with insider trading may be indicative of illegal information exploitation, they also may result from outside market participants' response to news of insider trading, such that it is perceived as a leading indicator, triggering a wave of transactions which subsequently increase returns to insiders. Givoly and Palmon's analysis revealed that abnormal returns to insider trading were primarily due to price changes resulting from market response to news of insider trades and suggested relatively low incidence of exploitation of privileged information by insiders.

In a recent article, Lakonishok and Lee[37] examined insider trading activities of all companies traded on the NYSE, AMEX, and NASDAQ during the 1975–1995 period. In general, very little market movement is observed when insiders trade and when they report their trades to the Securities and Exchange Commission (SEC). Insiders in aggregate are contrarian investors. However, they predict market movements better than simple contrarian strategies. Insiders also seem to be able to predict cross-sectional stock returns. The result, however, is driven by insider's ability to predict returns in smaller firms. In addition, informativeness of insiders' activities is coming from purchases, while insider selling appears to have no predictive ability.

7.3 Event Studies and Return Predictability

Event studies are now indispensable tools for corporate finance and investment decisions. The intent of these studies is to examine abnormal returns surrounding significant economic/financial information. In recent years, a body of evidence on security returns has presented a sharp challenge to the traditional view that securities are efficiently priced to reflect all public information. Researchers have identified quite a few economic and financial events to which the financial market may either over-react or under-react.

When we say that the financial market under-reacts to an event, we mean that event-date average stock returns are of the same sign as average subsequent long-term abnormal returns. In other words, if an event brings good news and the stock price rises at the event day, the average post-event long-term returns will be positive; if a bad event occurs and the stock price drops at the event day, the average post-event long-term returns will be negative. Similarly, market over-reaction means that event-date average stock returns are of the different sign as average subsequent long-term abnormal returns.

Researchers find evidence that the stock market under-reacts to the following events.

Stock Splits[38]

In theory, stock splits alone should not cause higher rates of returns because they add nothing to the value of a firm. Under the efficient market hypothesis, one would expect no significant price change following a split because any relevant information (such as earnings growth) that caused the split would have already been priced. Evidence presented by, for example, Grinblatt, Masulis, and Titman, however, suggests that stock prices, on average, respond positively to stock-split announcements that are not contaminated by other contemporaneous firm-specific announcements. Furthermore, their analysis documents significantly positive excess returns on and around the ex-dates of stock splits.

Open Market Repurchases[39]

Open market repurchases often send a positive signal to investors — stocks could have been under-priced. For this reason, there should be positive reactions to stock prices following open market share repurchase announcements, but these reactions should be done in a quick manner under the efficient market hypothesis. Ikenberry, Lakonishok, and Vermaelen's study examined long-run firm performance following open market share repurchase announcements in the years 1980–1990. The findings indicate that the average abnormal 4-year buy-and-hold return measured after the initial announcement is 12.1%. For value (low P/E) stocks, companies are more likely to be repurchasing shares because of undervaluation, the average abnormal return is 45.3%. For repurchases announced by glamour (high P/E) stocks, where undervaluation is less likely to be an important motive, no positive drift in abnormal returns is observed. Thus, at least with respect to value stocks, the market errs in its initial response and appears to ignore much of the information conveyed through repurchase announcements.

Seasoned Equity Offerings (SEOs)[40]

Loughran and Ritter found that companies issuing stock during the 1970–1990 period, whether an initial public offering (IPO) or a seasoned equity offering (SEO), have been poor long-run investments for investors. Firms conducting seasoned equity offerings have generated average stock returns of only 7% per year during five years after the offering date, following a sharp run-up in the year prior to the offering. The magnitude of the underperformance of the offering firms is large. An investor would have had to invest 44% more money in the issuers than in non-issuers of the same size to have the same wealth five years after the offering date.

Dividend Initiations and Omissions

Dividend initiations and omissions can send signals to investors about the operations of companies. Michaely, Womack, and Thaler[41] provided a study investigating market reactions to initiations and omissions of cash dividend payments. The study found that the magnitude of short-run price reactions to omissions is greater than for initiations. In the year following the announcements, prices continue to drift in the same direction, though the drift following omissions is stronger and more robust.

In corporate finance theory, dividend is viewed as irrelevant when there are no market frictions, such as corporate and individual taxes, transaction costs and any kind of market irrationality. As a matter of fact, it is even argued that dividend payments reduce firm value because dividend payments are taxed (until 2003) more heavily than capital gains — therefore, firms should maximize shareholder value with share repurchases and should not pay dividends at all. The arguments in favor of dividend payments are mainly as follows. First, the market is not perfect. Some investors have a natural preference for high-payout stocks. For example, trusts and endowment funds may prefer high-dividend stocks because dividends are regarded as spendable "income," whereas capital gains are "additions to principal," which may not be spent. Second, dividends provide a useful signaling mechanism. Think of a market in which investors are less informed than corporate managers. How investors in such a market separate marginally profitable firms from the real money-makers? One clue is dividends. A firm that reports good earnings and pays a generous dividend is putting its money where its mouth is. Accounting numbers may lie, but dividends require the firm to come up with hard cash. In the long run, only firms with sufficient cash flow will find that it pays to signal their good fortune by choosing a high dividend level.

Earnings Surprises[42]

Empirical studies found that earnings surprises are not fully priced in a quick manner. There are delayed responses to earnings announcements.

The stock market often overreacts to the following events:

1. Initial public offerings (IPOs)[43]

   Because of uncertainty about the appropriate offering price and the risk involved in underwriting such issues, it has been the prevailing hypothesis that the underwriters would tend to underprice these new issues. Historically, IPOs can offer investors an average initial return of about 15%. However, the long-term return performance of IPOs is not encouraging at all. Loughran and Ritter[44] reported that during the five years after the issue, investors have received average returns of only 5% per year for companies conducting IPOs, substantially below average stock returns to similar non-IPO firms. The hot market of Internet and high-tech IPO market in the late 1990s has taught many investors a hard lesson. Most Internet IPOs had an outstanding performance in their very first days of public trading, sometimes even tripled or quadrupled their offering prices. By the end of March 2001, however, many of these Internet stocks have been traded at prices significantly below their initial offering prices, and a significant portion of these IPOs have even become penny stocks.

2. Mergers (acquiring firms)[45]

   Although investors often react positively to the stock prices of bidding firms and target firms, the evidence indicates that most of the gains from a merger go to stockholders of the target firms, with the stockholders of the successful bidding firms earning little if any return.

7.4 The "Dogs of Dow"

Though not commonplace by any means, instances of persistent out-performance relative to the market are hardly scarce. We have already discussed two such examples, e.g., Berkshire Hathaway and Fidelity Magellan fund, in earlier chapters. Warren Buffet and Peter Finch rightfully belong to the investors' Hall of Fame, of course. Their stock-picking abilities are a legion. Exhibit 7.9 summarizes the results of another success story, actually a successful strategy, that anyone can replicate. Dow 10, popularly known as the "Dogs of Dow", strategy involves holding for a year the ten highest dividend-paying but most beaten down of 30 stocks in the Dow Jones Industrial Average (Dow 30) and repeating the same exercise every year. Dow 5 is a variant of this strategy and, as the name implies, limits the portfolio to the top five of Dow 10 stocks. It is also known as the "Fabulous Five" strategy, and for a good reason.

The statistics for total returns on these two strategies are compared in Exhibit 7.10 with the corresponding data for Dow Jones Industrial Averege and the S&P 500 index. Note that the Dow 10 strategy has not only significantly outperformed the market but has done so while reducing the risk substantially. The "Fabulous Five" strategy is appreciably riskier, but notice the returns!

Exhibit 7.9: How a $1000 investment of January 1970 would have grown in the "Fabulous Five" (Dow 5) and "Dogs of Dow" (Dow 10) strategies versus the Dow Jones Industrial Average (Dow 30) and the S&P 500 index.

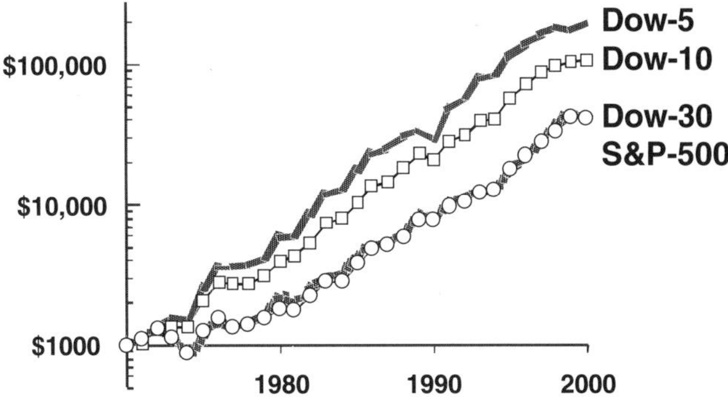

Exhibit 7.10: Comparing the annual performance data for Dow investing strategies (1970–2000).

	Dow 5	Dow 10	Dow 30	S&P 500
Annual return (%)	20.70	17.87	14.29	14.32
Annual volatility (%)	18.69	15.45	16.23	16.23
Beta (β)	0.71	0.73	0.94	1.00
Sharpe ratio	0.75	0.73	0.47	0.47
Treynor ratio	0.20	0.16	0.08	0.08

7.5 Select Stocks to Beat the Market: Concepts of Fundamental Analysis and Technical Analysis

We have introduced a variety of variables that predict future stock returns. These variables can be categorized into two groups: fundamental variables and technical indicators. Fundamental variables are concerned with the intrinsic values of firms or stocks and are often obtained from firms' financial statements. Most of the ratio variables mentioned earlier, including P/E ratios, price/sales ratios, and P/B ratios, are fundamental variables.

Fundamental analysts believe that, at any time, there is a basic intrinsic value for each security and these values depend on underlying economic and financial factors. Therefore, investors should calculate the intrinsic value of an investment asset by looking at the fundamental variables that determine the intrinsic value, such as current earnings, earnings growth, profit margins, and so on. An asset is undervalued if its current market price is below its intrinsic value and investors should buy the asset. In short, fundamental analysis provides a tool for helping to determine what to buy or sell, and assumes that the accurate determination of intrinsic value is possible indeed. If the fundamental analysis can generate abnormal high investment returns, the stock market is not efficient of the semi-strong form.

Properly used, the alternative approach, technical analysis can also be a powerful tool — especially so for determining when to buy or sell. The above mentioned predicting variables that do not directly determine the intrinsic values of firms, such as the past returns, the number of analysts following the company, and the company sizes, are examples of technical indicators that are often employed in the technical analysis.

The assumptions of technical analysis directly oppose the notion of efficient markets. Technical analysts often believe that stock prices move in trends that persist. They think that when new information comes to the market, it is not immediately available to everyone but is typically disseminated from the informed professional to the aggressive investing public and then to the great bulk of investors. Also, technicians contend that analyzing information takes time and therefore stock prices discount new information in a gradual manner, which causes trends in stock price movements that persist for certain periods until the new equilibrium is reached.

Technicians believe that nimble traders can develop rules to detect the beginning of a movement to a new equilibrium (called a "breakout"). Hence, they hope to buy or sell immediately after a breakout to take advantage of the subsequent price adjustment. Here are some popular indicators used by technicians.

Moving Average: A simple moving average is the average of the previous n-day number of closes. For example, a 10-day simple moving average (MA) is the average of the closing prices for the last ten days. In calculating the MA each day, the earliest day is dropped and the latest day is added to the ten being averaged. Thus the 10-day period being averaged moves forward each day.

The effect of a moving average is to slow down the price movement and filter out shorter-term noises so that the longer-term trend becomes smoother (or less volatile) and therefore more obvious. The longer the period of the moving average, the smoother the price movement is.

Moving averages can be calculated on either a simple or an exponential basis. For a simple moving average the values for each day are all given the same weighting. The formula for calculating the n-interval simple moving-average time series is given by

$$\text{MA}_n(i) = \frac{1}{n} \cdot \sum_{j=i-n+1}^{i} P(j),$$

where $P(j)$ is the stock price at time j, and n is the number of periods. Exhibit 7.11 provides examples of moving averages based on 50-day and 200-day intervals.

For an exponential moving average, the values for each day are weighted differently using an exponential factor that gives greater

Exhibit 7.11: 50-day and 200-day moving average lines, together with daily price changes, for IBM, for the February 7, 2001–February 6, 2002 period.

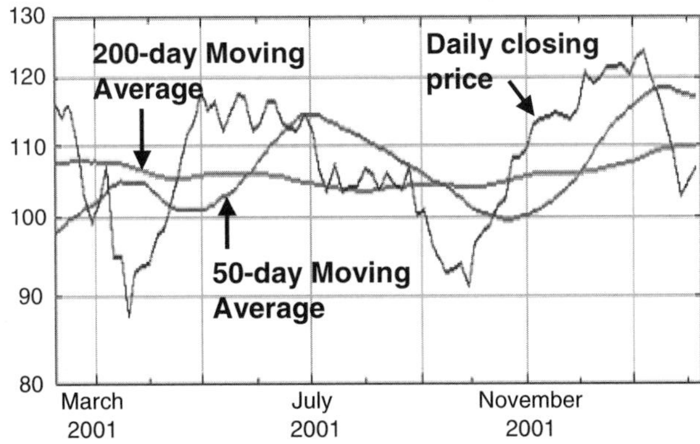

importance to the values of the more recent days. In either case, however, the moving average is interpreted basically the same way for analysis. For those who are interested, the formula for an exponential moving average (EMA) for n-days is:

$$n\text{-day EMA} = \left(\frac{1}{n} \times \text{new settle price}\right) + \left[\left(1 - \frac{1}{n}\right) \times \text{yesterday EMA}\right],$$

$$\text{e.g., 3-day EMA} = \left(\frac{1}{3} \times \text{new settle price}\right) + \left(\frac{2}{3} \times \text{yesterday EMA}\right).$$

There are many ways to use moving averages in trading. Among the most popular are: (1) moving averages as support/resistance levels; (2) moving average crossovers as buy or sell signals.

1. Moving averages often make effective support or resistance levels, that is, price levels at which the instrument should stop and reverse direction for some period of time.
2. Perhaps the simplest trading system involving moving averages is buying or selling when the price of an instrument moves above or below a particular moving average. For example, after an instrument has been trading below the 50-day moving average for several months, a trader may want to buy when the price crosses above that moving average. The significance of such a crossover is that the market has stabilized and turned higher and the instrument has thus been able to move above the average price seen over the past 50-days. This would indicate strength and that further price increases may occur.

Breakouts: Breakout is one of the most popular short-term trading strategies. Experienced technical traders do not buy or sell a stock before seeing indications that a stock may start a significant move. Then, monitoring a stock that has stayed in a narrow price range for some time, traders buy or sell the stock if it suddenly moves out of the range with significantly larger trading activities (larger volumes).

Put/Call Ratio: As we shall see in the next chapter, options are highly levered financial securities and therefore provide one of the effective ways in which traders bet on the financial markets. When a trader expects the price of a stock to go up, he can buy call options; otherwise, if he expects the price to decline, he can buy puts. The formula of put/call ratio is:

$$\frac{\text{put}}{\text{call ratio}} = \frac{\text{CBOE daily put volume}}{\text{CBOE daily call volume}}.$$

A *very* low put/call ratio is considered bearish because it shows that investors are trading heavily in calls and therefore the bullish activity may be overdone. The assumption is that a strong bullish market sentiment indicates that everyone is already bullish and therefore a correction is probably due. By the same token, a *very* high put/call ratio is bullish because it shows that investors are trading heavily in puts and that a bearish sentiment may be overdone.

7.6 The Problems of Active Trading Strategies

We have documented significant evidence that stock returns are, to some extent, predictable, and that certain trading strategies may bring abnormal investment profits, one must understand that active trading embodies substantial risk and disadvantages.

Execution Problem: The first, and also very important, is the execution risk. Whether a trading strategy is profitable on paper is one thing, and whether a strategy can make abnormal profits with it in practice is a different matter. To make a profit, one needs to execute a trading strategy effectively in a timely manner. This is not an easy task. Anxiety, emotion, negligence, lengthy decision processes, and so on, often cause execution errors, delays, and failures. As a result, most investors do not benefit from active trading activities.

Trading costs: The second problem that hinders investors from profiting from active trading strategies is trading costs. Active trading strategies could be very costly to implement. Stoll and Whaley[46] reported quoted (bid-ask) spread and commission costs of 2.0% for the largest NYSE size decile to 9% for the smallest decile. Bwardwaj and Brooks[47]

Exhibit 7.12: Commission schedule of stock trading.

Transaction amount	Commission
$0–$2500	$29 +1.7% of principal amount
$2500.01–$6250	$55 + 0.66% of principal amount
$6250.01–$20,000	$75 + 0.34% of principal amount
$20,000.01–$50,000	$99 + 0.22% of principal amount
$50,000.01–$500,000	$154 + 0.11% of principal amount
$500,000+	$254 + 0.09% of principal amount

found median quoted spread and commission costs of 2.0% for NYSE securities with per share prices greater than $20.00 and 12.5% for securities priced under $5.00. Lesmond, Ogden, and Trzcinka[48] estimated that average round-trip (buying plus selling) transactions costs are about 1.2% to 10.3% for large and small decile firms, respectively. Exhibit 7.12 reports the commission schedule determined using the discount brokerage schedule from CIGNA financial services, which is a standard (broker-assisted) commission schedule. The table shows that trading commission is particularly large for low price stocks. We must note that these costs have fallen rather significantly in 2003.

For stocks under $1.00 per share the commission rate is $38 plus 4% of principal. The overriding minimum commission is $38 per trade.

Transaction costs have been used to explain many well-known asset-pricing anomalies, including the January effect,[49] the small-firm effect,[50] long-run equity offering returns,[51] post-earnings price drift[52] and momentum trading profits.[53]

Here, we use the momentum strategy of Titman and Jegadeesh to analyze the importance of trading costs in implementing active trading strategies. Lesmond, Schill, and Zhou provided a model of market frictions and then used this model to infer trading costs from investor behavior. They found that the execution of standard momentum strategies requires extraordinary trading costs because of the type and frequency of securities traded. The evidence for positive trading profit net of transaction costs appears to be weak. The magnitude of trading costs, particularly for those firms which play an important role in generating abnormal performance, appears to be sufficiently large such that realizing net trading profits is elusive. Given the magnitude of transaction costs, there is little evidence to suggest that momentum strategies generate systematic positive trading profit across the variety of strategies they examined.

In short, trading costs may eat a substantial portion of profits one can make from active trading activities. When one decides to follow a active trading strategy to buy and sell stocks, one needs to consider whether profits of this strategy is expected to outweigh the related trading costs.

Data-snooping biases: The third problem is that the predictability pattern of asset returns may be spurious or unstable. The statistical inferences of return predictability by using certain publicly available variables are based on the extensive data analysis of many economists and financial analysts. Data-snooping biases, which refer to the biases in statistical inferences that result from using information from data to guide subsequent research with the same or related data, are virtually inevitable in this process due to the non-experimental nature of economics and finance. Lo and MacKinlay[54] for example, considered a large number of trading rules, applied the rules to 100 years to daily data on the Dow Jones Industrial Average, and determined the effects of data-snooping. They found that technical trading rules usually do not provide superior performance when used in the 10-year post-sample period. In a similar analysis, technical trading rules are applied to Standard and Poor's 500 futures contract. Once data-snooping effects are taken into account, there is no evidence that the best technical rule outperforms.

Sullivan, Timmermann, and White[55] contended that the presence of calendar effects in stock returns is a data-driven discovery and suffers significant data-snooping biases.

The evidence of calendar effects in stock returns has largely been considered without accounting for the intensive search preceding it. In terms of their analysis, although nominal P-values of individual calendar rules are extremely significant, once evaluated in the context of the full universe from which such rules were drawn, calendar effects no longer remain significant.

Of course, not all the evidence is discouraging to active trading rules. In a subsequent article, Lo and MacKinlay[56] constructed portfolios of stocks and of bonds that are maximally predictable with respect to a set of *ex ante* observable economic variables, and show that these levels of predictability are statistically significant, even after controlling for data-snooping biases. They disaggregate the sources for predictability by using several asset groups, including industry-sorted portfolios, and found that the sources of maximal predictability shifted considerably across asset classes and sectors as the return-horizon changes. Using three out-of-sample measures of predictability, they showed that the predictability of the maximally predictable portfolio is genuine and economically significant.

7.7 A Generalized Framework for Evaluating Stocks

We have introduced and identified several rules that may help investors to select good stocks to obtain high investment returns. Here is a summary.

Stock Screening Methods

Fundamental Screens

Fundamental screens compare price to intrinsic value implied in the firms' financial statements. Typical fundamental screens include:

Price-to-earnings (P/E) ratios: Buy stocks with low P/E ratios and sell stocks with high P/E ratios.

PEG ratios: PEG ratios provide a modification of P/E ratios. Buy stocks with low PEG ratios and sell stocks with high PEG ratios.

Dividend yields: Buy stocks with high dividend yields.

Price-to-book (P/B) ratios: Buy stocks with low P/B and sell stocks with high P/B.

Price-to-cash flow (P/CF) ratios: Buy stocks with low P/CF ratios and sell stocks with high P/CF.

Tobin's Q: Buy stocks with low Q and sell stocks with high Q.

Technical Screens

Some popular technical screens are:

Momentum screens: Buy stocks that have had large increases in sales, earnings, or stock prices in the recent past (past three or six months).

Contrarian screens: Buy small stocks following positive price movements in large capitalization stocks in the same industry group.

Inside-trading screens: Mimic the trading of insiders. The rationale is that insiders have inside information that they use in trading.

Neglected-stock and/or size screens: Buy stocks that are relatively small in size and are not analyzed by many analysts. The rationale is that these stocks are often underpriced and provide good long-term investment values.

Seasonal screens: Buy stocks at a certain time of the year, for example, in early January. The evidence shows that stock returns tend to be higher during these times.

Event screens: Buy stocks following positive events to which investors often under-react or negative events to which investors tend to over-react.

Other technical indicators: Moving average, put/call ratio, breakout signals can provide some technical information on the short-term trends of stock prices.

Risk Screens

Volatility: Buy a stock with low volatility.

Beta: Beta measures the systematic risk contribution of a stock to a diversified portfolio. In the CAPM, high beta means high-required risk premium. Therefore, one should buy a stock with a risk premium high enough to compensate the beta risk, or, with a positive alpha.

A Comprehensive Rating System

As such, there are a large number of stock selection screens that investors can follow. Of course, these screens do not always provide consistent recommendations. Consider a small-cap stock that has experienced a substantial price decline in the past six months and now has a low P/B ratio. Based on the momentum screen, one should sell the stock. But in terms of the size screen and the P/B screen, one should buy it. Naturally, investors will face the following question in making their investment decisions: for different stock selection screens, which one an investor should follow?

We recommend a rating system that may be implemented by any investor, no matter his/her bias and technical skills, in their investment decisions in three steps:

1. Assign a score (one to ten) to each screen summarized above. The more attractive a stock is in terms of a selection screen, the higher score the stock receives for that screen. For example, for the momentum screen, a stock receives a score of ten if its return over the past six months belongs to the highest 10%; it receives a score of nine if its return over the past six months is among the second highest 10%; and it should receive a score of one if its return belongs to the bottom 10%. For volatility screen, a stock receives a score of ten if its volatility is among the lowest 10%; and so on.
2. Assign a weight[57] to each screen based on one's investment horizon, market conditions, personal preferences, and investment objective. For example, certain technical selection screens, such as the contrarian screen and calendar screen, are mainly based on short-term trends of stock prices. If one has a short investment horizon, one can assign a relatively high weight to these screens. On the other hand, most fundamental screens, such as P/E ratios and P/B ratios, are often associated with the predictability of long term asset returns, investors with long-term investment horizons should assign relatively high weights to these screens.
3. Calculate the weighted average score of a stock and determine a stock selection standard. For example, buy a stock if it has a score above 7.5 and sell it if its score is below four.

Choosing weights in step two seems arbitrary, but is critical in one's investment decision making. Moreover, these weights do not have to be constant though time. As we mentioned, one could switch his/her emphasis between fundamental and technical screens based on investment horizon, market conditions, and personal preferences. For instance, a day trader typically makes trading decisions based on short-term technical indicators (possibly only one) and does not pay much attention to fundamentals. In fact, a day trader may be able to use only technical analysis. This is dictated by the facts that fundamentals usually do not change overnight but market psychology and order flows do. An investor who selects stocks for his/her retirement fund should, instead, pay attention mainly to the fundamentals of stocks. Market conditions can also play an important role here. For instance, when the market is very volatile, technical indicators can become very noisy and therefore active trading based on technical signals becomes very risky.

Exhibit 7.15 provides an illustrative example. It shows how an investor with one-year investment horizon evaluates the IBM stock using the technical and fundamental screens of his choice, based on technical and fundamental information of the stock as of March 22, 2001, as shown in Exhibits 7.13 and 7.14. Of course, an investor/trader does not have to use all screens mentioned above. The average score based on the investor's weight and score assignment is 6.14. If the investor requires

Exhibit 7.13: Daily price ($) and volume (million shares) charts of IBM stock.

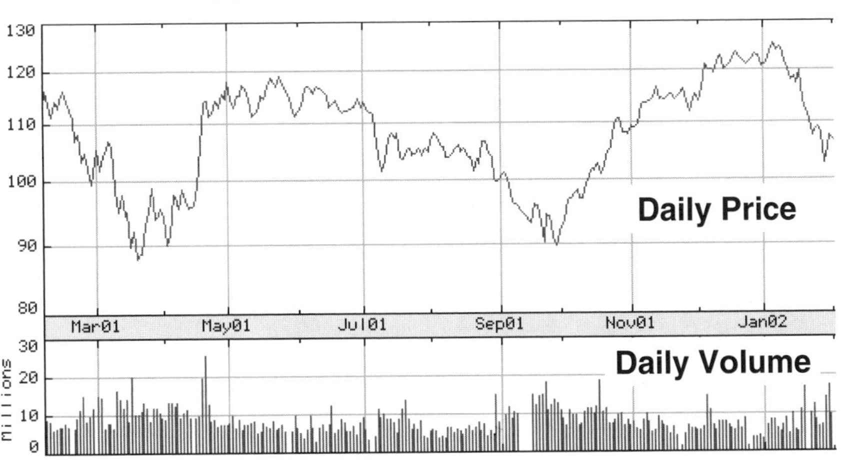

Source: finance.yahoo.com

Exhibit 7.14: Financial ratios and technical indicators of IBM as of March 22, 2001.

Dow Jones Industrials:	Computers
Market Cap:	156.9 billion
52-Week EPS:	$4.58
Estimated EPS Growth (Next 5 years):	13.0%
Book Value:	$11.69
52-Week High:	$134.94 on Friday, September 1, 2000
52-Week Low:	$80.06 on Thursday, December 21, 2000
P/E Ratio:	19.45
PEG:	1.63
P/B ratio:	7.62
Dividend Yield:	0.58%
Average Price:	105.81 (50-day) 107.58 (200-day)
Average Volume:	9,719,200 (50-day) 7,739,700 (200-day)

Exhibit 7.15: Scores of IBM stock as of March 22, 2001.

Item	Score	Weight	Weighted score
Fundamental			
P/E	7.00	0.20	1.400
PEG	5.00	0.10	0.500
P/B	4.00	0.10	0.400
Dividend yields	7.00	0.08	0.560
Technical			
Momentum	6.00	0.10	0.600
Moving average	3.00	0.05	0.150
Size	1.00	0.05	0.050
Seasonal	4.00	0.02	0.080
Risk			
Volatility	8.00	0.30	2.400
Total score		1.00	6.140

a score of 7.0 for buying, he should not buy the IBM stock under the current market condition.

IBM seems in this case neither a stock to buy nor to sell. It is a stock to "hold" if you own it already. We must stress that an investor may well choose different ratios and indicators as well as different weights. The framework we illustrate, however, will be a very helpful example to any investors, across different time periods and market conditions.

7.8 Conclusion

To conclude, we would like to re-emphasize the following points as a caution to active stock traders:

- To make a trading rule work, one must execute well. Poor execution will adversely affect investment performance, no matter how good a trading strategy is.
- High turnover of stocks will incur substantial trading costs. Determine whether the potential benefit of a trade exceeds its trading costs before you make a trade.
- The financial markets are very dynamic. A trading rule that worked historically does not necessarily work now. Update your information on the applicability of your trading rules constantly. Our framework (Section 4) shows you an easy, but rigorous way for doing so.

John Bogle, the founder of Vanguard mutual funds, claims, "After nearly 50 years in this business, I do not know of anybody who has done it (active trading based on fundamental and technical strategies) successfully and consistently." His view may be overly conservative, but it does tell us how difficult it could be to profit from active trading. The weight of the evidence is still with "buy-and-hold" for the "long run". But Keynes did warn us, "In the long-run, we are all dead."

Endnotes

[1] Kenneth R. French: "Stock Returns and the Weekend Effect", *Journal of Financial Economics*, vol. 8(1), pp. 55–69, March 1980.

[2] Michael R. Gibbons and Patrick Hess: "Day of the Week Effects and Asset Returns", *Journal of Business*, vol. 54(4), pp. 579–596, October 1981.

[3] Jeffrey Jaffe and Randolph Westerfield: "The Week-End Effect in Common Stock Returns: The International Evidence", *Journal of Finance*, vol. 40(2), pp. 433–454, June 1985.

[4] Stephen H. Penman: "The Distribution of Earnings News over Time and Seasonalities in Aggregate Stock Returns", *Journal of Financial Economics*, vol. 18(2), pp. 199–228, June 1987.

[5] M. Rozeff and W. Kinney: "Capital Market Seasonality: The Case of Stock Returns", *Journal of Financial Economics*, vol. 3, pp. 379–402, 1976.

[6] Eugene F. Fama: "Efficient Capital Markets: II", *Journal of Finance*, vol. 46(5), pp. 1575–1617, December 1991.

[7] G. Hawawini and D.B. Keim: "On the Predictability of Common Stock Returns: World-Wide Evidence" in *Finance* (Eds. R.A. Jarrow, V. Maksimovic and W.T. Ziemba) North Holland, Amsterdam, 1994. See also Robert A. Haugen and Philippe Jorion: "The January Effect: Still There After All These Years", *Financial Analysts Journal*, vol. 52, pp. 27–31, 1996.

[8] Paul Schultz: "Personal Income Taxes and the January Effect: Small Firm Stock Returns Before the War Revenue Act of 1917: A Note", *Journal of Finance*, vol. 40(1), pp. 333–343, March 1985.

[9] Charles P. Jones, Douglas K. Pearce and Jack W. Wilson: "Can Tax-Loss Selling Explain the January Effect? A Note", *Journal of Finance*, vol. 42(2), pp. 453–461, June 1987.

[10] J.Y. Campbell: "A Variance Decomposition for Stock Returns", *Economic Journal*, vol. 101, pp. 157–179, 1991.

[11] John Y. Campbell and Robert J. Shiller: "Stock Prices, Earnings, and Expected Dividends", *Journal of Finance*, vol. 43(3), pp. 661–676, July 1988.

[12] Eugene F. Fama and K.R. French: "Dividend Yields and Expected Stock Returns", *Journal of Financial Economics*, vol. 22, pp. 3–25, 1988.

[13] Robert J. Shiller: *Irrational Exuberance* (Princeton University Press, New Jersey, 2000).

[14] Eugene F. Fama and Kenneth R. French: "Size and Book-To-Market Factors in Earnings and Returns", *Journal of Finance*, vol. 50(1), pp. 131–155, March 1995.

[15] Louis K.C. Chan, Yasushi Hamao and Josef Lakonishok: "Can Fundamentals Predict Japanese Stock Returns?", *Financial Analysts Journal*, vol. 49(4), pp. 63–69, July/August 1993.

[16] Andrew Smithers and Stephen Wright: *Valuing Wall Street Protecting Wealth in Turbulent Markets* (McGraw-Hill, 2000).

[17] Andrew W. Lo and Craig A. MacKinlay: "Stock Prices Do Not Follow Random Walk", *Review of Financial Studies*, vol. 1(1), pp. 41–66, 1988.

[18] Eugene F. Fama and Kenneth R. French: "Permanent and Temporary Components of Stock Prices", *Journal of Political Economy*, vol. 96(2), pp. 246–273, April 1988.

[19] James M. Poterba and Lawrence H. Summers: "Mean Reversion in Stock Prices: Evidence and Implications", *Journal of Financial Economics*, vol. 22(1), pp. 27–59, October 1988.

[20] W. DeBondt and Richard Thaler: "Does the Stock Market Overreact?", *Journal of Finance*, vol. 40, pp. 793–805, 1985.

[21] Navin Chopra, Josef Lakonishok and Jay R. Ritter: "Measuring Abnormal Performance: Do Stocks Overreact?", *Journal of Financial Economics*, vol. 31(2), pp. 235–268, April 1992.

[22] See Endnote 19.

[23] Jacob Boudoukh and Matthew Richardson: "The Statistics of Long-Horizon Regressions Revisited", *Mathematical Finance*, vol. 4(2), pp. 103–119, April 1994.

[24] Matthew Richardson and James H. Stock: "Drawing Inferences from Statistics Based on Multiyear Asset Returns", *Journal of Financial Economics*, vol. 25(2), pp. 323–348, December 1989.

[25] Narasimhan Jegadeesh and Sheridan Titman: "Returns to Buying Winners and Selling Losers: Implications for Stock Market Efficiency", *Journal of Finance*, vol. 48, pp. 65–91, 1993.

[26] See Endnote 25.

[27] K. Geert Rouwenhurst: "Local Return Factors and Turnover in Emerging Markets", *Journal of Finance*, vol. 54, pp. 1439–1464, 1999.

[28] Narasimhan Jegadeesh and Sheridan Titman: "Profitability of Momentum Strategies: An Evaluation of Alternative Explanations", Working Paper, 1999.

[29] David A. Lesmond, Michael, J. Schill and Chunsheng Zhou: "The Illusory Nature of Momentum Profits", Working Paper, Tulane University and University of California, Riverside, 2001.

[30] Andrew W. Lo and Craig A. MacKinlay: "Data-Snooping Biases in Tests of Financial Asset Pricing Models", *Review of Financial Studies*, vol. 3(3), pp. 431–467, 1990.

[31] G. McQueen, M. Pinegar and S. Thorley: "Delayed Reaction to Good News and Cross-Autocorrelation of Portfolio Returns", *Journal of Finance*, vol. 51, pp. 889–920, 1996.

[32] Rolf W. Banz: "The Relationship Between Return and Market Value of Common Stocks", *Journal of Financial Economics*, vol. 9(1), pp. 3–18, March 1981.

[33] Eugene F. Fama and Kenneth R. French: "The Cross-Section of Expected Stock Returns", *Journal of Finance*, vol. 47(2), pp. 427–465, June 1992.

[34] Avner Arbel and Paul Strebel: "Pay Attention to Neglected Firms!", *Journal of Portfolio Management*, vol. 9(2), pp. 37–42, Winter 1983.

[35] Craig G. Beard and Richard W. Sias: "Is There A Neglected-Firm Effect?", *Financial Analysts Journal*, vol. 53(5), pp. 19–23, September/October 1997.

[36] Dan Givoly and Dan Palmon: "Insider Trading and the Exploitation of Inside Information: Some Empirical Evidence", *Journal of Business*, vol. 58(1), pp. 69–87, January 1985.

[37] Josef Lakonishok and Inmoo Lee: "Are Insider Trades Informative?", *Review of Financial Studies*, vol. 14(1), pp. 79–111, 2001.

[38] M.S. Grinblatt, R.W. Masulis and S. Titman: "The Valuation Effects of Stock Splits and Stock Dividends", *Journal of Financial Economics*, vol. 13, pp. 461–490, 1984. See also H. Desai and P. Jain: "Long-Run Common Stock Returns Following Splits and Reverse Splits", *Journal of Business*, vol. 70, pp. 409–433, 1997.

[39] D. Ikenberry, J. Lakonishok and T. Vermaelen: "Market Underreaction to Open Market Share Repurchases", *Journal of Financial Economics*, vol. 39, pp. 181–208, 1995. See also M. Mitchell and E. Stafford: "Managerial Decisions and Long-Term Stock Price Performance", Working Paper, University of Chicago, 1997.

[40] T. Loughran and J. Ritter: "The New Issues Puzzle", *Journal of Finance*, vol. 50, pp. 23–52, 1995.

[41] R. Michaely, K.L. Womack and R. Thaler: "Price Reactions to Dividend Initiations and Omissions: Overreaction or Drift?", *Journal of Finance*, vol. 50, pp. 573–608, 1995.

[42] V. Bernard and J. Thomas: "Post-Earnings-Announcement Drift: Delayed Price Response or Risk Premium?", *Journal of Accounting Research*, vol. 27, pp. 1–36, 1989. See also V. Bernard and J. Thomas: "Evidence that Stock Prices Do Not Fully Reflect the Implications of Current Earnings for Future Eearnings", *Journal of Accounting and Economics*, vol. 13, pp. 305–340, 1990.

[43] R. Ibbotson: "Price Performance of Common Stock New Issues", *Journal of Financial Economics*, vol. 2, pp. 235–272, 1975. See also Endnote 40.

[44] See Endnote 40.

[45] P. Asquith: "Merger Bids, Uncertainty and Stockholder Returns", *Journal of Financial Economics*, vol. 11, pp. 51–83, 1983.

[46] H.R. Stoll and R. Whaley: "Transactions Costs and the Small Firm Effect", *Journal of Financial Economics*, vol. 12, pp. 52–79, 1983.

[47] Ravinder K. Bhardwaj and LeRoy D. Brooks: "The January Anomaly: Effects of Low Share Price, Transaction Costs, and Bid-Ask Bias", *Journal of Finance*, vol. 47, pp. 553–575, 1992.

[48] David A. Lesmond, Joseph P. Ogden and Charles A. Trzcinka: "A New Estimate of Transaction Costs", *Review of Financial Studies*, vol. 12, pp. 1113–1141, 1999.

[49] Marc R. Reinganum: "The Anomalous Stock Market Behavior of Small Firms in January: Some Empirical Tests for Tax-Loss Selling Effects", *Journal of Financial Economics*, vol. 12, pp. 89–104, 1983. See also Endnote 47.

[50] See Endnote 46.

[51] Jeffrey Pontiff and Michael J. Schill: "Long-Run Seasoned Equity Offerings: Data Snooping, Poor Model Specification, or Mispricing? A Costly Arbitrage Approach", Working Paper, University of Washington and University of California, Riverside, 2000.

[52] David A. Lesmond: "Post-Earnings Drift: A Transaction Costs Perspective", Working Paper, Tulane University, 2000.

[53] See Endnote 29.

[54] See Endnote 30.

[55] Ryan Sullivan, Allan Timmermann and Halbert White: "Dangers of Data-Driven Inference: The Case of Calendar Effects in Stock Returns", Working Paper: 98/16, Department of Economics, University of California, San Diego, June 1998.

[56] Andrew W. Lo and Craig A. MacKinlay: "Maximizing Predictability in the Stock and Bond Markets", Working Paper: 5027, National Bureau of Economic Research, February 1995.

[57] The summation of total weights should equal to 100%.

Chapter 8

STOCK OPTIONS, WARRANTS AND CONVERTIBLES

8.1 Introduction

Stock options, warrants and convertibles are very effective tools to participate on the equity side of Corporate America. Stock and index options may be used to replicate a position in a stock or a portfolio of stocks. They may be used to enhance income on a portfolio or on a stock, a way to declare a "dividend" by and for yourself, or as a way to reduce the riskiness of a stock or a portfolio of stocks, or both. Options have proven to be very flexible and effective hedging tools across the spectrum of US stocks and are widely available on practically every stock that an investor may be likely to follow and ultimately invest in. They offer trading and hedging opportunities no matter the direction of the stock market and make the old adage: there is no such thing as a bad market, there is only a bad position in the market, more true and more realizable than ever. They effectively represent bridges across the rough terrain of risk and return that a stock (and only a stock) portfolio represents on its own.

The participation in the options markets, the equity options especially, has been growing dramatically as Exhibit 8.1 shows. The Options Clearing Corporation (OCC), which clears all transactions in options (also referred to as derivatives as they derive their economic legitimacy

Exhibit 8.1: OCC yearly cleared contract volume by product type.

Year	Options on equity	Stock index	Foreign currency	Interest rate	OCC total
1973	1,119,245	NT	NT	NT	1,119,245
1974	5,682,907	NT	NT	NT	5,682,907
1975	18,103,018	NT	NT	NT	18,103,018
1976	32,373,925	NT	NT	NT	32,373,925
1977	39,637,328	NT	NT	NT	39,637,328
1978	57,231,018	NT	NT	NT	57,231,018
1979	64,264,863	NT	NT	NT	64,264,863
1980	96,728,546	NT	NT	NT	96,728,546
1981	109,405,782	NT	NT	NT	109,405,782
1982	137,264,816	NT	3399	37,990	137,306,205
1983	135,658,976	14,016,726	194,041	186,332	150,056,075
1984	118,925,239	75,758,326	1,490,098	263,698	196,437,361
1985	118,555,989	110,044,331	3,873,740	436,487	232,910,547
1986	141,930,945	138,461,486	8,472,162	346,542	289,211,135
1987	164,431,851	129,696,209	10,807,879	232,996	305,168,935
1988	114,927,723	70,961,028	9,915,808	144,032	195,948,591
1989	141,839,748	73,897,486	11,050,855	228,571	227,016,660
1990	111,425,744	88,281,587	10,146,196	69,221	209,922,748
1991	104,850,686	83,053,082	10,847,721	50,111	198,801,600
1992	106,484,452	83,268,766	12,185,234	57,305	201,995,757
1993	131,726,101	87,736,349	13,135,109	64,536	232,662,095
1994	149,932,665	121,090,244	10,142,901	216,592	281,382,402
1995	174,380,236	107,874,016	4,977,555	65,102	287,296,909
1996	199,117,729	92,431,722	3,153,804	94,447	294,797,702
1997	272,998,701	78,182,725	2,566,175	75,517	353,823,118
1998	329,641,875	74,791,545	1,833,018	76,760	406,343,198
1999	444,765,224	62,263,239	820,464	42,556	507,891,483

NT: Not yet traded

from the cash (spot) market), tracks all options contracts that are not commodity related.

The discussion in this chapter may often seem laborious and technical. This is the nature of the beast. We have attempted to make it as accessible as possible. Some technical sections such as that dealing with the pricing of a stock option may be skipped without losing continuity and focus. That is, without changing the fact that options are a superb tool to manage risk and improve the risk/return tradeoffs for every investor, no matter her risk profile. Derivative contracts such as options perform fundamental economic functions. They permit investors to hedge and they allow for price discovery. The latter function derives from the fact that the transaction is consummated today and the delivery, should one occur, will take place in the future. The price of the option summarizes the expectations of the owner as to the future prospects of the underlying security in terms of risk and return.

8.2 Options

The Options Markets

Some Definitions

An option on a common stock is a contract between two entities, guaranteed by a third party. One party to the contract grants the other the right to buy (in the call case), or sell (in the put case), a specified number of shares, typically one hundred, at a specific price within a specified period of time. One party to the contract, the buyer of the contract (the long position), will have the option, i.e., the choice, to buy, or sell the shares while the other, the seller of the contract (the short), has the obligation to deliver the shares in one case, to take delivery of the shares in the other (the put case).

The option to buy the underlying shares is called a *call option*, while the option to sell the underlying shares is called a *put option*. The granted choice is not free. It is done for a price called the *option premium*.

Options are of two types: American and European. The above option described is the *American option*, which allows you to exercise your option anytime during its life. That is, if you own a call option, you can decide to exercise, that is to buy the underlying stock at the agreed upon price (the strike price), anytime during the life of the option. This, incidentally, is rarely done as investors simply sell their option (if they bought initially) instead of exercising them.

A *European option* allows for exercise only [buy the underlying (call case) or sell the underlying (put case)] upon maturity. The terms of delivery are exactly as specified in the contract except, as we discuss below, for adjustments because of dividends, distributions such as stock dividend, stock splits, recapitalizations, or reorganization with respect to the underlying security.

The short position carries a time-limited obligation borne against the premium received. The obligations of the short will have to be met depending on the choices made by the holder of the long position. Therefore the short has an obligation during the life of the option, the long has a choice.

Should a person sell a certain number of options and buy another number of options on the same security, she is then net long (if a net buyer) or a net short (if a net seller). The reasons for wanting to do so will become clear in subsequent discussions.

One can already see how an option can expand the opportunity set for an investor. Should the investor be interested in participating in the appreciation of 100 shares of, e.g., IBM, he could buy the stock itself for $10,000 (assuming 100 shares of $100 each) or buy a call option that would allow him to buy IBM at, e.g., $100 during a specified period (e.g., three months). For this right to have a choice, he would pay the option premium (e.g., $1000). The option would allow him to participate in the appreciation of 100 shares at IBM. If the investor had only $1000, he would be able to participate in only ten shares of IBM in the cash (spot) market. The option allows him to leverage his position and participate in 100 shares. One should be reminded that the entire premium can be lost if IBM does not appreciate or fall in value.

Types of Options

In addition to the stock options, described above, there exist many other types of options as well. They include the following, for instance:

1. Index options

   This is an option on the level of an index of stock prices such as the S&P index. Since deliverability is a problem because an index is not a deliverable security and its components could be fractions of securities, cash settlement became the necessary alternative. Here the short call will be required to pay the lon-g the difference between the current value of the index and the agreed upon strike price if the index has risen in value. The short put will pay the long the difference between the option's exercise price and the current market price if the index has fallen in value.

   The bet here is on the direction of a market index. The size of the contract is not in terms of numbers of shares, but rather the value of the index multiplied by a multiplier specified by the exchange where the option is traded.

2. Interest rate options

   The call and put options in this case cover debt instruments such as Treasury bonds and notes. The issue here is which of the many bonds or notes are deliverable against the position. The short will invariably look for "the cheapest to deliver" in the event a delivery is required.

3. Foreign currency options

   The underlying instrument here is a specified number of foreign currencies such as the Euro or the Swiss franc.

4. Options on futures

   The underlying instrument deliverable against the contract is not the security itself, but rather a futures contract on it. The long, upon exercising, will receive a long position in the underlying futures contract plus a cash amount equal to the excess of the futures price over the strike price.

5. Options on commodities

   The deliverable here is a commodity, such as a specified quantity (ounces or grams) of gold (ounces or grams), wheat, or oil, and not a financial asset.

Exhibit 8.2

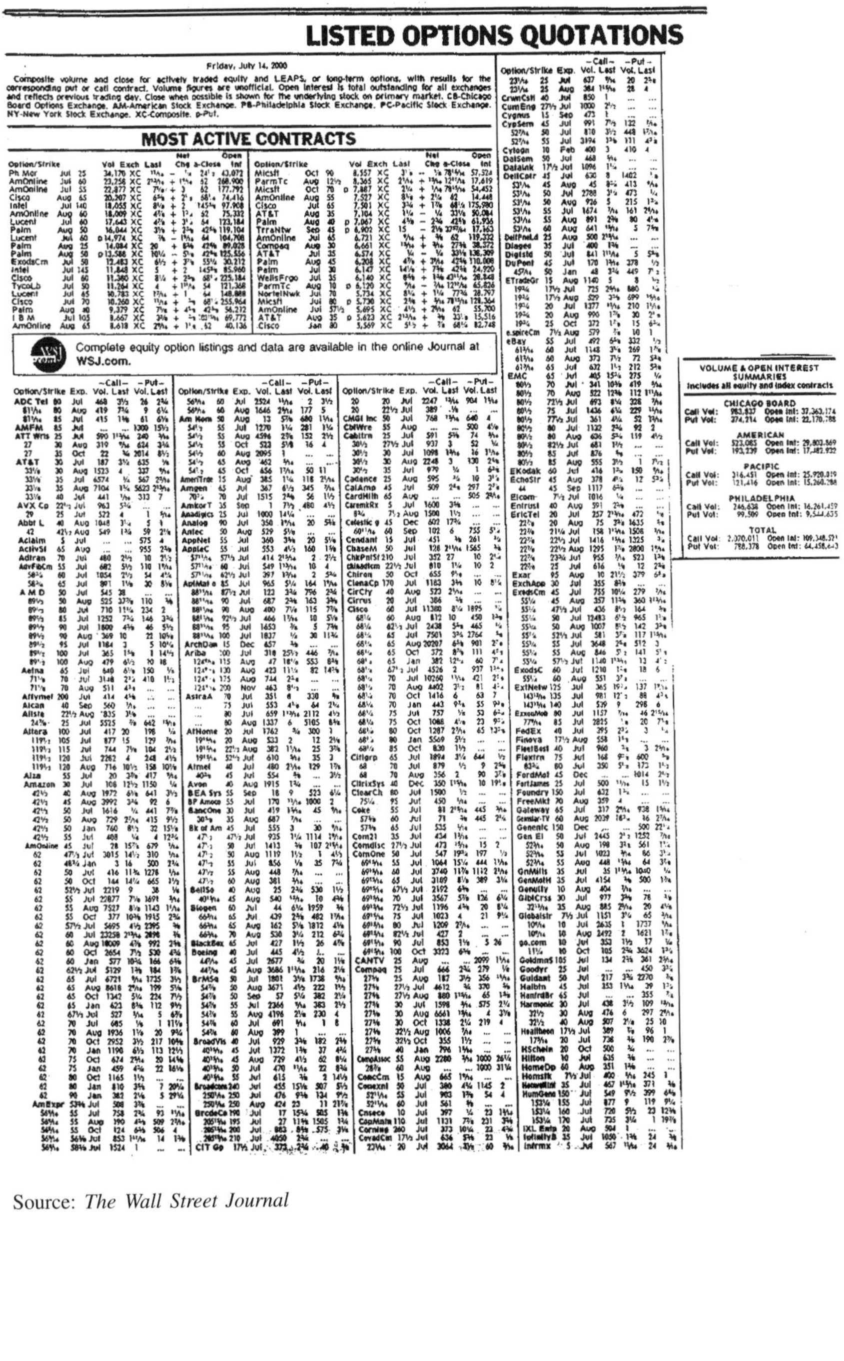

LISTED OPTIONS QUOTATIONS

Friday, July 14, 2000

Composite volume and close for actively traded equity and LEAPS, or long-term options, with results for the corresponding put or call contract. Volume figures are unofficial. Open interest is total outstanding for all exchanges and reflects previous trading day. Close when possible is shown for the underlying stock on primary market. CB-Chicago Board Options Exchange. AM-American Stock Exchange. PB-Philadelphia Stock Exchange. PC-Pacific Stock Exchange. NY-New York Stock Exchange. XC-Composite. p-Put.

MOST ACTIVE CONTRACTS

Option/Strike				Vol	Exch	Last	Net Chg	a-Close	Open Int
Ph Mor	Jul	25		34,170	XC	11/16	− 1/4	24 1/2	43,072
AmOnline	Jul	60		23,256	XC	2 13/16	+ 1 5/16	62	268,900
AmOnline	Jul	55		22,877	XC	7 1/8	+ 3	62	177,792
Cisco	Aug	65		20,207	XC	6 3/4	+ 2 1/2	68 1/4	74,416
Intel	Jul	140		18,055	XC	8 1/8	+ 2	145 3/4	97,908
AmOnline	Aug	60		18,009	XC	4 7/8	+ 1 3/4	62	75,332
Lucent	Jul	60		17,643	XC	4 7/8	+ 3 1/4	64	123,184
Palm	Aug	50		16,044	XC	3 7/8	+ 2 3/4	42 3/4	119,104
Lucent	Jul	60	p	14,974	XC	1/8	− 1 5/16	64	104,708
Palm	Aug	25		14,084	XC	20	+ 8 3/4	42 3/4	89,028
Palm	Aug	50	p	13,588	XC	10 1/4	− 5 1/4	42 3/4	125,556
ExodsCm	Jul	50		12,483	XC	6 1/2	+ 3 7/8	55 1/4	30,212
Intel	Jul	145		11,848	XC	5	+ 2	145 3/4	85,960
Cisco	Jul	60		11,380	XC	8 1/2	+ 2 3/8	68 1/4	225,184
TycoLb	Jul	50		11,264	XC	4	+ 1 11/16	54	121,368
Lucent	Jul	65		10,783	XC	17/16	+ 1	64	148,888
Cisco	Jul	70		10,260	XC	11/16	+ 3/8	68 1/4	255,964
Palm	Aug	40		9,379	XC	7 1/8	+ 4 3/8	42 3/4	56,212
I B M	Jul	105		8,667	XC	3 3/4	+ 3/8	103 15/16	69,772
AmOnline	Aug	65		8,618	XC	2 9/16	+ 1 1/8	62	40,136
Micsft	Oct	90		8,557	XC	3 1/8	− 1/8	78 15/16	57,524
ParmTc	Aug	12 1/2		8,365	XC	2 1/16	+ 15/16	12 11/16	17,619
Micsft	Oct	70	p	7,887	XC	2 1/4	+ 1/16	78 15/16	54,452
AmOnline	Aug	55		7,527	XC	8 1/8	+ 2 1/4	62	14,448
Cisco	Jul	65		7,501	XC	3 3/4	+ 1 7/8	68 1/4	175,980
AT&T	Aug	35		7,104	XC	1 1/4	− 1/4	33 1/8	50,084
Palm	Aug	40	p	7,067	XC	4 1/8	− 2 3/4	42 3/4	61,936
TrraNtw	Sep	45	p	6,902	XC	15	− 2 1/8	37 57/64	17,163
AmOnline	Jul	65		6,721	XC	9/16	+ 3/8	62	119,332
Compaq	Aug	30		6,661	XC	15/16	+ 3/16	27 7/8	38,372
AT&T	Jul	35		6,574	XC	1/4	− 1/4	33 1/8	138,309
Palm	Aug	45		6,208	XC	4 7/8	+ 3 9/16	42 3/4	110,008
Palm	Jul	30		6,147	XC	14 1/8	+ 7 3/8	42 3/4	24,920
WellsFrgo	Jul	35		6,140	XC	8 5/8	+ 1 3/8	43 11/16	28,848
ParmTc	Aug	10	p	6,120	XC	9/16	− 3/16	12 11/16	65,826
NortelNwk	Jul	70		5,734	XC	8 1/4	+ 1 1/4	77 3/4	28,797
Micsft	Jul	80	p	5,730	XC	2 3/8	+ 3/16	78 15/16	128,364
AmOnline	Jul	57 1/2		5,695	XC	4 1/2	+ 2 9/16	62	55,700
AT&T	Aug	35	p	5,623	XC	2 13/16	+ 3/8	33 1/8	15,516
Cisco	Jan	80		5,569	XC	5 1/2	+ 7/8	68 1/4	82,748

Complete equity option listings and data are available in the online Journal at WSJ.com.

VOLUME & OPEN INTEREST SUMMARIES
Includes all equity and index contracts

CHICAGO BOARD		
Call Vol:	983,837	Open Int: 37,363,174
Put Vol:	374,214	Open Int: 22,170,788
AMERICAN		
Call Vol:	523,085	Open Int: 29,803,869
Put Vol:	193,239	Open Int: 17,482,932
PACIFIC		
Call Vol:	316,451	Open Int: 25,920,019
Put Vol:	121,416	Open Int: 15,260,288
PHILADELPHIA		
Call Vol:	246,638	Open Int: 16,261,459
Put Vol:	99,509	Open Int: 9,544,635
TOTAL		
Call Vol:	2,070,011	Open Int: 109,348,521
Put Vol:	788,378	Open Int: 64,458,643

Source: *The Wall Street Journal*

Some Practical Details

1. Price and other quotations

   Exhibit 8.2 shows a cut out from a recent issue of *The Wall Street Journal*, and is intended to familiarize the reader with some of the terminology and nomenclature used in the options market. Here,

   - The option and NY close refer to the name of the underlying stock and its closing price.
   - The closing price is clearly determined by the market and not by the exchange.
   - The strike price is that price at which the option can be exercised.
   - The indicated months are the maturity months of the available options, calls and puts.
   - "*r*" indicates that the option, although available, did not trade on that day.
   - "*s*" indicates that the option has not been introduced and is therefore unavailable to be traded.

   The quoted price under each contract month is the option premium per share of the underlying stock. The full premium is, therefore, 100* per share premium. Option premiums are quoted in increments of 1/16th of a dollar. The volume refers to the number of options traded on that day. The open interest is similar to the number of shares outstanding for a corporation. It is the number of options available to be traded on a given date, but only a certain number (volume) does trade on that day.

2. Expiration dates

   The expiration dates are set by the exchanges that introduce a new set of options. The maximum maturity is typically nine months. Each class of options is assigned one of three expiration month cycles. The January cycle has the following expiration months: January-April-July-October; the February cycle has the following expiration months: February-May-August-November; and the

March cycle is: March-June-September-December expirations. Once listed, each option remains listed until the expiration date, which is 10:59 A.M. central time on the Saturday after the third Friday of the contract month.

3. Strikes prices

The strike prices are decided upon by the exchanges as well. The initial exercise (strike) prices will be set to envelop the prevailing market price. If the latter is $48, then the strike prices introduced will be $45 and $50. Other strike prices are introduced as the value of the underlying asset shifts. Contracts strike prices are introduced at $5 intervals for stocks prices under $200 (the interval is $2.5 for stocks under $25), and at $10 intervals for stocks above $200.

4. Trading

The trading rules and who trades depend on the exchange. The Chicago Board Option Exchange does not use specialists. Market makers are used instead and they act exclusively as dealers: buying and selling for their own account. They carry inventories of those option assigned to them. They must trade with floor brokers who handle the orders from the public, and they continuously quote bid and ask prices. Market makers may act as floor brokers in those options that have not been assigned to them. Limit orders submitted to the exchange, that is, orders to buy or sell an option at a specific premium flow to the order book officials. (The orders are executed through a system of open outcry in a double auction system: one on the sell and one on the buy side.) Both buyers and sellers pay a commission on the sale or purchase of an option, in addition to the spread (ask-bid). The size of these commissions has been shrinking rapidly primarily because of electronic trades through the Internet. The trading system is set up so the broker or the market maker does not take advantage of his privileged situation on the floor and hurt the position of Mr. Joe Public.

5. Position limits

The exchanges have, in order to prevent some traders from "cornering the market", set up trading limits for option positions on each stock. For large-cap stocks, this limit is 8000 options per trader. Long calls and short puts are considered to be on the same side of the market for the purpose of determining the limit.

6. The Options Clearing Corporation (OCC)

   The OCC interposes itself between every option buyer and every option seller (writer) in every option transaction. In so doing, it guarantees performance for the other side. Consequently, the seller of the option is effectively selling to the OCC and the buyer of the option is buying from the OCC. The creditworthiness of the ultimate counter party to the contract is, therefore, irrelevant. When a buyer chooses to exercise an option, the OCC will pick at random from those option writers who have not closed their position. Should the writer be unable to deliver the shares, the OCC guarantees their delivery.

   In addition, the OCC monitors the positions of all traders. The resulting net position will determine the exposure of the trader and the corresponding margin requirement that must be posted.

7. Margin requirements

   The margin requirements are the amount that must be posted by the party, which has the obligation to deliver. The delivering short (that person picked to deliver the shares to a holder of a call position electing to take delivery) is decided upon by the OCC and the brokerage firms. The margin is a performance bond of sort. It protects the OCC against non-performance by the short who is either obligated to deliver the stock in the case of a call or to pay the cash in the case of a put. The writer of an option may be "covered", that is she owns the underlying stock on which the option is written, or may be "naked", that is, she does not own the stock on which the option is written. The exposure of the writer and those guaranteeing the contract occurs in the latter case. The required margin to be posted is the higher of two figures both calculated by the OCC. One is the option premium plus 5% of the market price of the underlying stock. That margin is marked to market as the position of the short deteriorates. That is, additional funds will have to be put in the account of the short should her position in the option deteriorate. The purchase of an option, on the other hand, must be paid for in full. No portion of the option price may be borrowed.

8. Stock splits, stock dividends and cash dividends

   Stock splits are easily accounted for. An option on 100 shares becomes an option on 200 shares after a two-to-one stock split. The strike price will be split in half, consequently. A stock dividend is treated, effectively, the same way. A 50% stock dividend is equivalent to a 3 to 2 stock split. Every two shares are now worth three shares. The underlying shares in the option contract now number 150 shares (100*3/2), and the strike price will be adjusted by a 2/3 factor.

   There is no protection in listed call options for cash dividends. No adjustment is necessary, therefore, for either the number of shares covered by each option or for the strike price despite the fact that the price of the underlying stock drops by the value of the dividend on ex-dividend day.

9. Exercising an option

   The decision to exercise an option (not a common occurrence) is that of the long. When the decision is taken, the long notifies the broker who in turn notifies the OCC, which clears all trades. The OCC then selects randomly from the open short positions. The one who is short a call and has been "assigned" by the OCC will have to deliver 100 shares of stock, and the one who is short a put will have to buy 100 shares of stock. Once the exercise is completed, open interest will decline by one; that is, there will be one less option to trade. At expiration all options that are profitable to exercise must be exercised. The process could be short-circuited by the short delivering the profit to the long. The OCC would otherwise automatically exercise the options that are profitable by more than $0.75 per share if owned by individuals and by $0.25 if owned by institutions.

The Pricing Factors

The factors affecting option prices are:

- The current stock price.
- The strike price.
- Time to expiration.
- Volatility of the stock price.
- The risk-free interest rate.
- Cash dividend.

From the above discussions and from the contents of Exhibit 8.2, we can easily explain the connection between these variables and option premium. The only variable that may not be intuitive or apparent from the data is the risk-free rate. We deal with it first.

An owner of a stock is able to protect his or her position in the stock by marrying it with an appropriate number of short call options or long put options. A short stock position may be hedged by an opposite position in options, a long call or a short put. Once the position is fully hedged, the return on it should be equal to the risk-free rate. That is why the risk-free rate is relevant to option valuation.

To achieve a fully hedged position, the hedger will short the appropriate number of calls. This is determined by the hedge ratio as follows.

Suppose that for every dollar change in the price of the stock the call option premium changes by $0.20. This is equivalent (mathematically) to saying that the partial derivative of the call option price with respect to the price of the underlying stock is equal to 0.20. Therefore, it would take five short call options to hedge the risk of a stock position in one hundred shares. The hedge ratio is 1/0.20 or 5. Therefore, 100 shares of stock combined with five short call options will produce, theoretically, a net position similar to holding an equivalent position in a risk-free government bond yielding the risk-free rate.

All else being the same, the higher the risk-free rate, the higher the value of the call option.

From Exhibit 8.2, looking at Cisco we note that the market price of the stock is $68.14 and that there is a series of options available with different strike prices. The call and put options had strike prices ranging from \$60 to \$85. The August call option with the \$60 strike price is the most valuable. Looking at the same maturity (August) across higher strike prices, we observe that the price of the call option falls. That is because for each successive higher strike price the holder of the option receives less money (difference between strike and market price) if he chooses to exercise the option. We can say, therefore, that the August call option with the \$60 strike price is most in-the-money, that is, it will bring in the most cash in the event it is exercised. Clearly, the option with the highest strike price will bring in the beast, if anything. In fact, the August 70 option will lose money if it were exercised (option is said to be out-of-the-money). We will explain why it still trades at a positive stock below 70.

We know, consequently, that the higher the strike price, given a market price, the lower the value of option.

Should one check across stock, with different market prices in Exhibit 8.2, one would discover that the higher the price of the stock, all else being the same, the higher the price of the option.

We have, therefore, determined thus far that option prices (premia) are positively related to the market price of the stock and negatively related to the strike price given the market price of the stock.

Taking the Cisco options from Exhibit 8.2 with a strike price of 70, we find that the longer the maturity of the option, the higher the value of the option. The October 70 is more valuable than the July 70 option. Therefore, call option premia are positively related to their life (time to maturity). But, once the maturity is fixed, the passage of time will cause the time premium to shrink with most of the shrinking occurring in the latter part of the option life.

Since we already discussed that prices of stocks fall by the value of the dividends on a dividend day, we can safely conclude that dividends have a negative effect on option prices.

Volatility (σ) is the only remaining variable that is not shown in Exhibit 8.2. The higher the volatility, the higher the price of the option because more volatile stocks have a greater chance of being in-the-money which disadvantages the option seller, thus the higher option premium.

Upper and Lower Bounds for Option Prices

1. Basic assumptions

   Assume that, for market participants such as the large investment banks:

   - There are no transaction costs.
   - All trading profits (net of trading losses) are subject to the same tax rate.
   - Borrowing and lending occur at the risk-free interest rate.
   - There are no dividend payments.

   Assume the following notation:

   S: Current stock price.
   X: Exercise price of option.
   T: Time to expiration of option.
   S_T: Stock price at time T.
   r: Risk-free rate of interest for an investment maturing at time T ($r > 0$).
   C: Value of American call option to buy one share.
   P: Value of American put option to sell one share.
   c: Value of European call option to buy one share.
   p: Value of European put call option to sell one share.
   σ: Standard deviation of the rates of return on S.

2. Some preliminary conditions

   It is relatively straightforward to show that:

   $c \leq C$ The owner of the American call option has all the opportunities as the owner of the European option plus the right to exercise whenever he/she pleases.
   $c \leq S$ Stock price is the upper bound to the option price.
   $C \leq S$ Otherwise, you pay more for the *right to purchase* the stock than for *owning* (*purchasing*) the stock itself! This is clearly not possible.

3. The scenario

Let us now compare two portfolios. Suppose,

Portfolio	Comprises
A	One share
B	One European call option plus an amount of cash equal to Xe^{-rT} (the present value of the exercise price).

The following is the scenario that can be then envisioned:

	Portfolio A (the stock position)	**Portfolio B**		
		Call option	**+**	**Risk-free instrument**
	◀──	Value of the the portfolio		──▶
at $t = 0$	S	c	+	Xe^{-rT}
at $t = T$ (upon maturity)	◀──	Value		──▶
(a) $S > X$	S	$(S - X) > 0$		The value at $T = S$ (X is then used to exercise the option and acquire S)
(b) $S = X$	S	0		X
(c) $S < X$	S	0		X $(X > S)$

Therefore, since the investor who buys a call and makes the requisite bank deposit ends up being better off in some cases and equally well off in all other cases, it follows that the initial cost of taking this position should be greater than the initial cost of buying a share of common stock.

This also means that the following inequality should hold:

$$c + Xe^{-rT} \geq S \quad \text{or} \quad c \geq S - Xe^{-rT},$$

if, in portfolio B	**then, at time T**
• The cash is invested at the risk-free interest rate	→ it will grow to X.
• $S_T > X$, the call option is exercised at time T	→ B will be worth S_T.
• $S_T < X$, the call option expires worthless	→ B will be worth X.

If therefore follows that, i.e., at time T,

- Portfolio B is worth $\max(S_T, X)$, whereas,
- Portfolio A is worth S_T.

The upper and the lower limits on the option price are shown in Exhibit 8.3. Before discussing the graph in Exhibit 8.3, we introduce the major components of an option price.

option price = time premium + intrinsic value.

To understand these components we refer back to Exhibit 8.2. Let us consider the Cisco stock in Exhibit 8.2, in the development of a foundation for understanding Exhibit 8.3. Take the stock price of \$68.14 on July 17, 2000. Thus, S = 68. The range of strike prices available is from \$60 to \$85, typically at \$5 increments. The longest time to maturity option available on July 18, 2000 is January 2001.

Important Observations

1. For a given strike price, i.e., \$65, the longer the life of the option, the higher the premium. In fact, the premium rises from \$3¾ to \$12¼ per underlying share, or \$375 to \$1225 per call option contract.

Therefore, the increased life, from July to January, all else being the same, increased the price of the option by \$850. Time adds to the value of call options.

Option premiums for calls and for puts are positively related to time:

$$\frac{\partial c}{\partial T} > 0, \quad \frac{\partial p}{\partial T} > 0,$$

but not necessarily by the same amount.

2. Let us now consider call options with different strike prices.

The Cisco option with a strike price of \$60 and with August maturity has a premium of \$1000. The reason for this is that it is in-the-money, that is, if exercised today, it would bring:

$$S - X = 68\frac{1}{4} - 60 \text{ or a gross profit of } 8\frac{1}{4}.$$

This is the intrinsic value of the option. The difference between the option price and the intrinsic value is the time premium:

$$10 - 8\frac{1}{4} = 1\frac{3}{4}.$$

As X rises, e.g., to 65 for the call, the option with the August maturity is now worth only \$662.50. This is because the option is now less in-the-money. By exercising the option, i.e., buying the underlying shares at 65 (X) and selling them at 68¼ (S), one realizes only 3¼ per share or \$325 total. Therefore, the call option premium is inversely related to the exercise price. The higher the exercises price the lower the value of the call.

$$\frac{\partial c}{\partial X} < 0,$$

for given S. The opposite is true for puts.

Continuing into higher values for X, we discover that the call option premium shrinks further to only 3½ for a 70 strike price (X) with the August maturity. The 3½ is purely a time premium as the option is out-of-the-money, i.e., exercising the option would

Exhibit 8.3: A call option cannot exceed the price of a stock, nor sell below its intrinsic value.

Just prior to expiration

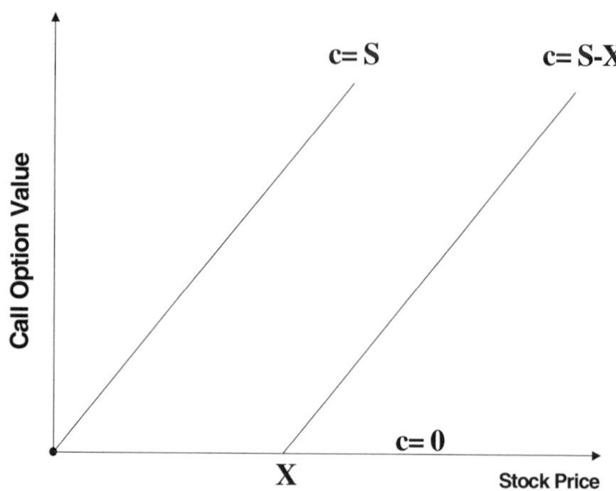

The highest valued option is the one with the longest life.

Tracing the option premium

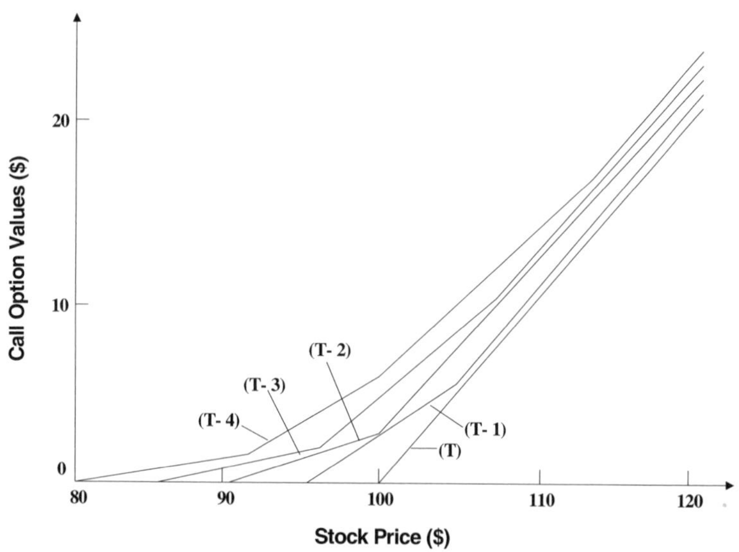

Exhibit 8.3: (*Continued*)

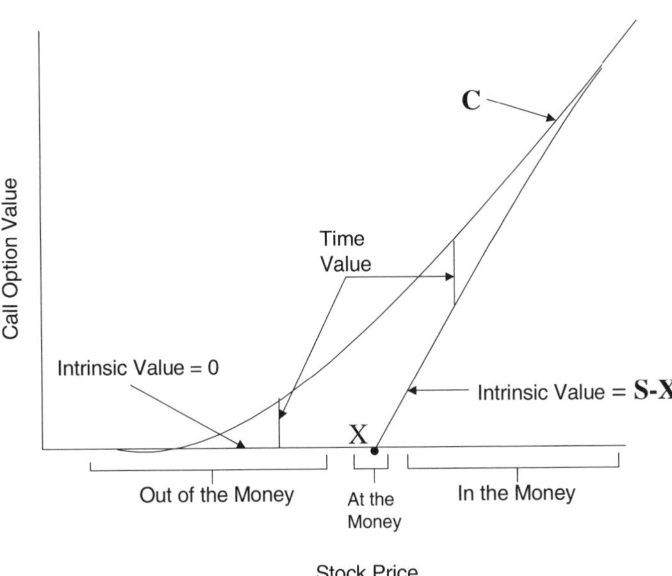

yield a loss as the long would be buying at a higher X and selling at the lower S.

It should be noted that the following inequality must be observed: $S - X \geq 0$. Otherwise, the option premium would be negative, that is, the call option writer would pay the long to buy an option from her. This is simply absurd. It is not possible in the market place.

Referring now to Exhibit 8.3, we can see that the broadest boundaries for the call value are in the first panel between $c = S$ and $c = S - X$ just prior to the expiration of the call option. A call option cannot exceed the price of a stock, nor sell below its intrinsic value.

The second panel shows the shape of the call option price as it travels between the price limits. The highest valued option is the one with the longest life (T-4), *ceteris paribus*.

The third panel shows a smoothed shape of the call option price for a given maturity. Below X, the strike price, the intrinsic value of the option is zero. The only value the call option has derives from the time premium. To the right of X, when the option is in-the-money, the time value begins to shrink toward zero where the option is well in-the-money.

$$S - X \ggg 0.$$

One must note the way the price of an option asymptotically approaches $S - X$, i.e.,

$$\frac{\partial c}{\partial S} \Rightarrow 1 \quad \text{for a call option},$$

but never reaches it. The partial derivative $\partial c/\partial S$ is referred to as the delta of the option:

$$\begin{aligned} 0 \ll \Delta < 1 &\quad \text{for call options}, \\ \Delta < 0 &\quad \text{for put options}. \end{aligned}$$

Option Pricing

The Black–Scholes Option-Pricing Model

The Black–Scholes (B&S) option-pricing model is possibly the most successful model in applied economics. It was first applied to stock options and then extended to options on other instruments, such as currencies. The model provides a closed-form solution for European options. The derivation of the solution is based on the following assumptions:

1. Efficient securities markets.
2. No dividends on the underlying stock.
3. No transactions costs and no taxes and all securities are perfectly divisible.
4. No restrictions on short selling.
5. The option is of the European type — exercisable only at maturity.
6. Stock prices follow a random walk. Stock prices are log-normally distributed so that the continuously compounded one-period rates of return are normally distributed with a known constant

variance. The variance rate is proportionate to the square of the stock price.

7. A known rate of interest. Investors can borrow or lend at the same risk-free rate.
8. R and σ are constant.
9. The price of the underlying asset is continuous.
10. The most important assumption behind the model is that the prices are continuous. This rules out discontinuous hedging argument behind the B&S model.

The statistical process generating the returns can be modeled by a geometric Brownian motion: over any arbitrary time interval, *dt*, the logarithmic return has a normal distribution with mean = $\mu\, dt$ and variance = $\sigma^2 dt$. The total return can be modeled as

$$\frac{dS}{S} = \mu\, dt + \sigma\, dz,$$

where the first term represents the drift component, and the second is the stochastic component, with *dz* distributed normally with mean zero and variance *dt*.

One can think of this as the return on a stock (*dS*/*S*) has a predictable mean value (average) expected value that is time dependent, or the return during a very short period of time (*dt*), and a draft component. The latter is unpredictable (the wild card factor) and is also time dependent.

Based on all the above assumptions, Black and Scholes[1] derived a closed-form formula for European options on a non-dividend-paying stock. Merton[2] expanded their model to the case of a stock paying a continuous dividend yield.

The price of an option should be set within reasonable boundaries.

$$C = \max(S - \mathrm{PV}(X), 0).$$

The boundaries for option prices were discussed earlier in this chapter.

The price of a call option should be set so that the price of the derivate asset should be consistent with that of the asset to which the option is linked, that is, the boundaries must be respected. Option prices on 100

Exhibit 8.4

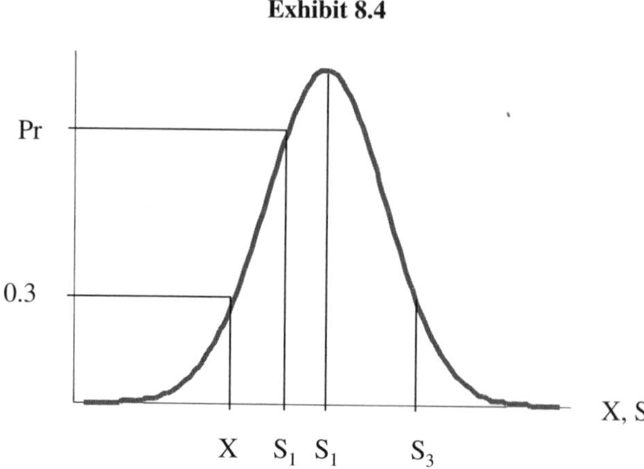

Exhibit 8.5

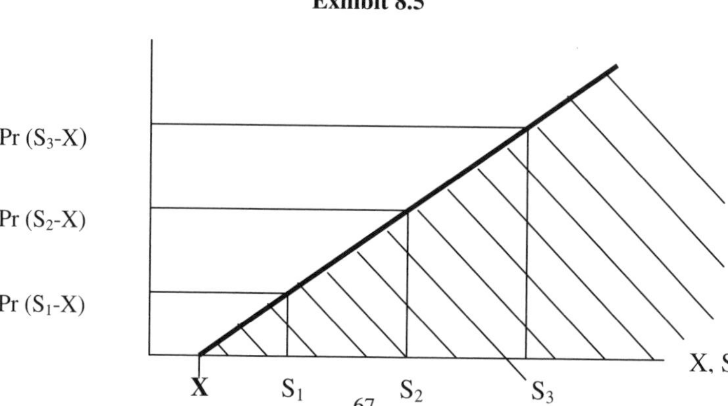

shares of stock cannot be priced in such a way as to induce the investor to buy the option while selling the underlying stock or vice versa.

Should this occur the investor would be able to earn a risk-free arbitrage profit. Arbitrage involves the sale of the overpriced asset and the simultaneous purchase of an under priced asset.

Consider a stock which is efficiently priced, and consider that asset prices are random and normally distributed. Assume in addition that for X and each S above X (making the option in-the-money ($S > X$, $S - X > 0$)), there is a probability attachable to them as shown in Exhibit 8.4.

Translating (mapping) the probability into the option price domain, for those values where the option has a positive intrinsic value, we get Exhibit 8.5.

The present value of the shaded region should constitute the price of the call option assuming $S \Rightarrow \infty$.

The mathematics of the shaded region (SR) are:

$$\mathrm{SR} = \left(\int_{S=X}^{\infty} (S - X)\,\mathrm{pr.}\, dS \right).$$

C = the call price = PV of SR.

Translated, it means that the call option price is the present value of all probabilistic outcome of the option being in-the-money with the stock price travelling from a minimum value of X to infinity.

Assume that stocks are correctly priced, as are options. Assume also that the delta of an option is known. Then it is possible to set a position, long in stocks and short in the appropriate number of call options, given the delta, that would be risk free and earning, consequently, the risk-free rate:

Value of hedged portfolio:

$$V_H = SQ_S + cQ\mu.$$

Q_S = No. of shares in hedged position.

$Q\mu$ = No. of options contracts in the hedged position.

- If the option's price should differ, an arbitrageur can produce, over the next instant of time, a riskless position with a return higher than the risk-free rate. Continuous rebalancing keeps the position riskless until the option expiration date.
- Arbitrage activity will eventually drive option prices in the market to equal the "replicating portfolio", i.e. their model values.

Why is it Difficult in Real Markets?

We must note that the dynamic riskless arbitrage strategy is difficult (albeit not impossible) to apply in real markets, however, because:

1. *Continuous rebalancing of portfolio*: This is not possible when markets are closed.
2. *No transaction costs*: In continually rebalancing a portfolio, the transaction cost can add up.
3. *Uncertainty in volatility*: To determine the value of an option one has to know the volatility of the underlying, which cannot be known exactly.
4. *Unlimited arbitrage*: Unlimited arbitrage does not dominate the market.

Pricing a Call Option

From the preceding discussion and based on the assumptions above, it can be concluded that the price of an option contract is determined as follows:

$$c = f\,(S,\ X,\ \sigma,\ T,\ r,\ D),$$

where

c = Option price of a European call.
X = Strike price.
S = Price of the underlying stock.
σ = Volatility of the stock price measured by the instantaneous variance of the rate of return of the stock.
T = Life of the options contract.
r = The risk-free rate of interest.
D = Dividend yield on the stock.

$$\frac{\partial c}{\partial S} > 0, \quad \frac{\partial c}{\partial X} < 0, \quad \frac{\partial c}{\partial \sigma^2} > 0, \quad \frac{\partial c}{\partial T} > 0, \quad \frac{\partial c}{\partial r} > 0, \quad \frac{\partial c}{\partial D} < 0.$$

But once T is fixed, $\partial c/\partial T < 0$ as the life of the option shrinks.

All variables are readily available from the pages of *The Wall Street Journal*. The only variable that must be estimated is σ, the measure of uncertainty about the stock returns in one year where the return is expressed using continuous compounding.

R_t = the return on the stock = $\ln (S_t/S_{t-1})$. The ln denotes the natural logarithm of the quantity S_t/S_{t-1}, which gives the continually compounded return.

We now calculate $\overline{R}_t$ = average rate of return on a stock.

$$\overline{R}_t = \frac{1}{n}\sum_{t=1}^{n} R_t .$$

The period variance, therefore, is: $\sigma^2 = 1/n - 1\sum_{t=1}^{n}(R_t - \overline{R}_t)^2$.

It is a per-period variance because its size is dependent on the length of time over which each return is measured.

$$\text{weekly returns} \Rightarrow \text{weekly variance},$$
$$\text{daily returns} \Rightarrow \text{daily variance}.$$

This relationship is negative because we assume that once the life of the option is fixed, the premium begins to decay (shrink) thereafter.

We need an annual variance, however. This is attained by multiplying the per-period variance by the number of periods per year.

$$\sigma^2 = 52s^2, \text{ where } s^2 \text{ is weekly variance}.$$

As a rough approximation, $\sigma\sqrt{T}$ is the standard deviation of the proportional change in the stock price in time T. Consider the situation where σ = 0.3 or 30% per annum. The standard deviation of the proportional change in one year is approximately 30%, the standard deviation of the proportional change in six months is approximately $30\sqrt{0.5} = 21.2\%$, the standard deviation of the proportional change in three months is approximately $30\sqrt{0.25} = 15\%$, and so on.

σ, we note again, is the only variable in the call option formula that needs to be calculated. The others are given either by the option details themselves (X, T), by the stock market (S), by the company (D) and by the money markets (r). A decision will still have to be made however, as to the appropriate r to use (issuer, maturity, etc.)

The estimation of σ assumes that it will be constant during the life of the options. We know, however, that when there is no trading on weekends, σ is not the same as when there is.

It must be remembered that we are working in trading time, not calendar time, and therefore weekends and holidays are not used. The accepted figure is that there are 250 trading days per year.

The second method for estimating σ is implied volatility. To find implied volatility, we use five variables of the Black–Scholes model (call price, stock price, exercise price, interest rate, and time to expiration) to back into the standard deviation. To solve for the standard deviation, we need a computer, because we need to search for the volatilities inherent in $d1$ and $d2$ that make the B&S equation hold.

For most stocks, several options with different expirations trade at once and all of these options may be used to calculate a *weighted implied standard deviation*, where the volatility is found for all the options and then each is weighted and averaged to find a single figure. While this appears to be a good idea, there can be problems with it. For example, some options trade infrequently which makes their prices less reliable for computing implied volatility. Additionally, options way out-of-the-money give questionable volatility estimates. Thus, almost all weighing schemes give the highest weight to options closest at-the-money. In other schemes or variations, at-the-money options are given the most weight because these options tend to give the least biased volatility estimates.

The Black and Scholes Formula

Black and Scholes took the total derivative of the equation $V_H = SQ_S + cQ_U$, using techniques borrowed from physics, to arrive at the call-valuation equation for a non-dividend paying stock.

$$C = SN(d_1) - Xe^{-rT}N(d_2),$$

where

$$d1 = \frac{\ln(S/X) + (r + \sigma^2/2)T}{\sigma\sqrt{T}}.$$

$$d2 = \frac{\ln(S/X) + (r - \sigma^2/2)T}{\sigma\sqrt{T}} = d1 - \sigma\sqrt{T}.$$

$N(x)$ = Cumulative probability function for a standardized normal variable, i.e., the probability that a variable with a standard normal distribution, $\phi(0,1)$, will be less than x.

S = Market price of the stock.

X = Strike price.

σ = Volatility of the stock price.

T = Time to expiration.
R = Yield on a T-bill having a maturity date close to the expiration date of the option.

Example

Calculate the theoretical value of an option on a security with a market price of \$40, a striking price of \$35, and a maturity of three months (T = 3 months or ¼ year). The annual risk-free rate is eight percent and the instantaneous variance of the stock price is equal to 20 percent.

Answer

$$\begin{aligned} d_1 &= \frac{\ln S/X + (r + 1/2\,\sigma^2)T}{\sigma\sqrt{T}} \\ &= \frac{\ln 40/35 + (0.08 + 0.2^2/2)T}{0.2 \times \sqrt{0.25}} \\ &= \frac{0.134 + 0.025}{0.1} = 1.59, \\ d_2 &= d_1 - \sigma\sqrt{T} \\ &= 1.59 - 0.2 \times \sqrt{0.25} = 1.49, \end{aligned}$$

where $N(d_1)$ is the cumulative probability from $-\infty$ to 1.59.

Thus,

$$N(d_1) = 0.9441,$$
$$N(d_2) = 0.9319.$$

And

$$\begin{aligned} C &= SN(d_1) - Xe^{-rT}N(d_2) \\ &= 40 \times 0.9441 - 35 \times e^{-0.08\times 1/4} \times 0.9319 \\ &= 37.764 - 31.964 \\ &= \$5.80 \text{ per share}. \end{aligned}$$

The value of the call contract[3] on 100 shares is therefore equal to \$580 (= \$5.80 × 100).

Put-Call Parity — The Way to Price a Put Option

For a non-dividend paying stock:

$$\begin{aligned} C &= c, \quad \text{American call} = \text{European call}, \\ P &> p, \quad \text{when } r > 0. \end{aligned}$$

What is the relationship between c and p?

Consider two portfolios:

A: One European call plus cash equal to Xe^{-rt}.
B: One European put option plus one share.

Both A and B are worth $\max(S_t, X)$ when the options expire.

At expiration,

	$\underline{S < X}$	$\underline{S > X}$
$A \Rightarrow$	X	$(S - X) + X$
$B \Rightarrow$	$(X - S) + S$	S

Therefore,

	$\underline{S < X}$	$\underline{S > X}$
$A \Rightarrow$	X	S
$B \Rightarrow$	X	S

In today's dollars, therefore:

$$p - c = \frac{X}{(1+r)^T} - S,$$

or,

$$(1+r)^T \times \{S + p - c\} = X$$

$$\text{Assume: } (1+r)^T \times \{S + p - c\} > X.$$

A risk-free arbitrage opportunity will present itself in the following way:

- Short stock;
- Sell put;
- Buy call;
- Net proceeds are used to invest in the riskless bond.

This arbitrage will continue until the inequality disappears. This assumes zero transaction costs. p, therefore, is equal to:

$$p = c + Xe^{-rT} - S.$$

The Pricing of a Put

From the previous discussions and using the same assumptions as in the call case, B&S derived the price of a put option.

$$p = Xe^{-rT} N(-d_2) - SN(-d_1),$$

where

$$d_1 = \frac{\ln(S/X) + (r + \sigma^2/2)T}{\sigma\sqrt{T}},$$

$$d_2 = \frac{\ln(S/X) + (r + \sigma^2/2)T}{\sigma\sqrt{T}} = d_1 - \sigma\sqrt{T}.$$

The variables are defined as before.

Exercising a Call Option: The Dividend Effect

1. Non-dividend paying stock and an American call

   An American call would be worth at least as much alive (not exercised) as "dead" (exercised), therefore, there is no compelling reason to exercise it.

   The value of the right to exercise the option prior to expiration is zero. Therefore, an American call option will have the same value as a European call option.

2. Dividend paying stock

   The larger the dividend to be paid during the life of the call option, the lower the value of the option. Stock prices fall by the size of the dividend on the ex-dividend day.

   There are conditions under which exercising the option prior to the ex-dividend date may in fact be profitable. In fact, it can be shown that some call options should be exercised only at expiration or immediately prior to the ex-dividend date.

   One extreme example, to dramatically illustrate the point, is if a firm pays all its assets as cash dividends. A call holder would want, therefore, to exercise prior to the ex-dividend date, since after the date the call will be worth zero.

   Exercising call options is appropriate only if the value of the call unexercised falls below the intrinsic value.

   Stated differently, if the maximum dividend is more than the interest earned on the strike price from the ex-dividend date to expiration, early exercise is optimal.

In terms of pricing an option, the following adjustments will have to be made in order to arrive at the price of what is referred to as pseudo-American option.

First, a few assumptions:

1. One dividend will be paid on the stock during the life of the option.
2. The ex-dividend and the payment date are the same.
3. The dividend's size is known with certainty.

We can, therefore, calculate c, assuming the option is held to maturity, using the following adjustment to the stock price:

$$S^* = S - \frac{D}{e^{rT}} \quad : X, r, \sigma, \text{and } T \text{ will be the same.}$$

Should the option be expected to be exercised prior to the ex-dividend date:

- Use S^* in the B&S model with the same T being the ex-dividend date instead of T.

- Use $X - D$ instead of X as the investor will receive the dividend by exercising just before the ex-dividend date.
- r and σ will stay the same.

Adjustments for Continuous Dividends — Merton's Model

The Black–Scholes model can be adjusted to account for dividends paid at a continuous rate. Merton's model applies when the dividend is paid continuously, with the adjustment for continuous dividends treated as a negative interest rate. This method works quite well for options on assets such as foreign currency and also applies fairly well to options on individual stocks. The formula for the Merton model is shown below:

$$c_1^M = e^{-\delta(T-t)}S_tN(d_1^M) - Xe^{-r(T-t)}N(d_2^M),$$

$$d_1^M = \frac{\ln(S_t/X) + (r - \delta + 0.5\sigma^2)T}{\sigma\sqrt{T}},$$

$$d_2^M = d_1^M - \sigma\sqrt{T},$$

where δ = Continuous dividend rate on the stock.

In this model, the current stock price is adjusted for the continuous dividend. If there is no dividend paid on the stock, the model collapses to the Black–Scholes model.

Option Positions and Strategies: Graphic and Vector Representations

Option Strategy — Some Helpful Reminders

The development of an investment strategy requires the setting of investment goals and the full realization of one's financial position. An investor with little cash reserves, poor health and minimal life insurance, an inadequate housing arrangement, and other glaring shortages should avoid the stock and option markets. Certainly, the latter should be totally avoided.

Exhibit 8.6: Characteristics of strategies.

Strategy	Nature of strategy	Desired action of stock at expiration	Risk	Gain potential
Write naked puts	High risk/ high return	Up (above strike)	Substantial but limited to price of stock minus premium received	Limited to option premium
Write covered call	Moderate risk/ moderate return	Unchanged	Substantial but limited to price of stock minus premium received	Limited to premium
Write naked calls	High risk/ high return	Down (below strike)	Unlimited	Limited to premium
Write covered straddles	Moderate risk/ moderate return	Band between strike prices	Limited downside	Dual premium
Write naked straddles	High risk/ moderate return	Band between strike prices	Unlimited upside but limited downside	Dual premium
Buy puts	High risk/ high return	Down	Limited but may lose entire premium	Limited but substantial
Buy calls	High risk/ high return	Up	Limited but may lose entire premium	Unlimited
Buy straddles	High risk/ moderate return	Above call or below put striking price	Limited but may lose entire premium	Unlimited

With the needed financial resources justifying entry into the capital markets, an investor is well advised to adopt a portfolio strategy in which options have a constructive role to play. The ad hoc arrangements and the "looks good" approach inevitably lead to financial setbacks. Furthermore, one cannot assume an option position and then "forget about it". It must be watched and managed aggressively (Exhibit 8.6).

From a portfolio perspective and with a certain attitude toward risk, the investor can best devise the option strategy most suitable for his or her needs and tax bracket. The characteristics of the most prevalent options strategies are summarized in Exhibit 8.6. The choice depends on the special circumstances of the investor and on the perceived risk of each position. The reader should remember from the discussions throughout the chapter that the options markets are so flexible that they allow the investor a wide range of possibilities in structuring the desired risk/return trade off: an income-oriented combination, a short put, and/or a short call.

These strategies, however, or the choice among them, constitute the second level in the investment decision-making process. There are several ways of acquiring an option on the stock. The first level in the choice process consists, therefore, of choosing between a long position in the stock (a stock being an option on the assets of the corporation), a long position in a convertible bond (an option — much longer-term option than is available with the listed options — on the stock of the company), a long position in a convertible preferred stock, and a long position in a warrant or in a stock right. These instruments will be discussed later in this chapter. We obviously assume that all or some of these instruments are available on each company that is being considered for investment purposes. After mentioning this, we should not lose sight of the fact that options offer much flexibility as well as a high level of liquidity and that they are available on an increasing number of stocks. Furthermore, options may be the least costly and the quickest, if not the only, way for hedging a stock position.

An investor seeking income from an investment should consider alternative income-producing vehicles such as government bonds, corporate bonds, dividend-paying stock, convertible stock, and others that offer good if not better risk/return opportunities in certain cases. Let us now consider the motivating forces for a call option position. The reader may well be able to infer the economic justification for other options and option strategies.

Fundamental Use of a Call Option

Call options are bought for several reasons, primarily for leverage and risk limitation.

Calls for Leverage

A call option on JAK (a hypothetical company) stock expiring in July with a striking price of $50, JAK/July/50 call, selling for $500 allows for substantial leverage potential. If the market price on the underlying stock is $55, the purchase of 100 shares will require a total commitment of $5500 or the equivalent of the cost of eleven options. If the stock advances to $60 and the option to $10, the profits are:

Stock Positions

Loss	Profit
	$6000 – $5500 = $500

Call Positions

Loss	Profit
	($1000 – $500) × 11 = $5500

To simplify the presentation, the profit figures ignore taxes and transaction costs. The rate of return on the stock position is $500/$5500 or approximately nine percent. That on the option position is $5500/ $5500 or 100 percent. Clearly the investor should prefer the option position under those circumstances. If, on the other hand, the share price remains constant or actually falls during the life of the option, the loss on the option position is 100 percent of the invested capital, while it is much smaller or negligible on the stock position. The leverage position must, therefore, be looked at very carefully.

The reader may already have observed that call buyers have a more complex task with regard to future predictions of movements in stock prices. Not only must they predict the direction of the market price of the underlying security but also the timing of the appreciation in the value of the security. The increase in the value of the security must occur during the life of the option and must be substantial enough to cover the cost of the option and to ensure the desired rate of return.

Calls to Limit Trading Risk

A JAK/July/50 call purchased for $500 becomes profitable (assuming conversion) if the stock trades at over $55, say $58 (see Exhibit 8.7). An investor watching the charts on JAK may arrive at the conclusion that the stock has hit a resistance level and may decide to sell his or her call (bought at 50) and simultaneously short the stock at 58. Using this strategy, however, the investor stands to lose a considerable sum if the price of JAK continues to rise instead of fall. The extent of the loss is theoretically unlimited. If, instead, the investor keeps the call option and goes short, the risk is reduced considerably. If the stock continues to appreciate, the call will appreciate in value, offsetting the loss on the short position. Once the price of the stock pierces the resistance level, the short position is closed. If the stock drops in price, the loss on the call is limited by its premium at the time of purchase ($500). The $500 is the maximum loss. Therefore, if the stock falls below 50, the gains on the short position will more than offset the losses on the call. The real value of the call, however, is increased through repeated trades against the protection it provides.

A short position at 58 followed by a cover and a simultaneous long position at 51, a sale of the long position and a short sale at 60 followed

Exhibit 8.7

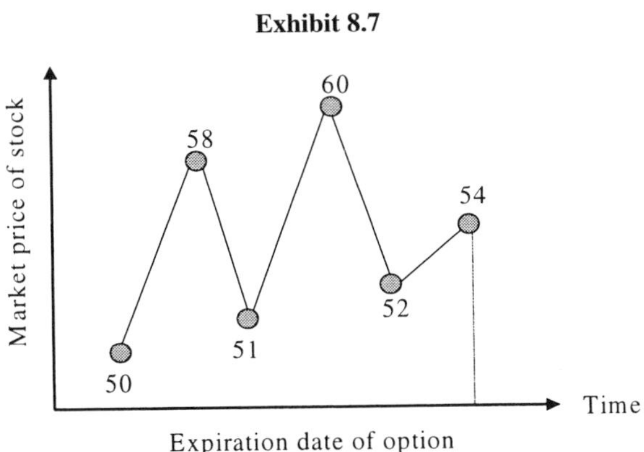

by a cover and a long position at 52, and finally a sale of the long position (optimal) and a sale of the option contact for 54 at its expiration date for $200 would produce considerable profits. This obviously assumes almost perfect foresight on the part of the investigator. Needless to say, the presence of the call emboldens the investigator to a great degree.

Call to Release Cash

An investor with 20-point appreciation in a security may wish to sell the security because of a cash need and replace his or her long position in the stock with a call in order to continue participating in the expected upside potential (see Exhibit 8.8). At 70, the stock is sold for $7000 (assume 100 shares). Simultaneously, a call is purchased for $800, reducing the gross proceeds (before deduction of taxes and commissions) to $6200. If the stock continues to appreciate, the investor would hope to recover the cost of the premium and even make a profit. If the stock declined instead, the maximum loss would be the price of the call.

Calls to Protect Principal

A call is a substitute, although potentially an expensive one, for a long position in the stock. Instead of going long on 100 shares of JAK selling at 50, an investor may choose to buy a JAK/December/50 contract for $500. The difference, $4500, will be kept in a bank, invested in money

Exhibit 8.8

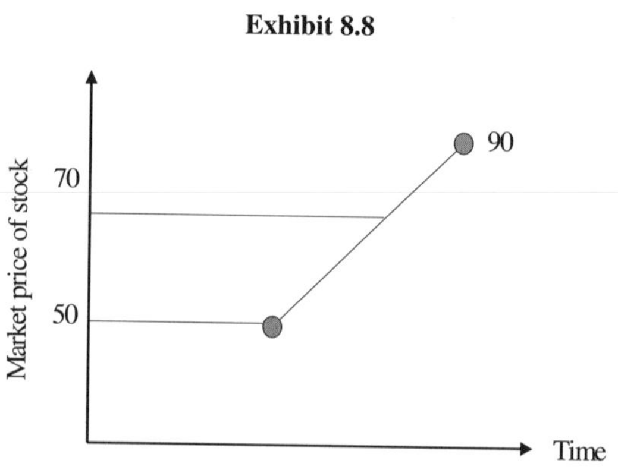

market instruments like T-bills, or used for other purposes. This advantage must be balanced by the following sobering considerations:

1. Unless the stock price rises by more than five points (assuming compulsory conversion, however unrealistic) there would be no profit in the call position, while a positive return would have been realized in a long position in the stock.
2. If the stock price stays at 50 during the life of the call option, the call position expires and is worthless, incurring a loss of $500. A long position in the stock would have zero loss unless the opportunity costs of typing up the principal (funds committed to the purchase of a stock) were announced for.
3. If a stock price falls by more than five points by the option expiration date, the loss on the call position is the maximum $500, but the loss limit on the long position in the stock could theoretically reach $5000. An investor wishing to limit this loss could, however, place with his or her broker a stop-loss order at 45, which means that if the stock trades at or through 45, the order becomes a market order and the stock will be sold at the next bid. This is true for securities listed on the New York Stock Exchange. Stocks listed on the American Stock Exchange will trade at the limit of the stop order. If that limit is passed and the stock is not sold, the investor would have to adjust the price limit if the stock were to be sold. Therefore, while the stop order offers considerable downside protection, it does not limit the maximum loss the investor would suffer. Given the trading rules on the floor of the New York Stock Exchange, however, a sale significantly below 45 is not likely.

Hence our conclusion is that a stop order does offer a reasonable level of protection when compared with a call.

Calls to Protect Short Positions

As discussed earlier in this section, a call is useful in keeping the loss in a short position to a maximum set by the call premium. The profit on the short position is reduced, however, by that premium. The profit on a

100-share unprotected short position in XYZ at 60 will be $2000 if the stock trades at 40 but $1400 if the position is protected by a call costing $600. With an uncovered position, the loss is theoretically unlimited if the XYZ appreciates in value (a limit defined by the investor's level of rationality and wealth does exist, however). The call limits the loss to the size of the premium. The reader should note that the options market permits various levels of protection at obviously different costs depending on the striking price of the call, the life of the call, and the relationship between the market price of the underlying security and the striking price of the call — that is, on whether a given call is out-of-the-money, at-the-money, or in-the-money. The protection sought should be thought of as an insurance policy. The more protection you seek, the more expensive the insurance, that is, the more in-the-money the option will have to be.

Calls for Psychological Sustenance

An investor with a long position in the JAK Corporation established at 60 may panic and sell the long stock if the market price drops to 50, for example. The psychological pains would be felt if the stock were sold only to return back to 60 and beyond. A call position, established on the basis of expectations at the time of purchase, would permit the investor to ride out downward slumps in the price of the underlying security for two major reasons:

1. The maximum loss that the investor can sustain, regardless of how low the price of the underlying security falls, is limited to the price of the option (the premium).
2. The fact that the price of an option does not fall to zero if the stock drops substantially in price — provided that a considerable portion of the life of the option has not expired — is an added advantage. The time premium will provide a cushion. More on this later.

The investor is therefore, more likely to "stick it out" if he or she owns a call option instead of a long position in the underlying security.

Calls to Fix the Price of a Security to be Purchased in the Future

An investor expecting a dramatic rise in the price of a security but unable to purchase it would buy a call on the security with a maturity coinciding with the date of receipt of expected funds. If the investor's price expectations materialized, he or she would purchase the underlying security for a total cost equal to the striking price plus the call premium plus the additional transactions costs. If the expectations did not materialize, the investor would simply sell the call option at a loss or allow it to expire.

Calls to "Declare Self-Dividend"

An investor in a stock that is not expected to move in the near future may decide to earn few dollars by selling (get short) a call option against the stock. His position will be a "covered call" position as he owns the underlying asset which can be delivered in the event the long (the owner of the option) decides to exercise. Should the option expire at- or out-of the money, the holder of the long position loses the entire premium, and, consequently, the short earns the entire premium. It is a zero sum game, after all. The premium earned by the short is a form of a "dividend" declared by the investor onto himself as a result of the understanding of the options market.

Technical Background to Strategies

Exhibit 8.9 illustrates graphically the payoff function from option positions. The short positions are assumed to be naked, that is, they are not covered by an underlying position in the stock (for the call) or by one hundred percent cash position in the case of a put.

The combinations are horizontal summation of the component parts. A straddle (a special case of a combination where the call and the put have the same strike price) is obtained, e.g., by horizontally summing a long call (buy) with a long put, by this representation is in the left middle of the page. Each graph has X (the strike price) and S on the horizontal axis, and profits (+) and losses (–) on the vertical axis. This

Exhibit 8.9

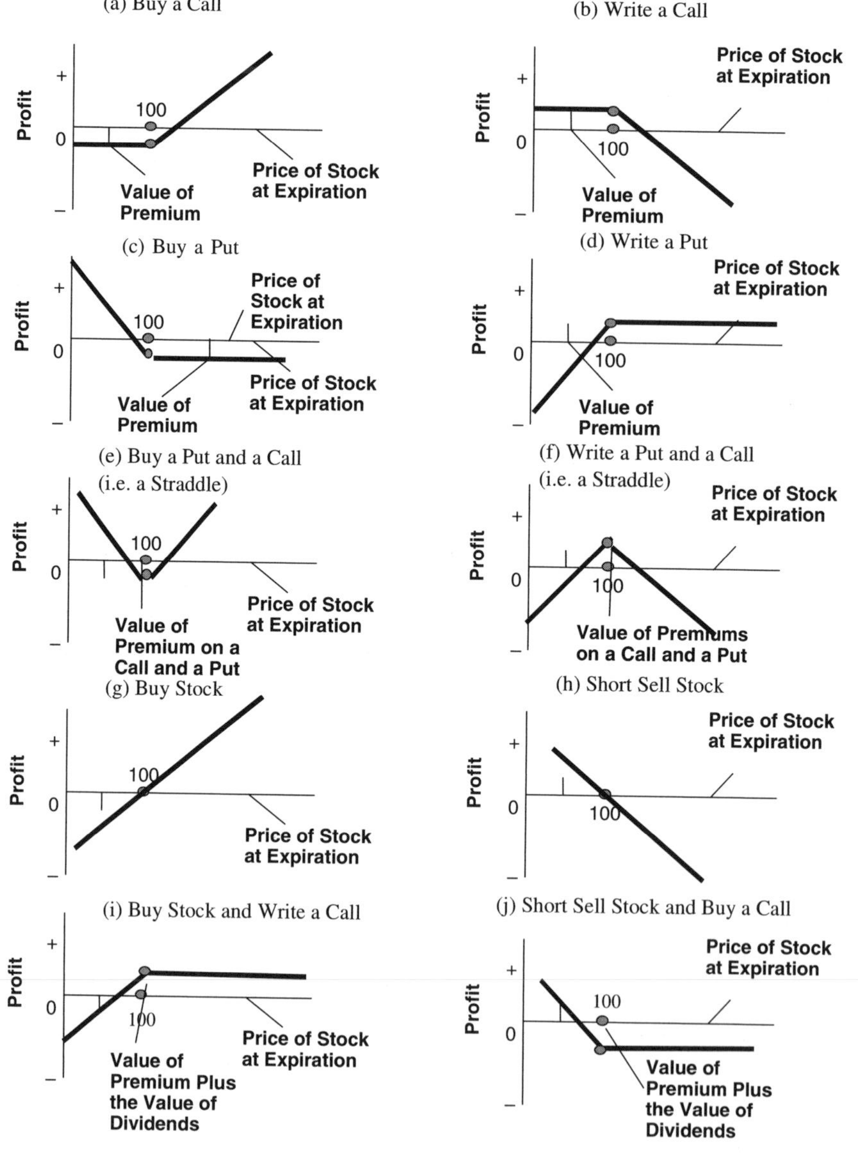
(a) Buy a Call
Profit
+
0
–
100
Value of Premium
Price of Stock at Expiration
(b) Write a Call
Profit
+
0
–
Price of Stock at Expiration
100
Value of Premium
(c) Buy a Put
Profit
+
0
–
100
Price of Stock at Expiration
Value of Premium
Price of Stock at Expiration
(d) Write a Put
Profit
+
0
–
Price of Stock at Expiration
100
Value of Premium
(e) Buy a Put and a Call
(i.e. a Straddle)
Profit
+
0
–
100
Value of Premium on a Call and a Put
Price of Stock at Expiration
(f) Write a Put and a Call
(i.e. a Straddle)
Profit
+
0
–
Price of Stock at Expiration
100
Value of Premiums on a Call and a Put
(g) Buy Stock
Profit
+
0
–
100
Price of Stock at Expiration
(h) Short Sell Stock
Profit
+
0
–
Price of Stock at Expiration
100
(i) Buy Stock and Write a Call
Profit
+
0
–
100
Value of Premium Plus the Value of Dividends
Price of Stock at Expiration
(j) Short Sell Stock and Buy a Call
Profit
+
0
–
Price of Stock at Expiration
100
Value of Premium Plus the Value of Dividends

presentation will be further reinforced and simplified through the vector presentation we introduce next.

Vector Representation of a Call Position

One easy way to track the effect of price movements in the underlying security on the profitability (or lack thereof) of a security or an option position is through the utilization of a vector notation. The vector here is a column vector with two of three possible entries: $+1$, 0, and -1. The first entry in the vector (the first row) represents the effects of a price rise in the underlying security. The second or last row represents the effect of a price drop in the underlying security. A long position in a stock is, therefore, represented by the vector $\begin{bmatrix} 1 \\ -1 \end{bmatrix}$, since the investment rises by one point when the stock appreciates by one point and falls by one point when the stock falls by one point. A short position in a stock has the opposite signs from those of a long position $\begin{bmatrix} -1 \\ 1 \end{bmatrix}$.

A long call position is represented by $\begin{bmatrix} 1 \\ 0 \end{bmatrix}$. If the market price of the underlying security increases, the call will realize a profit (gross profit), but a decrease in the price of the security will result only in a loss of the cost of the call (zero gross loss) without any further liability. The cost of the call is considered a sunk cost. The vector representation ignores the premium paid in any of the instruments. The vector notation for a call looks at profits in a call position resulting from a change in the price of the stock before accounting for the premium.

Vector Representation of a Put Position

A put buyer position is represented by the vector $\begin{bmatrix} 0 \\ 1 \end{bmatrix}$. If the stock appreciates, there is no loss on the put. The cost of the put is a sunk cost. If the price of the underlying security drops by one point, the put will appreciate by a point $(+1)$.

A long put position, it must be observed, is equivalent to a short position in the stock and a long position in a call option.

$$\begin{matrix} \text{Short Stock} & & \text{Buy Call} & & \text{Buy Put} \\ \begin{bmatrix} -1 \\ 1 \end{bmatrix} & + & \begin{bmatrix} 1 \\ 0 \end{bmatrix} & = & \begin{bmatrix} 0 \\ 1 \end{bmatrix} \end{matrix}.$$

Specific Vector and Graphic Representation

The put writer's position is summarized in the following vector $\begin{bmatrix} 0 \\ -1 \end{bmatrix}$, which indicates that the position would realize zero profit (before considering the put premium) if the stock appreciated by a point and would lose a point for every point depreciation in the value of the underlying security. This position is equivalent to a long position in the stock against which a call has been written.

$$\underset{\text{Covered Call}}{\overset{\text{Long Stock}}{\begin{bmatrix} 1 \\ -1 \end{bmatrix}}} + \overset{\text{Write Call}}{\begin{bmatrix} -1 \\ 0 \end{bmatrix}} = \overset{\text{Write Put}}{\begin{bmatrix} 0 \\ -1 \end{bmatrix}} .$$

A long straddle which consist of a long call and a long put will have the following vector representation:

$$\overset{\text{Long Call}}{\begin{bmatrix} 1 \\ 0 \end{bmatrix}} + \overset{\text{Long Put}}{\begin{bmatrix} 0 \\ 1 \end{bmatrix}} = \overset{\text{Straddle}}{\begin{bmatrix} 1 \\ 1 \end{bmatrix}} .$$

The reader should be able to extrapolate from then basic payoffs (assuming the price of the option is forgotten the moment it is made) other vector representation for other strategies and combination and spreads.

We now consider the representations for hedged positions, which are very relevant to stock investors

$$\overset{\text{Long Stock Position}}{\begin{bmatrix} 1 \\ -1 \end{bmatrix}} + \overset{\text{Long Put}}{\begin{bmatrix} 0 \\ 1 \end{bmatrix}} = \overset{\text{Hedged Position}}{\begin{bmatrix} 1 \\ 0 \end{bmatrix}} .$$

$$\overset{\text{Short Stock Position}}{\begin{bmatrix} -1 \\ 1 \end{bmatrix}} + \overset{\text{Long Call}}{\begin{bmatrix} 1 \\ 0 \end{bmatrix}} = \overset{\text{Hedged Position}}{\begin{bmatrix} 0 \\ 1 \end{bmatrix}} .$$

Thus far we have assumed through these representations that the price of an option moves on a one-to-one basis with the price of the underlying stock, but we know from Exhibit 8.2 that this will not be true as the behavior of the option will never track exactly that of the underlying stock, that is, the delta of the option is always less than one.

Using these structures (payoffs) we can look at a short call portion (naked).

The vector representation for writing a call is $\begin{bmatrix}-1\\0\end{bmatrix}$. An increase in the price of the security results in a loss on the sale of a call, while a decline results in no loss on a naked position.

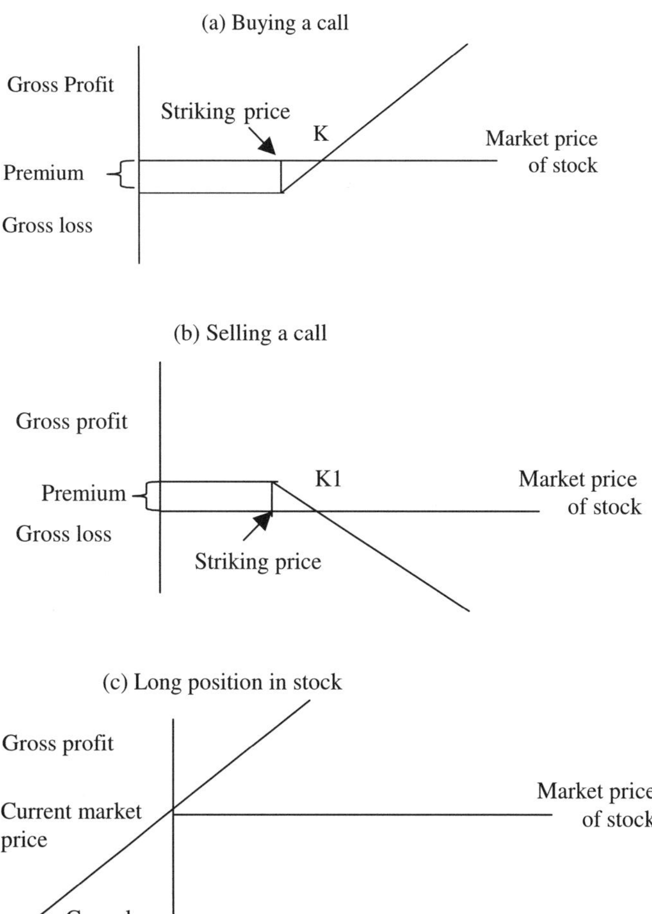

The call buyer will lose the premium (before commissions and other changes) in its entirety until the market price of the stock reaches the strike price. Beyond that point, the call buyer begins to recoup the premium on a one-to-one basis (one point appreciation in the market price of the security means a one point reduction in the cost of the premium). Once K is reached, profits continue to accumulate.

The writer of the call (panel b shown above) will earn the premium and will continue in an advantageous position until the stock price falls below K_1. At that point, the investor wishes that the option had never been sold or simply that a long position in the stock had been assumed.

Both option strategies should be compared with the long position in the stock market by contrast and extension, we can deduce the following:

1. Covered Call = Stock + short call.
2. Portfolio Insurance = Stock + long put.
3. Mimicking Stock = Long call + short put position with the same profit and loss at expiration as does the underlying stock.
4. Synthetic Stock = Long call + short put + bond.

   $$S_t = C_t - P_t + Xe^{-r(T-t)}.$$

   At T,

   $$\underline{S > X}$$

   $$\text{Call} = S - X$$
   $$\text{Put} = 0,$$
   $$\text{Bond} = \frac{X}{S}.$$

   Therefore, the synthesized stock will have the same value as well as an identical profit and loss pattern of the stock being synthesized.

5. Synthetic Put $\quad P_t = C_t - S_t + Xe^{-r(T-t)}.$

   Therefore: $\quad C_t > P_t,$

   $$C_t - P_t = S_t - Xe^{-r(T-t)}.$$

We now discuss other option combinations.

Exhibit 8.10: Position of the straddle buyer.

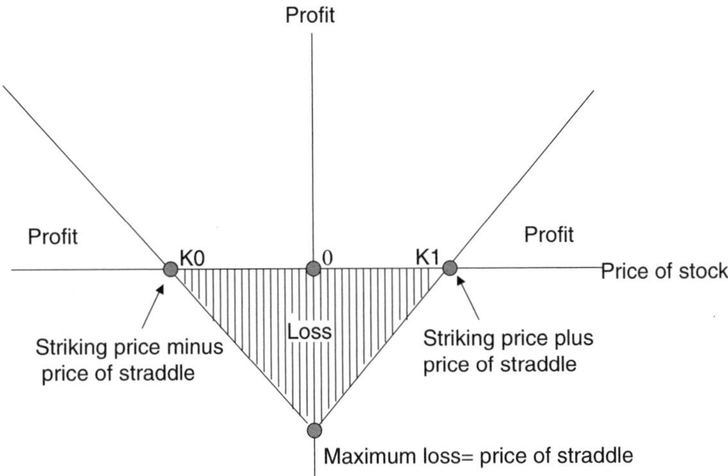

Vector and Graphic Representation of a Straddle

The vector representation of a straddle is as follows:

$$\begin{matrix}\text{Call} & & \text{Put} & & \text{Straddle}\\ \begin{bmatrix}1\\0\end{bmatrix} & + & \begin{bmatrix}0\\1\end{bmatrix} & = & \begin{bmatrix}1\\1\end{bmatrix}\end{matrix}.$$

A point appreciation in the price of the stock causes a point appreciation in the value of the call (before accounting for the premium); a point drop in the price of the stock brings about a point appreciation in the value of the put.

The position of the straddle buyer is shown graphically in Exhibit 8.10, which shows the straddle position realizing a gain beyond K_1 and below K_0. The maximum loss (100 percent of the premium) is realized at point 0, where there is no movement in the price of the stock (strike price = market price).

The vector representation of a straddle sale position is as follows:

$$\begin{matrix}\text{Write Put} & & \text{Write Call} & & \\ \begin{bmatrix}0\\-1\end{bmatrix} & + & \begin{bmatrix}-1\\0\end{bmatrix} & = & \begin{bmatrix}-1\\-1\end{bmatrix}\end{matrix}.$$

Exhibit 8.11: Straddle writer's position.

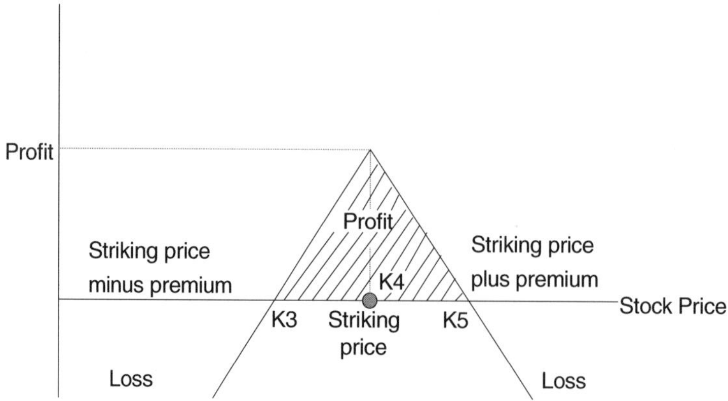

A one point movement (+ or –) in the price of the underlying stock would result in a one point loss on a short straddle position (before accounting for the premium).

Graphically, the straddle writer position can be depicted as in Exhibit 8.11, in which the put is exercisable to the left of K_3. The loss that could result from the newly established long position is limited (the stock could fall only to zero). Beyond K_5, the loss that could result from an exercised call is theoretically limitless. There is no upward limit to the price of a security.

The Strangle (Combination)

A strangle consists of a put and a call with the same expiration date and the same underlying asset. However, in a strangle, the call has an exercise price above the stock price and the put has an exercise below the stock price.

Thus, the strangle is similar to the straddle, but the put and the call have different exercise prices.

Cost of the Strangle

$$\text{Call} \Rightarrow X_1 > S\,,$$
$$\text{Put} \Rightarrow X_2 < S\,.$$

The cost of the long strangle *is* the cost of the call plus the cost of the put which is expressed as:

$$C_t(S_t, X_1, T) + P_t(S_t, X_2, T),$$

X_1 = the call exercise price,
X_2 = the put exercise price.

The cost of the short strangle is:

$$-C_t(S_t, X_1, T) - P_t(S_t, X_2, T).$$

The value of the long strangle at expiration will be:

$$C_t(S_t, X_1, T) + P_t(S_t, X_2, T) = \max(0, S_t - X_1) + \max(0, X_2 - S_t).$$

The value of the short strangle at expiration being:

$$-C_t(S_t, X_1, T) - P_t(S_t, X_2, T) = -\max(0, S_t - X_1) - \max(0, X_2 - S_t).$$

To more clearly explain the results of strangle use, assume:

- A call with an exercise price of \$85 and a cost of \$3.
- A put with an exercise price of \$80 and a cost of \$4.

The cost for the straddle is \$3 + \$4 = \$7.

Exhibit 8.12

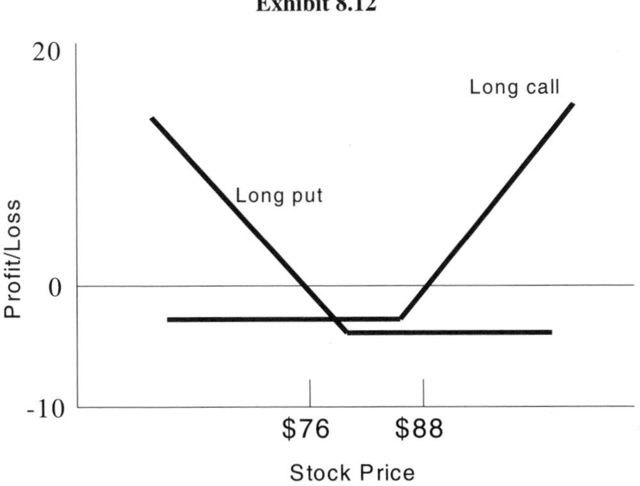

Payoff Diagram

Exhibit 8.12 shows the profits and losses for long positions in these two options.

As can be seen, the call is profitable above \$88 (85 + 3), and the put is profitable below \$76 (80 – 4). But for the strangle owner to make a profit on the overall position, the stock must either fall below \$76 or rise above \$88. Thus one establishes a strangle if one expects a vigorous price move up or down, but is unsure as to which direction will obtain.

Profit Diagram

If an investor were to buy and sell the strangle based on these two options, the graphical representation of the profit and loss is as follows: (Exhibit 8.13)

Exhibit 8.13

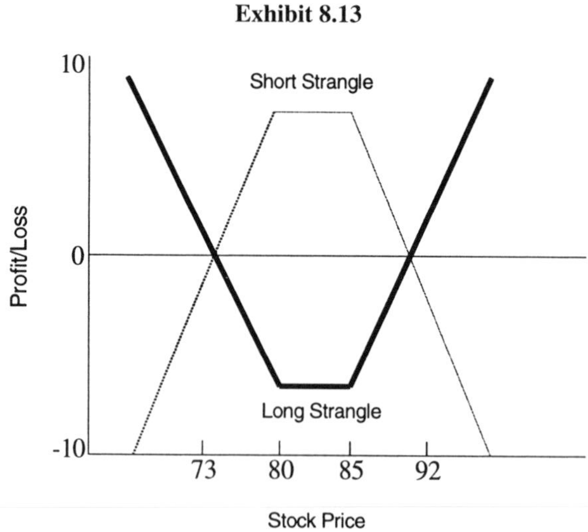

A short strangle (combination) position is established to earn a desired rate of return. The size of the return depends on the behaviour of the underlying stock, on the distribution of the combination premium between the put and the call, and on how far the two options are in- or out-of-the-money. A combination writer who is unable to predict the direction of the market, but who is willing to place a higher probability on a price decline, would want a lower limit on the profit range. This would obviously allow the writer to keep a larger portion of the premium if the price of the stock follows the expected direction. The wide range of combination opportunities that are available in the marketplace does allow the combination writer to set the desired profit range. The lower profit limit on a combination (the breakeven price on the downside) is equal to the striking price on the put minus the total premium received. The upper limit (the breakeven price on the upside) is equal to the strike price on the call plus the premium on the combination.

The sale of Amazon.com/August/45P and an Amazon.com/August/ 40 would produce the following range:

$$\left(45-\left(6+6\frac{1}{8}\right)\right)\text{to}\left(40+12\frac{1}{8}\right),$$

or

$$32\frac{7}{8}\text{ to }52\frac{1}{8}.$$

Below 32 7/8 or over 52 1/8 the investor loses money (Exhibit 8.14).

Exhibit 8.14

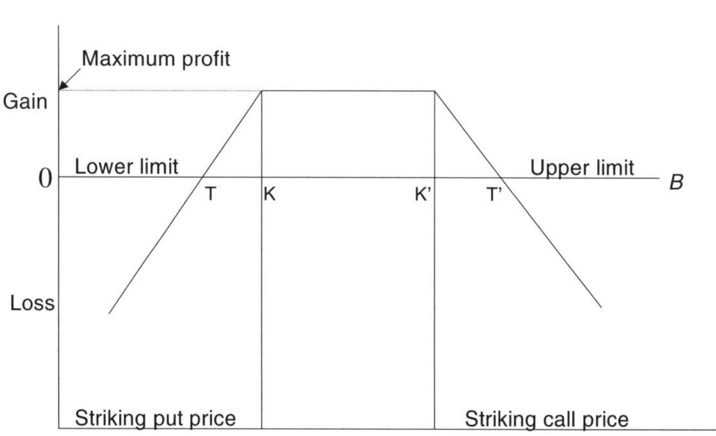

Spreads

A spread is the simultaneous purchase and sale of option contracts of the same class (put or call) on the same underlying security which a combination involves a put and a call, the spread involves only puts or calls. The option bought has a different striking price and/or a different expiration month from the options sold. The spread is the difference between the premium received and the premium paid.

Spreads can be vertical or horizontal. Vertical spreads involve different strike prices. Horizontal spreads involve different maturities. Either may be bullish or bearish. We now use a full example of a bull call spread.

Bull Spreads

A bull spread is established when the investor "buys" a spread, that is, the investor pays more (less) premium for the call (put) option bought than is collected in premium on the option sold. As its name implies, a bull spread is established when an investor expects an advance in the price of the underlying stock. In the call case, the bull spread results in a debit to the investor's account; in the put case, in a credit to the investor's account. In both cases, however, the investor is buying the option with the lower strike price and is selling the option with the higher strike price.

Bull Spread (Cells)

- Buy $X_1 < S$ in-the-money call option.
- Sell $X_2 > S$ out-of-the-money.

Intent: Profit from a rise in stock price.
Features: Limits trader's risk; limits profit potential.

The spread position is best understood using the vector notation:

$$\underset{\text{Buy Call}}{\begin{bmatrix} 1 \\ 0 \end{bmatrix}} + \underset{\text{Write Call}}{\begin{bmatrix} -1 \\ 0 \end{bmatrix}} = \underset{\text{Spread}}{\begin{bmatrix} 0 \\ 0 \end{bmatrix}}.$$

Exhibit 8.15

	July	August	October
AOL 50	11 _	*s*	14 _
AOL 50 *P*	1/16	*s*	1 _
AOL 55	7 1/8	8 1/8	
10 3/8			
AOL 55 *P*	3/16		
1 1/16	2 _		
AOL 60	2 13/16	4 7/8	7 _
AOL 60 *P*	7/8	3	4 _
AOL 65	9/16	2 _	5 _
AOL 65 *P*	3 _	5 _	7 _
AOL 70	1/8	1 1/8	3 _
AOL 70 *P*	11 1/8	9 _	10 5/8

P = put; *s* = no option offered.

The zero entries in the spread vector represent profits before the premium is accounted for. The size of the premium paid in a vertical bull call spread is the maximum amount at risk. The call spread, therefore, limits the risk to the differential between premium received and premium paid.

On a given day, we can observe all possible spread opportunities involving a certain stock, such as America Online (AOL) by merely inspecting *The Wall Street Journal* (Exhibit 8.15).

An investor bullish on AOL would have several vertical call spreads to choose from. The choice, then, would depend on the investor's level of risk aversion, on how bullish he or she is, and on the size of the financial commitment the investor wishes to make. With AOL trading at 62, the investor settles on the following:

Buy AOL/Jul/50	$1175.00
Sell AOL/Jul/55	– 712.50
Investment (maximum loss)	$ 462.50

Being bullish on AOL, the investor buys the option that tracks more closely the price of the underlying stock (the one more in-the-money), and sells the option with lower tracking (the one less in-the-money). This requires a net financial commitment. We now explore the impact of stock price movements on the spread position while we ignore commissions and tax consideration.

Stock Remains at 62

Since both options are in-the-money, they will be profitable for exercising or for closing out by entering a closing sale (purchase) transaction. The exercise would result in the following:

Profit in long call position	(6200 – 5000) = $1200
Loss on the short position	(6200 – 5500) = – 700
Gross profit	$ 500

Profit = 500 – 462.50 = $37.50 or a return of 37.50/462.50 = 8.11%

Stock Appreciates to 65

The results are as follows:

Exercise the long position at a cost of $5000 (striking price) + $1175.00 (option premium)	=	$6175.00
Short position is exercised against us. (The stock we now own (from the exercise of the long call) is effectively being sold at the strike price + option premium). $5500 (strike price) + $712.50. (option premium)	=	$6.212.50
Gross profit or a return of $8.11% (37.50/462.50)		$ 37.50

Therefore, the maximum profit in a spread position is established in advance. It is simply equal to: [(striking price on short position) + (option premium received)] – [(striking price on long position) + (option premium paid)].

Vertical Bull Call Spread Worksheet

		Option price	Stock price
Sell	AOL/Jul/55	7 1/8	62
Buy	AOL/Jul/50	11	62

1. Money at risk = 11 3/4 − 7 1/8 = 4 5/8.
2. Maximum profit potential = difference in exercise prices − money at risk = (55 − 50) − 45/8 = 3/8.
3. Risk/reward = (1.)/(2.) = 4 5/8 ÷ 3/8.
4. Breakeven point = money at risk + exercise price of option bought = 4 5/8 + 50 = 54 5/8.
5. Percent change in the price of the underlying security needed to reach breakeven point [54 5/8 (breakeven point) − 62 (price of stock)]/ 62 = 11.90% (decrease).

Butterfly Strike Price Spreads

A *butterfly strike spread* is established when two middle strike options are purchased (written) and two options — one on either side (of the strike price) — are sold (bought).

For example, consider a position consisting of buying two AOL August 60 call options and selling the AOL August 55 and August 65 contract (Exhibit 8.16).

Note that the payouts take the shape of a butterfly, hence the name. The sale of the butterfly involved the sale of two August 60 together with the purchase of one August 55 and August 65 call option. The expectation is for the stock price to remain almost constant. The sale of the butterfly spread produces maximum profits if the stock price remains unchanged. Note, however, that the maximum profit of the butterfly is $3 3/16.

If the middle is bought, sides sold,

Income = +10 11/16
Cost = +8 14/16
Net cost = −1 13/16
Net income = +1 13/16

Exhibit 8.16: Profit table for a butterfly strike price spread.

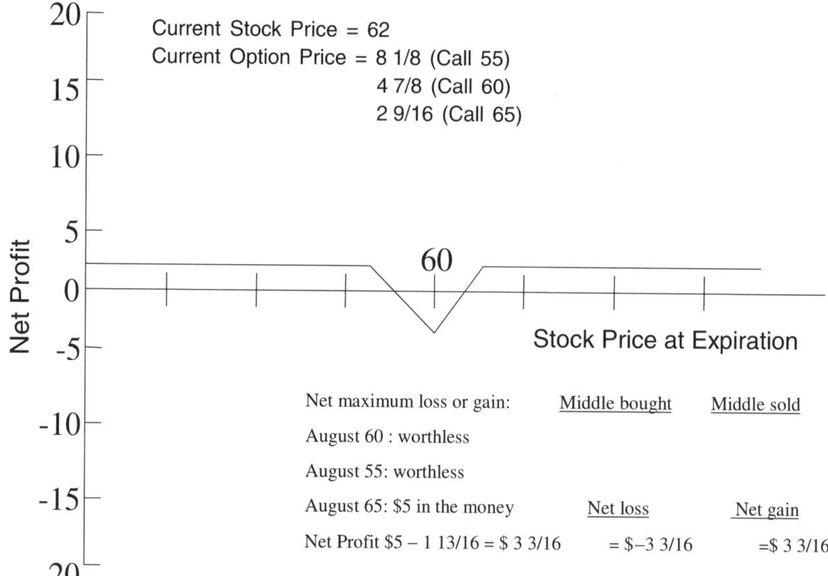

The middle is sold, sides bought,

$$\begin{aligned} \text{Cost} &= 10\ 11/16 \\ \text{Income} &= 8\ 14/16 \\ \text{Net cost} &= \$1\ 13/16 \end{aligned}$$

The Butterfly Spread with Puts

Similar to the call-based butterfly spread, the put-based butterfly spread can also be initiated. Using puts on the same stock all with the same expiration date, the long trader buys two puts with higher and lower exercise prices and sells two puts with an intermediate exercise price, while the short trader does the opposite.

The Box Spread

The box spread consists of a call-based bull spread plus a put-based bear spread, with the two spreads having the same pair of exercise prices, and the same expiration date.

Condor

A call-based Condor is like a butterfly with the middle made up of different strike prices:

Long	$C_1(X_1) - C_2(X_2) - C_3(X_3) + C_4(X_4)$
Short	$-C_1(X_1) + C_2(X_2) + C_3(X_3) - C_4(X_4)$

Puts based Condor:

Long	$P_1(X_1) - P_2(X_2) - P_3(X_3) + P_4(X_4)$
Short	$-P_1(X_1) + P_2(X_2) + P_3(X_3) - P_4(X_4)$

The Condor allows for a plateau (a range in prices), which varies with the width of the variance between the two intermediate prices.

The Greeks

The "Greeks" are Greek letters used by option traders to represent the behavior of an option price with respect to the determining variables listed earlier in the chapter.

Exhibit 8.17 summarizes all of the Greeks with respect to call and to puts and the signs of each Greek variable.

The delta of a stock is a measure of how the option price changes (ΔC) with a change in the price of the underlying stock (ΔS). The ratio $\left(\frac{\Delta C}{\Delta S}\right)$ is referred to in the mathematical literature as a "partial derivative" that is, how does the price of an option change given an infinitensional change in the price of the stock, given all of the variables are held constant such as σ (volatility), T (time left on the life of an option), etc.

The delta of a call or a put option is always less than one. That of the call is always positive (the call price will move in the same direction as the stock price) and that of the put is negative (the put price will move in the opposite direction from the stock price).

But delta is not stable throughout the life of the option. The way to measure its own rate of change is to look at the second derivative of the call value with respect to the price of the stock. This is summarized in the Greek letter gamma. An investor could think of delta as the speed of the call and of gamma as the acceleration. The gamma is positive for

Exhibit 8.17

Call sensitivities for Black–Scholes model

Name	Sensitivity	Sign of relationship
DELTAc	$\frac{\partial c}{\partial S} = N(d_1)$	+
THETAc	$-\frac{\partial c}{\partial (T-t)} = -\frac{SN'(d_1)\sigma}{2\sqrt{T}-t} - rXe^{-r(T-t)}\, N(d_2)$	–
VEGAc	$\frac{\partial c}{\partial \sigma} = S\sqrt{T-t}\; N'(d_1)$	+
RHOc	$\frac{\partial c}{\partial r} = -X(T-t)e^{-r(T-t)}\, N(d_2)$	+
GAMMAc	$\frac{\partial\, DELTA\, c}{\partial S} = \frac{\partial^2 c}{\partial S^2} = \frac{N'(d_1)}{S\sigma\sqrt{T-t}}$	+
Note:	$N'(d_1^M) = \frac{1}{\sqrt{2\pi}} e^{-0.5(d_1^M)^2}$	

Put sensitivities for Black–Scholes model

Name	Sensitivity	Sign of relationship
DELTAp	$\frac{\partial p}{\partial S} = N(d_1) - 1$	–
THETAp	$-\frac{\partial p}{\partial (T-t)} = -\frac{SN'(d_1)\sigma}{2\sqrt{T}-t} - rXe^{-r(T-t)}\, N(d_2)$	–
VEGAp	$\frac{\partial p}{\partial \sigma} = S\sqrt{T-t}\; N'(d_1)$	+
RHOp	$\frac{\partial p}{\partial r} = -X(T-t)e^{-r(T-t)}\, N(-d_2)$	–
GAMMAp	$\frac{\partial\, DELTA\, p}{\partial S} = \frac{\partial^2 p}{\partial S^2} = \frac{N'(d_1)}{S\sigma\sqrt{T-t}}$	+
Note:	$N(d_1^M) = \frac{1}{\sqrt{2\pi}} e^{-0.5(d_1^M)^2}$	

both calls and puts. It adds, therefore, to the reaction of the call option to changes in the stock price. A higher gamma will make for a more effective hedge as we demonstrate below.

The time or theta factor is negative for both call and put options. The value of either option falls with the shrinkage of time with most of the drop occurring towards the end of the life of the option.

One of the most significant of the "Greeks" is the vega. The higher the volatility, the higher the value of the option, put or call. High volatility stocks afford greater opportunity for the long position to be in-the-money ($S > X$ for the call, $S < X$ for the put). Looking at it from the perspective of the short position, one may understand the value of vega even better. The short loses when an option is in-the-money. The loss is exactly equal to the gain of the long position. Therefore, a higher premium would be required if the option has a higher probability of being in-the-money, that is, a higher volatility. Once again, it bears repeating, that the option-pricing model (B&S) assumes that the volatility of the option is constant throughout the life of the option.

Using the Greeks in Hedging

Assume that the delta of a call option on IBM is equal to 0.6 (indicating that the option is in-the-money) and assume that you have a short position in 100 shares of IBM.

To hedge the short stock position in IBM, that is, to protect yourself from a rise in the price of IBM which hurts a short position, you would "marry" your stock position to an option position that makes money when the price of a stock rises. This hedging tool is the call option. Assuming such an option is used, we now have:

Stock position		Option position
Short 100 shares	+	long a call.

$\Delta = -1$ (because the position is short), $\Delta = 0.6$.
Net delta $= -1 + 0.6 = -0.4$

The delta of 0.6 indicates, however, that the hedge is not perfect. Every time the price of the stock rises by a point you lost one point (one dollar per stock or \$100 per 100 stocks), but you only made \$0.60 per stock covered by the option or \$60. Knowing the value of the delta, and assuming it is constant, the "hedge ratio" should have been

$$HR = \frac{1}{\Delta} = \frac{1}{0.60} = 1.66.$$

That is, one must purchase 1.66 options in order to achieve a perfect hedge where the loss in the stock is "perfectly" offset by the gains in the call position. The problem, however, is that options are not divisible. The short stock position holder would then have to be satisfied with only one call position (be under hedged) or allow himself to be over hedged by buying two call options:

- With one call, the net delta = −0.4; this is equivalent to having a net short position in only 40 shares. The delta of a stock position is multiplied by (−1) when the position is short.
- With two call options, the net delta = (−1) + (1.2) = 0.2.

The net position of 0.2 is equivalent to having a long position in 20 shares of IBM. Had we been able to divide the option and get a net delta = zero, we would then achieve a perfect hedge or a delta neutral position ($\Delta = 0$). There is still some risk exposure through gamma, as we see below.

Let us now assume that the following values for the "Greeks" are observed for IBM:

X	= 100
T	= 180 days
Put price (p)	= \$8
delta	= −0.30
Gamma	= 0.02
Theta	= −5.0
Vega	= 25
Rho	= −23

Assume further that we have a long position in 100 shares of IBM. To hedge this position, we go long the put or short the call. Assuming the former is used with a hedge ratio = 1/0.30 = 3.33,

	Long stock	Long put
	100	3 puts
Delta	1	$(3)(-0.3) = -0.90$

Net delta $= 1 - 0.90 = 0.10$.

This is an imperfect hedge and is equivalent to having a net long position of ten shares in IBM (*0.10 × 100 shares)

The gamma (ζ) value of the put options = (0.02) * (3) = 0.06. The gamma typically rises with shorter maturity. At-the-money options ($S = X$) have the highest gamma. A high gamma indicates that a delta hedge needs to be actively managed. The net gamma of 0.06 means that as S rises, delta will increase by 0.06. This effectively translates into a delta for the three puts equal to: 0.90 + 0.06 = 0.96, or a net delta of 0.04, almost a perfect hedge.

Note that the gamma of a put and a call are always equal and can be either positive or negative. The theta = $\partial c/\partial T = -5$ means that every day the value of the put option falls by five cents merely because time is passing.

The vega of 25 means that if one expects σ to shrink, one would construct a net short position (short volatility) using options, and if, on the other hand, σ is expected to rise, the speculator should be long the volatility. One can use similar logic to develop the net delta, net gamma, net vega, etc. values for combinations, spreads and other speculative or hedging positions.

Let us conclude this section with a cautionary note.

A net delta equal to zero for a portfolio of stocks and options would constitute a risk neutral position which can only be maintained with a strategy of continuous hedging. The price of an option does not change at the same rate as the price of a stock, thus the need for continuous adjustment.

Absent a policy of continuous hedging, we get the weak form of a risk neutral position, that is, a hedged position.

A hedged position speaks of what happens at expiration and does not consider infinitesimal, instantaneous changes in the price of the underlying stock and corresponding changes in the price of the option.

8.3 Warrants and Convertible Securities

Warrants

A warrant is equivalent to a call option issued by the firm. It creates new shares when it is exercised. It, therefore, has disruptive effects on earnings per share, and consequently, has negative effects on stock prices!

Warrants are issued as stand alone instruments, but are often attached as "sweeteners" to help sell a bond and to lower borrowing costs.

Pricing Warrants

IP = implied price of all warrants = price of a bond with warrants − straight bond value.

$$\text{Price per warrant} = \frac{\text{IP}}{\text{No. of warrants}}.$$

Warrants have a market value and a theoretical value. The difference between them is called the warrant premium.

Theoretical value of a warrant (TVW)

$$\text{TVW} = (P - X)\,N,$$

where

P = Current market price of a share of common stock.
X = Exercise price of a warrant.
N = Number of shares of common stock received from the exercise of a warrant.

Assuming: $P = 50$, $X = 40$ and $N = 3$.
TVW = (50 − 40) * 3 = $30.

The market value (MV) is determined by market forces and is invariably higher than the theoretical value. The two converge as we get close to the maturity of the warrant. The difference between a warrant and a call are captured in Exhibit 8.18.

Exhibit 8.18: Warrants versus call options.

Similarities	Differences
• Both specify the number of shares the holder can buy. • Both specify the exercise price. • Both specify the expiration date. • Warrants are typically detachable and tradable as call options are. • Value depends on — value of underlying stock; — time to expiration; — the risk-free rate of interest; — the volatility of the underlying stock; — the exercise price; • The decision to exercise depends on S (spot) versus X (strike).	• Warrants tend to be very long term, some are perpetual. • There is no clearing house for warrants and there is no performance guarantee of the contract or in the case of the call. • Call options are issued by individuals with the OCC interposing itself between them. Warrants are issued by firms. Their exercise dilutes earnings per share. • The exercise of an option has no effect on the number of shares outstanding. The exercise of a warrant increases the number of shares outstanding. • When warrants are exercised, the money paid goes to the firm.

Exhibit 8.19

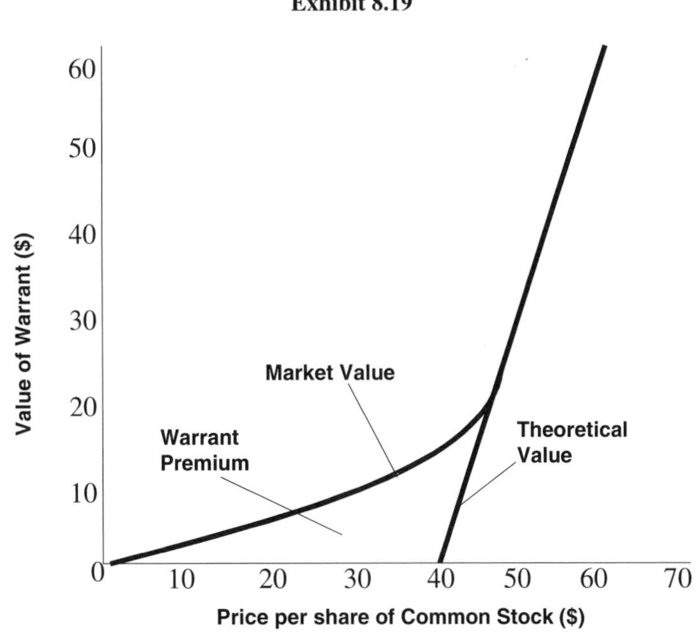

$$\text{Warrant Premium} = \text{TVW} - \text{MV}.$$

The warrant premium is captured in Exhibit 8.19 and is a function of investor expectations and the leverage opportunity warrants represents to their holders. Note the similarity of this graph to that of the call option.

The value of a warrant can also be arrived at using the Black–Scholes options pricing model without dividend payments and with considerable adjustments such as adjusting the market price of the stock to account for the effects of the exercise of the warrant on the earnings per share and consequently on the price of the stock.

Convertible Bonds

Convertible bonds are debt instruments that can be converted into equity securities at the option of the holder during a specified period of time. They are usually debenture bonds with no collateral pledged by the issuing corporation. They are effectively a straight bond with a call option or a warrant attached.

Elements of Convertible Bonds

A convertible bond represents a combination of a straight bond (non-convertible) and a warrant, a long-term option to purchase common stock from the issuing corporation under specified terms. An understanding of the convertible bonds requires knowledge of the following:

1. *Investment value IV* is the price at which a convertible bond would have to sell in order to provide a yield equivalent to that of a nonconvertible bond of equal maturity and risk. If the bond were to sell for this price, the value of the conversion privilege would be zero. Investment value represents a support level, a cushion in the event of excessive decline in the price of the common stock, assuming no accompanying changes in the bond risk.
2. *Conversion ratio N* is the number of shares to which a bond can be converted. This number is stated in the indenture agreement.

3. *Conversion price CP* is the reciprocal of the conversion ratio multiplied by face value (FV). It is equal to $1000/N$.
4. *Conversion value CV* is the market value of the bond if conversion takes place. It equals the conversion ratio multiplied by the market value of the common stock:

$$CV = N * MP^S,$$

where MP^S = Market price per common stock.
5. *Premium over conversion value PC* is the percentage difference between the conversion value and the market price of the convertible bond MP: $PC = (MP^B - CV)/CV$.
6. *Premium over investment value* is the percentage difference between the investment value and the market price of the convertible bond: $PI = (MP^B - IV)/IV$. PI measures the worth of the conversion privilege and concurrently the proportion of the market value of the convertible bond subject to risk resulting from the fluctuation in the price of the common stock.
7. *Price of latent warrant* represents the value of the conversion privilege per warrant that is, per each share to which the bond can be converted: W = price per warrant = $(MP^B - IV)/N$ (or number of latent warrants).

Example

The ASK Corporation issued an eight percent coupon bond at par convertible into 20 shares of common stock. The stock is currently trading at $40. Calculate the values of the relevant variables listed above, assuming the values show in the first two rows of Exhibit 8.20.

For the yield on this convertible bond to equal to the market yield 10.00% on a straight bond, the price must be $800: $80/$800 = 10.00%. This, however, assumes that the bond has an indefinite life. If, on the other hand, the bond had ten years to go before it matured, the market price (of a straight bond) should be determined using the following equation:

$$MP_0^B = \sum_{t=1}^{10} \frac{C}{(1+K_d)^t} + \frac{FV}{(1+K_d)^{10}},$$

Exhibit 8.20: Relevant data on a convertible bond.

Variable name		Value at time of purchase	Values if stock price appreciates by 25%	Values if stock price appreciates by 87.5%	Values if stock price drops by 50%
Market prince of bond	MP^B	\$1000	\$1200 (an assumed value)	\$1500 (an assumed value)	\$878 (an assumed value)
Current yield	$\frac{C}{MP^B}$	$\frac{8\% \times 1000}{1000} = 8\%$	$\frac{8\% \times 1000}{1200} = 6.66\%$	$\frac{8\% \times 1000}{1500} = 5.33\%$	$\frac{8\% \times 1000}{878} = 9.11\%$
Conversion ratio	N	20	20	20	20
Conversion price	CP	$\frac{1000}{20} = 50$	$\frac{1000}{20} = 50$	$\frac{1000}{20} = 50$	$\frac{1000}{20} = 50$
Assumed market price of stock	P	\$40	\$50	\$75	\$20
Conversion value	CV	$\$40 \times 20 = \$800$	$\$50 \times 20 = \$1000$	$\$75 \times 20 = \$1500$	$\$20 \times 20 = \$400$
Premium over conversion value	PC	$\frac{1000-800}{800} = 25\%$	$\frac{1200-1000}{1000} = 20\%$	$\frac{1500-1500}{1500} = 0\%$	$\frac{1878-400}{400} = 94.5\%$
Investment value	IV	878	878	878	878
Premium over investment value	PI	$\frac{1000-878}{878} = 13.9\%$	$\frac{1200-878}{878} = 36.7\%$	$\frac{1500-878}{878} = 70.8\%$	$\frac{878-878}{878} = 0\%$
Price of latent warrant	W	$\frac{1000-878}{20} = \$6.1$	$\frac{1000-878}{20} = \$16.1$	$\frac{1500-878}{20} = \$31.1$	0 (The price never actually drops this low unless the bond is approaching maturity.)

where

$$C = \text{Value of coupon.}$$
$$K_d = \text{Yield to maturity} = 10\%.$$
$$FV = \text{Face value of bond} = \$1000.$$
$$MP_0^B = \sum_{t=1}^{10} \frac{80}{(1+0.1000)^t} + \frac{1000}{(1+0.1000)^{10}},$$
$$= 80\,(PVDF_\alpha) + 1000\,(PVDF),$$
$$MP_0^B = 80(6.145) + 1000(0.386) = 878.$$

We observe from Exhibit 8.20 that the premium over conversion value moves in the opposite direction as premium over investment value. As the premium over conversion value *PC* shrinks toward zero, the convertible bond would behave (at zero) exactly like a common stock. Conversely, as *PC* rises, the convertible bond would approach its investment value and its behaviour would correspond exactly, when $PI = 0\%$, to that of a straight bond.

A conservative investor would, therefore, choose a convertible bond with a higher *PC* and a low *PI*, because the behavior of the bond under these conditions is less dependent on the behavior of the stock. An aggressive investor would choose a convertible bond with a low *PC* and a higher *PI* because its price more closely follows that of the common stock.

The following observations are also worth making:

1. The percentage increase in the market price of the bond lags behind that of the stock. The reasons for this and the extent of the lag will be explained below. For a 25% increase in the price of the stock, the premium over conversion value dropped by only 5%. For an additional 62.5% increase in the price of the stock, 87.5%–25%, *PC* dropped by 20% or a ratio of 20/62.5 = 0.32, as compared with an earlier ratio of 5/25 = 0.2. This simply indicates that the faster the price of the stock rises, the more quickly the behavior of the bond corresponds to that of the stock until the one-to-one correspondence is achieved. Again, aggressive investors would be most interested in convertible bonds with low *PC* because they offer higher appreciation potential.

2. The lower the premium over conversion value, the lower the yield.
3. The investment value represents a cushion of considerable importance in a bear market. When the market price of the bond is equal to its investment value, the convertible bond behaves exactly like a straight bond and its price is then determined by market rates of interest, supply and demand, and the financial position of the issuing company.

Our discussion, thus far can be summarized diagrammatically as shown in Exhibit 8.21 (assuming $MP^B < FV$).

The heavy line from IV through S to CV' represents the minimum market price of the bond. The bond cannot sell below its conversion value, otherwise investors would buy bonds, convert them immediately, and sell the stocks in the market. The conversion value curve CV to CV' is sloped as such because of the assumed constant geometric growth rate in the price of the underlying stick, $P_t = P_o\ (1 + g)^t$. This obviously excludes the 50% decline in the price of the stock discussed in Exhibit 8.20.

Exhibit 8.21: Relationships among the various values of a convertible bond. MP = market price of a convertible bond; IV = investment value of a convertible bond; CV = conversion value of a convertible bond.

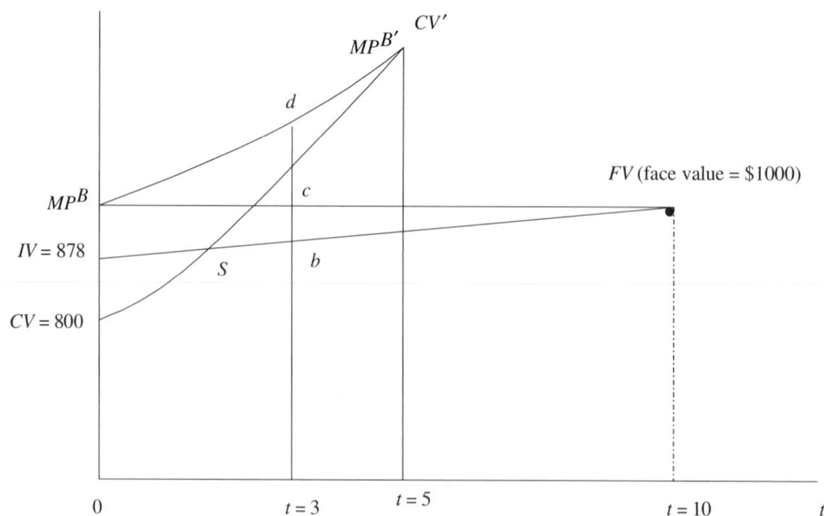

The curve from MP^B to $MP^{B'}$ represents the bond market value curve over a portion of the bond's life. This value is higher than the conversion value curve, initially because of the protection convertible bonds provide (in a bear market) through their investment value. The difference between MP^B and CV represents the value of the "safety net" that convertible bonds provide. This protection diminishes in significance as the price of the stock rises in value.

At $t = 5$, in this particular case, the market value of the bond is equal to its conversion value (premium over conversion value is equal to zero) and the bond is equivalent to holding 20 shares of the underlying security. The investment value of the bond is shown in Exhibit 8.21 to converge linearly to the face value of the bond as the maturity date of the bond approaches.

Determinants of the Market Price of a Convertible Bond

The pricing of a convertible bond is considerably more involved than that of a straight bond. The complications result from the unpredictability of future stock prices (and consequently the conversion value) and from the relationship between the conversion value and the investment value. If the convertible bond is callable, the pricing mechanism is complicated further.

The problem in pricing convertible bonds results primarily from the asymmetric effects on the convertible bond price when different conditions hold. This asymmetry can best be understood through a re-examination of Exhibit 8.21. The market price of the bond equals or exceeds the investment value because of the equity aspect of the convertible bond, that is, because of the price appreciation potential the convertible bond offers. This is observed at $t = 0$, where $MP^B > IV > CV$. The difference $MP^B - IV$ represents the value of the conversion privilege. Beyond point S, the market price MP^B of the convertible bond would exceed the conversion value. At $t = 3$, the difference $MP^B - CV$ is equal to cd and represents the value of the safety net provided by the investment value. This safety factor is nonexistent if the convertible bond is replaced by an equivalent number of common stocks; it becomes meaningless when the conversion premium equals zero. A stock position could theoretically fall to zero, but an equivalent convertible bond position would fall to the investment value. It is important to note, however, that the investment value is not constant. It is affected by changes in market yields and in the riskiness of the firm. A falling stock price is generally reflective of a deteriorating position within the firm. This increases the risk of a default and of bankruptcy. As this risk increases, the investment value falls. The safety net is not as strong as it may appear to be.

J. Walter[4] and A. Que[5] attempted to improve on the conventional model developed in the appendix by using the Monte Carlo simulation to forecast rates of return on convertible bonds conditional upon "the simulated behavior of the underlying stock". Their conclusion was that:

> Behavioral input derived for the simulation model attested to the powerful influence of the relationship between conversion values and straight bond values upon convertible bond premiums and to the asymmetry of premiums, depending on whether conversion values or straight bond values dominated.

If the range of expectations about the course of future stock prices is restricted to certain dimensions and if discrete time intervals are used, the calculation of market value will be considerably simpler.

An investor expecting the conversion value of the bond always exceed its investment value and the stock price to grow at a constant rate g, would calculate the market price of a bond as follows:

$$MP^B = \sum_{t=1}^{n} \frac{C}{(1+K_c)^t} + \frac{MP_0^S(1+g)^n * N}{(1+K_c)^n},$$

where

n = Length of holding period.
MP_0^s = Market price of stock at time of purchase.
C = Value of coupon = coupon rate X \$1000.
K_c = Cost of capital of the firm
$= W_d K_d + W_e K_e$.
W_d, W_e = The weights of long-term debt and equity in the capital structure, respectively.
K_d, K_e = Cost of debt and equity, respectively.
N = Number of shares to which the bond can be converted.

The deficiencies of this method should be obvious, we hope. However, it is very useful and easy to use.

The convertible bond could also be valued as a part bond plus a call option. The bond is valued using traditional bond valuation techniques, and the call option is valued using the Black–Scholes model with the adjustments suggested in the warrant case.

Features of Convertible Bonds

Convertible bonds are characterized by the following:

1. Fixed income set by the size of the coupon rate.
2. Appreciation possibilities resulting from increases in the price of the underlying stock and from a decline in interest rates.
3. Maximum downside risk defined by the investment value of the bond.
4. Generally lower commission costs than those incurred on an equal-size investment in the underlying stock.
5. Generally higher yields than those on common stock.
6. Dividend on common stock is earned only if the investor is holder of record when dividends are paid. The interest on convertible bonds, on the other hand, accrues from the day of purchase.

Investors holding convertible bonds must be alert to changes in the conversion privilege (e.g., different conversion price) and to the expiration date of this privilege. Also of great importance is the call date if the convertible bonds held are callable.

8.4 Conclusion

This chapter sailed through some very complex concepts/strategies and instruments that are related to common stocks. They are all mechanisms for bringing more consonance between the needs of investors and those opportunities available in the market place. Technical as the discussions were in certain sections of the chapter, the reader should be able to focus on the merit and the implications of the concept/strategy without allowing the technical details to disturb or to kill its promise.

Appendix

An Alternative Method for Pricing a Stock Option Contract

Call Valuation: An Alternative Approach — The Binomial Approach

A much simpler model for the valuation of call options on common stocks was developed by Rendleman and B. Bartter.[6] The model was dubbed the two-state option pricing model (TSOPM).

The understanding of TSOPM requires the understanding of the uses of call options and put option as hedging tools. A short position in the stock is protected either by a long call or short put. A long position in the stock is protected by a long put or a short call. The achievement of a perfect hedge depends on the use of the appropriate hedge ratio, that is, the appropriate number of options against a given position in the stock.

Assume that:

H^+ = Returns per dollar invested if the stocks rises in price between period $t - 1$ and t. This is the + state.

H^- = Returns per dollar invested if the stock falls in price between period $t - 1$ and t. This is the – state.

There are only two states + and –; the stock rising in price or falling. In both states:

V^+ = End of period value of the option if the + state obtains.

V^- = End of period value of the option if the – state obtains.

A = Number of option units to be held in the portfolio per \$1 invested in the stock. A can be positive (a long position) or negative (a short position).

W_{t-1} = Price of option.

A riskless portfolio in our construct would consist of a position in a stock requiring a commitment of \$1 minimally (or any multiple thereof) and the appropriate number of options a purchased at price W_{t-1}. If a is properly chosen, the portfolio payoffs would be the same whether the stock rises or falls in price.

Therefore

$$H_t^+ + aV_t^+ = H_t^- + aV_t^- . \tag{1}$$

Solving Equation (1) for a — the number of units of the option per \$1 invested in common stock, we get:

$$a = \frac{H_t^- - H_t^+}{V_t^+ - V_t^-} . \tag{2}$$

At time $t - 1$ the total value of the portfolio is simply the value of the stock (assumed \$1) plus the value of the options used to protect it: aW_{t-1}. This value must be the present value of the expected future value of the portfolio at time t whether the + state or the – state obtains. Therefore

$$1 + aW_{t-1} = \frac{H_t^+ + aV_t^+}{1 + r} . \tag{3}$$

The discounting is done at the risk-free rate because the position is riskless. Replacing a in Equation (3) by its value in Equation (2) we can solve for the price of the option

$$W_{t-1} = \frac{V_t^+(1 + r - H_t^-) + V_t^-(H_t^+ - 1 - r)}{(H_t^+ - H_t^-)(1 + r)} . \tag{4}$$

Equation (4) is the TSOPM. It can be used to price American call and put options as well as European call and put options. To see how both calls and puts are priced by TSOPM, a distinction must be made between the value of the option and its market price. At any point in time the value of the option is the larger value of its market price or its value exercised. In mathematical terms this value is expressed as:

$$V_t = \max(W_t, VEX_t), \tag{5}$$

where VEX_t = Value of the option exercised at time t.

Therefore

$VEX_t = S_t - X$ for all t in the case of an American call.

$VEX_t = X - S_t$ for all t in the case of an American put.

The value is determined by the extent to which the call or the put are in-the-money. To further understand the model, assume there are only two individuals in the option market, John wishing to sell an option and Jill wishing to buy. If both John and Jill can agree on the exact magnitude of the price change then they will definitely agree on the option price. To illustrate this, assume that current market price is \$50, the option matures in one period, and the current risk-free rate is 9%. John and Jill agree on the following:

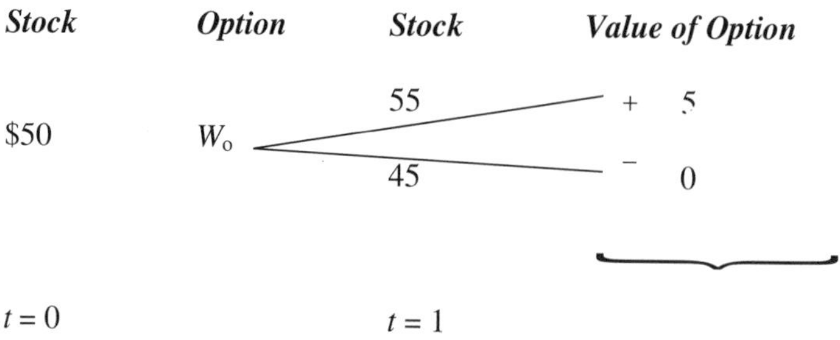

With the above scenario and value we can arrive at the price of the option using Equation (4):

$$W_0 = \frac{5(1 + 0.09 - 0.90) + 0(1.10 - 1 - 0.09)}{(101.0 - 0.90)(1 + 0.09)},$$

$$= \frac{0.95}{0.218} = \$4.35.$$

$$H^+ = \frac{55}{50} = 1.10, \quad H^- = \frac{45}{50} = 0.90.$$

The above model is deterministic and also unrealistic. John and Jill may not know the exact values for H^+ and H^-, which is typically the case, considering the behavior of stock prices. An estimation procedure for H^+ and H^- will, therefore, have to be devised. The proposed model by Rendleman and Bartter amounts to a (possibly biased, with a trend) two-state random walk process using a binomial distribution as an approximation procedure for arriving at option prices. That procedure can be illustrated using a two-period model.

Starting at period t the price of the underlying stock could rise or fall $\binom{+}{-}$. The probability of a rise is θ, of a fall is $1 - \theta$. At time $t + 1$,

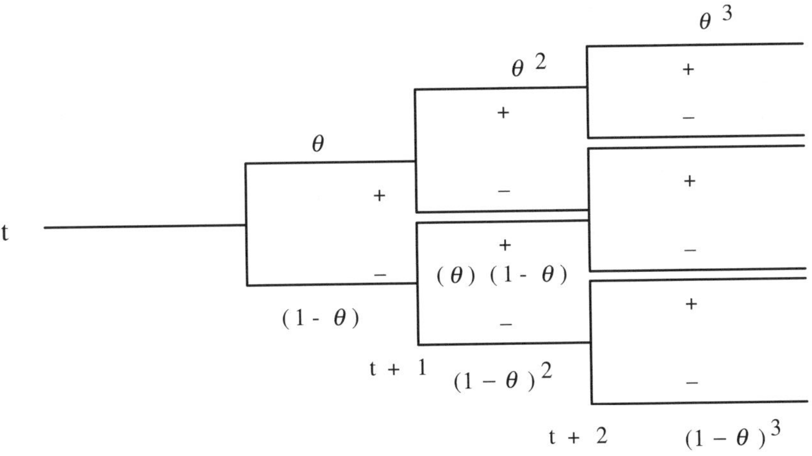

the stock price could again rise or fall if it has risen at time t or rise or fall if it had fallen at time t. However, the fact that it had risen or fallen at time t is assumed to influence in no way the probabilities of a rise or a fall at time $t + 1$. The probabilities are independent. Thus the probability of a rise-rise is θ^2, that a rise-rise-rise is θ^3, and that of a fall-fall-fall is $(1 - \theta)^3$.

In this construct, John and Jill will simply have to agree on the possible size of the + or − change in the stock price and on θ. If the option price consists of T periods, $T + 1$ possible stock prices would emerge which would be log-normally distributed (for large T's) with mean μ and variance σ^2.

The mean of the distribution of returns is calculated by

$$\mu = T[h^+\theta + h^-(1-\theta)] = T[(h^+ - h^-)\theta - h^-]. \tag{6}$$

The variance of the distribution of returns is calculated by

$$\sigma^2 = T(h^+ - h^-)^2\,\theta(1-\theta), \tag{7}$$

where

σ = Probability that the price of the stock will rise in any period.
$h^+ = \ln(H^+)$.
$h^- = \ln(H^-)$.

Given that John and Jill can agree on an H^+, H^-, and a θ value, and given a value for T, we can calculate the market price of the call or the put by using Equation (4). We must note that given the value of μ, σ, θ, and T we can arrive at the implied values of H^+ and H^- using the following equations:

$$H^+ = \exp\left(\frac{\mu}{T}\right) + \left(\frac{\sigma}{\sqrt{T}}\right)\sqrt{\frac{1-\theta}{\theta}}, \tag{8}$$

$$H^- = \exp\left(\frac{\mu}{T}\right) - \left(\frac{\sigma}{\sqrt{T}}\right)\sqrt{\frac{\theta}{1-\theta}}. \tag{9}$$

Example

Assume:

$H^+ = 1.10$
$H^- = 0.95$
$\theta = 0.50$
$T = 100$ (option life = 100 day is considered a period in this example.)
$h^+ = \ln(1.10) = 0.0953$
$h^- = \ln(0.95) = -0.0513$

Therefore

$$\mu = 100\,[(0.0953 + 0.0513)\,0.50 - 0.0513] = 2.20,$$
$$\sigma^2 = 100\,(0.0953 + 0.0513)^2\,(0.50)(0.50) = 0.54,$$

implied

$$H^+ = \exp\left[\left(\frac{\mu}{T}\right) + \left(\frac{\sigma}{\sqrt{T}}\right)\sqrt{\frac{1-\theta}{\theta}}\right]$$
$$= \exp\left[\left(\frac{2.20}{100}\right) + \left(\frac{0.54}{10}\right)\sqrt{\frac{0.50}{0.50}}\right] = e^{0.076} = 1.079,$$
$$H^- = \exp\left[\left(\frac{2.20}{100}\right) - \left(\frac{0.54}{10}\right)\right] = e^{-0.032} = 0.968,$$
$$W_o = \frac{V_t^+(1 + r - H_t^-) + V_t^-(H_t^- - 1 - r)}{(H_t^+ - H_t^-)(1 + r)}.$$

If we assume an $r = 9\%$ and a current market price of 50, the price of the call option will be

$$W_o = \frac{3.95(1+0.09-0.968)+0(1.079-1-0.09)}{(1.079-0.968)(1+0.09)} = \$4\,,$$

where

$$H_t^+ = 53.95$$
$$H_t^- = 48.4$$
$$V_t^+ = 3.95(53.95 - 50)$$
$$V_t^- = 0$$

We must note that W_o represents not the result of the interaction between a John and a Jill in the market place (as we have simplified), but the result of all the expectations of all the "Johns" and the "Jills" in the market.

As the number of periods in the binomial pricing model becomes very large, the binomial model converges to the Black–Scholes option pricing model.

Endnotes

[1] F. Black and M. Scholes: "The Pricing of Options and Corporate Liabilities", *Journal of Political Economy*, vol. 81, pp. 637–659, May/June, 1973.

[2] R.C. Merton: "Theory of Rational Option Pricing", *Bell Journal of Economics and Management Science*, vol. 4, pp. 141–183, Spring, 1973.

[3] For an easy access to the theoretical value of a call option, you could look up a website such as www.bankingtechnology.com.

[4] James E. Walter and Augustin V. Que: "The Valuation of Convertible Bonds", *Journal of Finance*, vol. 28, pp. 713–733, June 1973.

[5] See Endnote 2, p. 730.

[6] R.J. Rendleman and B.J. Bartter: "Two State Option Pricing", Working Paper, North Western University, Evanston, III., 1978.

Chapter 9

RETIREMENT PLANNING AND TAX MINIMIZATION

9.1 Introduction

Now that key strategies for profiting from investments have been thoroughly discussed, this chapter turns to retirement issues, how to increase after tax returns on investment, and how to keep control of the wealth that has been generated. In particular, this chapter focuses on income taxation and estate planning with an eye towards optimizing after tax returns and control. Keeping with the theme of this book, we focus on individuals who are investors, although the basic theory and many of the actual strategies are applicable to corporate investors.

We begin with a review of social security issues and supplementary retirement plans. We then present tax and estate planning, an overview of the relative importance of these topics, and then identify Web-based sources for updating and current events (which is important due to the constantly changing nature of taxation). Next, the Less Intrusive Alternative Planning Model® is described, with examples of how to use it to apply generic tax planning techniques to investment decisions. This is followed by an explanation of the key current US Federal income tax planning issues and rules. The rest of the chapter is devoted to an explanation of key current estate planning issues relating to the use of trusts to control investment portfolios.

9.2 Retiring Comfortably?

The dependence on the state for providing income safety nets, social security for retirement, and health care began in Bismarck's Prussia in 1889 when the state pension plan was introduced. These benefits defined the modern welfare state. Some states, like the Soviet Union, carried their income guarantee schemes to the point of bankrupting the system and eliminating property rights, others taxed their citizens excessively in order to expand the benefits on all fronts. Sweden spends 36% of its GDP on public social expenditures, for instance. In this respect, the United States lags behind Europe as yet, despite continuing to expand the social net. Even this limited expansion, especially of the Social Security (SS) benefits, has come with continuously rising taxes and rising income levels on which the tax is imposed.

The American people are notorious for their excessive spending. Consumption now versus tomorrow (saving) is the predominant option to the majority of Americans. Over 30% of America's workers have no savings for retirement and the SS system is scheduled to go bankrupt by the year 2030.

9.3 Social Security, US Style

The Social Security Act was passed in 1935 during the first Franklin D. Roosevelt Administration. It set up the SS system the payments out of which covered almost 46 million Americans in 2001 through three programs:

1. A Retirement Fund: The retirement benefits were distributed to 39 million recipients in 2001. These are individuals who have contributed to the SS system during their working years. Nine out of ten individuals over the age of 65 receive SS checks. The average monthly benefits per recipient in 2002 are $874.
2. A Survivors Fund: These benefits were distributed to 6.9 million recipients in 2001. The recipients are the survivors of a wage earner who died while working and contributing to SS.

The benefits represent equivalent of a life insurance policy of about $325,000 for a married person with two dependent children. For 2002, the average monthly benefits from the fund are $1764.

3. Disability Insurance: This is provided to those who become disabled and are unable to work. These benefits too were paid to 6.9 million recipients in 2001 and they represent the equivalent of $198,000 disability insurance. The average monthly benefits per worker are $815 and those per family are $1360.

Exhibit 9.1 summarizes the current revenues and expenses of the SS system while Exhibit 9.2 provides the details of SS benefits and Supplemental Security Income levels for 2002 and the related information.

The SS system is financed through the SS tax deducted from every paycheck. The tax is 12.4% with one half paid by the employer and the other half by the employee. This rate of taxation was recommended by the 1983 Greenspan Commission which also recommended, for the first time, that any surplus in the SS fund will be accumulated in a "fund". The tax is imposed currently on wages up to $80,400. The taxes are referred to as FICA (Federal Insurance Contributions Act) taxes. Since 1950, the SS tax or the base on which it is applied has increased annually

Exhibit 9.1: Some highlights of the SS system.

	Old age and survivors insurance	**Disability insurance**	**Hospital insurance**	**Supplementary medical insurance**
Income during 2000 (billion dollars)				
Payroll taxes	$421	$71	$144	—
General revenue	—	—	—	$66
Interest earnings	$58	$7	$11	$3
Beneficiary premium	s—	—	$1	$21
Taxes on benefits	$12	$1	$9	—
Others	—	–$1	$1	—
Expenses during 2000	$358.3	$56.8	$131.1	$90.7
Net increase in assets	$132.2	$21.1	$36.1	–$0.8
Assets at the end of 2000	$931	$118.5	$177.5	$44.0

Exhibit 9.2: SS benefits and Supplemental Security Income levels for 2002 and the related information.

Tax rate	2001	2002
Employee	7.65%	7.65%
Self-employed	15.30%	15.30%

Note: The 7.65% tax rate is the combined rate for Social Security and Medicare. The Social Security portion (OASDI) is 6.20% on earnings up to the applicable taxable maximum amount (see below). The Medicare portion (HI) is 1.45% on all earnings.

Maximum earnings taxable	2001	2002
Social Security (OASDI only)	$80,400	$80,900
Medicare (HI only)	No Limit	

Retirement Earnings Test exempt amounts

As of January 2000, the Retirement Earnings Test has been eliminated for individuals aged 65–69. It remains in effect for those aged 62 through 64. A modified set applies for the year an individual reaches age 65. (The Senior Citizens' Freedom to Work Act of 2000, signed into law by President Clinton on April 7, 2000)

	2001	2002
Year individual reaches 65	$25,000/yr. ($2084/mo.)	$30,000/yr. ($2500/mo.)

Note: Applies only to earnings for months prior to attaining age 65. One dollar in benefits will be withheld for every $3 earnings above the limit. There is no limit on earnings beginning the month an individual attains age 65.

Under age 65	$10,680/yr. ($890/mo.)	$11,280/yr. ($840/mo.)

Social Security disability thresholds	2001	2002
Substantial Gainful Activity (SGA)		
Non-blind	$740/mo.	$780/mo.
Blind	$1240/mo.	$1300/mo.
Trial Work Period (TWP)	$530/mo.	$560/mo.

Exhibit 9.2 (*Continued*)

Maximum Social Security benefit: worker retiring at age 65 in January	**2001**	**2002**
	$1536/mo.	$1660/mo.

SSI Federal payment standard	**2001**	**2002**
Individual	$531/mo.	$545/mo.
Couple	$796/mo.	$817/mo.

SSI resources limits	**2001**	**2002**
Individual	$2000	$2000
Couple	$3000	$3000

SSI student exclusion limits	**2001**	**2002**
Monthly limit	$1290	$1320
Annual limit	$5200	$5340

Estimated average monthly Social Security benefits	**Before and after December 2001 COLA**	
	Before 2.6% COLA	**After 2.6% COLA**
All retired workers	$852	$874
Aged couple, both receiving benefits	$1418	$1454
Widowed mother and two children	$1719	$1764

Monthly limit	$1290	$1320
Annual limit	$5200	$5340

Estimated average monthly Social Security benefits	**Before and after December 2001 COLA**	
	Before 2.6% COLA	**After 2.6% COLA**
All retired workers	$852	$874
Aged couple, both receiving benefits	$1418	$1454
Widowed mother and two children	$1719	$1764
Aged widow(er) alone	$820	$841
Disabled worker, spouse and one or more children	$1325	$1360
All disabled workers	$794	$815

Source: Social Security Administration at http://www.ssa.gov/pressoffice/colafacts2001.htm

with very few exceptions. The expected bankruptcy of the system by 2029–2038 may require, in addition to setting aside some of the budget surplus funds and to making SS an off-budget item (or placing it in a "lock box", so to speak), further raising the retirement age, raising taxes, raising the income ceiling subject to FICA taxes, or a combination of all these. The current political environment may preclude raising the SS tax as it is regressive and as it constitutes the highest tax paid by over 60% of Americans (higher for them than the income tax). It is worth noting that, already, the retirement age in OECD countries is 76 and rising, and the social security tax in Europe is 20% of the employee's gross income. It is expected to rise to 30% within the decade.

The regular collection of FICA taxes a produced a surplus in the SS fund in 1999–2001. Politicians are still finding ways to spend it despite repeated pledges to the contrary. This surplus, incidentally, accounts for the lion's share of the budget surplus and was expected to reach $2.4 trillion by the end of this first decade of the new century, until the disaster of September 11, 2001 changed the entire budgetary picture.

9.4 The Pressing Urgency for Supplemental Retirement Income

A number of factors have combined to exacerbate the need to supplement the SS benefits on retirement. The most obvious of these is the increase in life expectancy. As shown in Exhibit 9.3, in 1900 a 65-year old male was expected to live for another 11 years, and a 65-year old female for another 12 years. By 1950, these numbers had risen to about 13 and 15 years, respectively, and are expected to reach about 18 and 21 years by the end of this decade.

Assuming that the common retirement age today is 65 years, these figures require the stretching of the retirement nest egg in an average portfolio by at least 25% over what was needed about 50 years ago. Lest this may seem a societal rather than an individual burden, we should note that, already, today's retirees increasingly need to supplement their SS income by taking part-time jobs. It is not that the SS benefits are not adjusted for. As is evident from Exhibit 9.4, the SS benefits carry a built-in mechanism for Cost-of-Living Adjustment (COLA). The

Exhibit 9.3: American life expectancy has been rising and this trend is expected to continue.

	Life expectancy (years)			
	at birth		at age 65	
Year	**Male**	**Female**	**Male**	**Female**
1900	46.4	49.0	11.4	12.0
1950	73.2	79.7	13.1	16.2
1960	75.3	81.5	13.2	17.4
1970	77.9	83.5	13.8	18.6
1980	80.3	85.5	14.8	19
1990	82.2	87.1	15.8	19.6
2000	83.9	88.5	16.8	20.3
2010	85.5	89.8	17.9	21.2
2020	86.8	90.9	19	22.3
2030	88	91.9	20.1	23.4
2040	89	92.9	21.2	24.3
2050	90.1	93.7	22.2	25.3

Source: Social Security Administration at
http://www.ssa.gov/OACT/TR/TR01/V_demographic.html#136320

Exhibit 9.4: The 1975–2001 history of automatic Cost-of-Living Adjustments (COLA) received by the SS beneficiaries.

July	1975	8.0%	January	1985	3.5%	January	1994	2.6%
July	1976	6.4%	January	1986	3.1%	January	1995	2.8%
July	1977	5.9%	January	1987	1.3%	January	1996	2.6%
July	1978	6.5%	January	1988	4.2%	January	1997	2.9%
July	1979	9.9%	January	1989	4.0%	January	1998	2.1%
July	1980	14.3%	January	1990	4.7%	January	1999	1.3%
July	1981	11.2%	January	1991	5.4%	January*	2000	2.5%
July	1982	7.4%	January	1992	3.7%	January	2001	3.5%
January	1984	3.5%	January	1993	3.0%	January	2002	2.6%

*The COLA for December 1999 was originally determined as 2.4% based on CPIs published by the Bureau of Labor Statistics. Pursuant to Public Law 106–554, however, this COLA is effectively now 2.5%.

Source: Social Security Administration at http://www.ssa.gov/pressoffice/automatic-cola.htm

number of elderly poor has been rising, nonetheless, so much so that it is increasingly doubtful if the amount of SS benefits that today's boomers will receive when they retire will really allow them to live in anything but poverty. This entails having to build a large enough nest egg to generate adequate supplemental income during the retirement years.

Already, SS and Medicare comprised 6.41% of our 2000 GDP. Based on the projections of the Social Security Administration, and shown in Exhibit 9.5, they are likely to amount to about 11% of the GDP by 2030 and 13% of the GDP by the middle of this century.

The 2001 Annual Social Security and Medicare Trust Fund Reports thus estimate that the trust fund assets will be completely exhausted for Hospital Insurance in 2029 and for Social Security and Disability in 2038!

The second factor that adds to these worries is the continuous decline in retirement age, as computed from the work life expectancy data. Ordinarily, one might expect the rise in life expectancy to concomitantly raise the retirement age. But this is only seen at the age at which full

Exhibit 9.5: Number of workers per SS beneficiary (left scale) are likely to decline while the SS and medical benefits as % of GDP (right scale) are both likely to rise.

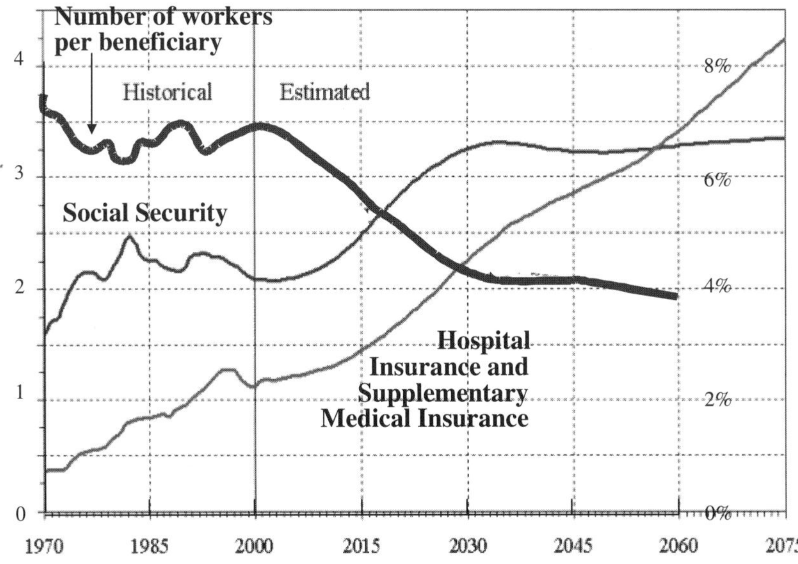

Exhibit 9.6: The increasing expectancy gap in the US (shown here) and other developed economies has meant that, with earlier retirements and longer life expectancies, we now need to build ever-larger nest eggs to survive the retirement years.

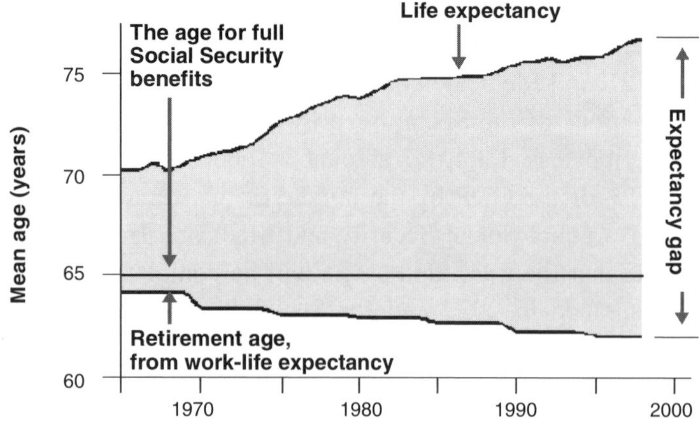

SS benefits materialize,[1] not at the age of retirement. Recent years have seen a persistent drop in retirement age in the developed countries,[2] except for Japan (Exhibit 9.6). Thus, compared to 64.1 years in 1965–1970, the average retirement age in the US dropped to 62.2 years by 1990–1995. In 1997–1998, a 20-year old American male had a work-life expectancy[3] of 36.9 years, and a 40-year old male: 20.6 years. The corresponding numbers for average American women are 31.6 and 17.1 years. Combine these two trends of rising life expectancy and declining work life expectancy and the result, as shown in Exhibit 9.6, is a rising expectancy gap that has significantly added to the number of years that one should expect to spend in retirement.

The third factor is the unmet need between the age of actual retirement and the age at which full SS benefits kick in. The statistics from SS Administration furnish part of the answer. They show that 62-year olds comprised 18.4% of men and 34.7% of women who received SS retired worker benefits in 1970. By 1996, these numbers had climbed to 49.9% for men and 57.4% for women. The benefits that these retirees receive are only partial, however. Clearly, as we start on this new millennium, the need for individuals to build their own retirement nest eggs has become increasingly critical. But this is occurring at a time when the choices for building this nest egg seem to be diminishing, save for the stock market. The fixed-rate instruments like the long-term government and corporate bonds have been the traditional mainstay for the retirees. As for the former, though, recent and projected surpluses in the Federal budget have produced the obviously well intentioned drive to retire the Federal debt. This has had the unintended consequence of effectively privatizing the long-term fixed-rate instruments. This may well render the risk-adjusted returns on fixed-rate market even less attractive than

Box 9.1: Americans and Their Preparedness for Retirement[4]

Americans today are living and spending more time in retirement but, financially, many are either unprepared or under-prepared for the reduced earnings that retirement entails.

"Will We Outlive Our Retirement Nest Egg?" asked the American Savings Education Council (http://www.asec.org) in a news release on January 16, 2001, having found from its 2000 Retirement Confidence Survey that:

- 55% of all current workers think they will be eligible for full SS benefits before they actually will be, and 17% do not know when they will be eligible for the benefits, although 38% of current retirees cite SS as their main source of income.
- SS Administration states that just 4% of today's retirees have saved enough and have enough income to have achieved financial independence, while 12.3% have incomes below poverty level after age 65.
- 45% of American workers have not tried to calculate how much money they will need to save for a comfortable retirement, and 69% of savers say they could save additional $20 a week or more.

Complimenting these results and inferences, a May 2000 survey by Keyport Life Insurance Company (http://www.aboutKeyport.com) found that:

- Most retirement savers have been "bystanders" to stock market boom — two-thirds of them have not gained much from the long-term stock market surge, and only 10% of individuals now working say their stock market gains will enable them to retire early.
- Many harbor contradictory attitudes and expectations about retirement financial needs and lifestyles — 75% of those currently working believe that their standard of living in retirement will be the same or higher than what they now enjoy, 52% cannot estimate how much money they will need to retire in the lifestyle they want (compared to 43% in 1995), and 26% believe that they have to save $100,000 or less to retire and maintain their current lifestyle.

they have historically been. As for the corporate bonds, it is doubtful if they are less risky or offer any better risk-adjusted returns than the stock market itself, particularly the dividend-paying stocks.

Investing in the stock market is the obvious choice, then. Indeed, the question whether one should be in the stock market at all or not may be already moot. With the participation of over 50% of US households in the stock market — a proportion almost comparable to that of the citizenry that voted in the 2000 Presidential Election, chances are that you are already in the market. These numbers are only likely to grow particularly because, as the results of recent surveys summarized in Box 9.1 reveal, many Americans continue to remain under-prepared for retirement.

The fourth factor deals with the burdensome intergenerational dependency. As the number of workers supporting a retiree has been shrinking over time (down to three already), the long term stability of the system without a massive increase in the SS tax rate, a reduction in benefits, and/or an expansion in the tax base remains very much in doubt.

In summary, there simply is no alternative to finding ways to supplement the SS system. We cover below some key provisions and strategies.

9.5 Supplemental Retirement Plans

The numerous privately financed plans currently available to the American wage earner have become so popular and so financially rewarding as to become the primary source of retirement income and turn SS benefits into the "supplemental" retirement income. They have also become very effective tax saving, income enhancing tools. Many Americans have awakened to the possibilities offered through Individual Retirement Accounts (IRA), Roth IRA accounts and 401(K) plans and consider the SS system as a necessary evil which will ultimately wind down through the political process, and the weight of the evidence against it. Many in the political arena believe that, no matter who is elected President in 2000, he will have to propose some privatization scheme to the American people as an integral part of reforming SS. But "31% of working adults in America are not saving for retirement at all". They may be required or may be induced through further tax incentives to change their saving patterns. The retirement saving plans available to them already have considerable incentives, however, as we demonstrate below.

We cover here three popular types of private retirement accounts available to practically every American with earned income.

The Classic IRA allows for a tax deduction of contributions and for non-taxability of income derived thereon. The maximum tax-deductible contribution is $2000 of earned income if the contributor is under age 70 1/2. Anyone with an earned income and who is under the age of 70 1/2 can open an IRA account. Each spouse in a one-income family under age 70 1/2 can open an IRA account. A spouse of a participant in an employer sponsored retirement plan can also make a tax deductible IRA contribution of $2000. The tax-deductibility of contributions in this case depends on one's income level (most Americans would qualify) and on whether the employee is already a part of an employer sponsored retirement plan. The deductibility is limited when the income surpasses the $150,000 mark. Withdrawals from an IRA account can be made without penalty for educational purposes, medical and health insurance purposes, and for the purchase of a home ($10,000 lifetime limit). Funds may be withdrawn without penalty after the age of 59 1/2 and must be withdrawn (at a rate determined by the participant, although there is a minimum distribution requirement) after the participant turns 70 years.

The Roth IRA, on the other hand, has no age limit for making the contributions and no age requirement for beginning the withdrawals of the funds. Anyone with earned income that meets the income caps can open a Roth IRA account. Each spouse in a one-income couple filing a joint tax return can open a Roth IRA if the couple meets the income cap. A contribution to a Roth IRA can be made even if the participant is a member of an employer-sponsored retirement fund. The maximum annual contribution is $2000 of earned income, if your adjusted gross income (AGI) is $150,000 or less and you are married and filing jointly, or $95,000 or less and you are single.

The contributions to a Roth IRA are not tax deductible. The earnings on the contributions can grow tax-free and the distributions from the Roth IRA account are tax-free as well. No single individual with AGI exceeding $110,000, nor a married couple with AGI in excess of $160,000, may contribute to a Roth IRA.

It is important to note that the $2000 per year limit per person applies to both Roth and traditional IRA's. The total contribution to both cannot exceed $2000 per year.

The withdrawals from a Roth IRA are tax and penalty free if the plan has been established for at least five years and one of the following occurs: attainment of age 59 years, first time home purchase ($10,000 lifetime limit), disability and death. Non-qualified withdrawals are subject to a 10% early distribution penalty, and to ordinary income tax.

Because of the interesting tax implications and the flexibility of a Roth IRA plan, some holders of traditional IRA plans are converting to Roth IRA plans. This is possible. There is no ceiling on the amount that can be converted. The rollover distribution is taxable, but the 10% early distribution penalty does not apply. The conversion is not allowed if the holder's income exceeds $100,000, both for single filers and for married couples.

The 401(k) plan, on the other hand, allows for greater flexibility than the IRA accounts and for larger contributions. It is the fastest growing and most popular retirement plan of all. The plan may be set up by the employer or by the employee through the employer. The plan that is set up by the employee allows him/her to decide how much to contribute and where to invest it. This is referred to as a "defined contribution" plan. The employer plan is a profit sharing plan where the employer sets up the plan for a designated set of employees regardless of whether they decide to contribute to the plan or not. This is called a "defined benefit" plan. This will translate, based on an agreed upon formula, into precise benefits to be received upon retirement. The funds are invested as per the directives of the employer or his agents. The size of the funds contributed to the plan is determined by profitability and a related formula. All employer contributions to the plan may be transferred to a plan set up by a new employer. The percentage that may be transferred depends on the vesting schedule.

A plan must be set up by January 1 of the year. The employer contributions must be made by the Federal tax-filing deadline. All contributions are protected under The Employee Retirement Income Security Act and invested within a trust account for the full protection of the participant. This protection is independent of who the money management company is, should one exist, as the company will not have access to the funds within the trust. Additionally, the employer has no access to the money deducted from your pay for investment in the plan.

The benefits from the personal 401(K) are no different from those of the traditional IRA plan. Fundamentally, they are: the ability to make contributions on a pretax basis, and to defer tax on the earnings thereon. Only individuals earning incomes may make pretax contributions to a 401(K) plan. This means that a husband cannot put money into the 401(K) account of his spouse, or vice versa. Generally, the participant in the plan may contribute up to 15% of annual income, up to a $10,000 limit per year. In about 80% of US corporations, employers contribute at least 50 cents against every dollar contributed by the employee. The maximum of the matching contribution is 6% of the pay of the employee. This translates into an instantaneous rate of return on contributions made by the employee equal to at least 50%. All contributions are vested instantaneously to the employee.

The distributions of benefits may begin, free of penalty by the age 59 1/2. Hardship withdrawals are also possible. Early withdrawals are subject to a 10% penalty.

An employee with a 401(K) plan may well decide to borrow from his accumulated contributions. Interest will be charged and will be paid by the borrower to the account.

Thousands of financial institutions compete with various management techniques and investment strategies for the 401(K) plan. One should be careful with the firm chosen to help one manage her/his future.

The above showed very popular and effective ways to save money for retirement, tax-free. All the plans afford the individual or the couple an opportunity to invest at least $4000 per year that is deductible from the current taxable income. We shall demonstrate below how such an invesment is vastly superior to the SS system within one's life and intergenerationally.

In the next section and chapter, we look at other mechanisms for building estates through tax planning, and controlling them even after death through estate (trusts) planning, that is, "A penny saved in taxes is a penny earned".

9.6 The Nature and Scope of Tax Considerations

It is altogether fitting and proper that tax related issues come last in a book about investing in stock, because it is important to recognize the subservient role of planning in this area. Tax and estate planning considerations should rarely dominate securities investment decisions. Instead, such planning should be viewed merely as "icing on the cake" that may generate marginal benefits once good investment decisions are made.

There are several reasons that prevent tax and estate planning from dominating portfolio decisions. First, estate planning — such as the use of trusts and similar devices to control property — rarely generates income tax savings, unless there is an irrevocable transfer of title to the securities to another taxpayer. This either entails a sale, which triggers income taxes, or a gift, which triggers the often-higher gift tax. In either case, to get tax savings, the investor usually has to give up significant amounts of control over the property. Successful investors, like most entrepreneurs, usually understand how important — and how difficult —- it is to amass working capital, and thus are reluctant to part with it.

Second, there is little need to worry about income taxes until one is making significant trading profits. There are several reasons for this. One reason is that gains on securities are tax favored especially after the Bush tax cuts of 2003. Profits on securities sold by investors are taxed at dramatically lower rates if the securities have been held for more than a year. More importantly, appreciation is not taxed until the securities are actually sold. Indeed, if an investor holds onto winners until death, the potential income tax on the appreciation of the investor's portfolio is never subjected to income tax. (Under current Federal law, this could change dramatically for many taxpayers in the year 2011.[5] However, whether the changes currently slated actually will be allowed to go into force is in question, and depends on a variety of political, economic, and social conditions which the country will be facing as 2011 approaches.)

Another reason is that losses on sales of marketable securities are tax disfavored. Such losses almost always are considered capital losses. These are of limited value. Investors are allowed to offset capital gains for the year with capital losses, but losses in excess of gains can offset other income only to the extent of $3000 per year. (Such net losses in excess of this limit are carried over to future years, however.) Although there have been proposals before the US Congress to expand this deduction, particularly in the case of losses on stock acquired through exercise of employer-granted stock options,[6] little has changed in this area for the past 50 years.

In addition, tax considerations should rarely dominate stock market transactions because investment-related expenses are of limited value as tax deductions.[7] For example, one of the largest — margin interest (as well as other investment interest) — is deductible, provided that it is not related to holdings of tax-exempt securities. But this deduction is limited to investment income for the year. In addition, although investors are allowed to deduct other investment related expenses — such as the cost of research reports — these expenses are classified as miscellaneous itemized deductions,[8] and thus rarely generate significant tax savings. This is because such deductions generate tax benefits only to the extent they exceed 2% of the investor's adjusted gross income for the year.

Even though tax and estate planning is subservient to profit making in stock market investing, it still is worthwhile factoring them in when tax and control strategies do not excessively alter basic investment decisions.[9] (Thus the plethora of publications and seminars on these topics.[10]) However, because of the overwhelming complexity of the details of income taxes and estate planning, the astute investor should seek just enough knowledge to understand and apply the key strategies available to optimize US Federal income taxes on the sale of marketable securities, as well as those available to allow investors to use trusts to control portfolios for estate planning purposes. (As part of this, one also should learn how to keep current.) This enables investors to factor in tax and estate planning considerations without excessive costs, and to be able to use consultants wisely when confronted with sophisticated issues.

Keeping Current: Web-Based Reference Resources

The law applicable to tax and estate planning consists of a bewildering array of Federal and State statutes, administrative regulations, and judicial opinions. Fortunately, a great deal of tax and legal information is available via the World Wide Web.[11] Some Web sources are proprietary, such as the Commerce Clearing House Tax Research Network.[12] Others are free. The advantage of the former is that they tend to be highly organized, well indexed, and more complete, along with being organized both by specific provisions of the law (e.g., Internal Revenue Code Section) and by topic. In addition, the topical analyses most often are present much like a text book, or a well written article, and thus are easiest to use by readers who are not experts in the topic.

The advantage of the latter is that they are free; the disadvantage is that they are less organized, less complete, and their addresses change too frequently. It is best to access them though a "gateway" website, such as www.taxsites.com, which provides some organization and keeps links to sites current. Using this, for example, one can easily access the Internal Revenue Service's site, which contains printable official forms, instructions, publications, and pronouncements. Sites for states and foreign countries are also readily available.

Because investors alone understand their own preferences among complex trade-offs involved in wealth preservation, it is worth quickly checking these sites to see basically what the law is on a particular idea. This also allows the investor to use tax and legal consultants more efficiently and effectively. However, to do so require that the investor have a critical mass of legal and tax knowledge sufficient to be able to identify opportunities. This chapter helps provide that critical mass. The first step is the development of a general model for planning in the area. The next chapter provides this — the Less Intrusive Alternative Planning Model®[13] of Tax and Estate Planning.

9.7 Conclusion

Retirement and tax planning are serious businesses. One must take into consideration the role of government that is invariably a partner in the process. The more the government role is restricted, the better the results. But, no matter, one must understand the limits of their portfolio flexibility either in terms of structure or tax implications, and work within the current constraints the market and the government present.

Endnotes

[1] As of now, persons born in 1960 or later will receive their full Social Security benefits at age 67, compared to the age of 65 years for persons born in 1937 or earlier.

[2] The data on work life expectancy are from Murray Gendell: "Trends in Retirement Age in Four Countries, 1965–1995", *Monthly Labor Review*, vol. 12, pp. 20–30, August 1998.

[3] These data are from James Ciecka, Thomas Donley and Jerry Goldman: "Work Life Estimates at Millennium's End", *Illinois Labor Market Review*, vol. 6(2), 2000.

[4] See also Gerda Gallop-Goodman: "Retire with Style?", *American Demographics*, August 2000.

[5] A comprehensive yet readable summary of current tax legislation can be found at http://www.smbiz.com/index.html.

[6] Compare the various proposals before Congress in 2002 to the actual bill which was forwarded to the President, *The Job Creation and Worker Assistance Act of 2002* (which contained only $40 billion of tax relief over the following ten years, primarily in the form of extended unemployment benefits and a temporary 30% of additional first year bonus depreciation).

[7] For a comprehensive discussion on this topic, see Karayan, Swenson and Neff: *Strategic Tax Planning for Managers* (Wiley, 2002).

[8] A glossary of business terms like this is presented at http://www.smbiz.com/index.html.

[9] Hjorth and Connelly: "Family Business Planning that Accomplished the Owner's Goals", *Estate Planning*, vol. 28(10), pp. 503–507, October, 2001.

[10] See, e.g., the websites listed at http://www.taxsites.com/publishers.html.

[11] For an excellent overview of tax research, see Raabe, Whittenburg, Bost and Sanders: *West's Federal Tax Research*, 5th Ed. (West Publishing, 2001). Richmond: *Federal Tax Research*, 3rd Ed. (Foundation Press, 2001), which provides detailed reference to various sources of Federal tax law.

[12] See, e.g., http:// http://tax.cch.com (CCH Tax Research Network); http://www.bna.com/products/tax/ (Bureau of National Affairs Tax Management Portfolios); or http://www7.checkpoint.riag.com/login (Research Institute of America Checkpoint).

[13] The term was first coined in a 1984 speech, entitled "Tax Planning for Middle Managers", given by John E. Karayan at the Informatics' Annual Finance and Administration Meeting in Los Angeles, California. For the economic, information systems, and legal foundations of the theory, see Karayan: "The

Economic Impact of a Tax Law Change: Publicly Traded Partnerships Under the 1987 Act", Unpublished PhD Dissertation (Peter F. Drucker Graduate Management Center, Claremont Graduate School, Claremont, CA, 1994). For a broader view of the decision-making implications, see Karayan, Swenson and Neff: *Strategic Tax Planning for Managers* (Wiley, 2002).

Chapter 10

HOLDING THE GOVERNMENT AT BAY: WEALTH PRESERVATION AND CONTROL

10.1 Introduction

The generation of wealth is not easy. Every dollar saved through tax reduction methods is a dollar earned. That may not be enough for many investors who need to make sure that control over their wealth is maximized, not only during their life, but after their death as well. This chapter deals with more tax strategies and wealth control strategies, primarily through trusts.

10.2 The "Less Intrusive Alternative" Model® of Wealth Preservation

Why attempt to tax plan, or estate plan, in the first place? It may seem obvious at first, but this is an important question, which is answered differently by different taxpayers and by the same taxpayers at different times.[1] This is because such planning requires changing operations, and doing so is not cost free. Nor are the rewards certain: one should focus on enhancing wealth before worrying too much about preserving it from creditors, even such dominant creditors as taxing agencies often are.

Further, one must consider the interactions of the myriads of often-conflicting and inconsistent tax and ownership rules from the multiple jurisdictions typically involved when dealing with even fairly modest levels of wealth. Because of these trade-offs, uncertainties, and costs, focusing on tax minimization should not be an over-arching goal. Nevertheless, optimizing one's total tax burden can be important to an investor's overall success. So can implementing strategies to control property in case of death or disability, or when being transmitted to less investment-astute or more risk-prone beneficiaries such as children or surviving spouses.[2]

The Less Intrusive Alternative Planning Model® is based on the idea that *optimal* — rather than *minimal* — levels of taxes and control should be the ultimate strategic goals in this area.

A good example of optimizing, rather than minimizing, taxes can be found when an investor is considering investing in tax-exempt securities. Unlike interest received on corporate bonds, that from a typical municipal bond is free of income tax. Thus, an investor focusing on minimizing income taxes would purchase municipal bonds instead of corporate bonds. However, as a quick review of current bond yields on the Web illustrates that tax-exempt securities tend to trade at yields of about 70% of those for equally risky taxable securities. For investors expecting effective tax rates of less than 30%, avoiding taxes by purchasing municipal bonds would result in lower after tax income than if equally risky taxable bonds are purchased.

Another example of optimizing can be found when an investor with children marries someone with their own children. Estate and gift taxes are avoided for estate left to surviving spouses. Many wealthy investors, however, do not do so. Instead, each spouse leaves "their" money to "their" children, thus subjecting some to estate and gift taxes. In this case, the non-tax goal of making sure heirs receive their rightful inheritance can dominate saving taxes.

A final example of optimizing can be found in the decision of successful investors who live in high tax jurisdictions like New York and San Francisco to continue living there, even though simply moving to live in El Paso, Nome, or Reno would free them entirely from state and local income taxes. In this case, lifestyle considerations (such as being close to legitimate theatre) dominate minimizing taxes.

As these scenarios suggest, optimization is the goal of good tax planning because taxes are only one factor, albeit often a major one, in the mix of costs (and supply of the factors of production) which generate profit and wealth, and which make life worth living.[3] The same thought applies to the use of trusts and other devices to protect heirs and beneficiaries of gifts. Instead of maximizing the investor's post-transfer control, it should be optimized based on non-control goals, such as liquidity.[4] Planning should focus on discovering ways to achieve tax and control goals, which distort investment decision making the least.[5] There are many reasons for this.

With regards to taxes, investments in general are made based on the risk adjusted net present value of expected *after tax* cash flows.[6] In addition, levies such as income taxes, Social Security taxes, sales taxes, property taxes, and estate and gift taxes often total to one of an investor's largest potential lifetime expense items. The cost of complying with tax rules (e.g., paying a tax return preparer) can be significant, too.[7] Not only can it be costly to figure out how much to pay, it must also be determined who to pay, and when to pay it.[8] In addition, similar taxes are often imposed by different states using similar but different definitions.[9] This could cause the same income to be 100% taxed.[10]

Another reason that tax planning can be important is that tax payments typically have a high legal priority claim on a taxpayer's cash flow.[11] That is, not only can taxes constitute a large expense item, but also they must be paid, and often paid quickly. In addition, investment targets themselves — such as multinationals publicly traded in US capital markets — can be especially sensitive to tax expense.[12] This is because earnings (which usually have a major impact on stock prices) must be reported to shareholders on an after tax basis. Net income is reduced not only by current taxes but also by expected *future* income taxes generated by such earnings.[13]

Furthermore, because senior managers' compensation often is tied to earnings via stock prices (e.g., through stock options), key decision makers in multinational organizations often have a high personal stake in optimizing taxes.[14] All in all, there are many factors which combine to motivate efforts to reduce taxes, provided the cost of doing so is not too high.[15]

Optimizing Rather than Minimizing Taxes or Maximizing Control

As noted above, optimizing, rather than minimizing, taxes and control should be the goal of tax and estate planning.[16] This is because taxes and control are only two factors, albeit usually the major ones, in the mix of costs and other factors which generate the amounts most often taxed: profits and wealth. Put simply, one can avoid many taxes — and need not consider control — merely by neither earning a living nor owning property, but most people do not aspire to a life of poverty, however tax free it is.

Furthermore, strategies undertaken to reduce taxes or maintain control rarely are cost free. If nothing else, when focusing on saving taxes, investors are not focusing on market research, trend analysis, or otherwise operating more efficiently. Tax strategies also are risky: changing operations to save taxes (e.g., by operating through multiple corporations) often results in an increase in long term administrative costs,[17] but only generates uncertain returns because tax laws can change (and, as the past 20 years has demonstrated in the US, change can occur dramatically, rapidly, and unpredictably),[18] and tax rules themselves all too often are, at best, obscure.[19]

The interactions of multiple taxes imposed by many jurisdictions also must be appreciated.[20] For example, consider an investor who seeks to reduce income taxes by building an office above the investor's garage. The cost of doing so may be deductible against Federal income taxes, but also most likely will increase the investor's local property taxes. If the cost is \$10,000 and the property tax rate is 1%, then the increased property tax would be \$100 per year. The income tax deduction would be based on the taxes saved by depreciating the \$10,000 cost, which would result in about a \$300 deduction every year. This would result in \$90 of income tax savings if the investor were in the 30% income tax bracket — for a net tax increase of \$10 — and \$120 of income tax savings per year if the investor's tax rate is 40% — for a net tax savings of $20.

Finally, tax savings strategies can be quite intrusive. Why is it, for example, that investors in the Los Angeles area — a relatively high tax location — do not all move to Las Vegas, a very low tax location?[21] One reason is that it is costly to move. Another (as noted at the beginning of this section) is that non-tax factors dominate the decision: many simply want to live in Southern California rather than Southern Nevada.[22]

Generic Tax Strategies

Tax strategies usually are based on either taking advantage of the time value of money (e.g., paying taxes later) or taking advantages of differences in tax rates (i.e., tax rate arbitrage).[23] These tax strategies usually fall into one of four families: creation, conversion, timing, and splitting.[24] The first is *creation*. This family involves plans which take advantage of tax subsidies, such as moving an operation to a jurisdiction which imposes lower taxes. For example, during the past quarter century many engineering firms have fled the City of Los Angeles, which imposes a gross receipts tax, and moved to the relatively tax free city of Glendale, which is located just a few miles away. Moves like this create tax benefits simply because the firms have left the jurisdiction imposing the taxes.

There are costs as well as benefits to creation strategies. Recall that in the discussion at the beginning of this section on optimizing as a goal, it was noted that successful investors who live in high tax jurisdictions like New York and San Francisco often continue living there, even though simply moving to live in El Paso, Nome, or Reno would free them entirely from state and local income taxes. In this case, lifestyle considerations (such as being close to legitimate theatre) dominate minimizing taxes.

Investors should be wary of schemes promoted as generating the benefits of low tax jurisdiction without a change of residence. This is particularly the case for foreign "tax havens". These rarely produce the benefits promoters claim. Investors should be aware that tax haven benefits typically apply only to citizens and residents of the jurisdictions, and not to transactions that occur outside the jurisdictions. US citizens and residents, for example, are taxed on their worldwide income. It makes no difference where it is earned. In particular, they are liable for income taxes on profits from stock trades made on exchanges outside the US, and for interest income from accounts in financial institutions located outside the US.

In addition, taxing authorities throughout the world are quite attuned to attempts to take advantage of tax havens, and quite hostile to them. Although some jurisdictions maintain the privacy of account owners, most have followed Switzerland's lead in co-operating more with foreign government investigations of their own nationals. US citizens and residents are required to declare ownership in foreign bank accounts, and those who set up foreign trusts must report this fact to the Internal Revenue Service (IRS). These reports dramatically increase the chances of being audited by the IRS. More intrusively, the US mandates detailed reporting for owners of closely held foreign corporations.

Creation costs and benefits can be expressed analytically as follows. Letting R represent the expected annual return on an investment and t_0 represent the income tax rate, the after tax return on a normal investment for n years can be expressed as: $[1 + R(1 - t_0)]^n$. Creation strategies, then, can be expressed as situations where $t_0 \to 0$.[25]

The second family of tax planning techniques is *conversion*. This entails changing operations so that more tax-favored categories of income or assets are produced.[26] For example, advertising in order to sell inventory results in ordinary income, which usually is taxed immediately, and at the highest rates. However, equally successful "image" advertising generates an increase in a firm's goodwill, which is taxed, if at all, only when the goodwill is sold, and even then is taxed at lower "capital gains" rates.[27] This can be expressed analytically as: $t_c < t_0$, where t_c is the favorable tax rate captured by the conversion strategy.

The third family involves *timing*. This involves techniques which move amounts being taxed (also called the tax base) to more favorable tax accounting periods.[28] A good example is accelerated depreciation, which allows more of an asset's cost to be a tax-deductible expense in early years, thus deferring the payment of taxes until later. Another example is contributing to an Individual Retirement Account.[29] This family can be expressed analytically as: $(1 + R)^n(1 - t_f) + t_f$ where t_f is the tax rate imposed in the future captured by the strategy.[30]

The final family is *splitting*. (Taxes also can be avoided through fraud, which is fairly widespread throughout the world outside of the US, but rather small in amount for non-criminal activities within the US. As alluded to in the discussion of tax haven schemes above, severe penalties and active enforcement strongly suggest that this is not a viable tax savings category for the legitimate investor.)

Splitting techniques entail spreading the tax base among multiple taxpayers to take advantage of differing tax rates.[31] For example, the top US income tax rates on individuals are nearly 40%, but the standard tax rate on the first \$50,000 of corporate income is only 15%. Incorporating a sole proprietorship generating \$200,000 in profits, and paying a \$150,000 salary (provided it is reasonable) to the proprietors, is a splitting strategy which saves about \$12,500 (i.e., 25% of \$50,000 split off and moved into the corporate tax return) of income taxes each year. This can be expressed analytically as: $(t_{e1} + t_{e2}) < t_0$, where t_{ei} is the tax rate imposed on the lower tax rate entities captured by the strategy.

Generic Asset Preservation Strategies[32]

The Less Intrusive Alternative Planning Model® discussed above in the context of taxation applies equally well in the area of wealth preservation. In this area, as with tax, it is important that strategies entered into with the object of controlling property do not unduly interfere with investment decision-making (and related tax planning.) Control strategies usually are based on limiting potential creditors' access to assets being given away, either during the giver's (also called a *donor*) lifetime — called an *inter vivos* gift — or as part of the giver's last gift, through his or her will or similar arrangements effective at death. (The latter is referred to as a *testamentary* gift, as well as an *inheritance*.)

Because control strategies tend to focus on keeping assets outside of the reach of creditors, one may be tempted to "park assets off shore", by secreting them in foreign trusts or financial accounts. This rarely generates tax savings in the long run. Instead, it can do just the opposite, by raising the frequency, scope, and intensity of tax audits.[33] Careful planning and assiduous reporting can minimize exposure to tax audit risk, however. Furthermore, although there are legal entities in the US, such as Wyoming statutory trusts — corporate entities usually are tax-disfavored for holding securities — privacy and protection from creditors can be enhanced to a greater extent with trusts organized in locations such as Jersey and the Isle of Man. The factors in making such a decision are so complicated, and so individualized, that no further blanket discussion is worthwhile in this chapter. Instead, investors considering these techniques should discuss them with a tax attorney experienced in this field.[34]

Control strategies also often are based on limiting the ability of a beneficiary to invest or spend assets received by gift unwisely.[35] (A *beneficiary* is someone who is, or will be, receiving a gift of an interest in property.) This gift can be outright ownership of property. However, in the control area, most often the gift is of a beneficial interest. A *beneficial interest* consists of the right to enjoy the use of property without actually owning it. Examples include such as the right to receive income generated by a portfolio without having the right to buy or sell the individual securities which make up the portfolio, or the right to use a residence for the rest of one's lifetime (called a *life estate*). Splitting the right to enjoy property from the right to manage it (and thus having the property subject to one's own creditors) most often is accomplished through the use of gifts in trust.

Trusts and Estates

A *trust* is a legal entity which is managed by a trustee on behalf of the trust's beneficiaries. The trustee, *qua* trustee, has no right to the use or enjoyment of the property held by the trust. A trust's property holdings also are known as the trust *res*. Instead, a trustee only has the obligation (known as a *fiduciary duty*) to manage the property prudently. Trustees are *strictly liable* for imprudent investments; that is, the trustee must reimburse the trust for any losses caused by actions which, via hindsight, were not prudent.

Trusts are established by *trustors* (also called *settlors*), by executing a valid *trust agreement* and contributing property to the trust. A trust can be established during the trustors' lifetimes; thus the appellation *inter vivos* trusts. Or it can take effect upon the trustors' death. Known as *testamentary trusts*, these most often are established through a valid will. A trust can be *irrevocable*, meaning that once the trustors establish it the terms cannot be changed nor can the trustor force return of the trust *res*. However, the most common form of trust is *revocable*.[36]

Known as a *living* trust,[37] this is a trust established by trustors who also are both the trustees and the beneficiaries during the trustors' lives. The trust is quite transparent until the trustors' death (or, most often, the trustors becoming incapacitated). At that time, a *successor trustee*, usually named in the trust agreement takes over managing the trust assets. Upon the trustors' death, the assets are held for the benefit of the *successor beneficiaries*. These almost always are the same natural objects of the trustors' bounty named in their wills.

The primary purpose of a living trust (also called a *grantor* trust) is to avoid the cost, delay, and publicity of probate.[38] Also avoided can be the pain and expense of a will contest, where survivors sue to prevent a document from serving as the dispositive guide to a decedent's testamentary desires.[39] Probate is the legal process of handling the property (called the *estate*) of someone who has died (called a *decedent*). Like a trust, an estate is a legal entity where property (sometimes called the trusters or *corpus*) is managed by an agent. This agent is called an *executor* if named in a valid will, otherwise, an *administrator*. The estate is managed on behalf of the persons[40] to whom the decedent desired to leave the property (i.e., decedent's *heirs*) as well as to the decedent's creditors (including tax agencies).

The executor/administrator has legal title to the property, and can thus exercise all the legal powers of other property owners. However, these powers can only be used on behalf of the decedent's heirs and creditors. That is, the agent does not have the right to enjoy the property, but instead is bound by a fiduciary duty to use his or her powers to manage it on behalf of the people who will be given (e.g., *inherit*) the property.

Avoiding Probate

In probate, a judge rules whether there is a valid will. That is, the judge determines whether it is probable that the document submitted to the court was intended by the decedent to outline how his or her property is to be allocated, and that the documents meets all of the requirements set by statute and common law for valid wills. If no valid will can be proven to the probate court, the decedent died *intestate* and his or her estate will be distributed according the jurisdiction's law of *intestate succession*. Normally this means the property is split up equally among the decedent's closest living relatives.

After ruling on the will, an executor (or administrator) is appointed, who has a fiduciary duty to *marshal* the estate — that is, identify the decedent's property and debts — notify potential creditors and beneficiaries, pay off debts and taxes, and then suitably distribute the estate. This can take quite a bit of time: two years is not unusual. It also can be expensive — fees often amount to 10% of the estate. Furthermore, all of this process is in public: anyone who asks can find out who got how much, where, and when, along with the beneficiaries' addresses. Many people do not wish to expose their heirs to this.

As noted above, probate can be avoided merely by putting one's property into a living trust. (Property can be put in a living trust after death, too. This can be accomplished by having a *pour-over will*, which is a will containing provisions which allocated property held by the decedent at death to the trust set up during his or her life.) Probate also can be avoided through the use of contractual relationships which mimic a living trust and taking effect upon death. This includes holding title to property in *joint tenancy* (which requires that a decedent's interest is split among all remaining owners), control property under a power of appointment (essentially the right to chose who gets to benefit from property set aside in trust or under a will),[41] life insurance policies (which require that proceeds be given to the persons named as beneficiaries by the policy's owner),[42] powers of attorney (which basically is the right to act as the owner of property)[43] and pension plans (which require that balances remaining at a pensioners' death be distributed to the persons named as beneficiaries by the pensioner).

Control Strategies Simpler than Tax Strategies

Control strategies are simpler than their tax counterparts.[44] Aside from limiting expenses and generating increases in asset values, the goal of control in wealth preservation is to assure that:

1. The benefits of assets go to intended persons.
2. Probate and other transactions costs (such as legal fees) are limited.
3. Investments continue to be astutely managed.
4. Access by creditors — especially those of less capable beneficiaries — is limited.

This typically can be accomplished by the investor using living trusts, and like contractual relationships, to avoid the costs, delays, uncertainty, and publicity of probate and *conservatorships*. (The latter is a legal proceeding, normally in a probate court, whereby the assets and life management decisions of an incapacitated person are made on their behalf by a person appointed for this purpose, called a *conservator*.)

Investors also can accomplish these goals by using *spendthrift* provisions in testamentary and *inter vivos* trusts. These protect the investor's intended heirs and other beneficiaries by denying them the privilege of being able to transfer any interest in the trust to another person. (Such other person most typically is a creditor.) Finally, investors can control assets by using lifetime giving and testamentary unified credit trusts to optimize estate and gift taxes.[45] These techniques are defined and explained in detail in the last section of this chapter.

10.3 Key Types and Uses for Trusts

Inter Vivos Trusts

Grantor Trusts: A trust where the persons transferring property into a trust also are the beneficiaries. They typically are the trustees, too. Also called a "living trust" or an *inter vivos* trust because it is set up during the grantors' lifetimes. It holds title to property, and provides for successor trustees and beneficiaries. No income or estate tax benefits are derived from this arrangement. For property transferred in, it acts as if it were the trustors' will. Thus it helps avoid the cost, publicity, and delay of probate and conservatorships. It also provides for management of assets during incapacity or absence, and as a receptacle for property being passed under a will. Being a revocable trust, it can be changed periodically to meet the varying needs of the trustors as their lives unfold. Should be used by most investors.

Insurance Trusts: These are irrevocable trusts which own life insurance policies. They are set up by the person who is insured. The beneficiaries are designated by the trust, which can identify them when it is formed. Thus a person who is insured can designate the beneficiaries of the policy. However, the insured cannot be a trustee. Their purpose is to avoid estate taxes on the proceeds of the insurance. Should be used by most investors, with the caveat that once set up the insured loses control over the insurance policy.

Crummey Trusts: These are irrevocable trusts set up for the benefit of the grantor's intended heirs. Income is taxed either to the beneficiaries or the trust, and thus may be subject to lower rates. Furthermore, appreciation and income is not subject to the grantor's estate tax. Contributions to the trust are considered *pro rata* gifts to the beneficiaries; existence of the Crummey power, which gives beneficiaries limited right to withdraw contributions, makes them a present interest. This qualifies contributions for the $10,000 per year per recipient gift tax exclusion.

Testamentary Trusts

Unified Credit Trusts: These are trusts established under a married person's will. They are funded with the maximum amount which will escape the decedent's estate tax by using up the remaining unified credit. Normally, the beneficiaries are the couple's children, and not the surviving spouse (who nevertheless can get the trust property in times of need). Because of this, the property also is free of the surviving spouse's estate tax.

Honorary Trusts: A trust set up to provide for the care of pet animals.

QTIP Trusts: These are trusts established under a married person's will. They are funded with the remained of a decedent's estate tax, and, because the life beneficiary is the surviving spouse, escape decedent's estate tax. Whatever is left when the surviving spouse dies usually goes to the couple's children, and, after considering the survivor's remaining unified credit, is subject to the survivor's estate tax.

In sum, investors should not see the goals of estate and tax planning in terms of maximizing control of assets being given away to heirs or beneficiaries, nor to minimizing taxes. Instead, as with tax planning, investors should seek to optimize control and after-tax accretions of family wealth by conscientiously considering non-control, and non-tax, costs and benefits when implementing tax and asset protection strategies. That is, even though total asset control (even after death) and elimination of taxes altogether should not be an investor's goal, it most often make sense to invest significant amounts of time and resources to implementing asset control and tax reducing strategies.

10.4 Tax Planning for Investments[46]

Income Tax Treatment of Gains and Losses on Marketable Securities

There are three key income tax issues to consider in dealing with transactions in marketable securities. These are: (a) the amount of gain or loss realized on an event, (b) whether the gain or loss will be *recognized* — that is, be taxable or tax-deductible — and, if so, (c) whether the gain or loss can benefit from favorable tax rates. As for the latter, income tax rates for *net long-term capital gains* can be half of that for interest, wages, or other ordinary types of income. (Net long-term capital gains most often result from the sale of securities by an investor who has held them for more than a year.) How much of a gain or loss is realized depends, in turn, on two factors: whether there was a realizable event, and, if so, the difference between the amount realized on the transaction and the *adjusted basis* of the property involved.

Adjusted basis is the income tax equivalent of net book value; for securities purchased by an investor on the open market, this consists of the taxpayer's total cost to acquire the securities. Total cost would include purchase price, sales commissions, and transfer taxes. Periodic fees, and expenses not related to specific sales — such as a subscription to an investment newsletter — are miscellaneous itemized deductions. As such, these only reduce income taxes to the extent the investor's total miscellaneous itemized deductions exceed 2% of adjusted gross income.

Even though economists may measure income by the increase in an individual's wealth or other ability to consume, there is no taxable income — and thus no income tax — unless there is a *realization event*. The mere fluctuation in value of assets is not such an event, nor is the receipt of property as a gift, inheritance, loan, or where there otherwise is an obligation to return the property involved. Generally, realization requires the transfer of title to property in exchange for bargained-for legal consideration, such as cash or a promise to pay. It can occur without a sale, however, such as when securities are exchanged.

Note that exchanges can be *tax-deferred*. Although a detailed discussion is beyond the scope of this chapter,[47] an exchange of property can be free of taxation in certain limited circumstances. These normally occur only when similar property is being swapped, such as in mergers and other business reorganizations. These exchanges are not tax-free: the gain or loss not taxed when the property is exchanged typically is taxed when the property received in the exchange is later sold. Another example is that securities which become *worthless* are treated as if they are sold for $0 on the last day of the year they become worthless.

Realization and Recognition

Selling securities almost always triggers realization. The gain or loss realized is the sales price (net of the cost of sales, such as commissions) less the taxpayer's adjusted basis in the securities. As noted above, the term "basis" refers to the remaining cost used for tax purposes. Most often this is the property's purchase price, including commissions.

In most transactions, calculating the gain or loss realized is simply a clerical matter. But issues can arise. For example, losses on sales to a *related party* (e.g., the taxpayer's sister) are not *recognized*. (Recognition means that a realization transaction triggers taxation. Almost all realizations result in recognition. As noted above, that exchanges can result in non-recognition of gain or loss at the time of the exchange.) That is, the losses are not currently deductible, although the loss disallowed can later reduce the related party's gain on the subsequent disposition of the property. In addition, the "wash sale" rules also defer losses.

A *wash sale* occurs when a security is sold at a loss by someone who is not a securities dealer, who also buys a *substantially identical* security within a short period. Securities can be "substantially identical" even if they are not the same; different classes of stock, and options most often do not but can fit this definition. This period begins 30 days before the sale, and ends 30 days after it. (If multiple blocks of a security are involved, the rules apply to transactions on a *First In, First Out* basis. That is, the stock sold is assumed to be from the first block of such stock which the investor acquired. If more shares are sold than the amount of shares acquired in the first block, the rest of the shares are assumed to come from the next block of shares in the same company which was acquired, and so forth.)

If a wash sale loss occurs, it is not tax deductible; wash sale gains, however, are taxable. The tax benefit of the loss is not lost forever: the amount of the non-deductible loss is added to the basis of the replacement security, thus reducing the gain or increasing the loss when this property is sold.

Similarly, certain hedging strategies discussed in Chapter 5, such as shorting against the box, forward transactions, and notational principal contracts, usually cannot be used by non-dealers to lock in gains on appreciated financial positions economically but defer their recognition for tax purposes. Instead, gain is triggered when the hedge (e.g., the short) occurs.

Identifying Cost

As noted above, a taxpayer's basis in his or her portfolio usually is merely a clerical matter over which there is little control. However, when a taxpayer sells off only part of an investment purchased at different times — such as 300 out of 500 shares held in a particular company of which 100 were acquired for $25 per share and the rest acquired for $90 per share — the taxpayer can chose whether the lower or higher cost applies. One normally wants to choose the highest cost, because this results in the lowest gain (or highest loss). Taxpayers can control this simply by *specifying* to the broker either the securities' certificate numbers or acquisition dates.

Without such specification, the IRS requires that taxpayers use the First In First Out (FIFO) method described above. FIFO can be disadvantageous because, in a rising market, the first block of securities purchased often has the lowest basis. Using such costs thus would generate the highest amount of taxable income. Individuals who sell mutual funds, however, are allowed to use their average remaining cost as their basis for calculating gain or loss on the sale.

Exactly what a taxpayer's *cost* is for tax purposes is not always clear. For the vast majority of market transactions, cost is merely the purchase price for the securities (including commissions paid on the purchase). Problems here most often arise with lost records, securities held for a long time, or where the taxpayer has begun to lose mental capacities such as memory. The latter most often occurs where there is a sudden debilitating injury or sickness, or due to the ravages of time. (This is one of the areas where taking precautions in wealth preservation, such as with the use of living trusts, can help assure that records are kept, and in order, in case an effective conservatorship is necessary so that the taxpayer's financial affairs can be managed properly.) Being unable to prove one's purchase costs can be Draconian: if a taxpayer cannot do so, the IRS uses a cost of $0, thus maximizing taxable income.

Tax basis is not always the actual cost of acquiring property. For example, basis is reduced by *non-taxable return of capital type dividends*. These are dividends distributed by a corporation which does not have either current or accumulated earnings and profits at the time. Such distributions are fairly atypical except in highly leveraged, capital intensive businesses such as utilities and airlines.

Another example is that, until the estate tax is eliminated in 2010, people who inherit property are deemed to have an initial basis equal to the value given to it in the decedent's estate tax return. (Even after this date, this rule will apply to up to $3 million of property being passed to a surviving spouse.) Known as the "step up in basis at death", this most commonly is the property's fair market value on the date of death. This is a tremendous tax benefit for property which appreciated a great deal while being held by the decedent; it is unlikely, for example, that Bill Gates and his family will ever have to pay income tax on their Microsoft stock.

A third example is for *gifts* which are received. A gift is a transfer of title to property without *consideration* being exchanged. Consideration consists of assets, relief from debts, or promises of future action or inaction. A giver is also known as a *donor*; *the* recipient of a gift is called a *donee*. For the purposes of calculating a taxable gain, a recipients' basis is the giver's basis (increased by a portion of the donor's gift tax, if any). For loss purposes, the basis of gifts received is the lower of the fair market value on the date of the gift and the giver's basis. This prevents taxpayers from shifting losses to related parties who are in higher tax brackets, but it does not prevent the shifting of gains, which is discussed in the following paragraphs.

Splitting Strategies to Transfer Cost

As noted above, a set of tax optimizing approaches which focus on realization are based on the generic strategy of splitting. To recap, splitting entails taxpayers taking advantage of lower marginal tax rates of related parties. Consider a taxpayer who has decided to sell stock in order to pay for a child's education, but because the stock has appreciated after its purchase, the taxpayer is facing a realization of gain. If, as is typical, the taxpayer expects to be taxed at a higher rate (i.e., is in a higher tax bracket) than the child, it might be better for the taxpayer to gift the stock to the child, and then for the child to sell it. Because gain basis carries over in a gift, the amount of the gain stays the same. But the tax rate can be lower.

For example, the Federal income tax rate on *net short-term capital gains* (e.g., an investor's profits from the sale of securities held for less than a year) is 31% for taxpayers with about $100,000 of taxable income, but only 15% for those with less than about $25,000. In addition, the maximum rate on net long-term capital gains (except on *collectibles*, such as art, where it is 28%) would be 20% for the former, but often is only 10% for the latter. As noted above, long term means the assets have been held for more than a year. The *holding period* for gifts generating gains includes both the time owned by the donor and the donee; property inherited is always long term. (Low bracket taxpayers qualify for an 8% maximum rate where the holding period is at least five years. A corresponding 18% bracket will be available for taxpayers above the 15% regular tax rate. Lower rates may apply in the future.)

This may seem too good to be true, and in many cases, it is; another provision — called the "*Kiddie tax*" — requires at the unearned income of children under 14 be taxed at their parent's rate. Thus, the attempt to shift income to the child's rate may not save any taxes at all. However, gifts to a college-aged child, or from a child to a parent (for example, to help pay for nursing home care), are not subject to Kiddie tax type restrictions.

Gifts can also be used to shift income streams, such as interest on bonds. The major caution is that in order for the resulting income to be taxed to the recipient's rate, the investor actually has to give up title to property. This can be disastrous from a non-tax standpoint. For example, the child may sell the bonds and spend the proceeds. Or the child may have to turn the bonds over to a creditor (such as following a traffic accident, bankruptcy, or divorce.) However, as discussed in the "Lifetime Gifts" section below, there are ways to mitigate this. Nevertheless, it should always be recognized that non-tax considerations might outweigh expected tax benefits.

Hold Winners, Sell Losers and Borrow to Eat

The above discussion suggests that the most important strategy for reducing income taxes on investments is to keep property that is worth more than it was purchased for, and, rather than selling it to satisfy cash flow needs, borrow against it. The opposite applies to property that has decreased in value. In other words, a good general strategy is to try to keep winners, sell losers, and generate cash flow through borrowing rather than by selling appreciated property.

For example, consider the purchase of 1000 shares of X Company at $7.50 per share on January 15, 2000. If the stock has risen to $30 per share, a sale would generate $30,000 of pre tax cash flow (ignoring commissions and other costs of sale). The tax most likely would be 20% of the gain on sale. The gain being $22,500 [that is ($30.00 – 7.50) × 1000], the cash flow would be reduced by a tax of $4500 [that is, (\$30,000 – 20% × \$22,500)] to \$25,500. The investor's wealth would also be reduced by \$4500.

The \$4500 reduction in wealth would not happen were the investor willing and able to borrow the \$25,500. The cash flow would be the same, but the investor's wealth would not be reduced by the \$4500 tax. (Note that were the investor to hold the stock until death, the potential income tax disappears. As indicated in the section above entitled "Identifying Cost", this is because the heirs are given a tax basis equal to the stock's estate tax value. This is known as the "step-up in basis at death". Should current law remain in place after 2011, the estate tax would disappear, and the only property revalued under the step-up rules would be up to \$3 million left to a surviving spouse).

There are limits to adopting a "hold winners" strategy. First and foremost, switching investments may be necessary to maximize returns. As noted above, taxes are an important factor in investment decisions, but are only one of many factors to be considered. A sale, even one which triggers taxation, may be necessary for non-tax reasons. The key is to balance the expected benefits from the sale with the tax costs, which often amount to 20% of profit made on the sale.

A good example of a non-tax factor which may mandate a sale is a significant change in the investor's risk preferences. This can happen for many reasons. Among them are a change in an investor's expectations for key macroeconomic variables, such as interest rates, economic growth, currency exchange rates, and political risk. Another reason for a change in risk preferences is a change in life style, caused by illness, retirement, marriage, divorce, or the birth of children (or financing their education).

Some of these events are typical transitions in an investor's life cycle, and thus can be anticipated. Others may be unexpected. Changes in wealth and expected cash flow, due to inheritance, sale of a business, or winning the lottery, also can suggest a need to further diversify a portfolio, or re-balance a portfolio into different sectors.

Also, investors have to eat: without selling property, one may have to borrow to generate desired cash flow. On the non-tax side, unhedged leverage is an investment strategy in and of itself, the wisdom of which does not extend to all investors at all times. Further, as investors increase their debt levels, the cost of debt usually rises. In addition, there often are practical and legal constraints to efficient borrowing. Finally, on the tax side, not all borrowing results in immediate tax benefit. The major reasons for this are discussed in the next section.

Deducting Interest

Margin interest, and interest on other loans used to purchase or carry investments, normally is tax-deductible, but is subject to several complicated limits. The threshold limit is that the loan must have a *bona fide* purpose. That is, it cannot be entered into merely to generate tax deductions. This is rare in normal market-related transactions, but has occurred. One such case was where a taxpayer borrowed money to purchase US Treasury notes under circumstances where there was no reasonable possibility of generating net income except through income tax deductions.

A second limit is that, for non-corporate taxpayers, investment interest is an *itemized* deduction. These are deductions reported on Form 1040, Schedule A. They do not reduce a taxpayer's adjusted gross income, and thus are of limited benefit to some taxpayers. For example, certain taxpayers — such as people who can be claimed as tax-deductible dependents on another's income tax return — are not entitled to itemize. Furthermore, one only itemizes when the amount spent on such expense exceed the *standard deduction* of about $5000–7000.

Investment interest saves no taxes in years when a taxpayer does not itemize. This is not a problem for many investors. But it can be for those who do not itemize because they live in low-tax states and are not paying mortgage interest. It also can be a problem for high-income taxpayers. This is because individuals whose *adjusted gross income* (basically, their taxable income before itemized deductions) exceeds a *threshold* — about $135,000 for marrieds filing jointly — can lose up to 80% of their total itemized deductions. This *cut back* is phased in by reducing most itemized deductions by 3% of adjusted gross income (AGI) in excess of the threshold.[48]

To illustrate this, consider an investor who is married and files a joint tax return for 2002. Itemized deductions for the year consist of

$18,000 of interest on a principle residence, $20,000 of state income and property taxes, and $8000 of charitable contributions. These total to $46,000. With taxable wages of $95,000, taxable interest of $17,000, taxable dividends of $22,000, and $34,000 of net short-term capital gains from stock sales during the year, the return shows AGI of $168,000. Because the cutback threshold for the year is (rounded) $135,000, the investor's deductions are reduced by $1000 [(= ($168,000 – $135,000) × 3%] to $45,000. However, if the investor also had $5000 of margin interest, this amount would not be reduced.

This limit cannot be avoided by investing through a corporation. Incorporating one's portfolio to avoid this limit, or to try to take advantage of lower corporate tax rates,[49] is rarely tax favored. This is due to the extremely complex *personal holding company penalty tax* rules. Discussion of these rules is beyond the scope of this chapter.[50] Similar, but different, problems arise if one attempts to use an *S corporation.* These are corporations which are eligible for and have made a valid election to be taxed like a partnership. As discussed in the following sentence, there is no "splitting" benefit involved when investments are held in partnership-like entities. It also is very difficult to use a partnership, a limited liability company, or a trust because the character of items of income and expense normally passes through to the owners of these non-taxable conduit entities.

A third limit is that no deduction is allowed to the extent the loan can be traced to investment generating wholly tax-exempt income, such as the typical tax exempt bond. Tracing is not always obvious. For example, the IRS has challenged portions of routinely deductible mortgage interest in years in which a taxpayer has sold a principal residence and invested the proceeds temporarily in a municipal bond fund.

Similarly, because life insurance proceeds normally are tax free, interest on loans to purchase or carry it rarely are deductible, nor is interest on loans against single premium life insurance or annuity contract, nor where there is a plan to systematically make tax-exempt withdrawals of increases in cash surrender values. On the other hand, this limit only applies to wholly tax-exempt investments. Thus, the fact that a taxpayer is making contributions to qualified retirement plans does not render margin interest non-deductible.

A fourth limit is that interest on debt incurred to purchase or carry commodity investments which are part of a *straddle* (as defined in earlier chapters) must be added to the tax cost (known as the "basis") of the commodity rather than being currently deducted. This effectively defers the deduction until the straddle is closed. In addition, it converts an ordinary expense to a capital one. This is detrimental because it acts either to increase a non tax-favored *capital loss* — after offsetting any capital gain for a year, only $3000 of capital loss can be used to offset other income for the year, such as interest or wages — or decrease a possibly tax-favored capital gain. Fortunately, normal hedging transactions are exempted from this straddle interest capitalization rule.

Fifth, for non-corporate taxpayers, investment-related interest is deductible only to the extent of *net investment income* for the year. The deduction for excess investment interest expense is not lost, however. Instead, the excess is carried over until the taxpayer dies to be applied in future tax years where there is net investment income. Net investment income is investment income less non-interest investment-related expenses (such as subscriptions or Web access fees). As with expenses, income is considered investment related if it could be traced to portfolio investment activities.

Generally, these are profit-motivated efforts undertaken by a taxpayer who is not doing so as part of a trade or business with respect to that undertaking. Examples are assets that produce interest, dividends, annuities, or royalties but are not derived in the ordinary course of business. Thus, royalties received on a book written by a taxpayer are not investment income, but those received by a taxpayer who purchases the copyright but is not in the publishing business do generate investment income. Net capital gain from the sale of investment property is not investment income, unless the taxpayer is an individual who elects to have the gain taxed at ordinary, rather than tax-favored capital gain, rates.

Thus, unless one is having a good year, investment interest may be of limited use in reducing current taxes. However, interest incurred in the course of an active trade or business — such as that on loans by a sole proprietor to purchase inventory — is not subject to the invest income limitation. Even better, it is deductible as a business expense, and not as an itemized expense. (The deduction may be limited by other rules, such as the "at risk" limitation and the passive activity loss rules discussed in the following paragraphs). Thus, if an investor can generate debt-financed cash flows through a business, rather than through margin loans, the deduction for interest may be free of the investment interest limitation.

Run-of-the-mill investment activity is not the type of business which would avoid these limitation rules. This is because buying and selling securities, even with significant volume or day-trading activity, rarely has been considered by the Courts or the IRS to amount to a qualifying trade or business for those buying for their own account. Usually, to qualify for tax-favored business interest status, the investor must also represent others (i.e., the investor also is a brokers or dealer).

However, investors who also own rental real estate may be able to dodge the investment interest limit in another way. This is because renting realty is considered a trade or business. Thus the decision to stay leveraged in one's real estate investments, rather than using other liquid assets to reduce mortgages, can be a source of tax-deductible debt. Of course, it may not be optimal to leverage one's real estate portfolio from a risk management standpoint.

One of the general limitations to all deductions referred to in the preceding paragraph is the *at risk* rule. These limit deductions generated by loans for which the taxpayer is not personally liable. This limits a taxpayer's ability to deduct expenses related to debt-financed acquisitions. However, to the extent the debt has commercially reasonable terms and can be traced to and is secured by real estate, the loan can be considered at risk. (As with the investment interest limitation discussed in the previous paragraph, excess interest is carried over to future years indefinitely, and becomes deductible then to the extent the taxpayers becomes at risk.)

Another limitation is the *passive activity* rule. Expenses generated by a passive activity are only deductible to the extent of passive activity income. A passive activity basically is a trade or business in which the taxpayer does not *materially participate*. There are a host of complicated rules which define what level of activity meets the "material" threshold, such as devoting at least 500 hours per year to the activity. Fortunately, most retail investors in securities are not involved in a passive activity unless they are doing so as a limited partner.

Using a home mortgage sometimes is considered as a means to be able to deduct interest on loans enabling market investments. This, too, may be a very poor strategy from a risk management standpoint. This is because qualifying loans must be secured by a taxpayer's personal residence, and thus market reversals can lead to foreclosure. On the other hand, mortgage debt often is a lower cost source of cash for many investors. In addition, in states such as California, lenders are limited to foreclosure on defaults of most residential acquisition mortgages. That is, if the borrower does not pay, all the lender can do is take the residence back: it cannot sue to recover an deficiency between what it nets when it resells the residence and what it was owned on the mortgage.

An itemized deduction is available for interest on up to $1,000,000 of qualified acquisition indebtedness which is secured by a *qualifying residence*. Qualifying means either the taxpayer's principal or one other personal residence. Note that such loans remain deductible if they are refinanced, but only to the extent the principal of the new loan does not exceed that of the old loan. Because the loan must be incurred to acquire, construct, or substantially improve such a residence, this tends not to be a source of new financing. Instead it merely allows the taxpayer to avoid committing liquid assets into a qualifying residence.

One source of new funds which generates deductible interest is *qualified home equity debt*. A loan is qualified to the extent it is not qualified acquisition indebtedness, and is secured by the taxpayer's principal or one other personal residence. An itemized deduction is available for interest on that portion of the loan, which does not exceed the lower of: (a) $100,000, (b) the taxpayer's equity in such residences, and (c) when added to qualified acquisition indebtedness, does not exceed the fair market of the securing residential property.

Although this source is easier to use to obtain investment capital, it may not be a good approach when taking into consideration the risks of cross-leveraging one's investment sectors. Nevertheless, interest on a qualified loan remains deductible even if the proceeds of the loan are used to purchase investments (unless the investment yields income which is wholly tax exempt, such as a municipal bond.)

Note that interest on other non-business debt, such as that generated by credit cards, rarely is tax-deductible.

Benefiting from Favorable Capital Gains Provisions

The last major class of tax-reducing strategies fits in the generic category of conversion. These are based on taking steps so that gains recognized will be characterized as long-term capital gains, but losses as ordinary ones. The latter is difficult to obtain for an investor who is not a dealer. Losses on most securities end up being capital losses, and, as noted above, if an investor's capital gains and losses net out to a loss for the year, only $3000 of the loss can be used to offset ordinary income (such as wages or dividends). The rest of the loss is carried forward, to offset capital gains (and then $3000 of ordinary income) in future years until the excess is used up or the taxpayer dies. Thus, to the extent of an individual's net capital loss, gains can be recognized as free of additional income taxes.

An exception to the net capital loss limitation is that the first $50,000 ($100,000 for taxpayers who are married filing jointly) of losses during a year which arise from certain direct stock investments in "small" corporations. Called "small business stock", the definition for this term is governed by Internal Revenue Code Section 1244. Almost no publicly traded stock qualifies, in part because Section 1244 only applies to stock issued directly to the investor by the corporation in exchange for money or property. Another reason is that it only applies to the first $1,000,000 of stock issued.

Emphasizing how complex and confusing tax law can be, the term "small business stock" is used, defined differently, and has different effects under several other Sections of the Internal Revenue Code. Of most relevance to securities investors is the definition under Section 1202. Individual who sell Section 1202 stock which has been held for at least five years can exclude 50% of their gain from taxation; the rest of the gain is subject to a maximum tax rate of 28%. Thus high-income taxpayers effectively are taxed only 14% of their total gain.

For example, consider an investor who purchases $10,000 in common stock of a fuel cell manufacturing firm which has just become profitable. If the stock is purchased directly from the company, and the other requirements of Section 1244 are met, profit on a subsequent sale of the stock would benefit from favorable capital gains status. On the other hand, a loss would be deductible as ordinary income and not subject to the $3000 per year limit on deducting net capital losses.

Furthermore, if the requirements of Section 1202 are met, the maximum tax rate on the profit would be 14%. Thus, if the stock were sold for $100,000, the maximum tax would be $12,600 [= ($100,000 – 10,000) × 14%]. This compares favorably with the normal 20% maximum on long-term capital gains, which would yield a tax of $20,000. Section 1202 treatment is even better than the $28,000 of tax which would result were the gain from the sale of art or other collectibles, and the roughly $39,000 maximum tax on ordinary gains.

As indicated above, ordinary rates are scheduled to drop over the next few years, with the maximum dropping to 35% in 2006. In addition, for taxpayers whose marginal income tax rate does not exceed 15%, the maximum rate on net long-term capital gains from non-collectibles is only 10%. For capital assets held for more than five years, this rate drops to 8%. Higher bracket taxpayers will benefit by a maximum rate of 18% on 5-year gains, but only after the year 2005. One final benefit is that gain is deferred — that is, the current tax rate is 0% — if a taxpayer disposes Section 1202 stock held for at least six months but elects to roll over the gain to Section 1202 stock of another company acquired within 60 days of the disposition.

There are limits, of course, to these benefits. This favorable treatment does not often apply to publicly traded companies. Only stock in regular domestic corporations with no more than $50 million of gross assets at the time of issuance qualifies, and the taxpayer must have acquired the stock at its original issue. The corporation must be engaged in an active trade or business, and not in professional fields such as engineering or certain other fields such as hospitality, farming, financial services, or mineral extraction.

10.5 Investing Through Mutual Funds and Other Pass Through Entities

Investments often are made through legal entities such as partnerships and mutual funds. The rules and tax savings techniques discussed above generally apply to such investments just as if the legal entities did not exist. Indeed, for tax purposes they are referred to as "pass through" entities because they do not pay income taxes themselves. Instead, their income is passed through to their owners on a *pro rata* basis.[51] In addition, the character of the income (e.g., long term capital gains) is preserved, just as if the investors had actually owned an undivided interest in the property sold.

Because of this, investors should monitor the tax aspects of the trading strategies undertaken by mutual fund managers. Some funds tend to generate more current taxable income than others. Good examples are certain "income" funds which focus on bonds or dividend paying stock. Because they are earning current taxable income, it must be passed through — and thus taxed to — the investors in the funds. Other funds, such as certain "growth" funds, do just the opposite. By investing in non-dividend paying common stock, the only income passed through to fund holders is the capital gains generated when the fund managers sell a stock. Some fund managers do a lot more selling, and thus generate a lot more current income which is taxed to the investors in the fund.

On the other hand, when fund managers are not doing a great deal of internal selling, the unrealized gains on their investments go untaxed until the investor sells some of his or her shares in the mutual fund itself. Further, as noted above, if an investor holds shares until death, the appreciation is never subject to income tax.

Real Estate Investment Trusts

Real Estate Investment Trusts (REIT) are a special, non-taxed flow-through entity. They have become increasingly popular in recent years. This entity's use is restricted to investments in real estate. An REIT essentially is a corporation which, if it meets certain requirements, is tax-free. The main requirement is that it distributes at least 95% of its income each year. For the income test, its income must not be from the sale of real estate (e.g., by a real estate developer or construction company). A number of holding companies are REITs, using the REIT to hold investments in office buildings, shopping malls, and apartment buildings, from which the REIT collects rental income. A number of hotel chains have also used this entity.

In the 1990s, a number of large corporations began using REITs to shelter their income from real estate. Accordingly, the IRS has attempted to place some restrictions on this entity. For example, the IRS issued a ruling on *step-down preferred stock* (also known as "conduit entities issuing fast-pay preferred stock"). Under the practice, the preferred stock issues were sold to tax-exempt investors such as pension funds. In the transactions the buyer and the seller would jointly create a real-estate investment trust, each contributing a large sum of cash (e.g., $100 million).

Through the REIT, the buyer would get inflated dividends which, because of the buyer's tax status, would be tax-free. After paying the oversized dividends for ten years, the seller would "buy out" the buyer's share of the investment for a nominal amount, liquidate the REIT and distribute the remaining (e.g., $200 million) assets to the seller. Under current US tax law, such liquidation is tax-free. But what really was happening, the Treasury declared, was that the seller was selling preferred stock and not paying taxes on $100 million of income. The IRS issued a notice declaring such transactions taxable, thus effectively eliminating this technique.[52]

Note that this is a common pattern with aggressive tax strategies. Quite often only early adopters and innovators reap tax benefits, with the IRS using its considerable legal powers to neuter such strategies as soon as they start to become widespread. This is a thought that underlies the basic idea of optimizing taxes, rather than minimizing taxes, as an astute investor's goals.

10.6 Taxability of Traded Stock Options

Except in the hands of a securities dealer, gains and losses from the sale or lapse of traded stock options are capital in nature. Because they rarely last for more than a year, gains do not benefit from the favorable tax rates granted to long-term capital gains. However, they can escape income taxation by being netted against capital losses.

For options on stocks, bonds, other securities, commodities, and commodities futures, gains or losses are triggered either by the sale of the option, lapse of the option, exercise of the option, or a closing transaction. However, for regulated futures contracts, foreign currency contracts, and certain nonequity options, gain or loss is recognized on the exercise of the options.

If a put is exercised, its cost offsets the gain or increases the loss on the accompanying sale of the underlying security. If a call is exercised, its cost is added into the basis of the underlying security which is being purchased.

Similarly, a shareholder normally (but not always) is not currently taxed when he receives a stock right declared by a corporation on its own shares. But sales of such rights trigger capital gains or losses.

Employer-Granted Stock Options

Some investors acquire securities in a somewhat involuntary manner. Aside from inheritance and gifts, the largest segment consists of employees who are granted stock options. Because of the size of this sector, the following discusses key aspects of employer-granted stock options. (As noted above, investors acquiring options on property through public markets, such as buying listed puts and calls, treat these the same as if the underlying securities were purchased.)

There are many non-tax factors which share stock option plans. Prime among them is the ability of an employer to craft incentives for executives which track increased shareholder value. Another is that cash flow is saved when wages and bonuses are shifted to stock options. A final non-tax factor is that under the Financial Accounting Standards Board's *Statement of Financial Accounting Standards* 123, employers are not required to reduce accounting income by option-based compensation.

Employer-granted stock options usually are designed to have a significant time lag between when the option is first granted and when the employee (usually an executive) exercises the option and actually becomes a stockholder. There also often is a significant time lag between the exercise and the sale of the stock obtained through the exercise. There are many reasons for this, including the desire to link employee incentive to increased stock prices, and an interest in creating "golden handcuffs" for key employees by delaying the rewards gleaned from incentives.

There also are numerous variations to option plans. Many of these stock-like incentive programs do not entail the executive actually owning stock. Examples include "phantom stock" and "stock appreciation rights" schemes.[53] Because stock is not actually owned, wealth generated by these plans typically is taxed simply as additional compensation.

Most stock option plans are "non-qualified". However, those which meet certain requirements, are treated more favorably for tax purposes. These are called qualified stock option plans, and are also known as incentive stock option plans, or simply "ISOs". To qualify, a stock option plan must be approved by shareholders, the options must be granted within ten years of the approval date, and the employee cannot own more than 10% of the corporation. Additionally, once stock has been purchased under an ISO, it cannot be sold within the later of: (a) the date the option was granted, or (b) the date the option was exercised. Further, the employee must remain so from the time of grant until at least three months before the option is exercised.

Under either an ISO or a non-qualified plan, the profit for the executive comes through sale of the stock. Tax deductibility and taxability generally have symmetric timing. However, this depends on whether the plan is qualified or non-qualified. The tax treatment for employer and employee, at the key dates involved, is illustrated on the following page.

As can be seen, ISOs are more tax beneficial to the executive, with two caveats. First, if substantial enough, the spread at the time of exercise between the exercise price and the stock's fair market value is potentially subject to the alternative minimum tax. The alternate minimum tax is

	Date of grant	Date of exercise	Date of sale
ISO			
Taxable to employee?	No*	No*	Sales price less previously taxed amount is taxed as capital gain or loss.
Deductible to employer	No*	No*	No
Non-qualified			
Taxable to employee	No, unless Fair Market Value (FMV) of option known.	FMV of stock less amount paid, unless taxed at grant, is ordinary income.	Sales price less previously taxed amount is taxed as capital gain or loss.
Deductible to employer?	Yes, in the amount taxable to employee.	Yes, in the amount taxable to employee.	No

*In almost all cases

discussed in the next section. It can be avoided with an election under Section 83(b), but at the cost of recognizing income at an earlier stage as well as possible limits on deductibility of losses upon lapse of the options or sale of the stock.

Second, there are time limits such as that noted above (*to wit*, the employee cannot transfer the stock within one year of sale). These, along with other reasons, result in a prevalence of non-qualified options among publicly traded firms. As noted above, tax treatment of non-qualified options are more favorable to the employer, but not as favorable to the employee. This is because the employer may be entitled to tax deductions, whereas the employee is taxed earlier and at the higher ordinary income rates.

Consider the following scenario:

Date of grant	Date of exercise	Date of sale
1/1/2000 for 10,000 shares at $50 each. The stock was worth $40 per share then. The FMV of the option was $2 per share.	12/31/2002 Projected market price = $70 per share.	12/31/2004 Projected sale at $75 per share.

If the option is an ISO, the firm gets no tax deduction and the employee would pay tax only after the option is exercised and the stock is sold. When this happens in 2004, the executive would then recognize $250,000 of capital gain (i.e., [$75 per share sales price – $50 per share purchase price on exercise] × 10,000 shares). At a 20% tax rate for long-term capital gains, this would result in tax of $50,000. There is no offsetting tax savings for the employer.

The results are different for a non-qualified plan. When the option is granted in 2000, the firm gets a tax deduction for $20,000, which is the value of the stock options: $2 per share × 10,000 shares. This also is the amount taxable to the executive. An executive in the 40% bracket would have a tax of $8,000 (i.e., 40% × $20,000). The deduction to the firm would typical save around $7000 (i.e., 35% × $20,000).

Note that the tax on the employee is about the same as the tax saved by the employer corporation. Because the transaction did not involve cash, and need not be reported as an expense on the employer's financial statements, the employer might see this as a superior way to provide incentive compensation to a key employee.

When the options are exercised in 2002, the executive recognizes $180,000 of ordinary income. This is calculated as ($70 per share value – $50 per share cost at exercise – $2 per share of income recognized at grant) × 10,000 shares. This translates into a tax on the executive of $72,000 (i.e., 40% × $180,000). The employer corporation gets a mirror deduction of $180,000, resulting in tax savings of about $63,000.

On the subsequent sale of the stock in 2004, the executive recognizes $50,000 of long-term capital gain (i.e., [$75 per share sales price – $70 per share previously taxed] × 10,000 shares). At a 20% tax rate for long-term capital gains, this would result in an additional tax of $10,000. There is no deduction for the employer.[54]

The scenario discussed above assumes that the employee will sell the stock at a gain. Were the employee to sell at a loss, the result can be disastrous. This is because selling the stock generates a capital loss. Although capital losses can be offset against capital gains for the year, and losses not netted this way carry forward indefinitely, only $3000 a year of ordinary income can be offset by net capital losses.

As reported in the financial press during the dot.com meltdown of 2000,[55] and again as such massive corporate collapses as Enron and Global Crossing, this is especially problematic for non-qualified options. This is because the employee is taxed at ordinary income rates when the options are exercised, but subsequent losses on the sale of the stock are limited in their deductibility.

Consider the following scenario:

Date of grant	Date of exercise	Date of sale
1/1/2000 for 10,000 shares at $50 each. The stock was worth $40 per share then. The FMV of the option was $2 per share.	1/31/2002 Market Price = $70 per share.	2/28/2003 Stock becomes worthless.

If the option is an ISO, the firm gets no tax deduction. The employee would not pay tax on grant in 2000, nor on exercise in 2003. When the stock becomes worthless, the executive would realize a $500,000 capital loss (i.e., $50 per share purchase price on exercise × 10,000 shares). Tax savings would be generated if (and when) the executive could realize capital gains – for example, by selling off other stock investments. Otherwise, only $3000 per year of ordinary income, such as wages, could be offset. This is not great, because the employee lost the $500,000 invested in the stock, but it is not as bad as the situation can be under a non-qualified plan.

If the option is non-qualified, when the options are granted in 2000, the firm gets a tax deduction for \$20,000. This is the value of the stock options: \$2 per share × 10,000 shares. It also is the amount taxable to the executive. An executive in the 40% bracket would have a tax of \$8000 (i.e., 40% × \$20,000). The deduction to the firm would typical save around \$7000 (i.e., 35% × \$20,000).

On exercise in 2003, the executive recognizes \$180,000 of ordinary income. This is calculated as (\$70 per share value – \$50 per share cost at exercise – \$2 per share of income recognized at grant) × 10,000 shares. This translates into a tax on the executive of \$72,000 (i.e., 40% × \$180,000). The employer corporation gets a mirror deduction of \$180,000, resulting in tax savings of about \$63,000.

However, when the stock becomes worthless in the same year, the executive recognizes a \$700,000 capital loss (i.e., \$75 per share sales price – \$70 per share previously taxed × 10,000 shares). There is no deduction for the employer. The \$700,000 capital loss is of limited value to the employee. Tax savings would be generated if (and when) the executive could realize capital gains — for example, by selling off other stock investments. Otherwise, only \$3000 per year of ordinary income, such as wages, could be offset.

The net result for 2003 is that even though the employee has invested \$500,000 in stock which is now worthless, the employee has to pay income tax on \$180,000 at the high ordinary income tax rates.[56] This must come from sources other than the stock which generated the income. Some former dot.com employees could be driven into bankruptcy by this obligation. It would seem to be fairer to let the employee offset the \$180,000 with the capital loss, but this is not the case under current law, and the investor is being treated just as if cash compensation had been earned and then reinvested in the employer's stock.

An astute employee may be able to hedge this risk through maintaining a tracking portfolio of exchange traded stock options of companies, or options with trading behaviors which correlate with the factors (e.g., crude oil futures for oil and gas companies) which drive the stock price of the employer corporation. It is very difficult to hedge with traded options of the employer corporation because of securities law restrictions on "insider trading".

Investing Through Qualified Retirement Plans

A significant portion of many investors' portfolios may be held in a qualified retirement fund. These can take many forms, ranging from traditional Individual Retirement Accounts (IRAs) or Roth IRAs to employer sponsored pension, profit sharing, stock ownership, or savings plans. The latter include 401(k) plans, and their equivalent for non-business employers, 403(b) plans.

The details about such investments would fill volumes, and thus are beyond the scope of this chapter. Each form has a host of complex rules to be followed.[57] There are extensive reporting requirements, as well as limits on who can administer such plans. Some rules set limits on the kinds of investments which can be made, albeit investments in publicly traded stocks and bonds usually are allowed. Of interest here is that many plans allow participants some choice in how the funds set aside on their behalf are invested. Other rules limit when funds can be distributed (e.g., after age 59 ½) or must be distributed (e.g., starting at age 70 ½). If a participant dies, the balance is paid to the people he or she designated to the plan as beneficiaries. These amounts are not only subject to estate taxes, but are also taxed (as *income with respect to a decedent*) to the beneficiaries.[58] However, amounts accumulated in a Roth IRA are not taxable until actually distributed to the beneficiaries. Thus, a Roth IRA can serve as a perpetual reserve fund for a family, accumulating free of income tax until needed.

Several features deserve highlighting here. All of these investment vehicles are highly tax favored.[59] Because of this, it normally makes sense to contribute as much as possible to qualified retirement plans, and wait as long as possible to withdraw the funds. Perhaps the most important tax benefit is that none of the retirement plan vehicles are subject to income tax on their current earnings. This is good when investments appreciate. However, losses incurred by these plans are not tax deductible. Investments grow at pre-tax rates until distributed to participants. At that time, distributions generally are taxed as ordinary income.

Taxation as ordinary income is not much of a problem when accumulated interest, dividends, or short-term capital gains are distributed.

This is because these items would have been taxed as ordinary income had the investor held them outside of the plan. It is an issue when long-term capital gains are distributed. There are two reasons for this. First, unlike holdings outside of a retirement plan, there is no "step up in basis at death" to the investor's beneficiaries for investments held inside of a plan. Second, capital gain distributions are taxed as ordinary income, too, rather than at their normally favorable maximum tax rates.

Therefore, all other things being equal, from a tax standpoint it may make sense to focus qualified plan investments on the safer, and current income generating, portion of the investor's overall portfolio, and leave long term — and riskier — investments outside of qualified retirement plans. As the major theme of this chapter indicates, however, tax planning should not be the "tail that wags the dog": it may not be optimal to limit long-term investment targets to holdings outside of a retirement plan due to diversification needs, asset protection strategies (property kept inside a qualified retirement plan is virtually untouchable by the investor's creditors, other than for personal support obligations like alimony), or cyclical trading or sector switching strategies which require frequent sales of investments.

Tax benefits for retirement plans extend beyond tax-free accumulations. For most, the amount contributed reduces the investor's current income. The traditional IRA, for example generates an income tax (but not Social Security) deduction when contributions are made. This may explain why there is a blanket maximum of $3000 per year as well as a prohibition for higher income employees who otherwise participate in an employer's qualified plan.[60] Roth IRAs do not enjoy tax deductions for contributions, but distributions are tax-free (providing certain holding period requirements are met).

Alternate Minimum Tax

There are a wide variety of other topics which might concern investors. State and local tax rules can vary greatly from the Federal; non-US citizens or residents can, in some countries, generate capital gains on securities sales tax free. The only further topic which should be discussed in this chapter, however, is the alternate minimum tax (known as AMT).

It fits here because one of the downsides for ISOs is the specter of AMT in the year of exercise.

As the name suggests this is a separate tax which only applies to the extent it exceeds the regular income tax. AMT is calculated by adjusting regular taxable income due to certain tax treatments. For example, 42% of a taxpayer's untaxed Section 1202 gain is added to regular taxable income, along with otherwise tax free interest on *private activity municipal bonds* (bonds whose proceeds are used for "business" like activities, rather than typically governmental ones) and the amount by which the value of incentive stock options exercised in a year exceeds the taxpayer's cost. Also added back are itemized deductions for state and local taxes. This expanded tax base is reduced by an exemption — which phases out for high income taxpayers — and then subject to tax rates which peak below those for regular income tax: 28% versus 40%.

The taxpayer is liable for the higher of this calculation or the regular tax. In recent years, an increasing number of taxpayers have found themselves in an AMT paying position. The numbers are expected to skyrocket as the lower tax rates of the *Economic Growth and Tax Relief Reconciliation Act of 2001* referred to above are phased in.

In sum, the following charts key tax strategies for investors in securities markets:

Key Tax Savings Strategies for Investors

Creation:	Retirement Plans
	Step-up in Basis at Death
	Identifying Highest Basis Stock on Sale
	Tracking Stock Basis
Conversion:	Holding to Achieve Long Term Capital Gain Status
	Investing in Section 1244 Stock
	Investing in Section 1202 Stock
Splitting:	Lifetime Gift Giving Program
	Using Employer Stock Options
	Avoiding Penalty Taxes on Incorporated Pocketbooks

Matching Tax Status with Mutual Fund/REIT Distribution Policies

Shifting: Avoiding Wash Sales
Identifying Deductible Source of Leverage
Adopting Hold Strategies
Avoiding AMT

Although there are many more tax rules, strategies, and pitfalls, which could be discussed, the above cover the most important and form a critical mass of tax knowledge for investors. These are the major considerations, which investors should have in mind when judging the expected net present value of future after-tax cash flows, and should help in the formation of investment strategic and the efficient use of tax professionals for detailed advice. Enough has been discussed on tax. The following addresses the last issue: control strategies to help preserve wealth.

10.7 Wealth Preservation Strategies

As with income taxes, strategies to preserve wealth — through control devices such as trusts,[61] and through plans to avoid estate and gift taxes — are not cost-free.[62] Most wealth preservations strategies entail drafting documents to set up new legal entities like trusts, resulting in significant professional fees.[63] In addition to increased administrative costs, the investor often must give up direct control of assets.[64] Accompanying this can be a reduction of liquidity and debt capacity, not to mention privacy.[65] Indeed, because of the importance of controlling a critical mass of capital, this often leads entrepreneurs to explicitly refuse to employ estate tax reduction strategies.

There are opportunity costs as well. In particular, the time and effort an investor spends on wealth preservation necessarily reduces that which can be devoted to generating it. Furthermore, the needs, and thus the rewards, for investors to plan in this area vary over time, due to the vagaries of time and changes in the investor's family situation[66] or lifestyle, not to mention market conditions.

Finally, the rewards of wealth preservation strategies are uncertain. Laws are rarely clear and immutable.[67] Although the legal doctrines and statutes which govern gifts, wills, and trusts are among the clearest and least subject to change in the US, they do change and sometimes in fairly unexpected ways.[68] Witness, for example, the possibility of same-sex marriage and the reality of quasi-marriage in the form of "life partner" registration in states such as California, as well as California's new way of holding community property in joint tenancy.

Tax laws are more likely to change, but the last 20 years has seen extraordinary amounts: four major US tax reform acts which have turned many good strategies into bad ones. The most recent of these — the *Economic Growth and Tax Relief Reconciliation Act of 2001* — proves this in the extreme, with its ten year phasing in of a variety of personal tax benefits such as the elimination of estate taxes in the year 2010 with their restoration in 2011. Because control strategies interact highly with estate and gift taxes, the following provides an overview of them.

Overview of Estate and Gift Taxes[69]

Basically, these are really one tax on the privilege of giving property away. The gift tax applies to donative transfers of property interests during the owner's lifetime. (Donative means that the transfer does not entitle the giver — called the donor — a right to receive something of legal value — called "consideration" in the context of contract law — in return.) The estate tax can be viewed merely as the gift tax on one's last gift: giving away all one owns at one's death.

As a further indication that these two taxes really operate as if they were just one, the same tax rates apply to each tax: the minimum rate for each tax is 18%, the maximum is 50%. The rates also progress through the same schedule at the same dollar amounts. Additionally, estate and gift taxes are based on lifetime giving patterns. This is unlike the income tax, which is based on annual income. Although paid annually, the amount subject to gift tax is imposed on the total of current year gifts plus all prior gifts, less a credit for previous gift taxes paid. Similarly, although only paid once — upon death — the amount subject to the estate tax includes all prior gifts (made after 1976, which is when the current system was put into place). This means that the more taxable gifts made during lifetime, the higher the tax rates on subsequent gifts. Similarly, prior taxable gifts increase the estate tax rates applicable to taxable property passed at death. These two taxes are larger, in theory, than income tax: rates vary effectively from 34–55% (although they are scheduled to drop in phases to 40% in 2009, and the estate tax eliminated for 2001) and these are imposed on the net fair market value of assets given away (rather than merely on income).

However, not all gifts are taxed, nor is all property passed at death. There are numerous exceptions. Transfers to spouses are tax free, deferring and eliminating a great deal of potential tax. There is a unified credit, allowing a combined $1,000,000 of taxable gifts and inheritances to be given tax-free during one's lifetime. Over the next few years, the estate tax unified credit is slated to increase (e.g., to $1,500,000 in 2004, $2,000,000 in 2006, and $3,500,000 in 2009), but the gift tax credit will remain at $1,000,000.

Furthermore, people can give tax-free up to $11,000 annually to as many donees as they want. (This amount is rose to $11,000 in 2002 due to inflation indexing.) Unlike the unified credit, this $11,000 per donor per recipient "small gift" exclusion can be used every year. There is only one unified credit to be used up either during one's life or at death. In addition, gifts and inheritances given to qualified charities and political parties are not taxed, nor are amounts spent paying for anyone's qualified tuition or medical expenses. Perhaps it is no wonder that the estate and gift tax has been labeled voluntary tax.[70] Indeed, people rarely actually pay the tax,[71] the exception usually being very successful people who unexpectedly die young.[72]

Finally, note that there is another tax — called the Generation Skipping Transfer Tax — which is hideously complex and subject to its own exclusions, which is intended to prevent estate taxes to be avoided merely by giving one's property to grandchildren rather than children.[73] This tax, too, is slated to disappear in 2010, and Congress may see fit to keep it from being automatically resurrected in 2011. The rest of this chapter weaves estate and gift tax considerations into each topic, rather than discussing these taxes separately.

To illustrate how all of these factors work together, consider a 50-year-old married investor with a 21-year-old daughter and a 12-year-old son. Let the investor have annual income of $100,000 with a securities portfolio worth $1,000,000, a home with equity of $400,000, and cash in money market accounts of $90,000. The investor can give $11,000 every year to each of the children, free of estate and gift tax. So can the investor's spouse. Thus, $44,000 can be given away by the couple tax-free every year.

Furthermore, the investor can give any amount to the spouse free of estate or gift tax. Thus, to the extent the investor's estate goes to a surviving spouse, there is no estate tax at that time. In addition, although gifts during lifetime, or upon the investor's death, made to the investor's children — or other people — may generate estate or gift tax liability, but the first $1,000,000 of this is offset by the unified credit. Thus, in addition to the $44,000 a year, which can be given to the children tax free, an additional $2,000,000 — $1000 from the investor and another from the spouse — can be left to the children tax-free.

10.8 The Goal of Wealth Preservation Strategies

As with income tax planning, the ultimate goal of wealth preservation strategies is to optimize, rather than to maximize, the investor's control over the wealth being generated. This requires efforts to identify costs, the balancing of the expected costs and benefits, the recognition that all taxes on all related parties ought to be considered, and that plans should be monitored to assure congruence with changes in the investor's situation.[74] This suggests that the focus of planning should be long term and strategic, and that the best approaches may be to find those control strategies which provide the most benefit with the least intrusion into the investor's wealth generation activities.[75]

With this in mind, the objectives should be to assure that:

1. Assets continue to be competently managed.
2. Income and principal are devoted to intended beneficiaries in intended amounts.

3. Taxes are not unduly incurred.
4. Administrative costs are not unduly high.

To accomplish this, investors normally should document assets and liabilities, adequately insure against legal liabilities and estate illiquidity, establish a living trust to avoid probate and conservatorship, maintain a valid will which effectively allocates assets to intended beneficiaries and maximizes the family's use of the unified estate and gift tax credit, and consider estate-freezing techniques such as a lifetime gift-giving plan.[76]

Lifetime Gifts[77]

A lifetime gift-giving program can accomplish many goals. On the non-tax side, for example, they can help avoid probate. As noted above, probate is a slow, expensive, and public process, which accomplishes little that cannot be done without it. All of this can be done without going through probate, for example through the judicious use of *inter vivos* trusts.[78] The use of grantor trusts to avoid probate brings no income or estate tax advantage.[79]

Property which passes by operation of law also is not subject to probate.[80] The same applies to property which has been transferred to an investor's beneficiaries, such as through lifetime gifts, avoids probate. Gifts can be made outright, or into trusts. (For beneficiaries which are minors, gifts can be made into custodial (e.g., CUGMA) accounts. In most states these allow the donor to retain control until the beneficiary reaches the age of 18, although some states allow this to be stretched out to 25.) The main advantage of a trust is that the beneficiary enjoys, but does not control, the assets.[81] This allows the giver to assure competent asset management, important if the beneficiary is aged, ignorant, or otherwise incapable of handling the gifts as the donor desires. A disadvantage is that maintaining a new legal entity like a trust entails administrative costs. A more important issue to many investors is that once property is given away in an irrevocable trust, it is difficult to change its operations so that it consistently reflects the investors changing desires.[82]

Of course, investors may not want to give property away while they are alive. First, once made, gifts are difficult to undo. Yet the investor's ability to make gifts, as well as the investor's intended beneficiaries and their needs, can change over time. Second, behavioral impacts should be considered. Entrepreneurs, rationally or otherwise, seem to strongly dislike reducing the capital which is so difficult to acquire. Ancestors also may fear "spoiling" descendants if money comes too easily.

Third, gifts may make them targets for "gold-diggers", creditors, and poor spending or investment decisions. Exposing the investor's hard earned assets to a beneficiary's creditors can be limited by making the gifts through the use of "spendthrift trusts". As alluded to above, a spendthrift provision allows a trustee to refuse to pay out to a beneficiary's creditor. A beneficiary cannot also fund the trust: one cannot avoid one's own creditors this way. Furthermore, as discussed below, in order to maximize estate and gift tax benefits, it may be useful to potentially expose the annual income of a trust to a beneficiary's creditors.

There are non-probate advantages to lifetime gift giving.[83] One is that the future income generated by the property given away is taxed to the beneficiaries who receive the gifts. (As noted above, this benefit is limited in the case of children under 14.[84]) Not only is this future income then excluded from the givers probate costs and estate taxes, but it is subject to the recipients' own income tax rates, which often are lower than those of the giver. Note that investors must give property away to get its income taxed to someone else: simply assigning cash flow is not sufficient. Also, as discussed above, the "Kiddie tax" rules effectively tax passive income received by children under the age of 14 at their parent's tax rates.

Gifts also may reduce the giver's estate taxes. This is important. Even though this tax is deferred until at least the investor's death, the rates usually are much higher than those for income taxes. They typically run between 35–50% of the fair market value of the net assets of a decedent. (As noted above, the maximum estate tax rate is slated to drop in steps to 45% in 2009, and 0% in 2010, but will snap back to 55% in 2011 unless changes are made in the interim.)

However, no tax is imposed on property passed to a surviving spouse, donated to a qualified charity, used to provide most forms of medical or educational support for children or unrelated parties. Furthermore, the "unified credit" amount remaining at death (e.g., $1,000,000 in 2002 and slated to rise in steps to $3,00,000 in 2009) will offset estate taxes dollar for dollar. (Note that gift taxes are not scheduled to be eliminated in 2010, but instead are being reduced so that the maximum rate will be 35%. Further, the unified credit for gift taxes will remain at $1,000,000, except to the extent changes are made in the intervening years.)

Gifts reduce estate taxes by reducing the size of the giver's estate, not only by their current value, but also by post-gift income and appreciation. This is not cost free: gifts (with a major exception being those to spouses) are subject to the gift tax, which is imposed at the same rates as the estate tax. But, unlike estate taxes, gift taxes paid reduce the giver's taxable estate.

Gifts not Taxed

Furthermore, some gifts are not taxed. There is not tax on donations to qualified charities. Indeed, they often generate income tax deductions. Educational or medical expenses which are paid directly to service providers are not taxed as gifts. Thus, a grandparent who pays for a grandchild's education, be it at the elementary, secondary, undergraduate, or graduate level, can do so free of gift tax.

This happens regardless of the donor's relationship to the person being benefited, thus allowing payments on behalf of "special friends" and "life partners" to be free of tax. This does not apply to other payments; whereas jewelry, house, cash, real estate, or other items of value given to a spouse are free of gift tax, those given outside of marriage are not. There does not appear to be an exception quasi-marital arrangements recognized under state law, such as "civil unions" and "domestic partners".[85]

Small gifts are not taxable. An individual can give $10,000 per year to anyone, and not be subject to gift tax. A husband and wife are not taxed if they give a combined $20,000 to any one person during the year. Thus, a married couple with three children could give them each $20,000 a year free of gift tax. This allows the couple to transfer $60,000 per year out of their estate, free of estate and gift taxes.

Note that this annual exclusion does not apply to gifts in trust, unless the giver gives up the power to reallocate ("sprinkle") the trust's income or principle among its various beneficiaries after it is created, and the beneficiaries are either under 21 or have a "Crummey"[86] power theoretically enabling them to withdraw their share of the trust's income every year.

However, gifts where the donor retains effective control — such as through revocable trusts, or by keeping the right to use the property for the rest of the donor's life — continue to be included in the donor's taxable estate, and the future income taxed to the giver. (The requirement that control be ceded is one of the key reasons why entrepreneurs tend to shy away from lifetime gift giving plans: capital is hard to amass.) Insurance is a good example of this.

Life Insurance

Life insurance owned by a decedent, or which is payable to his or her estate, is subject to estate taxes. However, insurance on a decedent's life which is owned by another party is tax free. Because of the moral hazard entailed were just anyone able to own life insurance on other people's lives, states have long limited such ownership to closely related parties, such as spouses or children. Because property passing to a spouse is tax-free anyway, there is no benefit to having the spouse own the life insurance. There is a cost, however: only the owner of life insurance can cancel it or change the beneficiaries. Because insurance companies typically limit the maximum amount of total insurance on any one life, giving ownership away can prevent the insured from getting coverage to pass benefits to other individuals — such as a new spouse after a divorce.[87]

Amounts gifted or willed to one's children, however, are not tax free. Thus, by setting up a trust for the benefit of one's children, and giving it both the ownership of life insurance as well as enough cash to pay necessary premiums, one can avoid estate taxes when the policy pays off. Note that no income taxes would be incurred, either. Interestingly, it is not uncommon to name one's spouse as the trustee of this kind of insurance trust.

Best Gifts: Assets Expected to Appreciate the Most

The best assets to give away are those expected to appreciate the most. (Of course, hindsight is 20-20: if an investor is lucky enough to choose the assets which actually do appreciate the most, this is better. For example, in 2000, an investor might have chosen Enron common stock to give away, on the basis of expectations that it would continue its meteoric rise. From the vantage point of the year 2002, this would have been a less than desirable choice.) This often is an ownership interest, such as common stock in a family business or a limited partnership interest in the investor's portfolio. (As noted above, penalty taxes such as the *accumulated earning tax* — a hideously complex area of tax law well beyond the scope of this chapter — suggest that maintaining a securities portfolio in corporate form is not preferable.)

As discussed in the previous paragraphs, these assets are likely to raise givers' greatest concerns over the loss of capital and control. Even though an ownership share has been given up, investors can maintain control by continuing to own a majority interest or by being a managing partner. And doing so can save taxes. This is because gifts of minority interests like these can result in reaping additional estate and gift tax benefits. This is because such gifts can benefit from reduced taxable value due to "minority" discounts. Discounts of 30% are not unusual; in such a case, the gift of 10% of a limited partnership worth $2,000,000 would be subject to gift taxes on only $140,000 of value.

Because of the problem that with lifetime gifts the giver must lose control in order to reduce estate and income taxes, many investors would rather "wait and see" what unfolds during the rest of their lives. Keep in mind that the state tax is slated to disappear in 2010, albeit to reappear in 2011. Thus, an investor who expects to live until 2010 might quite rationally decide to ignore estate and gift tax planning. Furthermore, because transfers to a spouse are free of estate and gift taxes, it also is rational to view these taxes as being triggered not when the first spouse dies but only when the second spouse (is expected to) die. Additionally, except for simple gifts (such as a check) or small gifts, legal fees can be significant. One "wait and see" approach, which is cheaper but not without its limitations, can be the use of joint tenancies.

Joint Tenancies

As noted above, probate is avoided to the extent that the property a person has when he dies is passed to his intended beneficiaries by operation of law. This can be done fairly quickly, privately, and cheaply through joint tenancy. A classic example is for a married couple to hold the title to their home and other assets as joint tenant with rights of survivorship. (In some states, a joint tenancy between spouses can be established by a tenancy in the entirety, which gives more protection to non-managing spouses.) Joint tenancy provides that at one joint tenant's death, the property passes by operation of law to the remaining joint tenant(s). No probate is necessary; estate taxes are avoided.

However, the ability to pass the unified credit amount to children and other beneficiaries is lost, as well as the "step-up" in income tax basis on half of the property. The latter is not much of a problem with bank accounts, but can be with assets which have appreciated (such as a home). In community property states, the step-up can be gained by recording property as "community property". The property passes to the surviving spouse just like joint tenancy, but probate — albeit usually a streamlined, less intrusive form — is required. Note that in California, a new form of title has been created: community property held in joint tenancy.

People other than spouses can form joint tenancies. A classic example is adding one's child or lifetime partner as a joint tenant. When this is done with financial assets, such as a bank accounts, it is known as a "Totten trust". Doing this avoids probate, and does not trigger gift taxes. It does not avoid estate taxes, nor is income from the underlying assets taxed at the child's rate.

More importantly to some people, joint tenancies similarly allow assets to be shared with other survivors who are not married to the investor, such as "lifetime partners" and "special friends". Indeed, due to uncertainties about the impact of state "civil union" or "registered domestic partner" schemes on Federal tax law, only explicit contractual arrangements, such as joint tenancies, partnerships, or wills and trusts, can generate a suitable degree of certainty under these conditions. On the other hand, the problem with these arrangements may stem from the very certainty involved. Once such a contractual arrangement is made, it may be very difficult to alter it if circumstances change.

Creating a joint tenancy is inexpensive — albeit recording is required for many non-financial assets, such as real estate and cars — but has its costs. Inflexibility is one: adding a joint tenant is easy; removing one requires their assent. More importantly, there is a loss of control: joint tenants have equal rights to the underlying property. This allows them to withdraw or sell some or all from a bank or brokerage account. Doing so creates a gift in the amount pulled out by the beneficiary. This may generate gift taxes on, but also removes it from the taxable estate of, the original owner, and also shifts future income on the amount to the beneficiary's income tax return.

A joint tenant also can force a judicial conversion of real property title to the tenancy in common form, allowing an independent sale of their respective part of the property. For these reasons, along with the fact that adding a joint tenant provides a financial benefit to them upon one's death, investor's should not use this technique except for people they greatly trust. A further caveat: even if a joint tenant would never abuse the relationship, his or her share is accessible to the joint tenant's creditors (including future ex-spouses). This suggests that other approaches, such as the use of trusts, might be preferable.

Other Contractual Techniques

Note that other contractual techniques can be used to mimic the best features of the above, and tailor them to the specifics of the situation. A classic example is a pre-nuptial agreement. These are costly, both in terms of professional fees and in their intrusiveness into relationships. Furthermore, they are not readily recognized for people for whom marriage is not an issue. Alternatives include a "lifetime partnership agreement", which is not clearly enforceable in all jurisdictions, the judicious use of life insurance, where it is available, and trusts, as discussed above. Because of the relative novelty and highly technical nature of such arrangements, it behooves investors considering them to retain an experience professional advisor.

10.9 A Classic Approach for Investor Control

The control strategies can best be summarized by looking at the classic approach for married taxpayers with children. First, they will have established a living trust, with themselves as beneficiaries and joint trustees and their children as successor beneficiaries and trustees. Suitable limits will be established on any possible distribution of principle to children (e.g., not before the age of 18), except as is necessary for their health, education, support, or maintenance. Title to their savings accounts, brokerage accounts, securities certificates, real estate, and other key assets will have been transferred into the trust's name. A list of personal property for which there is no state registry — such as jewelry and silver — will be identified as being part of the trust assets on a schedule attached to the trust. Either in the trust, or separately, they will have provided each other with a power of attorney for health care decisions. In addition, the trust will have provision for identifying if a beneficiary is no longer competent, most likely through the certification by two unrelated practising physicians.

Life insurance on one spouse will be owned and the premiums paid by an insurance trust, of which the other spouse as the trustee and the children as beneficiaries (with suitable limitations on distribution of principle).

Each also will have executed properly witnessed wills. Aside from specific bequests, their estates will pour over into a trust, with the proviso that it be split into two parts. The first part, known as the "bypass" or "unified credit" trust, will be funded when the first spouse dies by the maximum amount of that spouse's remaining unified credit. The surviving spouse will have the right to invade income and then principle as is necessary for health, education, support or maintenance. The second part, known at the Qualified Terminable Interest in Property (QTIP) Trust will name the surviving spouse as beneficiary, allowing access to all income and principal, payable at least annually, but names the children as successor beneficiaries.

Finally, lifetime trusts will have been set up for each child, and funded annually with the annual exclusions (currently $10,000) per year from each living parent. The children will have a Crummey[88] power to annually withdraw contributions during the year in amounts up to the annual exclusion. Otherwise, access to principle will be subject to suitable limitations as discussed above.

Is all of this worthwhile? Consider the following situation. T is a 51-year-old businessperson who is married and has two children, ages 12 and 20 attending private schools. From investments (made before marriage) of $200,000 he built up a portfolio of marketable securities worth about $1,000,000. Taxable income on T's joint Federal return has been averaging about $150,000 per year, which is pretty much all spent every year for family expenses and taxes. The mortgage on the family's home, which T bought while single for $145,000, is $200,000; the home currently is worth $375,000. T owns life insurance of $350,000 that is renewable to age 75 at an annual cost of $1300, and has $400,000 in an employer-sponsored 401(k) retirement plan. T has been so busy building a career, raising a family, and researching investments that there has been no time for lawyers, wills, trusts, or estate planning.

Were T to die today, T's probate estate would be $1,925,000 ($1,000,000 of marketable securities, $375,000–200,000 of equity in the home, $350,000 of life insurance, and $400,000 from the 401(k) plan). To the extent that the property is determined to be community property, half might be excludable from probate. This is unlikely, however, because the property was acquired before marriage, unless there was some agreement to covert it to community property. Furthermore, if the assets had been converted to joint tenancy (e.g., by changing the names on the brokerage account and re-recording the title to the home), or T's family designated as the beneficiaries to the life insurance and 401(k) (e.g., by filing proper forms to make the changes with the retirement plan administrator and the insurance company), these assets could be excluded from probate.

Attorney, court, and professional fees for probate would run around $35,000.[89] Except for certain allowances set by law to provide for families during the probate process, the assets would not be accessible by T's family for the two years or so that probate normally takes. There is one advantage to probate in that, provided adequate notice is provided, T's unsecured creditors are either paid off during probate or their claims extinguished. This may be of some help if T was a professional with substantial malpractice exposure (e.g., an anesthesiologist), although it is not clear in many jurisdictions whether probate cuts off liabilities unknown or contingent at the time of death.

This possible advantage must be balanced against both the cost, and the delay and publicity of probate. As to the latter, a list of all of the assets would have to be submitted to the probate court, which would become a public record. The probate petition, also public record, would show the names and addresses of T's family. This could all be avoided simply by using a living trust.

Without such a trust or a valid will, in most states[90] the investor's (non-community property) assets would be divided 1/3 to the surviving spouse and 2/3 to be divided equally among the children. (Community property would go to the surviving spouse, and thus be free of estate and gift taxes.) If this were the case, the children's share of the estate would be $1,125,000. Provided that there were no prior taxable gifts (which would have used up some or all of the unified credit), the first $1,000,000 would be free of estate tax due to the unified credit. The remaining $125,000 would be subject to estate tax of $31,300 [calculated as $23,800 + (30% × $25,000)]. Additional amounts to the children would be taxed at a 32% rate. The 1/3 of the property passed to the spouse would be free of estate tax, and because the spouse also has a unified credit, when the surviving spouse dies an additional $1,000,000 (more in later years) could pass free of estate tax to the children.

The use of an insurance trust would allow the life insurance proceeds to pass to the surviving family free of tax. This could save all of the estate taxes calculated in the previous paragraph, and even more if the investor's estate were larger. The use of the living trust pouring over to a spousal QTIP trust, but funding a unified credit trust to the amount of the unused unified credit, also would avoid the tax. Similarly, no tax would be involved has the investor used a will or living trust to pass all of the property to the surviving spouse.

10.10 Conclusion

Key strategies for profiting from stock market investments have been thoroughly discussed in previous chapters. This one turned to how to keep control of the wealth that these investments generate. In particular, this chapter focuses on some aspects of income taxation and estate planning with an eye towards optimizing after tax returns and control. Keeping with the theme of this book, the discussion dealt with individuals who are investors, although the basic theory and many of the actual strategies are applicable to corporate investors.

The Less Intrusive Alternative Planning Model® gives an innovative framework for integrating tax and control concerns with other strategic investing goals. Accompanying it were examples of how to use it to apply generic tax planning techniques to investment decisions. This was followed by an explanation of the key current US Federal income tax planning issues and rules. The rest of the chapter was devoted to an explanation of the most important control issues. In particular, the balance of the chapter described and illustrated the most important current estate planning issues relating to the use of trusts to control investment portfolios.

In sum, once one has made money, it makes sense to protect it from creditors. An important creditor is the tax collector. Tax reducing strategies should be employed, provided they do not unreasonably impinge on the investor's other goals. The same applies to asset protection. The above arrangement accomplishes this by avoiding probate and conservatorship, and taking advantage of the major estate and gift tax loopholes. These are the marital deduction, the unified credit, and the annual gift tax exclusion. Of course, the optimal plan for particular investors will differ, and may very well differ over time. Importantly, the tax tail is not wagging the investment dog: it is more important to make money than to fuss too much about losing part of it to taxes.

Endnotes

[1] For an in depth discussion of this issue, refer to Scholes and Wolfson: *Taxes and Business Strategy* (Prentice-Hall, 1991).

[2] For an example of how these factors are considered, and interact, in investment decisions, see Kohan *et al.*: *Planning Opportunities Under the New Tax Law* (PricewaterhouseCoopers, 2001).

[3] Karayan, Swenson and Neff: *Strategic Tax Planning for Managers* (Wiley, 2002).

[4] See Endnote 3.

[5] An astute application of this idea is found in Beatty, Beerger and Magliolo: "Motives for Forming Research & Development Financing Organizations", *Journal of Accounting and Economics*, pp. 411–442, March–May, 1995. The impact of goal suboptimization in general is summarized in Arrow: "The Economics of Agency" in *Principals & Agents: The Structure of Business* (Eds. Pratt and Zeckhauser), pp. 37–51 (Harvard Business School, 1985).

[6] Stiglitz: "The General Theory of Tax Avoidance", *National Tax Journal*, pp. 325–337, September, 1985.

[7] Slemrod and Blumenthal: *The Compliance Costs of Big Business* (The Tax Foundation, Washington D.C., 1993).

[8] Fellingham and Wolfson: "Taxes and Risk Sharing", *The Accounting Review*, pp. 10–17, January, 1985.

[9] Collins, Kemsley and Lang: "Cross-Jurisdictional Income Shifting and Earnings Valuation", *Journal of Accounting Research*, vol. 36(2), pp. 209–299, Summer, 1998.

[10] Double taxation is also an issue in multistate organizations, as aptly illustrated in Anand and Sansing: "The Weighting Game: Formula Apportionment as an Instrument of Public Policy", *National Tax Journal*, vol. 53, pp. 183–200, June, 2000.

[11] Willis, Hoffman, Maloney and Raabe: *Federal Taxation Comprehensive Volume*, Chapter 25 (Thompson Southwestern West's, 2002).

[12] DeAngelo and Masulis: "Optimal Capital Structure under Corporate and Personal Taxation", *Journal of Financial Economics*, vol. 8, pp. 3–29, March, 1980.

[13] Financial Accounting Standards Board, *Statement of Financial Accounting Standards # 109*.

[14] Hite and Long: "Taxes and Executive Stock Options", *Journal of Accounting and Economics*, vol. 4(1), pp. 3–14, July 1982; Holthausen: "Evidence on the Effect of Bond Covenants and Management Compensation Contracts on the Choice of Accounting Techniques: The Case of the Depreciation Switch-Back", *Journal of Accounting and Economics*, vol. 3(1), pp. 73–109, March, 1981.

[15] Ballard, Shoven and Whalley: "The Total Welfare Cost of the United States Tax System: A General Equilibrium Approach", *National Tax Journal*, vol. 38(2), pp. 125–140, June, 1985.

[16] Stiglitz and Wolfson: "Taxation, Information, and Economic Organization", *Journal of the American Taxation Association*, vol. 10(1), Spring, 1988.

[17] Mills, Erickson and Maydew: "Investments in Tax Planning", *Journal of the American Taxation Association*, vol. 20(1), pp. 1–20, Spring, 1998.

[18] An excellent example is presented in Wolfson: "Empirical Evidence of Incentive Problems and Their Mitigation in Oil and Gas Tax Shelter Programs" in *Principals and Agents: The Structure of Business* (Eds. J. Pratt and R. Zeckhauser) (Harvard Business School Press, 1985), who also provides a general theory in Wolfson: "Tax, Incentive, and Risk Sharing Issues in the Allocation of Property Rights: The Generalized Lease-or-Buy Problem", *Journal of Business*, pp. 158–171, April, 1985.

[19] Auerbach and Reishus: "Taxes and the Merger Decision: An Empirical Analysis" in *Knights, Raiders, and Targets: The Impact of the Hostile Takeover* (Eds. Coffee, Lowenstein and Rose-Ackerman) (Oxford University Press, 1987).

[20] One of the finest field studies in this area is presented in Wilson: "The Role of Taxes in Location and Sourcing Decisions" in *Studies in International Taxation* (Eds. Giovaninni, Hubbard and Slemrod), pp. 195–231 (University of Chicago Press, 1993).

[21] For an in depth analysis, see Swenson and Karayan: *Strategic Tax Planning*, pp. 340–369 (University of Southern California, 2001).

[22] Many other factors are at work. For more information, Swenson, Moore and Steece: "An Economic Analysis of the Impact of State Income Tax Rates and Bases on Foreign Investments", *The Accounting Review*, October, 1987.

[23] For a slightly different approach, see Jones: *Principles of Taxation for Business & Investment Planning* (McGraw-Hill, Irwin, 2001).

[24] Detail on this subject can be found in Karayan: *The Economic Impact of a Tax Law Change: Publicly Traded Partnerships Under the 1987 Act*. PhD Dissertation, Peter F. Drucker Graduate Management Center, Claremont Graduate School, Claremont, CA, 1994. Recall from Endnote 1 that removal of the copyright notice contained therein, without the prior explicit written consent of John E. Karayan, is prohibited. No such consent has been given as of March 7, 2002.

[25] For a more sophisticated derivation of an analytic formula, see Scholes and Wolfson: *Taxes and Business Strategy* (Prentice-Hall, 1991).

[26] A well-written, incisive analysis of one of the largest "conversion" transactions ever reported in the US business press can be found in Erickson and Wang: "Exploiting and Sharing Tax Benefits", *Journal of the American Taxation Association*, pp. 35–44, Fall, 1999.

[27] Ayers, Lefanowicz and Robinson do an excellent job of explaining this issue, and the tax status of goodwill in general, in "The Effect of Goodwill Tax Deductions on the Market for Corporate Acquisitions", *Journal of the American Taxation Association*, Supplement, 2000.

[28] Empirical studies of this phenomena range from studies of specific decisions, such as Frankel and Trezevant: "The Year-End LIFO Inventory Purchasing Decision: An Empirical Test", *The Accounting Review*, vol. 69(2), pp. 382–398, 1994, to general decisions, such as Maydew: "Tax-Induced Earnings Management by Firms with Net Operating Losses", *Journal of Accounting Research*, vol. 35(1), pp. 83–96, 1997.

[29] This is well illustrated in Sieda and Stern: "Extending Scholes/Wolfson for Post-1997 Pension Investments: Application to the Roth IRA Contribution and Rollover Decisions", *Journal of the American Taxation Association*, pp. 100–110, Fall, 1998.

[30] The scope of this generic strategy is manifest in a keen study by Wheeler and Outslay: "The Phantom Federal Income Taxes of General Dynamics Corporation", *The Accounting Review*, pp. 760–774, October, 1986.

[31] An intriguing example of this can be found in the use of an employer stock ownership plan (ESOP) to split dividend income into a tax-exempt retirement trust. ESOPs are astutely analyzed in Shackelford: "The Market for Tax Benefits: Evidence from Leveraged ESOPs", *Journal of Accounting and Economics*, vol. 14(2), pp. 117–145, 1991.

[32] For a comprehensive discussion of control strategies, see Rosen: *Asset Protection Planning*, Bureau of National Affairs Tax Management Portfolio No. 810 (BNA, 2002).

[33] Karayan: "International Tax Planning and Transfer Pricing", *Journal of the Institute of Regional and International Studies*, vol. 5, pp. 21–23, Spring, 1997.

[34] The most readable reference on international taxation is Outslay and Moore: *Taxation of International Transactions* (AICPA, 1997). The details can be found in Bittker and Lokken: *Fundamentals of International Taxation* (Warren, Gorham & Lamont, 2000), which is heavy reading.

[35] Because owners and beneficiaries often do not reside, or are not domiciled, in the same jurisdiction, the laws which actually control rights and obligations are often not certain. Similarly, because property, too, can be located, or considered located, in different jurisdictions, what laws actually govern such arrangements can be uncertain. This particularly is a problem when dealing with property, people, or legal entities having a connection with the United States of America.

This is because the laws of gifts, wills, trusts, estates, property, and support obligations are determined by the individual state having proper jurisdiction. But there is a wide variance among states as to these rules. For example, most of the Western states have adopted the concept of community property, which generally considers assets generated during marriage to be owned jointly by each spouse regardless of legal title or contribution. This often is not the case with most other states, which rely on British common law concepts.

However, during the late 20th century a variety model uniform laws (e.g., the *Uniform Gift for Minors Act,* and the *Uniform Limited Partnership Act*) were drafted and adopted, in whole or part, by most states. Thus there are commonalities which are fairly widespread. Keeping this in mind, the following presents key issues and generic solutions; actual implementation is unwise without consulting an experienced estate planner.

[36] A comprehensive view of both the non-tax and tax aspects of revocable *inter vivos* trusts can be found in Berall *et al.*: *Revocable Inter Vivos Trusts*, Bureau of National Affairs Tax Management Portfolio No. 468 (BNA, 2002).

[37] For a in-depth look at the pros and cons of living trusts, see Patrick: "Living Trusts: Snake Oil or Better than Sliced Bread?", *William Mitchell Law Review*, vol. 27, pp. 1083–1104, 2000.

[38] For a detailed discussion of probate, see Magowan: *Probate and Administration of Decedent's Estates*, Bureau of National Affairs Tax Management Portfolio No. 804 (BNA, 2002).

[39] An pithy yet comprehensive guide on this issue can be found in Collins: "Avoiding a Will Contest: the Impossible Dream?", *Creighton Law Review*, vol. 34, pp. 7–45, 2000.

[40] The decedent's intended beneficiaries can be natural persons (people), juridical persons (such as corporations), or other legal entities (such as trusts). Ways have even developed to effectively allow gifts to entities not recognized as person entitled to typical legal rights, such as pet animals. One is the *honorary trust*. For more on this, see Beyer: "Estate Planning for Pets", *Probate & Property*, vol. 15, pp. 6–12, July/August, 2001.

[41] For a discussion of powers of appointment, see "Scope and Exercise of Powers of Appointment", *Estate Planning*, vol. 28(9), p. 454, *et seq*, September, 2001.

[42] The breadth of strategies entailing life insurance is aptly illustrated in Nowotny: "The Use of Private Placement Life Insurance and Split Dollar to Transfer Post-Mortem Appreciation", *Trusts & Estates*, vol. 140, pp. 49–61, February, 2001.

43 An excellent source for more information on powers of attorney is Hook: *Durable Powers of Attorney*, Bureau of National Affairs Tax Management Portfolio No. 859 (BNA, 2002). The limits and opportunities for such a power to add flexibility is astutely explored in McLeod: "What are the Limitations on an Attorney-in-Fact's Power to Gift and to Change a Dispositive (Estate) Plan?", *William Mitchell Law Review*, vol. 27, pp. 1143–1167, 2000. See also Bove: "Powers of Appointment: More (Taxwise) than Meets the Eye", *Estate Planning*, vol. 28(10), pp. 496–502, October, 2001.

44 Compare, for example, Bost: *Estate Planning and Taxation* (Kendall Hunt, 2002), with *Federal Estate and Gift Taxes Explained* (Ed. E. Brown) (Commerce Clearing House, 2001).

45 For a more comprehensive overview, see Fithian: *Values-Based Estate Planning* (John Wiley, 2000). For useful language and detailed analysis, there are a few better sources from the California Continuing Education of the Bar treatise series. These include titles such as *Drafting Irrevocable Living Trusts,* 3rd Edition (C.E.B., 1998), *Capitalizing & Protecting New Businesses* (C.E.B., 1997), *Selecting and Forming Business Entities* (C.E.B., 1996), and *Forming and Operating California LLCs* (C.E.B., 1995).

46 For a comprehensive yet cogent exposition on family tax planning in general, see Rice and Rice: *California Family Tax Planning* (Matthew Bender, 2002).

47 An excellent source for more information on this and other tax issues discussed in this chapter, see the *US Master Tax Guide* (Commerce Learning House, 2002).

48 In particular, a person whose AGI exceeds the threshold set for the year must reduce most of their allowable itemized deductions by 3% of the excess. AGI, which is found on line 33 at the bottom of the front page of the US individual income tax return Form 1040, basically is an individuals' taxable income before itemized deductions and personal exemptions. Itemized deductions are items like qualified home mortgage interest, which are found on Form 1040's Schedule A. Most of these (including mortgage interest, taxes, and charitable contributions) are subject to the reduction. Medical expenses, investment interest, casualty losses, and gambling losses are not reduced.

The threshold is noted at the bottom of Schedule A on line 28, and is indexed for inflation.

49 At high levels of income, corporate tax rates typically are lower than those for individuals. For example, the marginal rate for $500,000 of taxable income is 34% for corporations but about 39% for individuals. (Under the *2001 Tax Act*, the top rate for individuals is slated to drop to about 38% in 2004 and

35% in 2006). At lower levels, the rate differential can be significant: the first $50,000 of corporate income is taxed at only 15%.

[50] For an excellent overview of these penalty taxes, see Karayan, Swenson and Neff: *Strategic Tax Planning for Managers,* Chapter 3 (Wiley, 2002).

[51] For a more detailed discussion, see Murphy and Higgins: *Concepts in Federal Taxation*, pp. 551–687 (South Western, 2001).

[52] For information on publicly traded partnerships, limited liability companies, master limited partnerships, and other flow-through entities, see Zwick: "Family Business Consulting Revisited", *The Tax Advisor* (January, 1999), Muhtaseb and Karayan: "The Impact of the Revenue Act of 1987 on Master Limited Partnerships", *Applied Financial Economics*, vol. 6(3), pp. 233–242, 1996, and Cruz and Karayan: "Should a Firm Operate as an LLC?", *Business Forum* vol. 1(3), pp. 16–21, Summer/Fall, 1996.

[53] For an excellent financial model in this area, see Scholes *et al.*: *Taxes and Business Strategy*, Second Edition (Prentice-Hall, 2002), p. 200, *et seq.*

[54] This example ignores the time value of money, which has no great impact due to the relatively short time horizon and low current interest rates.

[55] Matt Richtel: "Stock Option Blues: Slide Leaves Little But a Big Tax Bill", *New York Times*, February 18, 2001; Carrie Johnson: "Some Shocked at Tax Bills on Options", *Washington Post*, March 16, 2001 (http://www.washtech.com, December 19, 2001).

[56] This example also ignores the time value of money, which has no great impact due to the relatively short time horizon and low current interest rates.

[57] A readable, yet extensive summary can be found in the *US Master Tax Guide* (Commerce Clearing House, 2002) at paragraph 2168, *et seq.*

[58] For further information, see *Federal Income Taxation of Decedents, Estates, and Trusts* (Commerce Clearing House, 2002) at paragraph 15, *et seq.*

[59] For a comprehensive discussion, and excellent quantitative modeling, see Scholes *et al.*: *Taxes and Business Strategy*, Second Edition (Prentice-Hall, 2002), p. 211, *et. seq.*

[60] The *US Master Tax Guide* (Commerce Clearing House, 2002) at paragraphs 2168–2179 is an excellent source for further information on IRAs; paragraphs 2180–2193 do so for Roth IRAs.

[61] As noted above, trusts are legal entities which can hold property, make investment decisions, and even run businesses. There are three parties to a trust. The first is the trustor — sometimes called "settlor" — who creates the trust (by executing a trust agreement), and funds the trust by transferring the trust property — also called the trust *res* — to the trust. If this is done during the grantor's lifetime, the trust is called an *inter vivos* (lifetime) trust;

otherwise the trust must be set up or funded via the trustor's will. These are referred to as "testamentary trusts".

As with any of these parties, there can be multiple grantors. It is not uncommon, for example, for parents to set up a trust for their children. Furthermore, the parties can be the same person(s); for example, the parents might elect to serve as trustees of their children's trust.

The second party is the trustee, who is granted legal title to all trust property but has a strict fiduciary duty to manage the property prudently and in accordance with the trust agreement. The third party is the beneficiary, on whose behalf the trust property is managed.

Lifetime trusts can be revocable, that is, the grantor can change the terms or withdraw transfers of property to the trust. A good example of this is the "living trust", where people put property into a trust for their own benefit, and reserve the right to take the money back. (Property left in the trust at the trustor's death is then held for the benefit of successor beneficiaries named by the trustor.) Most trusts are revocable, being living trusts with the primary purpose of avoiding probate costs, as discussed below.

62 For a more comprehensive discussion, see Jones: "Family Limited Partnerships Achieve Tax and Non-tax Goals", *Taxation for Accountants*, pp. 33–40, July, 1994.

63 Bekerman, Engelhardt and Miranda: "Planning and Drafting from the Fiduciary's Perspective", *Probate & Property*, vol. 15, pp. 31–36, March/April, 2001.

64 Compare Lischer: "Domestic Asset Protection Trusts: Pallbearers to Liability?", *Real Property, Probate, and Trusts Journal*, vol. 35, pp. 479–600, 2000, with Shenkman *et al.*: "Trustee Removal Powers: How Many Strings are Too Many?", *Probate and Property*, vol. 8(4), p. 8, 1994.

65 See, generally, Fithian: *Values-Based Estate Planning* (John Wiley, 2000).

66 These include disabilities, see Rosenberg: "Supplemental Needs Trusts for People with Disabilities: The Development of a Private Trust in the Public Interest", *Boston University Public Interest Law Journal*, vol. 18, pp. 91–151, 2000, special interests, e.g., Pankauski: "To Sell or Cellar: What Fiduciaries Need to Know about Wine Collections", *Probate & Property*, vol. 15, pp. 6–11, March/April, 2001, and the impacts of the aging process, e.g., English: "The *Uniform Health-Care Decisions Act* and its Progress in the States", *Probate & Property*, vol. 15, pp. 19–23, May/June, 2001.

67 Park and Fox: "Evolution of the Charging Order Remedy Against FLPs", *Trusts & Estates*, pp. 22–25, August, 1997.

[68] Zysik: "Significant Recent Developments in Estate Planning", *The Tax Advisor*, pp. 500–510, August, 1997.

[69] Jones: *Principles of Taxation for Business and Investment Planning*, pp. 454–462 (McGraw-Hill, Irwin, 2001) does an excellent job of elaborating on these topics. Scholes *et al.*: *Taxes and Business Strategies* (Prentice-Hall, 2002) provides insightful quantitative models at pp. 463–489.

[70] Scholes *et al.*: *Taxes and Business Strategy*, Second Edition (Prentice-Hall, 2002), p. 464.

[71] Less than 2% of estates actually file an estate tax return. See Endnote 70.

[72] Schmalback: "Avoiding Federal Wealth Transfer Taxes", Unpublished Working Paper, Duke University Law School, April, 2000.

[73] One of the most cogent and concise expositions of this tax is Thornburg and Lowenhaupt: "Tips for Preparing Generation-Skipping Transfer Tax Returns", *Estate Planning*, vol. 28(5), pp. 208–216, May, 2001.

[74] This is presented essentially as an ethical duty for estate planners in California Continuing Education of the Bar, *Drafting Irrevocable Living Trusts*, 3rd Edition (C.E.B., 1998).

[75] For a fine overview of the art of estate planning, see Kess and Campbell: *CCH Financial and Estate Planning Guide* (2001), in particular Chapter 1.

[76] Wilson: "Providing Guidance to Executors and Trustees", *Journal of Accountancy*, pp. 1–4, October, 1997.

[77] For an excellent discussion of lifetime giving plans, see Mehigan and Potter: "Lifetime Giving Remains a Powerful Planning Tool for Family Business, *The Tax Advisor*, pp. 97–102, February, 1996.

[78] California Continuing Education of the Bar, *Drafting Irrevocable Living Trusts*, 3rd Edition (C.E.B., 1998).

[79] This is thoroughly discussed in Zaritsky: *Grantor Trusts*, Bureau of National Affairs Tax Management Portfolio No. 858 (BNA, 2002).

[80] The terminology and details of probate can be found in remarkably user-friendly language in Witkin: *Summary of California Law* (Bancroft Whitney, 2001).

[81] Trusts have long been used to separate control and beneficial ownership of property, and to avoid taxes. For example, the *Statute of Westminster*, which legitimized effective trusts — where law firms held title to manors to avoid fees owed to the King of England when property passed generations through primogeniture — was promulgated by Henry VIII in order to capture these "estate taxes."

[82] Meints: "Using Trusts to Provide Incentives, Rewards, Remembrances, and Other Benefits to Chosen Beneficiaries", *Practicing Tax Lawyer*, vol. 15, pp. 25–38, Winter, 2000.

[83] Gift giving which achieves the donor's often conflicting goals is an art, as aptly illustrated in Horn: "Transferring Wealth by Giving Different Interests and Powers but Equal Values to Different Children", *Estates, Gifts, & Trusts Journal*, vol. 18, p. 211, *et seq*, 1993.

[84] The are special restrictions on gifts to minors, which are perceptively outlined in Lischer: *Gifts to Minors*, Bureau of National Affairs Tax Management Portfolio No 846 (BNA, 2002).

[85] This does not mean that there are no techniques which mimic traditional approaches to family asset planning for non-traditional arrangements. An insightful overview can be found in Chasen: "More Estate and Gift Tax Planning for Nontraditional Families", *Probate and Property*, vol. 15, pp. 54–58, May/June, 2001.

[86] A "Crummey" provision can convert a future interest given in trust to a sufficiently present one so that the annual gift tax exclusion applies to contributions. Essentially, the trustor grants beneficiaries the right to withdraw any current contributions. This right normally is quite restricted as to time (e.g., during the last two weeks of December) and in procedure (e.g., in a notarize writing delivered to the trustee). A good overview of the power can be found in Wilson: "The Crummey Power and Inter Vivos Trusts", *Memphis State University Law Review*, vol. 22, p. 297, *et seq*, 1992.

[87] For an in-depth review of issues like these, see Grassi: "Key Issues in Drafting Life Insurance Trusts", *Estate Planning*, vol. 28(5), pp. 217–222, May, 2001.

[88] An illustration of the legal complexities involved can be found in Cavanaugh and Preston: "When Will Crummey Transfers to Contingent Beneficiaries be Excludable Present Interests?", *Journal of Taxation*, vol. 76(2), p. 68, *et seq*, 1992.

[89] E.g., California Probate Code Section 10,800.

[90] E.g., California Probate Code Section 6400.

INDEX